I HEAR FREEDOM

....
BLACK LIVES IN THE DIASPORA: PAST / PRESENT / FUTURE

BLACK LIVES IN THE DIASPORA:
PAST / PRESENT / FUTURE

EDITORIAL BOARD

Howard University
Clarence Lusane, Rubin Patterson, Nikki Taylor, Amy Yeboah Quarkume

Columbia University
Farah Jasmine Griffin, Frank Guridy, Josef Sorett

Black Lives in the Diaspora: Past / Present / Future is a book series that focuses on Black lives in a global diasporic context. Published in partnership with Howard University's College of Arts and Sciences and Columbia University's African American and African Diaspora Studies Department, it builds on Columbia University Press's publishing programs in history, sociology, religion, philosophy, and literature as well as African American and African Diaspora studies. The series showcases scholarship and writing that enriches our understanding of Black experiences in the past, present, and future with the goal of reaching beyond the academy to intervene in urgent national and international conversations about the experiences of people of African descent. The series anchors an exchange across two global educational institutions, both located in historical capitals of Black life and culture.

Isis Barra Costa, *Imagining the Past, Remembering the Future: Forms of Knowledge in the Afro-Brazilian Diaspora*

Nicole M. Morris Johnson, *The Souths in Her: Black Women Writers and Choreographers and the Poetics of Transmutation*

Jamall A. Calloway, *Imagining Eden: Black Theology and the Search for Paradise*

Wendell H. Marsh, *Textual Life: Islam, Africa, and the Fate of the Humanities*

Jarvis McInnis, *Afterlives of the Plantation: Plotting Agrarian Futures in the Global Black South*

Lauren Coyle Rosen and Hannibal Lokumbe, *Hannibal Lokumbe: Spiritual Soundscapes of Music, Life, and Liberation*

Laura E. Helton, *Scattered and Fugitive Things: How Black Collectors Created Archives and Remade History*

Sarah Phillips Casteel, *Black Lives Under Nazism: Making History Visible in Literature and Art*

Aïssatou Mbodj-Pouye, *An Address in Paris: Emplacement, Bureaucracy, and Belonging in Hostels for West African Migrants*

Vivaldi Jean-Marie, *An Ethos of Blackness: Rastafari Cosmology, Culture, and Consciousness*

Imani D. Owens, *Turn the World Upside Down: Empire and Unruly Forms of Black Folk Culture in the U.S. and Caribbean*

Gladys L. Mitchell-Walthour, *The Politics of Survival: Black Women Social Welfare Beneficiaries in Brazil and the United States*

For a complete list of books in the series, please see the Columbia University Press website.

I HEAR FREEDOM

The Great Migration, Free Jazz,
and Black Power

CISCO BRADLEY

Foreword by
GABRIEL JERMAINE VANLANDINGHAM-DUNN

Columbia University Press

New York

Columbia University Press
Publishers Since 1893
New York   Chichester, West Sussex
cup.columbia.edu

Copyright © 2026 Francis Bradley
All rights reserved

Library of Congress Cataloging-in-Publication Data

Names: Bradley, Francis R. author
Title: I hear freedom : the great migration, free jazz, and Black power / Cisco Bradley ; foreword by Gabriel Jermaine Vanlandingham-Dunn.
Description: New York : Columbia University Press, 2026. | Series: Black lives in the diaspora: past / present / future | Includes bibliographical references and index.
Identifiers: LCCN 2025036007 (print) | LCCN 2025036008 (ebook) | ISBN 9780231221566 hardback | ISBN 9780231221573 trade paperback | ISBN 9780231563802 EPUB | ISBN 9780231565370 PDF
Subjects: LCSH: Free jazz—History and criticism | African Americans—Music—History and criticism | Great Migration, ca. 1914-ca. 1970
Classification: LCC ML3508 .B73 2026 (print) | LCC ML3508 (ebook) | DDC 781.65/6—dc23/eng/20251216
LC record available at https://lccn.loc.gov/2025036007
LC ebook record available at https://lccn.loc.gov/2025036008

Cover image: *Albert Ayler Variant #2*. Painting by RA Washington. Courtesy of the artist.

GPSR Authorized Representative: Easy Access System Europe, Mustamäe tee 50, 10621 Tallinn, Estonia, gpsr.requests@easproject.com

To Imam Mutawaf Shaheed

CONTENTS

Foreword: Those Big Trees Over There, by Gabriel Jermaine Vanlandingham-Dunn ix

Introduction: Black Geographies, Networks, and Mobilities 1

PART I: BLACK NETWORKS AND LINEAGES

1. The Underground Railroad, Free Black Communities, and the Earliest Cultural Spaces in the Greater Ohio Valley 25

2. Post-Emancipation Mobilities: Reconstruction, Survival, and the Great Migration 42

3. Urbanization, Labor Struggles, the Blues, and the Great Migration: Industrialization and Cultural Space in the Early Twentieth Century 81

PART II: OLD AND NEW SOUNDS IN THE GREATER OHIO VALLEY

4. Cleveland: Jazz, Segregation, and Working-Class Aesthetics   117

5. Solidarity and Crisis in Detroit: The Detroit Artists' Workshop and the Forging of Radical Culture   156

6. "My Mind and My Spirit Were Liberated During the Riot": Faruq Z. Bey and Griot Galaxy in Detroit   202

7. Tribe: Collectivity, Self-Determination, and the Detroit Visionaries of the 1970s   237

PART III: OUTWARD MOVEMENTS

8. "Don't Be Scared to Tell Them the Truth": The Music of Albert Ayler in New York and Europe   257

9. Midwestern Drifter: Charles Tyler in California, New York, and France   298

10. Artistic Liberation Abroad: Frank Wright, Bobby Few, Muhammad Ali, and Alan Silva in New York and Paris   329

Conclusion: Legacies of Freedom in Sound   355

Acknowledgments   357
Notes   361
Bibliography   437
Index   467

FOREWORD: THOSE BIG TREES OVER THERE

For Mary, Mason, Michael, and Janice

It had to be 1993 or '94. Like many summers, my family packed into our vehicles and pulled out of 3805 Penhurst Avenue to start our long journey. We'd cut over to Coldspring Lane and turn onto I-83, which would take us to I-95. At some point, we'd end up on I-77, I-81, or I-85, depending on the weather, who was driving, and which route seemed the fastest from collective memory. If traveling by van, one of the uncles was driving, with my grandfather riding shotgun. My mother, aunt, and grandmother would be in the second row. The cousin section was always a mixed bag. I typically got dragged on these trips and didn't like going, while my older brother and our cousins his age stayed back in Baltimore.

Large chunks of the summers of my youth were spent in Gastonia, North Carolina, a small city just west of Charlotte. My mother and her siblings looked forward to the annual trip, while most of us who'd been born in Maryland weren't as excited. The weather was swampy; there wasn't much to do outside of church, funerals, and family get-togethers; and most of our southern cousins had a certain familiarity with us that we certainly did not have with them. However, something memorable did happen during the last trip we took together. My grandfather opened up a bit and spoke about a male relative who'd been chased down and tied to "one of those big trees over there" (pointing to a large field about a half hour away from our destination). As much as I didn't enjoy much of these road trips, I can say with certainty that this remains one of my deepest memories of my grandfather.

A few years later (I had to be in my late teenage years by then), our Gastonia family came up to Baltimore for a visit. There was food, talk of the Lord, and singing, as usual. On this special occasion, an elder relative (whom I'd never seen before or ever saw again) started preaching a bit. This wasn't common at our functions, save for someone who was a pastor or deacon (such as my grandfather). This gentleman had to be at least seventy-five years old and had a voice crossed between David Ruffin and Charley Patton (whom I'd not heard of yet). I remember being fascinated by the sounds coming from his small, frail body as everyone either joined in or encouraged him to keep going. I don't think I've heard such a powerful voice since that day in Owings Mills.

It wasn't until my early thirties that I began to think about my family within a historical framework. My grandparents were both born in the early 1920s and met relatively young. They moved to Baltimore after Bethlehem Steel launched facilities in the city, like so many folk who settled in the city. They were all looking for nicer living conditions, better employment opportunities, and, most importantly, a better life away from *the Klan*. My elders didn't speak much about their direct experiences with racism to us kids, but our parents were aware of the daily difficulties that the terrorist group brought to the doorsteps of Black folk just trying to live.

My teenage years were filled with concern over the increasingly dangerous landscape of Baltimore and my ever-changing identity as a young Black male. During these turbulent years, my soundtrack was mostly hip-hop, coming mainly from New York. Groups like KMD, De La Soul, and Gang Starr filled my head with digestible life lessons and well-produced rhythms. I'd had a familiar relationship with jazz through sample recognition, and I was quickly learning through collecting old records. When I started working at the Sound Garden (Baltimore's largest independent record store), my understanding of music, regionalism, and my relationship with it all was cemented. My first exposure to the New Thing (free jazz, avant-garde music, whatever) was through two CD reissues. John Coltrane's *Meditations* (Impulse Records, 1966) and Archie Shepp's *Mama Too Tight* (Impulse Records, 1967) both shifted my life path for the better.

Like many first-time listeners, I immediately became obsessed with Trane, devouring whatever releases I could find, regardless of format. This was not completely new for me since I'd been collecting records for years, but a fast-growing understanding of Black cultural production was emerging, and the passion spread to my expanding knowledge of other musicians. Through liner notes and personnel credits, I quickly developed lists of my favorites on their respective instruments and, most importantly, a timeline of cultural and musical events dating back to the early 1900s. I learned that musicians such as Trane, Thelonious Monk,

Max Roach, Bill Lee, and the illusive Lewis Worrell were all from North Carolina, and I developed a sense of pride for my family's Gastonia roots. With these folk traveled more than just memories and legacies but musical traditions dating back to *you know when and where* and a collective folk knowledge of how to create music that expressed the vastness of *all* our life experiences.

When my dear friend, colleague, and brother, Dr. Cisco Bradley, began his Migration Project, I was grateful that he shared with me so much of his research and freely asked my opinions on framing the narratives of musical luminaries and extensive historical networking. Our countless hours talking about figures such as the Ayler brothers, Charles Tyler, Charles Gayle, Bobby Few, Dave Burrell, Alan Silva, Frank Wright, Frank Lowe, Cecil Taylor, and William Parker gave me insight into how much he cared about the legacy of this music and, more importantly, the people and circumstances that produced it and what the current environment surrounding Black music looks like. Knowing that he was using the academic, professional, and personal resources afforded to him made the process that much more rewarding, demonstrating that there are concrete ways for non-Black folk to show up, compensate, and do the hard work in setting the American record straight. In the introduction to this book, he states: "Not only was music taught and passed down in families but an aesthetic value system was also inherited that defined music and its social place before and after the movement of people to the north. I argue, therefore, that Black families were the deepest reservoir and most important social unit for the maintenance, development, and transmission of American music before the rise of the record industry and radio broadcasting and that families have remained integral to the process up to the present time."

What should stand out to the reader is not just an emphasis on Black people being centered regarding the reclamation of art that has been created by us and our unique experiences (along with hyperspecialized skills) but also the wider measuring of the American landscape as our collective canvas, forced to toil on with little to no ownership of what we've contributed. In the liner notes for *Mama Too Tight* (1967), Archie Shepp wrote: "The point is that music which was endemic to and once was accessible to people (I mean the poor) has now been taken away and systematically moved to middle class, more commercially viable areas, with the result that many of today's youngsters in the ghetto situations are totally unaware of their own contribution to world music culture."

It doesn't sit well with me that this music that I hold so near and dear has been overrun with the white and the wealthy. Record labels, universities across America, and internet resellers all play a role in the continued gentrification of jazz, even going so far as to become gatekeepers of the output and product . . . while never lifting a finger for the community that created the music out of expressive necessity. In recent years, we've seen many of our musical heroes transition into ancestors, and many of them lived without reaping the full benefits of their work. Meanwhile, anyone (and everyone, it seems) with access to Discogs or eBay has the chance to make more money off of an album than its creator did without any thought or care for the community that the document might represent. And then there are the "improvisational music scenes" that have popped up in major cities around the world, using the expressive methods developed by Black Americans, who are rarely acknowledged as the creators as such.

This music was never meant to entertain the masses or become synonymous with or simplified to "technique" or dehistoricized "musical pedagogy" at Zionist-friendly institutions reserved for upper-class and international students. Nor were these creators satisfied with visions of sitting comfortably in seats at the tables of those forcing them into survivalist migration. The aim was to rip every door of the house from its hinges, bust out all windows of the building, and set the property ablaze, making sure that no one will ever again inhabit the place that kept us, the forced laborers of this stolen land, out in the cold in the first place.

Even though they've been gone for years, I often wonder if my grandparents would sway back and forth like I do while listening to *Spiritual Unity*... hopefully knowing that their hardships and sacrifices were not in vain.

Gabriel Jermaine Vanlandingham-Dunn
Brooklyn, New York
March 7, 2025

INTRODUCTION

Black Geographies, Networks, and Mobilities

This book began with a simple question: Where did the saxophonist Albert Ayler come from? I posed this query to myself during a research trip to his birthplace of Cleveland in June 2021. Of course, by asking this question, I meant much more than his immediate circumstances. What elements from his parents and community contributed to the formation of his unique musical aesthetic? Is it possible to find traces of influence going back deep into the history of American music and, if so, along what trajectories? And what did he and his contemporaries do with these inherited pieces of cultural matter in forming their own revolutionary approach to music?

In January 2022, I met the bassist William Parker for breakfast at the Remedy Diner on the Lower East Side of Manhattan. At some point during the meal, he slid his phone across the table with two tracks for me to hear. The first was Ayler's well-known piece "Music Is the Healing Force of the Universe," the title track from his last studio recording. The arcing saxophone lines are triumphant and prophetic in Ayler's characteristically bold and defiant way. Parker then played one of the Library of Congress recordings of a field shout from the 1940s. As Parker noted, there was considerable resemblance. Parker was not alone in this observation; prominent writers, critics, and scholars have detected a similar aesthetic in the work of Ayler and others in the same era.[1]

Ayler was born in the north, in Cleveland, in 1936, geographically far from where field shouts originated as a part of the daily lives of his ancestors and millions of other people in the US south. But how might we account for these features of his music if he never heard such things directly? What cultural and aesthetic inheritance was bestowed to Ayler and other practitioners of free jazz of his generation? And how were these bits of cultural knowledge, intuition, insight, process, tradition, and innovation transmitted? How were those echoes captured by the brilliant wave of creative musicians who emerged in the 1960s and 1970s? And what did they forge from these collected aesthetics?

To look for answers to these questions, we must examine how cultural production emerged out of migration, collective action, and community formation and dissolution. To see the broad, historical processes that resulted in the genius of free jazz in the 1960s and later, we must admit that the process of cultural production is complex and stretches far beyond the work of particular individuals, that their creative spark and vision were the final link in a chain of events that may trace back generations. This book seeks to follow the vital strands, some fragmentary, that inform our understanding of the complex web of geographies, mobilities, and networks that made the wave of free jazz in the 1960s and 1970s possible.

Since 2013, I have conducted nearly five hundred oral history interviews with musicians working in creative, improvised music, especially free jazz. The most striking thing to emerge from these conversations is how my interviewees came into contact with and began playing the music. Whereas the vast majority of white respondents had their first meaningful relationship with the music within institutions such as schools and universities or by listening to records, well over 95 percent of Black respondents cite family connections as the primary source of their musical interests and early training. Whether parents, grandparents, great-grandparents, aunts, uncles, or cousins, such connections have been central to the nurturing of America's musical culture over the past two centuries. In this book, I analyze Black musical-familial lineages as one of the primary repositories for the creation and reproduction of musical knowledge and aesthetics since the late eighteenth century. This legacy constituted, through a multigenerational process, the invention of free jazz in the mid-twentieth century. Not only was music taught and passed down in families but an aesthetic value system was also inherited that defined music and its social place before and after the movement of people to the north. I argue, therefore, that Black families were the deepest reservoir and most important social unit for the maintenance, development, and transmission of American music before the rise of the record industry and radio broadcasting and that families have remained integral to American music up to the present time.

MOBILITY AND MUSIC MAKING

The Great Migration from 1916 to 1970 constitutes the largest internal mass movement of people in the history of the United States, and it resulted in the production of most twentieth-century forms of American music, including blues, jazz, and gospel as national musical forms and the invention of rhythm and blues, soul, Motown, free jazz, rock and roll, funk, and hip-hop. Numerous literary, artistic, and performance movements also sprang out of the same migration. Thus, the Great Migration must be understood as the single most culturally productive process in the history of the United States.

The migration of at least six million African Americans from the US south to the north and west was a profound redrawing of the social fabric of the country. Not only did it create Black urban neighborhoods outside of the south, but it also populated them with people who formerly had lived in a diverse range of places, possessing a variety of cultural practices, aesthetic values, and political and social outlooks that could only have been fused through this unique migratory process.

Four particularly potent migratory zones emerged out of the Great Migration that contributed to the emergence of free jazz: from the deep south and the upper south into the greater Ohio Valley, especially Cleveland, Detroit, and Buffalo; from the Mississippi Delta, east Texas, and Oklahoma either to the West Coast, particularly Los Angeles and Oakland, or north to Memphis, St. Louis, and Chicago; from the Virginia-Carolina piedmont and northern Florida to Philadelphia, Baltimore, and Washington; and from the coastal regions of Virginia, Carolina, and Florida to New York and New England. Each of these zones possessed unique bloodlines of imagination, aesthetics, ideas, and politics, even if some elements were shared across zones. This book examines the first of these zones in depth: the greater Ohio Valley.

The greater Ohio Valley is defined not as a static geographical unit but rather as a fluctuating point of destination, a region defined and redefined by human mobility. As people moved north at different stages, they found refuge or built communities in a variety of locations. The southern edges of the greater Ohio Valley, primarily situated along the Ohio River, constituted many of the earliest sites of settlement, connected to both free Black and Underground Railroad networks emanating out of Kentucky, Virginia, North Carolina, and Maryland. But as time went on, it was the great industrial centers of Lake Erie, namely, Cleveland, Detroit, and Buffalo, that developed the greatest cultural gravity throughout the region.

The study of Black musical-familial lineages within this context reveals new historical unities outside of the industrial north that are informative for how we understand the development of free jazz. Rather than some random distribution of origin points, these lineages often lead back to common geographical pockets, especially in the Black Belt region from eastern Mississippi through Alabama to west-central Georgia. Three of the great tenor saxophonists to emerge in the greater Ohio Valley, Albert Ayler, Charles Gayle, and Faruq Z. Bey, trace their origins to a small cluster of counties in western Alabama, for instance, where their families dwelled for generations within a unique sociopolitical-cultural zone. Other common points of origin can be identified across the central Alabama Black Belt, in small towns in central Georgia, and in the eastern Mississippi city of Meridian. These southern geographical unities open avenues for understanding the multigenerational cultural processes that brought free jazz into being, and this methodology provides a blueprint for a much broader reexamination of the history of American music with Black lineages as a centerpiece of that development.

Beyond sound, the study of musical-familial lineages affords us the opportunity to examine a deeper social history of the music and its origins. As people moved from rural to urban settings and fought their way into the industrial working class, they also achieved new social unities through collective struggle. Through this process, a working-class consciousness arose that was the result of a matrix of forces that included unions, employment that afforded mobility, and a sense of solidarity with their fellows that sometimes extended across racial divides in the face of repression, exploitation, and violence carried out by state and capitalist forces. A history of resistance emerges from these harrowing struggles, journeys, and attempts at collectivism.

The cultural theorist Fred Moten advanced an acute critique, stating, "Performance is the resistance of the object. The history of blackness is a testament to the fact that objects can and do resist." Aunt Hester's scream, taken from Frederick Douglass's well-known account of witnessing gruesome violence against his aunt, roots Moten's analysis of what he terms "the transference of a radically exterior aurality that disrupts and resists certain formations of identity and interpretation by challenging the irreducibility of phonic matter to verbal meaning or conventional musical form."[2] Or, as Moten later wrote, "Aunt Hester's scream is diffused in but not diluted by black music in particular and black art in general."[3]

To understand the products of this irruption, Moten argues that "Blackness, in all of its constructed imposition, can tend and has tended toward the experimental achievement and tradition of an advanced, transgressive publicity. Blackness is, therefore, a special site and resources for a task of articulation where immanence is structured by an irreducibly improvisatory exteriority."[4] Thus Moten establishes that Blackness is a particular site of resistance that has developed particular vocabularies for its articulation, methods of survival, and codes of opacity. He defines resistance, improvisation, and incessant demands for autonomy as prevailing undercurrents in the formulation of Black sonic culture. This book carries this theoretical understanding through all the webs of its narrative.

Histories of violence and resistance may be uncovered in many ways, but an examination of lineages provides a spatial orientation and a personal tether to those narratives. Scales of violence varied from place to place, and they informed how resistance was articulated as people sought every means to combat lynching, Jim Crow, and restrictions to mobility and employment that were imposed by the prevailing power structures. Networks emerged, even across vast distances, to disrupt those scales and to formulate havens of autonomy. Music has been central to the public display of that resistance throughout the entirety of the post-Emancipation United States.

In particular, this book weaves together narratives of resistance articulated by freedpeople, spirituals, pre-blues, blues lyrics, and labor organizers with figures in the Black Arts Movement, Black Power movements, and other theorists of Black experimentality in the 1960s and 1970s. In so doing, I advocate for a broader historical understanding of the emergence of free jazz in the era of civil rights and Black Power. Musicians from that time had new visions but were very much in dialogue with ancestors who had forged paths of resistance over the previous century.

The study of lineages also reveals narratives of journeys. Local, regional, and national movements of people forged vast networks that facilitated mobility, communication, and social cohesion even against intense repression. Rivers and railroads were the means of escaping labor exploitation as people sought new realities. Families were the central, cohesive units that moved along these avenues, and they were the repositories of memory and music. When free jazz emerged in the mid-twentieth century, it spoke to the multigenerational journey people had undergone and fiercely demanded and displayed a greater freedom.

Migration and the emergence of free jazz communities in the greater Ohio Valley involved a complex network of families, communities, churches, semiautonomous spaces, and short- and long-distance communications from the time of the Underground Railroad up until World War II. The free jazz that emerged there possessed unique qualities not present in the free jazz of other zones of the United States where the music emerged during the same period in the 1960s and 1970s, especially in the aesthetics that its practitioners drew from the southern Black Belt. This book examines the deep historical processes that brought this musical movement to life in Cleveland and Detroit and the role that waystations such as Memphis, Louisville, and Indianapolis also played in the building of cultural networks.

These northern industrial cities were the destination of many thousands of Black migrants from the south who were escaping the exploitations of sharecropping, communal violence, landlessness, prejudice, and poverty. These mobile people, whether from rural areas or southern industrial cities, were urbanized and ghettoized in the north in a way that allowed for vital, dynamic cultural districts to emerge around the idiom of jazz, blues, and other cultural forms.[5] In traveling north, people carried music with them that included spirituals, blues, gospel, and various vocal and rhythmic traditions. In Cleveland and Detroit, these many strands mixed together, drawn from central and western Alabama, eastern Mississippi, the Georgia piedmont, the Florida panhandle, the Mississippi delta, and the Ohio River borderland. This fusion resulted in the formation of a dynamic cultural reservoir from which participants in the Civil Rights and Black Power movements could draw inspiration and models for being.

Mobility was at the heart of cultural change in the greater Ohio Valley. This stood in sharp contrast to the preexisting conditions south of the Mason-Dixon line, where movement was so heavily restricted.[6] As the historian Stephanie Camp argues, "That enslaved people were willing to risk gruesome punishments for the sake of a degree of mobility speaks volumes about its importance to them," and this demand for mobility continued into post-Emancipation society wherever people moved.[7] Existing scholarship on the earliest Black communities has focused primarily on political and economic outcomes. Joe William Trotter Jr. for example, examines the rise of the working class in these geographies while paying attention to flows of people and goods and the rise of industry along the Ohio River with a mostly east-west trajectory.[8] Keith P. Griffler offered one of the first detailed studies of Black involvement in the Underground Railroad throughout the greater Ohio Valley and showed how stations and flows of people were facilitated through a network of rural settlements.[9] Cheryl Janifer LaRoche offers an innovative leap forward with her study of networks and nodes as zones of resistance, particularly the involvement of free Black communities already present across the greater Ohio Valley in the building and maintenance of the Underground Railroad.[10] Darrel E. Bigham equates Black society to the growth of churches in the region before and after the Civil War.[11] Building on this scholarship, I consider a range of semiautonomous spaces where the genesis of culture was possible.

Mobility represented change on many fronts. At the forefront of these changes were power dynamics between Black workers and white employers; thus, the emergence of the music here is contextualized within broader labor history. The children of freedpeople and sharecroppers became railroaders, and a subsequent generation became industrial workers, fighting every step of the way for better pay, safer conditions, and collective power. Musicians, too, were in a constant fight for better pay and working conditions, but they were also in a position to publicly express the frustrations of the broader struggle. Black neighborhoods in

Cleveland and Detroit also allowed for some Black businesses to emerge and for a Black middle class to gradually take hold that ultimately produced some of the musicians. Still, the revolutionary politics that accompanied free jazz were almost always rooted in a working-class ethos that demanded deeper, more fundamental change than the middle class was willing to risk.

Mobility was a measure of freedom that allowed people to potentially evade violence and exploitation by moving and establishing community with other people in a new location. The process was fraught with peril, but it was one way people left sharecropping, other coercive labor, and violent white supremacist systems in the south. The way that musicians practiced their craft in the Mississippi Delta and many other parts of the south often demonstrated their own form of mobility and freedom. As the niece of the blues guitarist Charley Patton once stated about him, "He just left when he got ready, because he didn't make no crops.... He was a free man."[12] Yet mobility always positioned people to face other challenges in their new environs.

Mobility meant shifting loyalties and social obligations for people who moved north. Entire extended families often moved together but were reconstituted spatially in the industrial cities of the greater Ohio Valley. Within these shifting familial contexts, instrumental music became an even broader practice among the second generation, the children of the migrants born in the north. Access to education and musical instruments both from within the family and in schools and community organizations resulted in the most musically oriented generation in the history of the United States. By the time that many of the second generation were born between the mid-1930s and the late 1940s, the generation that would give rise to free jazz, this process had been somewhat institutionalized through schools, community centers, marching bands, churches, and night clubs.

Considerable research has examined the African origins of Black music and aesthetics over the past sixty years. One of the central aims of this book is to advance our knowledge of the process of this transfer via family networks in the full light of history, that is, in the century from Emancipation in the US south to the emergence of free jazz in the urban north in the 1960s, focused on the industrial cities of the greater Ohio Valley. Similar approaches could be employed to gain a better understanding of Black music across the United States in other regions and across all genres and may even provide clues as to how such transfers were maintained in earlier times.

Every major Black neighborhood in the United States had a jazz scene in the 1940s and 1950s. In Cleveland, Detroit, Buffalo, and other cities of the greater Ohio Valley, swing and bebop became the cultural vernacular of the first generation of migrants in the north. Clubs bred local talent and connected with other cities via touring networks that allowed for local scenes to be tightly connected to the national jazz culture. These sites were particularly vibrant and influenced the broader culture while also cultivating a multifaceted local milieu.

Spatial disruptions to jazz in the 1950s and 1960s, especially the building of the interstate highway system, cut through Black neighborhoods in most major US cities, tore the social fabric and upended the cultural dynamism present on the local level. The second generation, the children of the migrants, were to witness this, and it had a profound effect on their political outlook and cultural consciousness. Many had gotten a brief taste of the early jazz culture, whether it was late swing, cool jazz, or bebop, and watched it be dismembered by so-called urban renewal projects or suburban infrastructural changes that upended vital Black cultural districts. Or they witnessed desegregation, considered so vital for political reasons, destabilize urban Black cultural zones as people moved or were displaced through community transformations. These shifts spurred calls for revolutionary change in the years that followed. Thus, as political demands by Black residents crescendoed from the late 1950s to the mid-1970s as the second generation came of age, the free jazz that emerged reflected many of the same sentiments and aesthetics and even played a significant role in defining them. In what the historian Robin D. G. Kelley refers to as a "revolution of the mind," free jazz both contributed to and grew out of the Black Arts Movement and embodied the energy of revolutionary change.[13]

Free jazz was eclectic and multifaceted. African internationalism; other non-European influences, especially from the Middle East; the early roots of Afrofuturism; avant-garde modernism; and creative forms of composition all came together to form free jazz between the late 1950s and the mid-1970s. As the poet, essayist, and critic Larry Neal stated, "The so-called New Music represents at the core of its emanations the philosophical search of Black people for self-definition. Unlike the blues, its placement is more directed at our possibilities in the cosmic sense. . . . Max Roach and Donald Byrd showed the way; and there is still a lot of space left as [John] Coltrane, Pharoah [Sanders], and Albert [Ayler] indicate."[14]

As the Black Arts Movement grew, the music increasingly interacted with other performative arts, including dance, poetry, theater, and fashion. Throughout this time period, there existed regional variants that were on some level informed by the specific synthesis of communities in those locations but also were interconnected because of contemporary musical and artistic interactions and exchanges. In each of the sites discussed in this book, the music emerged contemporaneously with various Black Power movements, and many of its practitioners were deeply involved in Black nationalist movements wherever they lived. This symbiosis infused urgency and a specific political and social demand in the music as it developed.

FREE JAZZ IN CLEVELAND AND DETROIT

The Midwest has long been a site of musical innovation. From the 1930s to the 1950s, many of the defining jazz groups and big bands came out of cities like Kansas City, St. Louis, Memphis, Chicago, and Detroit. But by the late 1950s, much of the music was beginning to fall into a habit of repeating old forms and even repelling new ones. As the poet John Sinclair lamented rather dramatically in 1964, "the Midwest: where everybody's from and never stays," adding that the generation that was coming of age in the 1960s was searching for something distinctly new.[15]

Cleveland produced a fertile generation of musical visionaries, born in the decade between the middle of the Great Depression and the end of World War II. After gaining their earliest experience in Cleveland, most left for New York or Europe to gain recognition for their work. The most influential of these was the tenor saxophonist Albert Ayler (1936–1970), who made his first recordings in 1962 and burst onto the New York scene a few years later, an influence on and influenced by saxophonist John Coltrane.[16] His recordings of the mid-1960s, *Spiritual Unity*, *Bells*, and *Spirits Rejoice* on the ESP label were among the most influential free jazz records of that era.[17] Seemingly poised to carry the mantle of leadership within the community after the death of Coltrane in 1967, he met his own early death three years later, while leaving behind a monumental legacy.

Beyond Ayler, there were a number of important innovators who emerged around the same time or slightly later. The pianist Bobby Few (1935–2021), who knew Ayler in his youth, played in the Cleveland scene until around 1958, when he moved to New York to lead his own trio. Most of his innovative sessions came later when he worked with Ayler and after moving to Paris in 1969, where he was part of the group Center of the World with the saxophonist Frank Wright, bassist Alan Silva, and drummer Muhammad Ali.[18] Wright (1935–1990) was originally from Mississippi and grew up in Memphis but arrived in Cleveland as a young man. With roots in blues, rhythm and blues, and gospel, Wright forged his own voice on tenor saxophone as well. His recordings for the ESP record label in the mid- to late 1960s, as well as his involvement in Center of the World, established him as a significant innovator.[19]

The alto and baritone saxophonist Charles Tyler (1941–1992), originally from Indianapolis but who first met Ayler while touring as a young man in 1955, relocated to Cleveland in 1960 after a stint in the army. From that point on, he was a catalyst for things that were happening, as he commuted back and forth to New York, where he played with the saxophonist Ornette Coleman and drummer Sunny Murray and also appeared on some of Ayler's principal records at ESP. He made his own debuts as a leader on the label in 1966 but later moved to the West Coast, where he worked with the saxophonists Arthur Blythe and David Murray and trumpeter Bobby Bradford.[20] Returning to New York in 1974, he led a number of loft sessions and did additional important work with the pianist Cecil Taylor, drummer Steve Reid, and violinist Billy Bang.[21]

A number of additional, lesser-known musicians also made some key contributions to the music of the Cleveland circle. The trumpeter Donald Ayler (1942–2007) was a stalwart supporter of and contributor to his older brother's bands throughout the 1960s. Another trumpeter, Norman Howard (b. 1940) composed one of Albert Ayler's most well-known pieces, "Spirits," and made one recording as a leader that was released many decades later.[22] The alto saxophonist Arthur Jones (1940–1998) worked with Frank Wright and went to Paris with Sunny Murray, where he also worked with the trumpeter Jacques Coursil (1938–2020).[23] The bassists Earle Henderson (1937–2019) and Clyde Shy (later Mutawaf Shaheed, b. 1943) also worked with Albert Ayler at various points in the 1960s.

The greatest band to take root primarily in Cleveland itself was the Black Unity Trio, which came together in 1968. The group comprised the saxophonist Yusuf Mumin (b. 1944), cellist Abdul Wadud (1947–2022), and drummer Hasan Shahid (b. 1944). The group worked to extend the vocabularies started by John Coltrane but managed to establish their own perspective through the process before they broke up the following year.[24]

In Detroit, the community first formed around the writer John Sinclair and trumpeter Charles Moore in the Detroit Artists' Workshop. Collectivity and revolutionary politics surrounded the emergence of free jazz and other music at the time. But after corresponding fallout because of repression and political opposition, a second community formed after the Detroit uprising of 1967 and the social and cultural consciousness that occurred in its wake. Faruq Z. Bey and his band, Griot Galaxy, were at the forefront of the wave, contributing to the Afrofuturist avant-garde jazz movement of the city in the 1970s and 1980s.[25] The other significant development in post-1967 Detroit was the formation of the collective Tribe record label, led by the saxophonist Wendell Harrison (b. 1942), trombonist Phil Ranelin (b. 1939), and trumpeter Marcus Belgrave (1936–2015). In addition to the label, they published a quarterly magazine and issued a number of key recordings that displayed a different kind of free jazz, one that bore the influence of Motown and soul but was also rooted in the principles of avant-garde jazz.[26]

CHALLENGES

Given that the Great Migration was the watershed event in twentieth-century American social and cultural history, it may at first seem surprising that there has not been more written about it in the fields of history, migration studies, cultural studies, and ethnomusicology. But this is largely attributable to the fact that the data is immense and difficult to extract. Much of the recent scholarship has been spurred by the digitization of census data and other sources over the past twenty years, which has made it easier to analyze.

Studies of the Great Migration have not considered the long-term trajectories that informed free jazz or many other kinds of American music. James N. Gregory's work on what he terms "the southern diaspora" only examines its impact on jazz from the 1920s to the 1940s.[27] In James R. Grossman's definitive study of the Great Migration to Chicago, music is situated even more peripherally in the narrative.[28] Robert H. Zieger's study of race and labor in the United States, which covers the era of the Great Migration, does not include musicians in his scope of laborers during the period of great mobility or in its aftermath.[29] Isabel Wilkerson's book *The Warmth of Other Suns: The Epic Story of America's Great Migration* was a landmark synthesis that proved it was possible to capture the grand narrative of the migration while not losing individual stories in the process.[30] Following routes that led people to Chicago, Los Angeles, and New York, she subtly illuminates issues of class to show the complexities of the lives of people who were involved. Wilkerson has also spurred a broader cultural dialogue around the migration that extends well beyond the academy. Yet Wilkerson does not include music or jazz as central to her narratives of migration and redefinition.

Most existing studies approach the Great Migration from the perspective of demography in examining settlement patterns, sociologically in reference to family structures, or within the field of economic history as a means of charting the resulting change to Black financial outcomes. My approach makes use of social network theory in understanding how different flows of human movement intersected, conflicted, or supported one another. Or rather, I examine different parts of human movements that operated in tandem, even if the right hand did not always know what the left hand was doing. Broad networks spanning the

United States from south to north facilitated considerable human energy being translated into community building, social cohesion, and cultural production.

There is still a great amount of work to be done to understand the cultural impact of the Great Migration. This is for a number of reasons. Foremost among them is the general devaluation of Black culture within the matrix of American scales of value, both in terms of the prestige attached to such output and the financial remuneration to Black cultural workers. But there has been a particular and sustained disdain for Black experimentalists, rule breakers, and visionaries. This has had a deep impact on how free jazz has been received, judged, and rewarded.

Though there have been some critics who championed the music, the overwhelming response to Black experimentation has been delegitimization or exclusion. The bounds of legitimacy have often been girded by rules or structures that are meant to confine Black imagination, enforced often by white critics. *Down Beat*, for example, was the site of intense debate in the 1960s about what the musicologist Kwami Coleman terms the "aesthetic legitimacy" of free jazz.[31] Amiri Baraka, who wrote for *Down Beat*, was one of the music's champions, though Martin Williams and Nat Hentoff also supported the movement. Baraka identified the conservative tastes of the audience, "the listener who demands, even unconsciously, that every 'new' musician sound like someone he's already heard and digested."[32]

The majority critical reception was certainly negative. Those who attacked the music did it on a variety of levels, such as calling the ability or intent of the musicians into question.[33] Another common theme was to argue that the music had no value because it obstructed the rules, structures, or preconceptions of the jazz mainstream at the time. Black creativity was to be confined to particular tropes and to specific expressions within this thinking, bound by aesthetic laws imposed by a white power structure. At times, this systemic control was articulated quite explicitly, such as Taylor Castell's open letter to the readership of the magazine *Sound & Fury* in 1966, stating flatly to Baraka, "Yes, LeRoi, there is a white power structure."[34] Others took any critique of the white power structure as a violent act, displaying the fragility of whiteness when it was challenged publicly, with one writer describing Baraka's writings as a "venom-filled thrust from his dagger of hate."[35] The same writer also accused the saxophonist Archie Shepp of being a racial separatist bent on expressing grievances via identity politics.[36]

Ralph Gleason, one of the few champions of the avant-garde in the mainstream press, historicized the development of hostility, writing in 1968,

> Once jazz musicians decided that they needed new forms in which to work, they ran into incredible opposition. The parallel with the social revolution of black

people is obvious. When Ornette Coleman, John Coltrane, and Miles Davis opened up the scope of jazz and Archie Shepp, Albert Ayler, and Cecil Taylor began to define new musical concepts which were outside of the accepted framework of either the blues or the standard song form, and into a musical language based upon other assumptions, then the attack became severe. Jazz has been attacked since it began but this attack has resulted in the music getting very little exposure in person and almost none on the airwaves. The celebrated freedom of choice in music is paralleled by the political freedom of choice in many ways. It is hard for the neophyte to discover if he likes Cecil Taylor if he never hears him.[37]

As one enthusiastic fan wrote to the *Vancouver Sun* in 1969, "If only the uninformed general public's ears could be tuned to such worthwhile Canadian and American artists as Paul Bley, Albert Ayler, Cecil Taylor, and progressed to real electronic music such as the beautiful Stockhausen and Oliver Messiaen classical works, we would progress."[38]

Nat Hentoff was one of the few mainstream jazz critics who understood the sincerity of the intentions of the music. He wrote,

I remember conversations with John Coltrane, Ornette Coleman, Don Cherry, Pharoah Sanders, and Albert Ayler in which they kept emphasizing their conviction that music could be a liberating, a unifying force—a way of transcending present tensions and divisiveness by pointing toward a style and sound of life that would be natural, spontaneous, emotionally direct, and loving.... I've come to realize that what powered all these musicians was ... a belief in the perfectibility of man. And there was the further belief that music can be an essential way of energizing those listeners who also want more of life than existing in little boxes.[39]

Another writer put it more simply, stating, "The seeds of a cultural revolution are within the new sounds of people like John Coltrane, Ornette Coleman, Pharoah Sanders, Albert Ayler, and Sun Ra."[40]

If the negative and racist, "outsider" characterizations had been passing phases in communal thinking, the music might have moved on to better reception as the years passed. But many of these tropes only deepened as time went on. Picked up and repeated, the questions of aesthetic legitimacy have effectively remained at the forefront of the cultural dialogue surrounding free jazz up to the present time. The tenors of this debate reached a crescendo in the 1980s, with the critic Stanley Crouch working as what the writer Ishmael Reed has characterized as doing "hatchet jobs" for the neoconservative white establishment against Black artists, musicians, and writers they saw as "troublemakers."[41] Crouch used the *Village Voice* as a platform to attack a broad range of Black artists who strayed too far from the bounds set by the enforcers of aesthetic conformity. Over the course of his career, he attacked Amiri Baraka, Snoop Dogg, Alex Haley, Spike Lee, Tupac Shakur, Cornel West, and Cecil Taylor, among others. These reviews were not without their own context, the rise of the conservative jazz establishment embodied by Jazz at Lincoln Center, and are now seen as key building blocks in the legitimization of that institution at the expense of free jazz in New York. These narratives were further cemented with Crouch and Wynton Marsalis heavily advising Ken Burns's ill-informed and polemical documentary *Jazz* (2001).

It is also crucial to note that while free jazz generally faced opposition in the mainstream American press, it was often embraced and heralded as progressive, innovative, or genius in the mainstream press internationally in Canada, England, Australia, and elsewhere. These foreign outlets rarely questioned the music's artistic legitimacy. Many critics abroad also displayed a far more nuanced understanding of the music's historical origins, relevance, and new aesthetic expressions.[42]

At the time, some people understood one of the other problems that the music faced was that it required a new environment in which to be digested. There was a growing sentiment among musicians in the 1960s to be regarded as artists instead of entertainers. The trumpeter Bill Dixon stated, "Those who seek entertainment of the sort that has previously been indigenous to jazz will have to look elsewhere."[43] Club owners were generally not interested in the artistic merit of the music; they were just trying to fill their establishments with a well-trodden formula. Concert halls were sometimes too large for the relatively small audiences that the music initially drew. Or as Ralph Gleason observed, "The coffeehouses which flourish in the enclaves of bohemia and near the colleges are more important as incubation spots for the new jazz talent than the old jazz club and the off-night jam session."[44] Free jazz had new social implications, and because of this, it was deeply misinterpreted by the existing jazz establishment.

A number of studies of avant-garde music implicitly claiming universality have excluded free jazz altogether. The clearest case is the encyclopedic work edited by Larry Sitsky, *Music of the Twentieth-Century Avant-Garde*, which does not even include Ornette Coleman or John Coltrane, not to mention any of the other Black experimentalists of the 1960s or since. Positing the universal while excluding certain groups of people is a colonial method of establishing supremacy via spotlighting the self while silencing and devaluing the other.

Despite intellectual resistance to this branch of Black creativity, some recent studies have revealed some of the social and cultural processes that brought it to life, especially in New York. Michael Heller's book on the jazz lofts of the 1970s illustrates the setting for much of the experimental music of that decade, as he investigates issues of self-determination and the DIY movement in that era.[45] No comprehensive study has addressed either the 1960s free jazz movement or the Downtown scene of the 1980s to 2000s, though some have examined particular circles or individual artists or subscenes in those eras.[46]

While the reception of the music in New York often faced cold critics and jazz club owners, there have been very few studies of the reception of free jazz in other parts of the country. The musicologist and musician George Lewis's study of the Association for the Advancement of Creative Musicians, charting the rise of the organization in Chicago, remains the landmark study of American experimental music since World War II.[47] Meticulously researched, the book relies on his own connection to the community of musicians that he analyzed and his decades of experience in the music scene. Benjamin Looker's work on the Black Artist Group in St. Louis also sheds insights into another potent site of Black experimentalism outside of New York.[48] Steven Isoardi's social history of the music in Los Angeles, especially within the sphere of the Pan Afrikan Peoples Arkestra, is another landmark study of the development of the music on the grassroots level.[49] Yet none of these previous studies examine deeply the roots of the community before they arrived in northern or western cities.

Valerie Wilmer's vital book, based largely on oral history, remains the authoritative volume on the emergence of free jazz in New York in the 1960s.[50] Her methodology remains an inspiration on how to record and document the sociocultural dialogues around an art form and informs how I have conducted interviews for my own work. Amy Abugo Ongiri's work situates free jazz within the context of the Black Arts Movement but does not connect it to community development, migration, or geography.[51] In sociology, Philippe Carles and Jean-Louis Comolli's work and that of Ekkehard Jost's preliminary study remain some of the most insightful early studies of the music, but this scholarship was published in 1971 and 1975, respectively, and does not offer a substantial historical basis for its understanding.[52]

On the industrial Midwest, M. L. Liebler's collection *Heaven Was Detroit* stands out as a landmark, alongside a few other city-focused studies.[53] No monograph has been entirely dedicated to free jazz from the region. This is, at least in part, attributable to the economic decline of the region and the outmigration of both its artists and intellectuals in the period after 1970. Pairing this with the cultural elitism present in music criticism with a national reach that has always been situated in places like New York and Los Angeles, a systemic process has undervalued or ignored cultural production in places outside the metropoles.

Despite all of this, Cleveland and Detroit were the sites of the emergence of unique and innovative musicians who played a central role in advancing free jazz on a national and international level. This is the first comprehensive study to address the roots of this music in these cities and to look at them comparatively alongside each other.

Most histories of Black community formation in the greater Ohio Valley focus on political developments or labor movements. Beth Tompkins Bates, for example, examines the emergence of an industrial working class in Detroit but does not connect this history to cultural workers or music.[54] In a similar vein, Kimberley L. Phillips illustrates Cleveland's working class and discusses religious influence from the Black Belt but does not examine the emergence of jazz or any other music there that resulted from the Great Migration.[55] Musicians have generally not been included in discussions of labor, social movements, or political organization in these sites.

APPROACHES

Historically, most music that has been created in the United States has involved considerable human mobility. A band itself is a meeting place of people often coming from different points of origin. Migrations, whether small or vast, are often hidden in the prehistory of the music-making process and have been often ignored as a means for understanding the emergence of new musical forms in particular places. This book examines movements of people into the greater Ohio Valley and how they managed to form particular communities, how cultural autonomy became manifest in certain sites within those communities long before the advent of recorded music, and how those measures of autonomy were maintained and passed down through the generations. This constitutes the social and cultural inheritance of a network of communities over time and how they ultimately invented their own strains of free jazz in Cleveland and Detroit.

One of the blind spots of jazz studies is embedded in the idea that most cultural innovation is spurred by unique, individual genius, or "the big man."[56] This has distorted how we have interpreted cultural production on many levels in scholarly writing as well as in the popular press. Inherent in this way of thinking is the obsession in identifying the individual as the sole source of the creative spark; this fits within some of the larger national dogmas that undergird ways of thinking as pervasive as the American Dream. While this study is not in denial of genius-level thinking especially present in Black experimentalism in the mid-twentieth century, it seeks to look for the social and cultural influences that gave such ideas broad cultural capital in the period. In other words, the emergence of ideas in different sites cannot be merely explained by one artist influencing another. I try to understand each artist's social world as a way of delving into their thinking and outlook, and I consider what social and political contexts spurred experimentation. Was it a reimagining of the present? A rejection of convention? A declaration of autonomy or solidarity? Of revolution? Naturally the answers are no less diverse than the questions.

It seems that the answers to these questions cannot be found merely by looking at the cultural politics of the 1960s, and therefore this study searches for deeper undercurrents and networks of people who built and reproduced an array of social and cultural values over the century before the emergence of the revolutionary principles embedded in free jazz. Something as powerful and complex as cultural production cannot be easily reduced to the individual but rather must be seen as the product of a matrix of participants, values, spaces, and histories within which individual genius may manifest.

To examine the networks that gave rise to free jazz in the greater Ohio Valley, I draw upon a number of sources. First, to illustrate the voices and actions of the musicians themselves, I collected many dozens of oral histories with musicians and other artists, their family members, label owners, students, and audience members. Rich in detail and often relayed passionately, musicians spoke of their families and communities as sustaining entities that empowered them to act and contribute to the music. Furthermore, the oral histories are the vital link between migrations and family origins and the development of individual musical pursuits among the generation that gave birth to free jazz. These histories are vital documents of creativity and imagination and of social and political consciousness, and together they represent an archive never before assembled. The insights and observations of the artists form a counternarrative to the misunderstandings exhibited by critics about the music through the period. Because of the noncommercial nature of some of the music and how much self-production was involved, much of the music was not reviewed or recognized for its value in its own time; thus conversations with artists are particularly vital for understanding their aesthetic and artistic visions.

Furthermore, I project the value of the unique voices contained in oral histories forward into the writing process itself. While I naturally offer considerable commentary and analysis, there are many instances where I prefer to let the voices present in the oral histories speak for themselves without feeling the need to overanalyze or explain them. Many of the musicians discussed in this text were theorists of music and philosophers of life. They stand on firm ground and need not be hemmed in by overbearing hermeneutics. Whenever possible, I have placed musicians in dialogue with one another and also with writers, artists, and thinkers who contributed to related dialogues. My goal is not to always reach conclusions of finality but rather set to life voices upon the pages that follow and, at times, recognize the ambiguity or multiplicity present in these perspectives.

I have paired the oral histories with other archival materials such as censuses, newspapers, land deeds, tax rolls, military service records, court records, diaries, lyrics, poetic biography, and photographs gathered from local, state, and national archives that help illustrate the lives of the musicians and their families as they made the journey into and out of the greater Ohio Valley. This diverse set of data builds our social and cultural understanding of the world that existed around the music. Then to chart the work of the musicians, I drew from many out-of-print magazine interviews and other writings, often from the underground Black press of the mid-1960s to mid-1970s, that chart the intellectual conception of their own work. This tells a narrative quite different from the one created by mainstream critics. For complex and expressive music, these insider perspectives, too, are often vital in fully understanding the intentions of the artists.

OUTLINE: NETWORKS AND LINEAGES

Part 1 examines the social and cultural networks that allowed for the rise of Black creative music in the greater Ohio Valley. The first chapter traces networks to the late eighteenth century. The earliest sites of cultural production in the greater Ohio Valley linked to later developments were forged by people who had been manumitted or had escaped slavery and settled in the region before the Civil War. Though other Black communities preceded them, spreading westward from Pittsburgh along the Ohio River to places like Cincinnati, Louisville, and Evansville, these were often uncomfortably close to or within white settlements, where cultural autonomy was impossible. Autonomous networks may be traced to as early as about 1810 among small, rural, free Black communities in southern Ohio, many of which maintained connections to and directly sustained the Underground Railroad. Thus, the earliest vital cultural spaces were forged through a clandestine movement of people from south to north into and through the region, whether by passengers on the Underground Railroad or various free people who formed their own settlements. Though we often know very little about their specific cultural practices, nevertheless the measure of autonomy they gained, and the music and other cultural forms that they passed down to their descendants, is evidence that these early spaces were essential to later cultural developments.

Rural free Black communities were ultimately the most stable ones to form in the greater Ohio Valley before the Civil War. Most were sustained by more widespread land and property ownership than existed within small urban communities in the region during the same time period. These autonomous spaces allowed for the formation of a stronger social fabric, independent cultural forms and practices, and traces of a political culture. The free people of Roanoke, Virginia, manumitted en masse and relocated to southwestern Ohio in 1846, was one of the more visible settlements. Other smaller ones, such as Berlin Crossroads in southeastern Ohio, cofounded by descendants of Sally Hemings and Thomas Jefferson, as well as ancestors of the pianist Dave Burrell, were vitally connected to the Underground Railroad and became an early space for social, cultural, and political resistance.

Other free communities were more mobile and transregional while still connected to the greater Ohio Valley. These networks took root in southern Ohio by the 1810s, spreading northward, connecting to the Underground Railroad, and then creating satellites in the northwestern regions of the state by the 1830s and 1840s. There, a third-generation resident, Catharina Lucas, whose family had become successful hog farmers, married the prominent abolitionist Ezekiel Gillespie (1818–1892) of Milwaukee, forming a link between free networks across much of the Midwest. These networks continued to sustain communities after emancipation and proliferated gradually as other people migrated north and added additional layers to the social and cultural milieu.

Chapter 2 examines post-Emancipation networks. The flow of people from south to north, which had been a slow trickle before the Civil War, gradually increased in its aftermath but was not fully spurred until labor demands sparked widespread migration during World War I. The later free jazz communities that formed in the north traced their roots to a few specific geographies: a concentration of counties along the Mississippi-Alabama border, the west central Georgia piedmont, the Florida panhandle, the Mississippi delta, and the Kentucky edge of the Ohio River borderland. Each of these made its own imprint upon the community and their later aesthetics in Cleveland and Detroit.

Chapter 3 examines urbanization in the south and the emergence of waystations along the migration northward that allowed for the formation of communities and brought additional forms of social cohesion. Baptist and African Methodist Episcopal churches were paramount in the communal consciousness of people in the south and had a central impact on musicians in later generations in the north. One of the unifying factors was the process by which people survived, evaded, or escaped the violence of the Reconstruction era and its aftermath as white supremacy was revitalized across the former slave states.

The other unifier was the labor struggle, initially sparked in rural areas during Reconstruction where people worked as sharecroppers, often employing collective means to demand better conditions or pay. These early struggles were carried forward after a couple of generations into urban labor unions and campaigns by the early twentieth century in places like Mobile, Birmingham, Atlanta, Savannah, and Louisville, as well as rural struggles in the eastern Alabama Black Belt and southwestern Kentucky Black Patch, which were central to the formation of a working-class consciousness among people even before they migrated north. Places such as Indianapolis and Memphis, though not ultimately hubs of free jazz, nevertheless bore some imprint on a number of families that passed through them, even for generations, on their journeys north.

OLD AND NEW SOUNDS IN THE GREATER OHIO VALLEY

Part 2 takes a comparative look at the intersecting forces of desegregation, labor organizing, the rise of Black political consciousness, and how the formation of artist communities came together in different formations in each of the cities. A common working-class political ethos began to coalesce around a variety of approaches to Black liberation. Each city was a site for dynamic cultural change at an accelerating pace in the 1960s, though there were substantial differences in how the mechanisms of cultural production were ultimately harnessed in each of the cities.

Part 2 also focuses on the communities and movements that primarily remained in the region. Chapter 4 focuses on the formation of the Cleveland community and the emergence of Albert Ayler, Bobby Few, Frank Wright, and other musicians, set within the Black working-class politics of the post–World War II period. The chapter also provides a detailed analysis of the one great free jazz band, the Black Unity Trio, that remained in the city.

Chapter 5 examines the relationship between Black arts communities and labor organizing in Detroit in the 1960s. Figures such as the trumpeter Charles Moore and jazz poet John Sinclair were early arts organizers there, and they wed their practice with contemporary liberation struggles. All of these developments are understood in the wake of infrastructural projects that destroyed key parts of the Detroit jazz scene that had sustained the music in the preceding decades.

Chapter 6 then examines how Detroit after the 1967 uprising was a conducive space for the emergence of the saxophonist Faruq Z. Bey. Bey developed his own approach to the avant-garde in a series of different iterations of his band, Griot Galaxy, which defined the visionary Detroit sound of the 1970s and 1980s in clubs like Cobbs' Corner as well as the Detroit Institute of the Arts. The group advanced rhythmic innovations and its own brand of Afrofuturist imagery in their live performances and recordings.

Chapter 7 then turns to the other post-1967 development in Detroit, the collective record label Tribe, as it forged new sounds and built networks of self-determination and mutual aid in support of the community on a broad level. Musicians such as Wendell Harrison, Phil Ranelin, and Marcus Belgrave contributed to the collective, which established its own distinct sonic aesthetic, one bearing the influence of Motown and soul.

OUTWARD MOVEMENTS

Part 3 follows the movements and careers of musicians who chose to work primarily outside of the greater Ohio Valley region, especially in New York, Los Angeles, and Paris. Chapter 8 illustrates the rise of the tenor saxophonist Albert Ayler. He developed one of the most original sounds in the history of jazz, and this chapter considers how he reformulated field shouts, spirituals, blues, jazz, and rhythm and blues into his aesthetic. The chapter also follows his movement to New York and Europe as he sought audiences that were receptive to his innovations and how he developed a profound spirituality that informed much of his artistic vision.

Chapter 9 focuses on the saxophonist Charles Tyler and his move first to Los Angeles and then to New York and later Paris. Though Tyler mostly remained an underground figure, innovations in his work warrant a closer examination. His work in the jazz lofts in the 1970s, where he forged a unique sound on alto and baritone and built a community of collaborators around himself, was transformative. Curation and management of the Brook loft was also instrumental in projecting his work, and that of others, to a broader audience. The chapter closes with a look at his enduring legacy, one that is still playing out.

Chapter 10 examines the emergence of two other Cleveland musicians: the saxophonist Frank Wright and the pianist Bobby Few, who first went to New

York but spent most of their careers in Paris. In Paris they benefited from the cultural radicalism of post–May 1968 and found an eager audience (and several record labels) for their work. They joined with the bassist Alan Silva and drummer Muhammad Ali to form the band Center of the World, which had a major impact on the French and German free jazz scenes.

PART I
Black Networks and Lineages

CHAPTER 1

THE UNDERGROUND RAILROAD, FREE BLACK COMMUNITIES, AND THE EARLIEST CULTURAL SPACES IN THE GREATER OHIO VALLEY

THE EARLIEST BLACK COMMUNITIES IN THE GREATER OHIO VALLEY

The settling of the greater Ohio River Valley involved two intersecting human networks that both contributed to the formation of Black settlements in the region. The predominant one flowed east to west as settlers came from Pennsylvania, New York, New England, and Virginia into the river towns and the outlying rural areas. Pittsburgh was the key launching point for settlement of the region, and small Black communities developed in most of the early cities along the river almost from their inception. By 1810, for instance, nearly 4 percent of the Pittsburgh population was composed of free Black people.[1] From there, a network of cities along the Ohio River emerged. At the same time, Cincinnati and Evansville both witnessed the growth of small free Black communities.[2] Meanwhile, on the southern side of the river at Louisville, Kentucky, the city had approximately five hundred Black residents, though less than 2 percent of them were free. At the time of the emergence of these cities, the Ohio River simultaneously came to mark the division between free and slave states.

The invention of the steamboat accelerated the process of settlement throughout the entire region in the 1820s, leading to swifter westward migration and settlement and enabling regional trade networks to extend more readily to the Mississippi River and the Gulf of Mexico. Soon Cincinnati, which was 450 miles downstream from Pittsburgh, superseded the latter as the greatest of the river ports thanks to the trade that it attracted to its docks.[3] By 1832, a series of canals connected Cincinnati via the Miami River to Lake Erie and thus made it accessible for trade with East Coast American cities. It "brought the huge Hudson River and New York City markets within the orbit of Ohio River entrepreneurs."[4] But the canals declined as railroads became prevalent. By the 1840s, Cincinnati became the focal point of railway lines connecting it to St. Louis; the burgeoning Great Lakes industrial ports of Buffalo, Cleveland, Toledo, Detroit, and Chicago; and major ports of the East Coast such as Baltimore, Philadelphia, and New York via the Baltimore and Ohio Railroad.[5] Cincinnati was already a significant industrial center by the 1820s, when it became one of the centers of steamboat production and by the 1840s emerged as a major meatpacking center; by 1860, it ranked third among American industrial cities.

Louisville, just one hundred miles downstream from Cincinnati, also became a railway center, linked to Nashville and much of the deep south by the late 1850s, making it the largest industrial center in the south at the time.[6] Louisville, too, became a manufacturing and distillery center. Pittsburgh, Cincinnati, Louisville, and Evansville all saw meteoric rises in their populations by the mid-nineteenth century, driven by rural-to-urban migration as well as large-scale immigration primarily from Ireland and Germany but also from Wales, Northern Ireland, Switzerland, and France. Black communities in these early decades remained small, and many in Ohio remained rural until after the Civil War, when they began to move increasingly into urban areas.

Ohio was far from the Promised Land. At the 1802 constitutional convention, the proslavery faction only failed to legalize the practice by one vote. Nevertheless, Ohio's "Black Laws" passed in 1804, 1807, 1831, and 1838 institutionalized a second-tier status for Black people in the state, denying them access to the vote, barring them from serving on juries or in local militias, preventing them from serving in public office or testifying against white people, and denying them all of the basic civil services, including public education, asylums, and poorhouses.[7]

The east-west networks intersected and, at times, conflicted with the south-north networks that came to be collectively known as the Underground Railroad. These early networks of freedom and resistance were also the root of communities that would give rise to free jazz and were the genesis point for aesthetics of survival and resilience. Free Black people and people escaping slavery still generally viewed Ohio as preferable to Indiana or Illinois in the early decades of the nineteenth century because issues of slavery had not yet been fully solidified in the latter two states. By the time of the Civil War, Ohio had more Black settlements than any other state in the country.

THE EARLIEST CULTURAL SPACES 27

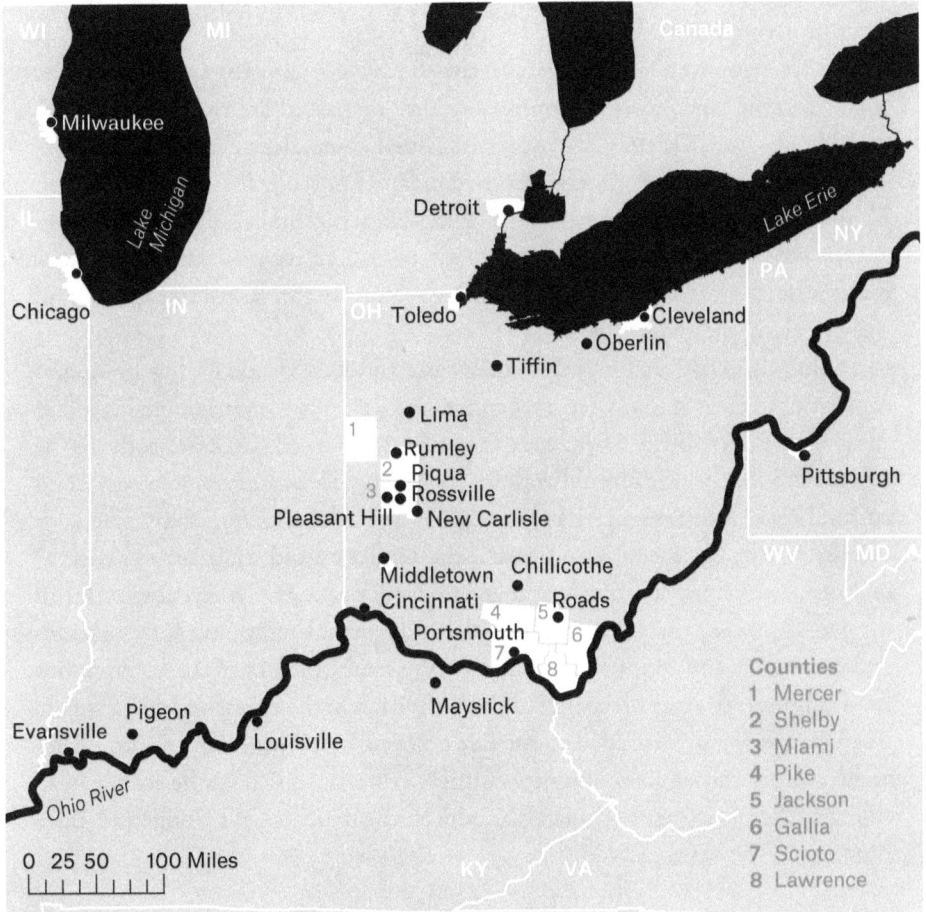

FIGURE 1.1 The Underground Railroad and free Black roots.

Source: Cartography by Alice Viggiani.

Black social networks in the greater Ohio Valley often stretched vast distances and connected people from not only disparate parts of Ohio but back into the south. These were tenuous networks in that they only managed to survive by the constant reinvigoration by dedicated members of the community, often at risk of their own peril. The Underground Railroad is of course the most prominent of these networks, but there were many others that grew out of free Black communities in the greater Ohio Valley as well that strengthened what would have otherwise been disconnected rural settlements. Overlaid upon one another, these intricate networks sustained these communities against systemic violence, economic and political encroachment, and consistent disenfranchisement and discriminatory laws.

By 1815, people escaping slavery in the south were entering Ohio and either began forging their own communities there or passed across Lake Erie into Canada. By 1817, Kentucky slave owners issued complaints that they were generally unable to recover people who had escaped north across the Ohio River. By 1820, some of the basic networks of the Underground Railroad had solidified in southern Ohio. By the 1830s, Lawrence County possessed some common routes for fugitives, and neighboring regions began to see an explosion of activity along the river.[8]

In this chapter, I will examine three case studies of particularly vibrant and important networks that were later connected to key musicians that emerged in the greater Ohio Valley. These were the earliest sustained Black networks in the region, and they set the groundwork for the emergence of autonomous social and cultural spaces throughout the region. The major development that came with the rise of free Black communities and the Underground Railroad was that, as opposed to the small communities that had developed in the cities, the rural farming communities possessed greater spatial and cultural autonomy. Or, as a member of one such community wrote in 1838, the establishment of the autonomous rural communities was a response to the "condition in the towns and cities" where Black people were "degraded to the last extreme."[9] In rural Black Ohio settlements, communities grew, and new cultural expressions and aesthetics began to emerge. These networks ultimately produced the pianists Call Cobbs and Dave Burrell and the bassist Clyde Shy.

FREE PEOPLE OF ROANOKE, VIRGINIA, IN MIAMI COUNTY, OHIO

Much of the pianist Call Cobbs's maternal side of the family arrived in west-central Ohio well before Emancipation, via a community of manumitted people from Virginia. Congressman John Randolph was an eccentric slave owner of Roanoke Plantation in Charlotte County, Virginia. His family had grown tobacco for generations, profiting off of enslaved laborers who worked the fields. Randolph refused to buy or sell any enslaved people during his tenure of ownership of the plantation, where more than one thousand people once were enslaved. In his own writings and speeches, he recognized the immorality of slavery and the slave trade, but he refused to relinquish his investiture in the system. He died in 1833, by which time the population of enslaved people on the plantation had dwindled to less than half their original number.[10] His heirs did everything they could to try to thwart his intention to manumit all of the enslaved people of Roanoke Plantation.

After much resistance, the 383 remaining enslaved people of the plantation were finally manumitted on May 4, 1846.[11] This group was described as primarily "old men and women . . . the proportion of able-bodied, middle-aged men and women to the children and old people was noticeably small."[12] Because Virginia law did not allow free Black people to remain within the state, Randolph made provisions in his will for them to be resettled elsewhere, leaving $38,000 of cash or real estate assets "to transport and settle the said slaves in some other state . . . giving to all above the age of 40 not less than ten acres each."[13] Judge William Leigh, the executor of Randolph's will, hired Samuel Jay of Mercer County, Ohio, to purchase land that was to be the site for the transplanted community. Jay ultimately obtained 3,200 acres in the southern part of the county by January 1846 with the aim of relocating them near to an already existent Black community of significant size.[14]

Setting out from Roanoke Plantation on June 10, 1846, Leigh accompanied the community first for eight days to Lynchburg via sixteen covered wagons. Then they proceeded through the mountains to Charleston and then to the Kanawha River, where Leigh chartered flat boats to take them to Cincinnati, arriving there on July 2, 1846, and then finally shifting to four boats on the Miami and Erie Canal that proceeded north toward their destination, passing through Dayton on July 7.[15] Throughout the overland trek, one of the leaders of the community, named John, "walked behind the procession with a staff."[16] Another of their number, Clem Clay, later recounted "going to the courthouse in Virginia, heard talk about [the freedmen] and telling them to pack their clothing, to go to Ohio. Had tents along, bought eatables along the road, sang songs in the evening, came on boats to Cincinnati from Kanawa."[17]

On July 5, 1846, the free people of Roanoke completed the five-hundred-mile journey at New Bremen but faced immediate opposition. Some of the hostility may have been sparked by reactionaries who were outraged by the fact that there was already a burgeoning Black settlement in the county, at Carthagena, with a population well over 250, with a school for their education, the Emlen Institute, founded by abolitionists.[18] Despite the fact that they had purchased land in advance for means of their own settlement and use, a white mob assembled by noon on the same day of their arrival, composed of "a large number of citizens" that "resolved that the contractor should remove them by 10 o'clock on Monday morning."[19] The opposition issued three resolutions:

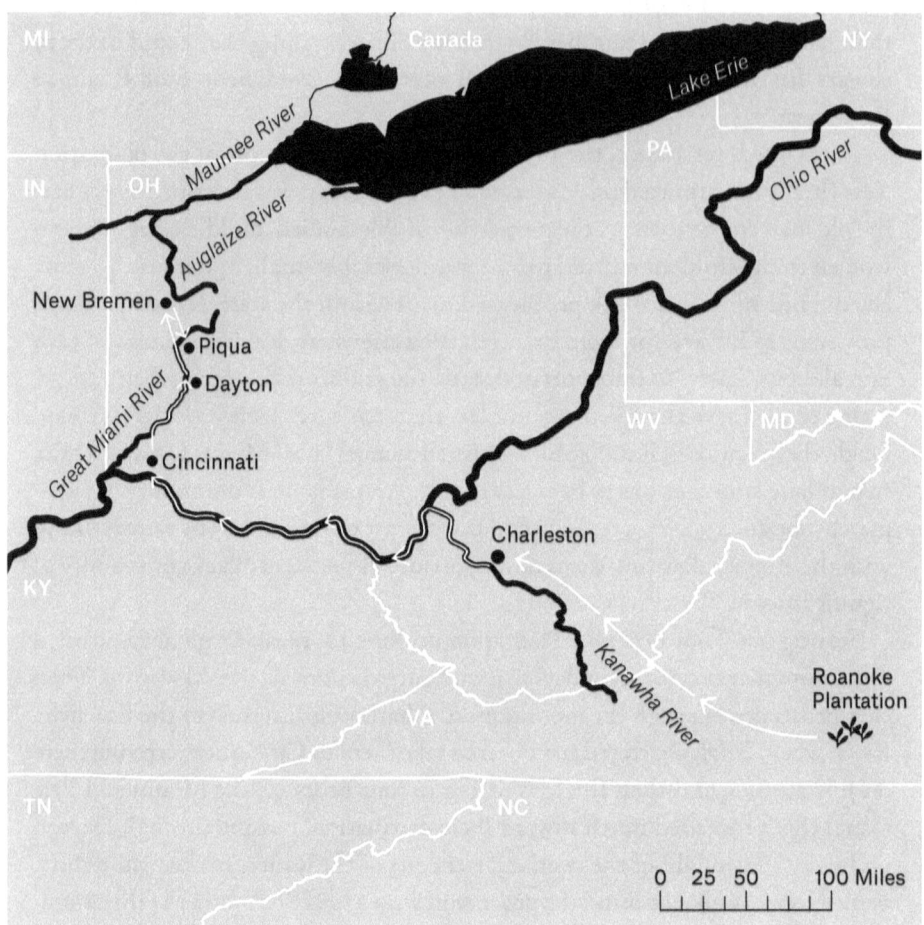

FIGURE 1.2 The journey of the freedpeople of Roanoke.

Source: Cartography by Alice Viggiani.

Resolved, That we will not live among negroes; as we have settled here first, we have fully determined that we will resist the settlement of blacks and mulattoes in this county to the full extent of our means, the bayonet not excepted.

Resolved, That the blacks of this county be, and they are hereby, respectfully requested to leave the county on or before the first day of March, 1847; and in the case of their neglect or refusal to comply with this request, we pledge ourselves to, remove them, "peacefully if we can, forcibly if we must."

Resolved, That we who are here assembled, pledge ourselves not to employ or trade with any black or mulatto person, in any manner whatever, or permit them to have any grinding done at our mills, after the first day of January next.[20]

The aforementioned custodian of the free people was Thomas Cardwell, who had been hired to bring them to their new land and who upon arrival requested three days to sort out the situation. Nevertheless, by that evening, the mob had grown and, "armed with muskets and bayonets, placed a strong guard around the camp, and took Cardwell into custody."[21] The people of Roanoke were forced back onto the boats and driven from the county by the mob. As one of the free people of Roanoke later stated: "It was with heavy hearts that we turned backward not knowing where we would be permitted to settle."[22]

One journalist observed at the time: "This part of Ohio has been noted for its abolition spirit. It appears, therefore, that while the abolitionists are very willing that the slaves should be set free in the South, they are not willing to receive them as neighbors."[23] Another journalist wrote: "These facts furnish a beautiful commentary upon the sympathy of the Abolitionists for the African race. No doubt, if these slaves had been runaways, the Ohio fanatics would have sheltered them without hesitation, and even resisted any attempt to restore them to their masters: but as they were free, their sympathies were at once congealed!"[24] Some Ohio newspapers spoke out, such as the *Cincinnati Herald* and *Anti-Slavery Bugle*, where an article appeared in mid-July 1846, exhorting the people of Mercer County and decrying the institution of slavery.[25]

From New Bremen, the free people of Roanoke retraced their route south on the river to the small town of Newport, "but meeting the same kind of reception, continued on down the canal to Piqua," where they disembarked.[26] Then they set up a camp "in a bend of the Great Miami river" and were allowed to "use as temporary camping grounds, part of what is East Ash St."[27] They again faced opposition by an armed mob of approximately one hundred men, and Judge Leigh had to flee to the nearby town of Sidney. However, there, "a public meeting was called that night at the Court House which was full, and without a dissenting voice, passed resolutions recognizing their right to settle—rebuking the exhibition of mob spirit, and pledging themselves to turn out if called on to sustain the laws and protect the negroes."[28] Nevertheless, throughout the ordeal, Leigh briefly entertained the prospects of resettling them much further afield, returning to Virginia, or taking them to Trinidad or Liberia, but ultimately he managed to settle about 150 of them in Miami County, with others "scattered at Piqua and Troy, with a few at Dayton."[29] Word eventually spread that Miami County was something of a haven compared to other parts of Ohio.

Many of them resolved to begin their new lives there or in the nearby area. Leigh, apparently, "with the ready money he had in his possession he bought small homesteads for the older members of the colony, in a suburb of Piqua, and found situations as laborers for the young men, and places as house servants for the young women—in many places securing homes for entire families on farms, and thus preventing, as far as possible, the separation of parents and children."[30] In some areas, Quakers played a role in obtaining homes and land for them.[31] The community was thereby fractured between four towns: Sidney, Piqua, Troy, and West Milton, in Miami and Shelby counties. More organic settlements eventually coalesced for the community and their descendants at Hanktown, Marshalltown, and Rossville, which they founded themselves, the last of which was the largest and most successful. A plot acquired in 1857 by William Rial, one of the leading figures in the community in Piqua, became the site of the first African Baptist Church and was the site of the African Cemetery.[32] Before the Civil War, Rossville was also an active stop on the Underground Railroad, and they had allies in some of the white Quaker communities of West Milton and the Wesleyan Methodist Church in Piqua.[33]

Political rights were hotly contested after the end of the Civil War. Despite having been a non-slave state, Ohio still had no intention of granting African Americans full or equal rights. In 1867, when an attempt was made to strike "white" from the Ohio constitution, it failed to pass, with about 54 percent of the voters opposed to the measure. Many public debates and newspaper articles of the time advocated for limited citizenship, especially around the issues of voting, representation on juries, and admission to schools.[34] Black political mobilization emerged as a force within the communities by the 1880s and ran several of their own candidates, but little more was possible when they constituted such a small minority within the overall population.

Informal schools opened soon after the arrival of the free people of Roanoke, but the first official Black school did not open until 1873. Schools emerged in the years after their arrival to these regions, and some of the younger members of the community had access to an education, first taught by white teachers but later by members, often women, of their own communities.[35] Much of the education focused on agriculture—the climate and crops of Ohio differed significantly from past labor they had done on tobacco plantations in Virginia.[36]

There is some trace in the record of the cultural practices that the free people of Roanoke brought with them. Some eyewitnesses noted that they danced "jigs" and sang songs, "while a 'hoe-down,' when one could be set in motion, was more fascinating.... I have seen boys of from 8 to 15 years dance and sing by the hour.... A refrain of one of their loveliest songs ran thus, repeated hour after hour, very monotonously, but without any apparent weariness:

> I Build My House in Baltimore;
> I Build My House in Baltimore;

I Build My House in Baltimore,
Three stories high."[37]

The singer stressed the word "three." Another song, usually sung by women, voiced a sense of melancholy and loss with the refrain:

Anymore, anymore;
Anymore, anymore,
I never come back, anymore![38]

"Day after day this refrain could be heard throughout the camp, almost without cessation, and far into the night," one observer noted during their initial arrival.[39]

Some of the people in the community survived the early decades in Miami County working as day laborers on nearby white-owned farms, but some did manage to acquire their own farmland over time. For example, one branch of Call Cobbs's family, going back to Geter Moton (c. 1820–1896), followed such a trend. Up until at least 1860, he hired out as a day laborer doing agricultural work.[40] But by 1880, he owned a small farm of ten acres, where he primarily raised hogs and chickens, as well as a few horses and cows, in addition to growing wheat, hay, and maintaining an apple orchard.[41]

Nearly all of the young men who were of appropriate age in the community enlisted in the Union army during the Civil War. Among them was Moton's eldest son, Pvt. Joseph Moton (1844–1913), who served in the 27th US Colored Infantry for about thirteen months in 1864–1865. During his term of service, he fought at the siege of Petersburg, Virginia, in the latter parts of 1864 and took part in the expedition against Fort Fisher, which aimed to cut off the Confederacy's last Atlantic seaport in late 1864 and early 1865, and the subsequent subdual of much of eastern and central North Carolina until the war's end. The man that was his future brother-in-law, Silas White, served in the famous 55th Massachusetts Colored Infantry, along with three other men from the community, but was killed during his service.

Joseph Moton, who had been brought to Ohio as an infant and later ordained as a Baptist minister, joined another of the Roanoke migrants, York Rial (c. 1837–1913), in initiating a case to attempt to recover the land or its value that had originally been purchased in Mercer County by Judge William Leigh on their behalf. They argued that Leigh had acted unlawfully in the original purchase and that future sale and possession of the land had also been done unlawfully. The defendants successfully shielded themselves with Ohio's twenty-one-year statute of limitations, and the Mercer County Court sided with the defense.[42] The fact that all of the documents pertaining to Leigh's transactions had been consumed in a fire in Richmond, Virginia, during the Civil War undercut the plaintiffs' case. The case, *Moton v. Kessens*, was appealed all the way to the US Supreme Court but failed to yield a different result.[43] Whatever happened to the money that Leigh subsequently procured from the resale of the land is unknown, but whether by conspiracy or fraud, the migrants and their descendants were denied any justice and received no benefit from Randolph's original bequest beyond paid passage to Ohio.

Rossville, which had been the most successful of the settlements made by the free people of Roanoke and their descendants, was largely destroyed in a flood in 1913. By that time, the population was declining sharply anyway, because the descendants of the original migrants had found few opportunities in the local area and began to leave for nearby cities such as Dayton, Cincinnati, or even farther north to Akron and Cleveland.[44]

Rev. Moton's daughter, Josephine (1869–1930), married the son of another Roanoke migrant, Albert A. Hill, and the two of them farmed in Pleasant Hill and Newton in Miami County until around the time of the flood, after which the marriage seems to have come undone.[45] Hill moved to Troy, working at different times as a sign painter, a cook, and a dishwasher until the 1940s.[46] Meanwhile, their eldest child, Ethel Hill (c. 1888–1960), married Harvey Call Cobbs Sr. in 1910, and after the couple united, they moved south to Middletown, where he worked as a janitor and she as a cook, allowing them to ascend into the small Black middle class of the city.[47] In 1911, their son, Harvey Call Cobbs Jr. (1911–71), was born and would become known professionally as the pianist Call Cobbs.

FREE BLACK COMMUNITIES AND NETWORKS IN OHIO

Another pianist, even more well known, Dave Burrell, also emerged from a related social milieu. His mother's family had deep roots in Ohio going back almost to the founding of the state. Following his maternal line back more than a century, we come to Rachel Roush (c. 1785–1870), who had been born enslaved on the plantation of William Cassels Sr., in Amelia County, Virginia.[48] More than half of the enslaved people on the plantation had been born in Africa and had been brought to the United States in the last decades of the eighteenth century.[49] While still an adolescent, Roush became Cassels's concubine, and they had a long, seemingly committed relationship, as he was not otherwise married; the two had fourteen children together. Out of a desire to provide better opportunities for their children, Cassels decided to sell his plantation in 1818 and relocate to Ohio, where he bought land. Unfortunately for them, as a mixed-race couple and family, they faced excessive violence, often directed at Cassels himself, and he supposedly survived three duels over the issue. Cassels eventually set out for Virginia but drowned in a river during the journey in 1823, perhaps from suicide. Roush's manumission appears in the Amelia County court records:

> Rachel Cassels, a free woman of colour, light complexion, aged about thirty three or thirty four years, height five feet five and a half inches with a mark on her left wrist just below her thumb of a dark complexion and was emancipated by the last will and testament of William Cassels deceased and admitted to record the 27th of November 1823. In Amelia County court March 27th 1824, the above named Rachel Cassels personally appeared in court and being examined was found to agree with the foregoing register which is ordered to be certified.[50]

Subsequent entries in the ledger record the manumission of each of her formerly enslaved children, omitting the younger ones, who had been born free in Ohio.[51]

Roush's land in Jackson County, Ohio, by 1826, was extensive, totaling approximately 2,500 acres, with each child receiving more than one hundred acres and a house, and the children divided Cassels's other possessions among themselves.[52] Her children seemed to experience varied success, some prospering to a certain degree as farmers, while others found their farms only providing a meager existence. Roush bequeathed most of her land to her children by 1860, after which she lived with one of her sons while "infirm."[53]

The family's farmlands became the vital nucleus of a Black community there. Roush cofounded the settlement of Berlin Crossroads in 1830 along with eight other families, including Thomas Woodson, who is believed to be the son of Sally Hemings and the slaveowner president Thomas Jefferson.[54] The families all attended church together at the Quinn Chapel African Methodist Episcopal (AME) Church, said to be "the first black Methodist church west of the Alleghenies."[55] They also founded their own school.[56]

Berlin Crossroads soon established itself as an integral stop on the Underground Railroad, and the Cassels were involved in its maintenance. From there people would move on to Chillicothe or Washington Court House, often traveling in hay wagons disguised as being sent to market. From there, fugitives were "taken to safety" in Ross and Fayette counties.[57] Because it was a relatively prosperous Black settlement, it became a significant destination for people coming north, and a number of residents opened their homes to fugitives. Doing so always came with a risk for local members of the community who harbored people there.

Two of Woodson's three sons were murdered for such involvement in 1846 and 1852, the latter by proslavery thugs from Kentucky, and both died because they refused to reveal anything about the fugitives they had aided.[58]

By 1840, the small farming community had grown to have blacksmiths, carpenters, clergymen, horsemen, merchants, schoolteachers, seamstresses, and shoemakers, as well as two hotels. The settlement grew to accommodate about thirty families, "with the older generation consisting mainly of formerly enslaved Virginians."[59] A local abolitionist noted that "most of them were children, as well as slaves of their masters."[60]

Berlin Crossroads served as a model for other Black settlements in Ohio emerging at that time and connected to the broader abolitionist movement via the Columbus-based newspaper *Palladium of Liberty*, which Woodson distributed locally. Woodson's only surviving son, Rev. Lewis Frederick Woodson, became engaged in ongoing debates about freedom and abolition and wrote of Berlin Crossroads, "Such a settlement would entirely alter our conditions, there we should be on perfect equality—we should be free from the looks of scorn and contempt—free from fraud—and, in time, free from all the evils attendant on partial and unequal laws."[61] Rev. Woodson cofounded Wilberforce University in Ohio in 1856 and cofounded the Pittsburgh Philanthropic Society, which assisted other fugitives coming north. One branch of the poet Langston Hughes's family traces back to the small community of Berlin Crossroads, further illustrating how these networks were crucial grounds for later cultural developments.[62]

Roush's third child, Fanny Cassels (c. 1805–1881), married Thomas Alfred Dyer (d. 1845), another "free person of color" who had settled in Jackson County by the mid- to late 1820s. Shoemaking was the family trade, passed from Dyer to his sons and grandsons.[63] The family was also connected to emerging Black educational networks in the region, with Fanny's sister-in-law founding the Rachel Cassel Education Center, with the aim of educating Black people in that part of the county. Fanny's nephew, Thomas Frank Cassels (c. 1845–1903), moved to Memphis and was elected to the Tennessee state legislature in 1880, becoming a significant figure in state politics there during the final two decades of the nineteenth century.

Alfred and Fanny Dyer's daughter, Eliza Ann, married John C. Tuck (1832–1915), whom they brought into the family shoemaking and repair business. Tuck's mother, Jane Ritchie Tuck (1797–1884), was from Rockbridge County, Virginia, born free and of mixed-race ancestry. Like many free Black people in Virginia and other slave states, they found little opportunity in their original environs, and after her husband's early death there in 1837, she led the family north to Ohio in 1841.[64] She was able to obtain small tracts of land along the Ohio River in Gallia County in the southeastern part of the state, though she was able to gradually expand her holdings over the decades that followed. Though it was a hard-fought existence, she eventually passed on land to her sons, where they raised small numbers of horses and cows while investing most of their time in growing wheat.[65] The family joined the AME Church, which at the time was expanding rapidly within much of the community across Ohio.[66]

Two years after the conclusion of the Civil War, John Tuck and his family moved north to Oberlin, Ohio, where he partnered with his brother-in-law to run a shoe shop right next to Oberlin College.[67] He had been drawn there because of the community's utopian goals and the potential opportunities it held, though as his son later stated, "you had to swear you were half white before you could vote," indicating that many barriers existed even there.[68] It was one of the first universities in the United States to admit African American students, beginning in 1835, and the first to admit women in 1837. This would prove fateful for Tuck's family, as it had been for a number of other free Black people in Ohio.[69] In the 1870s, his eldest child, Samantha Cordelia Tuck (1854–1908), enrolled in the preparatory school and English program at Oberlin, in 1878–1879.[70] Upon graduating, she taught school, first in Washington, Kentucky, for a year, and then for three years in nearby Mayslick, which lay on the south side of the Ohio River. It is there that she met her future husband, Alexander Vivian, and the two settled in New Carlisle, Ohio, in 1887.[71] They were drawn to the area northeast of Dayton because of its numerous Black rural settlements, like those previously discussed in this chapter, and they bought a farm there. They, too, were active in the AME Church.

Vivian's daughter, Bertha, met John Henry Washington (1890–1986) during his travels passing through Miami County, and they soon married. Washington had left Maysville, Kentucky, just fifty-five miles southeast of Cincinnati, as a young man and had moved another thirty miles north of there to Middletown, Ohio, in the 1910s, drawn by a job as a security officer at the American Rolling Mill, a steel manufacturing company.[72] It was there that Dave Burrell's mother, Mary Eleanor Washington (1912–1969), was born and grew up. The pianist himself was born in Middletown in 1940.

TRANSREGIONAL NETWORKS OF FREEDOM AND THE UNDERGROUND RAILROAD

The final network that linked free jazz musicians to the Underground Railroad is that of the family of the bassist Clyde Shy, who traces his origins to Mississippi via Wisconsin, but through broader free Black networks that connected and

FIGURE 1.3 Ezekiel Gillespie (1818–1893), abolitionist.

Source: Wikimedia commons.

influenced the communities of the greater Ohio Valley. On his mother's side, Shy descended from the prominent abolitionist Ezekiel Gillespie (1818–1892). Gillespie was born in Greene County, Tennessee, from the union of his plantation owner father and an enslaved mother.[73] They moved to Madison County, Mississippi, in the central part of that state, east of the delta and north of Jackson, in the 1830s, where according to one story Gillespie managed to purchase his freedom by the early part of the following decade for eight hundred dollars.[74]

From there, Gillespie seems to have followed the trickle of free people moving north and married a woman in Parke County, Indiana, along the Wabash River, in 1845, then moved a little south to Evansville by 1849, before settling in Pigeon, Indiana, where he worked as a huckster of groceries and small wares the following year.[75] With an exclusionary article added to the Indiana state constitution in 1851, he joined the exodus of other free Black people leaving the state, proceeding north to Milwaukee, Wisconsin, by 1852, where he resumed his grocery business, selling vegetables, poultry, and wild game at a shop on Mason Street between the Milwaukee River and Lake Michigan.[76] During that decade, when the economy crashed, he lost his business and worked for a time as a porter; he was employed by a banking and railroad magnate and gradually moved up to better positions within the company of the Chicago, Milwaukee, and St. Paul Railway.[77]

Meanwhile, Gillespie operated a branch of the Underground Railroad and developed a reputation as a vocal critic of slavery. As such, he was one of the principal figures involved in harboring the fugitive slave Joshua Glover, who sought asylum but was captured and taken to the Milwaukee jail. As part of a group led by the white abolitionist Sherman Booth, Gillespie and approximately five thousand other people broke into the jail, rescued Glover, and brought him in secret to Port Washington, on the west coast of Lake Michigan. From there Glover was taken by boat to safety in Canada. When the federal government attempted to prosecute Booth for leading the act of civil disobedience, a movement sparked in Milwaukee that ultimately pushed the supreme court of the state to declare the Fugitive Slave Act unconstitutional. Wisconsin thereby became the only state to formally refuse to enforce the act and afterward became more of a thoroughfare for fugitives on the Underground Railroad from the western slave states.

Refusing to remain idle, Gillespie did not wait for the federal government to guarantee his right to vote. With the support of Booth, he attempted to vote in the 1865 Wisconsin gubernatorial election.[78] He was denied a ballot and thereafter filed a lawsuit against the Board of Elections. The case, *Gillespie v. Palmer*, proceeded to the Wisconsin Supreme Court, where he attained a victory, the justices unanimously citing an endorsement of universal male suffrage in an 1849 referendum, and thus on March 28, 1866, the case resulted in Black male suffrage statewide, with Gillespie on record as the first Black person to vote in Wisconsin.[79]

After his first wife's death, Gillespie married the widow Catharina Lucas Robinson (1836–1874), whose family, much like those analyzed earlier in this chapter, came out of free Black networks in Ohio that trace back to the early nineteenth century. Robinson's father and grandfather had been manumitted or escaped in Maryland and moved north, first to "the Scioto bottoms" in Scioto County, just north of the Ohio River, where a burgeoning Black community had emerged before 1813.[80] One visitor to the region in 1789 described the ease of agriculture in the area: "Go to the banks of one of the creeks in the Scioto bottoms . . . scratch the surface of the earth and deposit there your wheat, your corn, your potatoes, your beans, your cabbage, your tobacco, etc., and leave the rest to nature. In the meantime amuse yourself with fishing and the chase."[81]

People involved in later movements out of Maryland cited the Lucas family, among others, as "their friends and acquaintances," suggesting a broader network of Maryland fugitives and migrants north to that part of Ohio. But Scioto had a history of Black residents being forced out by white vigilantes as early as 1818, so this may have played a role in the Lucas family's decision to move after less than a decade of farming there.[82] Nevertheless, the community of Houston Hollow, which did survive in Scioto County, was a crucial stop on the Underground Railroad for people crossing the Ohio River at Portsmouth, which was one of the major points of access.[83]

The Lucas family joined a broader movement of people in the community to Jackson Township in Pike County, just to the north of Scioto, by 1820, where they were able to acquire better farmland.[84] They were some of the earliest "free people of color" in the area, though they were soon joined by a larger group led by the Baptist minister and schoolteacher Thomas Walker, from Monroe County, in what is now West Virginia, in 1823. This latter group were quite poor, had walked the entire way, their only possessions being what they could carry on their backs; they founded a close-knit community that included a school and a church.[85]

Many of the descendants of these early settlers of Jackson Township later claimed Saponi or Catawba Native American ancestry, and it is quite possible that Catharina Lucas Robinson's native ancestry came through these links as she was said to descend generally from the Cherokee.[86] This further suggests the possibility of earlier, untraced generations of the family that may have been affiliated with maroon communities in the south and thus may have been free for several generations before migrating north. The Lucas family's strong devotion to the AME Church likely dates to the 1830s, when the aforementioned Thomas Woodson, of Berlin Crossroads, inspired the spread of the church into Jackson Township.[87] With the aid of the church, a number of figures in the community there became integral to the functioning of the Underground Railroad in the area, usually helping people reach Chillicothe for the next leg of the journey north.

By the 1840s, the Lucas family moved to northwestern Ohio: Van Buren Township, Shelby County. Like the community that they had been a part of previously in Pike County, the earliest settlements there were founded by people of African and Catawba descent.[88] They were also situated just six miles north of the site in Mercer County where the free people of Roanoke had been prevented from settling. The main settlement of Rumley had been first built in 1837, and by the arrival of the Lucas family at some point in the 1840s, a broader network of "free black villages" emerged in the county, including Carthagena, Middle Creek, and Wren.[89] Rumley reached a peak population of about four hundred residents in the 1860s.

It seems that Catharina's father, Zachariah Lucas (b. c. 1810), was able to acquire some of the best farmland within the Black community in Rumley, despite the fact that much of it was generally "too flat and wet" to be prosperous.[90] The Lucas family rose to some prominence, running a large hog farm and operating one of the smokehouses for which the town was then becoming famous.[91] Rumley appears to have had only a marginal involvement in the Underground Railroad, which ran through nearby Sidney. During the Civil War, however, the community did face considerable violence from proslavery sympathizers in the area, forcing some to leave. The Lucas family was among them; they sold their land and moved to a small town near Lima, Ohio. After that, Rumley dwindled, and in the 1930s it was abandoned entirely.

During its most prosperous years before the Civil War, Rumley was the site of an AME church that served many from the community and surrounding areas. There is no doubt that Zachariah Lucas and his daughter Catharina attended regularly as devoted members.[92] Thus it is fitting that after Catharina Lucas Robinson's marriage to Ezekiel Gillespie, the couple founded the first AME Church in Milwaukee in 1869.[93]

Some of Ezekiel and Catharina's children, however, returned to northern Ohio, settling in Tiffin, drawn back by their mother's extensive social network there and the family's elevated status among the Black community, which continued to grow after Emancipation. Their descendants married with other people who descended from free Black families that arrived in the area via the Underground Railroad by the 1840s or 1850s.[94] Their daughter Ida Mae Gillespie (1867–1947) married William Clinton McQueen (1858–1949), who ran a barber shop there from the late nineteenth century up until the Great Depression.[95] McQueen's father, Pvt. James Samuel McQueen (c. 1816–1896), had arrived in Tiffin by the 1850s and likely sought work in the flour mill, like other people at the time.[96] He enlisted in the 16th US Colored Infantry in March 1865, after the unit had taken some casualties at the Battle of Nashville late the previous year. He departed with the unit to central and western Tennessee and remained with it until the unit was mustered out at Memphis, April 30, 1866.[97] In early May, Pvt. McQueen witnessed white mob violence there but was among the Black soldiers who held the upper hand for a few days during the Memphis massacre, turning back the tide of police and vigilante violence before eventually fleeing the city.[98]

Many of these early Black social and cultural networks, both integral to and growing out of the Underground Railroad and the networks of free Black settlements that emerged in Ohio before the Civil War, were integral to sustaining the community in later generations. Many of the settlements did not prosper or survive but served as starting points for a network of people who would later gravitate to the industrial cities for work. Still, the legacies of freedom and autonomy that they achieved, in varying degrees, formed a backdrop for their social, cultural, and political outlook as new waves of people arrived from the south bearing other legacies of resistance.

CHAPTER 2

POST-EMANCIPATION MOBILITIES

Reconstruction, Survival, and the Great Migration

A majority of the musicians that emerged in the greater Ohio Valley come from families that trace back to the Black Belt, running from eastern Mississippi through Alabama to western and central Georgia, with some connections to the Florida panhandle. This region was the heart of Black culture, home to the blues, Baptist and AME church music, shout traditions, a variety of percussion practices, and many dance forms. The other major points of departure for musician lineages were in the Black Patch of southwestern Kentucky, the Ohio River borderlands of north central Kentucky and West Virginia, and the Mississippi delta. These regions provided further connections to the blues, church music, and the mobilities and boundaries associated with the Ohio River. People carried an assemblage of cultural practices, mobilities, music, religious beliefs, the practice of communal resistance to violence, and agricultural knowledge, even as they eventually fused these variants together to form something new and innovative in northern cities.

In these environments, emancipated people carried with them enduring social relations and a sense of place from slave society. These "neighborhoods," as the historian Anthony E. Kaye described them, were defined as adjoining plantations, and neighborhoods "encompassed the bonds of kinship, the practice of Christianity, the geography of sociability, the field of labor and discipline, the grounds of solidarity, the terrain of struggle. For slaves, neighborhoods served as the locus of all the bonds that shaped the contours of their society." Furthermore, "making places under the exactions of slavery and slave trading, which enabled owners to unmake neighborhood ties as readily as slaves made them, was a perpetual struggle," in what Kaye terms a practice of nonlinear freedom.[1] The historian Stephanie Camp, in her detailed study of spaces of slave resistance to the process of spatial control, argues that this process involved everyday gendered resistance in intimate, private, and public spaces as enslaved people harnessed whatever means they had to resist violence, bodily control, and movement.[2] This struggle for place, bodily autonomy, and the maintenance of social bonds, though evolving into new forms after Emancipation, would remain a constant struggle as people faced new forms of violent coercion, dislocation, and spatial control. Kaye's sense of place making and Camp's understanding of everyday resistance is ever-present in my analysis of social geographies not only in the south but across the expansive landscapes that people inhabited, organized, and transformed through mobility.

The end of slavery led directly to other kinds of coerced labor. As Saidiya Hartman argues, "Emancipation announced the end of chattel slavery; however it by no means marked the end of bondage. The free(d) individual was nothing if not burdened, responsible, and obligated. Responsibility entailed accounting for one's actions, dutiful suppliance, contractual obligation, and calculated reciprocity.... The exercise of free will ... was inextricable from guilty infractions, criminal misdeeds, punishable transgressions, and an elaborate micropenality of everyday life."[3] The carceral state was then (and is now) the response of the superstructures of the white supremacist American state system to advancements in Black freedom. People facing these manifestations of violence and control formulated staunch resistance from the Reconstruction period onward.

Emancipated peoples' first use of mobility and collective action after the Civil War was to move locations, searching for better conditions or opportunities and to forge solidarity in these aims in what the historian Thulani Davis has termed the "emancipation circuit."[4] She draws from Stephanie Camp's adaptation of Edward Said's concept of "rival geography." As Camp argues, "The rival geography was not a settled spatial formation, for it included quarters, outbuildings, woods, swamps, and neighboring farms as chance granted them. Where planters' mapping of their farms was defined by fixed places for enslaved residents, the rival geography was characterized by motion: the movement of bodies, objects, and information within and around plantation space."[5] Davis defines the Emancipation circuit as "a system of regional networks built on labor sites and shipping routes with local routes that created ties between communities as well as ties to other networks."[6]

Davis differentiates the "emancipation circuit" movements from the Underground Railroad and other preceding liberation movements because the former forged connections between sites in the south rather than serving as clandestine networks. "Importantly, though, it was a circuit born of abolition. It was made possible by the presence of the US military, during the war and after, and by the opportunity fugitive settlements provided for holding meetings and large assemblies, setting up schools, and conducting prayer meetings."[7] This book examines these spaces and networks during the post-Emancipation era and then considers their multigenerational outcomes over the century that followed with descendant communities emanating out and fusing with adjacent movements that came out of the Underground Railroad across the greater Ohio Valley.

BLACK BELT

Most of the territory of Alabama and Mississippi were held by the Creek, Cherokee, Chickasaw, and Choctaw tribes until the territory was invaded by Gen. Andrew Jackson, who carried out genocidal campaigns against the indigenous inhabitants. The defeat of this confederacy of tribes in 1814 forced them to cede most of their territory as they were tragically displaced westward. The outcome of this war led to the full-scale settlement of the lands by white planters and settlers, who brought many enslaved people with them to cultivate cotton.

The Black Belt came to form a distinct zone of Black American culture. As a region, it had some of the heaviest concentrations of African American population in the country, originally because of the cotton plantations' reliance on enslaved labor.[8] Not until the 1840s was there extensive cultivation in much of Mississippi, but from there on it gave way to rapid settlement by planters and enslaved laborers. In fact, African Americans constituted 55 percent of the overall Mississippi population on the eve of the Civil War. This set up a particularly volatile political landscape after the war, given that the state had not developed beyond a political system that was incredibly vertical and hierarchical, dominated by rich white planters, and, as the historian W. E. B. Du Bois noted, "it was suddenly required after the war that this state should not only assimilate a voting population of nearly 450,000 former slaves, but also that the mass of poor whites should have political significance which they had never had before."[9] The Civil War also deeply undermined cotton harvests for nearly a decade. The combination of these tensions played out quite violently during Reconstruction and its aftermath as planters worked to recruit and manipulate poor white populations as an effective means to subdue those who had been recently emancipated.

As numerous scholars have observed and debated since Du Bois, freedom was complicated and contested and often was suppressed or made minimal in terms

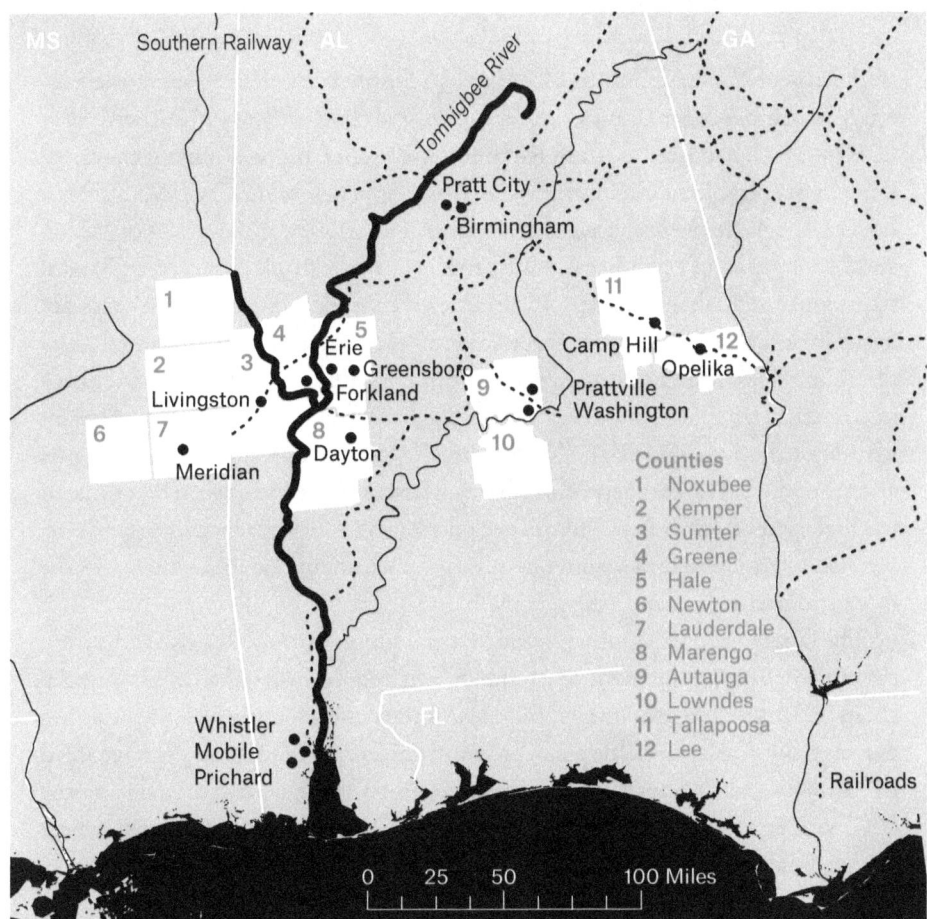

FIGURE 2.1 Alabama-Mississippi Black Belt and early migrations.

Source: Cartography by Alice Viggiani.

of a lived experience. After chattel slavery was abolished in 1865, many forms of coerced labor remained within the form of agrarian capitalism that emerged in the wake of slavery. This system kept many freedmen perpetually in debt or left them with no better option than to struggle to survive as sharecroppers in a system in which the planters and landowners held most of the power.[10] Nevertheless, the history we follow here in the Black Belt is one of constant resistance to oppression, manifesting in many different forms, from labor organizing, to the use of arms, communal solidarity, and migration.[11]

EASTERN MISSISSIPPI BLACK BELT

Both sides of the saxophonist Albert Ayler's family trace their roots to the eastern Mississippi border counties. Ayler's great-grandfather, Suther "Suthey" Ayler (c. 1838–1923), had been born in Richmond, Virginia, but was among the thousands of people sold or forcibly moved to Mississippi before the Civil War. In Mississippi, the Aylers were enslaved on a cotton plantation near the towns of Macon and Brooksville, in Noxubee County, in the heart of Black Belt eastern Mississippi along the Alabama border, where enslaved people outnumbered white inhabitants by a ratio of more than three to one.[12] The Ayler family remained there after Emancipation, dwelling in great turmoil as rumors of an armed freedman insurrection circulated but never materialized and facing the violence and intimidation of the Ku Klux Klan (KKK), which was active in the area in the years after the war.[13] The east central Alabama-Mississippi border region had some of the highest levels of violence in the period 1869–1871 of any place in either state, but the Aylers left before a subsequent surge of white supremacist violence in the 1910s and 1920s consumed the region.[14]

The family of Ayler's mother, Jessie Myrtle Hunter (1916–1985), also came from eastern Mississippi, the town of Meridian, situated in the southernmost Appalachian foothills in an area known for dense forests and limestone hills in addition to its agricultural land.[15] One poem or song from Lauderdale County was recorded in the 1930s. Sarah Snow, a freedwoman, claimed she had written it during the Civil War as a retort to being harassed by white children on the plantation where she lived. It spoke of President Lincoln and the advance of the Union army:

> Old General Pope had a shot gun,
> Filled it full o' gum,
> Killed 'em as they come.
> Called a Union band,
> Make the rebels understand,
> To leave the land,
> Submit to Abraham.[16]

The Hunter family continued to work fields in Lauderdale County in the decades after Emancipation while facing "a tidal wave of Ku Klux Klan activity."[17] KKK members from Alabama raided the county in the years following the Civil War and joined with a portion of the local white population in an attempt to violently overthrow the Republican government in Meridian; they burned down part of the town in what one freedwoman described as "one awful fire."[18] That observer, Nettie Henry, stated, "I was ten years old at the surrender, but I took notice. Them was scary times and when you is scared, you takes trigger-notice.... Things just kept getting worse and worse."[19]

Black residents formed armed militias in response to these aggressions and even paraded through the streets of Meridian in a show of force. Reconstruction also resulted in some freedmen taking new positions, as Henry stated: "After the surrender [Negroes] got mighty biggity. Most of them was just glad to be free.... They got to be all kinds of things... like being policemen and all like that."[20] The Black leaders were arrested and prosecuted in a process that escalated into white mob violence that massacred as many as 174 Black residents, raped at least four women, and burned down numerous residences in Meridian, March 6, 1871.[21] Though the incident was one of the catalysts for the federal government to pass the Enforcement Act of 1871 to combat the KKK, the moves by the federal government did little to abate local vigilante violence at the time.[22]

As one Mississippian soon after noted in a letter published by Frederick Douglass in the newspaper *New National Era*, "Do not be deceived, Ku-Kluxism is not dead, it but sleepeth; it is ready to wake at the first call of the 'Grand Cyclop.' I write this because as a colored man and living in the South I am fully acquainted with the rebellious spirit of a majority of the people in the midst of whom I live."[23] Indeed, other attacks on the Black community as well as white Republicans went unabated in Lauderdale County through Reconstruction and after.[24]

Vigilante violence by white minority populations in the wake of the massacre kept majority Black populations from realizing freedom and participatory government, even during the Reconstruction years.[25] As the freedman Berry Smith later stated, about the politics of Lauderdale County in that era, "I voted the 'publican ticket after the surrender, but I didn't bother with no politics. The Klu Kluxers was bad up above here... I heard tell of them whuppin' folks."[26] The situation intensified with the fully state-sanctioned white supremacy that came after the collapse of the Reconstruction regime. Lynching remained a serious threat through the 1890s and afterward continued at a lower rate into the 1920s around Meridian and throughout the rural parts of Lauderdale County.[27] These acts of violence formed the first step toward the systematic political disenfranchisement that came as the Reconstruction governments fell.

Meridian grew considerably between the 1850s and 1880s. Nettie Henry described the evolution: "I's seen this town grow from nothing. When us come here 'fore the war, they was hitching they horses to little oak bushes right in the middle of town where the biggest store is now."[28] It emerged in the late nineteenth century as the second-largest city in the state thanks to its position at the junction of five major railroad lines that together were linked to other cities and industrial centers across the eastern and central United States.[29] Manufacturing also emerged in the city with the founding of a cotton mill in the 1890s, and many more factories were built in the city in the 1910s, centered on textiles.[30]

Black freedmen from plantations in Lauderdale County had looked to Meridian railway companies as an opportunity for employment as early as the months immediately following the Civil War.[31] Despite the violence, the Hunter family moved into Meridian during the boom years of the 1880s, where Albert Ayler's great-grandfather labored in one of the numerous railyards.[32] Ayler's maternal grandfather, Will Hunter (b. 1891), grew up in the neighborhood just north of the railroad tracks in central Meridian, and he managed to secure a position as a fireman for the Southern Railway Company, as a part of a broader surge in Black hiring that the company initiated after the turn of the century.[33] Meridian became more segregated over time as it grew; by the time that the family left, it had several distinct Black neighborhoods.[34] Hunter's new position paid more than his father had made, and he joined a broader migration from eastern Mississippi and rural Alabama to Birmingham, where he settled with his family by the 1910s, just a few blocks north of the 16th Street Baptist Church.[35]

Several musicians who later emerged in Detroit originated from the same cluster of counties along the Alabama-Mississippi border. The drummer Elvin Jones (1927–2004), who was born near Detroit and was most well known for playing with John Coltrane, traces the maternal side of his family to Meridian, where they likely knew Albert Ayler's forebears. The trombonist Charles Greenlee (1927–1993), also born in Detroit and who is best known for his extensive work with the saxophonist Archie Shepp, had family that also came from the area. After Emancipation, Greenlee's maternal great-grandparents, Wesley and Dilsey Watts (b. c. 1837 and c. 1845, respectively), sharecropped in Newton County, which bordered Lauderdale County to the west, and by 1900, their son, Milton Watts (b. 1868), was employed as a teamster, but the latter was among the first to leave the area, arriving in Detroit during World War I, when labor demands drew him north.[36] Once in Detroit, he continued working as a porter and teamster, especially for Black-owned barbershops, and also developed his trade as a carpenter.[37]

WESTERN ALABAMA BLACK BELT

Three of the great saxophonists to emerge in the greater Ohio Valley all traced their origins to the western Alabama Black Belt. Ancestors of Albert Ayler, Charles Gayle, and Faruq Z. Bey all came from the cluster of Greene, Hale, and Marengo counties, situated about fifty to seventy-five miles east of Meridian. A unique pattern of settlement set the stage for the area. The three counties were the site of a settlement of French aristocrats, the final exiles from Saint-Domingue, where enslaved people had successfully revolted and cast off the slaver-planters to form the state of Haiti. These defeated French slavers had moved temporarily to Cuba before again moving north, this time to Mobile.[38] In 1817, they attempted to establish the Vine and Olive Colony on 92,000 acres of swampy lowlands in the three counties, which were stitched together by the Tombigbee River.[39] Only after the failure of the venture was it opened to cotton plantations in the 1830s, where the sonic cry of field shouts became a defining feature of social cohesion and a public declaration of resilience.

These foundational aesthetics in the western Alabama Black Belt gave rise to a particularly rich practice of music. Though before the 1930s we have only scant references in text, the emergence of a particularly strong blues and gospel music practice there at that time belies earlier developments. The vocalist Adel "Vera" Reed (c. 1902–1964) is one of the most well documented from the region, and many of the blues she sang are thought to have been evolved from earlier nineteenth-century forms.[40] Her cousins Dock Reed and Henry Reed were involved in maintaining and building a corresponding gospel corpus. Other figures such as Harriet McClintock, Clarence Davis, and Anne Grace Horn Dodson were also key figures in the blues tradition of the western Alabama Black Belt.[41] And the heavy concentration of musicians descending from Greene, Hale, and Sumter counties on the Alabama side of the border and from Kemper, Lauderdale, and Noxubee counties right across the border in Mississippi, discussed earlier, is additional evidence of potent musical roots that were passed down through oral tradition.

Albert Ayler's maternal grandmother's family, the Pryors, who had been brought from Virginia in the 1830s, struggled in Hale County in the aftermath of the Civil War. The pianist Dave Burrell's great-grandfather Henry Burrell also came from the county, working as a sharecropper in the years after Emancipation.[42] The region was one of the "most fertile and finest" areas for growing cotton in all of the US south. The area's large-scale plantations meant that the region's population was more than three-quarters African American at the time of the Civil War.[43] By 1867, a group of four thousand freedmen assembled in the county seat of Greensboro, where they elected delegates to the state Republican convention and made other resolutions. But the white response was swift, and the following month, a prominent freedman affiliated with the radical newspaper *Mobile Nationalist*, who had just been appointed voter registrar, was assassinated publicly in the streets of Greensboro.[44] In response, the freedmen organized a local militia, soon becoming an official Union League, numbering five hundred individuals under the leadership of the future congressman James K. Green to ensure mutual defense against potential attacks.

Many freedmen in Hale County refused to work the fields in the months that followed, and some claimed portions of the cotton harvests and local livestock such as hogs as their own, the end result being more decentralized tenant farming than what was typical in the Black Belt.[45] The KKK responded and became very active in the area in 1867 through 1871, though the freedmen were able to retain some of the gains they had made.[46] One observer wrote in 1869, "Many planters have turned their stock, teams, and every facility to farming, over to the negroes, and only require an amount of toll for use of their land."[47] Greater levels of autonomy were established by three mixed-race children of a white planter who founded the Free Town settlement in the county, where Black freedmen owned and ran their own farms.

Nevertheless, many people from Hale County began migrating west seeking better arrangements by 1873, including the Burrell family, which migrated to the Mississippi delta, where they continued to work as sharecroppers.[48] Out of the milieu of Hale County, Ayler's great-great-grandparents Ferdinand (c. 1832–1915) and Tempy Pryor (b. c. 1835) seem to have benefited little.[49] They lived with their children and grandchildren in the area for two or three decades after Emancipation working as domestics, hostlers, and cooks before at the turn of the century following many other people, moving seventy-five miles northeast to Birmingham, seeking industrial jobs.[50]

Charles Gayle's family came from the same region as that of Albert Ayler. The earliest traceable figures in the family, the musician's great-great-grandparents Joseph (b. c. 1820) and Harriet Gayle (b. c. 1822), were sold away from their parents and brought as children to Greene County from Virginia and North Carolina, respectively. After their arrival, they were bought by John Gayle, who came to the region in the 1820s, was elected governor of the state in 1831, and sold his house and the enslaved people who toiled there in 1834.[51] Other large plantations proliferated throughout the region in the 1820s and 1830s.

The flat, low-lying region had originally drawn settlers because it was situated at the fork of the Tombigbee and Black Warrior rivers. Pine pervaded the forests, with clusters of poplars and other hardwoods concentrated along the rivers that meandered through the swamp.[52] Surviving evidence of indigenous settlements also dotted the landscape, including numerous earthen mounds as well as a ruined fort just three miles southwest of Forkland, in Greene County.

After Emancipation, Joseph and Harriet Gayle worked as sharecroppers raising hogs and growing maize near Forkland.[53] They lived on the short stretch of road between Forkland and the town of Erie, which was on the opposite bank of the Black Warrior River cutting north-south through the area.[54] Erie was once a bustling river port where cotton grown in the area around Greensboro was stored before it was shipped downriver to Mobile. It had also contained a local market where "hundreds of slaves were disposed of at public auction during the years of Erie's existence," which likely resulted in the Gayle family's arrival there in the mid-1830s.[55]

In the aftermath of the Civil War, Forkland had a population of no more than two hundred people, and the settlement comprised little more than clusters of low-lying houses set around estuaries that wound through the swamp feeding into the Black Warrior River just to the east of the town. For a few years after the end of the war, the town had informal Black-run markets or roadside stands where farmers hawked their produce or cotton until white opposition forbid the practice in the mid-1870s as the gains under Reconstruction faded.[56] After that, much of the cotton grown in the area was transported locally to Union Springs or Eutaw or farther to Tuscaloosa or Meridian, and the prices became increasingly dictated by the manufacturers.[57]

The Black community in Greene County often organized dances on Saturday nights. One resident stated, "I was at my best in the job of picking the banjo. I . . . did love to pick that box while the other [Negroes] danced away."[58] Republican political organizing during Reconstruction led to the election of the Forkland freedman Lloyd Leftwich to the Alabama state senate, 1872–1876. He and his family also founded the Lloyd Chapel Baptist Church and an elementary school for Black children in the town, both of which the Gayle family attended in the early decades after Emancipation.[59] The graveyard at Lloyd Chapel dates to the 1920s, though the existence or whereabouts of earlier gravesites is not clear.

The first generation of freedmen built an African Methodist Episcopal (AME) church there by the 1880s or earlier.[60] Such churches were the primary autonomous spaces for the community in Forkland. In addition to church services, they gathered resources for communal meals and other gatherings, organized a drum corps, and sponsored baseball games for the community by the time that Charles Gayle's grandfather, Eddie Cato Gayle (1875–1938), was growing up there in the 1890s.[61] The Gayle family may have attended the Ebenezer Baptist Church, originally a small building with "a pot-bellied stove in the corner" for heat, which was closer to where they lived on the eastern outskirts of the town.[62] State or regional conventions drew together leaders of the churches on an annual basis.[63]

By 1910, the Gayle family managed to buy their own land, which set them apart from nearly all of their neighbors, who remained sharecroppers until the Great Depression.[64] The family continued to work the land there until Eddie Gayle moved the family north to Buffalo in the early or mid-1930s. They were not the only musical family to hail from Forkland. The Detroit blues guitarist, singer, and songwriter Bobo Jenkins (1916–1984) was born into a sharecropper family in Forkland and migrated north to the Motor City in 1944, where, in addition to making music, he worked in an automobile plant for twenty-six years.[65]

The saxophonist Faruq Z. Bey's family also came from the same region as that of Ayler and Gayle, though there is far less of a trace of them in the record. His paternal grandmother, Mary Lee Davis, lived in the town of Dayton, in Marengo County, just to the south of Greene and Hale, and her son, Jesse Saunders Davis (1908–1975), the father of Bey, grew up there. She moved the family westward first to Kansas City, Kansas, probably in the early 1930s, where he got to see the emergence of the saxophonist Charlie Parker at the Reno Club and other figures on the jazz scene there. Jesse Davis left in the late 1930s to eventually take a job at the Ford Motor Company in Detroit.[66]

NORTHWESTERN ALABAMA

One significant figure whose origins trace to outside of the Black Belt was the Detroit trumpeter Charles Moore (1939–2014). He was born in Sheffield, Alabama, next to Muscle Shoals and across the Tennessee River from the town of Florence in the northwestern corner of Alabama. The well-known blues composer and musician W. C. Handy was from Florence and wrote of the sounds of nature, including "birds of every variety" such as "whippoorwills, bats and hoot owls, with their outlandish noises."[67] Guitars and violins were commonly employed in music, though the latter would often be used in a percussive way, as Handy explained: "A boy would stand behind the fiddler with a pair of knitting needles in his hands. From this position the youngster would reach around the fiddler's left shoulder and beat on the strings in the manner of the snare drummer."[68] Foot stomping worked in the manner of a bass drum. Spirituals and breakdown dance tunes abounded within the community.

Moore's father's family had come from near Jackson, Mississippi, and had moved into the Delta after the turn of the century for work but then after World War I settled in a neighborhood of Sheffield called the Bottoms.[69] His paternal grandmother was a devout Christian and was deeply involved in the Baptist Church. His mother's family had sharecropped near Florence and acquired their own farm in the 1910s, but his grandfather, Robert Armstead (b. c. 1896), was jailed during the Great Depression for selling bootleg liquor.[70] Robert's wife, Betty, was a gambler, and "she knew how to play poker and she'd lay a gun on the table when she played."[71]

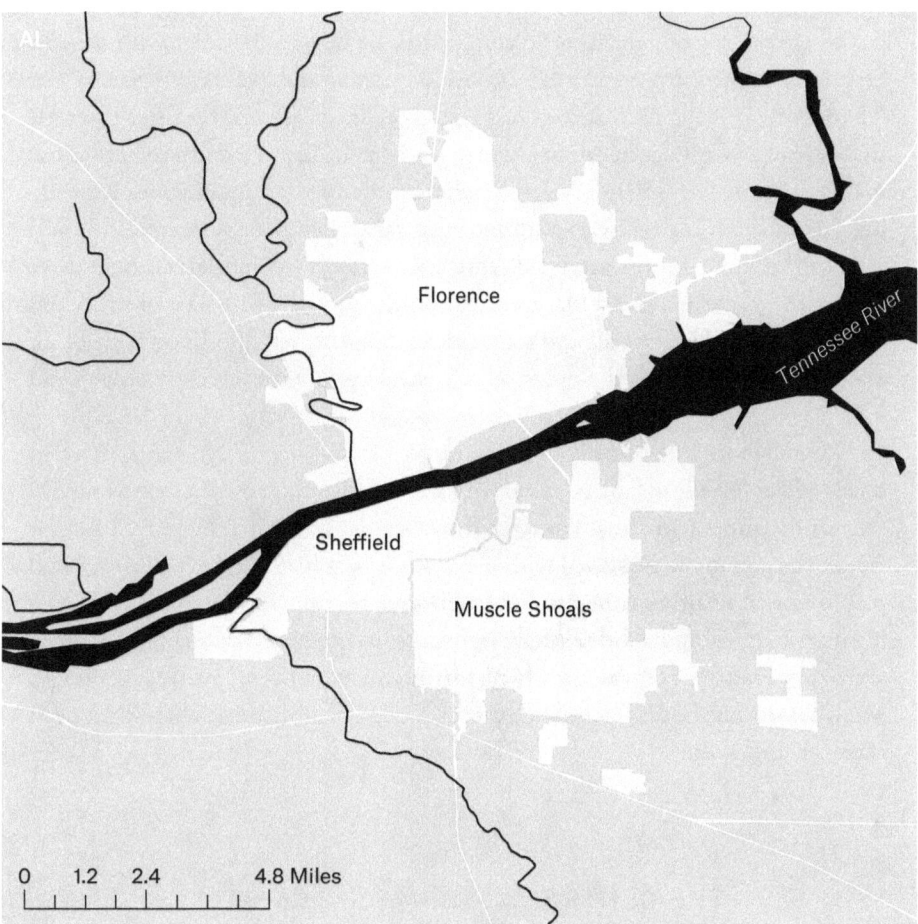

FIGURE 2.2 Northwestern Alabama.

Source: Cartography by Alice Viggiani.

After getting out of jail, Armstead managed to get a job at the Wilson Dam, one of the largest hydroelectric projects in the eastern United States, which spanned the river on the east side of Florence and was managed by the Tennessee Valley Authority (TVA). Moore's father, Eugene, spent his earliest adulthood working as a porter at the Sheffield Hotel, but in the 1940s he managed to join his father-in-law working for the TVA, which allowed them to ascend into the small Black middle class of the town. Moore's mother worked as a nurse's assistant, and Moore grew up picking cotton in the summers to earn a bit of extra money for the family.[72]

Eugene Moore was an adept dancer and went to local juke joints and later became president of a local social club, where he became familiar with jazz. In his home, he liked to play records by Louis Armstrong and Duke Ellington. When Charles was growing up, he developed a good ear for music, and his sister observed that even at an early age he "didn't have to read music, he just needed to hear music to be able to play it."[73] While Moore's father rebelled against his religious upbringing, his mother, Nettie, who had not been raised religiously, embraced it and sang in the choir. Moore attended segregated schools in Sheffield, though they happened to live in a small Black enclave on the mostly white part of town and as a youth played basketball and touch football in the neighborhood with Black and white kids. He was the oldest of five children and was an easygoing, jovial kid.[74]

When Moore finished high school, he set his eyes north. He briefly studied music at a college in Alabama, but it did not offer enough of what we wanted.[75] One of his aunts had already migrated to Detroit, and when he moved to that city in the late 1950s, he stayed with her while he got himself settled. Moore had played taps at military funerals and had been a part of the marching band during high school, but he did not have opportunities to play jazz regularly until he arrived in Detroit. He was already nurturing his interests by avidly listening to Miles Davis, but he also developed a broad taste that included blues, European classical, and opera.[76]

THE CENTRAL ALABAMA BLACK BELT

Some musicians can be traced to the central Alabama Black Belt as well. The drummer Hasan Shahid (b. 1944) had maternal relations who worked as sharecroppers near Lowndesboro, in Lowndes County, and near Washington, in Autauga County, in an area once home to the Autauga people, who were part of the Alibamu tribe.[77] The settlement of Washington inhabited the Autauga's former center of Atagi, meaning "pure water." They, too, were displaced by the invasions of the region under Gen. Jackson during the Creek War, which opened the region to cotton cultivation.[78]

At the center of Autauga County was Prattville, Alabama's first industrial center at its founding in the 1830s. By mid-century it had become the site of the Pratt Gin Company, which was the largest cotton gin production factory in the world, shipping its units to places as distant as Mexico and Russia.[79] Industry demanded railway facilities to distribute the cotton gins across the South, and soon the South & North Alabama Railroad Company connected the region to broader railroad networks of the mid- to late nineteenth century from the eastern seaboard to the Mississippi delta. Cotton production and manufacturing were particularly intense in the area, with dozens of collection and processing centers in Autauga County and the neighboring counties.[80] The railroads eventually facilitated greater mobility for some Black residents by the turn of the century as they moved to Montgomery, Birmingham, and other urban centers seeking employment in burgeoning industries.

By the late nineteenth century, African Americans numbered about 80 percent of the overall population in the central Alabama Black Belt. Lynching surged after the collapse of Reconstruction in the 1880s and 1890s, and Lowndes and Autauga counties had two of the highest rates of such violence in the state. The situation soon compelled Shahid's grandparents to leave sharecropping in rural Autauga and neighboring Lowndes counties for Prattville in the 1910s, drawn there during the labor shortage that occurred during World War I.[81] Miners and railroad workers in the Prattville area were actively organizing and carrying out strikes throughout the war and the immediate aftermath, though some of Shahid's relatives were forced to return to sharecropping as labor conditions deteriorated by the early 1920s.[82]

WEST CENTRAL GEORGIA PIEDMONT

Farther east, a number of musicians had families that came from the piedmont in the west-central Georgia Black Belt. Before the Civil War, the region was often the site of particularly large plantations of more than a thousand acres, which relied on between fifty and hundreds of enslaved people each.[83] These agricultural zones were most well known for producing cotton, but they also grew maize, wheat, potatoes, tobacco, fruit, rice, sugarcane, and various vegetables. Plantations also often bred horses, mules, goats, sheep, and hogs.[84] Much of the produce was shipped southeast to Savannah.

The pianist Bobby Few's family came from Upson County, which had previously been inhabited by the Creek tribe until their eviction by the Treaty of Indian Springs in 1821. Plantation settlement rapidly followed, with about half of the overall population being enslaved. The first cotton mill was founded in 1833, which spurred the earliest textile manufacturing in the area, producing sheets, shirts, and coarse yarn.[85] The Central of Georgia Railway had been built through the county partially by enslaved labor, from 1837 to 1843, allowing the local

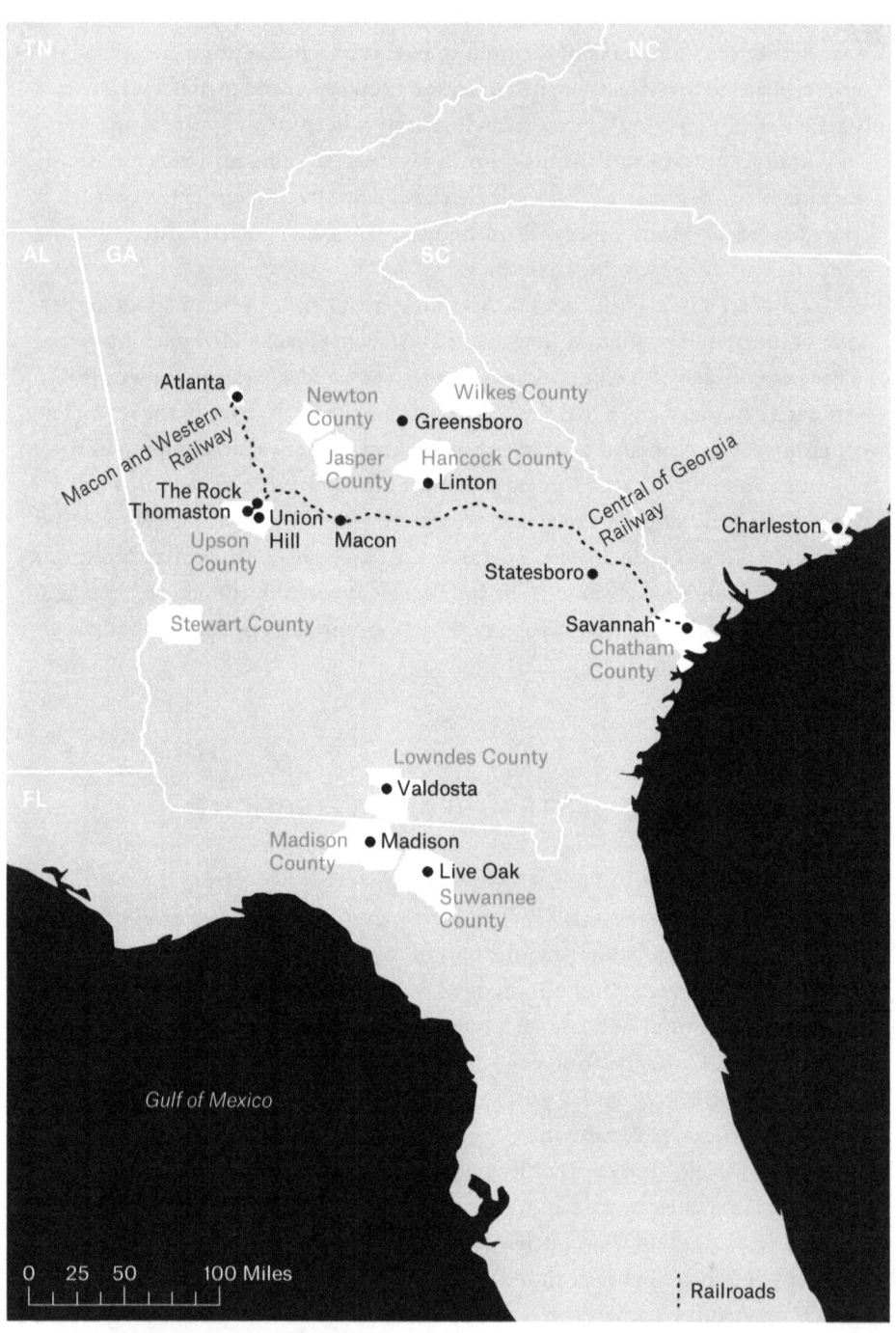

FIGURE 2.3 Georgia and Florida.

Source: Cartography by Alice Viggiani.

cotton plantations to export their produce farther afield. The railroad system became much more interconnected in the 1870s and 1880s, bringing some traffic and trade to the area. The region was cultivated primarily with cotton, but plantations and farms also planted maize, wheat, and some raised hogs or cattle.[86] Upson County was a particularly dangerous and hostile environment after the Civil War, with hundreds of freedmen being driven out of their homes and forced into immediate debt if they returned.[87] Armed white mobs attacked the freedmen as drought ravaged the area. These conditions compelled hundreds of freedmen from Upson County and some thousands from neighboring regions of the state to strike out to the west, seeking better fortunes, heading primarily for Kansas.[88] But most people persisted in Upson County, many of whom, like the Few family, looked north for opportunities in the twentieth century.

After Emancipation, the pianist Bobby Few's great-great-grandparents James and Ellen Few (b. c. 1821 and 1824, respectively) lived in the small town of Union Hill, in Upson County, where the couple and their children worked as sharecroppers.[89] The Union Hill area was covered in lush forests intersected by streams and was known especially as a peach-growing area, as well as a place for raising livestock. Various businesses had also sprung up around the railroad, including warehouses and transportation for dry goods and other merchandise.

Well before the Civil War, the enslaved people of Upson County had a particularly active practice of patting juba, a form of body percussion that people employed, maintaining rhythms from their musical past as well as innovating and creating new ones.[90] It was common to hold performances at annual cornshucking gatherings after the harvest, as well as at other times. One eyewitness account there from 1841 noted, "This is done by placing one foot a little in advance of the other, raising the ball of the foot from the ground, and striking it in regular time, while, in connection, the hands are struck slightly together, and then upon the thighs."[91] Solomon Northup, who witnessed the practice during his years of enslavement, described the rhythmic process of "patting . . . striking the hands on the knees, then striking the knees together, then striking the right shoulder with one hand, the left with the other—all while keeping time with the feet, and singing."[92]

The rhythms of patting juba were used to inspire dance, often accompanied by a violin. The dances and rhythms may be traced, in some cases, to similar traditions in the Congo and other parts of central Africa, while the melodies were sometimes influenced by Scottish or Irish reels. The rhythmic patterns catered to polyrhythms, or as one scholar observed, "patting juba is a particularly good example of how . . . multiple meters inform black dance in such a way that different body parts follow different meters and drummers."[93] The fusion of music with forms of patting juba occurred in different parts of the United States to produce local varieties, and the one that came to hold in Upson County probably developed in southern Appalachia in the late eighteenth and early nineteenth centuries after African drums were outlawed in most slave states.[94] Still, it has been speculated that patting juba, like the drum, was occasionally employed to send warnings, including forewarning of KKK riders after the Civil War.[95]

An eyewitness of the Upson County performance of patting juba in 1841 wrote, "They make the most curious noise, yet in such perfect order, it furnishes music to dance by.... It is really astonishing to witness the rapidity of their motions, their accurate time, and the precision of their music and dance. I have never seen it equaled in my life."[96] Robert Anderson, a formerly enslaved person who wrote an account after Emancipation, described the performances, "We danced some of the dances the white folks danced . . . but we liked better the dances of our own particular race in which we tried to express in motion the particular feelings within our own selves. These dances were individual dances, consisting of shuffling of the feet and swinging of the arms and shoulders in a peculiar rhythm of time developed into what is known today as the double shuffle, heel and toe, buck wing, juba, etc. The slaves became proficient in such dances and could play a tune with their feet, dancing largely to an inward music, a music that was felt, but not heard."[97] Juba is commonly referenced by musicians with origins in the region, perhaps most prominently in the saxophonist Marion Brown's record *Juba-Lee*.[98]

There is other evidence of members of the community possessing strong musical traditions, drawn from notices posted about fugitive slaves who are described musicians, especially singers.[99] The kazoo was invented by an enslaved man named Alabama Vest in nearby Macon, Georgia, in the 1840s or early 1850s.[100] Violins were commonly used by Black musicians in that part of the Georgia piedmont before Emancipation, and sometimes bands would travel through the area, especially around Christmas, playing music for plantation owners as well as enslaved people.[101] "Frolics" sometimes occurred in the communities "when they fiddled and danced all night."[102] One of the spirituals known to have been particularly popular in the area was "Glory to the Dying Land," dating back to the years before Emancipation but remaining popular for decades after the Civil War.[103]

There was also a brass band that was organized in nearby Thomaston by the 1850s. The Thomaston Sax Horn Band likely included a quartet or more of soprano, alto, tenor, or baritone saxhorns, which, like the saxophone, which had been invented by the Belgian instrument-inventor Adolphe Sax in the 1830s. So, within two decades of their inception, these instruments had found their way to the rural western Georgia piedmont, where one announcement mentioned such a band being "reorganized" and that public performances were being held in April 1859.[104]

Bobby Few's grandfather Simon Few (1872–1953), the eldest of eleven children, moved from Union Hill to the nearby town of The Rock in the 1890s.[105] It was a dangerous time, with numerous vigilante groups noted in the area.[106] Initially the family sharecropped, but they owned their own farm by the time Bobby Few's father, Robert Lee Few Sr., was born there in 1910.[107] Still, the injustice system aimed to thwart such advancement, using courts and policing to undercut social mobility, with a growing convict labor system on the local level around the dawn of the twentieth century that only escalated into the 1920s.[108]

Macon, about fifty miles to the east of Upson County, was a major music center in Georgia. The Douglass Theater, founded by Charles H. Douglass, was a major Black theater that catered to film, vaudeville, blues, and jazz.[109] Douglass Theater was quickly linked into national networks of Black performers, primarily through the interracial Theater Owners' Booking Agency (TOBA). TOBA stitched together a circuit of theaters in the south and Midwest and ultimately established a vast network that connected areas as far flung as Jacksonville, Savannah, Augusta, Atlanta, Columbus (GA), Bessemer (AL), Pensacola (FL), Birmingham, New Orleans, Kansas City, St. Louis, Memphis, Nashville, Chicago, Indianapolis, Louisville, Cincinnati, Chattanooga, Baltimore, Wilmington (NC), Charlotte, Winston-Salem, Spartanburg (SC), Columbia (SC), Philadelphia, New York, and Boston.[110] In a certain sense, this facilitated performances that would connect workers in cotton fields, workers in southern cities, and northern urban Black communities into one cultural vernacular. The TOBA network featured vaudeville, dance, comedy, circus acts, and often had a midnight blues performance as a part of its regular bills.[111] Figures such as Ida Cox, Bessie Smith, Ma Rainey, and many lesser-known musicians all performed at the Douglass Theater in the 1920s.[112]

There were many blues performers throughout the Macon area, including the slide guitarist Rev. Pearly Brown (1915–1986), who was inspired most prominently by Blind Willie Johnson (1897–1945). Rev. Brown was playing and touring through central Georgia, Florida, and other parts of the southeastern United States by the 1930s, though unfortunately there are no recordings of his early work.[113] The region would later produce some major figures, such as Little Richard, Otis Redding, and other key figures of soul, rhythm and blues, and rock, prompting Macon to be considered alongside Memphis and Muscle Shoals in its impact on American music from the 1950s to 1970s.

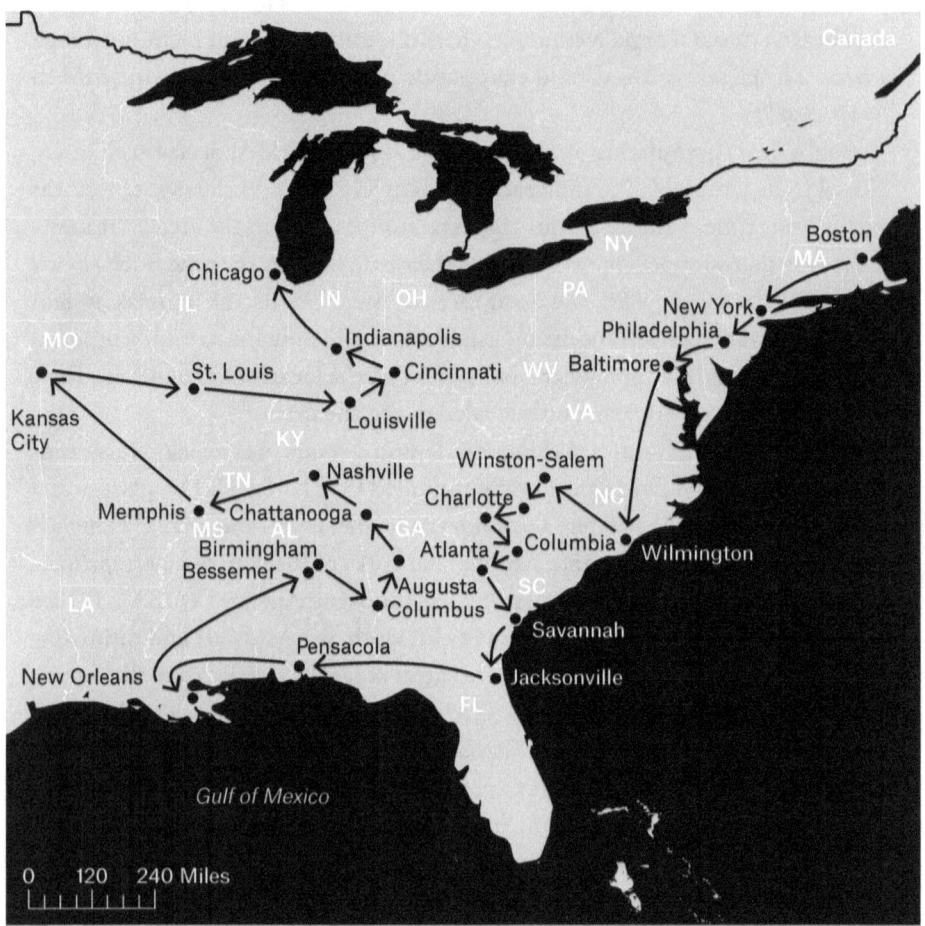

FIGURE 2.4 TOBA circuit.

Source: Cartography by Alice Viggiani.

In a controversy that erupted in 1921, a publication by Governor Hugh Dorsey leveled a scathing assessment of the conditions that African Americans were living under in Georgia at the time. Among the numerous injustices noted, the most common were mob violence, lynching, theft, police and other state violence, and an unfair legal system. The KKK, which was reaching a new peak in power, is cited numerous times as the perpetrators of much of the violence.[114]

The pamphlet included at least three cases in The Rock, including one where a relatively prosperous Black farming family was attacked. One member of the family, a community leader, was imprisoned, robbed, fined, threatened with lynching, and forced to work a chain gang, and other members of the family were driven out of the county.[115] The reaction by the white establishment to the pamphlet's publication in The Rock and other parts of the county was particularly vehement even in comparison to other parts of the state, and acts of public violence ensued in its wake.[116]

The Few family experienced something similar in the form of displacement. In March 1892, the pianist's great-great-grandfather James Few (b. c. 1821) and his family were forcibly evicted from the two-hundred-acre plot that they worked, and their harvest was sold at a sheriff's auction.[117] Though the details of the case are unclear, such occurrences were commonplace, especially for sharecroppers who had no recompense and were under constant threat of removal if they attempted to bargain for better contracts. In early 1922, Simon Few lost a court case in which he was sued for debts. He had four bales of his cotton seized, constituting the entire previous year; they were similarly sold at a sheriff's auction.[118] Having experienced the pattern of injustice and legalized theft without anywhere to turn, the Few family left for Cleveland.

The Buffalo saxophonist Paul Gresham's paternal grandmother and her parents and grandparents also trace to the west-central Georgia Black Belt in Upson and Pike counties. Gresham's great-great-grandfather Nathan Willis (b. c. 1835) registered to vote and acquired land during the Reconstruction period but lost those gains after the collapse of the brief Reconstruction regime.[119] The Willis family lived in Union Hill in the 1880s at the same time as the Few family, and the two families almost certainly knew each other in the small, tight-knit community.[120] Gresham's forebears generally worked as sharecroppers, often for so little that they could barely survive, though some people in the area did manage to organize and demand greater shares of the harvest. Still, it was meager living, and Gresham's great-grandparents, Peter and Anna Willis, migrated to Atlanta by the turn of the century in search of better opportunities.

Another musician who traces roots to the west-central Georgia Black Belt is the bassist Clyde Shy. His great-great-grandmother, who became known as Susan Shy, was born in Africa around 1795 and was brought to Georgia as a child during the last years of the slave trade before 1808. She was from "Upper Guinea," which at that time referred to the region that today stretches from Cote d'Ivoire to Senegal in West Africa.[121] Once in Georgia, she was enslaved on the cotton plantation of Samuel Shy in Jasper County. Jasper was on the north edge of the central Georgia Black Belt, about forty-five miles northeast of where Bobby Few's and Paul Gresham's families were in Upson County.[122]

After Emancipation, three generations of Shy's family sharecropped until after the turn of the century, and several of them served their community as Methodist ministers.[123] One great-great-grandfather, Rev. Paschal Showers, was even elected to be a presiding elder to represent his home district at a Methodist Conference in Atlanta in 1871.[124] Another branch of the family traced to Spencer Jordan (c. 1808–1886), who owned eighty acres of land in Jasper County in 1880, growing maize, wheat, and cotton and also maintaining a herd of fifteen hogs, a few dairy cows, and a dozen chickens, though he experienced problems with theft of livestock.[125] The Jordan family's modest success, however, came from the thirty acres they dedicated to cotton. Jordan's son, Lott (c. 1851–1918), left the farm after his father's death and moved south to Macon, where he worked at the C. B. Lane barber shop from the early 1890s until his death.[126] Various members of Clyde Shy's family held positions of leadership from one generation to the next within their communities wherever they lived, especially in religious capacities, before and after they migrated north.

The drummer J. C. Moses (1936–1977), who began his career as a bebop pianist in Pittsburgh but who later played a transformative role in the New York Contemporary Five with Archie Shepp, Don Cherry, and others, traced his paternal relations back to the same region. The family came from Stewart County, just seventy-five miles southwest of Upson County, where they lived for generations after Emancipation working as sharecroppers and blacksmiths.[127] They, too, attended "many frolics" where "everyone danced when banjoes were available"; one resident recalled a musician in the area playing "an improvised fiddle fashioned from a hand saw."[128] The biggest frolics were held right before spring planting, when "new ground was cleared, old land fertilized, and the corn fields cleared of last year's rubbish."[129] After decades of frustration with the sharecropping arrangements there, the Moses family moved east to Savannah by around the time of World War I, seeking jobs there in the growing industrial and shipping sectors.

FLORIDA PANHANDLE

Not far south from the Georgia Black Belt, the Florida panhandle region was another point of departure for some of the artists' families that migrated north to the greater Ohio Valley. The pianist Harold McKinney and trombonist Kiane Zawadi's paternal side of the family may be traced all the way back to a man who became known as Jacob McKinney Sr., who was born in Africa around 1790 and was brought to southern Georgia on the border with Florida as an adolescent in the early 1800s. He and his family were enslaved in or near Valdosta, in Lowndes County, Georgia, but after Emancipation, as the region's cotton production was undermined on a wide scale by a plague of caterpillars, they moved just twenty-five miles south across the border to Madison, Florida, where Jacob's son Rev. Ishmael McKinney (1832–1882) had a farm and where he was ordained as the minister of the Damascus Baptist Church.[130] On a political level, Madison County was a haven for Republican politics that even managed to survive the collapse of Reconstruction by a few years.[131] They later moved to Live Oak, in Suwannee County, where he served on the board of trustees at the Florida Institute (now Florida Memorial University) and was actively involved in the Florida Baptist Association.[132] Rev. Ishmael McKinney's son, Rev. George Patterson McKinney (1863–1933), became far more well known as the minister of the African Baptist Church in Live Oak. He also served two terms as president of the Florida Institute, which trained an entire generation of Baptist ministers who served across a number of states in the ensuing decades. He also worked as an editor and a writer of a number of Baptist magazines that were then just emerging and served in leadership positions within a number of regional, state, and national Baptist associations.[133]

FIGURE 2.5 Rev. George Patterson McKinney (1863–1933) and Sallie Richard "Tinesy" Ellis (1869–1951).

Source: Courtesy the Ashanti Drum, Home of the McKinley-Ellis Clan, https://www.theashantidrum.com.

Madison County and the surrounding area of the central Florida panhandle was known for the growing of Sea Island cotton, a rare type of cotton whose fibers were used in fine fabrics, laces, thread, and, later, automobile tires. The cotton generally garnered a price three times that of more common species.[134] In the period between the 1880s and the mid-1910s, there was a boom in demand for Sea Island cotton, leading to a rise in production throughout the area. But in 1915, the boll weevil struck the region and destroyed yields for three consecutive seasons, forcing many farmers to switch to other crops, such as peanuts, and pushing many sharecroppers out of work entirely.[135] Rev. McKinney's eight children all attended universities before moving north, a few to Atlanta but most of them journeying all the way to Detroit in the 1920s, among them Harold McKinney and Kiane Zawadi's father, who found work in the automobile factories that were then booming.[136]

KENTUCKY'S BLACK PATCH

Outside of the deep south, the other region that served as a point of departure for many musicians' families was southwestern Kentucky. Both the trumpeter Norman Howard and the saxophonist Charles Tyler came from families that trace back to southwestern Kentucky in a region known as the Black Patch, so-called because it was the leading worldwide supplier of dark, heavy-leafed, fire-cured tobacco used for snuff, chewing tobacco, and cigars.[137] Enslaved people had been originally brought there from Virginia in the first decade of the nineteenth century, though there was a second influx after 1840, which included most of Howard and Tyler's relations. On the eve of the Civil War, enslaved people composed about one-third of the overall population.[138] The northern border of the state had for decades before Emancipation represented the barrier past which one might attain freedom, and the pathways leading northward via the Underground Railroad left linkages that persisted well into the twentieth century.[139]

Norman Howard's family had been enslaved on a plantation in Christian County, which had the highest proportion of enslaved people in the state and some of the largest-scale plantations. The soil and climate supported widespread tobacco cultivation as well as hemp, maize, and wheat.[140] The county had also been home to slave-gathering farms and one of the most active slave markets in the entire region before the Civil War.[141] By the mid-1870s, the freedman community united around organizing and building schools. Though they were only

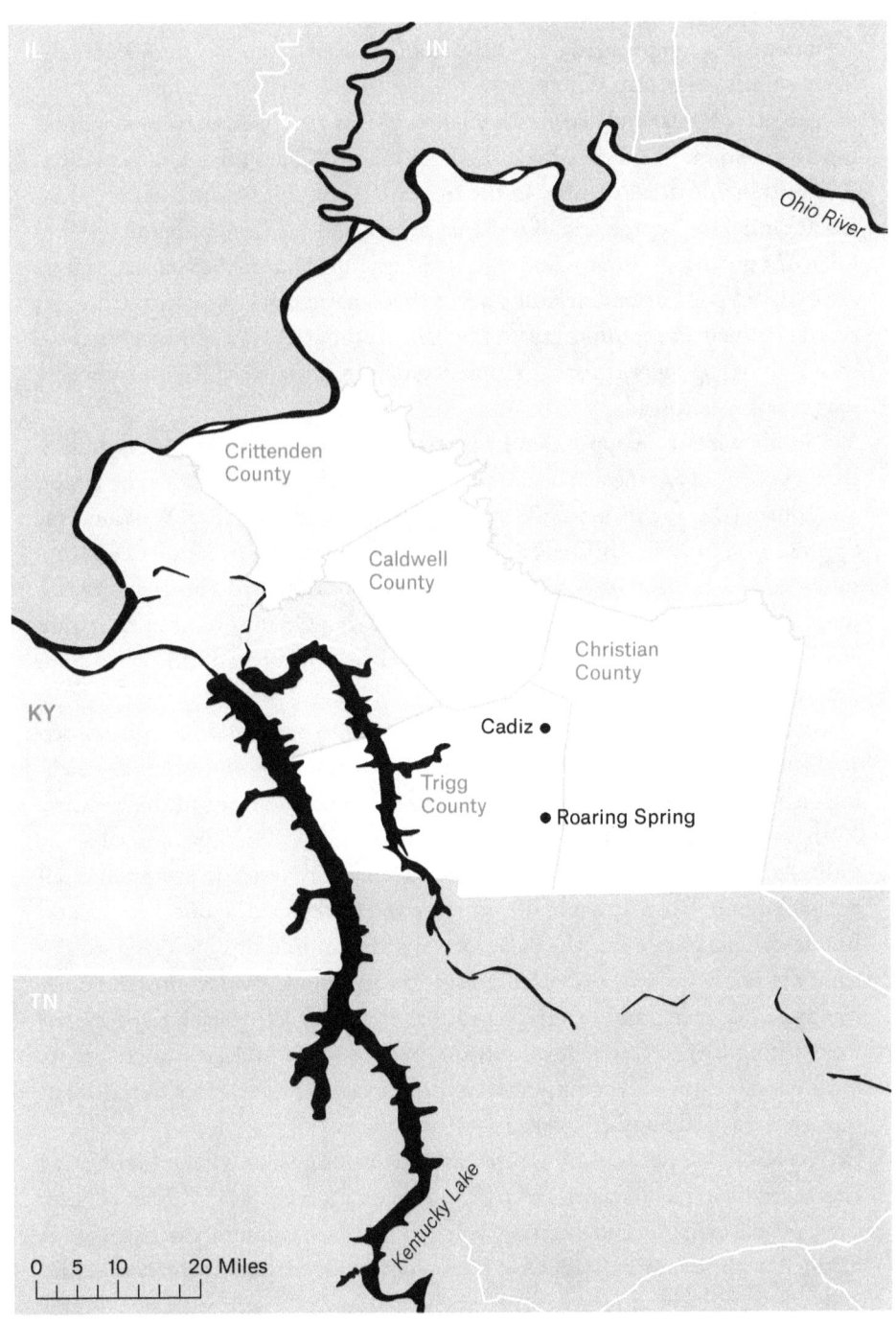

FIGURE 2.6 Kentucky Black Patch region.

Source: Cartography by Alice Viggiani.

adequately educating a fraction of the children in the area, the schools still were favorable when compared to other Black communities in southwestern Kentucky in the same time period.[142]

The saxophonist and clarinetist Charles Tyler's family came from neighboring Trigg County, and they lived there for many decades after Emancipation. There, as in Christian County in the late 1850s, paranoia by slaveholders about the potential for an uprising of enslaved people and the close proximity of free soil to the north led them to carry out lynchings and other public violence against the enslaved population, including a free charismatic Black preacher who was a central figure in the community.[143] Though Kentucky did not ultimately secede, there was strong support for the Confederacy in southwestern Kentucky, where slavery was widespread.[144]

Despite wide-scale opposition by proslavery factions in Kentucky, the Black Patch was one of the most concentrated sites of Black recruitment for the Union army during the war, including Tyler's great-great-grandfather, Pvt. William Tinsley (1846–1920), who enlisted in the 13th US Colored Heavy Artillery and was stationed as a garrison unit at various defensive positions in Kentucky in 1864–1865.[145] After the war, many slaveholders in Trigg County refused to release enslaved people until mid-1866, and only after being threatened with legal action did they concede.[146]

For two decades after the Civil War, Kentucky in particular "became associated with brutal behavior" that included "vigilantism, mob violence, and lynching on an unprecedented scale."[147] As one historian characterized the violence, "Gangs roamed at will throughout much of Kentucky, especially in rural areas, intimidating, beating, and murdering freedmen. They varied in size from small bands of four or five to gangs of fifty or more and represented, as one [Freedman's] Bureau official phrased it, 'the pulse' of the white community."[148] Vigilante violence did not begin to abate until segregation and Jim Crow laws institutionalized systemic racism and socioeconomic barriers and barred Black Kentuckians from taking part in the political process. Between 1866 and 1934, there are 353 documented cases of lynching, with a concentration in the Black Patch areas, though the actual number is certainly much higher.[149]

The KKK was particularly active in the area around Cadiz, the seat of Trigg County, which had a majority Black population after the war.[150] Even decades later, people remembered the spectacle of the lynchings and the fear that it instilled in the community. As one Black community member who was a child at the time stated bluntly from an eyewitness account, "There was a sign on this stake that said, 'Look out nigger, you are next,'" set next to victims' bodies along a roadside.[151]

FIGURES 2.7 AND 2.8 Pvt. William Tinsley (1846–1920) and Susan Coleman (1847–1941).

Source: Ancestry.com

Independent Black churches did not emerge in Trigg County until the 1870s, which was quite late even for southwestern Kentucky, but they were important for the community because they represented the only substantive Black-controlled public spaces throughout the region.[152] From that point on, however, churches grew exponentially as they attracted worshippers who had previously had no other option than to attend integrated services, which were held under the watchful eye of white church organizers. Such spaces were vital for the sustenance of the community. One former slave of Trigg County in the 1930s explained his dedication to religion in direct terms. "It enables you to have, though a slave, joy of the soul, to endure the trials," and then broke into song:

> We'll walk them golden streets,
> We'll walk them golden streets,
> Where pleasure never dies

And then shifted to another song:

> Oh! I's a-going to live always,
> Oh! I's a-going to live always,
> Oh! I's a-going to live always,
> When I get in the kingdom.[153]

Another of Tyler's great-great-grandfathers, Dick Tyler (c. 1825–c. 1870s), was likely enslaved in one of the ironworks sites just across the border in Tennessee or perhaps in connection to one of the many iron or lead mines concentrated in Caldwell or Crittenden counties in Kentucky.[154] Dick Tyler supported the family in the years immediately after Emancipation with his trade as a blacksmith at Empire Iron Works in Cadiz, a company that employed several hundred freedmen there in the late 1860s.[155] By 1870, he had a modest savings, but his death a few years later caused the family's fragile finances to collapse, and they turned to sharecropping in the area until after the turn of the century.[156] By 1910, Tyler's great-grandparents owned their own farm in North Cadiz, though his grandmother worked as a cook there, owned a small house, and rented out rooms to boarders to supplement her income through the Great Depression.[157]

Racist violence raged through Trigg and neighboring counties of western Kentucky well into the 1920s, forcing many Black residents out of the area, while it also undercut those who remained behind to build better lives. Many Black residents continued to work the same farms where they had formerly been enslaved well into the twentieth century. For all of these reasons, it became difficult for some sharecroppers to ever acquire their own land. Eventually the Tylers followed the steady stream of people who had moved northwest to Indianapolis, where Charles Tyler spent much of his childhood.[158] Indeed, the banjoist, guitarist, and vocalist Trevor Bacon (1907–1945), who first established himself in Indianapolis before being discovered by Lucky Millinder and going to New York, came from Roaring Spring, the same community where one branch of the Tyler family had lived for generations.[159]

OHIO RIVER BORDERLAND

Many of the musicians also traced their families back to the immediate Ohio River borderland itself, especially along parts of northern Kentucky and West Virginia. Positioned just across the Ohio River from free territory, people from this region were among the most numerous to migrate north into Ohio and other parts of the region after Emancipation. The saxophonist Rahsaan Roland Kirk, for example, came from these regions on both sides of his family. His father's family came from the town of Fairmont, in Marion County, West Virginia, arriving there from Louisiana during a brief period of urbanization just before the turn of the century. Fairmont was the site of major coal mines as well as intense labor organizing in the early twentieth century when the Kirk family was drawn there by employment opportunities.[160]

Kirk's mother's family, however, can be traced more effectively south of the Ohio River. They came from a rural area near Falmouth, in Pendleton County, Kentucky, and likely dwelled there for a number of decades before the Civil War. The region fell to the Confederates in the early years of the war, and it remained a centerpiece in the Confederate attempt to hold north-central Kentucky and exert control over the movement of ships on the Ohio River.[161]

Kirk's great-great-great-grandmother Lucy Duncan (b. c. 1795) lived to see Emancipation, working the years afterward as a domestic.[162] Her son-in-law Jack Broadus (b. c. 1810) somehow managed to acquire his own land in the years after Emancipation, which he maintained and passed down for at least four generations within the family.[163] His son, Pvt. Aaron Broadus (1842–1920), escaped behind Union lines and enlisted in the 100th US Colored Infantry, in which he served for about the final year of the war.[164] He helped run the family farm until after the turn of the century, when he moved into Falmouth, where he worked as a drayman; his wife worked as a nurse.[165] But their children, including Kirk's maternal grandfather, moved out of the area during World War I, heading north

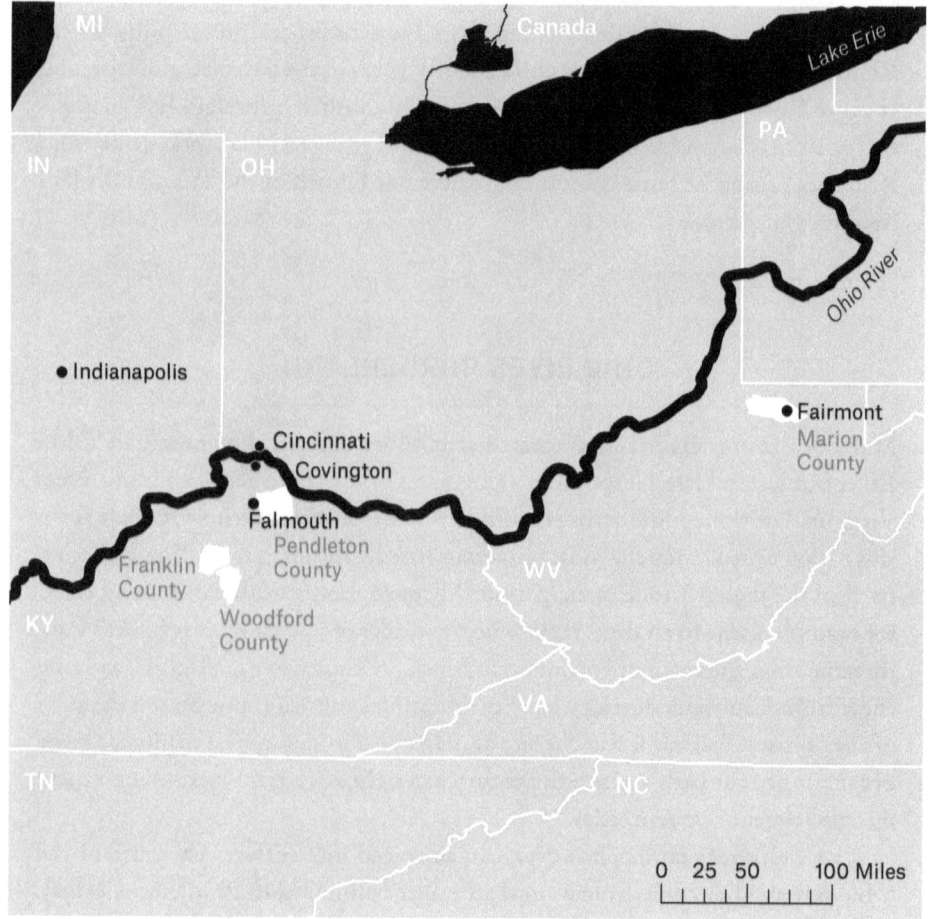

FIGURE 2.9 Ohio River borderland.

Source: Cartography by Alice Viggiani.

to Columbus, where construction jobs offered better pay and where Kirk's mother was born in 1917.[166]

Other musicians also followed a similar pattern. The trombonist Phil Ranelin, for example, had family who came from Covington, Kentucky, only thirty miles north of Falmouth, right across the Ohio River from Cincinnati. Covington was second only to Louisville in population among Kentucky towns on the south bank of the river, and before the Civil War, most of the small population of enslaved people in the town unloaded cargo on the docks.[167] After the war, a suspension bridge built across the river to Cincinnati in 1867 brought economic development. Many freedmen moved to Covington in the years after Emancipation for fear "that they [were] all going to be enslaved again. They ... complain bitterly ... that they are living in a regular reign of terror."[168] Upon arriving, however, they were restricted to living in "wretched old dilapidated ware houses, cellars, garrets and miserable shanties" located in the low-lying areas along the river or near the rail lines.[169] Some of these new residents of Covington eventually managed to secure employment in the expanding coal yards, glass factories, and wharfs. Public sector jobs excluded Black workers.[170]

Immediately after Emancipation, in mid-1865, the Black community elected a school board and set about raising funds from benevolent societies and the freedman's bureau to build elementary schools, though they were unable to afford a high school until the 1890s.[171] This urbanization process resulted in tightly knit Black neighborhoods in the town.[172] Ranelin's grandfather was born there in 1897; he eventually moved north to Indianapolis during World War I.[173] Similarly, portions of the pianist Dave Burrell's mother's family also came from the same north-central Kentucky region, around Mays Lick, in Mason County, where they owned and ran a farm in the early decades of the twentieth century before moving north to Middletown, Ohio, during World War I.[174]

The maternal side of the family of Harold McKinney and Kiane Zawadi may be traced back to Winny DeMar (b. c. 1780), who headed a household that included seven other "free people of color" including her young son, Hayden DeMar (c. 1805–75), in Woodford County, Kentucky, in 1810.[175] The record suggests that she was of mixed-race background and had left Virginia only a few years prior, though nothing else is known of her origins. By the 1820s, they had moved just north to Franklin County, where they lived on the outskirts of Frankfort and where Hayden established his own family by 1840.[176]

The small free community in the region centered on a prosperous grocer in Frankfort named John Ward and a small number of other free Black business owners.[177] In 1833, the community had formed an autonomous congregation, the Colored Baptist Church, and their minister, Rev. James Monroe, was described by one traveler as "the best preacher he had ever heard."[178] Rev. Monroe hosted the first meeting of the State Convention of Colored Baptists, which grew considerably after the war.[179] Schools appeared even earlier, with a Black day school first built in 1820, followed by additional schools in the 1850s, which were unusual even in that part of Kentucky.[180] Indeed, the historian Marion Lucas argued that free communities such as the one in Frankfort "created ... a life unto themselves" that operated like "segregated enclaves where they developed a strong sense of community."[181]

Kentucky's own abolitionist movement was centered in the capital, but it was weak and never progressed beyond the Frankfort Convention of 1849, which issued demands but was not able to build further support.[182] Worse yet, rumors of a rebellion by enslaved people there in 1856 brought the free community under intense scrutiny, leading to prominent figures being put on a list and threatened with violence if they did not leave the city.[183]

The DeMar family owned its own small farm near Frankfort; it was estimated to be worth six hundred dollars on the eve of the Civil War, growing tobacco, hemp, or grapes, which were common in the region.[184] Their plot of land was not very profitable but was enough for them to subsist on during those years, while a number of other members of the community faced lynching and other violence in the years right after the war.[185] They continued to farm there until Hayden DeMar's death in 1875.[186]

DeMar's son, Pvt. Washington DeMar (1846–1920), the eighth of sixteen children born to the family, made his way to Lexington in 1864 and volunteered for the Union Army after the formal authorization had been made to organize Black combat units.[187] Enlisting in the 5th US Colored Cavalry, he saw immediate action, and the company gained the reputation as one of the most notable and daring Black fighting units during the war. This all came despite their haphazardly assembled weapons and horses, given supply shortages. They were mounted on untrained horses and given Lee-Enfield infantry rifles, which could not be loaded while on horseback, unlike the more advanced Spencer repeating rifles that other units employed at the time.

Despite these challenges, in late September 1864 Gen. Ulysses S. Grant ordered the unit to proceed into southwestern Virginia and destroy the salt works near Saltville; they marched from Prestonburg on September 27 to perform the task. There was dissension within the Union ranks: White soldiers openly ridiculed many of their Black counterparts, at times stealing their horses or causing other confusion. This disarray contributed to the unit's defeat at the first Battle of Saltville, October 1–3. In the aftermath of the battle, the pursuing Confederates attacked hospital encampments and slaughtered Union soldiers in their beds, for which one of the leaders was later court-marshaled and executed. Through all of this, DeMar endured.

Two months later, in December 1864, the unit was again called into battle and joined other units from Union-allied eastern Tennessee for additional raids into Virginia. Through the course of this, the unit encountered pitched battles at Hopkinsville, Kentucky, on December 12; Kingsport, Tennessee, on December 13; and then entered into full-fledged fighting as they crossed into Virginia at the Battle of Marion, December 17–18; and at the Second Battle of Saltville.

At the Battle of Marion, Pvt. Washington DeMar's unit was positioned between two white units on the left flank of the Union line. Dismounting, they advanced toward the Confederate position but encountered heavy fire from Parrott riflemen, forcing them to retreat.[188] Gathering themselves together, they rallied and "with a mighty yell" made a second charge, eventually being forced back again, where they dug in as night fell, the healthiest in the company going out to carry back the wounded.[189]

The following morning, the 5th US Colored Cavalry awoke to cold rain and dense fog hanging over the battlefield. DeMar joined others in his company in a futile mission to rescue some white soldiers who had been trapped near a covered bridge on the left flank.[190] In a sudden Confederate counterattack later that day, one of the white units abreast DeMar's unit was almost entirely routed, and the 5th US Colored Cavalry was ordered to retreat. But many among them, including DeMar, "remembering the murder of their comrades during the first Battle of Saltville," broke ranks to rescue their wounded fellow soldiers. It was only Union reinforcements before sundown and a shortage of Confederate ammunition that caused the latter to retreat and for the Union to claim a costly victory.[191]

The 5th US Colored Cavalry pursued the Confederates back to Saltville, where they joined the 6th US Colored Cavalry, entering "a fray of cold vengeance," and there they definitively routed the Confederates. The unit hastily set about destroying the salt works and even portions of the Virginia & Tennessee Railroad in the area before retreating to avoid being surrounded by advancing Confederate reinforcements.[192] The cavalry unit remained active until 1866, by which point they had been drawn westward, with their final work being a memorial to the soldiers murdered at the First Battle of Saltville, which they built while stationed in Helena, Arkansas. Helena had been a major center of power for the Union army in the Mississippi delta in the last years of the war, and Black troops and white Union officers had occupied a number of plantations there that they turned into "places of learning, advancement, and compensated labor for former slaves" during the last war years and the aftermath.[193]

Having been discharged in Helena, Arkansas, Pvt. Washington DeMar decided to settle there, in Phillips County, right on the Mississippi delta, where in 1870 he and his family ran their own farm.[194] By 1880, they had moved twenty miles north to the river town of Marianna, where the family dwelled for four decades. DeMar's daughter Emma married a house painter who had migrated to the delta from Georgia.[195] Her husband died by the mid-1910s, leaving her to support six children there as a laundress before moving them all north to Detroit after her father's death in 1920.[196] By around the time that they left, Helena was just beginning to emerge as one of the main blues centers in the delta.[197]

MISSISSIPPI DELTA

Elsewhere in the delta, a part of the saxophonist Frank Wright's family may be traced to Grenada County, Mississippi, on the east-central fringes of the region, one hundred miles south of Memphis, on land that was once occupied by the Choctaw people. Grenada County stretched from the low-lying delta up into hill country straddling the Yalobusha River, along which cotton was grown and shipped downstream to the Mississippi River. In addition, small-scale farmers grew maize, potatoes, and sorghum, and laborers ran teams of oxen to carry logs from the interior to the river.[198]

Wright's great-grandmother Sarah Gary (c. 1850–1928) led the family from Emancipation through decades of sharecropping to owning their own family farm by the turn of the century.[199] But the family continued to struggle and within a decade had lost their land and were reduced to sharecropping once more.[200] In the decades after the Civil War, there were only dirt roads and the streams and rivers connecting Grenada to other parts of the delta.[201] Schools for Black children in the area were given paltry public funding, but there is evidence that some communities managed to improve upon them through their own donations and labor, such as the Mitchell Springs School in nearby Teoc.[202]

One local song survived that spoke of the difficulty of escaping enslavement in the Grenada area, written by enslaved people and maintained through oral tradition after Emancipation. The tune was typically accompanied by banjo or guitar:

> Run, Nigger, run
> The patrols'll get you.
> That nigger run
> That nigger flew
> That nigger bust
> His Sunday shoe.
> Run, nigger, run
> The patrols'll get you.[203]

Violins were also used in the area, and it was common for banjos and violins to be used together in small bands and occasionally rarer instruments like the mouth harp. By the turn of the century, the guitar began to supersede the banjo as the most widely used fretted instrument in the delta.[204]

The early blues tunes "Hop Joint" and "Good Morning Miss Carrie" both existed in the Grenada area by the turn of the century, and there was also

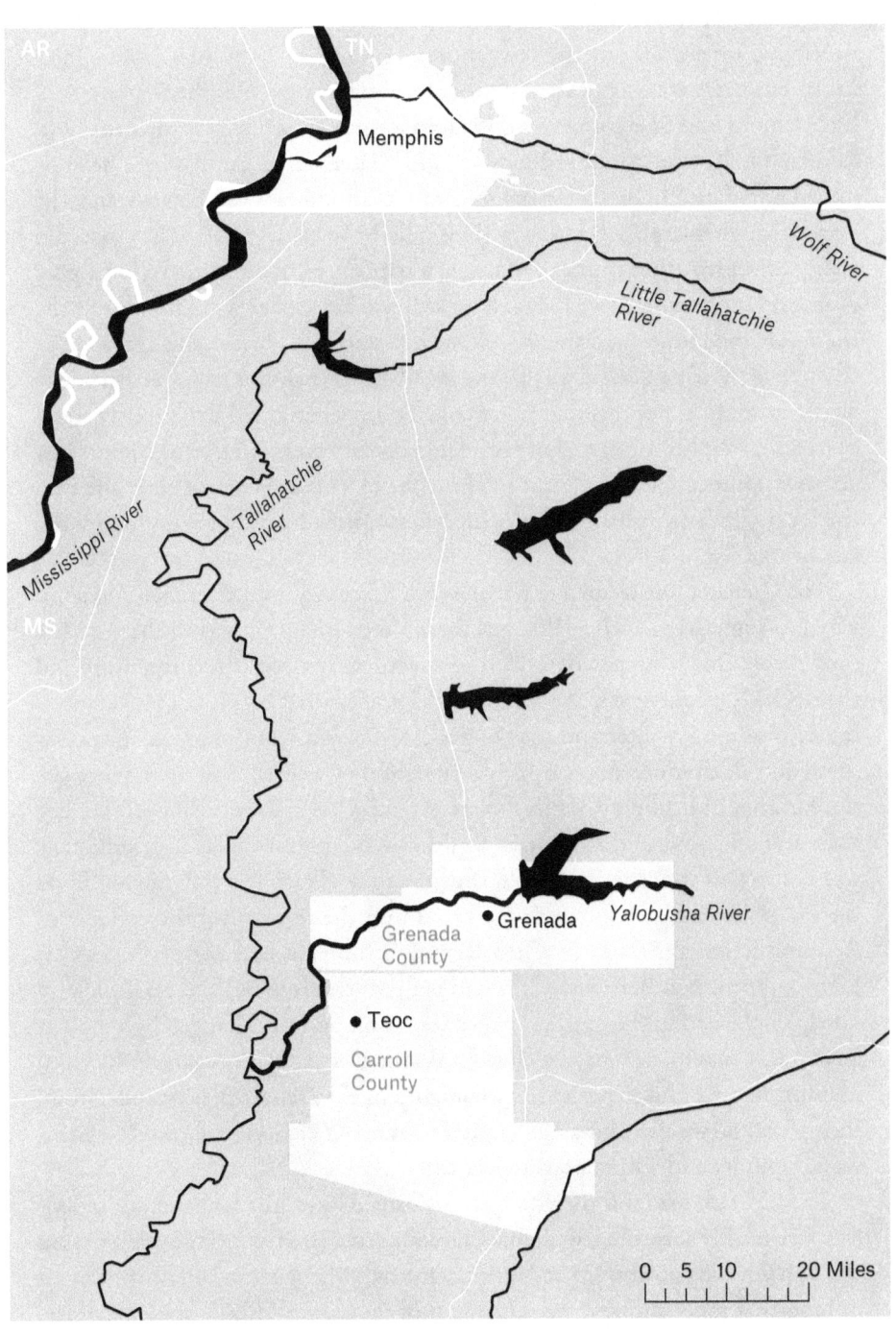

FIGURE 2.10 Mississippi delta.

Source: Cartography by Alice Viggiani.

"a ragtime consciousness" in much of the local music at the time.[205] Blues developed organically in the region, most prominently by Mississippi John Hurt, but there were a number of other local figures, such as the fiddlers Willie Narmour and Shell Smith, who played local dances and recorded the best-known hit, "Carroll County Blues."[206] Hurt later stated about where he grew up, "They danced the two-step, shimmie-shamwabble, breakaways and the slow drag. I remember the dance they called the camel walk. They also did some sort of trot that they called takin' a trip."[207] Hurt remained a local phenomenon for decades after his 1928 recordings, before being "rediscovered" by the recording industry in the 1960s. In the 1930s, the blues really exploded in the area as more people began playing locally and musicians from farther south began to settle in the region.[208] Grenada County remained dry after the end of national Prohibition, so local residents often traveled to the juke joints just across the line in Carroll County to hear the blues played live or else tune into the local Grenada radio station, which began broadcasting the music by the late 1930s.[209]

The Grenada area seemed to have less KKK activity after the Civil War compared to some areas of the delta, but there were some incidents in the 1860s to early 1870s. One freedman described an encounter between the community and the KKK: "Once after the War there was a lot of colored people at a prayer meeting. It was in the winter and they had a fire. The Ku Klux come up. They just stood outside the door, but the people thought they were coming in and they got scared. They didn't know hardly how to get out. One man got a shovelful of hot coals and ashes out of the fireplace and threw it out over them, and while they was dusting off the ashes and coals, the [Negroes] all got away."[210] Grenada was the site of lynching in the mid-1880s well into the 1890s after the collapse of Reconstruction.[211] In nearby Carrollton, lynching reached a feverish peak on July 30, 1901, when Betsie McCray and her two children Belford and Ida were falsely implicated in the murder of a white couple and were hanged by a mob in an incident that made national news.[212] As the Detroit labor organizer Michael Hamlin wrote of his experience growing up in the Delta: "Blacks understood their place and we also understood that if you got out of place, you could be killed with impunity and without any repercussions."[213]

The Grenada area was then being transformed by railroads that made mobility more readily accessible, with one line completed in the late 1880s that passed through Grenada northward and ultimately led to Memphis and another finished in 1900 that ran southwest into the heart of the delta.[214] Black residents of the delta had already resolved to seek better fortunes elsewhere, and by 1879 thirty thousand people had left, primarily to Kansas and Oklahoma.[215] Nevertheless, the Gary and Wright families persisted in Grenada, perhaps from a lack of means to leave, comforted by a turn to an ardent faith in God.

The Grenada area was particularly religious, and there are numerous accounts of religious revivals and traditions that were a part of everyday life. One sharecropper, Austin Parnell, described his earliest experiences:

> I can remember how my mother used to pray out in the field. We'd be picking cotton. She would go off out there in the ditch a little ways. It wouldn't be far, and I would listen to her. She would say to me: "Pray, son," and I would say, "Mother, I don't know how to pray," and she would say, "Well, just say Lord have mercy." That gave me my religious inclinations. . . . I try to pray and finally I learned. One day I was out in the field and it was pouring down rain. And I was standing up with tears in my eyes trying to pray as she taught me to. We weren't picking cotton then. I was just walking out. My mother was dead. I would be walking out and whenever I would get the notion I would stop right there and go to praying.[216]

People in the area sometimes sang a song with the chorus, "We will camp awhile in the wilderness / And then I'm going home," a variant of a song that existed in western Alabama and eastern Mississippi at that time:[217]

> My mother prayed in the wilderness,
> In the wilderness,
> In the wilderness.
> My mother prayed in the wilderness.
> And then I'm a-going home.
> Then I'm a-going home,
> Then I'm a-going home.
> We'll all make ready, Lord,
> And then I'm a-going home.
> She pled her cause in the wilderness,
> In the wilderness,
> In the wilderness.
> She pled her cause in the wilderness.
> And then I'm a-going home.
> Then I'm a-going home,
> Then I'm a-going home.
> We'll all make ready, Lord,
> And then I'm a-going home.[218]

Some of the religiosity within the Black community of Grenada seems to have been elevated by a particularly poignant revival that occurred there in the late 1870s or early 1880s, in the wake of the devastating yellow fever epidemic that killed five thousand people in Memphis alone and twenty thousand more throughout the delta region.[219] The town of Grenada was particularly hard-hit, with its population supposedly reduced from two thousand to two hundred in the span of a week.[220] Out of this terrible circumstance, a charismatic figure emerged, Cindy "Scinda" Mitchell, who led a powerful religious revival and built such respect that she still had followers who recounted her influence in the 1930s.[221] One stated that Scinda was "sent and called and picked and chosen" to be God's messenger on earth and, according to one report, "revealed it to the world that she had been inspired by God and was a servant of his to direct his people, both black and white."[222] She called for an end to racial violence, going from farm to farm preaching. According to one report, she gained respect in both communities, though her dedicated followers were Black.[223] In her role as a sort of prophet, she called a meeting of the entire community, to whom she preached in brightly ribboned attire with many handcrafted beads, rings on her fingers, and piercings in her ears. On her head, she wore a shoebox decorated with layers of ribbons, many detailed with religious symbols of her own craft.[224] By 1887, she had eight hundred followers in the Grenada area spread across at least one hundred families.[225]

Scinda's self-designed apron, which became a relic in the community, depicted a kind of procession of souls toward heaven and hell and was duplicated and worn by her followers. A description of one of the duplicates was recorded by an eyewitness in the early 1930s:

> On the lower right-hand corner of the apron are the goats, on the lower left-hand corner the sheep. This would seem to be the way people are born, into a category. Heaven, a little picture in applique, is directly above the good ones' heads, but the bad ones must follow a long path to get there. A black cloud is firmly stitched over them as they stand on the road, black with a tiny gold stripe that leads over a little hill. But just ahead to the left is an angel with a yellow heart whose arms are opened wide. The angel points above, where the tickets to heaven are tacked down like snowflakes over her head. A canopy of blue and white stripes is stretched there, on a little extension of which two chickens with golden eggs visible inside them sit on calico nests. Halfway along the path, the pilgrim is sewed on again as a half-and-half believer, with heart neither black nor gold, but speckled gray. Up there is ground to walk upon, but it is full of little holes, carefully cut out by scissors. If the pilgrim should heed the angel straight ahead and get their ticket to heaven, they may ascend where the sheep on the left ascend, and there watch Gabriel, white as a sheet, ring the red, blue, and golden Gospel bell by its long yellow cord.[226]

Other relics were sewn by Scinda that depicted a variety of biblical scenes.[227]

The community built a pine-log church about three miles from the town of Grenada. Sunday services commenced there at eight o'clock in the morning and often lasted all day.[228] White adherents sat in the back or outside by the windows if they attended the services.[229] According to one visitor who attended a Sunday service, "they danced and sung and played the banjo and shouted. When dancing begins they all stand up and as many as can join hands until a circle is formed. They march around and around, singing their own chants, occasionally stopping and each one goes through a 'shuffle' to the music of a banjo."[230] These ceremonial performances by the congregation preceded Scinda's pronouncements.

In one of her many sermons, according to one of her followers, Scinda declared, "Hell would be their bed if they didn't come and do right. Hell might rage and vent her spite, but God will save my heart's delight."[231] She further stated that God had selected her as "first shepherd of the judgment battle."[232] She accompanied her pronouncements with her banjo, often speaking of dreams while leading her congregants in "champing" (her word for dancing), because "God commanded her to pick while they moved their feet."[233] She commonly encouraged the faithful to pray, sing, or dance whenever they wished to do so, and members of her congregation improvised with guitar, bugle, and tambourine at the festive gatherings.[234] "At the close there is considerable ceremony," one participant noted. "It is marked by a procession, single file, each one carrying a symbol marked by design, moving under the music of the fiddle and banjo. After rounds of marchings they assemble in solemn awe around their priestess, Scinda, whose presence indicates she stands on the outer circle of divinity. Here, after singing their peculiar requiems, they disperse one by one."[235]

Scinda's following, referred to colloquially as "Cindy's Band," grew as she baptized each adherent in rivers or creeks in the area and they established several other churches in the post-Reconstruction period.[236] It was a staunchly oral practice, without textual reference to the Bible but heavily influenced by general Christian teachings. "Every member of the band was privileged to speak and pray and sing as long as the spirit moved them."[237] They often played out biblical scenes, however, like live action plays, with different members of the congregation playing figures such as the Angel Gabriel, King David, and others. They also carried out mock battles, symbolizing taking up arms against the devil, as part of worship services and processions. But as one observer noted, Scinda advocated very stringent codes of conduct. If one of her following was convicted of even a minor crime, they were immediately expelled from her band. In the years after the yellow fever epidemic, Cindy's band spread through Grenada, and they persisted for many decades. Frank Wright grew up around elements of this religious movement, and the earlier generations of his family were closely affiliated with the adherents and teachings. As a child, his family moved north to Memphis by the early 1940s, where he grew up.

The web of networks that emanated out of the Black Belt of the deep south, the Florida panhandle, the Mississippi delta, and the Ohio River borderland formed a second and more substantial flow of aesthetics, concepts, and social values from the south into the greater Ohio Valley and formed the initial movement of people from rural areas into urban sites within the South. These multi-generational lines of communication and inheritance facilitated a substantial flow of evolving cultural matter that would be employed by practitioners of free jazz in the mid-twentieth century.

CHAPTER 3

URBANIZATION, LABOR STRUGGLES, THE BLUES, AND THE GREAT MIGRATION

Industrialization and Cultural Space in the Early Twentieth Century

Before migrating north, many people first took part in urbanization movements to industrial cities in the south. This mobility separated such migrants from the majority who remained in rural areas, most of whom remained sharecroppers; thus urbanization represented spatial shifts as well as class stratification. The struggle to form labor unions and to demand higher pay and better working conditions in the face of state-sanctioned violence was a major part of the lives of these new urbanites, who a few decades later migrated to Cleveland, Detroit, Buffalo, and other northern cities.

In places like Mobile, Birmingham, Atlanta, and Savannah, workers faced racist opposition, attempts to divide workers along the lines of race, and labor organizations that either refused to organize Black workers or often inadequately did so. Cities in the greater Ohio Valley, such as Louisville and Indianapolis, were also the sites of labor struggles that shaped the community. But there were also corresponding struggles in rural areas in Alabama, Kentucky, and the Mississippi delta that faced even greater scales of violent repression. Through this, a Black working-class consciousness began to form that many would carry to the northern industrial cities of the greater Ohio Valley.

In these cities, the final two decades of the nineteenth century were a watershed moment in the formation of Black urban communities across the south. In Alabama, for instance, the percentage of the overall population employed in manufacturing more than tripled between 1880 and 1900, during which time the urban growth rate topped 200 percent.[1] This drew capital investment in a range of industries that spurred the spread of factories, primarily linked to the mining of iron and coal around Birmingham and the northern parts of the state, for which the Civil War was the catalyst. After the turn of the century, steelworks further spurred industrial growth. But the benefit of all of these developments was terribly uneven. Severe social tensions resulted between the few who profited from this gilded age and the many who toiled under dangerous conditions for the enrichment of the elites.

Networks of mobility facilitated the flows of people and information and spurred the formation of new communities. Railroads were at the center of the transformations at the time, knitting together every major city throughout the south and connecting them with the rest of the country. Though the earliest railroads to appear in the deep south were built in the 1830s, they were not developed on a broad scale until the decade before the Civil War. Many railroads were primarily built to transport goods and industrial raw materials, but after the war, freedmen and their offspring gradually made use of them for their own purposes in employment and to facilitate their own travel. First to southern cities and then north to the greater Ohio Valley's industrial cities, this mobility transformed nearly every aspect of life and its possibilities.

Throughout this period of urbanization, labor organizing, and increased mobility, communities formed that could not have come together previously. To varying extents, these cities became sites of cultural genesis, with the blues as the most widespread art form. It formed a cultural vernacular in most places, maintained by national and regional touring networks as well as local upwelling. These sites proved what was possible, despite the myriad challenges, exclusions, and violence that people faced in their daily lives. Music was itself moving, borne upon the lips and hands of guitarists, pianists, and preachers who were bearing witness to a world in flux.

MOBILE

The Ayler family sharecropped in Noxubee County, Mississippi, until after the turn of the century, before moving south to the Gulf of Mexico, where the saxophonist Albert Ayler's great-grandfather Suthers "Suthey" Ayler got a job working in a railroad machine shop in the small town of Whistler, Alabama, in the first decade of the twentieth century.[2] Many Black settlements were confined to the outskirts of Mobile proper, creating a number of protosuburban neighborhoods in small towns around Mobile.[3] Whistler was just seven miles northwest of the port of Mobile, which was connected to ports throughout the Caribbean, Central America, and the US Gulf Coast and had been the second-greatest cotton exporter on the Gulf after New Orleans before the Civil War.[4] Whistler had grown up around the land-grant Mobile & Ohio Railroad in the 1850s during a time of great speculation about the city claiming a greater portion of the trade emerging in the Gulf of Mexico.[5] The M&O Railroad had been used for military purposes and largely destroyed during the Civil War, then rebuilt such that by 1882 the railroad stretched north all the way to the Ohio River through Meridian, Mississippi; Jackson, Tennessee; Cairo, Illinois; and terminating at St. Louis, with innumerable connections to other cities throughout the eastern and central United States.[6] Though the railroad was initially built to facilitate freight traffic of cotton, other goods began to increase in the period between 1880 and 1910, such as maize, grain and alfalfa, vegetables and other refrigerated goods, livestock, coal, yellow pine, a variety of other industrial materials, and bananas and pineapples imported from Central America.[7] By the mid-1880s it also began to carry increasing numbers of passengers. With a total run time of just under twenty-four hours from Mobile to St. Louis, the increase in mobility was transformational in how people could construct long-distance social networks.[8] This railroad line would form the central artery for thousands of Black Alabamians, including the Aylers, when they eventually looked north for better fortunes during the Great Migration.

In Whistler, Suthey Ayler worked to build the new coaches, for which the M&O shops were just then developing a reputation "of the very latest designs," with interior panels of oak and ash, reversible red plush seats, polished brass fittings, French plate-glass mirrors, and gaslights.[9] Suthey Ayler and his sons who worked alongside him were prevented from joining the International Association of Machinists, the union that organized the white employees of M&O Railroad in the area. Though there had been attempts to organize Black labor throughout the Reconstruction era through collective actions, strikes, and occasional shows of armed force, it had not gained enough momentum to draw workers together across the region or beyond very specific trades or manufacturers.[10]

Organized labor in Mobile dated back to 1836 and was the earliest site of union formation in the state.[11] The shipping and railroad industries witnessed the most sustained efforts to build solidarity among workers. After the Civil War, most unions remained segregated or at the very least bore segregated chapters within the broader organization, though this did not prevent a group of Black longshoremen from striking there in 1867.[12] Still, the common result of segregation was that organized labor groups were often pitted against one another. In the late 1870s and early 1880s, a few integrated unions did emerge to encounter brief success. But prevailing racial politics more often ruled the day, and even within unions, Black workers were treated as second-class members.[13] Because of these tensions, the labor movement in Mobile was not effective in advancing the power of workers until the early twentieth century.[14]

A more substantial movement to organize Black labor emerged around the time that the Ayler family arrived in the city, led by the dockworker Ralph Clemmons, who organized his fellows into the International Longshoremen's Association.[15] Into the 1910s, this movement expanded to include a broader group of skilled workers on the waterfront as well as laundry workers and cooks, which drew a broader white response and led to Clemmons's lynching by the Ku Klux Klan in June 1918.[16] Though it seems that Suthey Ayler and his sons likely had an interest in the unionization that was then ongoing, there is no evidence there was ever one for them to join, and thus they were paid lower wages than their white counterparts and their positions were less secure.[17]

Whistler abutted the settlement of Prichard, which bore a unique African community, and strong bonds between the two small towns resulted in Whistler's eventual absorption into Prichard.[18] In 1860, just before the Civil War, the last slave ship to arrive in the United States, the *Clotilda*, illegally brought 110 ethnically Yoruba and Fon Africans, captured and purchased in Ouidah, the principal slave port of the kingdom of Dahomey, on the West African coast in what is now Benin.[19] The enslaved people were divided among the Mobile merchants and shipbuilders who had sponsored the venture, but after the Civil War, thirty-two of them returned and founded Africatown. As the scholar Sylviane Diouf has noted, it was the oldest African settlement in the United States.[20] The founders of Africatown made decisions collectively, appointed their own leaders, established their own system of governance, and bought land and built homes for the people of their community on the site right where the *Clotilda* had landed along the Mobile River, at Magazine Point just to the east of Prichard.[21] Their descendants maintained their languages and customs for about a century, transforming the Black culture of Prichard and the greater Mobile area.[22]

Baptist and Methodist churches proliferated throughout Prichard and Whistler in the early decades of the twentieth century as the population expanded rapidly and people like the Aylers were drawn there. Out of this rich cultural milieu came blues and R&B performers such as the vocalist Lil Greenwood (1923–2011), who performed with Duke Ellington and later the Texas blues guitar player and songwriter James "Thunderbird" Davis (1938–1992).[23] The character actress Ethel Ayler (1930–2018), who was the second cousin of the saxophonist and born in Whistler in 1930, starred in a number of Broadway performances over a forty-year career, especially new Black plays, achieving her greatest visibility as Carrie Hanks on the *Cosby Show*.[24]

The first Albert Ayler (1888–1935), along with his twin brother, were the last two of the ten children born into Suthey Ayler's family. Albert worked as a machinist for the M&O Railroad from the family's arrival in Whistler up until he enlisted briefly in the US Army at the end of World War I.[25] He was stationed at Camp Taylor, near Louisville, Kentucky, but was not deployed overseas.[26] Returning to the Mobile area in 1919, Albert apprenticed as a machinist in Whistler, though in the postwar period social tensions were high because of the difficulty many returning veterans had getting jobs.[27] As in other industrial centers throughout the Red Summer of 1919, during which the United States witnessed wide-scale vigilante violence against Black communities, Prichard was the site of physical attacks and the lynching of Black men.[28] Marcus Garvey's Universal Negro Improvement Association (UNIA) opened a small division of the organization in the wake of the lynching and was even more active in nearby Mobile through the 1920s.[29]

Albert Ayler married Augusta Thomas, who worked as a domestic in Mobile, in 1912.[30] The Thomas family had been enslaved in Mississippi but had moved to Mobile immediately after Emancipation, perhaps drawn, like some were, to work in the Union army camps near to the city, but afterward worked fields there into the 1910s.[31] The saxophonist's father, Edward Ceasor Ayler, born to Albert and Augusta in Whistler in late 1913, was taken north by his mother during the war years while he was still young.[32]

BIRMINGHAM

Birmingham emerged as one of the earliest industrial centers in the south as a center of the iron and coal industry. Though coal mining in the area dated back to 1844, there was a surge in the discovery and exploitation of iron ore, coal, limestone, and dolomite around Birmingham from the 1870s onward. By the turn of the century, Birmingham was competing on a global scale as an exporter of coal to places such as England, continental Europe, and Japan.[33] The earliest strikes by coal miners also dated to the 1870s, and there were 103 documented strikes from 1882 to 1900 alone.[34] The labor union United Mine Workers of Alabama formed in 1893, which in turn fused into the efforts of the national organization, the United Mine Workers of America, in 1898.

The region's mining industry made much of convict labor leasing, a system that exploited people mostly convicted of minor offenses to do hard labor in a variety of capacities. One estimate suggests that more than one hundred thousand convict laborers were drawn into the system of labor exploitation between the late 1860s and 1928, when it was finally abolished. It was a brutal system that continued many of the hallmarks of slavery: restricting mobility, whipping and beating laborers at the behest of the managers, killing or torturing those who attempted to escape, and not compensating laborers for their work. In many cases, laborers were worked to death, were killed in work-related accidents, or died from the deplorable conditions in the mines. Though exact records were not always kept of fatalities throughout the entire period, in 1913, for instance, there were 125 miners reported killed in the line of work in Alabama mines, of whom 56 percent were African American, and "as a result of . . . fatal accidents there were left seventy-one widows and 102 orphans."[35] Laborers were leased by the state and counties for use by mining companies.

The drummer Hasan Shahid's great-grandfather Augustus J. Gordon (b. c. 1861) worked at the Pratt mines, one of the most notorious sites of labor exploitation in the area. Gordon's mother, Eliza (b. c. 1839), had headed the family in Opelika, in Lee County, in eastern Alabama after the Civil War.[36] Eliza often worked as a cook, and Augustus worked as a porter for a couple of decades to support themselves before they sought other opportunities. There is evidence that they were involved in church communities at the local level and drew from the musical traditions of those spaces.

The enslaved people of the eastern Alabama Black Belt had generally embraced Christianity during the final decades prior to Emancipation and through this process developed a particular sacred musical tradition.[37] As Willie Collins, a scholar of the region, stated, they "could not invoke their God and spirit by striking a drum with a singular rhythm as in Africa; but they could strike a moan . . . and be consumed not by a Yoruban or Dahomeyan deity, but by Christianity's third Godhead, the Holy Spirit."[38] Collins defined moaning in these contexts as "singing with the lips closed and without the articulation of syllables," and it could take the form of chant or prayer that represented "the outward expression of an inward feeling."[39] One early observer of the moaning tradition among Methodists in Alabama in the 1830s stated: "There was among them in their worship a mixture of sighs, moans, and groans which made a peculiar sound, and which was peculiar to them and which it is impossible to embody in words . . . they were gifted in singing."[40]

Collins added that "moaning, because of its low amplitude, was responsive to the musical needs of the invisible church which demanded that the services be undetected." As one formerly enslaved person explained their own practice: "They couldn't go out and express themselves and they couldn't go out and sing so they would just hum and moan to themselves."[41] As Collins theorized, "In so doing,

FIGURE 3.1 Red Ore Mine, near Birmingham, 1908.

Source: Courtesy Alabama Department of Archives and History.

they developed a sound to accompany" their practices of worship, prayer, and self-expression.[42] These traditions became manifest in the AME Church as it grew in the region after Emancipation, though the practice was widespread. As Collins argues, "This genre of music, in all probability preceded the African-American spiritual song and the blues and forms the basis of their evolution."[43]

At some point in the 1880s or 1890s, Augustus Gordon moved to Birmingham and was the first in the family to work in the Pratt mines.[44] It is unclear whether Gordon arrived there as a convict laborer or was among the free laborers that also worked the mines.[45] The social geographer Bobby M. Wilson argues that "convict labor was ... a prime means of transforming the essentially agrarian work force into an industrial one. It was often the unfortunate situation of many former black tenant farmers who became skilled coal miners."[46] Even an estimated 15 to 50 percent of free laborers were former convicts.[47] In 1892, for example, one thousand convict laborers worked the Pratt mines, producing 38 percent of the overall yield of ore extracted there.[48]

The use of convict labor also allowed company bosses to keep pay rates low for free workers. As the historian Alex Lichtenstein wrote, the prominent industrialists of Birmingham "were the quintessential New South capitalist entrepreneurs, directors of industrial firms, railroads, banks and real estate companies. But they were also 'laborlords' as slaveholders had been before them, buying, selling, and exploiting the labor of convicts."[49] Augustus Gordon witnessed an intense struggle between the miners and company owners that took place between the 1890s and the 1920s. By the 1910s, Rev. Augustus Gordon began preaching in one of the Baptist churches built in the mining camps, while still working alongside his fellows in the shafts.[50]

Rev. Gordon's son Charles Preston Gordon (1887–1928) grew up in the mining camps. By the time he joined his father in the mines, the system had become brutally efficient in exploiting the labor of both prisoners and free miners. The Tennessee Coal, Iron, and Railroad Company (TCI) had been the main mining company in the area since 1886 and had gained a reputation for sacrificing laborers for the dangerous work; it maintained a cemetery of unmarked graves for the dead on mine hillsides.[51] Between shaft collapse, asphyxiation, beatings and other violence carried out by management, and disease, the miners had high mortality rates that sometimes exceeded 10 percent annually.[52] Death ledgers maintained by the Alabama State Convict Board indicate that many laborers died within weeks of arriving at the mines, while some managed to toil for years under horrid conditions.[53] Housing provided for the convict laborers and rented to free workers by the company were maintained at the barest level, referred to as "foul accommodations" with drinking water that "often passed through the mine waste dump."[54] Diarrhea, pneumonia, and typhoid were rampant, and "recreation was virtually absent." Residents of the housing could be evicted with only one day's notice if they refused to do work, thus adding to the difficulties of using strikes as a means of pressuring TCI.[55]

As early as 1893, the United Mine Workers of Alabama called for major changes to mining conditions at their first statewide convention in Birmingham. They pressured the state legislature to establish a bureau of mining statistics and pass laws that would protect the health of miners, enforce fair payment, prohibit the employment of boys under age ten, abolish the convict labor system, and provide free schools for the education of miners' children. None of these demands were accepted by the mining companies, and thus a three-and-a-half-decade struggle to fight against these dangerous and dehumanizing conditions was born.

In 1907, US Steel bought TCI, and the company chairman publicly promised to end the use of convict labor and to improve overall conditions. But records indicate that very little changed in the years after the merger. According to one report, mortality rates among convict laborers ranged anywhere from 3 to 25 percent on an annual basis, though mortality statistics for free workers are less well documented.[56] There were a number of strikes, attempts by convict laborers to escape, and attempts to organize for better pay and working conditions, though the company bosses generally used the convicts to break the strikes.[57] Racially integrated strikes in the 1880s had made clear the power of a united front. Or, as Wilson argues, the "attempt to unite poor people across racial lines convinced industrialists that they must act to avert social revolution," and so the company bosses took direct steps to pit the two races against each other.[58]

The first broad, coordinated strike occurred in 1894, which cut across racial divides. It was announced on April 14, and by May, mining companies employed violent coercion, placing "a vast number of armed deputy sheriffs" at the mines.[59] These shows of intimidation resulted in a "large body of men" who "attacked the mines ... blowing up boilers in a number of mines." TCI's main strategy was aimed at hiring a workforce to break the strike; the new workers were predominantly Black, which led to escalating tensions and occasional violence.[60] On July 9, thirteen companies of state troops arrived in Birmingham to quell the strike, but eight days later the tensions boiled over into open confrontation. At a pitched battle outside of the Pratt mines, striking miners again targeted Black workers, killing an estimated twenty people. More were killed in the week that followed, showing that racial divisions that sometimes ran along lines between strikers and strikebreakers had deadly consequences when the companies pitted one side against another.

During these struggles, one leader of the United Mine Workers of America stated, "Now fellow craftsmen let us all come together, never mind the color."[61] It was not uncommon for Black and white miners to make the same wages, which allowed for some solidarity over workers' demands, as everyone was paid poorly.[62] In the wake of the strikes, mining companies turned to hiring entirely Black teams of workers, whom they believed they could better intimidate against employing collective action.[63]

Despite all of the attempts to divide the miners, labor tensions culminated with the Alabama coal strike of 1908, which was a broad and coordinated action that crossed racial divides and was called in response to a 20 percent wage cut forced by the mining companies. The United Mine Workers of America announced the action by stating: "For many years the mine workers of Alabama have been poorly organized and in a demoralized condition. The natural result has been sweeping cuts in wages and the imposition of conditions of employment that should not be tolerated at any mining community in the country."[64] The union was criticized at the time for attempting to "establish social equality" across racial lines, and inflammatory journalists were hired by the opposition to stir up animosity within the striking miners, aimed at reminding white miners of their superiority vis-à-vis their Black comrades and conjuring images of the threat that Black men posed to white women in an equal society.[65]

During the course of the struggle, the union in Pratt City, which originally was composed of about four thousand workers, swelled to eight thousand (and in one report as high as 12,000), though TCI refused to recognize the legitimacy of the union.[66] The company bosses, with full support from the state government, moved to violently suppress the workers' movement. Through July and August, miners were threatened, attacked, and had their houses blown up, and leaders were assassinated by troops brought in to quell the strike.[67]

In other instances, striking miners blocked or attacked trains carrying strikebreakers. Pitched battles were fought in and around the mines; one observer described it as "a most exciting battle, which knows few equals in Alabama since the Civil War," as more troops armed with Gatling guns were brought in to attack the striking miners.[68] In another episode of the conflict, hundreds of striking miners surrounded a procession of convict laborers and "threatened to turn loose the convicts as they were being conveyed from the mines back to prison, and only strong reinforcements prevented this action."[69] The general tensions led to a number of Black miners being lynched whether they were members of the union or not.[70] Charles Gordon's future brother-in-law got a tip that company goons were coming to kill him, and he fled to Pennsylvania.[71] Ultimately the strike came to an end when Governor B. B. Comer made it clear that he was on the side of the mining companies and threatened strikers that he "would drive them either into the mines or out of their homes at the point of bayonets with the state troops."[72] The troops proceeded to destroy the tents that housed the striking miners, which forced the union to end the action.

The failure of the strike eroded the credibility of the miners' union. Nevertheless, Wilson argues that the whole process of organizing and uniting against the mining companies caused the Black workers to proletarianize.[73] One Black miner, B. H. Dillard, wrote in the newspaper *Labor Advocate*, that the biracial labor organizing had, briefly, promised conditions in which "all workingmen [might] live in peace and harmony together" and that the union's failed vision had nevertheless given voice to the idea of equal conditions and social rise for Black workers.[74] The destruction of the union led to a decline in prospects for labor organizing throughout the Birmingham mines, as new workers were forced to sign contracts that stated they would not join a union. Company agents, posing as union organizers, would be intermittently employed to draw out union sympathizers, who were subsequently fired.

Little is known of Charles Gordon's personal activity in all of the labor organizing of his time. But he did move to Greenville, Mississippi, at some point after

URBANIZATION, LABOR STRUGGLES, THE BLUES   91

FIGURE 3.2 Amos Franklin Gordon (1915–1992), saxophonist and clarinetist.

Source: Courtesy Hasan Shahid, private collection.

1910 just for a few years, suggesting that he had to flee the area because of the threats that many miners were then receiving or because he was blacklisted and therefore unable to find work.[75] It is also speculated that he then went north to Memphis, where he had a brother who owned a laundry.[76] Nevertheless, he eventually returned and again worked in the Pratt mines. The psychological impact of the violence and terrible conditions on Charles Gordon, however, was immense, and not long after his son was born, he abandoned the family and disappeared.[77] Little else is known of him other than that he died about a decade later, having only just reached the age of forty-one.

But born into the challenging environment and intergenerational trauma of the Pratt mines was a budding musical prodigy, Amos Franklin Gordon Sr. (1915–92), who was recognized from an early age as having talent, first on clarinet and later on alto saxophone.[78] He was raised by his mother and attended Industrial High School in Birmingham, where he was two classes behind Herman Blount, later known as the visionary artist Sun Ra. After graduating, he enrolled at what was then called the Tuskegee Institute (today Tuskegee University), where he met Booker T. Washington's daughter. He may have had intentions of courting her, but the relationship was discouraged because he came from a lower social standing than she did. He soon after met his bride to be, Lena May, and they enrolled at what was then called the Alabama State Teachers College in Montgomery.[79] After finishing their education, Gordon began playing music professionally, first at the Tuskegee army airfield with Erskine Hawkins.[80] Hawkins, who a few years later would write the well-known standard "Tuxedo Junction," led a big band there composed entirely of musicians from Birmingham, at least in part because jazz musicians from the city had a good reputation as sight readers. Gordon later toured extensively and recorded with Lucky Millinder. On a chance occurrence when the trumpeter Louis Armstrong was touring through Mobile and needed an alto saxophone player, he called Hawkins for advice, and the latter advised that he hire Gordon.[81] For a period in the early 1940s, Gordon was the first-chair alto player for Armstrong. Gordon's son, born Amos Franklin Gordon Jr., who later took the name Hasan Shahid after converting to Islam, was born in Birmingham in 1944 and was drawn into his father's musical world at a young age.

Birmingham was the site of other labor organizing as well. It is likely that the saxophonist Albert Ayler's grandfathers, both railroad men, were directly involved in the labor struggles of the 1910s and 1920s, since Black labor organizing was widespread after 1917. With assistance from the American Federation of Labor (AFL), Black railroad workers formed the Colored Association of Railway Employees, based in Memphis, for instance, which became one of the central forces for advocating for Black railroad workers throughout the south.[82] Unions for Black railroaders proliferated gradually in other cities. Major strikes during World War I demanded better wages, shorter workdays, racial equity in pay increases, and protection from violent racist attacks.[83]

By the years of World War I, the saxophonist Albert Ayler's maternal grandfather, Will Hunter, who had been working as a fireman for the Southern Railway Company in Meridian, Mississippi, moved his family to Birmingham. Southern Railway stretched from New York to New Orleans, passing through Birmingham, primarily transporting cotton, maize, wheat, oats, tobacco, potatoes, apples, peaches, livestock, coal, raw materials for munitions, and many manufactured goods, as well as passengers.[84] Labor struggles had been ongoing throughout the company's history but intensified by the early 1910s.[85] In the spring of 1918, the newly created US Railroad Administration established that "firemen, trainmen, and switchmen," such as Will Hunter, "shall be paid the same rates of wages as are paid white men in these same capacities."[86] In 1919, workers for Southern Railway demanded better wages as Black railroaders pushed to join existing unions or to form their own, despite constant attempts by company bosses and rival all-white unions to thwart or delegitimize those attempts.[87]

These labor victories led to a "substantial" increase in Will Hunter's wages from Southern Railway. Labor demands were more readily met because of national wartime needs and President Wilson's need to appease the AFL, though explicit attempts were made to roll back some of these gains in the postwar period.[88] Black railroaders had to contend both with the increased power of employers and white labor organizations, while train lines overall cut wages and staff throughout the 1920s. The Hunter family did not remain in Birmingham long, moving north to Cleveland in the early 1920s.

LABOR STRUGGLES IN THE RURAL EASTERN ALABAMA BLACK BELT

Farther east, one of the early bass players to work with Albert Ayler in Cleveland, Earle Henderson (1937–2019), traced his roots to Camp Hill, in Tallapoosa County, in east-central Alabama, before migrating north. There had been rising scales of violence in Camp Hill in the 1920s as white supremacist networks reacted to the labor organizing efforts that formed the Alabama Sharecroppers' Union, inspired by the Sixth World Congress of the Communist International, which had convened in Moscow in 1928 and recognized African Americans of the Black Belt region to be a distinct nation in need of liberation.

About 70 percent of the people working in agriculture in the eastern Alabama Black Belt were tenants or wage workers, the vast majority of whom were sharecroppers. Even by 1930, the depressed economy caused a crash in wages for many farm workers, with many in the region only being paid about $1.10 per day, which was the lowest for agricultural workers in the country.[89] On top of all that, boll weevils had been ravaging the region since 1912, causing an estimated $19 million dollars of losses, which were often transferred to sharecroppers.[90] The sharecroppers organized "to obtain the bare necessities of life."[91] Pamphlets from within the union "urged members to demand social equality with the white race, $2 a day for work, and not to ask but 'demand what you want, and if you don't get it, take it.' "[92]

The newspaper *Southern Worker*, published in Birmingham, became a central forum for Black farmers and sharecroppers to voice their discontent with the system of labor exploitation that they faced.[93] In the inaugural issue, the editors stated: "The Southern Worker is the voice of the Negro and white workers and farmers of the South crying in united protest against the state of starvation, suffering and persecution to which they have been subjected to by the white ruling class."[94] They went on to claim that it was the first real workers' paper published south of the Mason-Dixon Line. The editors also addressed the issue of race directly with this statement: "The Southern Worker is neither a 'white' paper, nor a 'Negro' paper. It is a paper of and for both the white and black workers and farmers. It recognizes only one division, the bosses against the workers and the workers against the bosses." The paper advocated unabashedly for proletarian revolution in industrial centers like Birmingham as well as in the rural Alabama Black Belt.

Southern Worker outlined what it saw as the primary problems facing workers of the time:

> Thousands upon thousands are unemployed. And yet not a cent from either the government or the employers for the unemployed workers although billions are spent for warships and armaments. The workers and their families are left to starve. And they do starve to death.
>
> The share-croppers and tenant farmers, "poor white" and Negro, face complete ruin. Many of the tenant farmers are losing their crops to the landlords because they cannot hold on long enough to harvest them. When a crop is finally raised the farmer finds that the prices have been kept so low by the agents of the buyers that he cannot get enough money not only to pay off his debts, but to keep going at all. Potatoes and cabbage is now the only food for many of the farmers of the South.
>
> The Negro worker is the most oppressed worker in the South. His lot is worse than any. Kept jim-crowed at every turn, working at lower wages than the white worker, subject to lynching and persecution, he is kept a virtual slave by the Southern white bosses. The Southern Worker is here to voice the rebellion against these conditions.
>
> The only way by which the Southern toilers can be victorious in their struggle is through firm and solid organization in militant unions. The unions we speak of are not the jim-crowed, weak-kneed unions of the American Federation of Labor. We stand openly and solidly against the treacherous,

FIGURE 3.3 *Southern Worker* political cartoon, January 10, 1931.

Source: Courtesy Alabama Department of Archives and History.

boss-controlled American Federation of Labor, which is closely allied with the K. K. K., supports bosses' candidates in election campaign. The unions we speak of are the militant, industrial unions of the Trade Union Unity League, which, like us, recognize only one division—the one between the bosses and the workers.

The Southern Worker stands unalterably for full social, economic and political equality for the Negro workers and farmers. The Southern Worker is published from Birmingham, Ala., despite the reign of terror directed by the Tennessee Coal and Iron Company, and supported by the A. F. of L. and the K. K. K. against the organizers and members of the Communist Party and Trade Union Unity League. That is a sign of our strength. Persecutions cannot drive us away.[95]

The Communist Party backed up its rhetoric by promoting an election slate in states such as Alabama, Georgia, and Tennessee that explicitly included both Black and white candidates, unlike any other political organization at the time, while also recognizing that Black citizens were prevented from voting across the South. As the writer Tom Johnson described, the prevailing power structures at the time worked "thru a whole elaborate system of Jim Crow laws, to keep the white and Negro toilers from uniting in common struggle."[96] The newspaper regularly reported on issues ranging from wages, work-related deaths, starvation, union organizing, and strikes both on a domestic and international scale, but it devoted more space to reports of and organizing against lynching, state and police brutality, and other racist violence than any other topic.[97]

For people employed to pick cotton at the time, most received about fifty cents per hundred pounds, which for the average adult worker meant that they would receive about $1 per day for twelve or more hours of work. Strikes in Arkansas in October 1930 demanded higher wages, and workers in some places managed to push the wage scale up to seventy-five or even ninety cents per hundred pounds, which still represented lower wages than any industrial work at the time.[98] Sharecroppers in Alabama began organizing around the same time, at least partially sparked by the *Southern Worker*, which provided space for solidarity building as people who were otherwise disconnected recognized they were involved in a common struggle.

In late 1930, one writer stated: "The tenant farmers, share croppers and small farmers are bearing the brunt of the crisis on the farms," referring to the collapse of the domestic US economy as the Great Depression was taking hold. "Most of the tenants and croppers turn their entire crop over to the owner who takes what he calculates to be his due for rent, use of implements, food and other advances out of proceeds of the sale. Result: the landowner has the entire crop, the tenant is left in great debt with nothing to live on for the winter, the cropper is bound over by contract in many cases becoming a peon."[99] According to one report, approximately 150,000 rural farm workers in Alabama were starving or in a state of near starvation in the winter of 1930.[100]

By that time, the Alabama Sharecroppers' Union had as many as five thousand members in Tallapoosa County alone, though violent forces were coalescing to oppose them.[101] One sharecropper in the movement stated that "we are ready to follow the Arkansas way," indicating that they had been inspired by the Arkansas sharecroppers and tenant farmers who had organized earlier that year. As the historian Robin D. G. Kelley argued, "Camp Hill, Alabama, became the scene of the union's first major confrontation with the local power structure."[102] An armed force of perhaps six hundred people eventually gathered to issue the union's demands; they were attacked by local police forces, who wounded and killed dozens of workers and tortured and killed the union leader. Mass arrests of rank-and-file members followed.

Other purges in Alabama occurred throughout 1931, with people facing lynching, assassination, arrest, and a wide range of threats if they continued to organize.[103] A bill had been introduced in the Alabama State Legislature on March 30, 1931, to outlaw the Communist Party in the state as a response to the Alabama Sharecroppers' Union's organizing efforts. In an attempt to counter this, the *Southern Worker* called on "white and Negro tenants and share croppers and small landowners to organize and fight for immediate relief" and that "farmers in the Black Belt [were starting] to fight against the starvation and the vicious system of persecution they suffer under."[104] The threats to life likely led to the Henderson family's flight from Camp Hill before the vicious 1931 massacre that left dozens of men and women dead and additional union members arrested on false charges, an episode of violence that further compelled people to leave the area for Cleveland and other northern cities.[105]

ATLANTA

Though the musician families that originated in Atlanta seem to have developed fewer proletarian roots there, it was an unparalleled fertile ground for music. The saxophonist Paul Gresham's paternal grandmother Pinkie Willis (b. c. 1887) arrived in Atlanta after the turn of the century, where the African American population in the final two decades of the nineteenth century had risen from nine thousand to thirty thousand.[106] She married a bricklayer named Force Gresham (b. 1875), who had come from Greensboro in northeastern Georgia as a young man the decade prior.[107] Gresham had then shifted into work as a fireman for the city crematory, while living near the railroad tracks in north Atlanta.[108] After they married, they settled first on Magnolia Street and later on Maple Street, in a neighborhood then known as Jenningstown. Force and Pinkie Gresham began a family there, and they soon welcomed their son, the saxophonist's father, Paul A. Gresham Sr., in 1910.

Jenningstown was the largest and most desirable Black neighborhood to emerge in post–Civil War Atlanta.[109] Located in the hilly western reaches of the city, at the neighborhood's center was Atlanta University, the city's first Black university, which had been built in 1867. One minister who served the community wrote a few years before the arrival of Force and Pinkie Gresham about the university: "Upon one of the many hills which surround the city of Atlanta, where battles were fought to keep the negro in bondage and ignorance, sets this grand institution."[110] Rents were rapidly increasing through the 1910s, pushing many

Black residents to the outskirts of the city, but the Gresham family seemed to rise with the changing times and managed to stay in Jenningstown. By 1918, Force Gresham was working as a drayman, and two years later he had purchased a wagon and was running his own business in an emerging Black commercial district.[111]

People living in the area of northeast Atlanta between Auburn Avenue in the north and Decatur Street in the south had developed their own blues scene by the 1920s, mostly composed of people who had migrated to the city from rural parts of Georgia to Atlanta in that decade. In particular, they came from north-central Georgia, around Newton County or nearby areas. This included Joshua "Peg Leg" Howell (1888–1966), the brothers Charlie and Robert Hicks (better known as Charley Lincoln and Barbecue Bob), Curley Weaver, and Eddie Mapp. Blind Willie McTell was born in the same general region but had grown up in southeastern Georgia. Still, despite being from the same region of Georgia, they all possessed a distinct voice on their instruments within the general piedmont blues style, in their vocal stylings, and in their orchestration. The Hicks brothers approach to twelve-string guitar was different than the more melodious style of McTell, for example, and Weaver and the harmonicist and guitarist Buddy Moss sounded much more contemporary than Howell's style, which descended more directly from pre-blues.[112]

Jenningstown became one of the centers of Black culture in the city, and the Beaver Slide slum bordered its southern edge. The community was later immortalized in the "Beaver Slide Rag," recorded by Peg Leg Howell and His Gang in 1927.[113] The guitar and violin trio fronted by Howell had a talking blues style over violin melodies, guitar rhythms, and occasional embellishments. "Peg Leg Stomp" was a dance piece that gained some popularity as Howell performed around Atlanta.[114] A talent scout for Columbia Records heard Howell playing with the mandolinist Eugene Pedin on Decatur Street and invited the former to record a series of sessions, which had at least modest commercial success.[115] Stints in a convict labor camp for bootlegging moonshine whiskey were the source of a series of tunes that he recorded, including "Ball and Chain Blues," "New Prison Blues," "Rock and Gravel Blues," "Skin Game Blues," and "Broke and Hungry Blues." The first of these spoke of the corrupt and violent justice system:

> They 'rested me, carried me 'fore the judge
> They 'rested me, carried me 'fore the judge
> Said the judge wouldn't 'low me to say a mumbling word
> (That's right! I know they give you a long time too!)
>
> I asked the judge what might be my fine
> I asked the judge what might be my fine

Said, "a pick and shovel, deep down in the mine"
Well I told the judge I ain't been here before (well you told him a lie, you know it)
I told the judge I ain't been here before (you can't fool him! you can't fool him)
If you give me light sentence, I won't come here no more
....

Mister judge, mister judge, please don't break so hard
Mister judge, mister judge, please don't break so hard
I've always been a poor boy; never had no job

(That's all I ever called you: poor boy!)

The next day, they carried this poor boy away
The next day, they carried this poor boy away
Said the next day, I laid in ball and chain
....

They put stripes on my back, chain found 'round my leg
Stripes on my back, chain found 'round my leg
This ball and chain 'bout to kill me dead!

Blues guitarists such as Fred McMullen (1905–1960?) were playing in places like Beaver Slide and other parts of Atlanta, with original blues tunes such as "DeKalb Chain Gang," based on his experience as a prisoner in a convict camp in DeKalb County near Atlanta:[116]

Eh, liquor and a gun caused me to ache and pain
Eh, liquor and a gun caused me to ache and pain
And they give me six to twenty years on DeKalb County gang
And I'll tell all you people, that ain't no place to go
And I'll tell all you people, that ain't no place to go
Well, they treat you cruel, dog you from morning to night
Well, they beat me and they slashed me, .45 in my side
Well, and they beat me and they slashed me, .45 in my side
I got dry from hot, mama, workin' all day long
Bring the rings, chains from around my leg
Take these rings and chains from around my leg
But I believe, me Lord, they's gonna kill me dead

The guitarist Hicks brothers Charley Lincoln (1900–1963) and Barbecue Bob (1902–1931), who learned to play from their fellow guitarist Curley Weaver's mother, Savannah "Dip" Weaver, were also active there in that period, also playing twelve-string guitar. Dip Weaver had been a central figure in their community, playing guitar and piano in their local church.[117] The elder Hicks was the first to move to Atlanta, in 1923, where he recorded "It Won't Be Long Now" and many other sides in the period from 1927 to 1930.[118] One scholar has argued that the Hicks brothers' distinct approach reveals that "a banjo tuning and strumming style had been transposed to guitar."[119] Barbecue Bob played a lot of parties within the Black community in Atlanta in the late 1920s, where people would dance the Charleston and the Black Bottom.[120] Barbecue Bob also commonly sang the tune "Atlanta Moan," which mentions living in Atlanta:[121]

> Lord nobody knows Atlanta like I do
> Lord nobody knows Atlanta like I do
> But the reason I know it
> I traveled it through and through

Barbecue Bob, the guitarist Curley Weaver, and the harmonica player Buddy Moss, as the Georgia Cotton Pickers, recorded four tracks in Atlanta in 1930.[122] Moss was the rising star of the time and recorded frequently until he was arrested and imprisoned for five years beginning in 1935.

Curley Weaver (1906–1962), the son of Dip Weaver, wrote originals such as "Leg Iron Blues" and "No No Blues" and later collaborated with McTell.[123] Weaver, interestingly, seems to have distanced himself from his mother's style and instead was mentored by two finger-picking guitar player brothers, Nehemiah and Judd Smith.[124] On the Smiths' farm, Weaver met the harmonica player Eddie Mapp in 1922, and the two spent the next several years finding steady employment playing dances and frolics in Walton County before they left for Atlanta in 1925. Weaver went on to record numerous sides and remains an underappreciated talent who had a significant influence on the Atlanta scene and beyond, especially after the early deaths of Barbecue Bob and Eddie Mapp and the withdrawal of Charlie Hicks.

Georgia's most well-known guitarist and vocalist of the era, Blind Willie McTell (1898–1959), was born in the northeastern Georgia corner of the Black Belt but grew up in Statesboro, closer to Savannah and the coast. He later penned what became his most well-known piece about his experience growing up:

> Yes now, wake up mama, turn your lamp down low.
> Wake up mama, turn your lamp down low.

Have you got the nerve to drive poor papa Taj from your door?
Woke up this mornin' baby, I had them Statesboro blues.
Statesboro Georgia, that is.
Woke up this mornin', had them Statesboro blues.
Looked over in the corner, well my baby had 'em too.
Mama died and left me reckless, Papa died and left me wild,
I ain't good lookin' baby, but I'm someone's sweet angel child.
Going to the country, baby do you want to go?
I know if you can't make it, your sister Lucille say she wanta go.
You know I loved that woman better than any woman I'd ever seen.
Yes I loved that woman better than any woman I'd ever seen.
She treat me like a king, I treat her like she was a doggone Queen.
Wake up mama, turn your lamp down low.
Wake up mama, turn your lamp down low.
Have you got the nerve to drive papa Taj from your door?

Both of his parents played guitar, and, according to his widow, "[McTell's] mother really picked the guitar and she wanted him to have a musical career... so that he would make a living."[125] In his early years and intermittently later in life he also played harmonica, banjo, violin, kazoo, and accordion. He played six-string guitar in his youth, but by the time he began working as a professional, he focused entirely on a twelve-string guitar. Attending a school for the blind in Macon and later in Michigan and New York equipped him with adept skills that he employed throughout his life to live actively and adventurously.

From his youth, McTell learned tunes from a variety of guitarists playing around tobacco markets in different locations before emerging to some recognition playing on the Atlanta streets.[126] He played regularly at a "car hop" barbecue restaurant called the Pig and Whistle on Ponce de Leon Avenue, sometimes joined by his wife, the vocalist Kate McTell. They would join medicine shows traveling through northeastern Georgia near where he was from and take part in shows that included blues, dance, and comedy.[127] Willie McTell first recorded in 1927, gradually establishing himself as one of the most prominent exponents of the piedmont blues style, though he added his own mark to it with his twelve-string guitar and laid-back tenor vocals.[128] He continued to record regularly until 1936, when the record industry collapsed, but resumed after the war. Beyond all of the musicians already mentioned, there were dozens more, most of whom recorded little or not at all and whose historical stature has been diminished even though they were active in shaping the sound of the Atlanta blues scene at the time.

The heart of Black culture in Atlanta was situated on Auburn Avenue.[129] The neighborhood had gradually grown from its roots around Big Bethel AME

Church, which had been founded in 1847, and various Black businesses that emerged and spread there in the decades after Emancipation and crescendoed into the 1920s, including barbershops, dry goods, drug stores, doctor and dentist offices, a haberdasher, a jewelry store, a bookstore, a furniture store, a bank, hotel, beauty shops, and many restaurants, including a barbecue restaurant called the Smokehouse and a café called Ma Sutton's, which served everything family style. The adjoining streets were clustered with shacks that gradually gave way to better accommodations as the community became more prosperous and became known as Sweet Auburn, because, as one resident who lived there at that time stated: "We could get everything we wanted, right there, in our own community."[130]

In the 1920s, cultural events were centered on the 81 Theater, where vaudeville, blues, jazz, dance, comedy, and other forms of music and entertainment occurred. Like the Douglass Theater in Macon, these theaters tapped into national touring networks of musicians and other performers via TOBA. Bessie Smith, Duke Ellington, and Ma Rainey performed there often, but it also catered to local blues guitarists and singers such as McTell, McMullen, Weaver, Moss, and Ruth Willis.[131]

And finally, McTell and others played in the Black Bottom neighborhood, an impoverished part of Atlanta that did not have electricity or paved streets. The scene was centered on Beale Street Alley, where people got together to sell corn whiskey and iron scrap liquor on the street during Prohibition. There was an active sex trade and gambling, and figures in organized crime socialized there. "Police were scared to go through there," McTell's widow later stated, which allowed for it to be a Black-only place, and the area had a late-night music scene of blues players.[132] One of McTell's lyrics referenced the place: "I lived down in Beale St. alley just as drunk as I could be...."[133] It was in such a place that the brilliant and still young Eddie Mapp was murdered on the streets in November 1931.[134]

But much of the Atlanta blues scene was less formal, thriving on street corners or at drive-in restaurants, with musicians playing for individuals or small groups. McTell's widow mentioned many times that he would walk around and get commissioned to play for people that he met, and Robert Hicks's sister and Buddy Moss both recalled a similar setting.[135] The blues guitarist Roy Dunn (1922–1988) mentioned the same thing after he first came to Atlanta as a young man in the 1930s and that he learned tunes from other players in that context, before later being mentored more substantially by Weaver, Moss, and McTell.[136] House parties, or "breakdowns," within the Black community were the most common place for people to hear music and to dance. The tune "John Henry" was one of the most popular in 1920s and 1930s Atlanta. Weaver, Moss, McTell, and Dunn all had careers that survived into the postwar period. So wherever the young Paul Gresham Sr., father of the saxophonist, found himself in Atlanta in the 1920s and 1930s, he was surrounded by the Georgia blues, and he carried that north to Buffalo when he moved there during the Great Depression.

SAVANNAH

Though located in the same state, Savannah was the product of very different cultural roots than Atlanta, with the former closely connected to the Sea Islands, resonating more with other Gullah Geechee cultural zones and port cities of the southeast coast, such as Charleston and Jacksonville, than the interior of the deep south. The city also saw an influx of Black migrants in the late nineteenth and early twentieth centuries who later moved north to cities in the greater Ohio Valley. In particular, the drummer J. C. Moses and percussionist Darryl Washington both traced their families to the city. The city had been Georgia's primary slave port and the center of the state's seaborne commerce. But Savannah had also been witness to a small free Black community dating back to at least the 1790s, which contained sites of resistance including a secret school that provided members of the community with education before the Civil War.[137]

Though there was a brief attempt to redistribute land to emancipated people in early 1865, which led some residents of the area to relocate to the coastal islands, thousands more moved into the city from rural areas following the defeat of the Confederacy. The Black population of Savannah and broader Chatham County grew dramatically, and by 1870 they constituted an outright majority in the county outside of the city and were approaching a majority in the city as well.[138] By that point, the city had already witnessed the violence surrounding the 1868 election, in which freedpeople were first able to exercise their right to vote. In the same year, Georgia had expelled its Black legislators, further adding to the volatile political atmosphere.

By 1870, Black politicians were routed citywide, and Black residents turned to other forms of resistance to survive. Between the upheaval of the early Reconstruction years and the turn of the century, Savannah continued to be a site of intense resistance. The 1870s, in particular, witnessed Black residents contesting existing conditions in the form of waterfront-worker protests, desegregation of the city's streetcars, establishing a Black press, and facing further intimidation when exercising the right to vote.[139] The community came together annually in public displays of celebration of Emancipation Day. Some independent Black churches had existed for decades before emancipation, but they grew stronger in the 1870s and 1880s as they began to organize themselves more openly and formally and hold annual conferences of church leaders.[140] It was into this atmosphere that J. C. Moses's grandfather Richmond Virginia Sutton (c. 1862–1934) stepped at some point in the 1880s or 1890s. He had been born into a sharecropping family in Wilkes County in northeastern Georgia but eventually set out to seek better opportunities in the port.[141]

After arriving in Savannah, Sutton developed a lifelong trade as a carpenter. By 1913, he also became a minister at Bethlehem Baptist Church, where he continued to preach until 1917, before moving to another Baptist church in the area. Thus, he joined the city's emerging class of ministers, educators, and intellectuals that included figures such as W. E. B. Du Bois's sociologist protégé Monroe Work (1866–1945), the businessman and writer J. C. Lindsay, and the writer Dr. W. G. Alexander.[142] They demanded greater access to education and deplored segregation in an era that began to give way to the NAACP as a new organizing force by the late 1910s.

Rev. Sutton's daughter, Annie Gertrude Sutton (1902–1966), married a more recent arrival in the city, Lemon Moses Jr. (1901–1985), who came from a sharecropping family in Stewart County just south of Columbus, Georgia, near the Alabama border.[143] He left while still in his teens to work in the emerging industrial sector of Savannah, developing a trade as an automobile mechanic. He carried this technical knowledge north when they settled in Pittsburgh around 1923. The youngest of their eight children was the drummer J. C. Moses (1936–1977).

The percussionist Darryl Washington, who was one of the early collaborators with the multi-instrumentalist Charles Gayle in Buffalo and younger brother to the more well-known saxophonist Grover Washington Jr., came from a family that followed a similar pattern. His grandfather Dolphus Washington (c. 1888–1932) came from a family of sharecroppers near Linton, Hancock County, in northeastern Georgia, eventually acquiring his own land by around the time of World War I but then moving to Savannah to work for a fertilizer manufacturer.[144] This allowed them to join the small, emerging Black middle class in the city. The family proceeded north to Buffalo during the Great Depression.

These various families witnessed the growth of blues culture in Savannah in the 1920s. Though the city's scene did not compare in activity or number of recordings to Atlanta, the locus of activity centered on the Pekin Theater. Many traveling vaudeville, blues, jazz, and comedy acts frequented the space via the TOBA networks. One of the most frequent was the guitarist Arthur Blake (1896–1934), known as Blind Blake, who sometimes joined with local bandleaders. Blake was from Jacksonville but likely had direct connections with Gullah Geechee culture from the Sea Islands. Blake toured the coastal region, going as far as North Carolina, Virginia, and New York, and recorded and performed as far west as Chicago, but he always returned to the southeast and may have spent his final years in Atlanta.[145] Another Savannah blues singer, Margaret Johnson's recording of "When a 'Gator Holler Folks Say It's a Sign of Rain," reveals even more direct Gullah Geechie influence in the intonations.[146] A few blues guitarists, such as Lord Randolph Byrd, better known as Blind Log, who later collaborated with Willie McTell, got their beginnings in Savannah in the late 1920s.[147]

The other important cultural development connected to music from the region was the emergence of the Charleston dance form. It may also be traced to the Sea Islands. As one bandleader and composer stated in 1926, "the 'Charleston' has been done in the South, especially in the little islands lying off Charleston, S.C., for more than forty years to my knowledge," and it had spread farther south along the Georgia coast by or just before the turn of the twentieth century.[148] Savannah also produced dance bands with little blues influence, such as the one led by Arthur Gibbs (1895–1956), who took his band to New York in 1913 and recorded his earliest sides in 1923.[149]

Jazz came to Savannah via touring networks and manifested along West Broad Street, which became the center of Black culture in the city by the 1930s. The Star, the Dunbar, and the City Auditorium were the key theaters that booked acts including Louis Armstrong, Ella Fitzgerald, Chick Webb, Duke Ellington, Erskine Hawkins, Billy Eckstine, Cab Calloway, Lucky Millinder, and many others.[150] The local trumpeter Cladys "Jabbo" Smith got his start in Savannah.

LOUISVILLE

Like its deep south counterparts, Louisville was also the site of early efforts to organize labor. Situated on the Ohio River, Louisville was the largest city on the southern side of the river. The saxophonist Marshall Allen (b. 1924), who became most well known for his lifelong involvement with the Sun Ra Arkestra, was born in Louisville to a family that had dwelled there since as early as the 1820s. His grandfather Nathan Allen Jr. (c. 1857–1928) worked in the years after the Civil War feeding and washing animals for the livery stable Able & Cummins. By 1877, he worked as a coachman for C. G. Davison, the president of the Louisville City Railway Company, which paid a little more.

But in 1877, Nathan Allen Jr. witnessed the Louisville general strike, first sparked by Black sanitation workers demanding better pay, though they were, in turn, inspired by the national railroad strike of that year, which had begun in

Martinsburg, West Virginia, and spread along the railways across the country. In Louisville, the strike expanded within days into a citywide action that included Black and white workers in tobacco factories, foundries, paper and woolen mills, furniture and plow factories, saddleries, and breweries.[151] Workers also wanted safer working conditions, and many Black workers demanded entry into unions from which they were barred on racial grounds. In a show of elite solidarity, both former Union and Confederate military officers joined together to lead a militia to put down the workers, recruiting several hundred local men and urgently requesting arms and ammunition from Frankfort.[152]

Many workers in positions such as Allen joined the strike and were met with violence, arrest, and fines, with Black strikers who came from "reputable black families" with connections to white society often facing increased fines because they were viewed as an even greater threat.[153] Allen's shift in employment in the wake of the strike seems to suggest some affiliation or involvement in the movement. The demise of the labor strike set the path for Louisville as an anti-labor town, where a smaller number of workers were unionized in comparison to other cities of the region.

In the years after the strike, Nathan Allen Jr. worked in a variety of capacities connected to Louisville's railways. He worked alternatively as a hostler for the city railway stables, a driver for the Louisville Transfer Company, or a laborer for one of several rail companies, including the Louisville City Railway Company and the Central Pacific Railroad lines through the period of 1878 to 1906. He was unable to join the unions that were then organizing white workers, such as the Brotherhood of Locomotive Firemen, which excluded Black workers.[154] By 1910, he shifted more toward the transport of goods ranging from groceries to lumber.[155]

During World War I, Nathan Allen Jr. found employment with the Louisville and Nashville Railroad, one of the largest employers in the state, likely as a baggage handler, as the labor shortage had opened opportunities.[156] Black labor organizing in Louisville faced insurmountable obstacles right up into the Great Depression; they were excluded from most unions and discriminated against in the few that did admit them. In the 1920s and 1930s, Louisville musicians began to organize, but they were racially segregated and unsuccessful in advocating for better opportunities or pay.[157] Allen's son, Nathan Allen III (b. 1896), followed in the same line of work as his father, working in transportation ranging from ice delivery to paper and box delivery. The latter's son, Marshall Allen, grew up in that environment, the fifth of seven children, before he enlisted in the US Army and eventually studied alto saxophone in Paris.

RURAL KENTUCKY LABOR STRUGGLES

Like areas of rural Alabama, southwestern Kentucky was another region that witnessed rural labor struggles in the face of state and vigilante violence. The saxophonist Charles Tyler's father, having learned to professionally cook from his own mother, began an amorous affair with Inez Argleo Tinsley, in 1941, and the couple wed in early 1941 after she got pregnant and later gave birth to Charles. The Tinsley family had sharecropped near Roaring Spring and Cadiz, Kentucky, until the 1940s.[158] The demand for the region's unique tobacco had declined after 1900 given the different demands of the emerging cigarette market, resulting in economic decline across the Black Patch region. The American Tobacco Company set prices as the monopoly buyer, which pushed a majority of the planters to form the Dark Tobacco District Planters' Protective Association of Kentucky and Tennessee (PPA) in 1904.[159] When pressure on the buyers' monopoly failed to yield results, some members of the PPA demanded stronger and swifter action, moving to suppress organizing by Black and white farm laborers to try to make up their losses to the buyers. The few local farm labor unions that formed were segregated, so Black sharecroppers were doubly marginalized and were the hardest hit economically.[160]

Soon class warfare became the premise for communal violence against Black landowners and sharecroppers by a group called the Night Riders, which grew out of the PPA.[161] Their first goal was to intimidate remaining independent farmers to join the PPA, which often did not protect the interests of Black tobacco farmers even if they were members.[162] But soon the PPA began committing communal violence against Black landowners and sharecroppers alike, and it even threatened white planters who worked with Black sharecroppers, such as one letter that appeared in a Christian County newspaper stating: "Know that you are not to have any negro croppers for next year."[163] In Trigg County, some members of the PPA spoke out against Night Rider violence against sharecroppers, but only out of self-interest in preserving a cheap labor force that they feared would migrate elsewhere.[164]

Though technically unrelated to the KKK, the Night Riders adopted their regalia and tactics and began threatening to lynch people in Trigg County. In 1908, the group attacked Black farmers who inhabited some of the best land and "fired off hundreds of shots, wounding several blacks," giving them ten days to leave or face additional violence.[165] In other cases, they invaded towns, orchestrated lynchings, destroyed warehouses, and caused millions of dollars of damage, for which sharecroppers had no recompence.[166] At times, the Night Riders committed acts of violence that had no direct connection to the dispute over tobacco prices as the situation spun out of control into banditry, smuggling, acts of revenge, and casual vigilantism.[167]

One eyewitness Black resident of the area recounted how Night Riders burned down their houses, barns, and storehouses; stole their livestock; and stalked local residents, especially sharecroppers, who were forced to flee from rural areas to Cadiz and then farther north or west in such numbers that "these refugees sometimes made up long rumbling night trains out of the tobacco patches."[168] Another source described the situation: "There is war in Kentucky. In a score of towns what is virtually a state of martial law exists. In the farming districts cellars have been fortified and loaded arms stacked within easy reach."[169] Whereas the conflict had begun as violence directed toward poor farm laborers, both Black and white, the violence eventually became racialized, and Black sharecroppers were arming themselves to fight back. Many other instances of vigilante violence appear in the records of that time.[170] The KKK was also responsible for a significant number of murders and disappearances in the small towns and rural settlements of western Kentucky in the 1910s and 1920s.[171] The Tinsleys persisted through all of these struggles, still sharecropping, until they finally left in the early 1940s.

INDIANAPOLIS

Indianapolis was the most important of the northern waystations in the migration. The city was founded on land that had been previously inhabited by the Delaware, after the latter had been displaced from areas farther east. By the late 1840s, railroads made the city grow, and it was in that decade that the first, small Black communities appeared in the city. During and after the Civil War, Indianapolis gained greater significance as a military base and industrial center, more than doubling its population between 1860 and 1870. By the 1880s, it was the world's third-largest pork packing city and the second-largest railroad center in the United States. It also was an early automobile manufacturing center as well as one of the earliest sites of mass labor organizing.

The trombonist Phil Ranelin's family first arrived in Indianapolis shortly after the Civil War. His great-great-grandfather Isaac N. Kimbrough (c. 1830–1902) had been enslaved on a plantation in Davie County, in central North Carolina. The slave master's son befriended him when they were just seven or eight years old, and the two grew up together. When the master died, the son promised to send Kimbrough enough money and materials to build five homes in Indianapolis "as partial payment for all of the pain and agony prior to that."[172] So when Kimbrough traveled west and north to the city around 1871, he came with an unusual amount of resources to establish himself. He acquired land right next to Crown Hill Cemetery and built all five of the homes right next to one another. Around 1885, when the city wanted to expand the cemetery, "they paid him good money to buy him out."[173]

Kimbrough then moved his family to the Brightwood neighborhood on the east side of the city, building six homes there for himself and his children.[174] Brightwood was a mostly white community with a predominantly Black section west of Dearborn Street. Kimbrough emerged as a construction entrepreneur and a leader in the community.[175] He formed the firm Kimbrough & Berry with his business partner Salathiel Berry, which sold "flour and feed" in Brightwood.[176] He also built the Mount Carmel Baptist Church at the end of the same block, which became a vital center of the community in the late nineteenth century.[177] Kimbrough then became the church's first minister, and he preached there through the 1890s. The family members were active in the church until the time of Ranelin's youth.

Isaac Kimbrough built one of the homes for his son, Arthur W. Kimbrough (1869–1943), and the latter inherited most of the other properties.[178] He continued in the same line of contracting work as his father but did not possess the latter's entrepreneurial spirit, eventually losing most of the houses.[179] Just one remained, at 2418 North Oxford Street, where the trombonist Phil Ranelin grew up in the 1940s. Brightwood was still segregated then, and Ranelin recalled that "we never went to downtown Brightwood after dark because it was not safe for us."[180] Arthur Kimbrough's daughter, Helen Kimbrough Ranelin (1898–1961), was to have a profound impact on her grandson, encouraging him to play music and connecting him with some of the jazz scene that his conservative parents would not have otherwise allowed.

Ranelin's mother's side of the family arrived in Indianapolis just after the turn of the century, coming north from Warren County, Kentucky, in rural areas outside of Bowling Green. His great-grandfather Ferney J. Hayes (1863–1939) had left the family and gone north to Indianapolis alone. But after his wife died unexpectedly at age thirty-two, four siblings made the trek themselves, with the oldest perhaps just fifteen years of age caring for the younger ones during the journey. Ranelin's grandmother Camilla Hayes (1896–1986), the youngest of the four children, was just nine at the time of their harrowing move north. They eventually found their father there, laboring in a cement factory, and he took them back in.[181] She married Wix Smith (1892–1974), who had moved north from Clay

County, Tennessee, and the two worked in a variety of capacities, from advertising to custodial work to restaurants. They, too, lived on the east side of Indianapolis but were Pentecostals and had a disdain for blues, jazz, and the other popular music of the time.

Raised as ardent Christians, Ranelin's parents kept him "away from the fast women and fast cars of Indiana Avenue" where most of the jazz was happening in the city.[182] But his paternal grandmother, Helen, encouraged him to be a musician. She had a piano in her house and used to host "legendary parties that lasted a whole weekend," drawing together musicians and other people from the community. Music was always at the center of what was happening. She also frequented the club Sunset Terrace on the avenue from the late 1930s to the early 1950s, where Duke Ellington, Count Basie, Charlie Parker, Miles Davis, Max Roach, and other national jazz figures performed, as well as the most high-profile local acts. Her stories were tantalizing to the young Ranelin.

Helen Kimbrough Ranelin also built a substantial record collection that included the jazz figures of that era; this allowed Ranelin to explore the music on wax. Since Ranelin's father had "refrained from his passion" to be a musician, Ranelin seemed to fulfill his grandmother's desire when he joined the school band. "She practically insisted that I become a musician," Ranelin recalled.[183] Despite his desire to be a saxophonist, like many young musicians of the time, the only instrument the school had left when he made his selection was the trombone, so that is what he studied, and it became a lifelong commitment.

Another figure to arrive in Indianapolis was Charles Tyler, who came at about age two or three with his family from Kentucky's Black Patch. His family settled in the Lockefield Gardens public housing projects, which had been built a few years before their arrival, and remained there until Tyler left home.[184] Tyler is said to have been almost identical in appearance to his mother and was "a happy go lucky kid."[185] One of his childhood friends from Lockefield Gardens, David Williams, who later became a historian, stated, "At that time, we didn't know how blessed we were. The community was more cohesive. We had a burgeoning commercial area with Black businesses with grocery stores, restaurants, doctors, dentists, lawyers, two movie theaters, and our schools were all right there. We could conceivably not need to leave that two-block radius for anything."[186] Still, segregated schooling was a constant reminder of systemic racism and exclusion.

Tyler was mobile even early in life. He spent most of his summers as a kid either visiting maternal relations back in Cadiz, Kentucky, or with paternal relations in Chicago Heights, Illinois.[187] Growing up, Tyler would avidly watch the Chicago Bears and then go out and play football with other kids from the neighborhood on the Lockefield Gardens green.[188] The future basketball star Oscar Robertson (b. 1938), who played with the Cincinnati Royals and Milwaukee Bucks, grew up in the same community. "I started to take an interest in the piano at home when I was young," Tyler later recounted. "Like a toy. As I seemed to have gifts, around six years old I was given an old clarinet, then, for my eighth birthday, my parents gave me an alto saxophone."[189] Because he was ten years older than his next sibling and his mother adored him, Tyler was a bit of a spoiled kid, and she seemed to instill a sense in him to pursue his interest in music, no matter the cost.[190] The Tyler family were Baptists.

Tyler attended Crispus Attucks High School, which was near Lockefield Gardens. From the very beginning, Tyler later recalled there was a distinct discrepancy between what was taught at school, primarily classical and marching band music, and what he was listening to at home, which was primarily jazz and rhythm and blues, especially Charlie Parker, Miles Davis, and Dizzy Gillespie.[191] Nevertheless, among his peers at Crispus Attucks High School were a number of figures who would go on to have major jazz careers, including the saxophonist and flutist James Spaulding and the drummer and vocalist Paula Hampton. But the most propitious encounter for Tyler in his years there was with the trombonist, cellist, and jazz educator David Baker, who had attended the school a decade earlier but who had returned to do student teaching as part of his own education.[192] Baker would later mentor Tyler, and the two would also record and perform together.

In the early 1950s, Tyler encountered the vibrant blues and jazz scene on Indiana Avenue, which ran abreast to Lockefield, where local musicians and touring bands combined to create distinct sounds. The Cotton Club and Sunset Terrace, run by two brothers, were the biggest stages. The Hampton family was the driving force on the scene at the time that Tyler was growing up there. Clark "Deacon" Hampton, his son the trombonist Locksley "Slide" Hampton, the Hampton sisters, and other members of the family performed there regularly and toured through a circuit that stretched from Chicago through Cleveland and Pittsburgh out to New York in the late 1940s and early 1950s.

Of particular note, saxophonists such as Alonzo "Pookie" Johnson, Bill Penick, Duke Hampton, Jimmy Coe, and Cleve Bottoms (who also played clarinet) and the pianist Erroll Grandy likely were early inspirations for Tyler. He played in the Indianapolis Junior Symphony Orchestra from age thirteen to fifteen. The guitarist Wes Montgomery was also fully establishing himself in the mid- to late 1950s, and Tyler managed to sit in with him on several occasions around age fifteen.[193] Though many of the figures of the Indianapolis scene other than Montgomery were under-recorded purely because they were not in New York, Chicago, or Los Angeles, they nevertheless left a significant mark on the music in Indianapolis and along the touring circuits where they performed.[194]

Tyler began playing music professionally in his early teens in Indianapolis, which allowed him to follow well-traveled touring networks and brought him to Chicago, Cleveland, and New York in the summers in the mid-1950s. He claimed to have randomly met a young Albert Ayler on the street during one of his journeys, identified by the distinct pink birthmark on his chin where he later grew a white spot in his beard.[195] The two later reacquainted themselves in Cleveland. Tyler joined the US Army band in 1957–1958, which may have played a role in his getting a scholarship to the School of Music at Indiana University around 1958–1960. "The exercise of playing with the army band was good for me," Tyler later reflected, "but the music there was similar to the high school curriculum, it wasn't what I wanted to play. The high school band was a little better, but in terms of me being able to release anything emotionally, they were blanks." When he was discharged from the army, he thought to himself, "What else could I do other than play music? So I must follow it to the end. There wasn't anything else I could do that would hold my interest."[196] Tyler then moved to Cleveland in 1960; his uncle got him a job at one of the hospitals there, and he was yearning to pursue music more seriously away from his parents, who had never approved of it as a career.[197]

MEMPHIS

From Grenada, Mississippi, the saxophonist Frank Wright's family moved to Memphis, where he spent some of his formative years from the late 1930s to the 1950s. By the late 1940s, when Wright was coming of age, Memphis was a flourishing center of the blues. As one writer noted, it was the site of the "Memphis synthesis," which drew heavily from the Chicago blues scene but was smoother and had a wider appeal, especially among Black audiences.[198] The scene was centered on Beale Street, which had been a haven for Black culture for decades. In 1949, the Memphis radio station WDIA also shifted to broadcasting entirely Black music in a city that was nearly 50 percent African American. WDIA was later described as the "Mother Station of the Negroes" and claimed by 1954 to be reaching 10 percent of the national African American population.[199]

WDIA and Beale Street became launching points for the guitarist B. B. King (1925–2015) in 1949. "Beale Street was where it all started for me," King later recalled, and one of his earliest performances there was a solo show at the radio station. Soon after, he began a group that was variously called the Beale Street Blues Boys, Bee Bee King's Original Band, Bee Bee's Jeebies, and finally the Beale Streeters. Various people were involved with the band over the next few years, and the group was described as "the premier band of Memphis throughout 1950 and 1951."[200] Via WDIA, many of the Memphis blues bands gained national exposure, opening up recording and touring opportunities.

Wright came of age in Memphis, steeped in the blues scene of the early 1950s. His first professional playing began on electric bass, where he backed up B. B. King as well as some other well-known figures in King's milieu.[201] For example, he played with the pianist and vocalist Rosco Gordon (1928–2002), in the years after the latter's hit tune "Booted" came out in 1951.[202] Thus Wright was exposed to Gordon's piano playing, which exhibited an emphasis on the offbeat or "afterbeat" rather than the downbeat and which was broadly influential, including in Jamaican popular music, reggae, and ska.[203] It is unclear but seems unlikely that Wright was still working with Gordon when the latter toured the Caribbean or South America in the late 1950s.

Wright also played with the vocalist Bobby "Blue" Bland (1930–2013) just as he was emerging to success in the late 1950s. At that time, Bland was recording hit singles including "Farther Up the Road" and "Little Boy Blue."[204] Bland's music managed to knit together the spirit of gospel and R&B with the authentic feel of a juke joint.[205] Playing with King, Gordon, and Bland would have a deep impact on Wright as he developed his aesthetic on the saxophone in later years, bearing something of a fiery preacher style, tinged occasionally with a groove or a dance step. Wright also knew fellow tenor player Charles Lloyd in those years, though it is not known whether they played together.[206] It is unclear when exactly Wright arrived in Cleveland, but he moved there by at least the early 1960s, when he was in his mid- to late twenties. Unlike many of the other Cleveland musicians, Wright arrived already with years of experience, while the others had grown up there in the Cleveland jazz scene. Wright was to be a catalyst both there and beyond.

In each of these sites, the prehistory of free jazz was being forged through working-class consciousness, increasing mobility, and the building of autonomous or semiautonomous cultural spaces. It was a struggle, but vast networks of people forged these spaces and built communities over time. By the time that migrants arrived in the bustling industrial cities of the greater Ohio Valley, they were already in the process of developing cultural attitudes that were in contrast to their kin in the rural south. The harrowing practice of freedom, the search for autonomy, community formation, and resistance to violence would all inform the aesthetics of free jazz in the decades to come as it emerged in Cleveland, Detroit, Buffalo, and other northern cities.

PART II

Old and New Sounds in the Greater Ohio Valley

CHAPTER 4

CLEVELAND

Jazz, Segregation, and Working-Class Aesthetics

For many of us in the Black nationalist movement, this music was part of the revolution because it was going against the status quo.... Everything was in flux and everything we did was rebelling against the system. From the arts to politics, there was no division. The whole process was about freedom.

—Clyde Shy (Mutawaf Shaheed)

Many pathways led people north to Cleveland in the twentieth century. Each migrant brought with them family and other social networks that continued to link them to the south and to other urban centers in the north. Each person also brought with them skills and trades that they attempted to use to gain employment in the quickly expanding industries of Cleveland. The variety of cultural and religious practices that they carried with them would form a unique synthesis that would manifest in a Cleveland aesthetic that would culminate in the work of Albert Ayler, Bobby Few, Frank Wright, Charles Tyler, and others.

By the turn of the twentieth century, Cleveland was on the rise as a major US city and was one of the largest manufacturing centers in the world. Situated on the southern edge of Lake Erie and connected to the numerous industrial centers of the Great Lakes, Cleveland was home to a plethora of early automobile manufacturers and oil refineries, and it supplied industrial goods that were integral to most other areas of American industry. As in burgeoning manufacturing centers in the south during the same time period, Cleveland's labor organizing and strikes were used to fight against the greatest excesses of the capitalist class, though given that 30 percent of the population in 1920 was foreign-born, the situation was even more complex in terms of forging solidarity.

THE MAKING OF BLACK CLEVELAND

Station Hope, as Cleveland was known in the Underground Railroad networks, had been a major stop for people escaping north to Canada. A slow trickle of African Americans moving from rural Ohio and from other parts of the upper south since the time of Emancipation were suddenly joined by tens of thousands more during World War I, from across the south. These newcomers, in particular, came from the deep south: from west-central Georgia, Alabama, and the eastern borders of Mississippi, seeking employment in the factories of Cleveland.

Cleveland had a small Black community almost from its beginnings as a city. Its numbers slowly increased after the Civil War, as did the resistance among the white population to Black access to jobs, education, and other aspects of public and private life. By the 1910s a small Black political class had emerged that vied for power in the city and fought to gain the support of the growing community. World War I drastically transformed Black Cleveland, with thousands of migrants arriving from the south to take industrial jobs that had previously been filled by immigrant labor from Europe. Many of the workers were drawn to Cleveland by labor agents, and regular articles in the *Cleveland Gazette* criticized the segregated south and claimed that the northern city held better opportunities for Black workers in its rapidly expanding industries.[1] The primary draw was economic: Wages sometimes rose to as high as six times what people were able to earn in the south.[2]

Just in the late 1910s, Cleveland's Black population increased by over 300 percent, to a total of 34,000 people; it more than doubled again by 1930. The migration required the effort of entire families and extended kin networks. At times, families moved up in parts, with men going first to secure a job and then the rest following. But the migration as a whole was also often intergenerational, with parents or extended family joining their adult children and grandchildren as they looked to make new lives.

As the population increased, Cleveland became more segregated along both lines of race and class. The initial heart of the Black community was situated between East Thirtieth Street and East Fifty-Fifth Street up to Euclid Avenue in the north and the Cuyahoga River to the south, an area known as the Cedar-Central neighborhood. Through the 1920s, the community continued to grow eastward; on the eve of the Great Depression, it stretched all the way to East 105th Street and down to Woodland Avenue to the south, even as the white population began to move farther out into the suburbs of Cleveland Heights, Garfield Heights, and Shaker Heights.[3] Wealthier Black families also began moving out from the center of the city. Black Clevelanders faced continuous housing exclusions and shortages and often paid higher rents than white residents, which resulted in Black neighborhoods becoming the most densely populated in all of Cleveland.

The core of the Black community developed in the Cedar-Central neighborhood, north of the train tracks on the east side of Cleveland. That part of the city had been settled and built by Southern and Eastern European immigrants, especially Jews and Italians, in the late nineteenth and early twentieth centuries; they had been poor and had inhabited housing that was of low quality. By the 1920s and 1930s, when most Jews moved further east or west and it became increasingly a Black neighborhood, many of the tenement houses "were basically shacks" and in a state of terrible disrepair.[4] Extended families often shared rooming houses with grandparents, aunts, uncles, and cousins living in the same building or nearby one another. "That is where Black life in Cleveland began," one longtime resident declared.[5]

The Cedar-Central neighborhood changed dramatically between 1915 and 1920. For one, there was a steady influx of Black tenants who moved into the area. Simultaneously, the city's racist policies pushed brothels out of white neighborhoods and into Cedar-Central. The mayor explicitly urged them to relocate there, which led to the devaluation of property throughout the area and created a stigma for the Black working-class people who lived there.[6] For decades after, the city used the area's association with crime as justification for so-called urban renewal projects, slum clearance initiatives, and home demolition.

The Communist Party was one of the most committed forces in the area to fighting discrimination in the early 1930s, forming organizations like the Unemployed Council in Cedar-Central, where unemployment rates ranged from between 54 and 91 percent in different parts of the neighborhood.[7] Interracial protests that they organized often faced direct and highly violent attacks by police. The Communist Party's popularity at that time caused one local minister to warn, "Communism and communistic leaders with their program of criticism, fellowship, and sharing, are far more popular than any church or minister. In fact, their membership is increasing far more rapidly than that of all the churches combined.

Thousands of once devout readers of the Bible have closed the book of books to read communistic literature."[8] Class politics were central to the evolving community on Cleveland's east side.

The city became increasingly segregated, with the west side and the far east side beyond East 105th Street effectively off limits to African Americans. Cedar-Central, and other parts of the community as it expanded, became a dynamic site of Black cultural production most visible in jazz and blues clubs. Most people from the community began to get jobs in the steel mills, which were nearby. "It was dangerous work," one resident cautioned. "Many Black people died in the steel mills."[9] From the time of World War II through the mid-1950s, household income for Black families increased at a rate 30 percent faster than white families, but less than 1 percent of newly constructed homes were sold to Black families for a complex variety of reasons, creating a constant shortage of good housing available to the community.[10] The community expanded eastward both as a result of economic uplift as well as a result of evictions, slum clearances, and home demolition. Much of the shift was also a result of subsidies given to building contractors, as the city abandoned its former commitment to public housing. As houses were built, the people who managed to ascend the social ladder began to move out along Quincy, Central, and Cedar avenues, which were nicer and of better quality. Class stratification thus had an eastward push.

The poorest members of the community, who could not afford renting tenement houses, settled south of the tracks in shantytowns along the Cuyahoga River near a polluted canal called Kingsbury Run.[11] Initial small settlements were bolstered by an influx of people who had been evicted by city officials from shanties along Lake Erie in 1934 through 1936.[12] The community was, by necessity, a diverse one, including not only Black migrants from the south but also Czech, Hungarian, Irish, and Slovak immigrants, who had either fallen on hard times or been evicted from nearby areas and had to take refuge along the canal.[13] There were a number of separate camps and shantytowns there, though all in close proximity, linked together socially and economically. The community achieved its greatest visibility in the Cleveland press in 1936 through 1938, when a serial killer with medical training plagued the community with grisly murders and dismemberment of victims that continued unhindered until the so-called city safety director authorized a raid against the shantytowns, which resulted in three hundred evictions and about one hundred shanties being burned down.[14] Despite this state-sanctioned violence, the community of Kingsbury Run revived and rebuilt itself in the wake of the attacks.

"The first step up for Black folks was moving into the projects along East 40th Street," the trumpeter Kamal Abdul Alim recalled. "My grandfather and my parents got homes there. When they were brand new, they were nice, and a much better place to live than the tenements."[15] Public housing in Cleveland was some of the first in the nation and became a blueprint for other cities. Public housing was also built and orchestrated in a manner to enforce racial segregation; the Outhwaite Homes were designated for Black residents, while the Cedar-Central Apartments were reserved for white inhabitants. One local resident, Pearl Mitchell, organized and wrote against the segregation of what had been up to that time the most racially integrated neighborhood in the city.[16] Nevertheless, when the Outhwaite Homes were first opened in 1937, numerous tenants commented on their quality, highlighting various amenities such as refrigerators, ranges, closets, ventilation, and ample space.[17]

In addition to factory jobs and club owners, gambling was one way that some people made their living. In a system called "the numbers," people would select numbers and if they came up in the draw, they would win money, like a lottery. One resident stated, "No exaggeration, it's a way that a lot of people moved further east and got better houses, playing the numbers."[18]

East Fortieth Street also became the cultural center of the community in the early years. "My grandfather had a club there," Abdul Alim recalled.[19] A community center there, the Friendly Inn, was a gathering place for musicians to jam, to learn from the older members of the community in art, music, and dance, and then, as they developed, to teach the next generation that was coming up after them. So much of the early music training for people happened within the community, supported by members of the community, because they did not have city-supported institutions where they could learn. "The community was tight. We were confined to that part of Cleveland, so everyone knew each other, people didn't leave except to work, so that's how culture developed," Abdul Alim stated.[20]

In the community centers, local bands often performed, and touring musicians played there and sometimes even gave workshops. Decades later, people recalled a wide number of performers, ranging from Duke Ellington, Fats Domino, Ray Charles, John Coltrane, and, later, Stevie Wonder, performing in the community centers, even in the projects, which disseminated knowledge of the music directly to the people. "Other than Central High School, musicians didn't go to school to learn to play. It was hands-on. Someone would school you if they saw that you had the capacity and interest. You could get great training right within the community," Abdul Alim observed.[21] The availability of musical mentors is clear evidence that the general level of musical ability and knowledge were at such a degree that sharing that cultural wealth and passing it down from one generation to the next was not only readily possible but also at least somewhat systemically stable, from the 1930s until the 1960s.

Black churches proliferated in Cleveland during the period of heaviest migration, increasing from just seventeen individual congregations before World War I to over 140 churches by the early years of the Great Depression.[22] Built on East Fortieth Street, St. John's AME Church was one of the most important and influential spaces for the community where other forms of music developed and the community gathered regularly.

Out of the social transformations of Cleveland grew a distinct Black consciousness that had roots in race, religion, and class.[23] This was heightened by Marcus Garvey's Universal Negro Improvement Association, which had a small chapter in the city by the early 1920s. The *Negro World* newspaper became widely read, especially among the working class, as it addressed issues that were of importance to them, ranging from racial unity and pride to economic uplift.

JAZZ ON THE EAST SIDE

Central High School was essential for developing most of the city's local jazz talent. For example, the vocalist Noble Sissle (1889–1975) was one of the earliest jazz artists to be educated there who emerged to prominence. Others included the trumpeters Harry "Pee Wee" Jackson and Freddie Webster (1916–1947), the latter of whom was a key bebop figure and an influence on Miles Davis and Dizzy Gillespie. The composer, pianist, and arranger Tadd Dameron (1917–1965), composer Emil Boyd, saxophonist Joe Alexander (d. 1970), trumpeter Bill Hardman (1933–1990), and bassist Bob Cunningham (1934–2017) all attended Central High School.

Cleveland's jazz talent was most prominently fostered in the club scene. The corners of many blocks had a club, and some areas had two or three as a local scene sprung up around a cluster of spaces. Woodland Avenue, for instance, near Thirty-Eighth Street, had three clubs that not only staged local talent but also touring bands. One musician recalled seeing the Jazz Crusaders play there in the 1950s, for example.[24] On Euclid Avenue and East Fifty-Fifth Street, Leo's was another long-lasting jazz club that featured local and national musicians from the 1940s until the mid-1970s. Gleason's on Woodland at East Fifty-Fifth Street was a famous rock and roll club that by the 1950s also booked jazz to attract Black customers.

Cedar Avenue was one of the most important cultural thoroughfares, and it was replete with a string of clubs that stretched from where the Black community had begun across Cleveland out toward the far east side. The Black

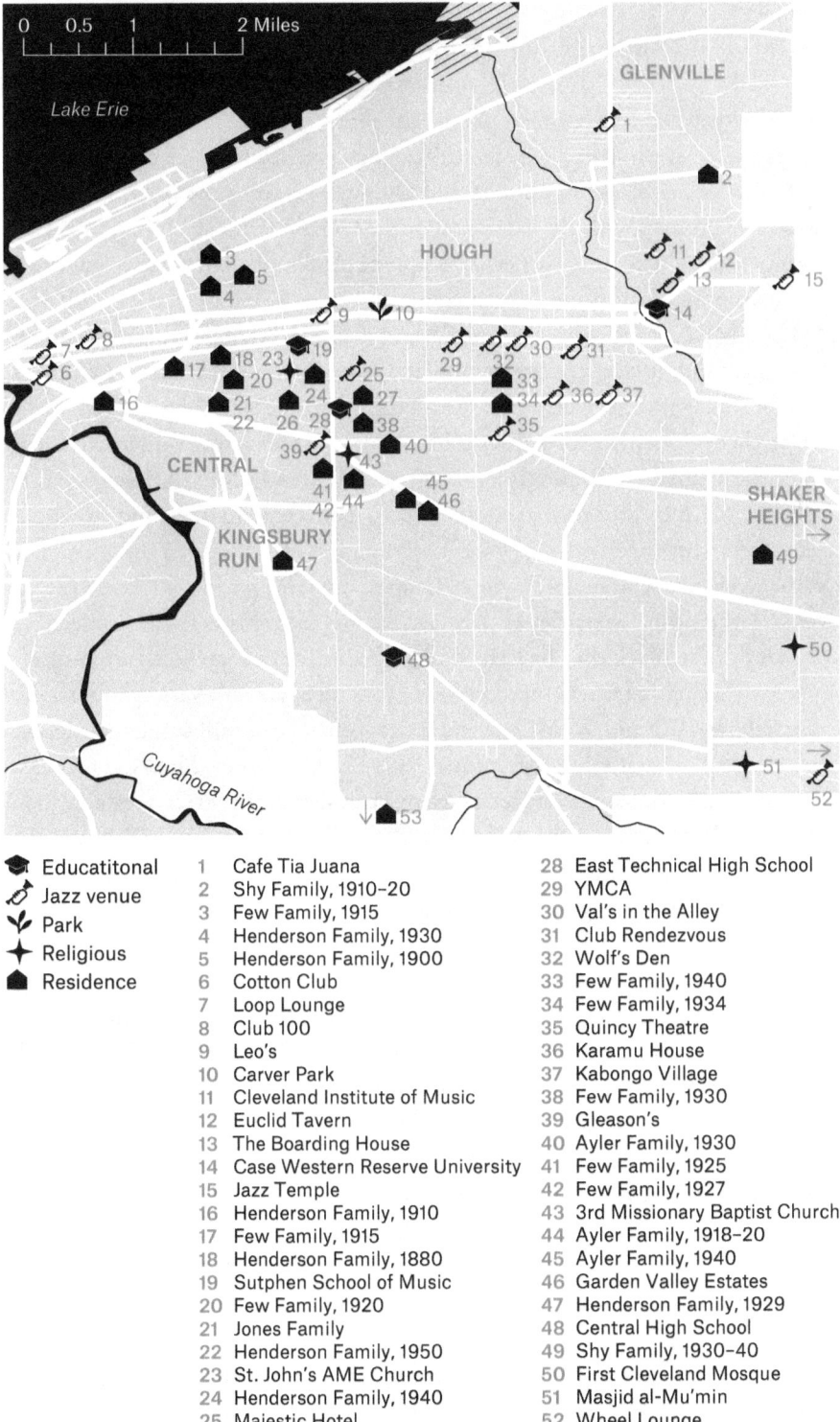

FIGURE 4.1 Sonic landscapes of Cleveland.

Source: Cartography by Alice Viggiani.

community expanded that direction by the 1950s, and it had a strong club scene through the following decade. It remained segregated, with Cedar as the northern border of the Black community and Quincy Avenue to the south as a purely residential district, with the exception of the Cotton Club at Quincy and East Seventy-First. There were bars every couple of blocks all along Cedar, making it the center of nightlife for the entire community.

The YMCA at the corner of East Seventy-Seventh Street was both a community center and a place where a lot of Black musicians stayed because they could not rent rooms at segregated hotels. Around East Eighty-Sixth to East 105th along Cedar, there was a string of clubs, the best known of which was Val's in the Alley, where the pianist Art Tatum (1909–1956) played extensively in the late 1930s and early 1940s. Club Rendezvous and the Wolf's Den were situated amid late-night restaurants where people would listen to jazz and blues, sometimes going very late on the weekends. Country's House of Grapes was a cheap wine bar where people would gather; the owner would play jazz records from his extensive collection. The city's first Black disc jockey, Walkin' Talkin' Bill Hawkins (1909–1975), broadcast a range of Black music in the 1940s and 1950s on a variety of stations, especially WABQ and WJMO, where he was central to establishing them as the first two stations entirely programmed for a Black audience. He also broadcast from his own record studio at Cedar Avenue and East 105th Street, around which a substantial community formed.[25] Another radio station, WCUY, broadcast regular jazz programs and even turned to an all-jazz format in the mid-1960s, before eventually ending jazz programming in 1971.

By the early 1960s, what remained of the club scene had moved much farther east along Euclid Avenue, to between East Ninety-Fifth and East 105th, as small numbers of Black middle- and upper-class people also began to move into the area. Club 100, for example, was one of the most active venues; Rahsaan Roland Kirk played there regularly when he was in the city.[26] Tia Juana, the Howard Johnson Club, and the Red Carpet Club were other key venues that sustained the scene in that area. The music also happened up through the Case Western Reserve University area to East 115th Street, including places like the Jazz Temple, which in 1962 through 1964 hosted national figures like the Miles Davis Quintet, John Coltrane, Les McCann, and others as a major stop along touring networks. The Boarding House was another venue in the area, featuring mostly local talent through the mid-1960s. The Euclid Tavern, a beatnik teahouse with more of a white audience, was where college students went to hear local jazz bands perform. It was also one of the few venues that later was receptive to free jazz.[27]

These areas adjacent to the university were the last surviving examples of jazz club life in Cleveland. There were forces beyond the music that were coalescing to push the clubs out. Local elitist and white supremacist development planning organizations saw them as a threat to their own goals of keeping the adjoining neighborhoods white. In the nearby neighborhood of Hough, the mayor had employed "the roughest, toughest men on the force" as police against the Black populace, and in the late 1950s they were openly referred to as a "goon squad" by city council members, employed for "skull-cracking attacks."[28] A later report on policing in 1966 stated clearly that racial profiling was a part of the everyday function of Cleveland's police department and that such tactics were most severely enforced in areas viewed as dividing lines between white and Black neighborhoods. In Glenville, jazz clubs and other spaces for Black culture that had "a high incidence of vice and rowdiness" were thought to be in the way of more powerful institutions, such as Case Western Reserve University and the Cleveland Clinic. Glenville and Hough would be the site of the most severe attempts at suppressing expressions of Black freedom and liberation in the 1960s.

LIBERATION MOVEMENTS

Cleveland was integrally connected to the national Civil Rights movement throughout its history and was often at the forefront of the struggle. It was a particularly segregated city, and the systemic violence of mid-twentieth-century America was clearly evident throughout its landscape, community formation, and ongoing politics.[29] A variety of organizations and movements shaped Cleveland's trajectory.

The Nation of Islam grew in popularity in Cleveland in the early 1960s. It was the door that some people took toward a variety of outcomes: Afrocentric cultural movements, Black nationalism, and conversion to orthodox Islam. Charismatic figures such as Malcolm X and Muhammad Ali gave the organization legitimacy, and they became its most effective advocates. By the mid-1960s, it was one of the most popular organizations advocating for the advancement of Black society in various forms. Many of the Cleveland musicians were part of the Nation for periods in the 1960s, with some, like Malcolm X, moving toward orthodoxy later, while some never converted. The strength of the community was pervasive and provided an environment where many people met, formed friendships, and found purpose in those years, which further fueled the music. The musicians Charles Tyler, Norman Howard, and Yusuf Mumin all joined the Nation of Islam in the early to mid-1960s.

A number of forces coalesced in Cleveland around 1963–1964 that produced an increasingly dynamic movement. Desegregating schools was a central issue, alongside economic struggles on the east side. School overcrowding only exacerbated issues at the time, and poor city planning failed to address the grievances in neighborhoods such as Hough and Glenville. Police brutality was commonplace. The United Freedom Movement (UFM) became the focal point at the time, composed of thirty-two organizations that ranged from churches, community groups, local chapters of national organizations like the National Association for the Advancement of Colored People (NAACP) and the Congress of Racial Equality (CORE), and local organizations such as the Freedom Fighters, Defenders of Human Rights, and the Afro-American Institute.[30] UFM's primary focus was desegregation of schools; in February 1964, the organization delivered an ultimatum to the school board.

In the wake of this, CORE invited Malcolm X to speak at Cory Methodist Church in Glenville, where he gave an early version of his "the ballot or the bullet" speech, demanding immediate change and progress. He professed his adherence to Islam but argued passionately against any divisions within the Black community and called for unity:

> I'm not here to argue or discuss anything that we differ about, because it's time for us to submerge our differences and realize that it is best for us to first see that we have the same problem—a common problem—a problem that will make you catch hell whether you're a Baptist, or a Methodist, or a Muslim, or a nationalist. Whether you're educated or illiterate, whether you live on the boulevard or the alley, you're going to catch hell just like me. We're all in the same boat and we all are going to catch the same hell from the same man. He just happens to be a white man. . . . If the white man doesn't want us to be anti-him, let him stop oppressing and exploiting and degrading us. If we don't do something real soon, I think you'll agree that we're going to be forced either to use the ballot or the bullet. It's one or the other in 1964. It isn't that time is running out—time has run out![31]

REVOLUTIONARY ACTION MOVEMENT

By the time of Malcolm X's speech, there were already movements developing in Cleveland that were articulating new approaches to liberation. At the forefront was a twenty-four-year-old junior high school social studies teacher, Don

Freeman. Freeman grew up in a jazz milieu of peers including his younger brother, the trumpeter Kamal Abdul Alim, and the saxophonist Arthur Jones. Freeman later wrote of his childhood experience: "Jazz music, America's most superlative twentieth-century art form, remained a significant component of my psyche and consciousness. This sublime Black innovation enhanced my appreciation of African Americans' merit and incalculable contribution to human/world culture. It motivated me to be culturally rebellious and was a prime impetus for the spirit that resulted in me subsequently becoming a political radical."[32] He added, "I was blessed to know and associate with Max Roach and Abby Lincoln, who were the most militant political advocates for African American liberation in the music."[33] When I visited him at his home in Cleveland in June 2021, his otherwise spartan apartment had only two pictures prominently displayed; one was of John Coltrane.[34] The bassist Clyde Shy observed, "In Cleveland, Coltrane was the icon of Black nationalism."[35]

Between 1960 and 1963, Freeman integrated himself into a national network across the Midwest and eastern United States advocating for substantial change.[36] His political thinking evolved quickly from advocating for the formation of a third party to abandoning electoral politics altogether in a call for revolution.[37] Freeman met Malcolm X in New York in 1962 and shared the stage with him at the Grass Roots Conference in Detroit in November 1963. Freeman, together with his college friend Max Stanford, cofounded the Revolutionary Action Movement (RAM). Freeman and Stanford were initially inspired by an essay written by Harold Cruse, "Revolutionary Nationalism and the Afro-American," which stated: "From the beginning, the American Negro has existed as a colonial being. His enslavement coincided with the colonial expansion of European powers and was nothing more or less than a condition of domestic colonialism. Instead of the United States establishing a colonial empire in Africa, it brought the colonial system home and installed it in the Southern states."[38]

Freeman became the leader of the Cleveland branch of RAM, and around the time of Malcolm X's speech in Cleveland in March 1964, they began working together. Malcolm X had just broken ties with the Nation of Islam and warned them against involvement. RAM was the first organization in the United States to synthesize the thought of Karl Marx, Vladimir Lenin, Mao Zedong, and others with that of Malcolm X to form a dynamic theory of revolutionary Black nationalism.[39] Stanford wrote that RAM advocated "mass rebellions and national black strikes as forms of struggle for the black nationalist movement. Its goal was to create an independent black republic through a socialist revolution."[40] Freeman often used jazz as a metaphor for political action, saying to his comrades in the organization that "we need to implement politically what jazz did musically in terms of revolution, raising peoples' consciousness, and providing an impetus for people to struggle for total liberation politically, economically, socially, and culturally."[41]

A month after Malcolm X's speech in Cleveland, Freeman, Stanford, and RAM-affiliated students at Fisk University held a conference to form a Black Nationalist Youth Movement. They labeled a broad range of organizations, such as the NAACP, CORE, the Student Non-Violent Coordinating Committee, and others, as "bourgeois reformism" that would ultimately fail because they still worked within a capitalist context, referencing W. E. B. DuBois's statement that "a system that enslaves you, cannot free you."[42] Furthermore, they saw "re-Africanization" aimed at aesthetic, intellectual, and spiritual development as necessary before Black nationalism could have any chance of success. And to build their network they sought ties with the nonaligned nations that had emerged from the Bandung Conference in 1955, especially, via their associate Robert F. Williams, with Cuba.[43] The conference enabled them to begin to "radicalize" the SNCC and gain influence in the south that eventually manifested in figures such as Stokely Carmichael. Beyond Cleveland, the organization's main chapters were located in Detroit and New York.[44] Nevertheless, Freeman and Stanford did not intend for the group to be a large movement known to the general public. For strategic reasons, they saw their role as "a vanguard group that will disseminate revolutionary ideas and will remain in contact with revolutionary forces everywhere."[45]

When in the fall of 1964 Freeman wrote an article in *Black America*, RAM's periodical, published in Detroit, describing the Fisk conference in detail, he immediately became the focus of the FBI's COINTELPRO program as well as "the tentacles of the CIA."[46] They surveilled him and conspired with police and Cleveland city officials to have him publicly fired from his teaching position in February 1965; he was one of the first targets of covert operations against Black Americans advocating revolutionary change in the United States.[47] Freeman subsequently withdrew from the frontlines of the movement, and RAM's presence in Cleveland began to fade. However, RAM was a direct source of inspiration for the Black Panther Party in Oakland a year later through their contacts with cofounder Bobby Seale.[48]

Years later, Freeman wrote in his autobiography,

> I have strived to foster a realization that American/global capitalism must be uprooted via political, socio-cultural, and economic revolution and supplanted by a post-secular spiritually based, classless, and genuine human community

thereby engendering a new, higher, more advanced civilization. As a resolute Black radical, I regarded it as essential to inspire African Americans to understand the profundity and uniqueness of their oppression has prepared them to occupy the forefront of this dialectic. Therefore, in order to fulfill our destiny, it is imperative that we be the vanguard in the long, protracted March till Victory is won.[49]

BLACK SEPARATISM AND THE REPUBLIC OF NEW LIBYA

Street-level violence only increased through 1965 and 1966, especially along the borders between the Hough and Glenville neighborhoods and the adjoining white areas. Poverty, substandard housing, police brutality, and lack of employment fueled these tensions. In July 1966, anger and frustration erupted in an uprising. Some of the people involved were RAM members trained in guerilla tactics and coordinated targets. As one eyewitness journalist observed, "Stores with a reputation for exorbitant prices or flagrant discourtesy to Negro customers, especially those on relief, provided most of the targets."[50] Subsequent police crackdowns in Hough only made the situation worse.[51]

A second surge came in the summer of 1968, in the wake of the assassination of Dr. Martin Luther King Jr. and the mainstreaming of Black nationalism in the political ethos of those who demanded revolutionary change. The new figure emerging in Cleveland was Ahmed Evans, who had formerly been a part of RAM and established himself as an eccentric figure advocating revolution and Black separatism. His organization was called Black Nationalists for New Libya or, alternatively, the Republic of New Libya (RNL), referencing the international organization, Republic of New Afrika (RNA), another separatist group that sought to establish a Black state composed of territories in the southeastern United States.

RNL coalesced by February 1968 and had drawn FBI and city police surveillance by July. With police at his doorstep, a fight eventually broke out between Evans and police on the evening of July 23. Other simultaneous incidents of police brutality further contributed to the clash. This led to a wide-scale uprising across Glenville over the four days following. It drew from many corners of the community. Mutawaf Shaheed noted that once the uprising had been sparked, someone went to his home, where he was hosting a gathering of poets, and said, "The pot is on," which meant that the uprising had commenced. Many hundreds of people took to the streets. Much of the music that emerged in the 1960s came out of these times of revolutionary politics, and some of the practitioners considered themselves to be preachers of liberation through their music.

THE BLACK MUSLIM MOVEMENT

Alongside the political movements, religious conversion was a major thread of African American cultural transformation in Cleveland through the 1960s. American Islam in the mid-twentieth century grew considerably and diversely, with more than a dozen different organizations shaping the growth and evolution of Muslim religious practice. By the 1960s, and in tandem with growing Afrocentric cultural movements and the influence of figures such as Malcolm X, there were substantive Black Muslim communities in places such as Brooklyn, Philadelphia, Pittsburgh, Jacksonville, and St. Louis.[52]

The First Cleveland Mosque had been founded by Wali Akram, himself an African American convert, in 1937.[53] Most of the early teachings and writings that informed their practice came from India and South Africa.[54] A subsequent, second wave of growth of the community in Cleveland in the 1960s extended how the religion was implemented in the community. As Imam Mutawaf Shaheed stated, "The first generation put a lot of emphasis on Arabic language. My generation focused more on community relations and spreading word about the faith within the Black community." Speaking of his own personal transformation, Shaheed added, "Black people needed a structure of some kind that was different from the one that was oppressing them since they got here. I saw Islam as a form of national government; it offered us the kinds of structures that we needed as a people."[55]

Most of the converts in Cleveland came out of the Black nationalist movement and the Muslim community that grew from it and embraced and synthesized the politics of that era. This second generation of the community in Cleveland had a greater interest in institutionalizing broader aspects of the faith, particularly those rooted in the *hadith*, the teachings and guidance of the Prophet Muhammad that governed much of the day-to-day lives of Muslims. This ranged from economics to personal moral conduct, from leadership to human relationships and interactions. "This gave us the ability to work against many of the customs and behaviors that the oppressor had himself," Shaheed observed. "It was a fresh approach to organization. Islam elevated us and moved us away from Western culture towards a spiritual culture and a moral framework."[56]

The first mosque had been located in the southeastern reaches of the city. A second mosque, Masjid Al-Mu'min, was built at what is now Martin Luther King Jr. Drive and East 116th Street, a location much more accessible to the east side community. The movement absorbed many elements of the preceding nationalist movements by about 1974. As the Muslim movement pushed for a more orthodox adherence to the faith, there was some friction with the remaining members of the Nation of Islam, who were connected to the Moorish Science Temple. According to Shaheed, leaders in the Nation of Islam instructed their members to stay out of the uprisings in the years 1966 to 1968, and it caused them to lose credibility.[57]

In the latter half of the 1960s, the Black Muslim movement grew considerably, with more than two thousand converts by the end of the decade. They joined the Black-led Dar Islam movement, which had originated in Brooklyn and was just then gaining national footing in Cleveland, soon spreading to Long Island, Philadelphia, Baltimore, Washington, Tallahassee, Atlanta, Birmingham, Detroit, and other parts of the country. In Cleveland there was a strong push to resist outside control, including international or foreign control of how Islam was practiced on the local level, with elements of earlier liberation movements continuing to demand autonomy and to focus on building a Black nation.[58]

COALESCENCE OF A COMMUNITY

The families of the musicians that contributed to free jazz in Cleveland arrived in the city between the turn of the century and the Great Depression. The saxophonist Albert Ayler's father, Edward Ceasor Ayler (1913–2011), was brought to the city as a small child by his mother, Augusta. She had fled her husband, the first Albert Ayler, and had entered into a relationship with a man named Wright Ceasor in Mobile by the mid-1910s; he helped the two travel north to Cleveland, where they first lived near Kingsbury Run, which Edward Ayler described as "so terrible down there that they had to move away."[59] They eventually managed to move two doors down from the Third Missionary Baptist Church, near Woodland Avenue and East Fifty-Fifth Street. Ceasor worked as a cement finisher for Hunkin-Conkey Construction Company; Augusta worked as a domestic to support their family. The children took the surname Ceasor up until their high school days, though it seems that Augusta and Wright split up by the late 1920s.[60]

Albert Ayler's mother, Jessie Myrtle Hunter (1916–1985), arrived in Cleveland slightly later. Her parents moved north in the 1920s, with her father joining thousands of southern Black railroaders who had been recruited for the New York Central Railroad and other related industries in Cleveland at the time.[61] Will Hunter died a few years after their arrival, leaving his widow, Lula, to head the family with Jessie and the other children in Cleveland while working there as a laundress.[62] After the saxophonist's parents were united in marriage in 1933, Edward Ayler worked as a chauffeur, but at some point during the war years of the 1940s he got a job working at the rocket and aircraft company Thompson Products, which pushed the family into the small, emerging Black middle class of Shaker Heights, a suburb on the outskirts of Cleveland.[63] Edward Ayler learned to play the alto saxophone but also played the violin and sang in local clubs. On his horn, he had a style that was "somewhat like Dexter Gordon."[64] His greatest exposure was with the Bob McKelby band.[65] "He was local and wasn't known widely," Albert Ayler later stated. "That's why when I was born he wanted me to be known all over the world."[66]

The pianist Bobby Few's grandparents Simon and Betty Few fled eviction and violence in The Rock, Georgia, and moved north to Cleveland around 1922.[67] They settled on East Fifty-Third Street as the community was expanding eastward, and Simon switched between labor jobs and working as a night watchman for a demolition company.[68] They moved residences every couple of years, seeking better housing, staying in that general area, near East Technical High School. Their second son, Robert Lee Few Sr., attended East Tech and married a stenographer, Winifred Raephena Towe, the daughter of a Barbadian immigrant, Thomas Lafayette Towe, who had arrived in Cleveland by the early 1910s, and his wife, Anna, who had deeper Ohio roots. Towe and his family first lived in the heart of the early Black community, on East Thirty-Fourth Street, but he managed to secure employment as a porter for the Firestone Rubber Company and soon moved eastward.

Robert and Winifred Few moved to East Eighty-Fourth Street after they married, where he worked at a country club, allowing their son, Robert Lee Few Jr., known all his life as Bobby Few, to grow up in close proximity to the vibrant jazz clubs that existed along Cedar Avenue in the 1940s and 1950s.[69] Bobby's mother, who played violin, encouraged him to pursue music instead of sports as a boy, and the family paid for him to take private lessons. Few also grew up with the bassist Bob Cunningham. Cunningham's father had died when Bob was quite young, and he looked to Robert Few Sr. as a second father and to Few as a brother. The two played music together and entered the professional world as jazz musicians together, playing in some of the same groups in the 1950s.

The bassist Earle "Errol" Henderson's family, having survived and escaped the violent repression of the Camp Hill, Alabama, labor struggles, settled on East

Thirty-First Street in 1929 in what was quickly becoming a slum.[70] A decade later, the neighborhood was deemed the poorest part of Cleveland. Earle's father, Jesse Lee Henderson, worked in a laundry, though his parents came from exceedingly different circumstances, largely dictated by skin color. His mother, Mary, was the daughter of a mixed-race couple, her mother being the child of Irish famine immigrants who had settled in Cleveland in the 1860s; her father, George Edward Fairfax (1868–1950), was light-skinned and sometimes passed as white in public records.[71] Their marriage in 1895 was rare, but they lived in the same part of Cleveland, even as it later transitioned to a Black neighborhood, while their children, including Mary, were generally considered white when they were growing up. But the family dynamics seem to have made it possible for Mary to marry a newly arrived migrant from Alabama and to build a family with him in the 1930s as a more obvious mixed-race marriage. Their son, Earle Henderson, grew up as a musician, embracing the Black jazz culture of Cleveland.

The family of the alto saxophonist Arthur Jones (1940–1998) also came north during the late 1920s. His mother's family came from the west-central Alabama Black Belt around Selma, where his great-great-grandmother Sabray Gordon (b. c. 1812) and her descendants led the family in the years after Emancipation through the collapse of Reconstruction and decades of sharecropping.[72] Arthur's mother, Adele Gordon (b. 1914), the youngest of eleven children, came north to Cleveland with one of her siblings and met his father, James Edward Jones (1911–1989), who had migrated north from near Lewisburg, Tennessee, around the same time. The newly formed family settled in the heart of the Cedar-Central slum on East Thirty-Third Street, where James managed to acquire a skilled labor position paving streets for the Works Progress Administration.[73] Arthur and his older brother, the tenor saxophonist Ernest Jones, had an extensive record collection growing up, and they lived within the orbit of the jazz culture along Cedar Avenue before moving to Glenville by their early teenage years.[74]

The trumpeter Norman Howard's maternal grandfather, David Sebree (b. c. 1896), was a railroader, working on the lines in Christian County, Kentucky, where the effort to segregate the trains in the state, along with most other public spaces, had begun in the mid-1890s.[75] Regular protests and numerous acts of civil disobedience failed to change the inadequate accommodations of the separate and unequal train cars. After working there in the late 1910s and 1920s, the family joined the exodus north, where he labored for an oil manufacturing company in Cleveland.[76] Sebree's daughter married a newly arrived immigrant from Guyana, James Howard (c. 1901–1958), who moved in with the family on East Forty-Third Street, having acquired a carpentry job working in building construction.

FIGURE 4.2 Peter Shy family in Cleveland.

Source: Courtesy Mutawaf Shaheed, private collection.

The family of the bassist Clyde Shy (later Mutawaf Shaheed) was the first of the free jazz lineages to arrive in Cleveland. Freeman and Miranda Shy and some of their grown children, including Peter Shy (1875–1940), left sharecropping in Jasper County, Georgia, in 1900.[77] Upon arriving in the city, they settled in northeastern Cleveland, in an area that would become the Glenville neighborhood. Peter was resourceful and managed to work his way into the plastering trade and in less than a decade was running his own business there, getting steady work building new homes as the city expanded. Peter's contracting business survived until the Great Depression. The steady income allowed them to raise eleven children, and when the economy crashed, Peter's wife, Frances, ran a lodging house that provided homes for "county wards." The second-youngest of their children, Pvt. Clyde Elmer Shy Sr., would eventually train to be an attorney after serving in World War II.

Glenville was initially a more integrated neighborhood but began to transition to a middle-class Black neighborhood in the 1950s after white flight to the suburbs. But the transition was met with considerable resistance, with violence not uncommon. When a Black church attempted to buy property on Magnolia Drive, for instance, it was bombed. There were also concerted efforts to resist all attempts at integration of schools, pools, parks, and other public spaces. An organization calling itself the National Association for the Advancement of White People was formed, temporarily, to oppose such measures. White students protested the matriculation of Black students at Patrick Henry High School in 1954. Assaults, bomb threats, and other forms of physical and psychological violence against new Black residents in the neighborhood were not uncommon. And much of this was spurred by the fear that the area might be redlined by mortgage lenders if it became marked as being in a process of racial transition. From the mid-1950s into the late 1960s, Glenville became the site of the most intense race-based violence in Cleveland.[78]

BOBBY FEW AND FRANK WRIGHT ON THE JAZZ CLUB AND DANCE HALL SCENE

Of all of the musicians who emerged from Cleveland who later contributed to free jazz, the pianist Bobby Few was the one with the most extensive earlier career as a bebop player. The evolution of his career tells something of the story of the jazz scene in Cleveland in the 1950s and 1960s. According to his widow, Simone Few, he began playing professionally in 1952 at the age of seventeen.[79] His earliest documented association was in 1954, with a group alternatively called the Sheltonaires or the Dick Shelton Quintet, playing at the Cotton Club in central Cleveland and at Café Tia Juana out on East 105th Street. Even in these early performances, Few was said to be "a musician with a splendid talent and some very unusual piano gymnastics."[80] The only other notable member of the group was Few's close friend, the bassist Bob Cunningham; the group generally backed up vocalists for cabaret or lounge-style jazz, as well as a few fashion shows.

From there, Few gradually established himself as a significant figure on the Cleveland scene through the last half of the 1950s. In 1954–1955, he played with an otherwise obscure group called the Metronomes at the Quincy Theatre, but by 1956–1957, he had assembled a quintet in his own name that frequented Club Congo and the Flamingo Lounge, where he appeared on bills with exotic dancers and comedians in entertainment variety shows, playing for Black audiences.[81] His holiday concerts at the latter venue in late 1956 were particularly crucial in solidifying demand for his groups in Cleveland, and the band managed to book a "highly successful" Midwest tour out to Decatur, Illinois, with numerous stops along the way.[82] Few also studied classical music at the Cleveland Institute of Music in the mid-1950s, refining his playing and also learning how to compose.[83] His teacher at the institute noted, even then, that Few "would never just play things as they were written, he was always doing something different, something uniquely his own."[84]

By 1959, his efforts had solidified around a trio that played weekly at Bill Lynch's Mirror Show Bar; they were regularly described as playing return engagements "by popular demand."[85] In 1960 and 1961, the trio was in demand at a variety of clubs in Cleveland including the Shaker Bar, the Poodle Lounge, and Club Downbeat.[86] The last of these, for instance, had "a unique new Parisian atmosphere," on bills that included magicians, comedians, exotic dancers, chorus lines, and other acts.

But Few also had an interest in other types of performances and was drawn to the plays of Langston Hughes. The latter debuted his new play, *Simply Heavenly*, at Karamu House, which today is the oldest Black-run theater in the United States and has been a major site for mentoring actors in Cleveland over many decades. As another Cleveland musician, Yusuf Mumin, noted, the institution was "conceived out of the principles that the individual is not wholly determined by their environment but has the capacity to transcend it"; the name was taken from Swahili, meaning "a place of joyful gathering."[87] At the opening performance in May 1959, Few held the role of the barfly pianist "Bob," providing much of the onstage music for the play as well as working as the assistant director of the music. Few appeared again when the play returned later that year and again in 1961.[88]

By 1963, Few's trio work evolved into what became known as the East Jazz Trio, with the bassist Cevera Jeffries and drummer Raymond Farris; this was a sustained group that played over the decade following.[89] Their first known performance was back at Karamu House, signaling that the trio was rooted in the community and that they were being taken more seriously as artists, rather than just as entertainers.[90] One critic at the time noted that Few had previously performed with the poet and playwright Langston Hughes in "poetry and jazz" concerts, and it seems that their meeting in 1959 may have prompted additional collaborations in a jazz poetry setting.[91] For their performance at Karamu House, the program was hosted and narrated by a student of Emil Boyd, a long under-recognized composer from Cleveland's east side. The East Jazz Trio played original works by Few and Jeffries, as well as tunes by Boyd, Thelonious Monk, and Bud Powell.[92]

From there, the trio played most of the jazz clubs of Cleveland, often in extended residencies, such as the Corner Tavern, Tangiers Lounge, Shaker Bar, Copa Lounge, Left Hand Jazz Room, Wrong Club's Place, Americana Supper Club, Kay's Casa Blanca, the Howard Johnson Club, and back at Karamu House. Even after Few was playing with the Frank Wright Quartet in Europe, he would return, in gaps between his other work, and play for a few months with the East Jazz Trio in clubs in Cleveland as late as 1972.[93] Though Few found his fullest artistic expression in free music, he enjoyed playing standards and found steady work doing it.[94]

Like Few, Frank Wright also played for a few years on the Cleveland scene, but not as extensively, and he never garnered the same kind of popularity as his counterpart. By early 1963, he organized the Frank Wright Organ Combo with the brothers Sam and Billy Blackshaw on organ and drums, respectively; they played for a month at the Royal Tavern, where a local critic described Wright as "talented." The band soon after found regular work at the Shaker Bar, Toast of Town, and the Wheel Lounge through mid-1965.[95] He also led the Frank Wright Orchestra at clubs and dance halls, such as the B&B Club, where people could "dance to the music."[96] But when he followed Albert Ayler to New York, it seems that he left his jazz club and dance hall days behind as he focused on his creative work.

EARLY LIFE OF ALBERT AYLER

In their home, the Ayler family had "a big radio," from which Albert, by the age of three, grew up listening to the music of the vibraphonist Lionel Hampton.[97] He later claimed to have developed the sentiments of an artist "because of my father."[98] By age four, he would bang his footstool to the beat of Benny Goodman and Lionel Hampton tunes, causing his father to declare that "he has the talent of an artist and I'll start him to play music."[99] He also developed a love for the music of Bud Powell and Horace Silver during his childhood and adolescence.[100]

Ayler began to study alto saxophone with his father at age seven, and if he tried to go outside to play with other kids, his father would beat him. His father wanted him to stay and work on music. Ayler claimed to have been considered a child prodigy a year later, after winning first prize at a talent show in Cleveland where he played "Ave Maria" and the Lord's Prayer.[101] But free improvisation began even at this age; as Ayler later recalled, "I always had thought of free music, even when I was still small. I'd be playing a ballad and my father would say, 'get back to the melody, stop playing that nonsense.' But I knew something was there. I'd be standing in a corner playing and trying to communicate with a spirit that I knew nothing about at that particular age."[102] Throughout his childhood, his mother always dressed him in short pants, "because she wanted me to be special, she always kept me special," and he would get teased by other kids.[103] He maintained a distinctive, hip style throughout his life, which was regularly mentioned by colleagues, critics, and audience members. This aspect of standing out from the crowd at an early age was definitive in pushing Ayler to think of himself as unique.

By age nine, he could play advanced jazz and classical music from memory. His father had him listen to a lot of the tenor saxophonist Illinois Jacquet, whom Ayler considered to be "one of the first people to get that humming sound in his horn."[104] He also listened to Lester Young, whom he considered influential in "the way he connected his phrases. The freedom with which he flowed and his warm tone. When he and Billie Holiday got together, there was so much beauty. These are the kind of people who produce a spiritual truth beyond this civilization."[105] Ayler and his father played alto saxophone duets in church, which allowed him to learn a repertoire of spirituals that he would carry throughout his life. The Ayler family were deeply religious people; as Beaver Harris would later observe, "Everything they did was based on spirituality. Albert's mother would sometimes go into a trance and speak in tongues."[106] Ayler even joined his father's band to play at funerals.[107] These early musical experiences were deeply influential on his worldview, instilling spiritual yearnings that were to be at the forefront of his artistic expression throughout his life.

By the age of eleven, Ayler stated, "My father could teach me no more," and he began to study formally at the Academy of Music with Benny Miller.[108] Miller had played with Charlie Parker, Miles Davis, and others at the club Tia Juana in Cleveland. Ayler studied there for seven years, until he graduated high school, earning the nickname "Little Bird," after the saxophonist Charlie Parker, for his facility with bebop styles. Among many contemporary influences, Ayler held a particularly high regard for the reedist Sidney Bechet, and the latter's vibrato style seems to have manifested in Ayler's playing as it developed. "I was crazy about [Bechet]. His tone was unbelievable. It helped me a lot to learn that a man could get that kind of tone. It was hypnotizing—the strength of it, the strength of his vibrato. For me, he represented the true spirit, the full force of life."[109]

The Ayler family lived in Shaker Heights well before it became a predominantly Black neighborhood a decade later. Ayler's parents would admonish him if he played too loud because they were worried he would disturb their white neighbors, so Ayler would practice in a closet with a sock stuffed in his horn to muffle the sound. "That's how he developed such a strong tone," the bassist Clyde Shy stated. "If he was playing behind me, I could feel the wind on my back."[110] Ayler introduced many of the younger musicians to the music through listening sessions at his home. "The first time I heard Ornette [Coleman], *Change of the Century*, was in a small room at their house where they had a record player," Shy recalled from listening sessions that the Ayler brothers hosted there in 1961–1962. "That was my beginning with that kind of music. When I heard it the first time, I heard freedom."[111]

By 1952, Ayler began sitting in with local musicians and others who passed through on tour, such as the blues harmonica player and singer Little Walter (1930–1968) and R&B singer Lloyd Price (b. 1933). In the summers of 1952 and 1953, while still in high school, Ayler toured with Little Walter, and from that point on, "I began living a different life," he later said, though "I had to carry my food in a bag because there wasn't much money."[112] It also introduced Ayler to the musician's lifestyle of late nights and club culture, and he also began sneaking into bars while underage to listen to music. As one childhood friend recalled, "We'd see all the horn players, all the good ones, the bar-walkers and everything. We had a good basis because that's all we did—music, music, music."[113]

As for Little Walter's music, Ayler reflected, "The country soul was different from where I was from. Where I grew up, there was a middle class, but these people were a little different from me. In the country, they were living with the music right there. [Little Walter] wanted me to hold the notes longer. Before I knew it, I fit right in."[114] Nevertheless, Ayler later confessed, "That wasn't for me. I had to think of a way out but it was all part of the development. It was important to my musical career to have been out there among those deep-rooted people."[115] He later claimed that through this circle of musicians, he had met the blues musicians Howlin' Wolf and Muddy Waters.[116]

Though Ayler excelled at golf and worked as a caddie, Ayler noted that "music was in my heart," so as he finished school, he knew that he needed to follow that forward. In 1955, Ayler began his own R&B band playing locally, sometimes just playing on street corners, but it was not financially successful, and he worked for a few years alongside his father at Thompson Products, where he won an award for being the fastest blade polisher at the plant.[117] Around 1956, he switched to playing tenor and began to sit in with groups in local clubs and bars, such as Esquire, but he "was forcibly ejected from the stand" by local musicians, Rahsaan Roland Kirk among them.[118]

In 1958, Ayler enlisted in the US Army to play music. While he was there, he first learned to read notated music, while completing his switch to tenor saxophone, stating, "It seemed to me that on tenor you could get out all the feelings of the ghetto. On that horn you can really shout and tell the truth. After all, this music comes from the heart of America, the soul of the ghetto."[119] The band regularly practiced "six hours per day," and then Ayler would practice alone late into the night, playing scales, drones, diminished chords, and becoming even more familiar with his instrument than he had been previously.[120] While stationed in Fort Knox, Kentucky, he jammed with the tenor saxophonist Stanley Turrentine (1934–2000) and drummer Beaver Harris (1936–1991) and also played in a regiment band with the composer, drummer, and poet Harold Budd (1936–2020) and conductor and composer Jimmy DePriest (1936–2013). Budd later observed, "Albert Ayler was the first guy that I ever met who absolutely put his life on the line every single time he picked up his horn and played."[121]

Harris stated of these early encounters,

I could tell immediately that he had something different because his tone was so large. He would come by the mail room where I worked and we would just sit and play together. We played a lot, that was my beginning. I was inspired to continue with music and get out of baseball because I felt that there was room in his music for the new breed. He was a natural horn player, he had a large tone, and full control of the instrument. He was louder than everybody else. He could play a march like nobody else and he could make it swing. I had never heard anybody play with that much authority.

Furthermore, Harris noted,

Albert understood his roots, spirituals, the blues. These are the roots that made musicians of that era great. It was natural for him to do what he did because he could play so much in different areas [of the music]. He had a jazz concept, he'd improvise, he understood the big sound of Coleman Hawkins, Pres, the music of Louis Armstrong. He had a traditional jazz feeling, but he wanted to expand upon it and utilize different musics. To change the music, he had to do something a little different.[122]

Marching band music became another major influence on his developing sound. Stationed in Orleans, France, he was able to find occasional opportunities to play in Paris, often with the bassist Lewis Worrell, who was in the same unit. As one fellow soldier noted, Ayler "was getting into his modern jazz then, and he was very different; he even played blues different: real hard sound, just a sound that was all his own—big sound, strong sound, with a lot of air support."[123] Of Worrell, Ayler stated, "All of the guys—and Lewis Worrell was one of them—were just as interested as I was in getting deeper into ourselves musically."[124] Ayler sat in (often uninvited) with one local jazz group but played whatever he wanted, sometimes at direct odds with the kind of harmonies or rhythms the other musicians were employing. Audiences did not accept his style, generally. Worrell observed, "It made him play that much harder."[125] Ayler had just started listening to the music of Ornette Coleman, and that opened the gates to new forms of expression in his own music, though he was set to go in his own direction. He told the clarinetist Perry Robinson, whom he encountered in Barcelona around that time, "I have something to say as well; I have my own thing and I'm going to do something special."[126] As Ayler would later write to one of his friends from this period, "I hope everything is fine, and you are still *blowing*, because this is the only way we can express ourselves."[127]

Playing in Sweden in 1960, one producer noted that "[Ayler] plays very straight on the statement of the theme. But as soon as he goes into the choruses, one by one all the musicians stop until the point where he's only playing with the drummer.... And it goes on and on, and the other musicians don't come back. Half of the audience is holding their ears, and the others are flabbergasted and fascinated: We've never heard anything like that."[128] One of the players who shared the bandstand with Ayler then remarked, "He was so alone doing that at this time. But what was clear to us was that he was a jazz musician, no doubt about that."[129]

After being discharged from the army, he spent a year or two trying to find opportunities to play in Cleveland and Los Angeles, but he was generally not welcomed because of his unique style. Still, he had one encounter with the comedian Redd Foxx, who told him, "If you believe it, play it!"[130] At the time, Ayler told a friend that he had "found the real music and the real religion, and it had a lot to do with God."[131]

As two writers later lamented,

> One of the great tragedies about Cleveland is that while it may nurture talent up to a point, it does not provide an expansive base sufficient to allow an avant-garde to develop. If an individual artist shows any promise of growing into a major stylist or innovator, he or she has to get out because often we are not ready to give them the necessary recognition and opportunity for expression of new ideas. Albert Ayler tried to expose us to his music and he lost the battle more than once. We simply were not ready.

They added, "Why was Cleveland not ready for a musician who was in a short time able to record four albums in Europe and three in New York, even before his name was mentioned in the U.S. press? That's a question that America will have to answer, because Cleveland is only a little less guilty of squelching a major innovator in the only form of music native to America."[132] Ultimately in Europe and in New York he would find more kindred spirits.

MUSIC, COMMUNITY, AND LIBERATION

Many of the Cleveland-born musicians had met while attending John Adams High School, though the school did little to cultivate their later music. Albert

Ayler, Donald Ayler (c. 1942–2007), Clyde Shy (b. 1943), Donald Strickland (1943–2017), and Larry Hancock (b. 1946) were the locus of that circle, and they brought other people together over time, including older figures like Bobby Few, as well as new arrivals in the city like Charles Tyler and Frank Wright.[133] Shy, Wright, and Donald Ayler were all mostly self-taught or learned on the bandstand.

Shy, who traveled and worked abroad in Sweden after high school, for instance, tuned his bass in fifths, like a cello, rather than fourths, like a typical bass. One of the features of Shy's playing is that he would often solo underneath horn solos while still holding the bottom line, the pulse, and the cohesion together. At other times he would hold the strings with his left hand and play above that with his right hand into a microphone in a way that almost sounded electric. "Even when I was playing with musicians with more training, like Charles Tyler, I just trusted my ear," Shy explained. "I could hear what they were doing and I could play in the same key. It just happened because it felt natural. Some of the trained musicians had to break out of the mode, but I didn't have to do that. I always told people at the time, these sounds already existed before we played them, we just reached out and got them. It was freedom of sound and the ability to express it together with other people."[134]

Donald Ayler took a few private lessons but also had "an especially good ear," according to his contemporaries.[135] Tyler was "quiet and often kept to himself," Shy recalled.[136] Tyler's wife was very dedicated in the Nation of Islam, though he was more loosely involved. His political outlook was framed in much of the group's rhetoric, and at that time he often referred to the white man as "the devil."[137] Tyler lived in the Garden Valley Estates public housing projects on Kinsman Road at East Seventy-Second–Seventy-Fourth Streets in southeast Cleveland while working at a hospital, and the trumpeter Norman Howard lived in a house across the street.[138] The two soon began playing together.[139]

Tyler and Howard had previously met in the US Army and played in the army band.[140] Though Tyler felt his creativity suppressed playing in the army, at one point he was ordered to play the baritone saxophone, which first introduced him to the instrument.[141] Referring to the instrument, he stated, "The saxophone is such a physically demanding instrument. My stomach muscles, lungs, and teeth all have to be in good working shape in order for me to play well. And I have to be especially fit to play the heavy baritone horn which takes a tremendous amount of energy to control."[142] The drummer Larry Hancock met Tyler around 1961, and the two began to jam together.[143] Tyler also played in a few rock bands, from time to time, to make some extra money, but he was driven toward free, improvised music because "the music I heard around me did not satisfy me."[144]

Hancock also came up through the same milieu and learned how to play from family as well as in school. He began playing with Shy, Donald Ayler, and others in the early 1960s. "We would get together and play some tunes," Hancock explained, "and then to get a lot of frustration out, we would play free. We would try to play together, in the moment, with whatever we had in our heads, out of the group inspiration. It was another form of expression; it was really liberating to play like that." He added, "We were encountering everything at once: Ornette Coleman, Malcolm X, James Baldwin, African independence. We were experiencing pan-Blackness with connections not only across this country but around the world. After Malcolm X was killed, the frustration kept rising and rising, and that came out in the music. Revolution was in the air, and the music was an expression of life at that time."[145]

Tyler regularly organized jam sessions at his home around 1964 or 1965. "[Tyler] invited us to come down to his house," Shy recalled. "There was one guy who played a flute, piccolo, and violin, I played bass, and we never had a drummer down there because the place was small. We would just get together and play. We would experiment with different sounds and see if we could make things fit. And we would hit grooves. But then [Tyler] would later compose based off of what we were playing. In fact, he wrote the tunes called 'Poppy' and 'Lamont's Lament' during that period."[146]

Frank Wright had a good-paying job running a dry-cleaning business during the early 1960s that allowed him to push his music into free jazz. He regularly attended jam sessions where people played standards but began playing free in those settings around 1963. The trumpeter Kamal Abdul Alim, who witnessed Wright in his earliest phases of experimentation and development, stated, "He had a big, open sound, and he had a very strong vision for his music that he was deeply committed to doing."[147] The pianist David Durrah recalled Wright as "the heavy weight of the Cleveland avant-garde scene."[148]

Shy had bought a used tenor saxophone, but after hearing Albert Ayler play, he switched to bass. Shy incessantly practiced at home during the day and hosted regular jam sessions in the evenings with the Ayler brothers, the drummer brothers Chuck and Sydney "Syd" Smart, Few, the flutist and tenor saxophonist Albert Rawlings, the flutist and violinist Jordan Frary, Wright, Howard, and Tyler. This circle of musicians began to jam there, at Shy's apartment in Glenville and at the Ayler residence in Shaker Heights in 1965, after Albert had returned from time in Europe and Los Angeles.[149] "Sometimes we would set up a gig in a bar somewhere, but they'd usually run us out," Shy stated. Tyler and Chuck Smart would often set up gigs for them around that time and even managed to secure one at the Gestalt Institute of Psychotherapy. "There were a lot of high rollers there, they only paid us $5, but we got lots of free wine. I took a bunch of bottles and put them in my bass case since they weren't paying us anything. They were astonished at what we were doing trying to figure out how we could play like that without rehearsing."[150]

Cleveland did not have a lot of places for free jazz musicians to play, but the most active one, Kabongo Village, at East 105th Street and Quincy Avenue, founded by a former boxer, was active nightly through the summer of 1967. It was built on stilts on an embankment and had a piano in the club with a capacity for about thirty audience members. "It was the young, hip place to be at that time," Larry Hancock stated.[151] Clyde Shy and Kamal Abdul Alim recalled hanging out there and jamming regularly, and Albert Rawlings would play there sometimes. Aside from the circle of musicians already discussed, the pianist David Durrah, alto saxophonist Otis Harris, flutist Charles Jack Roulette, bassist Walter Cliff, reeds player Donald Strickland, and Walter Massingale also played there regularly.[152] One time, Lionel Hampton's band—without their leader—came to the club and jammed.[153] "There were a lot of conversations happening there with individual players, a lot of exchange," Shy recounted. "A lot of people had something to say in the manner in which they said it. And they communicated. Everybody who was anybody in this city played there. It didn't pay anything, people just went there and jammed, often until one or two in the morning. Then a place called the Dome Club opened up down the street, and people began going back and forth between those two places, jamming. People didn't bring in tunes. We just got together and played."[154]

Shy further elaborated, "For many of us in the Black nationalist movement, this music was part of the revolution because it was going against the status quo. The same thing was happening with poetry and figures like Russell Atkins. Everything was in flux and everything we did was rebelling against the system. From the arts to politics, there was no division. The whole process was about freedom."[155] As the jazz historian Leslie B. Rout observed at the time, "There exists a . . . number of 'left-wing' avant-gardists who consider their music as a kind of socio-political weapon."[156] But Shy observed that Albert Ayler was noticeably different. "Ayler never talked about politics. If you started talking about that, he'd change the subject or just walk away. He was into what he saw and what he heard. He was focused entirely on the music all of the time," Shy recalled. "When we played together, he talked about putting all of these new sounds together that we were working with."[157]

BLACK UNITY TRIO

The Cleveland scene reached a peak in activity in 1968. The Black Unity Trio had the most sustained impact on the Cleveland scene because they chose to remain in the city after so many others had left for New York. The saxophonist Yusuf Mumin, cellist Abdul Wadud, and drummer Hasan Shahid formed the Black Unity Trio at the height of political tensions in Cleveland in mid-1968, but the band was many years in the making. The family of Yusuf Mumin (b. 1944) had migrated north from rural central Kentucky during the Great Depression. Born Joseph Phillips, he grew up around Cleveland's jazz culture of the 1950s. Mumin had befriended Abdul Wadud as kids in the Carver Park housing projects, in an environment that Mumin described as "working-class families with respect for each other. The residents took pride in the environment. Outside of the projects on Central Avenue and East Fifty-Fifth it was filled with businesses run by Afro Americans. Leo's on Central at Forty-Ninth and the Black-run Majestic Hotel were where jazz was happening all the time."[158]

But Phillips's family had come from Cleveland's poorest slum. "It just so happens," he explained, "that the house I was born in was right next to Kingsbury Run and the swinging bridge. As a boy I had to cross the bridge each day going to Todd Elementary School, and I passed over what we called 'the dump.' It was a walking bridge with wood planks that was always in need of repair and made spooky sounds. Beneath the bridge hobos dwelled and erected shantytowns along the river. Me and my young playmates found this the ideal place to have fun, but it terrified my parents. As a kid, crossing that bridge could be scary, especially on cold, windy days."[159]

Mumin described moving to the Carver Park housing projects as "night and day" and that Kingsbury was "something out of a bad dream." Trash and polluted water formed the environment where kids grew up, which he further described as "a bridge and a dump screaming with terrifying tales." By contrast, "Carver Park was basically a vibrant creative community that in my younger years I didn't know existed. It was fast moving and upbeat. Looking out at Fifty-Fifth Street from the projects, I was amused just looking at all of the people. It was like seeing the world for the first time or you might say my trip from Plato's allegory of the cave. I was only eight years old when we moved there, and music was everywhere."[160]

Abdul Khabir Wadud (1947–2022) was born Ronald DeVaughn, the youngest of twelve children in a family that had left sharecropping in southwestern and south-central Georgia to work in manufacturing jobs in Cleveland.[161] His parents had settled in the Central neighborhood on the east side and followed the general movement eastward; his father worked as a porter and later a truck driver for the city sanitation department.[162] His family moved into Carver Park near Mumin in 1957, and as a kid everyone called him "Cash."[163] Wadud's father played trumpet and French horn in local jazz bands and had an interest in big bands, which he exposed his children to at home via records. Several of Wadud's siblings sang or played trombone or other instruments.[164]

Wadud's first musical experiences occurred in the Cleveland public schools, which he described as "dynamite for the arts. Coming up, we had the all-city orchestra, various string programs throughout the city. I took part in them and that's when I was introduced to the cello . . . in the fourth grade. It wasn't an affluent neighborhood, it was the projects, as a matter of fact, but the schools were furnished with instruments."[165] Wadud began taking private lessons in junior high school and then received a scholarship to the Sutphen School of Music, where he studied with Martin Simon, a cellist for the Cleveland Orchestra. He also received a scholarship to the Chautauqua Music Camp in upstate New York, where he got his first concentrated experience working in chamber music. In high school, Wadud played alto, baritone, soprano, and tenor saxophones, as well as bass, and began listening to records by John Coltrane and Lee Morgan, among others. His main touchstones on cello were Fred Katz, Ron Carter, and Oscar Pettiford. Wadud became the principal cellist in the high school orchestra and in the all-city orchestra at that time. Thus, Wadud grew up with exposure to chamber and orchestral music, and he began improvising on saxophones as well as cello in the high school jazz band in 1963.[166]

In the mid-1960s, Phillips joined the Nation of Islam, attracted to its precepts of Black liberation and spiritual awakening, and changed his name to Yusuf Mumin.[167] His first significant musical inspirations came

> in the late 1950s listening to recordings by Yusef Lateef where he was playing bottles, penny whistles, and flutes, and creating sounds of nature. I began in my own normal walk of life to discern sounds around me such as automobiles, doors opening and closing, people walking up steps, birds chirping, and the loud cries and outbursts of children. I found that the inside of a piano had some interesting sounds, especially an old one with notes missing. Singing in the project hallways was a great resonating chamber. All of these different sounds went great with poetry and art.[168]

In 1962, Mumin moved out to Los Angeles to help his brother run a sign-painting shop for several months. There was a vibraphone in the backroom where Mumin slept.

I would play the notes and listened to the tones as they hung out in the air until the very last vibration. I laid back on my sleeping mat and went to sleep listening to the sound of the air. I also learned about harmony and chords with the vibes. Also, around that time, I read something in a book that I forget the title to, something to the effect of, "the responsibility of the musician is the different aspects of music and the cosmic sound of the universe which is always in a hum." I became interested in the nature of sound. Sound could move through the tiny pores of solid objects. Focusing on this, I thought of the idea of cosmic music transcending three-dimensional space and time. In my mind sound was a bridge from the known to the unknown.[169]

"From then on," Mumin added, "I attached a different importance to music. I was young and full of adventure because music could do something that I could not. But yet I could create something that could move through walls. I thought about that for a long time and added that to my music ideology and termed it cosmic music, communicating with the unseen." When Mumin returned to Cleveland in late 1962, he got a job working at a clinic and used that money to build an inventory for a record store, Cosmic Music, which he operated for four years. "I had food to eat and a place to lay my head," he recounted, "but sometimes I would go down onto millionaires row and bartend."[170] Meanwhile, throughout that period, he began to experiment on the alto saxophone, "to see if I could do anything with it. For me it was about sound control from the high register down to the low notes."[171] Mumin was entirely self-taught. Cosmic Music became a vital place in Cleveland where people could acquire records on ESP and other labels that were then catering to free jazz.[172] As a customer who was a teenager at the time described the store, "Most of the music was avant-garde, some was progressive jazz. Also featured in a showcase counter were selections of poetry and literature dealing with current events and world news, particularly information pertaining to the Black community."[173] The Cleveland-born dancer Dianne McIntyre (b. 1946), who has had a prolific career as an improvising dancer and choreographer working with a range of jazz artists in New York, noted that her first encounter with free jazz, the music of Albert Ayler, happened at Cosmic Music.[174]

Wadud first encountered the music through Albert Ayler in 1962, when the latter returned from Europe, and Wadud noted that the latter had hired the cellist Joel Freedman in the period 1965–1967, and he began to imagine how the cello could contribute to the music.[175] "Yusuf Mumin was partially responsible for getting me interested in the avant-garde," he recalled. Mumin and Wadud were both friends with Ayler's younger brother Donald and connected to that part of the Cleveland community through him, which is how they met Bobby Few and Frank Wright. By 1963 or 1964, Mumin, Wadud, and Donald Ayler were regularly meeting to listen to music; they also practiced together. "But it wasn't bebop," he observed. "We were interested in creating our own styles and situations."[176] Mumin was also drawn to the music of Igor Stravinsky, *The Rite of Spring*, and "Siegfried's Funeral March" from Richard Wagner's *Götterdämmerung*.[177]

John Coltrane, Eric Dolphy, and Cecil Taylor were paramount influences for both Mumin and Wadud. Wadud first studied music education at Youngstown State, in 1965–1967, but then transferred to study music performance at Oberlin College and began to work in the symphonies in Youngstown, Canton, and Akron. While attending Oberlin, Wadud met the alto saxophonist Julius Hemphill, and they began working together.[178] Around that time, Wadud, Mumin, and Oberlin's bass instructor, Oliver "Olly" Wilson (1937–2018), began playing at Oberlin and around Ohio, mostly featuring pieces written by Wilson and Mumin.[179] The group played a gig as the Black Unity Quartet with the drummer Chuck Smart at Oberlin, February 21, 1968.[180] "We would get college gigs and halls, little theaters, mainly college gigs," Wadud explained. "Young college kids came mainly."[181] In 1968, he converted to Islam and changed his name, which translates as "servant of the all-loving."[182]

But Wadud's approach was revolutionary, even early in his career. As he noted in an interview in 1980, "I approach the instrument in its totality," as opposed to adhering to a regional school or only thinking of cello strictly as either an orchestral, chamber, jazz, or solo instrument. "I don't believe in the cello being necessarily limited to being an accompanying instrument, or a rhythmic instrument, or a so-called lead instrument. The cello can be anything I want it to be. It can be a drum. It can be a horn. And out of this philosophy evolved a concept of ensemble playing [that] as far as I'm concerned . . . that is the essence of music."[183] Wadud's totality is evident even on his earliest recordings, displaying a wide range of vision and technique.

By 1967, Mumin was also playing in the trumpeter Norman Howard's quartet. They contacted Sunny Murray in New York but were not able to afford to bring him to Cleveland, so they hired a local player, Cornelius Milsap, instead, and "we were grateful for bassist Walter Cliff . . . who was known and liked around Cleveland." Mumin's earliest compositions appeared on the record they recorded in November 1968, such as "Sad Miss Holiday," which was "a mournful dirge reflecting the life experiences of the great singer who pleased audiences worldwide while at the same time being ensnared by systemic injustices and bad circumstances like what heroin was doing to communities."[184] Howard added the lyrics, and they each wrote half of the pieces that they recorded.

"*Burn Baby Burn* came about during a dark period when all of the problems of the 1960s came out not only in art and poetry," Mumin explained. "Music was also a vehicle for making a statement that spoke to the times."[185] The piece, "Time and Units," was about all of the various grassroots organizations that were springing up across the country advocating for rights, power, and cultural awakening. "Sound from There" spoke to the "unfavorable aspects of my younger life, memories fading into some other unreal place." And the piece "'NXJX' used X to signify the end of something, an entity whose existence is over, past, dead, and gone. X as a sign of the cross where Christ was crucified. It was the result of the slave trade, the Afro American untethered from his roots and his identity unknown."[186] Cliff and Milsap soon left the band, however, and they asked Wadud and the drummer Oscar Hood to join them, but the subsequent group did not stay together either.

Meanwhile, Mumin and Wadud soon formed a trio with the drummer Hasan Shahid, whose background in Birmingham, Alabama, I discussed at length in chapter 3. Shahid began playing with rhythm and blues groups at age fourteen, playing with Bobby Day, who later recorded "Rockin' Robin" and recorded with Little Brenda Duff at FAME Studios in Muscle Shoals.[187] Shahid left Birmingham in 1961 to attend Howard University, where during his freshman year he attended a debate between Malcolm X and Bayard Rustin, one of the trusted advisors of Dr. Martin Luther King Jr. Through that process he met his fellow student Stokely Carmichael, and the two got involved in the newly formed SNCC. "I would say that the Malcolm X debate," Shahid later recounted, "was the experience that changed my life and started me on my journey toward Islam. The second was the bombing of the 16th Street Baptist Church in Birmingham. Carol Robertson, one of the four little girls who were killed, was a cousin."[188] Shahid returned to Alabama in 1964 to work on voter registration in Lowndes County and other parts of central Alabama, where his family had previously dwelled for generations and where advocating for rights came with constant threats of violence. Shahid eventually took his *shahada* to convert to Islam not long after arriving in Cleveland in 1968.

Even then, Shahid was looking beyond bebop and swing.

I knew when I first heard *My Favorite Things* that this was different. I then got back to Birmingham in 1964 and met a tenor player by the name of Jessie Taylor. Jessie was a music major graduating from Tennessee State University and fresh out of the army. He was a Trane disciple and he really got me into Trane which helped me improve how I was doing things rhythmically. We started noticing a different thing that you could do, getting away from 4/4. We did not play Brubeck's 5/4 "Take Five" because we were entering into the Black nationalist mode. At this point we were into Trane's *Live at Birdland* album with "Afro Blue" and "The Promise." These were our march out the door tunes to fight the revolution. Trane's "Alabama" was inspiring even living in Alabama. Then there was "Out of This World," "Africa," "India," with Eric Dolphy, "The Inch Worm," "After the Rain," "Wise One" and so many more.[189]

Shahid graduated from Miles College in January 1968 and then was admitted to the New School for the MA program in sociology that spring, but on his first day of classes, when he realized he was the only Black student in the program out of approximately two hundred people, he recalled thinking, "This is not about *me* and so I withdrew."[190] Being in New York intermittently in the mid-1960s had exposed him to the Nation of Islam and much of the Afrocentric culture of the time, but he stated, "I was looking for something more spiritual." Shahid was offered a months-long gig and a drum set by the vocalist Countess Felder in May 1968 in Cleveland and there he happened to stumble upon Mumin's shop, Cosmic Music. It happened that Mumin and Wadud were looking to reform the band and needed a drummer, so they invited Shahid to play with them. Shahid stated, "We just hit it without needing any direction and boom! After we got through playing, for about thirty minutes, fierce, nonstop, blistering we knew that this was Allah-given, it was much greater than we were. That was the beginning."[191]

For every member of the Black Unity Trio, the primary inspiration was the late work of John Coltrane. Mumin observed, "When Brother John transitioned out of the tunes he was playing, the freeform music was already happening. But Brother John became its Apex, a gathering Force, the Vedas taught by the scriptures. He shifted out of the realm of bebop and into the Psalms of the Hebrew Bible. He also directed his attention toward Eastern philosophies and belief systems, as well as balance through meditation. When thinking about the book of Psalms, harp music comes to mind, and Alice Coltrane's in particular."[192]

Shahid referred to Coltrane as "a spiritual father and mentor. He was very humble when I met him, but he completely took over people with his music when I saw him play. He could relate to people and bring them so much joy."[193] When John and Alice Coltrane released *Cosmic Music* in 1968, "people became a little more friendly [with the music] and started saying things like, 'Hey Brother, right on, I can dig it.' Brother John came to the rescue in the music, he gave love supreme a new meaning, may the holy one forever be his cosmic guide."[194]

The band generally congregated at Cosmic Music and practiced in the shop after it closed for the day, though people who lived in the apartments above the store complained, so the band "had to go down underground" into the basement for most of their sessions, including the eventual recording. The tight improvisations that the band eventually recorded were only possible because they had met every day for six months and practiced. "We got to the point where any one of us could begin a phrase and without anything on paper," Shahid observed, "we knew the rhythm or phrase that they were going to play. We were that connected."[195] The aspiring saxophonist Hasan Abdur-Razzaq first learned about the music at the shop by witnessing the band practice. He wrote of the experience, "Especially important was the cosmic forcefulness of Yusuf Mumin's horn, either alto or soprano. It could blend seamlessly with the lyrical beauty and harmony of Abdul Wadud's cello while the thundering drums of Hasan Shahid rumbled the concrete and brick walls of that basement space. Those sessions were almost telepathic."[196]

Wadud noted right away that "it was really challenging playing with a drummer as strong as Hasan" because the band always played acoustically without amplifiers, which is particularly difficult to do with cello.[197] Shahid described his own playing as "I had my drums tuned in a descending pentatonic scale with my bass drum in C. And I had my cymbals tuned in an ascending chromatic scale."[198] Cellos are tuned in fifths, so Shahid noted, "Abdul and I could do some things with mallets that blended phenomenally. And Yusuf did it with the highs and the lows of the alto. What we were trying to do was blend this all together with the rhythm, where it became one heartbeat, one sound, one motion, one expression."[199] Shahid's process flowed organically from that. "So, when I heard either Abdul or Yusuf playing, my goal was to play something harmonious with them. I wanted to keep the momentum, power, and complementary harmonics going, but also trying to sound like Niagara, continuous water flowing and falling. I was trying to think and make people think. To detoxify. To heal."[200]

Most of the Black Unity Trio's performances were booked through Black student unions on college campuses. Members of the band obtained a list of about 125 such organizations and wrote to them. Almost all of their work came through that effort.[201] When they performed live, they played for forty-five minutes nonstop through various segues, took a thirty-minute break, and then returned to play a second set of similar length, going through various moods and tempos. Between mid-1968 and the end of 1969, they played at Wayne State University, the University of Chicago, the University of Toledo, Case Western Reserve, multiple times at Oberlin, and at Antioch College. They would often hand out a paper with their explanation of Cosmic Music and burn incense beforehand to set the atmosphere. They netted at least $1,500 per concert.[202]

The title of the record, *Al-Fatihah*, is a reference to the opening prayer of Ibrahim (Abraham), which says, "I'm turning myself upright. I'm not among the polytheists, I'm of those who submit. My prayers, my sacrifices, my life, and my death are all for Allah, Lord of the world." Shahid added, "We started with an explosion. What we were seeking to do was to commune with the spirit, the spirit dropped light down to us, and we dispersed it for the betterment of the people. Without that, it didn't mean anything to me."[203] In 1980, Wadud reflected, "I haven't experienced a total situation like that since then, the combination of music and philosophy and life all in one ... it was very powerful."[204]

Much of the music was biographical. As Mumin explained, "My early life near Kingsbury Run had a lot to do with the composition 'Birth, Life and Death,'" which opened and closed with call and response.[205] Shahid further elaborated that the piece charted "the child as an embryo, the child being born, the child crawling, the child walking, the child speaking, then ... with all of the struggle that's going on with living, all the stress, all the turmoil, all the hatred, all the evilness, all the violence, everything that has been done to the people for 500 years. At the end you hear Abdul and myself play the last heartbeats. And it's gone."[206]

The piece "In Light of Blackness" featured Wadud's articulation and versatility on cello.[207] But Mumin explained, "If all of the primary colors are mixed together you produce black. The so-called Black people of America are comprised of all the people on Earth. In my case alone, I have Irish, African, Asian, and Native American mixed. With all of these continents flowing through my veins, I could only reach out to the world in compassion, anything else would be self-destruction. Music is a mercy to the soul."[208]

Mumin wrote the piece "John's Vision," in reference to John the Apostle and the Book of Revelation, which depicts 144,000 people rising from their graves; he interpreted this as an uprising of the masses.[209] Shahid, however, viewed the piece as "that's what Trane saw," but it did not stop there. As Shahid stated, "We were saying to the world, we were so confident with everything that John Coltrane gave us that we actually thought in our hearts that [we] could go beyond Trane."[210]

A second record, *Mystic Vision*, recorded live in Dwain Hall at Case Western Reserve University on February 10, 1969, was never released because they ran out of money to produce it. The tapes have unfortunately been lost.[211] The aim was to move to New York and try to sign with the ESP label, but the band broke up before they could make the move. One piece they never recorded, "West Pakistan," featured Shahid on rim shots and mallets.[212] There was another piece intended for the first record that they were unable to record because they ran out of tape. On that piece, Shahid "was trying to imitate automatic weapon fire. And the bass drum, I was trying to get the feeling of an explosion," because of the uprisings going on in "Cleveland, Detroit, Watts, Philly, everywhere."[213]

Speaking more generally of the band, Mumin stated, "The Black Unity Trio and the music we produced dealt with extremes. Assassinations, police attacks, and government violence. But we resolved problems and offered solutions. The extremes were tempered with compassion throughout the album. Seeking refuge in the Lord of dawn was the ideal alluded to on the back cover of *Al-Fatihah*. The music was prescribed for a particular time and condition."[214] Wadud echoed these comments, reflecting a decade later, "We had some difficult times in this country, and we are still having them. [We made the record at] a time in this country... when things were being challenged and changed and preferences were being made as to what we wanted to do in life."[215] Shahid added, "The music was about our youth, our determination, our psyche... about seeking something new. But when Trane died, it looked like everybody made an about face, like they were scared to go on."[216]

After their rehearsals at Cosmic Music, the band often hung out at the nearby Shabazz Café, which was run by the Nation of Islam.[217] Shahid was not interested in joining the Nation, becoming more dedicated to orthodox Islam. This caused some divisions within the band, especially between Mumin and Shahid. Ultimately, Shahid left the band, though the latter stated many years later, "I have cried for fifty years making that decision which broke up the greatest chance that I've had to do something musically."[218]

After the band split up, the musicians of the Black Unity Trio scattered from Cleveland. Mumin moved to Los Angeles, where he played with Butch Morris, Charles Tyler, Will Connell, and Horace Tapscott, as well as the Watts Poets.[219] Wadud moved to New York to study performance at the State University of New York at Stony Brook and played in the jazz lofts through the 1970s while also playing in the New Jersey Symphony. Shahid refused to be drafted for the Vietnam War, and he was surveilled by the FBI. For a period in the summer of 1970, he took refuge in the Cleveland mosque. On July 13, federal agents apprehended him and "took me out of the mosque in chains and brought me back to Alabama for trial," Shahid described. "I got three years of probation. My case was quite similar to Muhammad Ali."[220] Shahid was not allowed to leave the state of Alabama and could not find other musicians playing the new music. So he turned his focus to Islam and became the imam at the Birmingham mosque.

EVOLUTION OF THE CLEVELAND SCENE

The rise of Black arts festivals in Cleveland, sponsored by the city, universities, churches, high schools, freedom schools, and other grassroots organizations, represented a cultural shift in the city.[221] Events happened in parks, at churches, in cultural centers, and street festivals, sometimes even somewhat spontaneously, outside of barber shops or other locations. Karamu House, for instance, sponsored some events, though a bit more within the musical tradition and for a middle-class audience than the new wave of music that was happening. The Republic of New Libya as well as the African Cultural Center would often put together jam sessions when people would gather and just play together.

Some observers recalled people just carrying around African drums wherever they went on a daily basis and just playing wherever and whenever they felt like it. It became fused to daily practice. Mutawaf Shaheed, for instance, recalled *bimsheas* (gatherings) where "people would sit in open fields, people would bring pots and pans, bottles and whistles, saxophones and whatever they had and just play. And it was African music or at least what we considered to be African music, all based around drums, gourds with beads around them."[222] Sometimes *bimsheas* were organized but at other times happened rather spontaneously.

Unlike in Buffalo, where free jazz found a foothold in the festivals, in Cleveland, there was a different strain of Afrocentric culture that pushed into African rhythms. Shaheed, for instance, began playing with bongo and conga players and even played bass like it was a hand drum, using his thumbs to thump the body while also playing the strings with all of his fingers in different positions to get a range of sounds. But he was moving away from the high-energy free improvising that he had been doing with Ayler and others. There were many other groups, troupes of dancers, bands, poets, and visual artists who took part in various events, with African clothes prominently displayed. "It was part of the cultural development in the community," Shaheed said. "It was our rebellion, speaking out against the status quo."[223]

Shaheed was among the converts to Islam, having first become interested while reading Malcolm X's autobiography. It was not initially a spiritual drive for him but rather "something that Black people would be able to improve themselves by," he later recounted, "and it provided a blueprint for our nation. It provided a set of rules and regulations, a whole structure, for the nation that we, as Black people, were envisioning at the time. Everyone was to be held accountable and held to the same standards."[224] After getting shot in late 1968, Shaheed converted, taking *shahada* on December 29 and changing his name. He had already gotten deeply involved in the Muntu Poets Workshop led by Russell Atkins and was also committed to Black nationalism. He found poetry to be more effective in expressing what he thought about the police and the many other injustices of those times. In 1970, he was elected the imam of Cleveland's Masjid al-Mu'min mosque, and he took up the mantle of leadership in the community, in which role he has remained up to the time of this writing.[225] Shaheed has spent many years working in prisons and advocating for racial justice initiatives to transform the Cleveland community.

For the visionaries of free jazz who came out of Cleveland, most of them had to find their opportunities elsewhere. Cleveland exported its artists more readily than Detroit, sending its greatest musicians especially to New York and even to Paris. It seemed not the exception, however, that Black arts went elsewhere to thrive; the newspaper, *Call and Post*, so regularly noted how members of the community had to go elsewhere to "make it."

CHAPTER 5

SOLIDARITY AND CRISIS IN DETROIT

The Detroit Artists' Workshop and the Forging of Radical Culture

The seeds of rebellion and resistance are deep in this city, generation after generation. From being the last stop on the Underground Railroad, to Ossian Sweet, from independent black caucuses to revolutionary politics in the auto industry and beyond, each era has added something new to the legacy that has not dissipated.

—Michael Hamlin

THE ORIGINS AND GROWTH OF BLACK CULTURAL SPACE IN DETROIT

Detroit began as a French fur trading port on the straits of the Detroit River in 1701 and grew to become the great entrepot of the colonial Great Lakes economies. Enslaved Africans and Native Americans dwelled in the city from its foundation. Despite attempts at the prohibition of slavery in the Northwest Ordinance, the practice was allowed to continue for much of the existing population, and, in fact, the slave trade boomed for several decades after the Revolutionary War. In the earliest manifestations of what became the Underground Railroad, a protracted struggle ensued around the turn of the nineteenth century, as enslaved people exploited the contested borderland of the Detroit River to plan escapes in both directions.[1] By the 1810s, the flow of people turned indefinitely northward as people sought freedom in British Canada.

The founding of the Second Baptist Church in Detroit in 1836, by people affiliated with the Underground Railroad, was significant in that it constituted the first public institution where Black music was openly performed with regularity.[2] This church was integral in fusing music to long-distance networks of resistance that tied the upper US south to Detroit and British Canada. In 1846, leaders from the Second Baptist Church and the Bethel African Methodist Episcopal Church formed the Colored Vigilant Committee, which served as the vanguard of Black militancy in subverting the Fugitive Slave Act in Detroit and providing sanctuary to several thousand escapees in the city, securing passage for many across the border in the years leading up to the Civil War.[3] This thoroughfare became the most active path to freedom for people escaping slavery in the United States.

Music began to proliferate in Detroit just before the Civil War. Theodore Finney's thirty-three-piece orchestra, founded in 1857, was innovative in syncopated music and led to the proliferation of brass bands throughout the Great Lakes in the following decade. With the increase of the Black population in the city to over two thousand in 1870, concert halls and theaters opened that catered not only to the white population but also to the emerging Black elite. Brass bands continued to grow in number such that they eventually contributed to some of the roots of blues and ragtime, attracting composers such as W. C. Handy and others to visit the city. Saint Antoine Street in the Paradise Valley neighborhood became the most vital center for music and performance after the turn of the century.[4] Still, much of the Black community lived interspersed within neighborhoods that included Germans, Russians, and Jews.

With the emergence of the auto industry in Detroit during the first two decades of the twentieth century, immigration from Poland, Canada, Germany, Great Britain, Austria, Italy, and Hungary was joined by a national migration from across the United States. During the early phases of the Great Migration, 34 percent of people leaving the US south settled in Detroit, which increased the Black community in Detroit eight-fold, from just over five thousand people in 1910 to over forty thousand in 1920 and tripling to 120,000 in 1930.[5] Migrants survived through networks of mutual aid, as Michael Hamlin experienced: "The ones who had already arrived would take in the new ones and help them get established."[6] A previously more dispersed community became firmly concentrated on Detroit's east side and began expanding northward. Systematic segregation became more prevalent after pressure from the real estate industry and banks from the 1920s onward.[7] These forces were further spurred by white neighborhood associations and skyrocketing membership in the KKK to restrict settlement in exclusively white parts of the city.⁸ By 1930, African Americans constituted 8 percent of the city's population.⁹ At that time, nearly three-quarters of them lived on the east side of Detroit, in the overcrowded and overpriced neighborhood of Black Bottom, which formed the heart of music and culture in the city until the 1960s.

Cass Technical High School was critically important for generating much of Detroit's music culture. As a racially integrated magnet school, it drew students from around the city and had well-established jazz programs and a singular program in the study of harp. "Cass was a phenomenal high school with great teachers. They had great programs in construction, metallurgy, engineering, printing, music, drama, across the board and pooled students who were Black, white, and Jewish together," the playwright Bill Harris, who attended the school in his youth, noted. "The school was doing hip, contemporary jazz there when I attended in the 1950s."¹⁰ The clarinetist Elreta Dodds regarded the structures of the curriculum at the school to be closer to a university than a standard high school in that it allowed her to focus more deeply on music at an earlier age. "It was an extraordinary school," she said.¹¹ "We are still feeling the effects of the earlier years of great public education," the saxophonist Marcus Elliot reflected, having come of age in the 2000s, "even though that infrastructure has completely collapsed. The spirit of mentoring the next generation is still going."¹²

Among the many jazz luminaries that emerged from the school from the 1930s to the 1960s include the trumpeters Howard McGhee, Gerald Wilson, and Donald Byrd; the saxophonists Wardell Gray, Lucky Thompson, and Billy Mitchell; the trombonist Frank Rosolino; the pianist Hugh Lawson; the harpist and pianist Alice (McLeod) Coltrane; the bassists Al McKibbon, Major "Mule" Holley Jr., and Paul Chambers; and the drummer J. C. Heard, not to mention other areas of music and the arts. People came to call a method of training, with older generations of artists, inside and outside of school, mentoring the next generation and preparing them with the life skills they needed for the world, "the Detroit Way."¹³ As a result of this cultural infrastructure, Detroit had one of the most active jazz scenes in the 1940s and 1950s, though after 1958, as performance opportunities began to diminish in Detroit and the Midwest in general, many of them began to move to New York.¹⁴

LABOR AND RACE

The first significant attempts to organize industrial labor in Detroit dated to the 1880s but took more serious steps forward with the formation of the International

Workers of the World union in 1912 and even more so with the socialist-led Auto Workers Union in the late 1910s. In the early years of the Great Migration, Black workers in Detroit were often left to work the worst paid and most dangerous jobs, being restricted to being production assistants, janitors, and foundry workers. From the beginning, they contributed to the labor movement, though their interests were inadequately represented. Still, many Black workers faced racist attacks and violence from their white counterparts throughout the decades of early settlement.[15] Meanwhile, the Detroit police force expanded rapidly in the 1920s to contain the growth of the community and to suppress strikes. At that time, Michigan came to contain the largest number of KKK members of any state, with at least 32,000 living in Detroit itself, with significant representation in the police force, which set the groundwork for Detroit to have particularly violent and racist policing in the ensuing decades.[16]

Some measure of cross-racial solidarity was born out of common struggle as embodied in the United Auto Workers (UAW) union, beginning with the sit-down strikes of 1936–1937; its tactics quickly spread to much of southeastern Michigan's other labor movements. The National Negro Congress actively organized Black workers, and together with the UAW they successfully resisted Ford's attempts at breaking them along racial lines during the walkout of 1941. Given the demands for continuous production during World War II, some of the potent militancy of the unions was pacified, but the UAW used strikes to successfully secure significant wage increases in the years immediately after the war.[17]

Even in Detroit's golden years following the war, there were seeds of destabilization. The Red Scare set in motion processes to disassociate the working class from leftist politics. Anti-labor legislation such as the Taft-Hartley Act undermined collective bargaining power, and suburbanization introduced new racial dynamics that spatially separated workers along lines of race.[18]

The National Negro Labor Council, led by future Detroit mayor Coleman Young, demanded labor protections for women and workers of color in 1951 but met resistance from conservative elements within the UAW, who conducted their own leftist purges. Automation within factories began to displace labor by 1952 and continued to be the specter of worker disenfranchisement. Black workers were commonly the last to be hired and the first to be fired within the factories and continued to be restricted to the most dangerous jobs, and their positions were the most vulnerable to redundancy brought on by automation.[19] The east side of Detroit, where the community was centered, lost ten factories involving 71,000 jobs between 1954 and 1960.[20] Despite the general economic boom, the seeds of discontent were being sowed.

URBAN DESTRUCTION AND THE NEW RADICALS

Detroit, like Cleveland, Buffalo, and many other cities in the United States, issued so-called urban renewal projects in the 1960s that decimated Black cultural spaces. The Black Bottom and Paradise Valley neighborhoods, situated in eastern and southeastern Detroit, had been the vital heartbeat of jazz, blues, and R&B music in the city from the 1930s to the early 1960s and had fostered several major poets.[21] Hastings Street, which had been the home to many jazz and blues clubs, was also targeted for destruction to make way for infrastructure to allow white suburbanites to commute into the city.[22] The poet Robert Hayden, who grew up in Paradise Valley, described the community as "people who retained ... a sheltering spiritual beauty and dignity ... despite sordid and disheartening circumstances."[23] The Nation of Islam was founded in Paradise Valley in 1931, which would grow to give significant voice to Black resistance against violence and oppression.

In the early 1960s, under the guise of slum clearance initiatives and to make room for the construction of Interstate highways 75 and 375, these areas, together with the dozens of clubs and concert halls that had been home to jazz and blues, were demolished.[24] This undermined the jazz scene in the city in a way from which it never recovered. Many of the cultural developments in the city in the following decade must therefore be understood as a reaction to this destruction, empowered by collective action and solidarity movements that solidified along lines of class and race in different configurations around the Artists' Workshop, the Tribe collective, and the work of Faruq Z. Bey and Griot Galaxy.

The earliest free jazz scene in Detroit in the 1960s was the result of relative newcomers to the city, who mostly came from neighboring parts of Michigan as well as from the south. Detroit was unique in that there were equal numbers of poets and musicians around the emergence of free jazz, but they worked together, wrote together, and often lived together in fellowship based on working-class concepts of fraternity, mutual aid, and collective advancement. The community in which free jazz emerged in Detroit at the Artists' Workshop was far more racially integrated than any other site in the United States. The poet and playwright Bill Harris, for instance, who was active there, felt comfortable presenting his work in that setting, though he nevertheless still felt a sense of difference with the community because it was predominantly white.[25] The Workshop was juxtaposed against a backdrop of racial tension, police brutality, communal violence, and mass-scale white flight to the suburbs.[26]

As segregated as Detroit was in the 1960s, it was still more integrated than Cleveland or Buffalo. "Detroit was somewhat unique," Harris observed, "in that a number of Black people had good jobs, they had money. When the

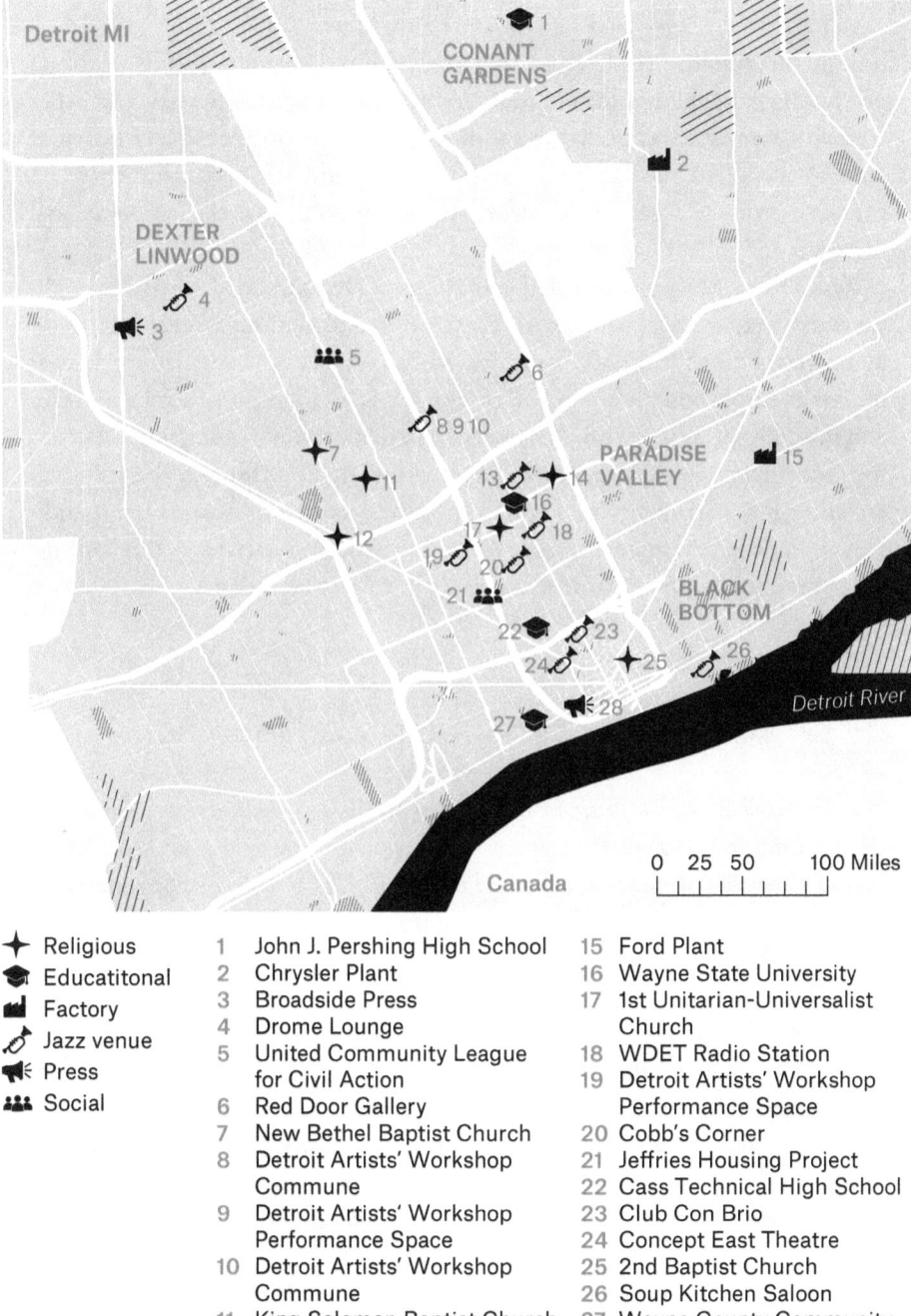

FIGURE 5.1 Sonic landscapes of Detroit.

Source: Cartography by Alice Viggiani.

unions integrated, people came out of that like Coleman Young who had power. Black people could get public sector jobs. At Ford, Chrysler, and other factories, we worked shoulder to shoulder with white people. The children of auto workers had time to study music. They could afford instruments and private lessons. People could afford to buy houses, but the city was still segregated."[27]

Wayne State University, located in the heart of Detroit, added a consistent radical presence to the Detroit cultural scenes. It had drawn considerable attention and investigations from McCarthyites in the 1950s; the latter also eyed labor unions as suspiciously left wing. Monteith College, aimed at general education and interdisciplinarity while "engendering a disposition to ask good questions towards understanding man in society and man in and through the arts" was searching for experimental new ways to nurture creative minds and cater to individual student development.[28] In the 1960s, students harnessed mechanisms such as the student newspaper to voice a new wave of radicalism.

JAZZ AND THE DETROIT LITERARY TRADITION

The immense literary culture of Detroit, especially its poetic tradition, is one of the defining and ever-present features of the free jazz culture that emerged in the 1960s. The roots of this may be traced to Robert Hayden (1913–1980) and Dudley Randall (1914–2000) in the 1930s and was further nurtured at Wayne State University by figures such as Chester Cable and the Miles Modern Poetry Workshop. There was a strong working-class element in these circles; many poets, such as Randall, worked in the Ford foundry by day and wrote and collaborated with other writers by night. Concept East debuted plays by figures such as Leroi Jones (later Amiri Baraka) throughout the 1960s, Boone House became an important incubator for Black poets at the same time, and Broadside Press spotlighted much of the scene's work. Articulating a counterculture, Black and white, became the staple of many Detroit poets of that era.[29] The connection between poetry and jazz seemed quite natural for many in Detroit "because they were both improvised art forms."[30] Or, as the poet George Tysh stated, "jazz was a central influence on everyone at the Workshop regardless of medium or artform."[31] The Black Mountain poetry of Robert Creeley, Charles Olson, and Denise Levertov and the New York school of Frank O'Hara, Leroi Jones, Allen Ginsberg, and the Beat poets were paramount influences on the Detroit community at the time, and many of these figures were also in touch with jazz.

Within the community of what was to become the Detroit Artists' Workshop, every artist was considered to be a writer capable of articulating their visions and creativity. And all of the poets and other writers had a deep interest in the music and its advancement as part of a broader progress for the avant-garde, or as the guitarist Ron English described it, a movement away from "familiar melodies, obvious rhythms, and background harmonies."[32] The poet John Sinclair and trumpeter Charles Moore often quoted Count Basie, from an interview in 1963, who said he served up "the same old beef stew," which was precisely what they wanted to leave behind. The poets in the community felt the same way about academic poetry, which they felt limited their expressivity.[33] Or, as the Detroit pianist Harold McKinney argued, Black music and broader culture was a kind of avant-garde, the cultural vanguard of the United States.[34] Radical change to Detroit's cultural landscape was sparked by their unity in the form of the Detroit Artists' Workshop Society in 1964, which became a centerpiece in articulating Detroit's counterculture.[35] But there were a number of pathways that led its most active members there.

A GATHERING OF ARTISTS

After moving to Detroit in the early 1960s, the trumpeter Charles Moore was introduced to the music of Ornette Coleman, and a whole world opened up to him.[36] As so many other people were getting drafted, Moore managed to avoid being conscripted into the military because of a physical he had failed while still in Alabama.[37] He finally settled on a program at Monteith College at Wayne State University via a scholarship.[38] Though he was situated in the music department, he was able to explore dance and visual art in a way that expanded his scope of music, especially at a time when Western classical music dominated the curriculum.[39] Professor Otto Feinstein, who taught at Monteith, was a mentor and inspiration for many in the community; he was an early anti–nuclear weapons activist and the editor of the left-wing periodical *New University Thought*.[40]

Many other musicians from Detroit and nearby towns and cities came together there to form the community in 1964. The guitarist Ron English was from Lansing but traveled to Detroit regularly as a teenager, where he saw Duke Ellington, Stan Kenton, Miles Davis, Dave Brubeck, and many others, while also developing an interest in Ornette Coleman. "Many of us at the time, as much as we loved Miles Davis," English noted, "we realized that Ornette had a new way of looking at things that really moved us."[41] He played with many local musicians, including the drummer Danny Spencer and the Flint-based organist Lyman Woodard, while studying comparative literature at Michigan State University. "Woodard was white," English observed, "but he had absorbed a lot of aspects of Black culture."[42] In the fall of 1964, English began commuting to Detroit regularly, while Spencer and Woodard moved to the Motor City. They had already met John Sinclair in Flint. Sinclair had become infatuated with Black culture in his youth via records and radio, and the poet and organizer preceded them to Detroit by the summer of that year to pursue graduate studies in American literature at Wayne State University.[43] The bassist John Dana, who was from Mount Pleasant and had studied at Central Michigan University, moved to Detroit around the same time. In Detroit, the Minor Key coffeehouse was the vanguard venue at the time, featuring the music of John Coltrane, Miles Davis, Duke Ellington, Art Blakey, Jimmy Smith, and many others.[44]

The drummer Ronald Johnson lived in the Jeffries Housing Projects on Warren Avenue in Detroit; he was attending Cass Technical High School when he first got involved in the community, and he continued his studies with Danny Spencer. The saxophonist Larry Nozero was also from Detroit. The pianist Stanley Cowell, who was from Toledo, was pursuing graduate studies in classical piano at the University of Michigan and frequented Detroit at the time. The trumpeter Pierre Rochon was originally from Montreal, relocated to Windsor, Ontario, and then came to Detroit to study music theory and composition at Wayne State. The saxophonist Brent Majors was also a student at Wayne State, while he honed his abilities on a range of reed instruments. This milieu comprised the regular musicians who shaped the Detroit free jazz scene; they were, at times, joined by others from the local area and from afar.

Leni Sinclair (b. 1940) was the primary photographer of the Artists' Workshop's activities.[45] Born Magdalene Arndt, she grew up in East Germany listening to jazz artists such as Louis Armstrong, Benny Goodman, and Ella Fitzgerald before emigrating to the United States in 1959. She became affiliated with beatniks in the Detroit area, which connected her to the cultural scene at the time. She soon after enrolled at Wayne State University to study geography, where she became involved with the SNCC as well as working as Otto Feinstein's publishing assistant.[46] She also met John Sinclair and began to attend jazz in the clubs there, as he was covering them for *Down Beat*. Her involvement in the short-lived Red Door Gallery brought her further into the circle of artists that soon after founded the Artists' Workshop. "I was an observer who documented what I participated in," she noted. "I never aspired to become a photographer, but it was just necessary at the time and I was the only one with a camera. Then I became more purposeful about it."[47]

THE FORGING OF THE ARTISTS' WORKSHOP

Detroit lacked organic art spaces in the early 1960s to nurture the next generation. The poet George Tysh's Touchstone had been a brief storefront gallery for artists but had not lasted long because of a lack of financial support. Tysh then joined efforts with the painter Carl Shurer to operate the Red Door Gallery in September 1963, a center of avant-garde film, painting, jazz, and photography, but it closed in June 1964.[48] Charles Moore first connected with the community of artists in the space and would play John Coltrane's records there and practice with them. The Red Door served as an early blueprint of an artist collective for the growing community in Detroit.

By that time, Charles Moore had become frustrated with the existing Detroit jazz scene. There were opportunities for people who wanted to play bebop in the approximately twenty jazz clubs that existed at the time, but free players and those who wanted to break new ground had few chances to play.[49] And Moore felt shunned from after-hours jam sessions, where a lot of the social connections were made, when people would say, "you play the wrong notes."[50] Sinclair met Moore through Tysh in May 1964, and during their first encounter they stayed up all night listening to records and talking about the music. Moore had few possessions and kept his cornet in a paper bag at the time.[51] "The next day, [Moore] moved into the house where the Artists' Workshop formed later that year," Sinclair explained. "We were close friends and race meant nothing to us, except as something that was oppressed by white people."[52]

Conversations between Moore and Sinclair that summer sparked the idea of creating their own performance space. "John and Charles were the architects of the idea," Leni Sinclair observed. "They became very close when they began talking about making things happen for avant-garde jazz in Detroit."[53] At the time, Sinclair articulated his frustrations with this poem:

>   the decay of a culture
>   permeates the day:
>   false rotting smiles
>   bring no light, the day
>   not safe, generations of innocence
>   blight the too-perfect forms
>   of a mother-and-child in a
>   toothless stare:
>   it's hard to believe people can hate so much,
>   or in the wrong direction.[54]

FIGURE 5.2 John Sinclair (1941–2023), poet and organizer.

Source: Courtesy Leni Sinclair.

Sinclair was already envisioning the transformational power of the avant-garde. He expressed how he saw the music as the answer to the ongoing social and cultural tensions of the 1960s in his poem "This Is Our Music," in honor of the record of the same name by Ornette Coleman:[55]

> how to get out
> side these chords: listen
> to Coltrane, Ornette or
> anyone
> who can tell you
> what you are.
> listen to me.
> Listen
> to yrself. if

you can still hear
anyone.
or our music
(if you can hear it)
will destroy everything
you have made yrselves
think you are.

From Sinclair's letters, we have the rare opportunity to delve into the rich intellectual history of a music scene. Sinclair wrote actively about the music throughout the period from 1964 to 1967 and was the driving force behind the many publications that were produced by the Artists' Workshop Press. His correspondence, which includes approximately seven hundred letters from the period, is a window into the myriad perspectives, politics, and organizing efforts present in the Detroit scene in the mid-1960s.

On October 2, 1964, Sinclair wrote to Leroi Jones,

A group of young artists of all persuasions here in Detroit have started to band together in a sort of makeshift community against the anti-art forces of the world. We are in the final stages now of getting a beautiful second-story sort of loft as a center for our community. There is now a lot of activity going on in Detroit that *can* be somewhat consolidated to the immediate benefit of everyone concerned—we're trying above all to create an atmosphere . . . that will be stimulating and conducive to maximum artistic involvement here. The concrete workshop is really the first step. Now we'd like to establish communication with people who are really doing it in New York to let you know what's going on here.[56]

In another letter, this time to Pauline Rivelli, an editor at *Jazz*, he described his vision: "An Artists' Workshop, non-commercial, supported by subscription by the people—musicians, writers, painters, filmmakers . . . a place that will be for sessions, rehearsals, poetry readings, film screenings, meetings—a real WORKSHOP."[57] By "subscriptions," Sinclair was referring to them splitting all costs evenly between participants. Free rehearsal space was aimed at eliminating the financial problems many musicians faced at the time.

The workshop was to function as a community center, publishing center, and a place for artists not only to create and rehearse on a daily basis but also to present their work.[58] The formation of the Artists' Workshop came as the merging of Sinclair and Moore's concept of a performance and creation space with poets, writers, and other artists coming out of Monteith College who wanted to create a grassroots publishing house.[59] From the very beginning, Sinclair advocated for the organization and publicized it through his reviews and writings. He became the Detroit correspondent for *Down Beat* in October 1964 and had begun writing criticism for *Jazz* the previous summer.[60] By the following year, he was also writing for *Coda*, *Spero*, and *Sounds & Fury*.[61] Though Sinclair was to find *Down Beat* to be less receptive to writings on the avant-garde, given what he referred to as its "middle-class-ness and insipidity," all of those magazines played a role in establishing a name for himself and for his becoming a visible figure to the musicians' community, especially in New York and Chicago.[62] Sinclair also incessantly attempted to submit reviews about Detroit avant-gardists for consideration in other publications around the country, including Leroi Jones's *Kulchur*.[63]

Sixteen artists were involved in the forging of the Artists' Workshop, and they articulated their vision with a manifesto that expressed a clear sense of collectivism, antiauthoritarianism, and a decisive move away from the mainstream.[64] It began with them defining what community was and why it was necessary for artists in particular—for fraternity, communication, and mutual advancement:

> Why a community of artists? We believe that one of the most important things to a young, formative artist is having a group of his peers (in the best sense of the word, taking into consideration his advanced level of consciousness &c) that he can be a part of, that he can talk to, work with, work out ideas &c and can give him support. Modern society has succeeded to a frightening degree in alienating artists from each other (and of course from people in general; or at least *vice versa*) and atomizing what could be a vital, active community into a group of lone, defensive, hungup people who are afraid to talk to and/or work with anyone but themselves and (maybe) three or four friends.
>
> A *community* of artists means that a group of highly conscious people have resolved their individual ego problems and can *help* each other in real ways—by giving support, stimulation, &c. The artist working alone is cutting himself off (tho not consciously I'm sure) from sources of inspiration and influence that can help him immeasurably in his work. The lone artist has no one to *listen* to his work (LeRoi Jones: "how you sound"), no one to offer criticism, ideas &c that would bring his work into sharper focus with itself. He stumbles along, hung up in his own ego & his work, no perspective, he can only listen to the generations before him & those who are getting exposure now (if he knows where to find them on his own) to get his inspiration & perspective—solitary, at best an artificial situation. Hard to get as excited, as completely involved in his work by

himself; when he can talk about it with/to others who are trying to do the same thing as himself (i.e. create some poetry (read: beauty) "out of the garbage of their lives" (LeRoi) and communicate it to others) he can achieve and maintain the state of consciousness Henry James called "perception at the pitch of passion." And who better to communicate to than those few people who are operating at the same level of awareness and involvement as oneself?

Poetry (or any art) does not need to be "sullen" (solus: alone) anymore. We are now in a period of expanded consciousness in all the arts, the most immediately important aspect of which is the transcendence of what is understood as the "ego" (in the accepted—worst—sense of that word). Left alone, without any real criticism (i.e. "constructive" criticism from those who are involved in the same thing you are, not from dilletantes & culture/vultures, "art lovers" &c), the artist's peculiar ego swells, he becomes deadened to his mistakes, he after a while can't bear real criticism, he's defensive, gets more atomized, separated, alone, can't talk to anyone, everyone else is crazy; becomes (alas!) the old "romantic" figure, misunderstood, one man against the world—no good. NOW is the time to find out what's wrong with your work, NOW, at least get an inkling of what other real people think about it, how it communicates, &c.

Another vital aspect of community thinking: each individual involved must (—has to—) learn a sense of personal responsibility: must take an active role in the life of his community, assume its problems and (this too is difficult anymore) its rewards & achievements, as his own, pitch in and help those around him who are trying but who haven't succeeded in getting themselves together as soon as he has. This is not like trying to work with (convert?) straight people (i.e. non artists)—they have far to go anyway, hard to really help them, they aren't in the supportive environment, they have to go home at night, no good, they really have not got a chance to make it. Artists, conversely, do have the very best chance to achieve higher & more productive levels of consciousness: they exist, for the most (& best) part, outside the existing social system, aren't as hung up by pettiness, have a chance to really get into their work, the best chance—by virtue of their distance from what its pitiable inhabitants call the "real" world (bombs, bureaucrats, greed, politics, "what filth deals consummated in what lavatory to take what is not yours"—Burroughs), artists *can* transcend that swamp of artificial reality and have a chance at putting love and help into action in making their *own* reality.[65]

Central to the manifesto was the refusal to see society as everyone competing against one another and instead that there was a shared fraternity: This was the very definition of community. The idea of mutual responsibility and collective advancement bore a heavy influence from the labor organizing that had come to define the city and much of Michigan's political and social consciousness. The manifesto targeted social alienation and isolation as distinct problems and as the first obstacles that needed to be overcome if an arts community was to have any chance of doing something dynamic that went beyond individual actions.

But the manifesto's discussion of the destruction of the ego went beyond working-class consciousness. Some of this was brought on by members of the community experimenting with LSD. "Acid made us fearless," Sinclair declared. "We weren't even scared of death. We lived in a trembling society where everyone was terrified of the government, the police, the FBI, the CIA, and the army. Everything was crashing down on us trying to make us be one way. LSD blew our minds open."[66] He added, "Doing acid made me realize that everything around us was a lie, that the people in power were corrupt. And most importantly, it made me realize I didn't want to be a part of all of that, that I didn't have to obey authority or work a regular job, that I could do whatever I wanted."[67] LSD also had an impact on how people processed music, such as when Sinclair later listened to Shepp's *Fire Music*: "I got a whole new sense of the music that way, we actually felt ourselves passing from a listening state into a state of total unity with the music, to a point of becoming the music itself."[68]

Finally, the manifesto described how the community would function as a mostly noncommercial entity, welcoming people regardless of financial background and bound together by an interest in a variety of the arts. As Eichele and Sinclair later stated, they were intent on "working as independently as possible from the economic framework that the established order left us. We saw Detroit as essentially virgin ground—there was everything to be done, the raw material was at hand, and we started working to exploit the situation in the best interests of every artistically-oriented individual in the community. . . . the Artists' Workshop is not simply for artists, in the strictest sense, but is a community by artists designed to give any human being disenchanted or, more honestly, humiliated and disgusted by the present order a means of, first, surviving in a dangerous world, and then creating something meaningful from what is left."[69]

There is at least some evidence that as the organization grew over the following year that they took at least some inspiration from the Jazz Composers' Guild, which had been founded by Bill Dixon and others in New York around the same time.[70] From the outset, the Artists' Workshop was designed to be interdisciplinary:

> So: what we want is a place for artists—musicians, painters, poets, writers, filmmakers—who are committed to their art and to the concept of community

involvement to meet and work with one another in an open, warm, loving, *supportive* environment (—what they don't get in the "real" world)—a place for people to come together as equals in a community venture the success of which depends solely on those involved in it. To this end we have acquired a "studio" workshop which will be maintained (rent, electricity, heat) by the artists themselves, through individual subscriptions of $5.00 each (i.e. initial investment—the pledge will be adjusted, on a monthly basis, and probably downward, as the workshop program is totally implemented and we have a concrete figure for maintenance costs). This method of supporting the Artists' Workshop is necessary, we feel, because:

1) Each member of the Workshop is to assume an equal responsibility in the project's success;

2) Members have to go into their already near-empty pockets, thus the project cannot be treated lightly;

3) We feel that any commercial means of support, at least (& especially) in the beginning, would tend to create an *artificial* community hung together on money, rather than a genuine community built on mutual need and support and interest;

4) No "outside" pressures, hangups, interferences;

5) The *Workshop* ideal can be maintained, i.e. there will be no pressure on artists to produce work that would have commercial success, rather than integrity and aesthetic honesty, as its ultimate purpose.

We do believe, however, that commercial ventures will come into being as logical and desirable outgrowths of the Workshop, as it has been conceived and as it is now operating. For example, we can see in the future a coffeeshop where musicians would present their work; a gallery for painters and other graphic artists to exhibit their work; a small printing and/or publishing concern through which poets & writers could introduce their work; an operating film society that would enable local filmmakers to produce and possibly market their cinematic ideas.

Other individual projects that are being planned as part of the Workshop's total program: lectures on modern music, painting, poetry and film, by the artists themselves, that would serve to introduce & enlighten an often-puzzled public to the artists' aims, purposes & finished work; free jazz concerts & workshops, featuring in particular the work of Detroit's musical "avant-garde," with commentary on their work by the musicians themselves and by enlightened critics & students of the music; interpretive poetry readings, with background and explanatory commentary by the poets; screenings of films by Detroit experimenters and by independent filmmakers from New York & San Francisco who are involved in what has been called the "New American Cinema," and whose work is not readily available, via commercial theatres, to its eager audience. All these will be "free," non-commercial affairs that are planned, programmed, & produced by the artists themselves.

We sincerely believe that our Artists' Workshop Society can and will succeed: the time is over-ripe, the people are ready to convert their ideals into real action, there is no real reason why we can't make it. We need all the support we can get, especially your spiritual support & blessing; we are trying to establish ties with the isolated groups of artists that exist in this country and throughout the universe, and we sincerely wish to cooperate with everyone who will let us. Please help.[71]

The manifesto embeds an interest and commitment to the avant-garde from the outset, even identifying some specific scenes and movements around the United States that they intended to connect with while establishing a seat at that national table for Detroit's artists.

The artists involved in the collective rented a line of houses near Wayne State at 4825–4867 John C. Lodge Service Drive, which became the Artists' Workshop. Artists lived upstairs, and the downstairs had seating and could accommodate an audience. They had an additional space a block away, where the poet Robin Eichele lived at 1252 West Forest Street; this became the performance space. *The Fifth Estate* anarchist periodical was produced in the same building.

On November 1, 1964, the Workshop held its inaugural event in a manner that would become a tradition.[72] Sunday afternoons became the time that the community would gather to present live music, poetry, visual art, and film. On that particular day, the Workshop gave their stage to the Detroit Contemporary 5 (DC5), a newly formed group that at that time included the trumpeter Charles Moore, guitarist Ron English, pianist Hach Grjegian, bassist John Dana, and drummer Danny Spencer. They displayed their interpretations of a range of contemporary standards by Thelonious Monk, McCoy Tyner, John Coltrane, Miles Davis, Prince Lasha, and Grachan Moncur III.[73] Sinclair observed that the band "is firmly committed to John Coltrane's brand of music, i.e. right to the deepest emotions, and they all had the people cooking with them."[74] In another way, he wrote, "The DC5 is in the Coltrane thing, ie. instant involvement at the deepest level and immediate emotional smash, and Charles is slowly turning the other cats onto Ornette's music, which is really a breakthru for Detroit."[75]

Of the inaugural event, Sinclair wrote: "It was a bigger success, artistically and otherwise, than even I'd dreamed. We had close to a hundred people in our Workshop—a house, a whole house in the Wayne [State] University area—and as an audience we couldn't have asked for anything better. *Everybody* dug the music—and it's supposed to be hard to get to, this avant-garde stuff."[76] The DC5 would go on to be the most featured band throughout the existence of the Workshop. A week after the inaugural event, the DC5 returned to play more pieces from the same milieu, including "Impressions" by Coltrane.[77]

"At the time it was something for white people to accept a Black person as their leader. Charles Moore was our leader. That was radical then," Sinclair explained. "He showed us how things were supposed to be, how to be himself and to do what he wanted artistically and in every other way. For those of us who were interested enough, he showed us some ways of how to go about getting there. He was supremely confident in his beliefs, he had no reservations, nothing could stop him, he never trembled in the face of opposition. My entire life is dependent on what I learned from him."[78]

One unifying factor at the Workshop was a mutual love and admiration for John Coltrane. They had circulated Coltrane's record *Sound* within their circle.[79] But their interest surged when a number of them drove together to see him play at the Plugged Nickel in Chicago on October 23, 1964.[80] The poet Jim Semark was one of the most dedicated Coltrane followers in the circle, and he would transcribe and analyze his solos.[81] "Much of the poetry that people were presenting at the Workshop," George Tysh noted, "was aiming at that apocalyptic screaming that Trane was getting at with his music."[82] Sinclair's younger brother, David, also a poet, who affiliated with the circle considerably, once hitchhiked seven hours to see Coltrane perform in Boston, where Tony Williams took Elvin Jones's place for that evening.[83]

On November 22, 1964, the pianist Pierre Rochon led a quintet with the saxophonist Brent Majors, along with Moore, Dana, and Spencer, to put on a concert as a homage to Coltrane.[84] They played a range of Coltrane pieces including "Dahomey Dance," "The Inch Worm," "Tungi," "My Favorite Things," "The Promise," "Miles' Mode," and "Impressions," as well as Rochon's own tribute to McCoy Tyner. At the event, Sinclair presented Leroi Jones's *Birdland* liner notes, a couple of the latter's reviews, a review of Coltrane by A. B. Spellman that had appeared in the magazine *Kulchur*, and two of his own reviews. The artist Larry Weiner also supplied action drawings that he had done of the John Coltrane Quartet from the concert they had all attended in Chicago.[85] Sinclair presented the title poem:

HOMAGE TO JOHN COLTRANE

*all (beyond win
and lose*

—e.e. cummings

"You are sorry you are born with ears"
yr ears. how it can become
the stuff of such lies.
or its inexhaustible
truth. how a man
can stand, & fall. stand.
"a coil around things"
a sound. his sound. a test
of what music can
bear. a scream
for the time.
an irrevocable beauty
"John Coltrane can do this for us"
teach us to stand / like giants
in the face of the most devastating
insensitivity. can
touch us. where the hand
or mouth or eye can't go.
can see.
can be a man, where boys
have forgotten
what a man is about.
can love. make a love
from centuries of unplumbed music
& a common metal tool anyone can misuse.
can make you think of

1

"a lot of weird & wonderful things:"
yrself.
beauty.
love.
gold & miles
of trees. elvin jones.
murdered dreams. a-
pocalypse.
Turtles.

armageddon.
the moon.
& beyond.
ornette.
grapefruits.
silver pendalums.
music.
& (when you've for-
gotten it:
time. screaming,
jumping up & down, & crying
for a new dignity
out of the ruin
/of my lack
before anyone can listen. before
time. before the hatred & ugliness
of this world.
before promises,
& lies. before it all collapses on our heads.
before its all too late

2

"If you've ever sat in a Coltrane audience, you'll understand what I mean."

—a.b. spellman

it cd happen
to you, too, a loss
of control, a be-
ginning. a reshaping
of what they've always told you
to believe. the old forms
& "music," that we've been fooled with,
the "songs" they taught you.
& lied
when we begin to understand that
what we've been told is

> how they can put us exactly
> where they have to believe
> we have to be.

3

> —man
> If you can't *hear*
>   what *can* you do?
> you're *born* with ears

The Artists' Workshop Press soon began putting out small magazines and volumes of poetry for national and local distribution.[86] Some would focus on poetry and others on jazz, though they generally insisted on all of them being interdisciplinary and having both musicians and poets write about the music to avoid the dynamic of detached cultural critics handing down their proclamations to artists.

Another poet of the Workshop, Bill Harris, who had befriended George Tysh when they were students at Wayne State, penned this tribute to the music and its personal meaning:

> Im *great* things:
> Birds horn
> Pres/ lid
> Ornette & Archie & Eric & Booker at the same time!
> Im
> a poem by LeRoi
> Caroles eyes
> a Beatle movie
> Orson Welles (in his prime
> an African nation
> Monks mind
> A Giocometti figure
> New York
> John Sinclair
> A Jim Semark rhythm ballad
> Sophias bra
> peace[87]

FIGURE 5.3 Bill Harris, poet.

Source: Courtesy Leni Sinclair

Harris had begun listening to jazz when he was thirteen and stated that jazz had influenced the rhythms of his writing both as a playwright and as a poet.[88]

By December 1964, Sinclair was actively trying to build connections with the free jazz community in New York. He was particularly interested in Coltrane, Cecil Taylor, Ornette Coleman, Don Cherry, Bill Dixon, Charles Mingus, Albert Ayler, Sonny Simmons, Billy Higgins, Archie Shepp, and John Tchicai.[89] Sinclair wrote to Shepp on December 14, inviting him to play a two-week stint at the Unstabled Theatre in Detroit, stating, "I can offer a free place to stay at the Workshop and a free open place to rehearse, play, jam, or whatever—we're hoping that this combination will help cats with bands come here for a modest price—to help jazz and art, not like clubs." He then asked him how much he would want for the performances for between one week and a full month at the venue.[90] He made a similar offer to Charles Mingus, John Tchicai, and others to entice these musicians to perform in Detroit.[91] Mingus showed no interest and even seemed a little paranoid about being approached by an enthusiastic promoter.[92] Other musicians were gradually receptive.

Undeterred, John and Leni Sinclair visited New York over the Christmas holiday; his aim was to spread word about the Workshop and make connections with a number musicians. As Sinclair wrote, they "propagandized for Artists' Workshop with Diane DiPrima, LeRoi Jones, musicians, everybody."[93] Jones was the prime inspiration for Sinclair, who admired him as a poet, playwright, critic, and activist.[94] On a practical level, the most influential experience during their trip to New York was spending time at Jones's loft at 27 Cooper Square, which became a model for an artist-run space. Upon their return, they "moved our whole menagerie next door . . . spent two weeks and more painting and restoring the place to a livable condition, and now it's beautiful!"[95]

Situated at their four-building line of houses, the Workshop also organized a cooperative housing program to provide space for all of the members to live together and for guest artists visiting Detroit to stay.[96] Artists interested in becoming members of the Workshop made an initial contribution of $5 and then continued to pay $3 per month.[97] All members met on a monthly basis. "We ran everything on a shoestring," Leni Sinclair observed, "and we divided all of the expenses equally between the members."[98] One small grant from the Dramatic Arts Center of Ann Arbor allowed them to set up their publishing operations, though they got much of their logistical knowledge from Eichele and Tysh, who had served as editors of *Monteith Journal* during their college years, where they became familiar with mimeograph machines.[99] On a functional scale, Sinclair was the primary driver behind the organization's day-to-day activities, building networks with like-minded people elsewhere and managing the fragile finances to keep it all afloat.[100] By November 1964, the Workshop had thirty-four members, and their numbers swelled over the year that followed.[101]

As the year progressed, the Sunday afternoon events attracted as many as one hundred attendees each week, mostly from the student beatnik artist community that existed around Wayne State. As Bill Harris observed, "The combination of the radical student newspaper, the Workshop, the hippie movement, and elements of the Black Arts Movement all at Wayne, these various groups began to comingle and find common ground."[102] Leni Sinclair, who was still a student there, began an affiliated student group that helped sponsor events and channel funds toward their activities. John Sinclair penned a letter to *The Collegian*, the campus newspaper, in which he stated, "The most independent artistic venture in the country has received no recognition nor support from the *Collegian*. I am speaking of the Artists' Workshop Society. . . . The Artists' Workshop is first a place where Detroit artists can meet and work together in a community situation, free from academic and other institutional interference."[103] He then elaborated on all of the free educational opportunities that they offered as well as the group's publishing wing of operations.

The Artists' Workshop began offering classes for what they called the Free University of Detroit. Everyone who wanted to teach a class offered something in the arts, ranging across music theory, composition, music ensemble workshop, music and philosophy, jazz criticism, poetry, prose, theater, acting, drawing, painting, photography, and other areas of the arts. One class engaged with anticolonial movements through the writings of Frantz Fanon, Che Guevara, and Mao Tse-Tung. Another course taught organizational methods of the New Left, and some provided space for discussion of sex and LSD experiences.[104] The collective goal was "to offer an alternative or extension to the present university curricula" and to build "a permanent community of committed artists and scholars in the area."[105]

The Artists' Workshop had revolutionary aspirations, as articulated in a utopian manifesto written by the guitarist Ron English, who stated that if they could form a separatist cooperative economy, spread literacy, increase access to birth control and sanitation, enact nondestructive community redevelopment, break the power of landlords and reduce rents, establish nonprofit local manufactures, and establish a baseline of well-being, "then the revolutionary society may come about. Should the revolution succeed, it will usher in a golden age of arts and letters." But then he added that such a thing would likely be short-lived, given the crushing response of the capitalist economy; slide slowly back into the status quo; or ultimately perish "with the rest of society."[106] To this, Eichele and Sinclair added, "We at the Artists' Workshop are not crazy enough to believe that this [revolutionary society] will happen tomorrow, if ever; but we do believe that it *can* be done, if enough of us are willing to start at the bottom, recognize the walls that our general society has put up for us, stop beating our heads against these walls, organize, and get to work."[107]

In late January 1965, the Workshop drew up plans for their own jazz club. It was not a separate entity but rather one to be incorporated into their ongoing operations. Their goals were clear: to provide a space for regular concerts by its two house bands, the Detroit Contemporary 5 and the Workshop Arts Quintet. They hoped also to cultivate connections with other aspiring free jazz bands. And they wanted to cement its presence by inviting figures from other parts of the country, with specific interest in Archie Shepp, Cecil Taylor, Bill Dixon, and the New York Arts Quartet, whom they saw as aesthetic touchstones for what they had in mind.[108]

Their performance space remained the primary site for public events until Memorial Day 1965, when the house burned down. Then for nearly six months, they relied on public venues, especially via the Artists' Workshop Society student affiliation at Wayne State, to hold events. Then in November 1965 they reopened their own space at 4857 John C. Lodge Street, which remained the base of operations until the Workshop ended. In 1967, the buildings were condemned and slated to be torn down to make way for the university's new football complex.[109]

DETROIT CONTEMPORARY 4 AND 5

The DC 4/5 first formed between a meeting of the trumpeter Charles Moore and drummer Danny Spencer in the early fall of 1964.[110] "Charles was the ultimate perfectionist," his longtime partner Kathleen Beaufait stated. "I saw him practice, and he worked on each little detail and technique over and over until he mastered it before moving onto the next thing."[111] Between November and March, Moore experimented with different lineups, including the guitarist Ron English and reedist Brent Majors, the latter of whom was then replaced by the saxophonist Larry Nozero. When the tenor saxophonist Charles Lloyd was in town with Cannonball Adderley in early 1965, he came to the Workshop and sat in with the band, "cohering quite naturally."[112] In the early months of the band's activity, during which time they played at the Workshop at least twice each month, they mainly played tunes by contemporary jazz artists as they built their own repertoire. Work by Coltrane, Eric Dolphy, Ornette Coleman, Jackie McLean, Grachan Moncur III, McCoy Tyner, Prince Lasha, and Sonny Simmons were central to their development.

When Nozero was drafted for the war in Vietnam, Moore settled on a quartet formation for a few months, but in June 1965 he invited the pianist Stanley Cowell to replace Ron English in the lineup. In addition to putting on concerts at the Workshop, the DC 4 managed to secure gigs at Michigan State University, Flint Junior College, and at Wayne State, where they began to refine their approach to group improvisation and a commitment to equality in participation and expression.[113]

"When you listen to Moore's compositions," one observer noted, "you were often hearing a sonic representation of a visual concept. Like dropping a pebble into water and watching the reverberation outwards, the interplay of sound and silence, the various qualities of pitches."[114] Moore often told the members of his band to "put a variation on it. Twist it. Look at it a different way. Make it become something else. Turn the time over," whenever they were working on a musical idea.[115] "Listening to Charles Moore," Leni Sinclair stated, "was like ecstasy. It

FIGURE 5.4 Charles Moore and the DC5 at the Detroit Artists' Workshop, 1965.

Source: Courtesy Leni Sinclair.

totally opened my mind. He had this way of riffing behind the saxophone player getting tighter and tighter and then they would play together."[116]

The DC4/5 also began debuting compositions by other members of the Workshop. For example, in January 1965 they presented "Adolescence: a musical reality for cornet, saxophone, and rhythm," by Sinclair, which he dedicated to Eric Dolphy. The piece was inspired by the idea of "adolescence as wildly turbulent, schizophrenic times for young human beings—we're put thru so many changes at these times by the brainwashers and evil mindcroppers that we're lucky to get out alive in any sense."[117] The piece juxtaposed cornet and saxophone in drones trading space with arco bass, vibraphone, and drums playing "out of time" but sustaining forward flow with decreasing durations. Then, "when the notes approach staccato, the piece suddenly and wildly bursts into chaos: the horns start screaming weird dissonant blasts at each other, the bassist can tear violent double-stops out of the bass, the drummer beats his instrument as hard and as non-musically as possible, the vib[raphon]ist makes as much irrelevant noise as he can. What is needed here is a violent cacophony."[118] This was followed by resolution in 4/4 time, solos, group improvisation, and finally a return to the opening aesthetic. In March, the band presented an early version of "Concerto for Charles

Moore," written by Jim Semark, which they would continue to refine and eventually expand into a larger Workshop ensemble later in the year.[119]

Only a few live recordings have ever been released of the DC4, and only in 2022 through the efforts of John Sinclair, since all of the members of the band had passed away by that time.[120] Cowell's composition "Effi" shows the band adhering to a theme, with billowing piano chords forming the buoy for the piece while Moore displays agile, vertical lines that cut through the soundscape with pristine articulation. Moore's own composition, "Three Flowers," showcases his most exploratory improvising with stark, turbulent imagery.[121] Their recording of Coltrane's "The Promise" shows the group's most daring interplay and soloing that pushes the music further out.

Moore and others in the band were committed to operating in a leaderless format in terms of what they did on stage and to working on a group sound. At the Detroit Jazz Scene conference in 1965, Moore stated, "Now out cats who were good musicians started getting together and thinking in group terms rather than as only individuals, they could get to make some music. And that's what we're trying to do, with the Contemporary 5. Everybody can be an integral part of the group. That's the only way to approach it."[122] The DC4/5's bassist, John Dana, added, "The only way these musicians are going to reach [a high level] is through group playing and group thinking. I don't think it's so much something that's 'new' but something that's your own, something that you've gotten together yourself and not just taken from somebody else. [We] try to make music in equal shares, and the more equal you can get it, the better the music is."[123]

The DC 4/5 began to gain attention outside of Detroit in 1965 and 1966. They played several concerts on the East Coast in New York and Newark. Locally, they also presented concerts at the University of Michigan and at Michigan State University, as well as at the Detroit Jazz Conference and at Antioch College in Yellow Springs, Ohio.[124] And occasionally, when other musicians were passing through Detroit, they added them as guests to their concerts, such as the alto saxophonist Byron Pope and trumpeter Warren Gales. Meanwhile, they constantly presented new material on a monthly basis at the Workshop, where they split bills with poets.[125] The Lansing radio station WKAR began broadcasting music by the DC4/5 in the fall of 1965 in an effort to broaden their local audience.[126]

In October 1965, Moore wrote of the band's progress, "We've played through different levels of the music so far, we've covered modern music starting with [Thelonious] Monk and going through Miles [Davis] and [John] Coltrane, but now we're trying to get into our own thing. We're trying to push the Contemporary 4 to a point where we're out of the tonal aspects of the music and more into the reality aspect. In other words, we want to portray the human . . . how a man talks, feels, thinks, moves."[127] Then Moore added, "What we want to do is come up with a more positive approach to music. The idea is to simulate, on an abstracted level, the human being, the human mind. Really think about how you feel and apply it musically on your instrument. And if we can get into what we feel ourselves, we can cover a lot of music, put it to work toward an ultimate end, and then I think we'll be satisfied with ourselves."[128]

When Moore expanded from the DC4 to the DC5 once again in the fall of 1965, it was to include John Sinclair reading poetry. At Wayne State on October 14, the band played a range of pieces by Coltrane, Grachan Moncur III, and Jackie McLean while also presenting pieces by Moore and Cowell. The apex of the performance was when Sinclair joined them on stage to read his poem "The Destruction of America," which they dedicated to Malcolm X:[129]

> When the form begins to go. Crumbles. Shattered, some lack of precision, blasted thru the end of intellection. Where gut is law, the only law. Where what is left, is not worth saving. Where we can start, now. The shape, bent out of recognition, smeared on the page, on their wavy faces. The Social Order. Anarchy. Murder. Where the breath runs off the page, into some silent jungle of compromise. Where the race, you can see. Race. The ends, of logic. Where what was left, is gone. Wiped out. What song, is left to sing. Who, to sing it. The story is there, in the man's blood, on the streets of real america. Where they left it.
> (How to blame them, or anyone. To keep from murdering them, in their senseless sleep. What slap, to wake them. What eyes, are theirs. Lies, they can't help but tell. How to get out of it. Thru what forms, can we make it. What music is left, for our ears. Where we can take it. The music, of the voices we have left. The form it puts to us, for our use.
> how to use them. how to get
> to that point, counter-
> point, where words move
> into melody. Song. Music,
> where the sense comes dancing
> thru. to feeling, the sense of
> feel, how to build it, the
> harmony, how the changes, the
> progressions, move us, to you,
> people, killers, anyone, left,

> to preserve. Advance, on each
> other. Dance. Sing[130]

The DC5 also sometimes edged into R&B or "contemporary folk forms," with Charles Miles joining on alto saxophone and Kenneth Schooner on harmonica.[131] Sinclair described the process as "the most forward musicians here going back into their roots."[132] Of the experience, Sinclair wrote to the alto saxophonist Marion Brown, "I've been reading with them as part of the group each time, which is a beautiful thing for me, and has been very successful both artistically and in terms of audience movement."[133]

In January 1966, the DC4 invited Brown to join them for a tour between New York and Detroit.[134] At that time, Brown had just recorded his first quartet record for ESP and had worked with Coltrane, Archie Shepp, Sun Ra, Pharoah Sanders, Paul Bley, and Grachan Moncur III. The tour began with the Jazz Art Music Society in Newark, New Jersey, which also included Pharoah Sanders, Burton Greene, Rashied Ali, and other musicians as guests. Sinclair wrote that "Burton Greene literally [tore] the Society's piano up trying to keep up with Charles, Marion, [Pharoah], and Ronnie Saturday night, finally crawling around on the floor beating two blocks together to add to the energy section of John Dana and Ronnie Johnson when the piano proved too fragile for him. And Sunday night brought the lovely sight of LeRoi Jones hopping up and down, dancing, a big grin on his face, while the musicians took him out of his troubles for a while."[135]

The DC4 together with Brown then went across the border to Toronto, where they played another three nights at the Bohemian Embassy, and then returned to Detroit, where the Workshop sponsored a concert for them at Wayne State on January 21.[136] Sinclair wrote of Brown at the time, "He has come in what seems a very short time to make a very personal music, a music that moves straight out of his self, right there, where he lives. There seems to be very little preconceived 'formula' noise that gets in the way of his own music, a situation that is, unfortunately, a rarity still among modern musicians. Marion is able (equipped) to produce any kind of sounds, including what the formula people would have him do, but it is his strength that he persists in making a music that is as much his own as is humanly possible."[137] Brown wrote autobiographically in a poem titled "Wordsong":

> sound, what we hear, is
> a transistor, how nature feels
> her own way of saying . . . I live, breathe,
> in time-space-distance
> I'm eternal, as the lake at Nomi,
> or spring in Guernavaca.[138]

Sinclair also penned his poem "Fire Music" in response to Brown's playing on Archie Shepp's record of the same title, which he read to introduce the DC4 with Brown as a guest for their performance at Wayne State:[139]

> who begins
> with this record
> to tap a possibility
> heretofore only hinted at
> to make a music of
> the materials of
> his instrument
> "a common metal tool"
> a source of music that has
> with few exceptions
> (& on alto saxophone—even fewer
> in the sense I mean to put to you
> i.e. in Marion Brown's sense)
> up to this point in time been
> only & occasionally momen-
> tarily
> made use of.
> The strength & breadth of
> his breath
> (& the sources of it, in his own
> physiology
> brought thru a metal saxophone
> & registered with our own sources
> thereby.
> May he realize
> thru his work in this raw direction
> all the beauty & love
> that is due him

The New York sojourn for the DC4 seemed to initiate a new phase of experimenting with personnel, such as a sextet version that included a tenor saxophonist and a second drummer.[140] In November 1965, they invited the Chicagoan Joseph Jarman, whom Sinclair referred to as "the beautiful one," to perform with them, and he played reeds as well as bells with the group.[141] Jarman became a Detroit regular and split bills with Workshop musicians. "Jarman brought an energy that fit right in," English noted, "but also expanded what we were doing at the Workshop."[142] For instance, in March 1966, Moore and Danny Spencer played with the bassist Charlie Haden at the University of Michigan on a split bill with Archie Shepp and a big band that Jarman led that combined Haden with Chicago and Detroit musicians.[143] Jarman penned a poem in honor of the DC4:

> THEY PLAY THE LIFE THEY SING
> the 4 from
> Detroit; together
> bounce thump moan
> tear
> laugh.
> outside the workers
> in space age speed
> on freeways
> head home unaware
> of joy[144]

Over the course of 1966, the DC4 played at protests, many Workshop events, and at the Festival of People in August, which was also sponsored by the Workshop to celebrate the release of John Sinclair from prison, where he had been incarcerated on a narcotics charge.[145] At times the band drew crowds of one hundred or more, even at club gigs.[146] But as the Workshop itself began to splinter apart toward the end of the year, the band also disintegrated, and Moore began to turn his attention to other projects.[147]

In reflecting on his own development, Moore saw moving away from bebop as essential to find his own voice and to play liberated, autonomous Black music. Free playing was the sonic demonstration of that act of freedom. He referred to that freedom as "his bushman thing"; it got him away from the patterns of the past and would ultimately lead him to making "plain, beautiful music."[148]

WORKSHOP MUSIC ENSEMBLE

A mini–big band emerged organically out of the Workshop in 1965 that became known as the Workshop Music Ensemble, conceived of by Jim Semark, Lyman Woodard, and Charles Moore in the winter of 1964–1965, as a cooperative unit that was "dedicated to the performance of new music by young Detroit composers and arrangers."[149] The group naturally shifted in composition and at different times included the cornetist Charles Moore; trumpeter Pierre Rochon; alto saxophonists Gene Moore, Jim Guinness, and John Sinclair; tenor saxophonist Anthony Harris; trombonists George Garnett and Jim Semark; organist and pianist Lyman Woodard; pianist Clarence DeMyers; bassists John Dana, James Calhoun, and Doug Riggs; drummers Ronald Johnson and Byron Lyles; and occasionally a poetic choir.[150] They played compositions such as "The Pimp's Vision," by Woodard; "Adolescence," by Sinclair; and "The Emotional Organ" and "Concerto for Charles Moore," by Semark.[151]

The last of the pieces by Semark became the Workshop Music Ensemble's most visionary project, and they continued to work on it throughout the year. By late November 1965, when the Workshop organized the three-day Festival of Avant-Garde Music in Detroit, it had evolved into a nine-part suite that chronicled the rise and corruption of human civilization through the stages of ancient music and eventually through swing and bebop to free expression, which symbolically represented freedom from the past and from the strictures of society.[152] The apex was a solo by Moore, "the Free Will of Charles Moore," straddled by two group improvisations, "The Mechanics of Social Exploitation" and "The Consummate Hope of Civilization." The first of these group improvisations included a reading part for a chorus of fourteen voices lined up in two groups facing each other shouting dichotomies such as "life/death" and "love/hate."[153] It was the debut of Semark's extended compositions and was presented with the idea that "the audience may participate in this performance by understanding that it is symbolic consciousness-expansion, a kind of symbolic satori."[154]

Of the performance, Moore wrote:

> Since the very beginnings of the music the emotional profoundness of the black man has always been expressed on one hand and felt on the other. Over a period of three and a half centuries the music has changed in its structures, form, sound texture, but in its essence, it still has had the personal quality of Raw Blackness, meaning simply that although the Black himself acquired the knowledge to master the musical instruments he in his agony still expresses the essence of his emotional being. This period of 3.5 centuries would point out the Black's period of sufferance. From the early to the late fifties, he went through a very profound transition in his means of expression by trying to cling to something or someone to give him his lost identity. The Black emerged from this garbage, the stink and filth that he was brainwashed into creating because of his lack of recognizing his own mental prowess; his own mind, to bring about a music (NOW) that is so threatening that it will be a major force in the destruction and death of this useless society.[155]

Moore went further to describe that what he participated in was

> a Fire Music; a searing, scorching, controlled utterance; personal, stronger in its performance than any other musics . . . before it. This would then be Black Music—a cry for freedom; an utterance so powerful that it shatters the ears with pure Brute Black emotional force. A Force that is more powerful than the decibels that make the energy (the sound energy) surrounding the nucleus of this utterance. A wave of energy that refuses to remain hidden in the dark recesses of the mind. Being propelled by the force of its own energies. Raw in its energies/ fresh in its forms/ profound in its aesthetics/ The New Music/ The New Wave.[156]

The Workshop Music Ensemble was active through 1966, including a performance at the Festival of People, but they, too, split up when the Workshop disintegrated. In some ways, the Lyman Woodard Ensemble comprised the surviving pieces of it in the years that followed.[157]

At the Festival of People, Jim Semark presented an extended poem:

> there were COLORS they'd
> never seen before
> & there were SOUNDS they'd
> never heard before
> they saw young-people living in
> mansions & old-people living
> in play-houses with make-believe
> doors & windows & chimneys & streetsigns
> without streets   & sidewalks
> that went off in to
> no-   where.   & they ran
> down the streets & through the fields
> & past the trees & houses & shouting:
> "EVERY ONE DOES
> WHAT HE DOES!"
> & when they stopped
> to catch their breath they
> heard the sound of the ENERGY MUSIC.
> how strange it was!!
> —they heard
> the sound of ENERGY MUSIC

in all the plants & trees
the sound grew louder
. . . .
they heard the sound of the ENERGY MUSIC
coming from the sky & from the ground
& plants & trees & rocks & even from all the
cells in their bodies[158]

OTHER BANDS TO EMERGE FROM THE WORKSHOP

Another active bandleader at the Workshop was the trumpeter Pierre Rochon. He was from Windsor, situated right across the Canadian border, but he regularly participated in events at the Workshop. His bands had a variety of names, first appearing under the name Workshop Arts Quartet, which seems to reference the New York Arts Quartet, but the group downsized to the Workshop Trio, with the bassist Tommy Dorsey and drummer Ronald Johnson, in June 1965.[159] He also led a group simply called the Pierre Rochon Quartet. Unfortunately, there is no surviving documentation of his work, though other Workshop participants recalled Rochon's music as being less experimental than that of Charles Moore.[160] Rochon's involvement with the Workshop faded in 1966.

The other significant bandleader and organizer was the organist and pianist Lyman Woodard (1942–2009), who as a composer was influenced significantly by Charles Mingus.[161] Aside from co-leading the Workshop Music Ensemble, he led several other groups. He regularly played with the alto and soprano saxophonist Charles Miles in a duo format.[162] By early 1966, the Lyman Woodard Ensemble was playing regularly at the Workshop and was described as having "developed ensemble playing into a consciousness-expanding emotional and intellectual experience."[163] The band included Miles and Moore, as well as the tenor saxophonist David Squires, trumpeter Ed Hood, bassist John Dana, and drummer Ronald Johnson, in varying lineups. "Johnson was a gifted, intuitive drummer," Ron English noted.[164] Like the other Workshop bands, Woodard's ensemble was featured at the Festival of People.[165] The band continued to perform within that milieu until the Workshop came to an end in 1967.[166] Woodard would remain a central figure in the Detroit music scene for decades after, extensively recording with Motown acts and serving as the musical director for Martha and the Vandellas, though he is best known for his record *Saturday Night Special*.[167]

NETWORKING WITH THE NATIONAL SCENE

The Workshop built a national profile by establishing and maintaining communications with artists, writers, and publishers around the country to inform them of their activities. A mailing list of January 1965 indicates they were sending their announcements to a broad range of people including musicians such as Charles Mingus, Archie Shepp, Jimmy Garrison, Cecil Taylor, and John Tchicai; poets and writers such as Leroi Jones, Allen Ginsberg, Robert Creeley, Ed Dorn, Diane DiPrima, Lawrence Ferlinghetti, and Nat Hentoff; and label owners such as Bob Thiele (Impulse!) and Bernard Stollman (ESP). Together, this placed them at the center of a Detroit–Ann Arbor–Windsor network that included many cities and towns in Michigan, as well as New York City, Chicago, Pittsburgh, Cleveland, San Francisco, Berkeley, Los Angeles, Seattle, Houston, Atlanta, Washington, Tampa Bay, Toronto, Calgary, Vancouver, and smaller towns across the Midwest and in Alabama, California, Connecticut, Idaho, Massachusetts, Nevada, New Mexico, upstate New York, North Carolina, and Oregon. They also maintained communications with artists and writers in England, France, West Germany, Italy, Mexico, the Netherlands, Peru, and Poland.[168]

Thus by the end of 1965, the Workshop had elevated itself to a national and international profile with especially strong connections with New York, Chicago, Los Angeles, and San Francisco.[169] In a letter to Jamey Aebersold, Sinclair outlined their plans, stating, "We want especially to consolidate forces here in the Great Midwest and get some kind of circuit going."[170] As he stated later, "We wanted to put Detroit back on the map. It had been the second city of bebop but that had all ended in the early 1960s."[171] They had limited funding, so they could not invite all of the acts they wanted from other cities, but they began programming people who did respond from New York and especially from Chicago.[172] Plans were formulated to bring Albert Ayler to Detroit and Ann Arbor in early 1966, with Bernard Stollman stating, "Albert Ayler's group would be a very appropriate opening salvo judging by the tumultuous reaction he has received here," but the concert never materialized.[173]

The particularly strong connection between Detroit and Chicago grew out of a proposal by the writer and promoter J. B. Figi to John Sinclair to do a series of exchange concerts for the DC4 to go to Chicago and for Joseph Jarman, Roscoe Mitchell, Phil Cohran, and Richard Abrams to come to Detroit.[174] In March 1966, Jarman brought to the Workshop his quintet, which comprised the tenor saxophonist Fred Anderson, trumpeter Bill Brimfield, bassist Charles Clark, and drummer Steve McCall, along with special guest pianist Richard Abrams.

Ultimately Abrams was unable to play because no piano was available, but he did join the band for a subsequent concert in Ann Arbor.

This was the beginning of a number of collaborations that the Workshop initiated with the newly formed Association for the Advancement of Creative Musicians (AACM). In fact, the growth of the Workshop and AACM should be seen as happening alongside each other. Members of the two groups were in constant communication, especially Joseph Jarman, Leni Sinclair, and John Sinclair. They saw that they had mutual interests and offered support to each other as they envisioned creating apparatuses to bridge their communities.[175]

Jarman's band had grown organically out of the AACM community. In December 1965, they had worked with the composer John Cage's experiments in electronics and were gaining a reputation for ardently striving toward new sonic breakthroughs. To explain their intentions, Jarman penned, "The Quintet *loves* every musician that ever played, big or little. We are influenced by every sound we ever heard. We are not angry. We want PEACE."[176]

Jarman returned in June 1966 with a different quartet lineup that still included Clark, but this time with the pianist Christopher Gaddy and drummer Thurman Barker; they invited Charles Moore to join them as a guest.[177] At that time, they were working on material that ultimately appeared on Jarman's debut record, *Song For*, which included the masterpiece of jazz poetry "Non-Cognitive Aspects of the City," alongside three other original works.[178] Jarman remained in the city for the summer and brought his band to the Festival of People in August.[179] The close relationship that Jarman forged with the Detroit community found him invited back for additional concerts. In November, he guested with the DC5, playing reeds and bells, and in early 1967 he performed at several concerts there on split bills with the MC5, a rock band managed by Sinclair.[180]

The Workshop had grand plans to invite all of the vanguard free jazz figures to the city. Though lack of funding prevented many of those aspirations from manifesting, the collective did manage to program an impressive array of concerts over the course of its existence that connected them to the national scene. The pianist Andrew Hill played in concert at Wayne State University in December 1965 with the rhythm section of John Dana and Ronald Johnson, then traveled to Toronto the following February for three nights at the Bohemian Embassy.[181] At the time, Hill privately expressed the need for musicians to stop entertaining and instead "create their own forms of public expression."[182] The pianist Paul Bley put on a concert in February 1966 with the same rhythm section of Dana and Johnson supporting him.[183] The Workshop also formed the link in getting the Archie Shepp Quartet, with the trombonist Roswell Rudd, bassist Charlie Haden, and drummer Beaver Harris, invited to perform at the Creative

FIGURE 5.5 Andrew Hill (1931–2007), pianist, in Detroit.

Source: Courtesy Leni Sinclair.

Arts Festival at the University of Michigan in March 1966 as well as a performance at Wayne State.[184] The festival included a panel discussion on the significance of free jazz in the broader context of Black music in the United States led by many of the performers, and they were joined by Roland Kirk, who happened to be in the audience.

Initial plans to have the pianist Burton Greene join the DC4 in Detroit for a concert in March 1966 of that year did not come to fruition, but they did bring him in November, when he played in solo, duo, and trio formations with local musicians.[185] Around that time, Greene wrote:

> When one finds his core truly or analogously, the pebble thrown into the mainstream of life, the widespread expanding circles happen of their own accord, promulgating an ever-increasing, myriad-faceted self-expression. Thus, we find that the apt practitioners of this new music are essentially positivists, great practitioners of life itself. The music is so intense, so complexly diversified and far-reaching, that it entirely demands an almost holy, a daily dedication to its principles. What is truly beautiful to me is that because the basis of the music is so

human, simple, and direct, that it cannot happen, cannot be successful unless the practitioner himself is all these things. This may be said about all great art but is directly in evidence here because there is no other arbitrative "glue" to pull the music together.[186]

BUILDING A DIALOGUE AROUND FREE JAZZ

The Workshop's deepest impact on free jazz came through the dialogue that it created via its publications, which were nationally and internationally distributed. This was particularly important because most jazz critics rejected free jazz. Sinclair joined Leroi Jones, A. B. Spellman, and Frank Kofsky as the few who supported and embraced the music. In February 1965, Sinclair wrote a letter to the Canadian poet Victor Coleman in which he articulated his view of free jazz. "The music comes out of the whole way of looking at the world, now, and is a logical and necessary opposite choice, the music that is, it stands in relation to the old music the same way as these men stand to the old style of men. Archie [Shepp] and [the other musicians] are the hangmen, or assassins, as Leroi [Jones] called Trane, they have to get rid of the old order."[187] Sinclair also composed the poem "the whip," taking Robert Creeley's title, dedicating it to Charles Moore, to express the significance of this new era:

> how to lead a band
> of men, to where they are. Shepp
> showed the 'mean' streak
> of the lash: Whip
> backs, hands, to bone. Poke
> holes, in their sloth. Scream.
> stick yr tongue out, jump
> up & down, stone
> where the slop
> slips in. (slip up, & yr gone.
> wasted noise. music, where you climb
> up their backs,
> crunching silence.
> browned stalks of feeling, snapped
> at the neck. Lead them anywhere,
> they can go. Rocks,

> in the head, point
> the way. Where the song
> must go, by the bridge
> of memory, where the head
> gives up. Ignore ignor-
> ance, jab, shove, men (not
> sheep) to the head of where
> they are. You are. Waiting[188]

Put another way, Sinclair declared, "Audiences have to be educated to a certain degree, and the artists are supposed to be at a higher level of awareness and able to show the audiences where it's at. It's their responsibility."[189] Moore echoed this: "This is a good thing for the musicians and the audiences . . . they want to see the musicians get into their own thing, the more the better."[190]

At the conference Jazz 1965, held at the University of Michigan on a series of Fridays between April and June, members of the Workshop led panels to engage in public discussion about free jazz. John Sinclair opened the discussion with a panel titled "Jazz in America Today: What It's Doing and Why."[191] Charles Moore led a conversation about Ornette Coleman and another about Cecil Taylor and Archie Shepp, Danny Spencer discussed the music of Coltrane and Elvin Jones, Lyman Woodard talked about Charles Mingus, Pierre Rochon discussed the music of Booker Little and Eric Dolphy, John Dana led a conversation about Scott LaFaro and other bassists, and Ronald Johnson talked about Tony Williams and Miles Davis. The DC4 and DC5 performed at several events through the course of the series and were sometimes joined by the Pierre Rochon Quartet for indoor or outdoor performances. In their own space but affiliated in many ways with the series, the Workshop held a symposium, "Contemporary Social Issues and the Artist," led by Sinclair, Moore, Robin Eichele, and Bill Harris.[192]

Through 1965, Sinclair came to view free jazz as pure music unhindered by contrivance. He wrote, "Men like Archie Shepp, Marion Brown, Albert Ayler, Charles Moore, and other contemporary workers who are bringing their music (again) straight out of themselves, no artifice at all, but pure form (pure feeling). I do not know where this new music might lead, but as I feel it now it is leading me into myself, what I am, again without artifice at all, but as pure as the saying will have it, and the cleanness this saying brings, the sense of purification."[193]

The Workshop established itself and built an audience for free jazz in Detroit by self-producing many events. Sinclair stated in December 1965, "We are thinking now that exposure under the proper conditions is the first step toward making the music popular and that's what we are doing lately at Wayne [State]. We set up a group there (a front organization called the WSU Artists' Society) which enables us to get auditoriums free, pass out propaganda on campus, sell magazines there, etc. So we get at a lot of people we would otherwise miss that way and I'm sure it can be done on enough campuses to start turning people's heads (minds) around."[194]

At a concert at Wayne State on October 14, 1965, before an audience of three hundred people, Sinclair introduced the bands by saying, "[These musicians] propose to impinge on your consciousness through their own personal machination, not by replaying a music or musics you already have with you—that is to say, they mean to move you *out* from where you are, into areas of your being you may never have thought possible. If you are at all interested in their progress, of discovery and invention, then these men are playing for you. They are not here to play 'weird,' or show off, or to 'prove' anything except the single fact of their existence, as men and musicians—artists—and the uses they have made of themselves."[195]

In December 1965, Charles Moore wrote an angry letter to the periodical *Jazz*, responding to Don Ellis's critical review of Coltrane's *The John Coltrane Quartet Plays*. He articulated how often white reviews show "utter contempt for Black creativity." Then he addressed the need for Black musicians to be more than just entertainers. "The Black artist is playing almost entirely about, of, and from the way he feels. If a Black artist stoops one iota to the listening standards of the audience this music will die, the Black artists will die and the only creative music in this hemisphere will die."[196]

The Workshop's most influential dialogue on free jazz was via two issues of the magazine *Change* that they issued in 1965–1966. It was the world's first publication devoted entirely to free jazz, predating publications like *The Cricket* by three years.[197] *Change* was coedited by Sinclair and Moore, and they had a global network of correspondents that included Marion Brown (New York), Tam Fiofori (London), George Tysh (Paris), Ruggero Stiassi (Bologna, Italy), Art Williams (Newark), and Mort Maizlish (Los Angeles).[198] The magazine printed correspondence on the music from readers in Hanover (NH), Pittsburgh, Lincoln (PA), Washington (DC), Selma (AL), Lansing, Chicago, San Francisco, and the Canal Zone, as well as general observations from England, Germany, Australia, and Vietnam.

The same networks also distributed the magazine at local record stores and bookshops in many of these locales, drawing a number of regular subscribers to *Change*.[199] The heaviest concentration of subscribers was in cities and towns in Michigan, Indiana, Ohio, and Pennsylvania, especially in Pittsburgh, as well as Chicago, Louisville, and the University of Wisconsin, but also in California, Delaware, New Jersey, New York, Oregon, and internationally in England,

Denmark, Poland, and the Canal Zone. The editors courted relationships with relevant record labels like ESP and Impulse! to send them review copies in exchange for advertisements.[200] The original plan was to have quarterly issues, but Sinclair's imprisonment in 1966 prevented more regular releases.

In the inaugural issue, Sinclair stated their vision clearly:

> The purpose is to create a forum for the new music, to make up for the lack of same in the other "jazz magazines." ... We take as example the huge forum that exists for contemporary poetry in the "little magazines" ... usually edited and printed by the poets themselves, who have realized that the established communications media are not even interested in what is really going on ... and take the job of getting the work out themselves, as it should be anyway. *Change*, then, proposes to take on the job of providing such a forum, and to encourage those writers and musicians who would attempt to register their responses to music verbally. *Change* will have to do entirely with those musics and those musicians its editors hear as the *real* voices of America, the strong and useful artists of this time.... *Change* is what is needed, on all levels. Things cannot remain as they are.[201]

They further cited the idea of self-determination in their work as first inspired by the Jazz Composers Guild.

Change included extensive reviews of a broad range of well-known and lesser-known figures of the music, including Ornette Coleman, Sun Ra, Charles Mingus, John Coltrane, Cecil Taylor, Andrew Hill, Eric Dolphy, Archie Shepp, the New York Art Quartet, Steve Lacy, Pharoah Sanders, Wayne Shorter, Paul Bley, Booker Ervin, Burton Greene, Byron Allen, and Giuseppe Logan, sometimes employing poetry as a means of commentary. The magazine also included personal essays by musicians, interviews, and discographies. Each of the field correspondents reported on concerts, record releases, and the growth of audiences in the places that they observed. Official correspondents also often served as local distributors for the magazine. In general, the reports were optimistic about the growth of a national and global audience and sometimes gave voice to their own personal transformations as a result of the music.

POLICING ARTIST COMMUNITIES

From the very beginning of the Artists' Workshop, the community faced challenges from the police. In 1964, John Sinclair had been charged with the sale of marijuana but eventually pled guilty to the reduced charge of possession in December. For that, the state gave him two years of probation, though the maximum penalty at the time was life imprisonment. On August 16, 1965, he was again arrested, along with two others, by an undercover police officer who posed as a marijuana buyer and then carried out a raid with two dozen other officers.[202] The police viewed Sinclair as "the chief marijuana supplier in the campus area."[203] "Sinclair was constantly being harassed by police," Robin Eichele observed. "He had his chin out, he was confrontational, he was not intimidated by them and he let them know that."[204] Over the next two days local newspapers printed statements by Sinclair to the police, which he claimed he never made, using them to create an environment of fear and distrust between the artists and the broader Detroit community.[205] This second arrest would have graver consequences for both Sinclair and ultimately for the Artists' Workshop when, in February 1966, he was sentenced to six months at the Detroit House of Corrections.[206]

Many of the musicians that had worked with Sinclair had sympathy for his cause and supported the actions that he had taken. Burton Greene, for example, wrote in a letter to Leni Sinclair,

> He's got the right idea, the right motivations. All he has to do is be able to dig the fact that he must be clever and cope with the insecurity or the strong reactions to all of the shit he is stirring up. When people go from apathy to an acknowledgement of beauty, I'm afraid they first get reactive or angry to the state that they've been in which is often further clouded by their projecting their own uptight state onto you. He should continue without compromise; but a little diplomacy, a little judgment or carefulness will certainly pay off in the long run. I've found that a little humility is a groove in certain tight situations also. After all, isn't what we anarchists [are] doing is disarming all of the land mines we come across without detonating them into a harmful explosion—but eventually into a positive one—an uplifting eruption for all?[207]

The strain of Sinclair's imprisonment was felt by everyone in the Workshop, since he had been the primary organizer of events, as well as promoting them regionally and nationally. Some members stopped paying their dues almost immediately after his incarceration.[208] An emergency meeting on March 16, 1966, resulted in some contributions and a recommitment from many of the core members.[209] In May 1966, the board members met to discuss whether to keep it going. Though they ultimately decided to do so, the organization itself was in tatters.

There was talk of the DC4 breaking up, and both Charles Moore and Ronald Johnson were considering moving to the West Coast. Danny Spencer moved

FIGURE 5.6 John Sinclair (1941–2023), poet.

Source: Courtesy Leni Sinclair.

back to Lansing.[210] Sinclair wrote a terse letter to Moore, chiding him to keep "the music thing" going at the Workshop.[211] Then, after hearing that Moore had gone to San Francisco, Sinclair wrote a second, angry letter saying that the Workshop would be finished if he did not return.[212] In July, Joseph Jarman moved to Detroit and lived at the Workshop; Leni Sinclair wrote, "he says he'll do what he can to keep the Workshop going."[213] Though the Workshop did survive for the moment, Moore had moved out of the communal living space, and it was clear that the community was beginning to fall apart.[214]

As Sinclair neared his release from prison, he began to make plans to reformulate the community with the feeling that he had not been adequately supported while in prison. On July 19, 1966, he sent a plea to the members of the Workshop asking for financial contributions and subscriptions to their new newsletter, *Vortex*, and requesting volunteers to teach at the Free University and offer other volunteer labor. It was a way of testing how the community might continue.[215] In November, Sinclair attempted one final time to draw together people at the Workshop, but things had splintered to the point of no return.[216]

Some members of the Workshop viewed police hostility toward them to be attributable in part to the fact that it was a racially integrated community. "Detroit was pretty segregated, but the Workshop was different," Leni Sinclair noted. "The police really didn't like that, they wanted us separated.... We were for a new way of doing things. I would hesitate to say we were participating in a revolution because the broader society resisted all of this change."[217]

On January 24, 1967, the police raided several locations operated by the Artists' Workshop looking for marijuana and LSD.[218] The operation was led by Vahan Kapagihan, who had infiltrated the Workshop, posing as "Louie," attending events and even assisting with publishing logistics. A twenty-two-person squad, including FBI agents, carried out the raid. They arrested fifty-six members and others visiting at the time, including John and Leni Sinclair; the drummer Don Moye; the saxophonist Joseph Jarman; the members of the Detroit Edison White-Light Band, "a new-consciousness rock-jazz-music band" led by Sinclair and Jim Semark; about two dozen Wayne State students; and a few high school students; among others. The band had been rehearsing and were playing

FIGURE 5.7 Joseph Jarman (1937–2019), saxophonist, in Detroit, 1965.

Source: Courtesy Leni Sinclair.

Coltrane's "A Love Supreme" at the moment the raid began.[219] Sinclair was charged for giving away two joints a month earlier and would be immortalized by John Lennon in the song bearing his name: "They gave him ten for two, what else can the bastards do?"

The members of the Workshop saw themselves as integral to broad changes then happening in the city and penned a response that stated, "In order to understand the significance of this latest police action against the Artists' Workshop community, you will have to understand that Detroit is going through an intense period of spiritual awakening, for the first time in its history, and that the Workshop people are beginning to furnish effective leadership in this cultural revolution."[220] Sinclair declared in a public statement, "They weren't interested in marijuana. They're just against our way of life. They're harassing us."[221]

GOING IN OTHER DIRECTIONS

The Workshop began to disintegrate while Sinclair was in jail, and it continued to do so through early 1967. The hippie movement had emerged in Detroit in 1966, and when Sinclair was released from prison, he found solace in it and became a leading figure there. While still interested in jazz, he began to draw blues and rock bands into his milieu, and the community evolved into a kind of hippie collective. Having become frustrated with Detroit at that time, he relocated to Ann Arbor in 1967.[222]

After the Workshop ended, Charles Moore started a large unit named Shattering Effect that had saxophone and trombone in the front line, keyboards, guitar, bass, and three drummers, including Ronald Johnson.[223] He also ran a radio program at WDET that featured a wide variety of music and sounds, free jazz and African music to whale calls.[224] But he found his most regular work with Kenny Cox's Contemporary Jazz Quintet in the late 1960s and recorded two records with them. That drew him into the circle around Strata Records, and though the band had the freest elements presented on that label, most of the music they put out was modal, post-bop, or funk-infused jazz. Moore also established a persistent presence among the musicians who recorded with the Tribe label. Moore commuted to Oberlin College to teach jazz improvisation for some years in the 1970s.[225] He remained in Detroit until 1977, when frustrations with lack of opportunities finally forced him to leave for Los Angeles. He wrote a letter to Leni Sinclair in which he stated, "Detroit is a dying city. It's so hard on artists.

The sooner I get out the better."[226] He later spent time in Ghana and received a doctorate in ethnomusicology from the University of California–Los Angeles.

John Sinclair moved to Ann Arbor and managed the MC5. In November 1968, he cofounded the White Panther Party to support the Black Power movement and to push for social and cultural revolution. "We wanted to organize white people," Sinclair declared, "especially young people, because white people were the problem. I wanted to unite the people on the Left against the government at the time and support Black revolution."[227] Many of the other artists that had been involved in the Workshop continued their work in Detroit in a variety of capacities inside and outside of free jazz. The bonds formed at that time remained strong throughout their lives through many collaborations, records, and publications.

CHAPTER 6

"MY MIND AND MY SPIRIT WERE LIBERATED DURING THE RIOT"

Faruq Z. Bey and Griot Galaxy in Detroit

When I started playing saxophone, music became a functional metaphor for a way to live. And that's what I was trying to do then, affect life, my life and the life of people around me, using music as a metaphor. Some kind of magical system of dealing with things.

—Faruq Z. Bey

SOLIDARITY MOVEMENTS IN DETROIT IN THE 1960S

The early phases of the deindustrialization of Detroit laid the groundwork for new resistance movements in the 1960s.[1] Between 1947 and 1967, metropolitan Detroit lost 47 percent of its blue-collar manufacturing jobs as new employment opportunities rapidly moved to the suburbs.[2] Young Black adult residents were particularly hard hit, with at least a quarter of them unemployed, with occasional spikes in joblessness reaching as high as 76 percent.[3] The city has never fully recovered from this deterioration as capital was carried by the same currents that resulted in white flight to the suburbs. Between 1950 and 1960, the city's Black population increased by 180,000, while its white population decreased by 350,000. These changes coincided with company executives making aggressive moves to destabilize workers' ability to organize effectively for living wages, benefits, and middle-class livelihoods. The institutionalization of power relations between the UAW and the corporations also caused the union to lose touch with significant portions of its membership, especially Black workers, by the 1960s as the latter began to increase their demands.

Malcolm X, who had formerly worked at the Lincoln-Mercury plant in Detroit, delivered his well-known "Message to the Grass Roots" speech at King Solomon Baptist Church in Detroit on November 10, 1963, in which he called for Black unity. As Michele Gibbs observed, the impact was that "he placed the objectives of the Black Liberation Movement in the United States as necessarily revolutionary," and she added, "It signaled the shift from 'speaking truth to power' to actually taking power ourselves."[4] Another member of that audience was Jesse Davis, later to be known as Faruq Z. Bey.[5] There was a proliferation of nationalist groups in Detroit through the 1960s in various forms, including the Nation of Islam, the Revolutionary Action Movement, the Black Panthers, and the Republic of New Afrika, and the city became the epicenter for many of these groups.

Attempts at cross-racial solidarity also continued in Detroit within the labor movement. Michael Hamlin, one of the leaders of the League of Revolutionary Black Workers, noted:

> My experience was that the most advanced, i.e., those who had done the most work, were struggling to find a common approach. For a lot of us that was Marxism, many others embraced Black Nationalism. Marx, Lenin, Mao [Tse-Tung], Nkrumah, Lumumba, Nyerere, Ho Chi Minh, Fidel [Castro], Che [Guevara], C. L. R. James, and Frantz Fanon were some of the influences convincing us to organize our people for power.... At this time the notion of "picking up the gun" were very attractive to both black men and women in the context of Robert Williams' and Malcolm X's call for self-defense and self-determination. But for me, a feeling of collectivity and being responsible for our people's overall well-being led me away from adventurism.... In Detroit, it led us to organize our organic base, black industrial workers who were strategically placed to shut the system down.[6]

The social dynamics in Detroit led Gibbs to argue that "with 'identity politics' cresting in the 70s, Detroit was one of the only urban contexts in which blacks and whites were able to work together and where whites accepted black leadership" within various activist movements.[7]

Every person I interviewed who grew up in Detroit in the 1940s to 1960s referred to the police as a white supremacist organization that brutalized the Black community. Black neighborhoods faced extralegal harassment, beatings, and killings meted out by rank-and-file police officers. Just in the years from 1958 to 1961, twelve Black residents of Detroit were killed with impunity by the police.[8] The police were also connected to the FBI's COINTELPRO program, which aimed at undermining and attacking Black power groups. Police brutality only increased through the 1960s. The poet and playwright Bill Harris characterized the situation as: "The police were still a constant problem for us, with their hit squads."[9] Michael Hamlin wrote, "The police were, by and large, white ethnics who wanted to be cowboys and they operated as a terror force."[10] By the early 1970s, racist policing in Detroit enacted a program called Stop the Robberies Enjoy Safe Streets (STRESS), which employed decoys to entrap and murder Black men. Over the course of the three years of the program, twenty-two men were killed by police without any repercussions.[11] The election of Coleman Young, the first African American mayor of Detroit, in 1974 would eventually "make the streets safe *from* police."[12]

THE 1967 UPRISING

Early on the morning of Sunday, July 23, 1967, undercover police officers made arrests at a community social club at 9125 Twelfth Street (later renamed Rosa Parks Boulevard) that had formerly been the site of the United Community League for Civic Action (UCLCA), an organization aimed at mobilizing Black political support in local elections.[13] After the group had become defunct, it continued as a social club, or "blind pig," which sold alcohol and permitted gambling without city-issued licenses, though such practice was not uncommon. The club bred a feeling of commitment to the community, of brotherhood, according to William Walter Scott III, who had worked as a bouncer at the club and was the son of one of the founders. He wrote:

> I developed a feeling toward my people. I began to care about what happened to them, as well as to myself. I think this made the whole difference in my life because people have got to care about each other if they are going to live together without hurting themselves. And for the most part this all they knew ... when people hurt and don't have any way to stop it, and the only people they're around is each other, then they're going to direct their anger at whoever and whatever is present or nearby at the time. Usually, the wrong people ... never the cop, or the white, and the negro store owners who cheated us out of every cent we had. No, not them, the keepers of the poor.[14]

The club was a refuge from the depredations and atrocities of everyday life. As Scott explained, "People were frustrated, they were tired, tired of police, tired of fighting and killings. It just got to their heads. It was just too much. So they danced. In the club."[15] He added, "The dim atmosphere, loud music, talking, and dancing made the club a family gathering each time we congregated. The whole affair was a brotherhood, composed of people who cared about happiness and the sharing of their mirth. Everyone was dancing, laughing, having a nitty-gritty-funky good time.... The club was trembling from the clapping of hands and the stomping of feet in rhythmic syncopation to the intoxicating music of Mr. James Brown."[16]

In the darkness before dawn on July 23, resistance to police presence outside of the club on Twelfth Street quickly erupted.[17] William Walter Scott III had been arrested in a previous raid, during which he had been beaten by police. Recalling the earlier incident, he wrote, "I wanted to fight back and hold my stand.... The cop was wrong for hitting me."[18] So in those early hours of July 23, when he approached the club and saw police arresting his father and sister, he found a bottle in the street and threw it, thinking, "I didn't care right then if they killed me."[19] Inside the club, the police had smashed the jukebox and wine bottles and had done considerable damage to the club itself, all without a warrant. Scott reflected, "I felt powerful and good inside for being a part of those who finally fought back regardless of fear" and admired the "unification of the rebellious spirit of man; a fearless spirit ordained for complete liberation of the self, combined with and supported by a community at large. Guess one could say it was like fighting and gaining your citizenship, after having given it away to obedience of the law—police law—which was a one-man judge and assassin that ruled black people."[20]

Scott's initial act of resistance was quickly joined by a chorus. From the early morning hours into the bright light of day, thousands of people joined what exploded into a mass uprising in Detroit. Despite attempts by police, firefighters, city officials, and some Black community leaders to stem the tide, the movement grew. From its epicenter, the revolt spread into neighboring streets and by the evening had moved downtown in the form of arson, looting, and destruction of businesses and residences. The Michigan National Guard, state troopers, and two US Army airborne divisions outfitted with tanks were called in, and a curfew was instituted to quell the uprising that was noted for having "no organized leadership" but was rather a wide-scale and spontaneous insurrection with considerable popular support. Pitched battles and sniper fire between residents and the authorities spread north into Dexter Linwood, east toward the North End, and further into the midwestern part of the city, reaching an apex by Tuesday and Wednesday and finally dissipating by the beginning of the following week. Approximately 40 percent of the 7,200 people arrested during the uprising were employees at the city's auto plants, and though it was Black-led, many working-class white workers, themselves southern migrants, also took part in what one scholar has called "a working-class rebellion."[21] Forty-three people were killed, thirty-three of whom were Black, at least twenty-nine slain by state forces. The Detroit uprising was the largest rebellion in the United States since the Civil War.

The poet and percussionist Sadiq Muhammad Bey, who was an eyewitness to the events, stated plainly that the prevailing mentality of the uprising was "Take what you can get."[22] Scott added, "It was a free day for everybody to do and be what he wanted, regardless of the world and its laws.... The rioters and looters did have one common interest: lack of respect for the law, the law that had abused them and their right to live."[23]

In the aftermath of the Detroit uprising, solidarity within the community continued to coalesce. One of the centerpieces was the new newspaper *Inner City Voice*. The people who had founded it came out of a decade or more of activism, including the SNCC; the all-Black Freedom Now Party, which had gained ballot access in Michigan; the radical action group UHURU; the Revolutionary Action Movement; and other organizations.[24] Some had traveled to Cuba to meet with Che Guevara. The masthead declared the paper to be Detroit's "Black Community Newspaper" and "the Voice of Revolution."

The inaugural issue began with the editorial headline "Michigan Slavery" and advocated for forward movement building out of the uprising:

> In the July Rebellion we administered a beating to the behind of the white power structure, but apparently our message didn't get over.... We are still working, still working too hard, getting paid too little, living in bad housing, sending our kids to substandard schools, paying too much for groceries, and treated like dogs by the police. We still don't own anything or control anything.... In other words we are still being systematically exploited by the system and have a responsibility to break the back of that system. Only people who are strong, unified, armed, and know the enemy can carry on the struggles which lay ahead of us. Think about it, brother, things ain't hardly getting better. The Revolution must continue.[25]

The paper bore heavy influence from Che Guevara and Malcolm X, reproduced articles by Robert Williams, published essays by the Detroit labor leader James Boggs, and reprinted speeches by C. L. R. James. The readership of the *Inner City*

Voice rapidly expanded such that within the first year of operations, they averaged ten thousand copies in their press runs.

Inner City Voice adeptly fused revolutionary ideas on a local, national, and international scale with a united front approach to contextualize the struggle in Detroit. As Dan Georgakas and Marvin Surkin observed, "The unifying ingredient in all *ICV* material was the sharp emphasis on defining the strategy and tactics of the ongoing black liberation struggle and how it might prefigure and trigger a second American revolution."[26] One of the leading figures behind the paper, John Watson, worked "to present complicated ideological analyses of capitalism in a popular style which made the leap from theory to practice," as in this statement: "To struggle in our own interest means that black people of the ghetto must struggle to overthrow white capitalism. The struggle against capitalism is world wide and the revolutionary struggle of the ghetto is crucial and essential in the over all world revolution. If the Koreans and Vietnamese can overthrow imperialism in Asia then Asia will be free. But if the Black Revolution can overthrow capitalism and imperialism in the U.S., then the whole world will be freed. This, then, is our role."[27] Even when covering local grievances with housing, jobs, and education, the paper framed them in a way that critiqued the entire American social order.[28]

The strong revolutionary sentiment of *Inner City Voice* quickly attracted reactionaries, whether from the American Legion or the John Birch Society spinoff group Breakthrough, which carried out physical attacks against antiwar protesters. The FBI began to intimidate and harass print shops that produced the paper, eventually pushing the editors to move production to the same Chicago print shop that produced *Muhammad Speaks*, the paper of the Nation of Islam. One of the primary foci for the people involved in the paper manifested in the Dodge Revolutionary Union Movement, which formed in 1968, calling for major strikes and fundamental changes to the relationship between labor and production in Detroit.

Within the Black nationalist movement, the Republic of New Afrika had a central presence in Detroit in the late 1960s and early 1970s. On March 31, 1968, the RNA formed a provisional government at a convention of over five hundred people that drafted a constitution, declared independence from the United States, and elected Robert F. Williams as its president in exile. The organization aimed to inform people of African descent that an alternative state existed and to implement economic, diplomatic, and political strategies designed to free the diaspora "from the captive control of the United States." A year later, on March 29, 1969, after a police officer was killed in what the RNA claimed to be an attempted assassination of their vice-president, Gaidi Obadele, there was a shootout at Detroit

New Bethel Baptist Church, which resulted in injuries and the arrests of the 142 people gathered there, who were only released after an intervention by Rev. C. L. Franklin (father of Aretha Franklin) in the aftermath. The RNA then moved its primary base of operations to land they owned in Hinds County, Mississippi, where, on August 18, 1971, the FBI pursued them and attacked its leaders, imprisoning many of them for decades on trumped-up murder charges. Amnesty International considered those imprisoned to be political prisoners. The RNA was formative in the consciousness of many young Detroiters of the period who were then coming of age, some of whom were also involved in the music scene.[29]

ARTISTIC SELF-DETERMINATION AND THE DETROIT UPRISING OF 1967

From the fires of the Detroit uprising, there emerged one of the city's most profound artists: the saxophonist and music theorist Faruq Z. Bey (1942–2012). Music had been stirring inside of him for some years, but in 1966 and 1967, two pivotal events formed a turning point that compelled him to embrace the avant-garde for the rest of his life. The first was hearing the John Coltrane Quintet with Pharoah Sanders play at the Drome Lounge in Detroit during their residency there, June 17–26, 1966.[30] "It impacted me to the core," Bey reflected many years later. "I had never heard any music that deep or profound before. It shook me to my root. My entire attitude about music changed."[31]

Bey was born Jesse Davis and grew up in the Conant Gardens neighborhood on the northeastern side of Detroit, a highly educated community that traced its roots all the way back to the milieu that surrounded the Detroit Anti-Slavery Society, which had been founded there in 1837. His father was an auto plant floor worker and later a city bus driver. Bey's parents sang in gospel choirs, and he developed his earliest harmonic sense with his two cousins, the bebop musicians Charles Rowland and Sherrell Rowland, whom he jammed with while he was growing up. He also grew up near the R&B singer Eddie Floyd, who performed with the band the Falcons. Known as "Big Jesse Davis" because of his tall, broad frame, Bey studied bass with James Tatum at Pershing High School and had been writing poetry since age thirteen. He later studied mathematics and existentialism at Wayne County Community College.[32] His first horn was a euphonium.[33] He switched to tenor saxophone after spending a brief period in the US Air Force, and after returning to Detroit he became a disciple of the Moorish Science Temple, changing his name first to Malik and then to Faruq Zinji Bey.

FIGURE 6.1 Faruq Z. Bey (1944–2010), saxophonist.
Source: Courtesy Leni Sinclair.

Bey had already become a dedicated follower of Coltrane back when he played with the Miles Davis Quintet and became even more interested after he released *My Favorite Things*. "I was approaching music entirely from one angle until I heard Trane play at the Drome. It affected me intellectually and spiritually," Bey explained. "That's when I realized that the real expression of what has come to be called music is a totally unifying force, a unifying energy that brings every aspect of your existence and being into play. I saw that clearly when I saw Trane and Pharoah."[34] He added, "When I first heard Trane, I knew that was what I wanted to do."[35] He regarded Malcolm X to have shaped his political vision and Coltrane to have focused his spiritual yearning.[36] In the ensuing years, Ornette Coleman, Sun Ra, John Gilmore, Anthony Braxton, and Roscoe Mitchell would also serve as significant influences, though Bey did not see what he was doing as purely a linear development from them.[37]

The other major spark for Bey was the Detroit uprising. The night before it broke out, Bey and his friends had gathered for a celebration of the life of Coltrane, who had passed away just five days earlier, and they stayed up all night. In that moment, the music gripped Bey, and he realized he needed to play saxophone and pursue that course with his life. "Detroit had all kinds of oppression and repression entrenched in it," Bey stated. "The uprising was a reaction to that, the police violence, the unhealthy political attitude of the city. It was inevitable. My mind and my spirit were liberated during the riot."[38]

Bey further observed, "The people who were rioting in the street, they moved like one mind. It was almost like a hive of insects moves. It was like a wave; it just moved, but that whole episode put me in a frame of mind of thinking about our position here as a subculture, and how to deal with that. And since music was always an interest of mine and seeing how our music defined itself and our relationship to the greater environment as well . . ."[39] Bey's frequent early collaborator Sadiq Muhammad Bey noted, "It was post-riot Detroit. It was all wide open. We were brand-new people. Whatever we wanted to be, we could be. We were making jewelry, making art, performing. It was a renaissance. Everybody was a renaissance man. It was incredible."[40]

In a material way, Bey "liberated" his tenor saxophone during the uprising and began to play regularly.[41] The doors to self-expression had been blown open. One of his first teachers was Leon Henderson, the older brother of the alto saxophonist Joe Henderson, who, Bey stated, "really opened me up to all of the theoretical and technical possibilities of the horn. And he exposed me to people like Joseph Schillinger."[42]

One writer from Detroit noted that in the aftermath of the uprising, "it was a time of heightened social consciousness and artistic innovation."[43] Bey's first collaborators were people he knew in the community around 1968 including Abdul Jalil Bey, Abu Ishak, Sadiq Muhammad Bey, and Marcus Townsend. At the time, Bey used the name Aindido, and the group mostly played hand drums when they gathered. "It was such an incredible connection that we just decided to live together as a commune sort of thing. It just grew from that. Guys brought their girlfriends in and people started having kids, and it was just this huge family, and we all decided to be Beys," Sadiq Muhammad Bey explained.[44]

"Faruq was our leader," Sadiq Muhammad Bey stated, "even though Abdul Jalil was older, Faruq was the chief of our tribe. We depended on each other to be other, to be far out, so that we could go far into ourselves."[45] Faruq Z. Bey was a charismatic figure, encouraging other musicians around him, and emboldening them as they worked toward artistic envisioning. They lived together communally with their families and were regularly joined by activists, painters, jewelers, musicians, poets, and fashion designers, bound together by a common life philosophy, identity, and a commitment to Black cultural revolution.

Their music developed organically from that point, with musicians bringing in other instruments as the group crystallized as the First African Primal Rhythm Arkestra, comprising the tenor saxophonist Faruq Z. Bey, alto saxophonist Abdul Jalil Bey, bassist and poet Abu Ishak, and euphonium player Sadiq Muhammad Bey. They would invite different bassists and drummers to join them for gigs around Detroit within the community connected to the Moorish Science Temple, especially at the Concept East Theater, where they performed as the orchestra for Leroi Jones's play *A Black Mass*, among other things.[46] Performing at Concept East placed them at the center of Detroit's thriving theater scene, which was at the cutting edge of Black theater nationally, with many local, accomplished playwrights debuting work there. When the First African Primal Rhythm Arkestra was joined by numerous other people in the community, they called themselves the Bey Brothers or Bey Family. "It was wild, a lot of free stuff," Bey remarked nearly a decade later.[47] They played free and searched for harmony together in sound.

The Bey Family studied Sufism as part of a mutual spiritual commitment. This often involved the study of Islamic poetry such as the *Divan of Hafez*, by the fourteenth-century Persian poet Khwāji Shams al-Dīn Muḥammad Ḥafeẓi Shīrāzī (c. 1325–90), known commonly as Hafez. Hafez practiced theosophy, writing mystical ghazals that were entirely inspired by Muslim holy texts culminating in the Quran. Music was sometimes woven into mystical practice in Hafez's verse:

> Brave tales of singers and wine relate,
> The key to the Hidden 'twere vain to seek;
> No wisdom of ours has unlocked the gate,
> And locked to our wisdom it still shall be.

Or as in this verse:

> What instrument through last night's silence rang?
> My life into his lay the minstrel wove,
> And filled my brain with the sweet song he sang.
> It was the proclamation of thy love
> That shook the strings of Life's most secret lyre,
> And still my breast heaves with last night's desire,
> For countless echoes from that music sprang.[48]

The group also studied works by the Sufi mystic and poet Jalāl al-Dīn Muḥammad Rūmī (1207–1273), who was gaining in popularity at the time. These shared interests in Islamic mysticism and literature played a role in deepening their mutual spiritual commitments, and they began to pray together, and gradually they became Muslims as part of a wider-scale conversion within the Black community around 1970–1971.[49]

The group also shared a love for the music of John Coltrane, John Tchicai, James Blood Ulmer, the Art Ensemble of Chicago, and especially Archie Shepp, because he worked poetry into his music. They also closely followed a local group composed of the trombonist Patrick Lanear, alto saxophonist Billy Higgins, bassist John Dana, and drummer Doug Hammond. "We were anti-bebop at the time," Sadiq Muhammad Bey noted. Faruq Z. Bey, Abdul Jalil Bey, and Sadiq Muhammad Bey wrote their own poetry, composed pieces drawn from their improvisations, and combined them into their live performances. They played around Detroit until the mid-1970s but never released any recordings. "It was orchestral music, set up for small ensemble," Sadiq Muhammad Bey explained.[50]

Bey was direct in expressing a desire to move away from bebop in his own playing:

> They've turned [bebop] into a classical, crystallized form. And consequently killing it. It can't live and grow, because every step you make toward locking the form in is a step toward killing the form itself because it's no longer spiritually alive.... The crystallization of a form to me represents the form at its least effective, because at that point the form itself has ceased to grow and change. It has ceased to be affected by other forces around it. So consequently it's locked in. It's dead. Life is motion, death is stasis.... In terms of being translated into working metaphors for living people, living forces, that is no longer useful except as a reference. In my estimation, since I'm alive and caught up in the thralldom of living, I'm only interested in those things that are alive. I will take time out to observe crystallized forms as reference, but I can't spend my life studying death.[51]

Then turning to his own approach, Bey stated:

> I see what is called "improvisation" as the process of making living music. I only see that as a metaphor, and the more you can stretch that metaphor the more meanings you can give it in a positive way.... I see that any piece of music I write I try to make it a microcosmic equation for the macrocosmic equation that I'm living in. I try to have it reflect my own existence in terms of my environment. So all of the forces in my environment are brought to bear on it. Consequently, in terms of the "classical" approach to composing music, I have to break a lot of laws. Because that approach to make music does not apply to the times that I'm living in.... So consequently my music is constantly changing, and I hope that

it continues to until I die, and that shows me that it's still alive and capable of responding to the environment itself as I live in it.[52]

Bey was very much in dialogue with thought contemporary to the Black Arts Movement in the early 1970s, such as the ideas that were gathered together in the landmark book *The Black Aesthetic*.[53]

EARLY FORMATIONS OF GRIOT GALAXY

As much as he had learned through these early musical explorations, Bey wanted to have a band that he could work with to refine musical concepts more directly. In 1972, he gathered musicians around him to form the group Griot Galaxy, taking the name from the French word for the Manding term *jali*, the West African tradition of praise singer–historian-musician-poets who passed down knowledge, law, and historical memory over the generations. The band name also referenced what Bey referred to as "infinities of space and music."[54] "We were griots," Sadiq Muhammad Bey stated, "in our galaxy."[55] Or as Jaribu Shahid observed, "It was Faruq's way of saying 'Ancient to the Future' like AACM."[56]

Bey further explained, "There was a lot of great free playing going on, but I wanted to put that together with traditional elements. I was influenced by what Roscoe Mitchell was doing; I wanted to explore new compositional forms."[57] When Bey heard something, he could quickly reproduce it, in his own way, which informed his approach to developing compositions that were steeped in his own imagination. "He had a carefree mind," Sadiq Muhammad Bey explained, "so he was always open to new things."[58] The earliest formation often consisted of a trio, with the bassist Dauud Abdul Khafiz and drummer Tariq Abdul Samad, who were all part of the Moorish Science Temple community. Abdul Samad "sounded like water and walked around in a constant state of prayer."[59] The alto saxophonist Charles Miles and percussionist Barbara Huby (known then as Mama Hoodoo) also participated in early sessions.

By the mid-1970s, Faruq Z. Bey's vision for Griot Galaxy was shifting; he wanted to trim down the group to allow the music to grow in new directions.[60] He became acquainted with a new wave of musicians who were about a decade younger, such as the bassist and bass guitarist Jaribu Shahid, clarinetist Elreta Dodds, flutist and harpist Patrice Williams (who later changed her name to Kafi Patrice Nassoma), drummer Darryl Pierce, and percussionist Mubarak Hakim, while also retaining Sadiq Muhammad Bey, on congas and poetry, and Abdul

FIGURE 6.2 Faruq Z. Bey (1944–2010), saxophonist, in Detroit, 1977.

Source: Courtesy Leni Sinclair.

Jalil Bey. They were occasionally joined by other musicians, including the bassists Kuumba Kyo and Shoo-Bee-Do, pianists Abdul Rauuf and Ken Thomas, and electric guitarist Horace Harlaque.[61]

Shahid's introduction to jazz was through Coltrane's *Ascension*, and he had gained experience playing around Detroit with Kamal Kenyatta, Kenny Cox, Phil Ranelin, and Wendell Harrison. Shahid also liked fusion and listened to Miles Davis and Wayne Shorter. He had previously met Bey in the First African Primal Rhythm Arkestra. Shahid was also coming of age with organizations like the Republic of New Afrika and the Pan-African Congress. "The music was inseparable from the politics and other culture of the time. I approached music in the same way, as rebellion," Shahid stated, "like Sun Ra said that within every people there are a few who are responsible for maintaining their ethnic structure, so I thought that was something we had to do. Every generation has to do that. Jazz had changed throughout its history with influences from everything happening around it and at that time we were pushing it further ahead."[62] Shahid went to Philadelphia and lived at the Sun Ra house for a period in 1978, during which time he absorbed some of the latter's philosophies and aesthetics. Shahid became familiar with Islam primarily through Bey, Abdul Jalil Bey, and others of the Griot Galaxy circle.

Dodds, who was both classically trained and influenced by gospel, had studied at Cass Technical High School, where she was a classmate of the pianist Geri Allen.[63] While attending Wayne State University, she met Bey and soon joined the band. "I felt like we were all equals," Dodds stated. "It wasn't until years later that I realized how unusual it was to have two female instrumentalists in the band at that time and that was due to Faruq's leadership."[64] Nassoma had grown up in a musical family and had been inspired at age seventeen, when she witnessed a live performance by the harpist Dorothy Ashby. She acquired her first harp in 1972 while also later playing flute with Griot Galaxy.[65] She had become enamored with the music of Sun Ra and felt that Bey was working in a similar aesthetic.[66] The band held most of their early sessions at a private residence in nearby Pontiac, at the home of the bassist and vocalist Reginald Fields, known as Shoo-Bee-Do, occasionally at Wayne State University, and at Bey's home on the western edges of the Dexter Linwood neighborhood. The group played music during their rehearsals, of course, but Nassoma recalled that some sessions were entirely devoted to philosophical discussions and that sometimes they were listening sessions that covered everything from Andean pan pipes to Balinese chanting.[67]

At the core of the group's concept was polyrhythms and unusual meters, though it was commonly bass line and melody driven. The only nonoriginal compositions the band played were Charlie Parker's piece "Scrapple from the Apple" and Ornette Coleman's "Law Years."[68] Bey liked to employ a variety of scales and modes, and as the scholar Kofi Natambu has argued, "What distinguished Bey's individual contribution to the recent tradition was an equally committed and creative appropriation and extension of ancient traditional modes, expressive forms, and structures culled from North and West African sources as well as 'Middle Eastern' ideas and modes from Arabic and Islamic traditions."[69] Bey saw himself connecting his present existence in Detroit with ancient Africa, Egypt, and Mesopotamia through a kind of "rhythmic consonance."

As Bey noted, he became aware of direct connections to West Africa at an early age. "When I was thirteen, my great-grandmother told me for the first time that on her side of the family we were Bantu people," Bey said. "I wanted to find out more about those people. Both of her parents were Bantu and she was born in slavery but the library claimed that there were no such books, no such things about African history." Through the years, he had studied the history privately, which contributed to his consciousness. "There were an awful lot of Muslim brothers over in Africa stolen illegally. Once you know the real story of things you have a better idea of who you are."[70]

DECOLONIZING BLACK MUSIC

Bey was decolonial in his approach and conception. In 1983, reflecting back, he stated,

I've heard music that they call "primitive" from Africa and other parts of the world, South India, the Aborigines, the so-called "primitive people," and in terms of the production of the music, in terms of the emotional feelings that are expressed in the music and the response of the people, this is the most perfect music that you can conceive of. I think this attitude is another effect of the elitism of certain social groups to set up a hierarchy of standards and then compare the works of entire cultures to some arbitrary standards that were set up by people who don't even understand the cultures that they're commenting on. In other words, to say that this music is primitive and therefore substandard, say the music of the Bantu people, which is some of the most highly evolved harmonic, melodic and most definitely rhythmic music in the world or that the world has ever seen, and then to compare it to European symphonic music and say that the Bantu music is inferior to European music is just sheer arrogance and racism.[71]

Bey aimed directly at critics and scholars, especially when they applied European standards to what music was or what a performance was supposed to be:

Most "critics," most "pundits," most so-called "scholars" have no idea of the composer's or the performer's or the improviser's intent. The only person you can really ask what his objective is in terms of something that is close to a person's entire life force, his whole soul, his spirit, the only person you can really ask and establish any kind of measurement is the person himself.... They should ask them, "What are you trying to achieve?" ... I don't value the opinion of the scholar any more than someone off the street. Because I'm reaching at something deeper than a person's intellect.[72]

Bey further elaborated,

Personally I think music that's structurally based in improvisation speaks more to the reality of the times than a music that speaks to conditions and an environment that existed four or five hundred years ago. Any musician who is sensitive to the nuances of the music can tell you that the notation system is a very shallow interpretation of music ... the notation only gives you the skeleton of what the music really was. That music that was produced by Bach, Beethoven and those people is gone. It will never happen again. Any music that happens is gone and will never happen again, just like Eric Dolphy said. And what you got by the notation system is just a very meager reference to what happened. Because music is sound and not paper. People ... mistake the symbol for reality. If you mistake the symbol for reality, you wind up with a two-dimensional reality instead of the multidimensional reality that is given to us at birth. This is our birthright, our spiritual birthright.[73]

Pointing to the African roots of his thinking, Bey wrote a poignant poem titled "Mizimu," a Swahili word meaning "souls, ghosts, or spirits."

> He is here
> The one who looked beneath
> The gleaming shell of ether
> Behind the deceptive shade
> Of the matrix
> and saw there
> The shining eye of God
> He has arrived . . . we
> Have smuggled him in by night
> Wearing the hateful garb
> of your derision bearing
> the awful weight of your
> threats and boasts, in the dark
> morass we conjured
> like fifty year old Brazilian
> Pickaninnies huddled around the
> cauldron
> making Gnagna the spirit
> we make and we make
> but we do not remake
> and so we called him
> the one you called the primitive . . .
> savage
> and you worked other such
> sad and hollow juju
> and you bellowed, belching
> anguishes and swamp gas
> because he was not like you
> But we called him anyway
> and He came
> The GrandFather
> Mizimu the watcher

> Mizimu the wielder of past
> and futures like great and fiery
> swords
> Mizimu soul of glass
> hard with this sheen
> untouched by your grey
> incredible dullness
> Mizimu we are here
> in brilliant and florid death
> we are Mizimu ... here[74]

"My music sounds conversational because music is derived from speech," Faruq Z. Bey stated.[75] He was influenced by Amiri Baraka's idea that languages are infused with logic. Bey argued, "Language is a logic you speak. And when you get into ... music, you get into a different language. With a different logic you deal with different syllogistic principles and different conclusions."[76]

> There is a linear evolution from African tonal languages to jazz. Changing the tones lends meaning to the vowel-consonant. If you listen to English as a tonal language, often when a question is asked, the voice of the speaker goes up by a tritone. A tritone or a flat five is a sonic question mark. When we return to the one, it is inflective of peace, correctness, or resolution. An interval has a different meaning in a musical environment than it does in a language. In music it is abstract and is divorced from meaning, it is pleasant or unpleasant. The flat five always indicates instability. In wave form, the flat five challenges the tonic. It is exactly antithetical to the tonic, it challenges it. So that is what a question does, it challenges the reality as you present it. It asks, are you sure?[77]

BUILDING A BODY OF WORK

"Faruq was the type of bandleader who allowed everyone in the group to express themselves musically, in playing and composition," Dodds explained. "Faruq had no problem allowing other group members to contribute original material. He encouraged it."[78] Shahid, Dodds, Nassoma, and Sadiq Muhammad Bey all contributed pieces to Griot Galaxy's expanding corpus of material. Dodds's piece "Time Capsule" was composed in a 10/4 meter, for example, and other pieces were in 5/4 or other odd meters, though many did have grooves.[79] Band members brought charts to the group, and they worked them out together, usually first with the horns, then adding percussion once they had the melodies and harmonies worked out. "It's a collective," Bey stated in reference to the band's process. "And in any state that you see that collective in, it just reflects whatever that equation is calling for at that time."[80]

At the time, Bey noted, "The music has kind of changed. It's more rhythmic now with a lot of odd meters, Oriental modes, a primal kind of music."[81] As Natambu stated, "Through engaging in deep collaborations and creative exchanges with . . . members of Griot Galaxy . . . Bey created the basic compositional and improvisational template that subsequently became the structural and spiritual foundation of the powerfully original, hypnotic, and electrifying music"[82] The band first played at a coffee shop that Bey and other members of the Muslim community operated, and their first significant concerts came at the Afro-American Festival in Detroit in March 1976.[83] Their music was alternatively referred to as avant-garde, urban folk, and percussion jazz by contemporary critics.[84]

The band often played at events connected to the Muslim community of Detroit, such as one concert on September 4, 1976, as part of the celebration of Ramadan. One attendee described the impact as

> the spectators . . . were transformed into spiritual oneness. . . . The only high winds on this pleasant day were from Patrice Williams' flute solo, swirling melodically together with Elreta's merciful bass clarinet in Viking II-like orbit. The thunder and enlightenment caused by Brother Abdul Jalil Bey's alto saxophone was to be expected, while the loping and subdued conga playing of Brother Saleem provided more than enough gravity for the violin section, which featured Brother Mansu from Pontiac. Together with the continuously creative drumming of [Tariq] Abdul Samad, creating sound of earthquake-like proportions, the double basses of Abdul Nur and Brother Dauud [Abdul Khafiz] did not let up—plucking, throbbing.[85]

During the last half of the 1970s, Griot Galaxy got regular work in Detroit, especially at Cobb's Corner, situated at Cass Avenue and North Willis Street. It evolved from a rough dive bar with a reputation for fistfights to the premier jazz venue in the city and booked the band weekly on Monday nights for nearly two years.[86] It was there that they built a strong local following, and as Shahid noted, "Cobb's gave us a place to develop what we were doing. We went from raw to really good there."[87] Griot Galaxy developed its original repertoire at the venue; Bey composed a majority of the pieces for the group. The music was laden with visual and musical cues and bore spiritual commitments. Sadiq Muhammad Bey referred to their music as "an act of worship" bringing Muslims and Christians together in spiritual oneness.[88] They developed a dedicated following that aside from the general public included "a lot of artists, painters, a lot of poets, a lot of writers [who] were interested in the band."[89]

Of one gig at Cobb's Corner, a critic wrote:

> The drummer takes off softly on his own. The flute picks up what sounds like a chant and is joined by the string bass stroked by a long bow. The sax moves in with its incisive bite, and the three additional percussionists begin to pound, shake and rattle their hardware with a varied pulsating beat that glues the whole thing together. The unusual makeup of Griot Galaxy allows for sharp contrasts and deep changes, Faruq Bey, spiritual and musical leader of the group, softens sax for a duet with the sweet flute or turns it harsh to match the dry clarinet. A soprano sax and bowed bass duet is as daunting as Debussy, and the harp speaks gently, but they also take off like startled birds and crow wildly in their flight.[90]

At Cobb's Corner, the band also often asked figures like the trumpeter Marcus Belgrave, saxophonist Donald Walden, and guitarist A. Spencer Barefield to sit in with them.

Though the band was not overtly political in its general practice, they did perform at a fundraiser to support the gubernatorial candidate Zolton Ferency in May 1978.[91] Ferency had previously run unsuccessfully in 1966 as a Democrat but had split off to form the socialist-oriented Human Rights Party in 1970 in protest of his former party's support of the Vietnam War. Ferency was again unsuccessful in 1978 but had broad support from within the Black community. Griot Galaxy retained an activist presence, performing at benefits to express solidarity with the people of El Salvador against right-wing US-backed paramilitary groups in 1984 and to raise money to oppose Apartheid in South Africa in the later 1980s.[92]

Occasionally Bey invited others to sit in with the band, such as the guitarist Horace Harlaque, alto saxophonist Anthony Holland, bassist Eric Anderson, drummer Darryl Pierce, and others. The band also sometimes played at the First Unitarian-Universalist Church and various theaters, concert halls, and libraries in the city through the late 1970s.[93] Their residency at Cobb's Corner came to an abrupt end when one of the owners, Henry Normile, was shot on January 27, 1979.[94] The band managed to secure a regular Wednesday night gig at Club Con Brio through the following summer and, in the fall, played regularly at the Soup Kitchen Saloon, which was situated in an old building in the riverfront warehouse district.[95] But for the most part, Griot Galaxy never really had a strong presence in the Detroit bar or club scene after about 1980 and mostly played at regional festivals and at arts institutions from that point forward.[96]

Around the same time as the decline of the scene at Cobb's Corner, Griot Galaxy was booked for the Detroit Jazz Artists on Tour program, funded by the Michigan Council for the Arts to tour through different parts of Michigan outside of Detroit, which brought them to Ann Arbor, Lansing, and elsewhere. Around that time, one writer described the band as "immense, towering over you and throwing out shafts of light to the far reaches of your mind."[97]

GRIOT GALAXY BECOMES A QUINTET

In late 1977, the drummer and tabla player Tani Tabbal began playing regularly with Griot Galaxy, and he had an immediate, transformative presence.[98] He had grown up in Chicago, where his mother introduced him to the music of Sarah Vaughan as a child, which exposed him to the drummer Roy Haynes. His father introduced him to Thelonious Monk, Charles Mingus, and Miles Davis, and by high school he was learning to play funk and rock music, and, as he noted, he "got to see how all of these kinds of music came from each other."[99] His earliest professional experience came at age fourteen, with the singer-songwriter, playwright, poet, and activist Oscar Brown Jr. (1926–2005). After some concerts with Brown in Philadelphia, he met musicians who played with Sun Ra, and he soon after joined the latter's band and toured with him for a year and a half.

But through his teenage years, Tabbal became acquainted with many of the figures in the AACM, especially Phil Cohran, Muhal Richard Abrams, Wallace McMillen, and Roscoe Mitchell; he also had family in Detroit and New York, so he frequented those cities in his youth as well. He was eventually drawn to Detroit around 1976 because "there was time to hang with cats there and to really develop the music that I wanted to do."[100] He first joined a group called Pyramid, a trio with Bey and Shahid, which functioned as a collective workshop for them to experiment with odd meters and with a variety of non-Western scales. By 1978, they also began to include the saxophonist and flutist David McMurray, which they called Pyramid +1. This band eventually became the basis for the new Griot Galaxy. Bey retained Shahid and Tabbal and added the alto and soprano saxophonist Anthony Holland in 1979. Barefield had a brief stint with the group before McMurray also joined in mid-1980, giving the band a three-saxophone front line.[101] This new formation allowed them to weave three-part free harmony over the rhythm section.

Anthony Holland had studied at Michigan State University and met A. Spencer Barefield there in 1971. They were both losing interest in fusion and had a shared interest in the Art Ensemble of Chicago and Cecil Taylor. The Creative Arts Collective (CAC) grew out of mentorship from Roscoe Mitchell during the years that the Art Ensemble of Chicago moved to Lansing. The CAC then moved to Detroit. Tabbal soon gravitated to the CAC orbit as well after working with Sun Ra.[102]

McMurray was an eclectic musician who had grown up listening to a range of music, from Anthony Braxton and John Coltrane to Frank Zappa and the MC5.[103] At the time that he met Bey, he was studying at Wayne State University. "I think Faruq appreciated my openness to many different kinds of music. When I joined the band," McMurray explained, "they already had the group, their songs, and their concepts worked out, so I just melded into it. It was the most adventurous music that I had ever played." In reference to Bey, McMurray noted, "He had a big personality, but not a big ego. He was very approachable."[104]

"There were too many variables when the group was big," Bey stated, referring to the previous lineups he had employed in the band between 1972 and 1980. He felt that with a smaller group, he could "better manipulate the forces."[105] "When Tani came we were really able to refine what we were doing," Shahid stated. "He had learned a lot from playing with Sun Ra with odd meters and different modes and when he joined it became easy musically to do what we had been trying to do before."[106] When Bey wanted the bass in five and the drums in seven (with the rhythms meeting on one in each bar), such as for the piece, "Song of the Kente Nobles," Shahid and Tabbal could easily implement that structure, allowing the horns to, at times, play free melodies over the top. They also explored music with no discernible beat at all, which one poet observer referred to as "ecstatic energy space."[107] As much as their meters are generally classified as "unusual," Tabbal noted, "that's just how we were hearing things. That's why we got together to make music. It felt quite natural to us."[108] This kind of rhythmic complexity became one of the defining features of the Detroit sound.

"Our music was about rebellion, but it was also about extending Black music forms," Shahid explained. "Regardless of what we were doing with time, there was still groove."[109] As their former bandmate Sadiq Muhammad Bey wrote of the band in 1980, "Griot Galaxy . . . is a group of musician/composers that have survived the insurrection and pacification of contemporary music in the last decade. Their force at times is something to contend with, their style is not reminiscent of any one composer, although an influence of several modern contributors is heard in their music. The power to incite the emotions to outright pleasure, pain, and indifference has erupted in the scientific writing of Faruq and

Griot Galaxy."[110] Griot Galaxy established itself as one of the most rhythmically complex bands of the 1980s. Bey wrote most of their pieces, though Shahid, Tabbal, and occasionally Holland also composed music for the group. Many pieces that they developed were never recorded.[111]

The band members also began donning silver face paint and branded themselves as a "new wave science fiction band," which Bey explained as "a response to a modern environment speaking about androids and robots and that sort of thing," as opposed to the Art Ensemble of Chicago's performative focus on African ritual and history. Indeed, as much as the members of Griot Galaxy admired Sun Ra and the Art Ensemble of Chicago, they resolutely advocated for their own aesthetic both in their music and their theatrics. It was a different brand of Afrofuturistic performativity, one rooted in the Motor City, which owed so much of its supposed glory to technological innovation and advance. "Chicago had AACM, we had our own thing," McMurray explained. "Our thing was very visual, earthy, it was all coming out of Detroit. Even for people who didn't really understand our music, the visuals clued them in."[112] Even in his personal attire, Bey shifted from African-style garb in the 1970s to biker's leather in the following decade. At other times, the band was described as "polytonal space funk."[113]

Their former bandmate Sadiq Muhammad Bey wrote of their performativity in 1980, "Before their performance, one notices galvanized garbage cans, buckets, assorted saxophones, and percussion instruments scattered about the stage. But the silver painted faces that appear behind the instruments set the environmental mood for exploring human emotion. The listener is immediately grabbed up into the arms of Griot Galaxy and sped off into other worlds of innovation. Some call it Jazz, some call it avant-garde. Some even (ambiguously) call it new wave . . . Space Music."[114] Bey added his own perspective: "I call it the logical extension of urban folk music. While I'm not particularly carried away by designations, the term 'urban folk music' closely approximates what we're trying to do and has even more profound implications for the future."[115]

In further explaining their stage theatrics, Bey stated:

> In the old sense, ritual is a form of sympathetic magic. . . . In that sense, the ritual is to remind the people of the analog nature of the world that we live in. Like the Hindu say, "All is Maya, or illusion." And we have to remember that: Everything is an illusion. And by remembering that and being conscious of that, then the illusion falls under our manipulation, it falls under our sway. We thereby gain a certain amount of control over the nature and the direction of the illusion. So we can use that analog to describe certain things. There will always be ritual in human existence, because ritual is the symbolic analog to an activity that's going

on, on another level. The reality . . . has all these different layers from the microcosm to the macrocosm. And like these analogs hold throughout that whole structure and that whole hierarchy. This process of relating one level of concreteness to one level of metaphor until you arrive at the core of truth.[116]

Bey commonly rooted his understanding of music in mathematics. In fact, he often saw no separation between the two. "Old cultures never differentiated between music and mathematics. What Griot Galaxy is trying to accomplish is a recognition of spiritual technology as well as physical." In a way, he saw Griot Galaxy as the meeting place of this spiritual and physical fusion, noting that primary influences were, "spiritually, Coltrane, Sun Ra, Ornette Coleman, and Roscoe Mitchell. Physically, Schillinger, Stravinsky, Darius Milhaud." Bey considered improvisation to be a paradox, in that "in order to improvise properly, one must bear in mind the original theme, as well as whatever new data one is trying to bring to the form. . . . It's impulsive. It is predicated by one's total experience. . . . Intuition is the facility that synthesizes *apriori* knowledge with the unknown."[117] Improvising, for Bey, was a spiritual experience.

In the early 1980s, tensions existed within the band on how and where to grow. Bey generally had a more laid-back approach to getting gigs and openly expressed a disinterest in trying to take the band to New York, stating, "I've been to New York a couple of times. I've looked around. But, I'm from [Detroit]."[118] Shahid and Tabbal, who had both played more in New York and elsewhere, wanted to push harder to get beyond Detroit. The band primarily played in Detroit, elsewhere in Michigan, and regularly in Windsor, Toronto, and other places in Canada.[119]

Bey also ran a popular radio show on WDET called *Met-azzthetics*, which featured free jazz and other kinds of music. "It was the pipeline for adventurous music in Detroit," McMurray noted, "and at that time I joked that Faruq was a rock star. He was one of the most popular people in the city then."[120] Through the show, he met the producer and promoter Ron DeCorte, who began recording the band's live performances and ultimately set up the recording sessions for the group's debut record, *Kins*.[121] They did not have access to an established studio, so they set up their own studio and effectively recorded the sessions live.[122] The critic Kim Heron noted that "just as one of the saxophones is peaking in a solo the other two come back with a fragment of the melody shoving the soloist even harder. It's a technique that is both effective and accessible."[123]

The record opened with Bey's piece, "Xy-Moch," which placed simple, interlaced melodies over bass and drums that were set at different meters, giving the horns light forward movement. Tabbal's piece, "Zycron," in many ways takes this further, with more repetitive melodies that involve more dissonance, but also takes on an ethereal, evaporative quality. Shahid displayed brilliant arco playing both in group interplay and in his solos. "Zenolog Aintro" offered more driving, unison melodies over a groove beat. Shahid's piece, "Androgeny," was the contemplative core to the record; it patiently adds ideas to the growing musical organism, though at times the piece isolates a few elements amid ample use of space to drive home its ideas. These various themes coalesce in Bey's title track, where the band exhibits its most playful interaction.

Heron further argued that "few bands have had as much success as Griot Galaxy in packing the energy of the avant-garde jazz movement into a compact and individual style." Heron attributed much of that to the rhythm section of Shahid and Tabbal and described the latter as "an original stylist with an affinity for blasting out long, jagged rhythmic patterns."[124] At the time, Bey still considered Coltrane, Sun Ra, Indian ragas, and some classical composers to have led him toward employing unusual or complex meters.

The quintet came together in time to play at the inaugural Montreux-Detroit International Jazz Festival in September 1980, a recurring event that continued through the decade, highlighting many bands from the greater Detroit area, as well as bringing bands from Switzerland, Finland, England, and elsewhere.[125] Griot Galaxy was one of the featured bands at the festival and presented their music together with poetry. Griot Galaxy appeared annually at the festival until 1987, and their live sets were recorded in 1980, 1981, and 1983. With the release of *Kins* and the live recordings, the band began to get radio play not only in Detroit and Windsor but on National Public Radio and at college and public radio stations in other parts of the country, such as in Tallahassee, San Francisco, Tucson, Missoula (MT), Indianapolis, La Crosse (WI), Berkeley, San Mateo (CA), Ithaca (NY), Pittsfield (MA), Jackson (MS), and Boston, reaching a peak in 1984.[126]

Griot Galaxy integrated many poems into their music over the years. Bey described the intent of their music and poetry in visual terms: "painting metaphorical frame-scapes . . . doing a giant painting, with all these subtle inflections, and all these little shadings and colorings."[127] For example, this one, by Bey, spun an autobiographical narrative in "The Myth of the Rhythm of the Times":

> Captain Ra Bey alias Reggie Brown
> he fly high over in ghetto myth wisdom
> he be sourcery
> his Ka be straight
> he be Ma Akheru

he be Kun Fiya Kun
He hooked up straight baàk to Heliopolis
Possessor of the sho nuft magic
carpet ride the sunshine magic-child
ride low thru chaos big chops
& elephant ears he hears everything & he don't make
sense
he lean hard against the tense
of the black bubble
could be four-eyed & ready.
lives of the music
the sun being
won't be Buckstar
that drifting image him
Mister Melody the deadly avatar
he didn't hear the "choon" but speaks
of the rhythm
of the times
we sought an informal god
all us scufflin
Baraka, Tolson, poets, painters
plumbers, pimps copped Out
to the grey worlds
to the mists all
of us scuffhin shufflin
again to the rhythm of the times
to dialectical mammyism
to uridialect anything... all that
scorin and capping of that movement past yesterday,
ten years ago
Pharoah, Wayne, Miles
"we reserve the rite
to wear silver lame &
fag scarves & spout spiritchul
platitudes, to dip around
the corner & snort P coke
in short to change our minds"
we all sought an informal god
for the form had betrayed us

>   so we tried to slide
>   heralded but unnoticed into
>   the rhythm of the times

The critic Wilbur Mackenzie argued that in the 1980s version of Griot Galaxy, "AACM-inspired experimentalism and abstraction combined with a sense of groove and pulse that was uniquely Detroit. Though dancers and poetry had always been a component of Griot Galaxy's work, this version of the band significantly upped the ante, adopting futurist science-fiction imagery, wardrobe and theatrics. This look, combined with the blistering intensity of the playing and the futurist vibe of Shahid's effects-laden bass, resonated with local audiences drawing huge crowds."[128] Heron argued that "with their theatrical edge and their penchant for hypnotic, layered rhythm, they were an avant-garde group for people who didn't particularly like the avant-garde, or maybe even jazz."[129]

Occasionally Griot Galaxy collaborated with visiting musicians playing in Detroit, such as when the violinist Leroy Jenkins presented four concerts at the CAC in January and February 1981. Jenkins led the session with pieces such as "Through the Ages Jehovah," with Bey, Barefield, Shahid, and Tabbal backing him through compositions and improvisations.[130] Jenkins returned one year later and worked with many of the same musicians working on new compositions.[131] The band was flexible in that they could accommodate other musicians and play in a variety of settings.

All of the musicians in Griot Galaxy worked in related formations, sometimes hiring one another for performances.[132] In one such instance, Holland and Bey presented their composed work at the Detroit Institute of Arts (DIA) on May 15, 1982. The music critic Ray Waller noted the strong "African folk" elements of their music, arguing, "Holland and Bey prove, through their compositions, that it would never be wise to forget that 'jazz' is a hybrid of African and Western forms, and that the African gene is the dominant one. Jazz can at least be partially defined as the African sensibility expressed via Western instrumentality.... The music of Holland and Bey relied heavily upon the elements of African form: group melody, portamento, interlocking microtonality, call and response, cross rhythms, and improvisation."[133] This particular concert featured a saxophone choir that in addition to Holland and Bey included Kamau Kenyatta (tenor saxophone), David McMurray (tenor, alto, and soprano saxophones and flute), and Wallace McMillan (baritone saxophone).

In reference to the performance, Waller observed, "While Kenyatta, Bey and Holland displayed amazing power and depth of tone, David McMurray demonstrated remarkable versatility in a wide range of emotional stances; his more frequent movements from one instrument to another was done with a fine sense of demarcation, and the growling force of his sax solos were a beautiful contrast to his more subtle and flutteringly sharp flute which never got lost in the brawnier sounds going on around him but embellished him."[134]

Waller further wrote of Bey, "[His] solo on the first piece of the second set displayed ominous emotional undertones, and each of the players excelled in the ability to evoke powerful emotional states in every composition played. Most notable of the compositions played was 'Steen' . . . It began with a haunting intro, broke into a long process of embodying the 'idea' of steam with its pitch and its 'breathy' sectional repetition peppered with incipient homophony. . . . McMurray embellishes, his flute floating in and around key phrases. . . . The group as a whole is playing up to 600 or so beats per minute, the number of beats being divided among the players. Such a technique takes a very sophisticated sense of rigor and precision."[135]

On January 29, 1983, Griot Galaxy gave a historic performance at the DIA that was recorded but was not released until twenty years later.[136] Though it does not contain any poetry, the recording captures the band's sound at the peak of their talents as an improvising group. The record included "Zenelog" from *Kins* but otherwise features work from their growing corpus at that time that was never recorded in the studio. It is a masterwork of improvisatory interplay, showing that this band had developed a sophisticated group sound in the live setting, felt the energy of the moment, and could produce highly spontaneous, brilliant music. Whereas the music on *Kins* at times feels restrained, on *Live at the D.I.A.*, Griot Galaxy is fully free to explore ideas in a more extended way; show great range in rhythm, harmonies, and volume; and fill the ample space of the room with their sound. It is their most experimental recording of theirs that has been released. The record features compositions by Bey, Shahid, and Tabbal, especially Bey's "Fosters," which Heron described: "It starts off with a braying horn line, a sort of allusion to blues so old they creak, works into a hum-along mid-tempo stomp, then raises the tension and ante each time it circles back to the theme."[137]

The record also displayed guests Fahali Igbo on djembe and Sadiq Muhammad Bey on percussion and dance on the piece "Marz Society," which pushed the ecstatic energy to a high point. "Sadiq had the best hands," Shahid stated of the latter's hand drumming. "He was one of the only conga players who could draw on hundreds of years of tradition while also playing with the music that we were making, this improvised, polyrhythmic complexity of the 1980s."[138] On the recording, the band also engaged directly with some of their roots with two Sun Ra pieces, "Spectrum" and "Shadow World." Heron noted: "At times, collages of instrumental sounds float as if in search of a larger picture to attach themselves to and finally coalesce in dramatic shapes and structures."[139] The recording also captured the enthusiastic response of the audience. "The peak of the band really came when we were all acting intuitively," McMurray stated. "Most of it was written, but we got to a place where we could anticipate each other so well."[140]

The other major feature that the band received was at the African World Festival, in Detroit in August 1983, which featured music and other culture from across the diaspora and the continent. Griot Galaxy shared bills with groups such as Taj Mahal; Mandingo Griot Society, led by musicians from Gambia; the Izulu Dance Theatre, which combined South African and Detroit performers; and many others.[141] They also played at the second annual festival the following year, which was even more ambitious. The 1984 festival bill featured many of the groups that had played the previous year but also included groups and figures such as Afrika Bambaata, Soulsonic Force, and James Blood Ulmer.[142] The second festival also included numerous panels that spoke to issues of the economics of the African diaspora, international relations, the challenges facing Black families, a fashion show, a photography exhibit, and food from across the continent and diaspora. Griot Galaxy displayed that they had absorbed a significant amount of ideas from the broader diaspora while pushing their own synthesis, compositional concepts, and improvisational techniques forward as visionaries of new aesthetics.

Finally in 1984, the band embarked on its first European tour, playing in Groningen, Netherlands; several concerts in Italy; Salzburg, Austria; and then at Nickelsdorf Konfrontationen on July 1, 1984.[143] A live recording was made, and it was soon released as *Opus Krampus*, the band's final and most well-developed recording.[144] The record caught the band and its most refined sound in the live setting, in what sound like effortless yet driving and searching pieces that are stretched out so that every idea is thoroughly explored. As Heron noted,

> Bey and Holland play shouting jazz ragas over the swinging treadmill patterns of bassist Jaribu Shahid and drummer Tani Tabbal. Meanwhile, guest percussionist Prana Ananda adds an extra layer of polyrhythms on one cut and Bey and friends delve into an elliptical poetry recitation. As with all great combos, the musical chemistry of its members make Griot something more than the sum of its parts. Fine as the musicianship is, the group's impact is inseparable from a direct style of composition that builds on the dynamic interplay between the instruments and uses easily discernible rhythmic motifs as launching pads for improvisations.[145]

Another review simply referred to the music as "surreal and African."[146]

BEY'S ACCIDENT AND THE LATE VERSIONS OF GRIOT GALAXY

As Griot Galaxy emerged to some critical recognition and seemed on the verge of wider success, Bey wrote that that he was experiencing "a rough period for me socially and artistically and every other way... there was just a lot of confusion."[147] On September 28, 1984, while under the influence of alcohol, Bey endured a nearly fatal motorcycle accident that left him in a coma for over two weeks and from which he never fully recovered physically.[148] Sadiq Muhammad Bey wrote in a thinly veiled fictional account of the aftermath, "I saw Jesse sprawled on the roller bed. His dreadlocks scattered like black yarn over the pillow. There was a majestic, regal quality about him. He jerked and struggled a little, almost like he knew we were there... He had every imaginable tube and needle in his body. A fucking Frankenstein Monster sniffing the flowers of death. A 6'4", 185 lb. black grass eater reduced to a sleeping menace. A menace to our love for him."[149] The story alluded to the Egyptian myth of the god Osiris being betrayed and dismembered but eventually regaining wholeness.[150]

The poet, writer, friend, and Malcolm X biographer Kofi Natambu dedicated the poem "We Think We Know You or Roving Enigma Blues" to Bey as the latter lay comatose in the hospital, intended as a public prayer for his full recovery:

> So strangely we think we know
> you. I've even heard it said after
> Griot has lain waste to yet another
> dying empire. We know this Myth that
> calls itself Man. We know this man that
> calls itself Musician.
> But what is it that we know? That the shining grey
> mask you seem to wear is an affirmation of our
> fears? That the melodies you ponder and furtively
> reveal are cultural readymades for us to wear then
> discard when the houselights come on?
> Is this our history you sing as your grinning groupies
> crawl in for the delicious kill? What about the painters
> who buy you too much beer as we finger that aching saxophone
> sweating between sets in the corner?
> Do the critics feel your rage when they go to sleep at night
> whistling "Fosters"?
> And the poets, we of nagging words, do we offer more than

fat platitudes as we stroke yr growling locks? The dreads that
bring revolutionary dope addicts to yr concerts and neoclassical
composers in search of the perfect rhythm
So strangely we think we know you.
As you beat despair away with a Song.
Fly down crooked avenues in metal wings kicking
yr spinning wheels. (Vaporize cynics with a sullen laugh.
Cut thru pretense with a wicked look.
What is it that we know?
That the beboppers shudder when you do something that
you're not supposed to do, something all yr own, and you do it so well
that they look away whenever your name is mentioned? That the
youngbloods stand in Hart Plaza and give each other sly looks
as they recite every line from "Zinjanthropus" over the slashing
energy called the Science Fiction band? That you love to
hide and seek in public especially in
front of thousands of beings
who call themselves "lovers of jazz?" That you shoot down
expectations whenever you feel like it (which is all the time)?
That the men and women who say they need you and love
you also listen to and sometimes participate in
the ugly and beautiful gossip
surrounding yr name?
That we burst out chanting whenever Tani and Jaribu
Go into their Graucho and
Harpo stage-act, and you bent
back chortle before breaking into that famous half-step of yours?
The one that undulates when the Music takes over completely and
We see just how strong yr Love really is as it defies
the sentimentalists who applaud only when they
recognize some harmony they
think they've heard before (and will hear again)?
So strangely we think we know you.
So strangely we think we know you that we tell Zapman stories
    whenever
We get bored and wonder aloud why you always tell the best ones. That
the bodyguards of the flesh that houses your soaring
spirit mistake their desires for your needs. That the
concrete and the metaphorical

> merge in the space that surrounds sound and silence.
> You are that
> space: a wandering Interval lost to your demands but
> loyal to that Instance of passion that sends yr soul
> racing thru air
> So strangely we think we know you
> that we play games in the shadows
> of yr pain and call it concern
> that we stand in the dry well of
> yr flight from us and call it fate
> that we pay tribute to yr image
> and call it compassion
> that we cry and moan and thrash and curse and freak and
> posture and grieve
> waiting waiting waiting (Yeah) Waiting for yr return
> for the return
> we swear we deserve
> o so strangely we think we know you
> so strangely we think we know you
> so strangely we think we know you
> that we would risk our heavy ignorance
> to love you (Again . . .[151]

Bey's recovery was to be arduous; as the left side of his body was paralyzed in the accident. He would eventually regain movement after years of physical therapy. He also eventually worked to overcome alcoholism. It constituted something of a new spiritual awakening: "I came away with another knowledge, another knowing about this condition we call life."[152]

Bey wrote a poem after his accident:

> Tales of Zinjanthropus
> galacticus
> pararealities
> grey-brear on g-erz
> roiling vapor mists
> scudding across the face of the nascent sun rising as if from an electric
> toaster
> in gods shirt pocket
> Sir-real counts dinars

as prayer beads contemplative the pilot of g-erz has
cursed this vessel
tho he be an unlikely
candidate
vain dark androgenous
waddling contemptuous
toward singularity a saint absurd
Sir Real annotates vector rises
for instance under acceleration particles behave
strangely colliding
assuming identity yinyangularities
the analog physique
another grey-break
washed pastel tonalities
witnesses dark osirian
travels
nites of pulsing genitalia union of dissolution
g-erz prime myth drama
black october
dark roiling masses
with no blue promise
today I saw a great "U"
in the sky
the sun too caught repose in that
well is it midnite yet
are our fears to go
ungrounded
when are the demons
to present themselves
the witches ride souls
where are the demons our fears
the illuminati
masonics
rothschildren
our captors
is it midnight yet
for this we abandoned
love & Chalie Smith
African to entrophy Blk oct dark roiling

>   masses harsh & hurting
>   blue[153]

The Detroit avant-garde scene had been growing in the early 1980s. Bey had been central to that development, though many people contributed to its success. "The whole scene was happening, it was a good time for the music," McMurray observed. "Faruq was the leading figure in all of it. His voice was a powerful voice. The accident changed everything."[154]

Griot Galaxy never recovered. In the wake of the accident, it took many years for Bey to return to being able to play at a high level. Griot Galaxy attempted to continue without Bey, but after some gigs in 1985 through 1987, the band went on hiatus for some years. They tried to reunite with Bey later, but he could not play at the same level as they had in earlier years. The band also tried to fill the void with the then-emerging saxophonist James Carter in the early 1990s, including a European tour, but that was short-lived.[155]

THE MUSIC THEORY OF FARUQ Z. BEY

In the years that Bey struggled to recover from his accident, he began to write considerably about musical theories that he had previously practiced and discussed with his collaborators. I will not attempt to cover them comprehensively, for this should very well be the subject of a separate and longer study, but here I wish to make some preliminary observations. Bey was deeply interested in sonic aesthetics, the relationships of intervals, and the language of music as an expressive form. He was also concerned with the dialectic, or the lack thereof, in relation to the avant-garde.

In relation to Coltrane, he stated,

> John Coltrane's use of the "natural scale" i.e., the scale which is the product of tonal physics and mathematical ratio relationships and its harmonic consequences, obviously received some popular acceptance because of its scientific and physical "correctness," yet because there was neither a science of tonal aesthetics nor a codification of the principles thereof, there has been no transposition to semantics nor the evolution of a functional dialectic. The advances made by the logic of Coltrane's "inner ear" and its acceptance by the "inner ear" of the audience led not to any substantial advancement in tonal engineering, but the emulation of "aspects" of his playing by saxophonists who sought only to mimic

his popularity and deceive an unsuspecting audience. The measure of John Coltrane is an increment on the scale of courage. The realities of the natural scale are implicit to the saxophone (as to the human voice). While it is unlikely that he was the first saxophonist to hear these "plateaus of congruence," he was the first to make them a part of his "public" expression.[156]

Furthermore, Bey observed,

> While to the practicing musician correct intonation is of the utmost importance, the "harmonic" tones present in wind and stringed instruments while popularized by musicians such as John Coltrane, those "harmonics" are in the physics or natural scale. In other words they are "partials" of the fingered fundamental and as such are part of the overtone series and subject to those mathematical consequences and the attendant psychological meanings to say nothing of being slightly out of tune with the equally tempered system. Again, the natural scale is a physical phenomenon and as such is subject to the laws of wave-theory no less concretely than the observed laws that govern gravity.[157]

Bey saw larger-scale conflicts playing out in music itself, the repercussions of colonialism and enslavement and the cultural hegemony of Western music over other forms and practices:

> Though there was much interfacing of culture and cultural traditions, among them tone-forms, in the southern part of North America during the slavery period, and while there was much oppression of the cultural expression by invading Europeans of the Africans and the indigenous natives, both groups (Africans and Natives) though from different parts of the world could claim the pentatonic mode as part of their cultural heritage. And while there was an effort by Europeans to supplant any and all evidences of cultural tradition other than their own, in spite of those efforts the pentatonic mode survived. While there are certain parallels and points of congruence which approach the "tonic" model sequence of the overtone series because of the congruences or points of similarity the displaced Africans were able to use the pentatonic mode as a substitution or derivative mode in whatever tonic environment. A mode is a logic.[158]

Bey conceived of the survival of African cultural elements across this vast stretch of time and geography and saw them alive not only in Coltrane but in his own work and that of some of his contemporaries.

AFTER GRIOT GALAXY

The musicians that took part in Griot Galaxy all went on to do other major projects. Bey did not play saxophone publicly until the mid-1990s. One of his consistent collaborators in the later portions of his career was the poet M. L. Liebler. The two began to work together in the late 1980s in poetry settings, and when Bey returned to playing his saxophone, Liebler formed the Magic Poetry Band, which featured him alongside the guitarist Ron English and others. By 2001, Bey was also working regularly with the Northwoods Improvisers, with whom he put out a series of seven records. Bey also became part of the house band at Detroit Art Space, which was run by the bassist Hakim Jami. Along with Jami, the group also included the saxophonists Michael Carey and Skeeter Shelton, pianist Kenny Green, and drummers Alan "Ali" Golding and Ajaramu. The band focused primarily on presenting Bey's music. Bey led other groups that explored polyrhythms and modes with this circle of musicians, which also included the bassist Joel Peterson and several musicians from Ghana and Nigeria.[159]

Shahid worked extensively with Roscoe Mitchell; returned to playing with Sun Ra in the late 1980s; and recorded with Geri Allen, James Carter, David Murray, and numerous others up to the present time. Tabbal also worked with Mitchell, Carter, and Murray and led his own groups. McMurray led many of his own sessions, often more in a mainstream jazz vein, while delving into funk, soul, and smooth jazz in a variety of forms. Holland continued to collaborate with Barefield through the 1980s.

Griot Galaxy was a defining band of the Afrofuturist wing of free jazz. The band bore a unique sound, and its refined use of polyrhythms set them at the forefront of musical innovation in the 1980s. No band to emerge out of Cleveland, Detroit, and Buffalo had a greater influence on the next generation of musicians in the region, primarily because Griot Galaxy committed to remaining based in Detroit, and fostered a wave of talent that is still manifest to the present time.

CHAPTER 7

TRIBE

Collectivity, Self-Determination, and the Detroit Visionaries of the 1970s

If you create something, you should be able to control it. You should be able to own it.

—Wendell Harrison

The desire for artistic and cultural autonomy in music had a long history in Detroit.[1] The entrepreneur Joe Von Battle opened his store, Joe's Record Shop, in 1945 and then founded the J-V-B Recording Company in 1947, making it the first post–World War II–era independent Black-owned record label in the United States.[2] The recording studio and record shop was located at 3530 Hastings Street, the main thoroughfare in the Black Bottom neighborhood, home to many jazz clubs, and it experienced initial success in recording, producing, and selling blues, gospel, R&B, and early rock and roll records, including a vast array of figures such as John Lee Hooker. But in the 1950s, Interstate Highway 75 was built directly through the neighborhood under the guise of so-called urban renewal, which destroyed one of the most vital Black cultural districts of the city. Joe's Record Shop was torn down in 1960. Despite this catastrophe, Von Battle moved his store to Twelfth Street, where he continued to conduct business until it was burned down during the 1967 uprising. J-V-R Recording Company contributed significantly to forging what would become identified as the "Detroit sound."[3]

The 1967 uprising generated a new phase of people searching for artistic independence and self-determination in music. Motown Records was still booming then, but the company executives were already contemplating a move to Los Angeles. When they finally departed in 1972, it was a major blow to the Detroit music scene; many musicians working across a range of jazz styles had supported themselves working as session musicians in the Motown studios even while they developed their own music.[4] This led to a significant number of musicians following Motown westward, leaving behind stalwarts who were intent now to forge their own paths.

The establishment of Tribe Records just as Motown was departing came as no coincidence. Musicians were now forced to work collectively and to realize their musical visions through their own efforts, or as the saxophonist Wendell Harrison recalled, they said, "To hell with that, we're going on and doing our own thing. We were tired of backing folks up anyway."[5] Motown Records had often been constraining for musicians who wanted to explore their own ideas. As the trombonist Phil Ranelin noted, Motown Records had "used a tight, almost paint-by-number approach. The black-owned label's musical assembly line hadn't allowed much room for quirky ideas."[6] Nevertheless, the lasting influence of Motown Records was audible in the unique Detroit avant-garde sound, which was often deeply steeped in Motown, R&B, soul, and funk.

Tribe joined a broader movement across the United States among experimentalists who were creating their own record labels. Alton Abraham and Sun Ra were at the vanguard of the movement when they founded El Saturn Records in Chicago in 1957. On the East Coast, Leroi Jones founded Jihad Productions in Newark, New Jersey, in 1965, and the drummer Rashied Ali founded Survival Records in New York in the early 1970s. In Detroit, Kenny Cox led the way when he founded Strata Records in the late 1960s. Many other labels began appearing in different cities throughout the 1970s.

SMOKE STILL IN THE AIR

The community that eventually came together to form the Tribe record label coalesced in the wake of the 1967 uprising in Detroit. The pianist David Durrah had first come to Detroit in early 1967 to play with Charles Moore and then frequented the city regularly. On the night of the uprising, July 22, he happened to be playing in a neighboring town. He returned the next night and found that his apartment had been partially burned down. He later reflected, "In America, racism is so thick that I am surprised that more people didn't get killed immediately. It was really bad then. For the first time since the riots there in the 1930s, the police really didn't know what to do."

Durrah nearly lost his life in the days that followed. At one point, he was standing by a window looking at the helicopters that were overhead when a national guardsman shouted from the street, "If you move, I will kill you," while another guardsman told him to open the door to the building. Eventually Durrah opened the door. The officers stormed the building, physically assaulted him, and held him with a bayonet to his neck while they unsuccessfully searched for guns. They arrested his friend, who was doing yoga on the roof, and Durrah claims that they attempted to plant a gun on him so that they could arrest him as well, all the while keeping an M-16 rifle pointed at him. "I'm glad that my wife wasn't there at the time because that would have made them kill me. She's a German Jew. If they had found me with a white woman, they probably would have shot me right there," Durrah stated.[7] His friend witnessed the officer trying to plant the weapon on him and convinced the commanding officer to intervene.

In the aftermath, Durrah remained in Detroit for about three years before touring with B. B. King and the Rolling Stones. He played in Detroit with figures such as Leon Henderson, Charles Moore, John Dana, and Danny Spencer, but he felt that Detroit was disintegrating.[8] The automobile companies began moving jobs elsewhere, and the downtown clubs, such as the Detroit Repertory Theater, the Twenty Grand, the White Horse Lounge, and many others, which had provided so many musicians with steady gigs, began to close. So Durrah departed for Oakland, California, but would later be drawn back into the Tribe milieu via collaborations with his fellow pianist Doug Hammond.[9]

"Because of the position I was in, as a Black man in America," Ranelin stated, "going from Indianapolis to Detroit was like night and day. I was able to express myself more in Detroit because there was a cultural awareness there and it was way less conservative." He moved there in 1968 at the invitation of the alto saxophonist Sam Sanders, whom he had encountered in Indianapolis. Sanders told him he could get steady work in Detroit, which enticed Ranelin to move.[10] "When I got there, you could practically still smell the smoke in the air," Ranelin noted. "Many businesses and residences had been burned down. King had been killed and Nixon got elected. It was a lot to take. We were trying to remain as positive as possible and still fight the battle through our music. The arts have a healing effect."[11]

Within days of arriving in Detroit, Ranelin was hired to tour with the Temptations on a ten-stop Midwest tour. He then spent his early years in the city doing Motown session work, which added to the experience he gained playing with

Eddie Harris, Freddie Hubbard, and Pharoah Sanders.[12] He later toured with the soul singer Joe Simon and filled one dry spell with a short stint on the assembly line at Ford. But by 1969, Ranelin was getting enough steady work to play full time.

METROPOLITAN ARTS COMPLEX AND THE BIRTH OF TRIBE

In 1971, the pianist Harold McKinney, a central figure on the jazz scene in Detroit for over two decades, invited Ranelin to work at the Metropolitan Arts Complex. The organization had been funded by the city as a response to the 1967 uprising, and they put on workshops for aspiring musicians with the goal of keeping kids off of "the streets."[13] McKinney served as the music director of the organization. Ranelin joined McKinney's group, Creative Profile, which also included the trumpeter Marcus Belgrave and saxophonist Wendell Harrison, among others.[14] "It was straight ahead," Ranelin observed, "but progressive." An early recording of the group, with Ranelin, was made but never released.[15] Belgrave, like Ranelin, had gotten a lot of Motown session work in the late 1960s but was now developing his own work with more focused rigor.

Wendell Harrison was born in Detroit, October 1, 1942, to a middle-class family. His grandfather was a doctor, his father was a professor, and his mother had a graduate degree in education. Harrison began playing piano at age five, and at age seven his grandfather gave him a clarinet so that he could play in the school band. Later, while attending Northwestern High School, he worked a newspaper route and stocked shelves in a supermarket to earn money to buy a tenor saxophone, which became his primary instrument for the rest of his life.[16] Harrison rebelled against his parents' desire for him to pursue a profession such as a doctor or lawyer. "The more they discouraged me," he explained, "the more I pursued music to prove them wrong."[17]

Harrison began studying the recordings of Charlie Parker closely and then began formal music education with the pianist Barry Harris; he began playing professionally at age fourteen and had early gigs with Marvin Gaye and Choker Campbell. After graduating, he moved to New York in 1960, where he worked with Grant Green, Jack McDuff, Lloyd Price, Chuck Jackson, Big Maybelle, Betty Carter, and Sun Ra. "It was good to work with Sun Ra," Harrison reflected. "I had been playing a lot of bebop, but he blew my mind. He said he didn't want me to do any of those other exercises, he just wanted me to deal with sound and imagery. I had to deal with other sounds, street sounds, birds, he wanted me to listen to nature, to emulate stuff that was more organic."[18]

Harrison's first extensive tour came with the alto saxophonist Hank Crawford in 1965, and they traveled through Alabama and Mississippi, where he saw firsthand what Harrison termed "American Apartheid." He added, "We had to be careful there, so we didn't get into trouble."[19] They were not able to stay in hotels and relied on church connections or Black rooming houses for accommodations. Bebop and free jazz were both seen as northern musical developments, so during the tour they played R&B tunes that were popular in the south at that time. Belgrave was also in the band, and this environment allowed them to forge a lasting friendship and a shared commitment to cultural expression in their music. Harrison also met Ranelin while on tour with Crawford in Indianapolis; both of these encounters were integral to their later collective work with Tribe.

While Harrison was in New York, he began to develop a social and political consciousness. It began as he developed connections to the Nation of Islam, though he never joined the organization. Seeing Malcolm X speak transformed his perspectives. By the late 1960s, "Nixon was in office. We were pursuing self-determination. It was happening everywhere," Harrison declared. "It was a rebellion against the status quo. We were searching for change."[20] After a two-year stint in California, where he went to detox from heroin, Harrison returned to Detroit in 1970, where he was drawn into the circle of Harold McKinney and began teaching at Metropolitan Arts.

The encounter in Creative Profile sparked conversations between Ranelin and Harrison. Ranelin recalled, "We talked and decided that we wanted to record our own music. At the time, we were both writing a lot of music and didn't have an outlet."[21] He added, "We discovered that we shared some of the same dreams. We both had a burning desire to lead a band and perform and record our own original music. We were developing a sound."[22] Harrison observed, "We wanted to do all the stuff that had been bottled up inside of us for many years, give ourselves a chance to put this stuff on wax.... We respected each other's music."[23] The drive to create Tribe also reflected a broader feeling among the musicians' community that Black art was not being recognized. Take, for example, the statement by the Audubon Society, which was founded by colleagues of Ranelin and Harrison in 1972: "We intend to make our youth aware of this phenomenal gift of Black music which is jazz. The community and America in general, is less aware of this Black art form than the rest of the world."[24]

Tribe began by organizing live concerts, including a series of quarterly shows at the Detroit Institute of the Arts, occasionally at the University of Detroit, and at other venues.[25] The first major event was titled "An Evening with the Devil." It was held at the DIA and featured work by both Ranelin and Harrison that would later appear on the inaugural Tribe release, *Message from the Tribe*, coupled with poetry and drama, in a performance that one observer noted as "spiritual and militant."[26] Many of the early gigs did not pay well, so they began a small self-produced newsletter that announced their concerts and included advertisements for local businesses, especially on Gratiot Avenue. Harrison's wife was a graphic artist and oversaw the production of the newsletter. Soon it grew into the magazine *Tribe*, after the historian Herb Boyd suggested that they expand the newsletter, which they distributed locally and gradually developed a roster of subscribers.[27] Most of the articles they published were written by the musicians, though they wrote about a wide range of issues concerning the community beyond the arts.

Building on their concert production and newsletter, Harrison and Ranelin founded Tribe Records in 1971, as Harrison stated, "with all of these Motown musicians who were distraught and disgusted, but they were skilled musicians. Everybody had a little money, so we did things differently from how record labels were generally structured at the time and everyone owned their own product. We invested in the product. We owned our own publishing company for our own material. And we made connections with deejays and journalists, and they welcomed us and promoted us."[28] The label quickly expanded to incorporate a cadre of figures including Harold McKinney, Marcus Belgrave, Doug Hammond, David Durrah, and Ron Brooks. John Sinclair advised them in setting up the structure of the homegrown corporation.

As the critic Grant Martin observed, "In order to be able to try and make a living for himself and family many of the musicians playing jazz music today have collectively organized to form record companies such as the Tribe label. This will not only allow the artist to earn a livelihood but also give him more exposure in his own community and more importantly he begins to learn about the business aspect of music. For example, how to promote, market, and distribute his product. In other words, the musician of today has become more sophisticated to the degree that he has become involved in business and politics to survive."[29]

"The philosophy we had," Harrison explained, "was that if you create something, you should be able to control it. You should be able to own it. In the existing system, you were forced to give away most of it up front. We thought of that as the second plantation. If I work and work and give my recording to a major label and they only give me five percent and then they tell me how to record and where to play, I have no control over my life. And they'd set it up where on paper it was a loan to you and you'd pay it back through record sales, which was more like a sharecropper deal."[30] Or, as the Detroit writer and critic Grant Martin stated plainly, "It is becoming increasingly clear that in order to play the music that is close to the artist's heart he must have control over his product/music in order to create, record, produce, and market this great American music born out of the Afro-American Experience."[31]

Harrison's basement became the warehouse that held the stock for the label, and they mailed out their orders from there. Harrison worked as the president of the label, Harrison's wife, Pat, worked as editor-in-chief, and Ranelin was the director of public relations.[32] Ranelin was particularly focused on getting airtime for records, especially at local and regional radio stations, and he also networked with other independent labels to share information about distribution. For a self-produced record label, Tribe did well, and by 1976 they had as many as thirty distributors working with them to sell their line of albums across the United States in Chicago, Washington, New York, Los Angeles, St. Louis, San Francisco, and elsewhere.[33] Through their San Francisco distributor, the records found their way to Japan, China, and the Pacific Rim, while via New York, they made their way to Europe, with particular interest in Poland and the United Kingdom.[34] Several decades later, when there was a resurgence of interest in the Tribe catalog, they began licensing the records through other labels as reissues.

PHIL RANELIN

The label's first release, *Message from the Tribe*, appropriately was a split record with Ranelin presenting music on one side and Harrison on the other.[35] As the liner notes, written by the vocalist Jeamel Lee stated,

> The Tribe is an extension of the tribes in villages of Africa, our mother country. In Africa everyone has a talent to display. There were no superstars, just people, and collectively all the people of the village played a vital role in shaping that culture. We see all the black communities within this country as villages and the tribes are people residing within them. The Tribe is composed of creative artists from the Metropolitan Detroit area who have traveled extensively with many well-known musicians and have returned with the intention of sharing these experiences with our people in order to broaden the cultural base of the city.[36]

Lee's liner notes further explained the collective's view on the purpose and social function of art.

> We hope to bring out points, situations, and events that are happening in our communities by way of music, poetry, dance, and rapping in the people. Pure music must reflect the environment that we live in if it is to be educational and beneficial to our culture. It must portray our way of life. At this point in our history, harmony for the most part is not reflected in our communities. There's a lot of rebellious tension and discord, even though we have some groovy or harmonious moments along the way. This is evident when one listens to the music of composers like the late John Coltrane, Archie Shepp, Ornette Coleman, and the late Albert Ayler. These guys understand the relationship between art and culture and they took the total vibrations, positive and negative, of the whole culture and served as amplifiers or speaker systems through the arts. You cannot divorce art from its roots culture and expect it to be relevant for both the artist and his culture.[37]

The bands on the record were different, but the two leaders played in each other's bands. Both composers included material that was socially and politically aware. For Ranelin's band, he assembled the trumpeters Charles Moore and Marcus Belgrave, pianist Charles Eubanks, bassist William Austin, drummer Ike Daney, and vocalist Jeamel Lee. The music exhibited myriad influences ranging from bebop and R&B to Motown and free jazz; it was innovative at the time for bridging together all of these traditions that had been central to the Detroit sound for many years but had never previously coalesced in this way.

Ranelin's half of the record was titled "What Now? (Freedom Suite)" and included three individual pieces, all of which were based on R&B rhythms but with the musicians making freely improvised instrumental statements. The first, "What We Need," honored his own generation and their social, cultural, and political consciousness, with lyrical lines spun by Lee:

> For four-hundred years we sweat and we strained to be like the white man
> If that was our aim, but now a new generation has taken his place in this nation.
> We used to believe to better our arts we had to do and to think like the whites.
> It's plain to see now this was untrue because the Blacks of today want what's now due.
> We need knowledge and education. We need books with Black history.
> We need togetherness and love for our fathers. We need freedom within ourselves.

We need love and understanding. We need trust and peace of mind.
We need good times for our people and land and property, too.

The optimistic tone of the opening piece then gave way to a more ominous dirge titled "Angela's Dilemma," which was in honor of Angela Davis, who was imprisoned at the time of the recording. Shafts of defiant light erupt from Moore's trumpet that eventually meld with Ranelin's trombone and Eubanks's electric piano. Then Harrison cuts indigo hues across the simmering sounds in a searching trajectory that erupt into brighter statements, with Lee returning to express solidarity with Davis's facing injustice. "How Do We End All of This Madness?" was written with environmental concern about the growing nuclear and pollutive threats to the survival of Earth. Opening bass statements by William Austin are quickly encircled by buoyant piano lines to which Belgrave and Moore later add additional layers of harmonic interplay.

Whereas the first two tracks are relatively simple in structure, this final piece contains many layers of sound that Ranelin uses to depict the complexity of Earth and its impending environmental disaster.[38] Ranelin sings the lyrics on the final piece, drawing questions of human survival toward a look within the human spirit and the quest for human unity in common purpose. The second and third tracks, which each were about nine minutes long, were later cut into separate instrumental and vocal tracks, to make them more tailored for radio play.[39]

"Everything I wrote had lyrics, and they were basically protest and black-struggle-oriented songs," Ranelin explained. "I didn't deliberately set out to write those lyrics; they were inspired by the times. All of those songs had revolution written all over them. I couldn't separate the things that were taking place socially from what I was doing musically."[40] As one critic at the time wrote, the music "swirls though the brain, enters the bloodstream and disturbs the senses," indicating that it was meant to awaken listeners.[41]

Ranelin's second release on Tribe, *The Time Is Now!*, reveals the maturation of ideas that he started on the first record. The group itself had evolved and now included Harrison, Belgrave, the pianist Keith Vreeland, bassist John Dana, drummers Billy Turner and George Davidson, and noticeably no vocalist this time. "The Time for Change Is Now" opens with one of Ranelin's great solos on record, and the rest of the band gradually joins him into forthright, ascendant lines that speak to the demands of liberation. "Time Is Running Out" is an aesthetic counterpoint to the opening track, adding the somber realism of the long march toward societal progress through interwoven lines from guest trumpeter Charles Moore, the alto saxophonist and percussionist Haroun El Nil, and the bassist Reggie Fields (known as Shoo Bee Do).

"Of Times Gone By" serves as a historical tether within the record that grounds it in the tradition while remaining innovative and progressive as it builds toward the record's climax in the next track, "Black Destiny." The final two tracks each feature Ranelin in a more contemplative mood in his solos, pushing a bold narrative forward that keeps the energy elevated, like the final stages of a long-distance run. *The Time Is Now!* gives a clearer indication of his abilities, and his compositional strengths are on full display. Ranelin's third and final record on Tribe, *Vibes from the Tribe*, pushes further into a funk aesthetic, while retaining some free elements in Ranelin's solos, and he explores his own vocals on the songs "Wife" and "For the Children."[42]

Aside from his recordings and involvement in the Tribe label, Ranelin also founded Time Is Now Productions, a short-lived company that produced concerts in the Detroit area. For example, on March 21, 1976, he organized a bill at the Langston Hughes Theatre, where he presented the work of Kim Weston, Tribe, Griot Galaxy, and the Sharon Edmonds Dancers. The purpose was to present Black art: "We are striving to preserve the deep rusted cultural aspects of Afro-American life by reflecting the past, present, and future through a means of communication that has become international Afro-American improvisational music. Time Is Now aims to focus on and bring forth the real significance of the various forms of music that are called 'jazz' and the music and musicians' role in influencing and representing the lifestyles of Afro-American people, as well as other people of the world."[43]

WENDELL HARRISON

Harrison's contributions to *Message from the Tribe* added a slightly different aesthetic. Ranelin, Moore, and Belgrave all appeared on the record, as well as the bass clarinetist Aaron Neal, pianist Keith Vreeland, bassist Reggie Fields, drummer Billy Turner, and two poets, Oba and Vajava, who were associated with the Black Messengers, a Detroit theater group.[44] Fields's opening arco bass solo sets the stage, with ominous cuts across the sonic landscape. Then Harrison begins intoning a poem that begins with familiar lyrics from "Mary Had a Little Lamb" but quickly departs to tell of the current challenges facing the community, including war and local threats like "dope," while admonishing society at the time for accusing the protagonist of having an abortion. The instrumental interactions are the most intense on the record, with Harrison emitting particularly emotive lines while Moore spars with him, and the rhythm section elevates the contest with constant energy for the remainder of the piece, only diminishing slightly toward the end.

Harrison's second piece, "Where Am I," paints a fascinating dreamscape with electric piano and cymbal-led percussion adding accents to a flitting bass solo. The simmering piano lines eventually center the piece before Harrison emerges with a somber, slow-moving melody followed by the other instrumentalists. His final piece, "Angry Young Men," was an extended piece of storytelling about contemporary social movements of the time, featuring free solos over cymbal-heavy rhythms. Horizontal electric piano lines serve as the tether for the more exploratory elements from the horns, while the piece returns to a bebop-oriented theme at several points. Harrison's side exudes a confidence that is textured with forward movement and sonic unity.

The three pieces were reissued on Harrison's own record, *An Evening with the Devil*, which appeared in 1973, which also included two additional works.[45] The provocative cover of the record, designed by Pat Harrison, displayed a naked man holding a scale in each hand, one containing a skull and, as Harrison explained, the other containing

> the foot of the systems or establishment that we live under in this country. One stands for the head of the system and the other stands for the foot of it. The skull represents the intellect and the skillful intellectual propaganda that's going down both internally and externally. Included within this category is the businessmen on Wall Street who own and operate all of the major corporations within the country. With their finances and influences they dictate the governmental policies which create the negative vibrations that are oppressing, disabling, and killing millions of people in Viet Nam, Africa, Latin America, and America by means of war in the name of democracy. War is profitable from an economical standpoint and therefore the economy of the country is dependent upon it to survive. You have the cunning intellectual ways of the law, by way of its Supreme Courts that legislate against the true rights of the people and deny them an equal opportunity with smokescreen issues like housing, civil rights, and bussing.[46]

Harrison further explained,

> This is balanced on the other hand or scale by the foot of the system. This brings into play your police forces likes STRESS (Stop the Robberies Enjoy Safe Streets) in Detroit, a special detachment, who harass black people without a justifiable cause. Then there's the total rip offs that happen within the prisons like Attica in N.Y. and the underground things like dope, prostitution, numbers racket, and

abortion. Actually what it is saying is that you have your upper and lower structure of the system. All these things are represented by the man in the nude and directly above him is the all-seeing eye that symbolizes the Creator of the planet observing all of these things that are taking place below. These lifestyles and forces are placed in the center of an astrological chart of myself which is symbolic of every black person within the community trying to balance this hell of a monster.[47]

"Consciousness" opens with the line "The revolution broke out all around me" and then tells a story from the first-person perspective about a man involved in a revolutionary struggle that evolves from naïve optimism to the realities of the struggle, including violence and injury. "The pitfall of integration turns into the pitfall of separation," Harrison states, "the pitfall of a separate Black nation where I can really be free, where I can really be free, and all around me people are screaming: Nation time! Nation time! Nation time! Nation time!" The story ends with an arrest by police for another matter entirely, pointing to the carceral forces that were at the disposal of the white supremacist state that could be employed to thwart positive transformations in the community. The closing track, "Rebirth," is a triumphant statement, full of light and vitality in its imagery. Polyrhythms are present throughout the record, even though there are regular grooves.

The Tribe collective began playing with some regularity in Detroit in 1972–1973, especially at the Strata Gallery, assembling in a variety of formations that included Harrison, Ranelin, Belgrave, Eubanks, Lee, and other artists such as the bassist Rod Hicks and drummer Leslie Daniels.[48] It was a constantly evolving circle of musicians playing music composed by the different members of the collective. Interestingly, in some of his live concerts at the time, Harrison billed the group's work as "jazz-rock."[49] By 1974, Tribe was playing regular Sunday evening concerts at Alvin's Deli, just north of Wayne State University.

MARCUS BELGRAVE

The trumpeter Marcus Belgrave released *Gemini II* on Tribe in 1973. It represents one of the most experimental and exploratory recordings in his discography; it was also his debut as a bandleader. He had grown up just south of Philadelphia in the town of Chester, Pennsylvania. He had been tutored by the trumpeter Clifford Brown and toured extensively with Ray Charles, Charles Mingus, Max

Roach, and McCoy Tyner, among others, and had moved, like Ranelin, to Detroit to find work in the Motown studios.[50] He had also spent time in the Bahamas and had been inspired by musicians there, who seemed to be performing and recording with greater freedom of expression than was generally possible in the United States.[51] Like Tribe's earlier recordings, *Gemini II* features Harrison and Ranelin, along with the pianist Harold McKinney, synthesizer player Darryl Dybka, bassist Ed Pickens, drummer Billy Turner, bongo player Lorenzo Brown, and Roy Brooks on musical saw. Centered on a science fiction theme, the opening track, "Space Odyssey," is framed by the effects of Dybka's Mini Moog, before funk-oriented beats gracefully propel radiant, vertical trumpet lines and cool electric piano soundscapes.

The title track draws the greatest number of elements, explored elsewhere in the record in small doses, into a cohesive whole, with Brown's bongos rooting the piece in an organic feel. While Belgrave's playing is rooted in the post-bop idiom, he harnesses a free energy in his solos, stretching out over the six pieces. Like Harrison and Ranelin, he began featuring his work at Alvin's Deli, where he had weekly gigs throughout 1974.[52] While less overtly experimental than many of the other records on Tribe, *Gemini II* nevertheless represents the forward-looking aesthetic of the early 1970s Detroit sound, exemplifying a core different from what was present in Cleveland, Buffalo, Chicago, or New York during the same period.

HAROLD MCKINNEY AND CREATIVE PROFILE

One of the most visionary records on the label came from the leadership of the pianist Harold McKinney, *Voices and Rhythms of the Creative Profile*, in 1974.[53] McKinney came from one of Detroit's great musical dynasties, which included several of his brothers, including the trombonist Kiane Zawadi (born Bernard McKinney), bassist Ray McKinney, drummer Earl McKinney, and vocalist Clarence McKinney, and later generations of the family have carried on this legacy up to the present time.

McKinney was also a significant jazz educator in Detroit and occasionally presented lectures at music festivals about the history of "Afro-American improvisational music."[54] Like Belgrave, McKinney was more of an inside player throughout his career, and in the latter's case, he had been a central figure in the Detroit scene since emerging in the late 1940s, having also played with figures such as Kenny Burrell, Wes Montgomery, and John Coltrane.[55] Despite his experience, he was terribly under-recorded, and this record served as his debut as a bandleader. Creative Profile had been a central force in drawing together the creative energies that manifested in Tribe. Aside from playing at Metropolitan Arts Complex, the group also played in local clubs such as Abstention Coffee House near the Oakland University campus, among other places, between 1971 and 1974.[56]

McKinney's record is an astounding accomplishment for a debut record, fully realized and orchestrated by McKinney's confident leadership and recorded live at Bert's Blackhorse Saloon, September 16–18, 1973.[57] Though Creative Profile included a variety of musicians during its years of activity, the record includes Harrison, Belgrave, Dybka, Pickens, and Turner, as well as the drummer Ron Jackson, conga player Charles Miles, and a choir of Detroit vocalists, led by McKinney's wife, Gwen. On the final evening, the pianist Kirk Lightsey, soul singer O. C. Smith, and drummer Bobby Battle also sat in with the group.[58] The opening piece, "Ode to Africa," roots the record in an eclectic aesthetic ranging from West African rhythms through progressive jazz to Detroit funk and McKinney explores these elements throughout the rest of the record. The critic Grant Martin characterized the piece as one that "was a soul shouting, hand clapping, foot tapping number that embraced the many rhythms of the Afro-American Experience from Detroit to Alabama to Africa, the Motherland."[59]

Sometimes the influences in the record are made explicit, such as "Out of the Blues," though there are occasional searing solo blasts that emerge quickly and then meld back into McKinney's swaying, aqueous chords and plaintive lines. Again, Dybka transforms the architecture of the record with "In the Moog," making more angular cuts than his work with Belgrave. An imaginative cover of Eddie Harris's "Freedom Jazz Dance" serves as the apex of the record, with high-energy group work pushing the pace, which carries into another cover, Herbie Hancock's "Dolphin Dance," with lyrics added by McKinney. In the live setting, Creative Profile often played pieces by other members of the band such as Belgrave, Sam Sanders, Jimmy Allen, and Ed Pickens.[60]

The critic Grant Martin argued, "As today's artist becomes more in control with presenting his art form in the manner that he created it rather than play it the way some business executive instructs him to, then there will be more groups such as Creative Profile doing their own musical thing. Then and only then will the masses of people in the universe definitely benefit from that total experience."[61] This invaluable record documents McKinney's compositional vision, already matured to a great degree, and blends myriad musical strains seamlessly into his own version of the Detroit sound.

DOUG HAMMOND AND DAVID DURRAH

The two synthesizer players Doug Hammond and David Durrah came together to record *Reflections in the Sea of Nurnen* for Tribe, in 1975.[62] As noted earlier, Durrah had arrived in Detroit in 1967 and had subsequently moved to Los Angeles. Hammond was from Florida, had worked the Detroit scene from 1965 to 1970, and had then left for New York. Through connections with Belgrave, Tribe obtained the recording and decided to release it. In many ways, it is the outlier on the label, as it is the only major release that did not include Ranelin, Harrison, or Belgrave. The band includes the alto saxophonist Otis Harris, violinists Charles Burnham and Trevis Mickeel, and percussionists Frederick Boon and Thomas "Turk" Trayler. It is set within the funk–science fiction aesthetic resonating with some of the other Tribe material but explores moments of dissonance that reveals a free jazz mentality. "Space II," for instance, mimics a police horn woven through synthesizer to give it a futuristic feel. This is then immediately juxtaposed against the cool R&B-laced tracks "Wake Up Brothers" and "For Real," with vocals that drive home the message of self-determination and liberation more explicitly, such as the line "Who's to blame that the brothers are running a game on each other ... We are dying for crumbs and cars, our family starves." These forays are then bookended by "Space I," which returns to space-age dissonance. In brief statements, the saxophone and violins ground the otherwise futuristic narrative into a historical dialogue with the musical past. The label's final release, *Mixed Bag's First Album*, was more fully situated in the funk-soul-jazz idiom, though it features familiar Detroit figures such as Danny Spencer and Larry Nozero, among others.[63]

SETTING THE CONTEXT: *TRIBE* MAGAZINE

Tribe magazine became a focal point for a community and framed the musical events that the label organized by placing them in the milieu of Black history, contemporary political and social struggles, and music and arts happening both locally and across the United States. In many ways, the magazine responded to the call that Faruq Z. Bey, Phil Ranelin, and others had made regarding a need for resources on Black history. For example, in the 1973 third-quarter issue, the scholar and historian Herb Boyd penned an article that charted the history of the struggle from Frederick Douglass to Malcolm X and the various organizations that were currently advocating for political power, social change, and cultural autonomy.⁶⁴ Boyd and other writers also regularly reported on anticolonial and anticapitalist movements throughout the developing world with the locus set on Africa and Black America.⁶⁵

Other feature articles articulated solidarity with Black political prisoners held in American prisons, linking them to a longer history that stretched from the assassinations of Dr. Martin Luther King Jr. Malcolm X, and Patrice Lumumba to the coup against Kwame Nakrumah in Ghana, the deportation of Marcus Garvey, and even the crucifixion of Jesus Christ.⁶⁶ *Tribe* also directly confronted police violence in Detroit and featured articles about and interviews with Detroit's first Black mayor, Coleman Young.⁶⁷ On an international scale, the magazine highlighted ongoing anticolonial movements and locally raised issues of unemployment.⁶⁸

Tribe also took an interdisciplinary approach to the arts by publishing engaging interviews and artist features with a range of figures such as the filmmaker Melvin Van Peebles (1932–2021), who discussed his foundational blaxploitation films. The magazine regularly featured articles concerned with the potential for Black-produced and -directed television that had been growing nationally since 1969.⁶⁹ The editors and writers regularly examined growth in other areas of the arts, both locally and nationally.⁷⁰ The magazine also featured a regular column that highlighted advances for Black women in radio broadcasting.⁷¹

Situated in this milieu was coverage of jazz in Detroit and the Great Lakes region that both historicized the music and promoted contemporary developments, especially concerts happening at the Strata Concert Gallery.⁷² Extensive interviews with well-known Detroit jazz figures like the trumpeter Donald Byrd (1932–2013) deepened the magazine as a resource for building a community knowledge base.⁷³ Connecting Tribe's music with other creative musicians of the time formed another part of the context for the work of the label, such as feature articles and reviews of John Coltrane, Sun Ra, Kalaparusha Maurice McIntyre, and Anthony Braxton.⁷⁴ Other articles, like one penned by the Detroit pianist Kenny Cox, argued for the decolonization of the American music industry, especially within jazz, and cited the long history of exploitation and poverty that had surrounded "America's only native art form."⁷⁵

IMPACT OF TRIBE

As Larry Gabriel wrote, "Tribe was about cool grooves and creative music, but it was also about community, rebellion, and black self-determination."⁷⁶ Belgrave stated, "Tribe was just an expression of what we felt about the music business. It was sort of like a rebellion. There was too much dictation going on; the company executives weren't jazz musicians. The musicians went underground to present their own music and cut out the record companies; it was a notable and historic thing that happened. Music gained a lot more freedom."[77]

The Detroit avant-garde as documented on the Tribe label was a vital contribution to the broader development of the music across the United States. For one, the sound that pervaded the label, which coupled free improvisation and polyrhythms with the pulse of R&B and funk, was a unique and organic one. During an era where the most pervasive aesthetic in almost every site where the music was being invented bore the towering imprint of John Coltrane, Tribe departed in surprising ways. Tribe documented one more phase in the evolution and advancement of the Detroit sound.

END OF TRIBE

In 1977, the Tribe collective began to break apart as its members began to take an interest in pursuing their own work in other capacities. Harrison remained in Detroit and founded Rebirth Records in 1978 and later founded WenHa Records, which he used to feature jazz coming out of the city over the following decades. McKinney and Belgrave remained towering figures not only as regular performers on the Detroit scene, and both played central roles in jazz education in the city. Belgrave toured extensively both domestically and internationally. Ranelin moved to Los Angeles in 1977 and later worked with his childhood friend, the trumpeter Freddie Hubbard, and he eventually had much of his work reissued on Hefty Records. As for the Tribe recordings, they experienced a rebirth in interest beginning in the 1990s and especially in the 2010s, when they began to get reissued primarily through the efforts of Harrison, appearing on labels in Detroit, the United Kingdom, Japan, and elsewhere, making the hard-to-find records once again available to the public.

PART III
Outward Movements

CHAPTER 8

"DON'T BE SCARED TO TELL THEM THE TRUTH"

The Music of Albert Ayler in New York and Europe

It's late now for the world and if I can help raise people to new plateaus of peace and understanding, I'll feel my life has been worth living as a spiritual artist.

—Albert Ayler

When explaining his decision to embark for Stockholm, Sweden, in 1962, Ayler stated that he had fallen in love with the Swedish "clean, simple way of life . . . where there are no slums and everybody's working."[1] A local party put on by his parents bid him bon voyage. His mother did not want him to leave Cleveland, but he recalled thinking, "I need to go somewhere where somebody understands me because I didn't quite understand myself because the music hadn't quite formed in my head yet. I was playing it but it was slow."[2] During his previous visit, when he was stationed in Europe while in the army, he recounted that people said to him, "This is what you feel, this is beautiful!" He wanted to return to that warmth and reception as he ventured more seriously into making music.[3] His first gigs were playing what he described as commercial music, including calypso, and a stint with the blues pianist and singer Candy Green, but he hated it. He only stayed for eight months.

"Whenever I could, I would go to the old town and play for the young people," Ayler recalled. He eventually met the producer Bengt Nordström, who invited him to record for Bird Notes. Nordström regularly took Ayler to jam sessions and private gatherings where "young modernists" were open to new sounds. Hearing Ayler was an awakening for the producer, who declared, "That was a decisive moment for my realizing the possibility to make use of my imagination in more unconventional and unbounded ways."[4] Another Swedish observer, Nils Edström, who witnessed Ayler playing at the Golden Circle in Stockholm, stated,

> Precisely because of Ayler's presence, it was an absolute necessity that you were present when he played, placed in front of him and confronted by his playing, to be forced into trying to grapple with the realization that this experience was totally unfamiliar and devoid of references to anything that had gone before . . . he saw to it that the sound streamed out of his saxophone in all directions, roaring from every acoustic aperture as well as from the sides and the bell, and the mouthpiece too . . . he wanted everybody to be reached by the physical substance and body of the sound.

Though Ayler certainly made many references in his playing, the way it coalesced for him was startlingly new. Edström continued, "His sound was described as coming from nowhere, like an archetypal raw blast from the primordial forest and this simply has to do with the fact that people were so shocked by his physical tone, his actual intensity of sound. . . . The effect was rather like a massive snowplow clearing a through way and pushing aside everything it encountered, including all those personal prejudices you collect when you listen to music a lot."[5] Other witnesses appreciated Ayler's "non-intellectualized, expressionist way of playing."[6]

Not everyone was receptive, for as Ayler later recalled, "I remember one night in Stockholm, I started to play what was in my soul. The promoter pulled me off the stage" and according to other eyewitnesses threw the saxophonist to the ground. So instead Ayler went to play for Swedish children in the subway and observed, "They heard my cry." In a more cogent statement, Ayler explained, "I've lived more than I can express in bop terms. Why should I hold back the feeling of my life, of being raised in the ghetto of America? It's a new truth now and there have to be ways of expressing that truth."[7]

These first tracks as a bandleader sound more self-conscious than what he would be doing just a short time later.[8] His lines are more jagged, more pronounced, and less flowing but no less bold and defiant. Ayler had found a deep cache of sound within himself, and he was beginning to mine it, to trust himself, and to announce his presence, despite the fact that his bandmates at the time clearly did not know what he was doing or why. Even the audience can be heard expressing disbelief or even horror at his playing. From this point on, Ayler could not be ignored, his artistry would become increasingly controversial, and most critics would not bother to even try to understand his perspective or where he was coming from aesthetically. Nevertheless, he would forge ahead.

Ayler was hesitant to make the record at the time, with the mentality, "I wasn't developed like I wanted to be," but Nordström convinced him to do it. He recorded it in front of an audience of twenty-five people at the Stockholm Academy of Arts. By this time, Ayler's visionary ideas had progressed beyond his ability to articulate them on his instrument. That would come with time. As one South African colleague who was in Sweden then observed, "He was looking for new sounds and ideas. He spoke about them, he said he heard what he wanted but could not play it."[9] Ayler's first record showed hints of all of this development, but it would take two more years before he was able to fully demonstrate these manifestations of his imagination.

Ayler also first encountered other elements of the African diaspora in Sweden in meaningful ways. He played with musicians from South Africa, Trinidad and Tobago, and other places. But his friendship with the South African alto saxophonist Harold Jefta was the most substantial. Ayler began to take an interest in what was happening in South Africa, saying, "[White men] are afraid of the truth. Tell them the truth, don't be scared to tell them the truth."[10] Jefta recalled "the truth" being constantly in Ayler's vocabulary at the time, adding, "His political consciousness was an inheritance since childhood. This was noticeable in the course of our many conversations. He reminded me of a man of pride whose music always came first."[11] Still, Jefta noted, as others did, that Ayler rarely talked about anything other than the music and was reticent to discuss politics or social issues.

After he made the record in Sweden, he was invited to play for Danish radio. Once he arrived, he was invited to make a second recording with Debut Records. The label had attempted to arrange a recording with Ayler sitting in with the Cecil Taylor Trio, which was visiting with Jimmy Lyons and Sunny Murray. Over the previous couple of years, Taylor and Murray had made major strides in adapting new rhythmic approaches to playing; thus Ayler stepped into one of the most innovative groups in the world at the time. Ayler joined the front line beside Lyons, and it was personally transformational. As Ayler exclaimed, "I finally found somebody I could play with!"[12] From a television studio tape, we have evidence of what Ben Young has noted as "the first recording from anywhere in the jazz spectrum of a long-form improvisation with no overt synchronization—of time, structural harmony, or song."[13] Ultimately, Taylor elected not to record for the label.

Debut Records soon offered Ayler his own recording session, which was to include standards such as "Bye, Bye, Blackbird," "Billie's Bounce," "Summertime," and "On Green Dolphin Street," as well as one original by Ayler. "I was spacing sound and I developed a rhythmic space type of free form," Ayler noted. This recording became *My Name Is Albert Ayler*, which, Amiri Baraka stated, "had a deepness, a kind of 'gone behind himself' that summoned the close listener that there was something else yet to come. That same achiote sharpness characterized his person, so that whatever he said added to the 'challenge' coming out of his mouth, as if he was his horn!" He added, "That 'other' kind of wail that was promised underneath the standard bebop context of *My Name Is Albert Ayler* had sounded—the mouth of a different, stranger wail."[14]

As one writer noted, "The Danish musicians, though competent, did not understand his music. Albert was playing free and these musicians were still on a conventional track. The rhythm section played standards but Ayler soared into another space."[15] So the record became a kind of reinterpretation of bebop and post-bop. As another critic stated, "Ayler wrenches the melody of Charlie Parker's 'Billie's Bounce' inside out, shaping it into an abstraction of itself."[16] As one commentator wrote at the time, "[Ayler's] tone is still thin, not as developed as Shepp, but Ayler is so musical . . . he goes a lot of places . . . the rest of the quartet isn't playing the same music, but Ayler goes on without them."[17]

Jefta recalled playing "Billie's Bounce," in a co-led group at the Frid och Fröjd in old town Stockholm:

> Albert took the first chorus on that huge tenor and held it straight up in the air. His time had come, he was filling the place with a murderer's sound. He was telling the truth by singing through that horn. Now was the time to tell them. The people were coming out of their corners to find out who was being murdered. They all gathered in front of the band. The pianist who guided the 12-bar blues pattern was now lost completely. Albert was cursing out harsh sounds by which no harmonies could fit. The rhythm section who looked asleep were now wide awake like athletes ready for their off set. The choruses of Albert were only becoming more defiant; I could hear that he wasn't going to pull any punches. The horn was lifted still higher in the air while the audience stood paralyzed like dummy dolls in a dressing shop window. . . . The rhythm section with its musical doctrines and old habits were struggling and doing their best to cope up with this new phenomenon giving birth in the heart of Scandinavia. . . . I knew that this explosive event was coming because this man Albert Ayler was drowning in frustrations. All the humiliations on the street and public places of Stockholm and the United States which accumulated, came out of that horn with a handful of witnesses. They heard an unsung tune, a story untold.[18]

Through these appearances, Ayler became a featured freelance soloist with a variety of bands in Stockholm and other parts of Sweden during his extended stay there in 1962.

BACK HOME TO CLEVELAND

After spending time in Scandinavia, Ayler returned to Cleveland in early 1963, stating, "Our parents are very understanding. When the economics get to be too much, we've always been able to go back home, work out new tunes, and keep the music going."[19] His developing concept was at first a shock to the city, with one journalist describing it as "a totally new departure in jazz music."[20] When asked about his music, Ayler stated, "People are going to the moon. It's time for music to change too." Then, referring to the roots of the music, he stated, "Free music is a new blues, the new truth as seen by musicians who want to take a modernistic view. Geometric shapes and forms conveyed musically."[21] Ayler would later define improvisation as "an expression of one's feeling through a suffering pain that is injected on them that they know not of. They don't know what they are feeling themselves, but it is coming out of the bell of their horn."[22]

The saxophonist Yusuf Mumin was just beginning to experiment on alto saxophone when he first witnessed Ayler play around this time. He stated, "The consciousness of man is constantly expanding... I wouldn't term Albert's music as grotesque, but at first encounter 'startling' for some would be an appropriate word."[23] Ayler was mostly confined to playing at home or with friends, such as the bassist Clyde Shy and drummer Larry Hancock. "The music that he recorded later on *Bells* and other stuff for ESP," Hancock recalled, "he was playing early forms of that then. It was absolutely revolutionary."[24] Soon after, Ayler sat in with Sonny Rollins, Don Cherry, Henry Grimes, and Billy Higgins for a matinee performance on Easter Sunday at the Jazz Temple.

A lack of acceptance in Cleveland beyond the circle of musicians, however, spurred Ayler to look to New York as a haven for his musical expression, a city where the movement was growing more visibly, with figures such as Ornette Coleman and Cecil Taylor, both of whom he played with soon after his arrival. Of the move, Donald Ayler stated, "I felt that musically speaking it's best to get to the melting pot."[25] Albert Ayler recognized the challenges, noting, "It is undeniably time for a change, but you have to be ready for it. Everybody's not. Some people don't want to be free."[26]

When he went to New York, some of his first gigs were with Cecil Taylor at the Take Three, where they played for some weeks in a group that also included Jimmy Lyons, Henry Grimes, and Sunny Murray. Eric Dolphy and John Coltrane would often attend the concerts. They only got paid about one dollar per night, which was just enough for food the next day and to return for another night. Ayler found the experience with Taylor to be eye-opening, though he admitted that "Cecil Taylor is a great artist but he [played] too hard, I like smooth myself."[27]

The bassist Alan Silva witnessed Ayler when he was first in New York, playing at a club across the street from the Blue Note.[28] "Late one night, this saxophone player comes in, and I thought, that looks like Albert Ayler. And he says, 'Can I play a tune?' I said, 'Yeah go ahead, play a tune. What tune do you want to play?' And he says, 'Well, I'll play Ornithology.' So he plays Ornithology perfectly, really in a bebop mode, incredible. He takes this first, very strong bebop chorus, second chorus, and then he starts to do these fantastic things on the saxophone. Screaming qualities, and vocal qualities, on the lower and upper registers, and it was really cooking, we were really burning. With perfect pitch, his intonation was incredible. I said, 'This guy's brilliant, what is he doing?'"[29] Soon after, Ayler returned to Europe with Sunny Murray.

Ayler again returned and reunited with Taylor's band at the Philharmonic Hall at Lincoln Center on New Year's Eve, where the group was expanded to include the bassist Henry Grimes, on a shared bill with John Coltrane and Art Blakey. It was Ayler's broadest public exposure up to that point by far, as approximately 1,500 people attended, and Ayler was referred to as a "cautious, but promising follower of Ornette Coleman."[30] According to one eyewitness, "Albert was just playing this *staccato* stuff; he wasn't doing any of those long tones."[31] Taylor and Ayler's set was not received well, however, with half of the audience leaving in the midst of it. In the year following, his signature sound would finally become manifest.

AYLER EMERGES AS A LEADER

Spirits, Ayler's first recording to display his unique sound and approach in a setting that integrates the other musicians effectively, brought together elements of the Cleveland and New York scenes.[32] Ayler summoned the trumpeter Norman Howard and bassist Earle Henderson from his hometown and invited the New York bassist Henry Grimes and drummer Sunny Murray to join the session. The New York contingent had considerably more professional experience, but the

FIGURE 8.1 Albert Ayler (1936–1970), saxophonist, in Prospect Park, Brooklyn, 1969.
Source: Courtesy Elliott Landy.

recording feels unified and makes good use of the talents of all five musicians, even doubling basses on the title track. Ayler found his flowing, wailing, vibrato-infused tone on *Spirits*, and the fluid expressiveness that would come into full form in 1964 was born. And his collaborators felt his spirit and responded in a cohesive language for the first time.

The record introduced Ayler to the critic Amiri Baraka, then Leroi Jones, who wrote enthusiastically about the group, "Albert Ayler . . . is [getting] together . . . the most exciting—even frightening—music I have ever heard. He uses . . . a thick plastic reed and blows with a great deal of pressure. The sound is fantastic. It leaps at you, and actually assails you. . . . The timbre of his horn is so broad and gritty it sometimes sounds like an electronic foghorn. But he swings and swings."[33]

However, the other material recorded at the same session, which became *Swing Low Sweet Spiritual*, is, in some ways, an even more revealing record.[34] Generally dismissed by critics as a marketing gimmick, the record revealed Ayler's reinterpretation of a number of spirituals and is his most direct confrontation with this vast body of Black music. "Nobody Knows the Trouble I've Seen" had been composed by an enslaved person or persons during the first half of the nineteenth century and first appeared in South Carolina and Florida.[35] First published in

1867, the song became further popularized by the Jubilee Singers after 1872, as it spoke to the necessity of spiritual commitments to survive the long violence of slavery. "Deep River" and the title track, adapted from "Swing Low, Sweet Chariot," were of similar origins. "When the Saints Go Marching In" originated out of the gospel awakening of the early twentieth century, declaring a commitment to religious piety and a hope for salvation in its lyrics.

The noted addition to the session was Ayler's fellow Ohioan, the pianist Call Cobbs Jr., who functioned as the primary accompanist throughout the record. Ayler displayed much of his signature sound as he moved through a corpus of familiar tunes. But perhaps the most revealing thing about the recording is that it unveiled one of Ayler's most significant influences—the spiritual tradition going back well into the nineteenth century, a powerful root to his playing and thinking that many critics missed when hearing the more abstract work that soon followed. Ayler the preacher was on the ascent, showing his ability and interest in reinterpreting spirituals that cut to the core of Black experience and survival.

Baraka witnessed Ayler play with Coltrane in early 1964 and wrote of an

> emotional convergence [that] turned Albert into the horn he suddenly had in his hand. He began to stride out onto the stage. The horn raised high above his head, as if he wanted to take Pres *manqué* all the way out. The bell pointing as much as possible at the embroidered ceiling of the place. And then, Lord, with that pose as his heart's signature, he began to open a hole in the roof so his angels could descend, summoned by his exploding plaints. That sound Albert created then was of an actual frightening nature. It had no older reference; it was like a thing born then, that we all witnessed, flying out of the womb of his horn, screaming in it suddenness, with a thousand times more force than all those assembled around him. It was like a thing that you could hear and feel and be made "other" by, because it swallowed you![36]

After the concert, Coltrane famously queried, "What kind of reed you using?" and Ayler became the most talked-about and most controversial figure in New York.[37]

FINDING A SOUND: *PROPHECY* AND *SPIRITUAL UNITY*

Ayler's first sustained band, a trio with the bassist Gary Peacock and drummer Sunny Murray, took shape in mid-1964. Ayler later reflected on Peacock as "the best bass player I ever met."[38] Peacock, for his part, stated of Ayler, "He killed me, just fractured me—the quality of the sound, where he was coming from, his lack of censoring what he was doing. It was joyful, celebratory. He had a quality in his playing that allowed you to play from a place that you couldn't name, couldn't define.... With Albert's music, there wasn't anything to get at, nothing you could point to and say, 'That's where we're coming from.' It was beyond the verbal domain."[39]

Though *Prophecy* was recorded three weeks before Ayler's more well-known *Spiritual Unity*, it was not released until 1975, five years after his death. By that time, Ayler's importance was beginning to be recognized. One critic stated,

> It is a timely reminder of just how superlative, how unique and how advanced this particular trio was at that particular time. Ayler is once again revealed to be a master of melodic fluency of tonal and rhythmic variety, and of overall form and consistency. It is these abilities that stand out now, though at the time one tended to notice his complete break with stated time and his extensive use of properties of the saxophone that were probably not envisaged by Adolphe Sax; areas that had previously been explored in more limited fashions by Illinois Jacquet and John Coltrane, and which have since been extended by Peter Brötzmann and Evan Parker, among others. There was also that enormous vibrato used primarily on ballads that had not been heard in any serious context for thirty or forty years, something that nobody had expected to return. Complimenting all of this were the fast fragmented movements and the darting lines, involving wide jumps, of Gary Peacock, perhaps the best of the post-Mingus bassists, and at the top of his form. And underneath and above and around these two was the floating percussion work of the master of implied time, Sunny Murray, whose daring approach to rhythm makes him the Thelonious Monk of the drums. Amazing as these three individuals are, it is the way they act together as a group that is the most outstanding feature of this trio. Ostensibly, each piece begins and ends with a theme statement which frames a tenor saxophone improvisation and a bass improvisation (with drums). However, if one isolates each of these improvisational sections one is left with magnificent examples of free group improvisation in which all (or both) of the musicians play an equal role with little or no hint of the conventional jazz hierarchy of a soloist over a rhythm section.[40]

Spiritual Unity was Ayler's first masterpiece. It revealed a revolutionary group sound, or as Ayler stated of the session, "We weren't playing, we were listening to each other."[41] Ayler worked on variations of melodies, especially on the piece "Spirits," where he returns to the theme four times, each time improvising a different variation. The two variations of "Ghosts" revealed Ayler's ability to deconstruct a theme in ever more daring thrusts. The bassist Steve Tintweiss, who was studying with Peacock at the time, observed, "The system of organization that Albert used was to alternate between solos and ensemble playing with no preset arrangement or order of solos. It was different from how John Coltrane or Cecil Taylor were doing things then. Everything was on the fly, he wouldn't hesitate to play four or five melodies within one piece in the moment."[42]

At the time, Baraka declared, "This is the new jazz environment," in relation to the emergence of Ayler alongside Archie Shepp, John Tchicai, Sunny Murray, Don Cherry, and Pharoah Sanders. "I had a party at my place. I had four jazz groups playing. And 500 people showed up," he stated of one particular loft concert he organized involving them.[43] These concerts went on for several years. The bassist Clyde Shy, who occasionally worked with Ayler, recalled playing at Baraka's loft on Cooper Square in Greenwich Village around 1966 during his dozen or so trips to New York City: "We would play all night there until the daylight," Shy recalled, "with people such as Pharoah Sanders who would come to jam there."[44]

Spiritual Unity appeared on the new ESP record label. ESP would eventually develop a checkered reputation because, according to numerous accounts, the artists rarely got paid by its owner, Bernard Stollman. But the company's motto of "the artist alone decides what you will hear" was a stark departure from overbearing producers who confined artistic expression on other labels at the time. Stollman also understood the radical nature of the music, declaring, "No one connected the free jazz players with the radical movement. It needed language before anyone woke up to what was going on. The sound of that music was absolutely the most radical sound of its time."[45]

As the critic and producer Joe Pinelli wrote of the record, "The tunes are Ayler originals, open-hearted pieces reminiscent of hymns and military marches." He heaped praise upon Gary Peacock, in particular, whose playing "has an intelligence about it in the way he moves into a multiplicity of directions, achieving a kind of mystical, cosmic quality." And of Murray, he is "an innovator in his own right, [he] is also a very free player, [he] moves the pulse around in fresh and surprising ways with a richness of effect rare even among the newer drummers."[46] One other writer reflected in 1976 that *Prophecy* and *Spiritual Unity* "capture the major stepping stone between the initial breakthrough of Ornette Coleman and the now ten years old world of group improvisation."[47]

"That sound—the horn's timbre unbuckled, broadened, deepened—assumed a wolfsome, metallic, echoing bottom," Baraka wrote of Ayler's evolution.

And with each succeeding record, that signature thundering, Klaxonic, aerodynamic, keening, crack-edged blast, "Blahhwaonnkaad," released a sonic-born electricity, blown into ringing continuum as music. It was a drum, but blared. The hammer of Human Feeling against the Anvil of the Air! . . . That overwhelming sound was, I felt, the principal focus of Albert's musical intentions. That that brass "Waw" carried a new understanding, a *canto jondo* religious vision. And as such, provided both the overarching form and content of what he played. Every other feature of Albert's approach seemed to be shaped by, or the result of, that Sound! As astounding as they are, the recordings only get the tops or edges of the sound, but not the unnerving deepness of the sound's force! The actual human, physically aggressive wail of it![48]

Another commentator stated in reference to *Spiritual Unity*, "The open field at last. Open ended. Time: no longer 'sided.' Time down to biological 'feel.' The pulse no human can avoid, and I said 'heartbeat' but perhaps nerve-pulse would be more precise. Now the music can go anywhere the body/mind can . . . a music beyond memory perhaps."[49]

Much of the mainstream response to the record, however, was mired in writers' personal struggles to comprehend, as evidenced by accusations of chaos. To Ayler, it certainly was not chaos. But one writer offered a retort to such perceptions: "It doesn't take much listening to a performance such as Albert Ayler's *Spiritual Unity* to realize that the music does have a coherent, if flexible, pattern. Themes occur and reoccur, there is a constant give and take between the musicians, the music builds to instinctive climaxes and sharp mood changes."[50] *Spiritual Unity* documented Ayler finding the full expression of his sound, and it would form a powerful jumping-off point for the next stages of his evolution.

COLLABORATIONS WITH DON CHERRY

The soundtrack for Michael Snow's film *New York Eye and Ear Control*, commissioned by the experimental film for Ten Centuries Concerts, was featured at the Vancouver Art Gallery, among other venues.[51] Snow had just seen a concert by Ayler and "was completely knocked out," so he approached the musicians and let them know, "I wanted it as pure free improvisation as I could get."[52] Snow told them he did not want any previously played compositions and wanted group improvisation instead of soloing. The record that resulted bore some of the recent features of both leaders' work.

Ayler and Cherry had met in Copenhagen back in 1962, during Ayler's first trip there, when Ayler attended a performance by Cherry and Sonny Rollins. Cherry was immediately struck by Ayler, stating, "I had this feeling that I was in the presence of someone who was carrying the gift, the voice, and the reflection of God. It's only been a very few people in my lifetime that I have met that I feel have carried this light, and it's musicians."[53] After that performance, they all went over to the Jazzhus Montmartre, where Dexter Gordon, Don Byas, and Kenny Drew were playing, and they sat in with them. Ayler played his own version of "Moon River." "All of a sudden I heard this sound," Cherry reflected, "all the naturalness, all that love, it was like the Word had come back, and the Word was love." For Cherry, it was like the feeling of when he was young, in the Baptist church, when "everyone feels the spirit in the room. This feeling of bliss. It happened that night, hearing Albert Ayler play."[54]

There were already elements of a New Orleans style in Ayler's playing; he would confirm this in interviews two years later. The trombonist Roswell Rudd spoke of his experience in the band, "[Ayler] had that irrefutable sound and everybody joined in behind him. It was like having Louis Armstrong—a real lead. He made such a statement, that for me it was the ideal kind of accompaniment situation. In so-called Dixieland, trombone plays an accompaniment to lead trumpet, as does clarinet and everybody else in the band. And so Albert set up that old feeling, where he would play the call, and the band would play these responses."[55]

Archie Shepp saw the Ayler-Cherry band perform at the Jazz Gallery in the summer of 1964 when his band shared a bill with them. After departing the stage for his set, Shepp took a seat at the bar next to Amiri Baraka and then, "all of a sudden there was a sound like an explosion. It was Albert Ayler. It honestly sounded like a bomb had gone off. I thought I was avant-garde, but when they finished I realized they were avant-garde!"[56]

Expanding upon material he had recorded with the trio that summer, Ayler took the group, now with the trumpeter Don Cherry joining him in the front line, to Europe, with only one-way plane tickets. "With other musicians you have to talk about the music," Ayler observed, but with this group, "we just played."[57] The most developed piece they played regularly was "Ghosts," presented in two distinct variations. Cherry was so enamored with the piece that he stated at the time that "it should be our national anthem."[58] Nevertheless, the reaction from the Danish audience was mixed, though the band did receive some exposure on the radio there.

Recordings of the European tour document the high-energy sound that Ayler's quartet generated in the live setting.[59] Of the title track on *Ghosts*, Ayler stated,

I'd like to play something—like the beginning of *Ghosts*—that people can hum. And I want to play songs like I used to sing when I was real small. Folk melodies that all the people would understand. I'd use those melodies as a start and have different simple melodies going in and out of a piece. From simple melody to complicated textures to simplicity again and then back to the more dense, the more complex sounds. I'm trying to communicate to as many people as I can. It's late now for the world and if I can help raise people to new plateaus of peace and understanding, I'll feel my life has been worth living as a spiritual artist.[60]

New York Eye and Ear Control features Ayler attempting to share the front line with another horn, but Cherry often sounds a bit tentative next to Ayler's big sound.[61] Ayler sent *Spiritual Unity* and *Ghosts* to Coltrane after they were released, "to help give him the direction," Ayler recounted two years later. "He is a spiritual brother and one that can really hear music of all different kinds. After I sent him those records, the next thing I heard was *Ascension*, and it was so beautiful, everyone was building, everyone was screaming."[62] Coltrane questioned his own influence on Ayler in an interview with Frank Kofsky in 1965, stating, "I think what he's doing, it seems to be moving music into even higher frequencies. Maybe where I left off, maybe where he started."[63]

In reference to the idea of screaming, Ayler clarified, "We're just screaming about life in its different channels. The true artist feels the vibrations of what he is living around and this has held true all through the past, from Louis Armstrong and Lester Young up to Coltrane. We're not screaming against the 'system.' A man who's creating doesn't have time to hate. Whenever you hear our music you're hearing something fresh and that's pure art."[64] Around the same time, Ayler further stated, "Everyone is screaming 'Freedom,' but mentally everyone is under a great strain. But now a truth is marching in, as it once marched back in New Orleans, and that truth is that there must be peace and joy on earth. Music really is a universal language, and that's why it can be such a force. Words, after all, are only music."[65]

The musicians returned individually, but when Ayler got back, he expressed that he was "very frustrated, not understanding where everything was going, not understanding anything. All I knew was that I loved Charlie Parker, I used to listen to Coltrane in the army, this all I knew. I was living pure frustration like a madman."[66] On a visit to Cleveland, his mother told him that she did not recognize him, as he had changed considerably, and at the time, he felt that "nobody understood what music I was trying to do. I'm trying to understand it!"[67]

Once back in New York, Ayler sat in with Coltrane, Dolphy, and other musicians, and after the other two had taken their solos, he began to play his. At that moment, a member of the audience stood up and shouted, "No! Leave the club!" But after the concert, Dolphy consoled Ayler, supposedly saying, "You are the best I've ever heard! Stick with what you are doing. Let nobody stop you." Nevertheless, his moments playing with Coltrane were deeply inspirational. "He was a strong force," Ayler said of Coltrane. "So I figured I had to incorporate it all to say I was playing free form, to accomplish what I was born for."[68] Of Coltrane, he added, "This is a beautiful person, a highly spiritual brother. Imagine being able in one lifetime to move from the kind of peace he found in bebop to a new peace."[69]

MAKING AN IMPACT IN NEW YORK

Upon his return to the United States after the fall European tour, Ayler organized a new band that included the alto saxophonist Charles Tyler, Ayler's trumpeter brother Donald, and the bassist Lewis Worrell, the last of whom Ayler had met in the army. This band was documented for the compilation *The New Wave in Jazz*.[70] On an aesthetic level, the record was Ayler's first work with a cellist, in this case Joel Freedman, which he doubled with bass, and it marked the beginning of his extended foray into playing with multiple strings and, later, multiple basses. Freedman moved between front-line involvement in the melody and the backline rhythm section. "The New Black Music is this: Find the self, then kill it," Baraka wrote in the liner notes of the record. "Albert Ayler thinks that everything is everything. All the peace. All the motion. That he is a vessel from which energy is issued, issues. He thinks that he is not even here. Not even here enough to be talked about as Albert, except we are biological egos. Separate. Sometimes unfeeling of each other but Music joins us. Feeling. Art. Whatever produces a common correspondent for existence."[71]

By the spring of 1965, Ayler was entering a new phase of his work through encounters with Baraka. He put on a March concert at the Village Gate that served as a benefit for the Black Arts Repertory Theatre School (BARTS) that was about to open in Harlem. This project, spearheaded by Baraka, was aimed at creating a platform for Black art in New York that would "instruct young Negroes in the dramatic arts and related subjects. Its overall cultural program include[d] courses in remedial education, music, dance, photography, writing, painting, and history."[72] The central subject matter of the performances, which were often brought into the streets of Harlem, was aimed at "rallying blacks to fight white oppression" as well as centering the institution around a new cultural corpus that featured the work of the poets Larry Neal and Sonia Sanchez and musicians such as Sun Ra.[73]

Though the school only survived a year because of funding cuts, political opposition, FBI surveillance, and ultimately a raid by police, the organization was a landmark institution that "vitally influenced the development of black revolutionary art and black power politics" and was central to sparking the Black Arts Movement, "which spread to every major city in the United States from 1965 on."[74] As the scholar and poet Lorenzo Thomas noted, "The Black Arts Repertory Theatre/School ... was the ignition spark of a new nationwide movement that [was] much more energetic and extensive in its impact than the Harlem Renaissance of the 1920s had been, simply because this movement [was] completely controlled by black artists. The Black Arts Theatre represented a conscious decision to do art within the physical environs of the black community, utilizing the artistic and spiritual resources of that community."[75]

The opening weekend was centered on "new Black music, Black art, and Black revolution."[76] The Albert Ayler Quartet performed there twice, first as part of a parade celebration that also included the Sun Ra Myth Science Arkestra, Milford Graves, a troupe of dancers and drummers, and actors who were set to stage one of Baraka's new plays the next day. As advertisements stated to the community, "COME ON OUT ... SUPPORT BLACK ART AND BLACK FREEDOM."[77] A more formal concert followed, where Ayler also played as part of an impressive bill of musicians that included Sun Ra, Ornette Coleman, Milford Graves and Giuseppe Logan, Grachan Moncur III, the Rashied Ali Quartet, Roy Haynes and Wayne Shorter, J. C. Moses, Pharoah Sanders, C. Sharpe and China Linn, and the Dynatones.[78]

The literary elements present at BARTS had precursors in organizations such as On Guard for Freedom and Umbra, which had emerged during the first half of the decade. In fact, Umbra was invited to curate the opening weekend and included Baraka, Leroi Bibbs, Albert Haynes, David Henderson, Calvin C. Hernton, Larry Neal, Ojijiko, Charles Patterson, William Patterson, Ishmael Reed, Roland Snellings, Edward S. Spriggs, Lorenzo Thomas, and Steve Young.[79] The power of poetry was meant to be transformational, Neal observed of Baraka, such that poetry "is a concrete function, an action. No more abstractions. Poems are physical entities: fists, daggers, airplane poems, and poems that shoot guns. Poems are transformed from physical objects into personal forces."[80]

The events ended at an apex with Baraka's play *The Toilet*, followed by a panel titled The Black Artist and Revolution, which featured Baraka; Neal; Snellings; Sun Ra; Young; the essayist and historian Harold Cruse; the poet, editor, and sculptor Hobb Hamilton; the writer Selma Sparks; and the painter Rob

Thompson.[81] That night, Ayler went to Town Hall and played a sensational set that formed the live recording *Bells*.[82] According to Ayler, the march-type of idea came from his brother Donald, which formed the underlying theme throughout the record. "Then I put in the intricate parts between to carry it," referring to the saxophone lines over the top.[83] "When my brother started playing with me, that's when I really started stretching out. He was very far into it."[84] In this record, Ayler seemed to settle into a spiritual space. "We can get a divine harmony or a divine rhythm," he stated, "that would be beyond what they used to call harmony."[85]

Ayler reflected on the work that he had put out on *Bells*, as well as *Spirits* and *Ghosts*: "The scream I was playing then was peace to me at the time. That was the way that it had to go then. Whatever was inside of me, something was happening and I did not know exactly what it was. America was going through such a big change and I'd been traveling all over, seen it all, and had to play it out of me." But by the time he was asked about it in late 1966, he added, "But now it's peaceful. It's more like a silent scream." Still, he connected his music to what he saw as a prevailing truth of the time. "People are coming from every direction and appreciation of the truth is just a matter of time," Ayler stated.[86]

Ayler further noted, "We're not sitting down and trying to create beauty. We're making more than pretty melodic forms. . . . We're musicians and we are asking the whole world to listen—and understand. We're all together, everybody, and there has to be peace. That's what we're saying."[87] He later reflected, "America tried to say that [the music] was political and it had caused a lot of the riots, when I was affiliated with Leroi Jones, but that wasn't true at all. The music was very beautiful."[88] Ayler saw his music as including but going beyond the Black experience, making claims to the universal. As Donald Ayler noted, "We aren't selfish enough to limit it to that."[89] As the trumpeter Newman Alexander observed, "[Ayler] never engaged in the trivial or the superficial and exhibited the clear signs of advanced spirituality. A striking feature of this is exemplified by the fact that, although the prevailing mood of the time was one of sectarianism and ethnocentricity, ex. Black power, Albert's worldview stemmed from a deep conviction of the universal brotherhood of mankind."[90]

The material had evolved forward from his previous work, especially the final piece, "Prophet," where Ayler dispensed with his common melodic forms and, as one critic noted, produced "a fast-moving series of slashing horn effects . . . tightly executed at a dynamic level that never lets up. It's a fiercely joyous piece. . . . It plunges straight ahead into a shrieking love bombast."[91] But some sensed pain in the music; one writer noted that *Bells* was "wrung with incredible shrieks of pain. A visible anguish, that sees itself and can weep and laugh. . . . The music moves in the hearer's body, oddly in the stomach, belly song, through the tissue, vibrating you, the music plays you." He further observed, "Ayler's tone is much fuller [on *Bells*]. His first total breakaway I've heard. . . . There are silences in the music, like slices of flame. . . . No trace of an apology for the full emotionality of life-song."[92]

In the fall of 1965, Albert Ayler's quintet with his trumpeter brother, alto saxophonist Charles Tyler, and former bandmates Peacock and Murray joined Baraka for a tour, mostly in university concert halls.[93] The two acts "[toured] the national college circuit, presenting the new musical sound and Jones' plays."[94] Ayler featured the music he had just recorded on *Bells*.[95] Baraka, meanwhile, was debuting his new plays *The Toilet* and *The Dutchman*.[96] At the time, Donald Ayler stated that the group's goal was "to travel the globe—preach and play the word—bring[ing] understanding and peace to the world through their free, new sound."[97]

A SECOND MASTERPIECE: *SPIRITS REJOICE*

Spirits Rejoice marked a new stage in Ayler's evolution.[98] Whereas *Spiritual Unity* remained conceptually rather simple, this record included a lot more interplay and brought the march-like themes to fuller expression. With tenor, alto, and trumpet, along with arco playing from one of two basses, the band wove together harmonies that were at different times fluttering, ethereal, driven, and bold. The looseness of the tempo and rhythms allowed for the music to take on a folk feel while still retaining forward movement that pushed each melodic line to its conclusion.

Ayler revealed, again, his use of martial references, bugle calls, hymns, and anthems in his melodies, especially on the title track. He later revealed that much of the concept for the record came from the time he had spent in France while in the army: "I remembered a number of things, so I tried to incorporate certain things in the music to help the people understand more."[99] Henry Grimes mentioned that "it was just about me being able to adapt" to the two-bass lineup and relating to the music as it unfolded. "I just had to listen to [Ayler] to snap right into [the music]. The thing about that music is that it has an arhythmic texture. In all of music that is very rare, especially Sunny Murray because he is a drummer, and Ayler did something to the rhythm, too."[100]

The critic Joe Pinelli enthusiastically wrote of this record and the preceding *Bells*, "It's apparent that Ayler has brought together the strongest group on the scene," adding that this lineup "permits Ayler to execute the kind of musical conception necessary to the full expression of his vision."[101] Furthermore, Pinelli systematically dissected Ayler's innovations:

> Ayler's music [is] a fanfare to the joy of being alive. There's never been a music like it. It's a brilliant whirlpool of feeling, somehow pleasantly shocking, always exhilarating. It's a boldness of imagination and a strongly felt need to communicate the urgency of his feelings that permits the brain-reeling effect he creates: joy in piercing high notes several octaves above the traditional range of the tenor; a controlled low-note overblow effect, a jolting thing that wants to lift you out of your chair; vibrate effects, blown so hard and fast they rip out at you like the sound of a locomotive about to derail itself; and like a lot of the new players, he shifts the melodic line, but incessantly, often sustaining incredible tempos for periods of several minutes. But the one element that gives these aspects of his style such a rending impact is the sheer volume of his playing, a lyrical love feeling of immense power, breathtaking on record, overwhelming in person.[102]

Baraka echoed this when he wrote, "It was this wonderful sound that really marked Albert Unique! And live ... that sound was literally devastating. It Wailed and Wawed, not a scream, but something nature only sowed the seeds of, like the singing from a Black Hole, something very loud and very hard. It confronted, attacked, took hold. It was, nevertheless, touching, but its touch was 'past' aesthetic/psychological; it was bluntly physical, not just being heard, but being felt. It was not just the ears that dug Albert; the whole body became a field of sonic ideational penetration!"[103] The bassist Alan Silva, who got to know Ayler personally soon after the record was released, observed, "The records that Albert put out didn't really show his vastness as a musician. He had his feet in many areas. He could play Muddy Waters, he had a very strong bebop experience, he had a real interest in Dixieland, and the old spirituals, and spirituality."[104] Though most traditional jazz critics were dismissive or even hostile to the avant-garde, the jazz poll for the British newspaper *Melody Maker* declared Ayler to be the best new star of 1965, and a French magazine echoed this honor.[105]

Ayler's quintet, now composed of his brother Donald, Charles Tyler, the cellist Joel Freedman, and the drummer Charles Moffett, took the cramped stage at the Astor Place Playhouse on February 7, 1966. "Ayler's last concert there drew almost a full house and it looked like the thing was finally beginning to get off the ground," one audience member noted. "But the other groups rarely drew more than a handful of people and before that last concert Ayler's biggest crowd was about forty people."[106] The performance did garner one rave review, however, with

Rupert Kettle writing, "Ayler is the most important member of the contemporary jazz community, both as an individual player and as a leader. In the recent concert his mastery of his instrument was obvious, and his solos were intensely beautiful; his group, which sounded best when playing 'Tutti,' often had as many things going as there were men on the stage. [Ayler] has said that's it's no longer a matter of scales or chords or even notes, which would seem to indicate that he may be getting very close to something."[107]

As Baraka elaborated, "Albert meant it was the Sound and that force and, ultimately, that Spiritual Power that were the real purpose of the music. To bring and raise and spread the Force of Spirit. That fundamentally the music was—if comprehended and sincerely projected—a Holy Spirit, a Soul/ar Force, an instrument of Revelation, even Salvation."[108] More directly, Baraka stated, "John Coltrane, Albert Ayler, Sun Ra, Pharoah Sanders, come to mind immediately as Godseekers. In the name of energy sometimes, as with Ayler and drummer Sunny Murray. Since God is, indeed, energy. To play strong forever would be the cry and the worshipful purpose of life."[109]

BACK TO CLEVELAND

In the fall and winter of 1965–1966, the Ayler brothers spent significant time in Cleveland, where they made a concerted effort to spread their musical language to their hometown. It met with modest success but the great expenditure of energy did not produce a proportional result. Ultimately this resulted in a weekend at La Cave. As one local writer noted, "The date at the club attracted the entire jazz community of the city, Black and White, all of whom came to get their first taste of the new sounds that had only been something to read about before this momentous occasion."[110] To this group, he added the French violinist Michel Samson, who was in town to play with the Cleveland Philharmonic, and Donald Ayler's childhood friend, the bassist Clyde Shy.

For his part, Shy stated bluntly, "I thought of bebop jazz as the music of slavery. When I looked at a musical chart, I thought of the bars like bars of a prison that were keeping me confined and telling me where to go, what to do." He noted, "I wanted to do it my way, in my personal expression. That revolution didn't come out of the music, it came from the people in the street. The same attitude was coming out of the Black Nationalist movement, the same idea was in the Socialist Workers Party. It had the same spirit as our desire in the music. I wanted something that challenged the status quo."[111]

"Whenever I was playing free, it was always a relief to be in the midst of people who you could have a conversation with because we were having a conversation that other people were not having," Shy added.

> Before that time, the conversations people were having were structured in terms of the music. The conversation we were having made stuff happen and we communicated on a level where we didn't need to say much or anything at all. We were doing something that hadn't been done before and we were challenging the status quo. The establishment did whatever it could to turn us back because the people in control couldn't deal with what we were doing. But as Albert Ayler used to say all the time, when the music changed, the people changed; when the people changed, the music changed, it was interchangeable.[112]

Some have suggested that Samson brought a Roma music influence, especially on "Truth Is Marching In," "Change Has Come," and "Our Prayer." Ayler regarded Samson as a genius and gave him considerably free rein, especially for a player whom he had only met shortly before the concert took place. Samson had performed with Ornette Coleman in Amsterdam in 1965 and had become interested in free jazz.[113] "These three performances have a beautiful feel to them alternating moments of ecstatic serenity with sections of spirited extroversion—a dangerous mixture that others have attempted without much success," one critic noted a few years later.[114]

Ayler made one more attempt to bring his music to his hometown when he returned to Cleveland in January and February 1967, when he set about organizing a benefit concert for the Cleveland Music School Settlement, where he had taken lessons in his youth. Ayler chose to present the band in a sextet formation, with his brother in the front line, while bringing the harpsichordist Call Cobbs Jr., whom he had first worked with three years earlier, and the drummer Beaver Harris from New York, as well as unidentified local musicians. By this point, Ayler was citing his search for Black identity as one of his motivations and inspirations.

As Ayler had declared in late 1966, "I think it's a very good thing that black people in this country are becoming conscious of the strengths of being black. They are beginning to see who they are. They are acquiring so much respect for themselves. And that's a beautiful development for me because I'm playing their suffering, whether they know it or not. Beyond that, it all goes back to God."[115] On the level of pan-African solidarity, a year or two later Ayler was inspired by the people of Biafra in their attempts to secede from the state of Nigeria. He entered into an eleven-day fast "to see if I could get a little bit of the suffering that they were feeling."[116] He also remarked, "Maybe I had to suffer to develop such a strong tone."[117] A proud local paper stated, "They've been home for about three weeks and what a triumph their return is."[118] It was to be his final public performance in the city of his birth.

GAINING MOMENTUM IN NEW YORK

After the first Cleveland sojourn, Ayler returned to playing club gigs in New York, yearning for greater exposure and acceptance for his music. Between January and May 1966, he played several concerts at Slug's Saloon and in mid-June brought the band to the Cellar in Newark.[119] Live recordings from this period reveal that he was extending what he had done on *Bells* and *Spirits Rejoice*. The bassist Steve Tintweiss, who played with Ayler at an early Slug's gig, noted, "He was a very empathetic person. Contrary to how he played, in person he was relaxed and laid back. Albert listened to all of the musicians around him but when he got into his improvisations, he reached another plane like he was serving a higher calling. He maintained it on such a high level. This connection was not fleeting and it was a constant in all of his playing, shifting between free improvisation and some of his themes, organically creating structures on the spot without limit."[120]

Nevertheless, it was a time of yearning and anguish for Ayler. As his bandmate Samson recounted, they walked the streets of Manhattan together, "hoping that a crumb would fall their way. We brainstormed endlessly about commercial success. Albert didn't intend to cause confusion. He wanted to make it and be part of the establishment. This came with a certain degree of opportunism. I think that me being part of the band was because having a white violinist from Europe made it easier to gain a foothold with record companies and jazz clubs. Being famous was part of the 1960s. Albert wanted to tour in Japan and was considering incorporating Japanese themes that [they] would like."[121] That fall, Ayler would get the most exposure of his career, a period of his work that was better documented than any other.

AN EXTENDED EUROPEAN TOUR, NOVEMBER 1966

In the fall of 1966, the Newport Jazz Festival organized a European tour to bring their bookings abroad. Ayler's band was included among a wide range of jazz figures including Max Roach, Stan Getz, Dave Brubeck, Roy Eldridge,

Illinois Jacquet, Freddie Hubbard, and many others who flew and traveled by bus together to Berlin, Munich, Lorrach (Germany), Rotterdam, Helsinki, Stockholm, Copenhagen, Paris, Bordeaux, and London over the course of fifteen days. Ayler was included because of a specific demand from one of the European organizers.[122] "Albert's music was so different," observed Beaver Harris, "but the other musicians seemed to respect it. I never heard them say it was nothing."[123]

The series of concerts was one of Ayler's high points in the live setting, even though he received mixed reactions from audiences. At the Berlin Jazz Festival, Ayler's quintet was given enthusiastic applause.[124] At the Paris Jazz Festival held in Salle Pleyel, Ayler and his band played two twenty-minute sets. There was staunch audience resistance to the music, and a fight broke out in the audience between a larger group of detractors and a smaller, younger group of admirers. The second set, recorded around 2 a.m., was released as *Lörrach, Paris 1966*.[125] In France, Ayler claimed to have been robbed, losing most of the money made from the tour, though George Wein paid the band after they returned to make up for the loss.[126]

For the final stop on the tour, the band went to London, where they faced clear racism coming through customs. Folwell and Samson were processed without incident, but all three Black members of the band, the Ayler brothers and Harris, were pulled aside, questioned, and searched. This left them in an angry mood, and they spent the day in London, skipping the rehearsal for a television recording that was to be held in front of a live audience at the London School of Economics. Eventually, the three disaffected band members arrived and played the concert, but, according to Folwell, the producers "hated the recording" and later announced that the planned broadcast had been canceled because of "technical irregularities."[127]

"We are the music we play," Ayler stated to the critic Nat Hentoff after returning from the tour.

> And our commitment is to peace, to understanding of life. And we keep trying to purify our music, to purify ourselves, so that we can move ourselves—and those who hear us—to higher levels of peace and understanding. Every kind of music has an influence on the world around it so that after a while the sounds of different types of music go around and bring about psychological changes. We're trying to bring about peace. In his way, that's what Coltrane is trying to do. To accomplish this, I must have spiritual men playing with me. Since we are the music we play, our way of life has to be clean or else the music can't be kept pure. You have to know peace to give peace.[128]

Donald Ayler tempered these statements by commenting, "This music is one individual's suffering—through his imagination—to find peace."[129] Albert Ayler said of Samson, "Michel, too, is a man who spent a long time searching for peace."[130] Samson resonated with this feeling, stating, "You can look at Albert's music as some kind of church music. The titles of his compositions are quite religious. Our music is a religion, the majesty of the arts."[131]

Ayler hired a new bass player for the band's European tour, Bill Folwell. Folwell had previously toured with the Uni Trio but was otherwise fresh out of music school. "I just tried to create as much energy as I could," Folwell reflected.[132] Ayler liked Folwell's arco playing, so he encouraged him to do that through much of the music, which shifted the group sound of the band away from the pizzicato and terse plucking of earlier bassists in his groups toward a more fluid, sustained energy and multilayered, undulating harmony. The other new addition to the Ayler orbit was Harris, whom Ayler had met in the army, but when the two met again in New York in 1965, Ayler said to him instantly, "I want you to play with me." So when the opportunity arose to go to Europe, Ayler hired Harris for the tour. "We played so long and so hard that the drums would fly all over the place, that they nailed the drums to the floor," Harris recalled.[133]

Harris further noted, "What Albert did was very natural because of his spiritual upbringing. You notice that his music often goes into a drone, like a chant, it stays in one place and then evolves from that point. The use of so many strings gave [the music] a mysterious quality. The strings had a lot to do with him getting his feeling across. Everything had Biblical connotations. I could relate to it because my grandmother had the same type of thing going on. He would go beyond what was expected."[134] Ayler expanded on this point, stating, "My music is the thing that keeps me alive now. I must play music that is beyond this world. If I can just hum my tunes and live like, say, Monk does—live a complete life like that, just humming tunes, writing tunes and being away from everything—if I could do this, it would just carry me back to where I come from. I don't think you can ask for more than just to be alone and create from what God gives you. Because I'm getting my lessons from God. I'm trying to find more and more peace all the time."[135] The next day, Ayler brought his band to the Village Vanguard.[136]

ONCE MORE, NEW YORK

By early 1967, some perceptive critics were beginning to look more deeply into Ayler's music, though the attention still came largely from outside the United

States. The British journalist Ronald Atkins, who was responding to Ayler's London debacle, described the latter as "a young tenor-saxophonist building a reputation with another kind of jazz.... He might be the most progressive thinker around. His music seemed to presage the complete liberation of the solo instrumentalist... from predetermined melody and rhythm. Suddenly it changed direction: the ensemble passages grew longer; the solos contracted." Atkins detected a different sort of tradition in the Ayler brothers' playing, referring to Ayler as an "old marching-band saxophonist" and describing Donald Ayler as playing "the trumpet with a rough-hewn tone that predates Louis Armstrong." He added, "[Albert] Ayler is seeking to reinstate jazz as a polyphonic music in the face of its continual tendency towards individual expressiveness." As Ayler stated himself, "We are trying to rejuvenate that old New Orleans feeling that music can be played collectively and with free form."[137]

Furthermore, Ayler stated, "We're trying to do now what people like Louis Armstrong did at the beginning. Their music was a rejoicing. And it was beauty that was going to happen. As it was at the beginning, so will it be at the end."[138] Atkins added,

> Each item performed consists of a succession of themes, which are elaborated in an improvised contrapuntal style that rarely ventures beyond the simple New Orleans harmonic idiom. Only the solos recapture the wild cacophony previously associated with Ayler, and these are usually the briefest of interludes. In sharp contrast to such apparent conservatism, the drummer avoids any regular rhythm and the bassist never lays down his bow—without the need to cater for marchers or dancers, Ayler has been able to carry polyphony to its ultimate conclusion. The almost classic equilibrium attained by Ayler's quintet at his BBC recording caused as much controversy as the musical anarchy of his early days.[139]

After returning to New York, Ayler prepared for a concert at the Village Theatre, where he presented his septet, which was, at times, expanded to an octet that included the trombonist George Stell and bassist Alan Silva in addition to Donald Ayler, Samson, Freedman, Folwell, and Harris. Ayler invited Silva to play because he appreciated his upper-register bowing technique, among other aspects, and the two began to work out a language privately, often playing Beethoven sonatas together with Silva on cello. Ayler incorporated horns and stringed instruments into a kind of "string concept" that used the horns as strings conceptually.[140] Adding a dose of futurism, the program was titled "Music for the Year 2000!!"[141]

The tribute piece, "For John Coltrane," featured Ayler on alto saxophone, in a long, somber piece that celebrated the optimistic hope and peace represented in Coltrane's music.[142] The piece was a conglomeration of different ideas that Ayler did not bestow titles upon until after Coltrane's death.[143] The hymn and bugle call returned in "The Truth Is Marching In." As one critic noted, "Following stately renditions of variations on the theme, the Aylers escalate to playing sounds that make one think of whirling masses of dense energy flying through space. The level of tension they build to is deafening but compelling in its drama."[144]

The most innovative piece on the record was "Light in Darkness," which featured Ayler speaking in tongues through his horn.[145] "He could chant through the horn," Harris stated, "but he was using his own language in a chant. It was a chance for me to exploit all of these different rhythms, so it was a continuous flow of rhythms while keeping the melodic figure in mind. Everything I played related to that melody."[146] Samson explained the music differently in that they employed a

> form in the shape of freedom, to play a solo in which everybody is listening to each other. If you would take our form literally, it would become a very complicated form. Planned chaos? That sounds very distant from peace to me.... It happens intuitively because it's a unit. It's about listening rather than thinking of chords. We listen to each other rather than thinking of where to put our hands. It is like a conversation, sometimes there are days that you don't talk much. If I don't feel like it, I just don't solo. Albert... never struggles with technique. Albert has a fabulous technique, nobody but he can make such long strophes on a saxophone.[147]

If Ayler was to experience any kind of breakthrough in the American press, it was with *In Greenwich Village*. The critic Russ Wilson wrote of the record, "One of the true creators in this new jazz is... Albert Ayler. This is the best of the few albums Ayler has recorded and also is a good introduction to the 'new thing.' The four pieces on the album reinforce the belief that the saxophonist-leader has a deep feeling for form that some of his contemporaries lack, that his lyricism and rhythmic sensitivity are strong, and that he can create tremendous waves of emotion. The group's utilization of sounds—dense, shifting masses—and their skillful use of free improvisations are notable."[148] Another writer stated that the piece "Our Prayer" had "the genuine spirit of an old revival meeting with none of the pandering blues cliches."[149]

In the summer of 1967, Ayler took the stage at the Newport Jazz Festival. The critic Leonard Feather wrote of the performance, "The evening ended with a set by the tenor saxophonist Albert Ayler, whose quintet played what might be best called avant-garde gospel music. Though this was essentially a very abstract, personal extension of Ayler's emotions, the most persuasive moments were those provided by the tout ensemble, in provocative improvisation by a personnel that included a young Dutch violinist, Michel Samson."[150] Another critic observed, however, that the band's performance "brought either unfavorable or indifferent reaction from many of the spectators," though a third writer noted that all of the avant-garde bands at the festival were received better than Archie Shepp had been the year prior, indicating a slight shift in popular taste.[151] The concert marked the last time that Samson played with the band. The constant turnover of side people in the band finally alienated Samson, and he left jazz altogether.[152]

COLTRANE'S FUNERAL AND *LOVE CRY*

Love Cry must be understood as the first record that Ayler recorded after the death of Coltrane. "Bob Thiele called me and told me that Coltrane was dead," Ayler related, "I said, 'No, you're joking,' because he was so beautiful. He never got mad with anybody."[153] In another statement, Ayler said of Coltrane, "he was so truthful."[154] Ayler had visited him the day before his death but even then had no idea that Coltrane's passing was so near. Thiele then informed him that Coltrane's last request was for Ayler and Ornette Coleman to play at his funeral, at which point Ayler asked himself, "How can I do that? How can I play crying?"[155]

Coltrane, who was without a doubt the most visible and powerful force within the avant-garde movement, died of liver cancer on July 17, 1967. His death was an irreparable blow to the community and to the music on a national and international scale. "To the tune of a wailing sax and mournful trumpet, over a thousand jazz musicians, friends and relatives paid their last respects yesterday to John Coltrane, considered by many the most gifted modern jazz man of the decade," one writer observed. "As the mourners filed slowly into place at St. Peter's Lutheran Church on Lexington Avenue at 54th Street, two of 'Trane's' closest friends, Ornette Coleman and Albert Ayler, played 'The Truth Is Marching In' in the Balcony of the ornate church."[156] Both musicians also composed original music for the funeral proceedings.[157]

The funeral was held at St. Peter's Lutheran Church on July 21, where Ayler also played "Love Cry" and "Our Prayer," joined in different formations by

Donald Ayler, Richard Davis, and Milford Graves. The recording of Coltrane's funeral performances is the most important jazz bootleg recording ever made, as it captures the spiritual power of the music in tribute to one of the greatest visionaries of the twentieth century.[158] Thiele was in the audience and called Ayler soon after to invite him to record the piece for a new album.

"Albert knew that Coltrane really loved him," Beaver Harris observed.

> Coltrane had said that Albert was basically the next horn player in line. Albert was the most different horn player on the scene which made Trane dig him. They were both really searching in their music. I think Albert thought that he and Trane were the chosen ones. Trane needed Albert and Albert needed Trane, they were drawn together. Trane's death affected Albert so much that he felt alone. I heard Albert say, "I guess it's only me now." At the time, it was a great responsibility to follow in the footsteps of the masterful John Coltrane. His death affected everyone, but for Albert, being highly spiritual, it affected Albert even more deeply.[159]

So Ayler assembled a new band at Capitol Studios for a recording on August 31, which became *Love Cry*.[160] It was the crystallization of ideas, techniques, and philosophies that he had been nurturing over the previous five years and throughout his travels. He assembled a new rhythm section for the project by hiring the percussionist Milford Graves, who had released innovative records on ESP and other labels, as well as bringing back Donald Ayler, Silva, and Cobbs. As Silva noted, "This album was very important to Albert because it was on a major label, and John Coltrane had passed, and I think Impulse thought that [Albert] was going to be the next saxophone position. And me and Milford were like the next Elvin Jones and Jimmy Garrison."[161] For Ayler, the new contract finally made him feel like things were moving in the right direction and more opportunities were going to open up for him. He stated, "Everything was beautiful."[162]

Ayler achieved a new kind of aesthetic with *Love Cry*, which marked a significant stage in his evolution. The melodic lines were cleaner, which allowed the front line to interact in a less muddled environment where all of the components could be easily distinguished. This had the side effect of producing music that had less ecstatic energy than his recordings of the previous three years, and the recording seemed aimed at garnering a broader audience. The recording bore familiar pieces such as "Ghosts" and "Bells" while introducing Ayler as a vocalist in chant-like forms. It achieved a kind of classical beauty.

"This LP is notable for 'Universal Indians' which features such superlative solo and group improvisations by the two Aylers, Silva, and Graves that it must be considered one of Albert's very best performances," one critic reflected a few years later.¹⁶³ The remainder of the album's tracks comprised marches or ballads that were shorter and well suited for the radio, including two tracks on which "Albert's singing reflects his playing, in the tradition of Louis Armstrong, Henry Allen, and Dizzy Gillespie, among others."¹⁶⁴

Ayler never got a lot of radio play during his lifetime, but his presence in New York and the reactions from critics compelled some radio stations to begin to play his records. The first known broadcasts outside of New York occurred in Kansas City in August 1966.¹⁶⁵ His most sustained radio play, beginning around 1968, came from radio stations that covered the Hudson Valley or the central and northwestern parts of upstate New York.¹⁶⁶ University-affiliated radio stations began to show increased interest by early 1969 in places like San Francisco.¹⁶⁷ In the wake of his death, Ayler's music was finally included in a brief wave of broadcasts in a range of cities such as Knoxville, Madison (WI), Minneapolis, Ottawa, and Montreal in the period from 1971 to 1973.¹⁶⁸

"Ayler, for me, was one of the possible crossover artists, especially in this particular period, when rock was just beginning to formulate," Silva explained.

> And the group thing was more important than the individual, and the rock guys were able to create these groups. This was an important thing in this period, about what free jazz proposed, at the same time that rock music was being formulated. That free jazz proposed a group sound ... and that we could be a new music tool. I think Bob Thiele thought that Albert, with his blues base and his jazz base, could reach out to a broader audience. And Albert had a spiritual message; at the time of the Vietnam War and the whole anti-war movement, I felt that, as a social artist, he was very important. *A Love Supreme* had already made gold, and it was a spirit; I think Albert had a real accessible saxophone style at the time, and even the band we had was accessible.¹⁶⁹

As Thiele supposedly said to Ayler, "You've got to get with the young generation now and see what you can do."¹⁷⁰ According to Silva, Thiele believed that Ayler's music could have an impact on the rock and roll market, and so the record was structured with singles for radio play. "Albert had a mission," Silva observed. "He recognized that John Coltrane had made some steps with *A Love Supreme*. He felt the music was important for the time and that we could present it to young people. Jimi Hendrix was a fantastic blues guitar player, and he was reaching people. Albert also had that fantastic blues experience so we thought he could do it. He had an immediacy in his horn."¹⁷¹ There were plans to feature the band at the Fillmore West in San Francisco, which was establishing itself as a rock venue at the time, but it never happened.

In 1966 and 1967, Ayler was getting more attention domestically as concert promoters began to try to book him. Often the universities and arts organizations did not have enough funding to make such shows a reality. For example, the historian Frank Kofsky intended to bring him to the University of Pittsburgh in mid-1966 and even attempted to collaborate with the Artists' Workshop in Detroit to split the travel costs, but ultimately it did not happen.[172] Likewise, in the fall of 1967 a union of student organizations at Stanford University, Reed College, and Simon Fraser University formed specifically to bring Archie Shepp and Albert Ayler there for concerts, but their attempts did not manifest.[173] In Montreal, the Jazz Workshop attempted to book Ayler throughout the autumn and winter of 1967, but the concerts never occurred.[174]

Nevertheless, this band got some work in New York, including a week at Slug's in the fall of 1967, playing from 9 p.m. to 3:30 a.m. each night. "When Milford [Graves] was playing with the group," Ayler reflected,

> he passed out after two nights. We play energy music. Coltrane, Pharoah [Sanders], and Archie [Shepp] play space bebop, but we play an energy-type music and we really jump on it. [Milford] was so tired by the end of the week he could barely move. The people at that time didn't understand what Milford was doing. He was so natural. We decided then that we wouldn't play jobs like that anymore, we would wait for concert types of gigs. That's a suffering thing because the society of America tries to get one to do as it wants them to do: play in a club. If you have any respect or pride for yourself you stick to your belief. That's the most important thing. So, we will do that until we make it big, it's either big or it's nothing.[175]

RECEPTION WITHIN THE BLACK ARTS MOVEMENT

The poet, essayist, and critic Larry Neal hailed Ayler as "one of the driving geniuses of the Music." He elaborated further, "[Ayler] has clearly put forth a definite sound; a different and fascinating way of thinking about the world as sound; as movement; as the ghostly memory of the Spiritual Principle. Albert's sound at its best is the field holler and the shout stretched like a piercing shaft from

Alabama cotton fields to New York and on into some cosmic world of strange energies. At his best, Albert's voices buzz and hum with awesome deities."[176] The organic nature of his music was self-evident in Neal's view and drew right from the root of Black American music and history.

Neal further wrote, "When most of us first heard Albert, he really blew our minds, opening us up to not only new possibilities in music, but in drama and poetry as well. He was coming straight out of the Church and the New Orleans funeral parades. He had all kinds of Coon songs in his horn. He had compressed, in terms of pitch, all of the implied cycles in the blues continuum. His thrust was shattering."[177]

Baraka considered Ayler's music to be primordial, in a way. "He had a sound, alone, unlike anyone else's. It tore through you, broad, jagged like something out of nature. Some critics said his sound was 'primitive.' Shit, it was before that! It was a big massive sound and wail. The crying, shouting moan of black spirituals and God music. . . . Feeling all that, it touching us and us touching it, gave us that strength, that kind of irrevocability we felt. Like the thunder or the lightning or the ocean storming and mounting, crushing whatever was in its path."[178]

But like Neal, Baraka also noted its spiritual aspects, stating, "Albert's music, which he characterizes as 'spiritual,' has much in common with older Black-American religious forms. An openness that characterizes the 'shouts' and 'hollers.' But having the instruments shout and holler, say a saxophone, which was made by a German, and played, as white folks call it, 'legitimately' sounds like dead Lily Pons at a funeral, is changed by Ayler, or by members of any Sanctified or Holy Roller church (the black churches) into howling spirit summoner. . . . The instruments shout and holler just like the folks."[179]

On March 9, 1968, Ayler brought his quintet to the Albright-Knox Auditorium in Buffalo. It was a harrowing experience getting there, and their flight from New York was forced to land in Rochester because of thick fog, then the band drove west to Buffalo, arriving two hours after the concert was set to begin.[180] Nevertheless, an audience of approximately 125 people greeted them enthusiastically, including the saxophonist Charles Gayle. The band picked up a local bassist, Juini Booth, who was just twenty at the time. Donald Ayler, Cobbs, and Graves filled out the band. The concert was filmed for part of the Public Broadcast Laboratory television program under the title "Who's Afraid of the Avant-Garde?" though footage of Ayler was not actually included when it aired on April 21. One local critic described the performance emphatically as "anti-establishment" and "new culture" and then stated, "A new vocabulary must be invented to describe the type of sounds generated by the group, sounds which are becoming more and more prevalent in the world of modern music."[181] The band featured music from *Love Cry*.

NEW GRASS

Ayler had apprenticed in R&B bands in the 1950s, so his usage of related concepts in his own work should not have come as a surprise. Ayler also met his wife, the singer Mary "Maria" Parks, who began composing most of the music he would play over the final two years of his life; she also effectively became his manager. "It gives me a chance to sleep," he quipped. "I just sleep and take care of my music!"[182] Thiele supposedly urged Ayler to play with a younger pop group as a crossover band, but Ayler insisted on assembling his own lineup. Thiele also urged Ayler to sing. So Ayler began experimenting with that in New York clubs. At the time, Ayler thought, "In America I can play pop, I can play free, I can play a variety of things, so maybe it will be okay."[183] It was his way of giving the American audience another chance at appreciating what he was doing. "They deserve that."[184]

New Grass was an attempt at drawing together rhythm and blues together with free jazz. Ayler's voice is still his own, but the orchestra accompanying him added more popular and musical forms that the general public might recognize. In some ways, it had a similar feel to Ayler's earliest recordings as a leader, where, at times, Ayler felt misplaced with his accompanying musicians. But nevertheless, it felt like Ayler was attempting to reformulate elements of soul, rhythm and blues, and rock into his own vision.

One reviewer stated: "Ayler announces that through meditation, dreams and visions he has been made a universal man, sent to bring the peoples of earth a spiritual message. The power and strength of his tone, splitting strands of sound and setting them screeching and vibrantly jangling, is astonishing. The source of energy and light, his sound becomes the sun at the fervent opening of 'Sun Watcher,' only to leave a base guitar anti-climax before he returns. The more I hear this record, the more I marvel at it."[185] Another writer simply stated, "*New Grass* is an extraordinary piece of work, being a rock record by the master of gothic galosh."[186] His former bandmate, Alan Silva, lamented this direction in Ayler's music. "Me and Call Cobbs, we were more or less an avant-garde rhythm section, with a strong feeling for time. But if [Ayler] wanted to be a crossover artist, he had to get into a rhythm and blues number. Bob Thiele didn't need that real free rhythm that me and Milford were doing. But I believe we could have gone over.

I don't think *New Grass* worked very well, as a crossover."[187] Silva added, "*New Grass* was a compromise for the pop-rock market."[188]

Larry Neal wrote a particularly devastating review about the record, "We must acknowledge that anything that we say about this album must be seen against Albert's fantastic possibilities." Neal then suggested that Ayler was being manipulated by Impulse Records or out of some desire for popularity. Neal added, "This album is a failure. It attempts to unite rhythm and blues dynamic with the energy dynamic of Ayler. But in attempting to unite the two styles certain fundamental things have been overlooked. First, rhythm and blues is rooted in a popular tradition which has allowed for innumerable innovations in and of itself. It is a tradition that demands respect.... It's not cool to get to the Rolling Stones or the Grateful Dead to learn things that your old man can teach you. And this is the feeling that I get from listening to *New Grass* . . . This album strains at everything, even social consciousness."[189]

But Neal saw some value in what Ayler was attempting to do and urged him to continue.

> Albert's attempt is fundamentally correct. It just must be focused sharper. The music must find ways of reaching into the pulse of the people; ways of taking ordinary elements out of their lives and reshaping them according to new principles. In this procedure, therefore, the music moves us toward national unity and spiritual unity. A unity music. A music that is so total, so fully informed by a Black ethos that it meets a more collective and less specialized need. Music can be one of the strongest cohesives towards consolidating a Black Nation. The music will not survive locked into bullshit categories. James Brown needs to know Albert Ayler, Sun Ra, Cecil Taylor, and Pharoah Sanders.... Implied here is the principle of artistic and national unity; a unity among musicians, our heaviest philosophers, would symbolize and effect a unity in larger cultural and political terms. Further, there should be attempts to link the music to other areas of the Black Arts movement.[190]

The mainstream press saw the record as breaking down barriers between jazz, rock, and soul, but they did not embrace it beyond that.[191] "Jazz rock, this music might be called, were it not so sophisticated. 'Sun Watcher' suggests the ritual qualities of both American Indian dances and fundamentalist church music. 'Everybody's Movin'' and 'Free at Last' join a choir (the Soul Singers) with horns so that voices and horns become one sustained call for joy and freedom. This disk demonstrates contemporary musicians have come to terms with their roots in African and Afro-American music and have brought it all to bear on their playing."[192] To all of these various criticisms, Ayler replied, "You have to make changes in life just like dying and being reborn again, artistically speaking. You become very young again through this process, then you grow up and listen and grow young again."[193]

For years, Ayler had lived by the philosophy that "the better you are, the harder it is for you to make it. People will copy you. When you make it, you make it big."[194] He had dwelled in poverty throughout his years in New York before signing with Impulse. *New Grass* finally provided him with a measure of financial stability. In an interview in 1970, he claimed that the previous year he had made ten thousand dollars, which allowed him to pay off all of his existing debts, support his parents, and "to live the complete life of an artist."[195]

"THE TIME IS NOW": PROPHETS AND VISIONS

In 1968, Albert Ayler wrote an essay in which he detailed portions of his religious and spiritual beliefs, citing Bible passages:

> I saw in a vision the new Earth built by God coming out of Heaven. Years ago they called it New Jerusalem. It was a solid foundation built by God himself. It is not like the foundation that we have where men seek to kill each others spirit.
>
> The vision I had of Jesus coming again, it was at night again; large clouds forming in the east and something said to me this is the way Jesus is coming. The Son of God would be coming in his father's name, God Almighty. So be ready when that time comes, because it could happen in the blink of an eye. Remember he said you know not the minute or the hour, so let's be obedient children to God's laws. We live in darkness now; God Almighty is the God of lights. You see there are mighty angels from Heaven and they are very large. Bright as the sun. Another way to describe it is like the color of lightning magnified ten times. So you'd better get ready for the bright lights that will appear in the sky. It has been written on the wall of the universe by God Almighty for me to see and give you this message. So don't transgress any of God's Laws. The time is at hand. Make up leaflets and pass out to all people Revelation 14, verse 7 to 10. This is very important that everybody should know that this will save your soul and you will see a beautiful eternity. I'll have more to say next time. We must move this by chain letters and get it in papers in as many parts of the U.S.A. as possible. This is very important. The time is now.[196]

Ayler's ascent to the position of prophet seemed to happen in the wake of Coltrane's death as he took up the mantle of spiritual revelation and believed that he had been chosen to bring people to the spiritual awakening that he saw within his own music. It was a tremendous burden, in some ways, that isolated him socially, as he tried to communicate his message to audience members and other musicians. In some ways, the roots of Ayler's rise to revelation were embedded in his work going all the way back to 1963 or 1964. Baraka observed, "Ayler uses the older practical religion as key and description of his quest. *Spirits. Ghosts. Spiritual Unity, Angels*, etc. And his music shows a graphic connection with an older sense of self."[197]

As Ayler moved toward prophetic visions on a spiritual level, he became more reclusive. He became less trusting of his friends and began to isolate himself. He spent most of his time with Parks, and they made music together with her increasingly composing much of the work. "I seldom go to the Village anymore," he stated. "I live a very private life, me and Maria together," at their apartment in Brooklyn.[198] Ayler even began practicing less frequently, though he felt his music continued to be strong.

Nevertheless, Ayler continued to be productive. In early 1969, he began to reorient his music, evolving away from *New Grass*. He sought out a new drummer for the occasion. Sunny Murray introduced fellow drummer Muhammad Ali to Ayler around 1965 or 1966, and the latter invited Ali to sit in with one of his bands. "At that time, [Ayler] was playing at coffee houses down in the village because the clubs weren't hiring the people who were playing the avant-garde," Ali recalled of their earliest meetings. "So we were playing in those kinds of venues just to keep the music out there." They kept in contact with one another and, as Ali recounted, "we were always great friends and musical colleagues."[199] Finally in January 1969, Ayler called Ali for a concert at Town Hall in New York. Subsequently, Ayler retained Ali as he reconstituted the rest of the band for an extensive August recording date. "[Ayler] invited me to do a record date with him which turned out to be *Music Is the Healing Force of the Universe*. There wasn't a follow up from that because I went to Paris a couple months later and ended up staying over there for a while."[200] So Beaver Harris returned to the drum chair in Ayler's band.

Another big change was for Ayler to dismiss his brother Donald from the band. They played their last gig together at a place called the Black Mind, in Harlem, April 4, 1969.[201] Donald Ayler had been suffering from mental illness, which made his participation problematic. Ayler declared, "My brother was a very great artist in his own right. We tried to talk to each other but when we talked, he didn't hear me and I didn't hear him. We were screaming at each other like the music was."[202] Beaver Harris observed, "Albert knew that he needed to change to keep his thing going and I think he knew that he couldn't keep his brother with him and do that change. There were a lot of pressures on him."[203]

MUSIC IS THE HEALING FORCE OF THE UNIVERSE

Ayler's last studio record represented a final evolution for the artist. Ayler still had a big sound, at times, but it was tempered with layered accompaniments, especially Cobbs's, and also made more room for Parks's vocals. The record also featured the inclusion of the blues rock guitarist Henry Vestine, who, according to Folwell, "was in awe of Albert. He wanted to do anything he could to play with him."[204] Ayler remained the lead melodic voice on the record, but Vestine's guitar, at times, worked in a duet fashion as they dialoged together, while at others, Vestine lays down the top layer of the interlaced textures beneath Ayler.

"I believe that music is the healing force of the universe, it is a natural force," Ayler declared.[205] One critic observed that the record "spotlights Mary Maria who sings the sermon-like lyrics in almost cantor-like fashion."[206] Ayler played a bagpipe duet with himself, using overdubbing to create the effect. But many reviews of the record did not like the vocals or Ayler's experimentation with bagpipes and lamented that Ayler had turned away from his earlier powerful sound. Nevertheless, Ayler stated, "It's very beautiful when you can hear a number of bagpipes going at the same time, you can hear another kind of music altogether."[207]

Though Ayler never received steady work in New York, from late 1969 into 1970 it fully evaporated, mostly of his own doing. In mid-1970, he reflected, "I haven't played in New York in a long time. I believe the music that I am playing and other musicians of the same caliber like Ornette Coleman, the music we're playing is our own classical music. So, it doesn't make sense for us to play clubs like the Village Gate, the Village Vanguard, Slug's, and places like that because people will be drinking to the music and don't take time to listen to the music. The smoke and everything, it isn't a concert type thing."[208]

The greatest exposure of Ayler's late work came in France in the summer of 1970. The social transformations that occurred in post–May 1968 France meant that when Ayler played at Fondation Maeght in July 1970, he received far more positive reactions than he had during his previous visit in 1966. In fact, as the journalist Daniel Caux claimed, Ayler "was welcomed as a hero by the public."[209] Ayler had been invited to play at the Antibes festival but had turned it down to play concerts at Fondation Maeght because they were billed as more avant-garde, and the festival organizers wanted an exclusive appearance by Ayler.

The band was composed of Ayler and Parks and also included their longtime collaborator Call Cobbs, as well as the bassist Steve Tintweiss and drummer Allen Blairman. Tintweiss had previously played with Ayler at Slug's Saloon in 1966, but the two had not played since that time. The Pittsburgh native Blairman was a new addition to the Ayler circle. Donald Ayler was supposed to join the band for the festival but had been summoned to Cleveland to care for their ailing mother.[210] Cobbs was delayed in arriving, and thus he only appeared on the second night.

The concerts were the crowning achievement of this last phase of Ayler's career. "I live the music that I play in," Ayler stated in an interview at the time of this series of concerts. "This music keeps me going day to day. I try to live each day to its fullest."[211] Ayler was exploring the lower registers of his horn in contrast to the higher-pitched wailing that characterized so much of his earlier playing. The critic Val Wilmer detected a continuity with his earlier work through the spiritual themes, noting: "There is no escaping the religious nature of Ayler's music. It was not just that what he played could only have been created by a man of his spirituality. Many of the figures, themes, and the feeling itself, sprang directly, unadorned, from the black church. His saxophone punctuates Mary Maria's phrases on 'Music Is the Healing Force of the Universe,' as though they were side by side on the moaner's bench. It often seemed as if the church were the very place for which this music was intended."[212] In this vein, Tintweiss simply added, "The whole band would let the spirit take over and become a vessel for the music. You get to the point where you don't have to really think about it, it just flows through you. With Albert it was something he could summon through the strength of his playing. He had a singular direction with his raw sound that was transformational, especially when playing live."[213]

Before the concert, Ayler asked the band to walk with him out behind the villa where they stayed. They went into the forest, which was situated at the crest of a mountain. He turned to them, pointed at Tintweiss, and said, "'You start off with the bow and we will go from there.' That was his only instruction."[214] Throughout the performance, if Ayler wanted to start a new piece or change direction or mood, he would just start playing a theme or melody or shout something out to change tempo. There was no set list established in advance. Tintweiss, who was not familiar with Ayler's tunes and who'd had no opportunity to rehearse with the band, explained, "I just listened and tried to keep up." There were no stage monitors, so the musicians had to listen intently to one another. On the first night, Ayler attempted to play the bagpipes, but no sound came out, which is when he realized that they had been damaged during the flight, but he still attempted to produce sound for the entirety of the solo.[215] "We would have finished sooner," Tintweiss recalled, "but for the last three or four pieces on the second night, the audience was so intent with their encore that we kept going. Even on the first night, there was a lot of audience interaction and that's why we extended 'Ghosts' with a reprise."[216]

There were offers for the band to do some club dates in Paris, but not for several weeks after the festival performances, so Ayler ultimately declined. But the band did put on a house concert without Parks in a small hall at the villa where they stayed; Tintweiss recorded it on a mono boom box that he happened to have with him.[217] The managers of the villa did not want to let the impromptu concert happen there, but there was pressure from attendees, and they eventually capitulated. The batteries unfortunately ran out in the boom box, so the final pieces were not documented, including a version of "Summertime," for which Tintweiss supplied the vocals.

During this series of concerts, Ayler gave a definitive interview with the French journalist Daniel Caux, during which he stated, "For a long time, the mentality in [Europe] was much greater than in America because in America they were only after money, [Americans] didn't understand what the music was about, but now they are understanding a little bit. Now I notice a new generation in America, they are free minded, and they think like the music is. A number of the musicians, now they are playing the free music, they've incorporated certain ideas with pop music. So I see that the music was ahead of its time. I believe in the years to come it will be beautiful."[218]

Ayler did have some encouraging things on the horizon after returning to the United States. The record producer John Hammond was involved in arranging a tour for Ayler in Japan set for January 1971. These concerts would have expanded Ayler's audience considerably. Hammond was quoted as saying, "We are going to make him the next Miles Davis."[219] Ayler did not live to see it.

DEATH

On the morning of November 25, 1970, Ayler's body washed up on the Congress Street pier in Brooklyn. Earlier in November, after an argument with his mother, who felt that Ayler had abandoned his brother, who was dealing with mental illness, he smashed his saxophone into a television set and then left his apartment. He was never seen again. To this day, it is unclear what circumstances led to his death, as rumors told tales of murder, but most signs pointed to suicide.[220] Archie Shepp, in an obituary for the *New York Times*, wrote of his friend and colleague:

> In one of his final interviews, John Coltrane remarked to Frank Kofsky that Albert Ayler was one of the most promising new stars in contemporary jazz. Certainly that statement is true in retrospect as Ayler's music was truth: the soul embodiment of a boldly futuristic dream, rooted in a passionate, unyielding sense of morality and justice. For Albert Ayler was a charismatic man who in his time here on earth influenced many people. Perhaps all our lives have been enriched because we knew him—those of us who took the time to listen to his beautiful music and learn from him. Mr. Ayler was an Evergreen. A perennial child of the muse.[221]

Shepp continued, "[Ayler] was known for his fierce, almost other-worldly sound on the saxophone, and his unique, uncompromising concept, which from the outset could be described as a pure musical sound bereft of chords and banal melodies.... Ayler's genius lay in the fact that he revised the musical context with the result that many new sounds and effects were added to the legitimate range of the instrument." But then, in a final lament, he added, "I know I speak for brothers everywhere when I say we lament deeply the passing of this young, gifted black man. Indeed, the loss is greater than personal, it is national.... Brother Albert Ayler is not gone from us. He's somewhere now tellin' it like it is. And as his golden horn shrieks out the sound of his 'Ghosts,' the celestial host sways to the rhythm of Murray's thund'ring drum. Good spirits everywhere, rejoice!"[222]

Don Cherry remarked of Ayler: "In the West you reach a level where you are playing for money, but there are a few people that play for the love of God and as a reflection from God. Albert Ayler was one of these people."[223] But for Charles Tyler, he stated, "Al was really a sad person despite his charisma and everything. That 'old-time religion' was what caused his sadness; it was in his music. Al was a heavy guy, and there won't be nobody like him.... Someone said Al got depressed and jumped off the bridge. I wouldn't be surprised his religious background followed him through to the end."[224]

Despite the fact that Ayler did not receive wide acclaim within his own lifetime, ironically his death was announced in newspapers across the country, even in small-town and regional editions, in late 1970 and early 1971. Ayler's father commented after his death, "He represented the true spirit, the full force of life that many older musicians had and which many musicians today don't have. He was a true genius. He had all the title but not a dime."[225]

MEMORIAL FOR A NATIVE SON

Back in Cleveland, the Organization for the Development and Advancement of the Cultural Black Arts (ODACBA) organized what was intended to be the first annual Albert Ayler memorial fund program at Karamu House on April 11, 1971. ODACBA's aim was to educate the community about the historical contributions of Black artists to American culture.[226] Ayler's childhood friend, the pianist Bobby Few, flew back from Paris for the event. He composed extensive scores of music for the concert collectively titled "Sound Bomb," which he led with a twenty-five-piece big band composed of musicians from the Cleveland area.[227]

Ayler's fellow saxophonist Faruq Z. Bey penned a tribute to Ayler a decade later:

> they did not need you, Albert
> they did not need you and
> we could not bear
> the awful weight of
> your song Albert
> of Ancient Dynasties
> of occult, stellar
> communities, of Ausars
> insistent transmigration
> & cosmic parody they
> prefer to stare blank-eyed
> into the god-damned maw
> of intransigence, we
> could not hold nor protect
> you, Albert
> we who are raw &
> debauched would not
> suffer for your
> brutally olympian sweetness,
> the invocation of power
> ghosts, your timely
> candor, the burden of your
> martyrdom
> and so they come
> loudspeakers in the nite

with jarring angular
voices comes red mists
& sulfuric yellow rains
so we sweat pus &
languid oils from the east
comes prophets unacquainted
with sin
comes the anti-cristo
comes in halting
arhythmic steps, & we're
to assume them dancers
they come with stones
& equations they claim
to love the brilliant imago
if you are the dalai lama
then your light is dispersed
among raggedy-assed
saxophonists under the
evasive streetlights of
tomorrow[228]

LEGACY

One of the common statements that critics made about Ayler's music was that his music came out of nowhere. These claims may well have been, especially in Baraka's case, a genuine desire to recognize and champion the originality in his sound. But as a historical claim, these statements are faulty. As much as any musician of his time, Ayler drew from the deepest roots of American music. His imitation of vocals, whether from blues, spirituals, or a preacher's cadence, possessed at least some familiarity. His usage of religious sonics, like speaking in tongues, again possessed a forthright lineage and history. But his embrace of field hollers in the arc of his most ecstatic saxophonic cries, arguably his single greatest innovation, were perhaps unfamiliar to many listeners in the 1960s, though Black critics such as Baraka and Neal recognized them. These aesthetics had undergirded Black music's development since spirituals and the blues.[229] Ayler, more than any other twentieth-century artist, took the rich sonic matter of America and recast it in new, startling forms. Ayler stated, "I believe that all music must have roots, it must have rhythmic truth. I love rhythm just like Louis Armstrong and Coltrane. For you to really feel it, and to appreciate it, that has to be there."[230]

The misinterpretation of Ayler during his lifetime likely played a role in the alienation he felt on a personal level. His self-assumed prophetic stance seems to have only exacerbated that alienation and may have spurred his death. That Albert Ayler was a free jazz pioneer is clear, but his much more momentous claim—to reformulate not only jazz but aspects of soul, Blues, gospel, spirituals, rhythm and blues, speaking in tongues, and field shouts pushes him into the realm of being one of the most transformative, innovative, and challenging American musicians of the twentieth century. In many ways, Ayler seems to have exhibited much of what Fred Moten has theorized: A unique form of sonic resistance is present in his sound, employing a wide range of identifiable pieces of tradition and communal memory that are drawn together in a unique and profoundly new synthesis. There was no limit to the Ayler synthesis, and his organic, original voice offered some of the most forward thinking across these many genres ever accomplished.

CHAPTER 9

MIDWESTERN DRIFTER

*Charles Tyler in California,
New York, and France*

Freedom is what every man seeks, not only in music but in everything. . . . To play free music one must have a technique of one's own. Few men are fortunate enough to be free."

—Charles Tyler

Charles Tyler left a significant legacy as a musician and recording artist, and also through the many people who he mentored, but his perspectives on his own work remain elusive.[1] No substantive interviews with him appeared in print in English during his lifetime; those that did were in European jazz magazines in French or German. From a very early stage in his life, he exhibited a strong desire to learn, to study music systematically, and bring a trained ear to his own musical ideas. His financially poor background served as a nagging insecurity, but he developed an incessant drive to overcome that and attended universities wherever he lived, pursuing training in performance, composition, and improvisation. His desire for knowledge is embodied in his statement, "I wish I could live a hundred years and know that I will never be done learning and understanding."[2]

In Tyler's first known interview in 1965, he stated very clearly, "I think all music plays an important role in shaping the destiny of humanity and the world." Tyler was an artist that took his craft seriously, and he thought deeply about his role and its impact on broader society. But to this he stated his own purpose clearly: "Freedom is what every man seeks, not only in music but in everything. I believe that freedom in music is achieved when an individual can play what they feel and express their feelings properly. To play free music one must have a technique of one's own. Few men are fortunate enough to be free."[3]

FOLLOWING AYLER TO NEW YORK

By 1962, Tyler had become interested in playing free jazz.[4] "A lot of the musicians of my generation started the New Music because they didn't like the old lifestyle as well as some aspects of the older musical philosophies," Tyler explained. "Still, we all took from the jazz tradition, using these elements in new and different ways. Music is much more spiritual now. Many musicians didn't want to eat, drink, or dope themselves to death like Charlie Parker and others from his generation did."[5]

Tyler's first work came through his association with the musician's union, which would sometimes get him weekend gigs in Cleveland, but he found a new creative focus when he reunited with Albert Ayler. In 1963, the latter asked Tyler to come to New York to work with him.[6] Tyler lived near him, rooming with the Cleveland-born bassist Earle Henderson at 130th Street and Lenox Avenue in the heart of Harlem. Other musicians from Cleveland also stayed at the apartment, and Ayler came over several times a week to practice with them. Henderson stated of the sessions, "We young bloods, we bearers of the torch of certain tribal traditions, raised the skies over Harlem every night with the steam of our music."[7] Tyler would often say to friends that he and Ayler were brought together by "a spiritual force."[8]

Tyler rejected the notion that free music was not rigorous. He admitted that the music had attracted some charlatans, who "grabbed an instrument and started running." Rather, he argued, the musicians in his circle "had exactly the opposite approach. It was because we had assimilated the established techniques to the point of exhaustion, because we were frustrated to go around in circles in the codes of the previous generation that we were looking for a new way of expressing our ideas." But Tyler readily recognized the challenge that they faced. "Any innovation, any break with tradition is difficult to carry out. We come up against the listening habits of the public, the establishment, the dominant distribution circuits, the record companies, the timid spirit of producers whose only role is to exploit proven 'recipes' that have already managed to capture the attention of a mass audience."[9]

Tyler gained considerable experience in the Ayler circle and was soon hired for his band. The following two years would witness Tyler's rise to significance within that orbit, appearing on the groundbreaking records *Bells* and *Spirits Rejoice* as a significant counterpart on the front line with Ayler. For his involvement in the group, Amiri Baraka, then Leroi Jones, called Tyler "one of the best alto men on the scene right now" and added in more colorful language, "only Charles Tyler of the Ayler unit has the big wailing heavy alto sound that satisfies my particular need for flesh and blood."[10] Another critic stated, "Tyler especially is a tremendously original altoist. Like Marshall Allen, he's gotten away from playing in keys, moves with fire into an amazing variety of effects, always bursting through the melodic line, devouring freedom in huge, wild gulps. There really isn't enough of him in these two albums, but his contribution to the excitement of the music is indispensable."[11] Many years later another critic wrote, "Tyler lays out for an extended period on every track, allowing the principals to move from a lite pulse to a contrapuntal invention seemingly string quartet-like in beauty and solemnity."[12]

Tyler remarked about the work he did with Ayler, "In 1964–65 our music had a strong political coloring. This is because the social and racial struggles that shook the country were reflected there. Music is a means of expression and we were all concerned with what was happening. Everyone wanted to be a musician and at the same time, a preacher. Our music was really a discourse, a manifesto. That's why it was so hard-edged."[13] On a more practical note, Tyler later noted that the most profound thing that he learned from Ayler is that it was more important to express his feelings in the music than whether what he was playing was right or wrong.[14] It was a very freeing and liberating experience.

Tyler's departure from Ayler's band came only as the latter became determined to elevate his brother, Donald, into the front line on trumpet. For a short while, Tyler remained in the band, but by early 1966, when Ayler announced plans to include the violinist Michel Samson in the lineup for a concert in Cleveland, Tyler walked off the bandstand and never returned.[15] He was resistant to sharing the stage with a white musician at the time, though scarcely a year later he would hire a white musician for his own band.[16] But at that time in 1966, Tyler refused to appear at the concert out of principle. And aside from that, Tyler was restless and wanted to get out from Ayler's shadow and start his own band. He later stated of the period, "I needed to take a step back from the New York scene, so I withdrew."[17] He was already pushing in new directions toward his own unique vision.

FIRST RECORDINGS

For his first recording date as a leader, Tyler was joined by the vibraphonist Charles Moffett, cellist Joel Freedman, bassist Henry Grimes, and drummer Ronald

Jackson.[18] Tyler originally asked Moffett to play drums, but at that time the latter was trying to help his friend Jackson get started in New York, so he offered the gig to him instead; Moffett played orchestral bells.[19] They recorded *Charles Tyler Ensemble* in Indianapolis, on February 4, 1966, which bears, on the surface, some clear aesthetic influence from Ayler. The piece "Three Spirits" makes direct reference to the similarly named piece composed by Norman Howard and commonly played and recorded by Ayler.

But Tyler also exhibited some startlingly original ideas. The fluttering pitches on the opening piece "Strange Uhuru" are the most obvious example, but the way that Tyler orchestrates them is very different, allowing it to crystallize amid adornments of vibraphone and then evaporate into ethereal space on Freedman's cello. The melding of saxophone and cello sounds was another innovation. The piece is one of the most remarkable from that era of fiery saxophone in that he reaches a more subtle outcome while driving home a spiritual message of freedom and independence. In the other pieces that follow, Tyler's playing is a bit closer to Ayler's, but he maintains the same aesthetic often through Moffett's vibraphone playing and occasionally in the cello and bass parts. One critic used the German term *Klangfarbenmelodie* (melody of tone colors) as "a good expression for [Tyler's] playing" on the record.[20] Even with this first record, Tyler's approach to rhythms stood out, and others would comment on his unique rhythmic style throughout his career.

Tyler's second record, *Eastern Man Alone*, recorded eleven months later, also in Indianapolis, is a more daring record.[21] For this session, he hired local musicians, the bassists Brent McKesson (b. 1946) and Kent Brinkley (1949–2010), and of particular note, the cellist David Baker (1931–2016), whom Tyler had known since high school.[22] Tyler came to Indiana University and wanted to collaborate with Baker, who had previously played with Lionel Hampton.[23] Baker had had a "great influence on the technical development of Charles' music."[24] Tyler referred to Baker as "one of the most complete musicians I have ever known. As a teacher, he is profound."[25] While still a student at the university in 1959, Baker had directed the school's jazz band to a first-place finish at the Notre Dame Collegiate Jazz Festival. The school immediately started to offer jazz courses for credit and hired Baker soon after that, promoting him to chair of the jazz department in 1966.[26] As McKesson observed, Baker "made it blossom like a whole new universe from what it had been."[27]

Baker was deeply rooted in bebop and influenced by the pianist and composer George Russell, but "he loved Ornette [Coleman] and the avant-garde in general."[28] Baker explained, when he wrote in 1970, "Jazz is a black music, and its content mirrors the black experience. Because we are so regularly imitated and exploited, we are forced to invent new vocabularies in order to keep our language of music vital, authentic and safe within the vault of black culture."[29] Baker was particularly interested in the avant-garde for its creative rhythms and melodies. It avoided what Amiri Baraka referred to as "predictable regularity," and its uniqueness made it difficult to replicate easily. Baker was instrumental in recommending McKesson and Brinkley for the band.[30]

Tyler met with McKesson one-on-one to play together a couple of times, which was the only rehearsing that happened before the recording.[31] McKesson characterized Tyler as "so down to earth, it was really easy to work with him. He had such an amazing musical mind."[32] The bassist had recently gone with the Indiana University jazz ensemble on a State Department tour performing in India and Pakistan. During that journey, he "heard a lot of music from there and we got to interact with musicians, especially sitar players and percussionists. We learned about the scales they were using and about quarter tones. But the idea of freedom in the music was the most revealing thing," McKesson noted. "Music can come from a part of yourself that you aren't familiar with yet. There is so much more to do and to hear than what is written on the page. That tour opened the door to another world musically for me."[33]

Tyler, Baker, and McKesson then went to Indianapolis to a small space named Feature's Studio, where they met Brinkley for the first time. The latter was just seventeen and was trying to get work as a musician in the city. The two-bass lineup was likely inspired by Ornette Coleman's *Free Jazz* (1961).[34] As a reference point for them, Tyler talked briefly about the work that Henry Grimes was then doing with Ayler and others. McKesson had heard Ayler's record *Spiritual Unity*, was infatuated with Gary Peacock's sound, and bore considerable influence from Charles Mingus. "But Charles [Tyler] did not tell us anything else about what to do when we played."[35] McKesson described Brinkley as "almost like a drummer, he provided a very strong foundation rhythmically for what we were doing."[36] McKesson added, "I supported the alto and cello, responding to them or taking what they were doing a little further. The music was about forward motion, what we were doing in one moment, the next moment, and so on."[37] Tyler composed the piece "Eastern" with the idea of "an Eastern imagination functioning under Western circumstances." It was dedicated to John Coltrane.[38] The record title itself was a reference to Tyler's interest in Islam and the sense of origins in the East.[39] Tyler was musically declaring autonomy.

Tyler asked the writer and editor Lloyd Weaver to write the liner notes for the record because he felt Weaver understood his music and was a vocal Black nationalist.[40] Weaver wrote:

The craft of bearing witness to the crumbling system of Western Civilization and simultaneously to the culmination of the positive forces of the universe in such a manner that only the true, the honest, the compassionate, the wise can understand, is a virtuous skill that requires a certain alienation from matter itself. And if fleshful creatures surrounding such an entity, through some ephemeral understanding, master the craft, touching the person and bearing witness to his creation, his living-in-creation, they might also experience a wholesome recreation of their own transcendent lives.

Charles Tyler finds self. As a stellar spirit he consumes reality and commands as God commands. He is an integral and fierce voice, screaming the word of Allah. He explores the soul of the universe finding the first tenet: man has alienated himself from the forces which control him.

So, in this light Charles sings with and of a total self. A man whose involvement with the universe transcends Earth and is one with God. His song, on the other hand, encompasses and suggests the becoming of man, the "web of life." It is a hopeful tune which praises those who hear it, and hopefully welcomes them to meaning.[41]

Here Weaver speaks of transcending contemporary politics, the material world, and the self-alienation of Black modernity in America. But he also identifies Tyler's mission: to seek a sense of self and to root that self in something new, belief, philosophy, God. This outlook positions music as one of the processes to undo the wrongs of the world, the confusion, disorder, and injustice. Music was the interconnector, the very process of becoming that frees the spirit.

Though the record was generally dismissed by critics at the time, *Eastern Man Alone* was an aesthetic breakthrough on several levels. The aqueous string lines, often intersecting, melding together, or floating about one another, create a sonic palette unlike any other free jazz recording of the era. Tyler further explores his forays into melding his own alto tone with the cello again on this record, creating a subtle synthesis of strings and horn. A few critics who did praise the work were drawn to the textural ideas.[42] Three decades later, the saxophonist Elliott Levin's record *The Motion of Emotion* would garner comparisons to the "highly successful experiment" of *Eastern Man Alone*.[43]

The band never performed in public, nor did they ever assemble to play again, so this stage of Tyler's experiments in composition and bandleading came to a close. In an interview with *Ebony* magazine after the release of *Eastern Man Alone*, Tyler stated, "Music now has a political structure. That's why our music sounds so anarchic. The political atmosphere in the world is distorted and chaotic. But our music is simply suggesting what the world is like today. And the black musician has the most to say about it."[44]

Tyler had another band in Cleveland in 1967 that included the soprano saxophonist Dempsey Powell, bass clarinetist Donald Strickland, pianist Sigmond Raoul, and bassist Clyde Shy.[45] Raoul had been mentored by the Cleveland-based composer Emil Boyd. Tyler was initially quite excited about the prospects, referring to Raoul in *Jazz Magazine* in April 1967 as the most creative pianist since Bud Powell and Thelonious Monk, but the band soon disintegrated, which may have finally been the impetus for Tyler to return to New York.[46] His last known concert in Cleveland on February 9, 1968, was at an event organized by CORE advocating for the anniversary of Malcolm X's assassination to be recognized as a national holiday.[47]

Tyler moved to New York for some months in 1967, where he reunited with the bass clarinetist Donald Strickland and also met the bassist Ibrahim Abdul Wajid and drummer Majid Shabazz.[48] The four found solace in sharing a dedication to Islam and lived together in a modest apartment in northwestern Harlem, near Washington Heights. They invited the journalist and photographer Guy Kopelowicz, who worked for the French magazine *Jazz Hot*, to attend a jam session at their home in late 1967. "After having attended to their ritual prayers, they took their instruments and launched into tense yet catchy music where movement dominates the musical order but where lyricism still has its place."[49]

Kopelowicz was drawn to the frontline of Tyler and Strickland, the combination of which "forms one of the most endearing sounds of new music. The rhythms punctuate non-stop the contrapuntal improvisations of Tyler with his loose and leaping playing, and of Strickland's sound, shocking and forceful."[50] Tyler was unable to find much work for the band, however, putting on the occasional concert and playing benefits with Black community organizations. Tyler had another short-lived sextet group that included the trumpeter Arthur Williams around the same time, but it also failed to get traction.[51] "Tyler was clearly influenced by Albert Ayler at that time," the trumpeter Ahmed Abdullah noted. "And he had a way of using folk music for going into the avant-garde. He composed in that way also."[52] With Tyler's first attempt at establishing himself in New York having failed, Tyler soon set his sights elsewhere. He moved to Denver for the last half of 1969, claiming, "I had a family to feed and needed to prove to myself that I was capable of doing so with my musical talent alone."[53]

During that time, an agent suggested he start a rock band, which he named Tyler and the Vulcans.[54] Tyler sang and played harmonica and saxophone, with a backup band that included a guitar and keyboard. The band played a range of popular songs from that era including "Michelle" by the Beatles, songs by Jimi

Hendrix and Bob Dylan, and others of the time. Tyler admired Dylan especially, and much later in his career, when he chose to include vocals, they often revealed some aesthetic influence from Dylan.[55] The band did what Tyler referred to as "the cowboy tour," traveling from Albuquerque and Santa Fe through Texas, Oklahoma, Colorado and concluding in Cheyenne, Wyoming. They made some money, but he ultimately found it unfulfilling.[56] Tyler claims that they were offered a lucrative recording contract by A&M Records but that he refused because he did not like the music they were playing, and he expected the company producers to compromise their artistry.

Tyler later remarked of the experience, "I try to make music properly without betraying myself. I try to be honest and not sacrifice my unique voice. So, I have a certain repugnance for electrified music. It's not 'human' as it sounds. I like the lively sounds that come from natural, simple materials: wood, metal." He considered the natural elements of music "comparable to the need of the inhabitants of a hostile city like New York to have dogs, cats, a form of animal life, plants on their windowsills as substitutes for nature to ward off the concrete."[57] It is also likely that during this travel through the western United States, Tyler first encountered various elements of American Indian culture and spirituality, which he carried with him and treasured through his life.[58] With this all in mind and with new-found conviction to pursue his own organic sounds, Tyler moved to Los Angeles at the end of 1969. From that point on, he was committed to making his own music regardless of the financial consequences.

LOS ANGELES AND OAKLAND

Tyler arrived at a time when a mini-migration was bringing many musicians to Los Angeles.[59] His first important encounter was with the young trumpeter Lawrence "Butch" Morris (1947–2013) and his older brother, the bassist Wilber Morris (1937–2002). Most of the first wave of players in Los Angeles had already moved to New York, such as the saxophonists Ornette Coleman and Charles Brackeen, multi-instrumentalist Eric Dolphy, drummers Ed Blackwell and Billy Higgins, pianists Andrew Hill and Carla Bley, trumpeter Don Cherry, and bassists Gary Peacock, Scott LaFaro, and Charlie Haden.[60] A few figures, such as the trumpeter Bobby Bradford and clarinetist John Carter, were still forging music at the time, but at the heart of the community in the late 1960s was the Underground Musicians and Artists Association, which evolved into the Pan-Afrikan Peoples Arkestra, led by the pianist Horace Tapscott.[61]

By the time of Tyler's arrival, the emerging generation of improvisers under Tapscott's tutelage was beginning to take shape. Tyler attended the band's rehearsals for a short period and met a number of musicians through the process. The twenty-year-old alto saxophonist Idris Ackamoor was one such person, and Tyler soon became one of his mentors there. "He really opened up his musical world to me and took me under his wing," Ackamoor explained. "He was my first mentor out on the scene. He had a very rhythmical way of playing melody sometimes that I have carried with me for the decades since. He also played a lot of wonderful folk melodies such as a piece he titled 'Spanish Gathering.'" Tyler also led his own trio while he was in the city. "But Los Angeles was not a supportive place for us in terms of the police, the political situation at that time, and the lack of public transportation," Ackamoor observed. "And almost nobody could make a living as a musician there."[62] Tyler claims to have found some studio work in Hollywood, but it did not seem to last, and he left after about a year in the city.[63]

A lot of musicians began drifting north to the Bay Area around the same time, and Tyler was a part of that movement, initially going to visit an uncle in Oakland who subsequently helped him get an apartment. Then, with the provisions of the GI Bill, he studied at the University of California–Berkeley, where he obtained a degree in music education.[64] Tyler was there at the time that the curriculum was shifting from being staunchly focused on Western classical music and beginning to offer courses in Black music.[65] He attended courses such as "Afro-American Music," taught by the bassist Olly Wilson (the same figure who had mentored Abdul Wadud at Oberlin a few years earlier) and enrolled in "The Music of Black Africa." Tyler would have also had the opportunity to take courses on various Asian musics, especially those of South Asia, though the full extent of his education is unknown.[66]

While in the Bay Area, Tyler became an active bandleader, which was the impetus for Butch Morris to move there, and the two began playing together regularly.[67] Soon Tyler fronted the Charles Tyler Sextet (or Quintet), involving shifting lineups that included, in different formations, the Morris brothers, the alto saxophonist Arthur Blythe, drummer Jackie Prentice, and two Cleveland natives: the alto saxophonist Otis Harris and pianist and keyboardist David Durrah. Harris and Tyler had played together in Cleveland, but Durrah and Tyler met for the first time in Los Angeles shortly after the latter's arrival.[68] At that time, Tyler resumed playing the baritone saxophone, "finding that his bass-like instrument provided an effective foil for his more overtly melodic alto style."[69] Tyler's bands played weekly at the Native Son for stretches of 1971 while also playing at other venues in Berkeley, Oakland, and Palo Alto.[70] "The Native Son was a very small club," Durrah recalled. "I used to play there with Tyler and at other times with Sun Ra. It was amazing to me, how we would fit everyone in that club, with dancers and people moving around to the music. It was probably only supposed to hold thirty-five or forty people but we would get 120 in there!"[71]

Tyler also taught at several schools in the Bay Area. First, he was invited to do a residency at San Francisco State University, where he led an ensemble of students.[72] During that time, he met the clarinetist and saxophonist Roland P. Young, who was a student there. Young ran a show under his own name on the rock radio station KSAN-FM but had a four-hour late-night time slot where his aim was "to show the connections between all kinds of music from classical, avant-garde classical, native music from all over the world, jazz from all eras, just to break down the boundaries of the music to then break down the boundaries of people. That was the ultimate goal."[73] He regularly broadcast Tyler's recordings *Charles Tyler Ensemble* and *Eastern Man Alone* over the year preceding the residency.

Tyler and Young forged a musical connection almost immediately, playing together there and later reconnecting in New York. "We came together very well and quickly," Young reflected. "Our sounds merged quite lucidly. We sometimes used arrangements and written material, but most of the time we just tried to find connections through playing together. That was the era that we got as close as a people to ever having true power. Politically but even more so musically. People were hearing and feeling on a different level."[74] Soon after, Young was fired from KSAN for defending free speech by airing a speech by the Black Panther member David Hilliard.[75]

By the time that Tyler reached the West Coast, he had left the Nation of Islam but had joined other efforts to build and strengthen the Black community. Tyler soon was drawn into activities at Merritt College in Oakland, where Huey Newton and Bobby Seale were very active in trying to get educators hired who taught Black culture and history.[76] This movement was based around the Black Panther Party, which was organizing Black Students Alliances (BSAs) at Merritt, Grove Street College, Laney College, California State University at Hayward, and the University of California–Berkeley. Seale described these efforts: "[The BSAs] are based in the community at this time. They are working right now to raise funds and put funds together from the campuses and also the community and, whatever aid the [Black Panther] Party can contribute, to set up actual community survival centers where they have programs to aid students on campuses and also a program to directly aid oppressed people in the community. This group of brothers is very important because we have to get as many brothers who are into any kind of academic situation to regard their skills in terms of building a framework for black liberation."[77]

In 1971, Merritt College moved to the hills in eastern Oakland in reaction to the rising presence of the Black Panthers on campus, and what was left behind became Grove Street College, later named Peralta Community College. "The Panthers were making a political statement and wanted to show that they could hire qualified people," David Durrah stated. "Huey Newton and some others came to us and told us we were going to teach for them. They didn't really ask! So, we got letters of endorsement from John Handy, Charles Mingus, and Bobby Hutcherson because we didn't have advanced degrees, but we had the talent."[78]

The alto saxophonist Lewis Jordan attended Tyler's workshops at Grove because he knew of the latter's association with Albert Ayler. "I thought of Tyler and Ayler as twins in terms of sound, so to me he was pretty much on the highest level of the music that I wanted to be involved in. He would bring his own compositions in and have us work on them and play them together."[79] Other students at the workshops included the saxophonists Henry Peters and Michael Wilderman and trumpeters Sam Triplett and Reggie Colbert. A dozen or so others attended the series. Butch Morris and David Murray also joined Tyler in playing the pieces and demonstrating the improvisational and compositional concepts. "The students were at varying levels of being able to play," Jordan recalled. "Some were just learning to play the heads, while others were further ahead."[80] The workshop helped launch Jordan's career. For Tyler, it added significantly to his confidence and offered him a measure of financial stability for the first time in his life. He later remarked of the experience, "I knew then that I was not a prisoner of showbusiness, condemned to accept everything because I had no other way out. I felt freer, more serene."[81]

Tyler's presence at Grove thus came through the efforts of Newton and Seale, and he taught a history course titled "Jazz in American Culture" in addition to the workshop "Instrumental Ensembles," with Durrah serving as his assistant musical director.[82] Tyler and Wilber Morris also played at other Black Panther events for fundraising drives and community gatherings.[83] "Charles wasn't overtly involved in politics at the time, he was an artist and very dedicated to the development of avant-garde music," Durrah observed. "But he was also committed to making that happen within the Black community."[84] For example, Tyler led a quintet that formed part of the music in a play titled "Deep in My Soul," which was featured at a Black cultural festival that was organized by affiliates of Grove Street College at the East Oakland Development Center in the summer of 1971. The production chronicled "the black experience from Africa, through slavery and reconstruction, to the black ghetto and finally to the youth of today," featuring African, jazz, and gospel music.[85] The organization and funding of the festival was supported by the Black Panthers.

At the time he was teaching at Grove, Tyler's regular band was a trio with the bassist Wilber Morris and drummer Jackie Prentice, with whom students were invited to sit in.[86] Tyler's trio played regularly in Oakland and Berkeley and occasionally at colleges such as Santa Clara University.[87] Tyler also often played with the drummer Charles Moffett. "Charles Tyler and I became friendly through the workshops and then he invited me to join his trio at a performance in Berkeley," Jordan explained. "It was my first time playing in front of a live audience. He arranged his piece, 'The Queen,' so that we had a duet. The workshops and performance were a major point for me in my life as a musician."[88] Tyler's work in Oakland, like elsewhere, brought the music close to the Black community, to young, aspiring players, and served as an inspiration for people trying to get involved with the music on a community level. Tyler continued to teach there until he moved to New York in late 1973.[89]

Tyler would often meet with David Murray and improvise duets together around 1972. Murray was just seventeen, and the two would get together at his family's house in south Berkeley. They had a back house, basically a woodshed, where the two would play for four or five hours in the afternoon with some regularity. "He had that energy, like Ayler and he would talk a lot about Albert. He would show me things that he learned from Albert," Murray recalled. "He was always encouraging me to play freer and freer, to get off the regular notes and go to the multi-phonics, play harder or play softer, to really open up the horn. He definitely influenced me, at that time I was coming off Paul Gonsalves solos, Bird, all that bebop stuff. So, he helped open things up for me."[90]

In Oakland, Tyler encountered another aspiring player, the saxophonist Glenn Spearman (1947–1998), whom he hired. Spearman stated, "Charles was one of my first mentors, he believed in me right away. Charles loved my sound and that was good enough. He brought me into his band and we went to L.A. where I met Butch Morris." Spearman added, "He was well-schooled, more than people thought. He had beautiful compositions and scores, a very good composer. He was serious about the music, very spiritual, committed to Black mysticism. He's still to be discovered."[91] Even then, Tyler taught in California public schools to support himself, while putting together tours through Phoenix, Denver, and other western cities when he could.[92]

When back in Los Angeles, Tyler eventually found himself in the circle of the drummer Stanley Crouch and the group Black Music Infinity, which also included Murray, Blythe, Bobby Bradford, and the bassist Mark Dresser, as well as somewhat regular guest appearances by the clarinetist John Carter, flutist James Newton, Butch Morris, and Tyler. The band had been originally formed in Pomona around Claremont College. The band recorded a session, purportedly to be titled *Now Is Another Time*, but it was never released. Newton later commented that his encounter with Tyler in those years was one of the inspirations for him to pursue music more seriously.[93]

Crouch stated, "The music is avant-garde to the degree that it's unfamiliar and not workable in clubs. It's too electrifying. You can't pat your foot to it. People can move to it, but they'll have to learn to move another way. People will come around. We'll just have to wait." The drummer added, "People are wired to learn. Freedom always calls for greater levels of discipline. It requires you to diminish the fraudulent aspects of yourself so that the pure and stronger aspects can be made manifest. With freedom tied to the learning idea, both become a consistent, life-long quest."[94]

The band got considerable work through a circuit of colleges where Black student unions organized events. At one such event at the University of Santa Clara, they took part in a series of free public events under the theme of "Is This Black Enough for You?" By the time of Tyler's departure for New York in October 1973, the group had finally coalesced into a quartet of Crouch, Bradford, Murray, and Dresser, likely serving as the impetus for him to seek out opportunities elsewhere. He also soon stated that he wanted to return to teaching later in life, because it was one of the few means for practicing musicians to sustain themselves, but that at this moment he wanted to focus all of his energy on making music.[95] Tyler's California sojourn was a period of intense personal development. He wrote of it later, "During that time of reflection, I accumulated the energy necessary for a new beginning. My ideas had settled. That's why I felt strong enough to come back to New York."[96]

BACK TO NEW YORK: THE LOFTS

Tyler announced his arrival in New York in January and February 1974, leading a quartet on a series of Tuesday nights at Studio Rivbea, the city's most active loft run, by the multi-instrumentalist Sam Rivers.[97] The writer Stuart Broomer later referred to these performances as demonstrating that Tyler was a "direct descendant of Ornette Coleman's [1960s-era] quartet" with its natural transformation of bebop. Tyler also drew comparisons to many of the other altoists of the period, such as Oliver Lake, Julius Hemphill, and Luther Thomas. But really Tyler was forging his own sound and beginning to build a corpus of compositions that would gradually gain him the respect of his peers over the course of the decade. One figure took immediate notice: The eminent pianist Cecil Taylor invited Tyler

FIGURE 9.1 Charles Tyler (1941–1992), saxophonist, in New York.

Source: Courtesy David Glaubinger.

to participate in the Cecil Taylor Unit Core Ensemble's historic big-band performance at Carnegie Hall on March 12. His experience with the big band caused him to profess that he believed that Taylor's music was the future, that it possessed the next great concepts of human music, and that it would probably get recognition within a few decades as rising human intelligence and consciousness demanded the support of noncommercial music.[98]

"A bunch of us had been playing Tyler's piece, 'Lacy's Out East' in the lofts before we ever met him. We were hoping he would come back to New York," the bassist William Parker noted. "But when Tyler came back to town he had developed his own sound. If you heard him play without seeing him, you immediately knew it was Charles Tyler. It was almost a country sound, a blues sound, but a modern sound. Very different from what he had done on his ESP recordings. And he had developed a substantial body of work by that time, a stack of charts that he carried with him everywhere."[99]

Tyler wasted no time and began organizing a recording session for July 1974. Just before the recording, the band played two sets at the Rivbea Summer Music Festival, on June 30, where Tyler featured his New York band: the cornetist Earl Cross, bassist Ronnie Boykins, and drummer Steve Reid. Boykins had previously worked with Sun Ra and Rahsaan Roland Kirk. Cross had preceded Tyler in the Bay Area but had moved east to join Sun Ra in 1967. Shortly after the recording, Tyler stated that he and Reid "went back a long way," suggesting that they had met in New York in the 1960s, but it is not known how or when they first met.[100] At the festival, Tyler added two guests: the alto saxophonist Arthur Blythe and soprano saxophonist Roland P. Young, both of whom he had played with in California. Blythe also guested on the studio recording the following month.[101]

Tyler later admitted, "I found the money and paid the musicians who were my friends. Of course, I couldn't pay them union wages, but I managed to pay $40 or $50 per man to do it with me."[102] Each brought a unique sound to the group as Tyler recorded what many consider to be his masterpiece, *Voyage from Jericho*. The critic and scholar Ron Welburn wrote that the record exhibited "high caliber musicianship that will reaffirm and refurbish the vistas arrived at in the sixties."[103] Tyler stated of the record, "Politics come afterward from a self-defense point of view. It doesn't have anything to do with what I am trying to do with my music other than what is there naturally."[104]

The music on the record was a bold new statement by Tyler. For one, it was the first documentation of Tyler on baritone saxophone. The title piece had a folk melody but then built out in other directions as the band improvised. The title piece and the second track, "Return to the East," expressed spiritual connections to the Middle East, with Jericho as a metaphor for the Holy Land.[105] Though

Tyler never talked about his spiritual philosophy publicly, this record, like much of his other work, bore references to Islam and a desire to embrace spiritual origins outside of the West. This yearning is embodied not only by the searching quality in Boykins's brilliant bass solo but also through the triumphant statements by Tyler and Cross, contrasted by turbulent percussion from Reid.

As Ron Welburn noted, "On 'Surf Ravin' one can especially hear a contrast between Tyler and Blythe. Both have a similar way of sinuously delineating a line, but Blythe will use a vibrato more obviously than Tyler who in turn has that strange big tone that gives one the uncanny impression of being delicate at times."[106] Boykins had an early 1960s walking-bass-type of feel, while Reid's "execution is facile and one from which percussive colors emerge."[107] As another writer observed, "What really makes the music here is the interaction of the group and the sensitivity of the response between artists."[108] A third critic stated, "Distinctive, sharply contoured ensemble themes frame improvisations which weave looping, soaring lines or leap in guttural, angular fragments while retaining a solid, riff-based foundation and walking rhythmic drive."[109] Originally Tyler had intended the session as a demo tape for Prestige records, but they turned it down, so Tyler put the record out as the inaugural recording on his own label, AK-BA records. "We were a little bit too avant-garde [for Prestige]," Cross explained.[110] "Charles was one of the heroes for those of us who were a decade younger," William Parker stated. "He was the image of Black mysticism at the time. He had those records where all you could see was his face like he was coming out of the night."[111]

Throughout Tyler's career, reviewers would generally either compare him directly to Ayler or note his struggle to step out of Ayler's shadow. One reviewer of *Voyage from Jericho* noted that while the two shared some clear aesthetics, Tyler "leaned toward the meditative in his own music."[112] Though Tyler never recorded or published lyrics to his songs, William Parker recalled him regularly singing at gigs in the mid-1970s. "He would sing, he had lyrics to most of his songs, and he was a very good singer. He had a midwestern Blues kind of thing happening."[113] Over the eight years that followed, Tyler's bandmates from *Voyage from Jericho* would continue to be his primary collaborators.

The other substantial development for Tyler that coincided with the release of the record was the founding of the label AK-BA records. The label was just one of dozens of self-owned and self-produced labels that grew out of the music scene in the 1970s, coming out of the same philosophy of self-determination that had inspired the jazz lofts. Tyler declared at the time, "I am with the idea of controlling our own destiny in the music 100%."[114] Tyler pooled money together with his wife and brothers and founded the small record company, which worked in tandem with Steve Reid's label Mustevic Sound, their distributor.[115] Over the following eight years, the label released four additional records, one being a live concert by Tyler and the others coming from sessions led by the saxophonist Arthur Doyle and poet Barry Wallenstein. He originally had more ambitious plans, to sign European bands, to produce records by David Murray and others. He even dreamed that he might eventually find greater financial stability: "If I get signed by one of the bigger companies later on, I'll still keep my own company going by hiring other people. That's how I always invest my money in the music. In the end, it always boils down to musicians saving our music ourselves."[116] Like most of the small labels, the company never managed to turn a profit, and Tyler disbanded it in 1982.

Tyler's first substantive sideperson work at the time was with the trumpeter Ted Daniel, whom he had met at Studio We in 1974. By that fall, Daniel was running a composers' workshop at Studio We. People could bring material in, and they would work on it together over a series of rehearsals to refine what the band was capable of doing together. The band included the soprano saxophonist Hassan Dawkins; alto saxophonists Blythe, Oliver Lake, and Kazutoki Umezu; tenor saxophonists Daniel Carter and David Murray; trumpeter Ahmed Abdullah; French hornist Richard Dunbar; trombonist Charles Stephens; guitarist Melvin Smith; bassist Richard Pearce, and drummers Steve Reid and Tatsuya Nakamura. Tyler brought his piece "Folley" to the group, which Daniel considered to be "melodically quite typical of Tyler's compositions of the time with folk song elements and sound to them."[117] The group had their first concert at Brooklyn College on April 9, 1975, and then went into the studio to record three days later. A second session in May completed the record. At the time there were few labels supporting this kind of innovative big band work, and it was not released until Daniel put it out on his own label in 1997.[118]

Meanwhile, Tyler was active in pushing his own group ahead. In October 1975, he took a slimmed-down quartet with Melvin Smith, Ronnie Boykins, and Steve Reid to the Jazz Festival Umea in northern Sweden.[119] One review at the time spoke to the challenges that Tyler had faced in gaining recognition: "Tyler is a much overlooked jazz artist, eclipsed by giants like Coltrane and Ayler when he came up during the [19]60s, now overshadowed by the younger 'avant-garde' of the Chicago-St. Louis school," here referring to figures like Julius Hemphill, Oliver Lake, Roscoe Mitchell, and Joseph Jarman, who were steadily gaining recognition.[120] Another writer stated, "His sound and style have an immediacy that doesn't date. Why doesn't some capable company record him for he is a strong, developed, distinguished voice, both in playing and composition, and he has, perhaps as well as anybody who comes to mind, combined the styles and ideas of both Ornette Coleman and his old side kick, Albert Ayler into a derivative, but original and articulately, gutsy style of his own?" One might think there were several horn players playing simultaneously at moments on the live recording, but it was just Tyler issuing "shockwave after shockwave of shrieking high energy" in tandem with his bandmates.[121]

The Charles Tyler Ensemble continued to forge ahead. They had a residency at the Tin Palace in March 1976, where they presented new material that was well received.[122] By that time, Tyler had added a second bassist in John Ore, while retaining Cross, Boykins, and Reid. One critic stated that "on alto he was a player of great power and passion who was yet always dignified and controlled. His baritone was hard and muscular.... The compositions ... included a number of attractive marchlike themes and one Ayleresque line."[123] In May, they recorded *Saga of the Outlaws* back at Studio Rivbea, partly funded by a small grant from the National Endowment of the Arts.[124]

The music was largely inspired by the American film tradition of westerns.[125] Tyler's interest in the project had been inspired by his experience while touring with his rock band through the southwest and mountain west parts of the United States in 1969, when he got to see those landscapes firsthand. Tyler stated in the liner notes to the record, "I love Westerns, always have. I wanted to project a feeling of the daring, romantic Old West, like the Dalton gang or *Gunfight at the OK Corral*, which was a classic. I used to dig the background music in those films and the feeling that Frankie Laine used to achieve with his voice. Of course, this is quite different musically with modern overtones and instrumentation, but I was looking for the same sort of feeling."[126]

Much of the underlying, frantic energy of the films manifested in the dueling narratives of the two bassists, Boykins and Ore. They played excerpts of the theme, and like some other Tyler compositions, the bassists' rhythms were situated outside of the drum and horn parts. Tyler wrote, "I was specifically inspired by the possibility of finally using two basses. It gave me the opportunity to write four different melodies and put together something like two horn trios, bass and drums, except that they share the same drummer. *Outlaw* is a polyphonic work. In this, each musician uses the theme as a working motif. There is an organization, a harmony behind what I play."[127]

"I'm trying to develop another kind of sound that incorporates the two basic human characteristics of thinking and feeling," Tyler added. "While I'm certainly not emulating Ornette Coleman or Gerry Mulligan, I'm also developing a music that excludes a keyboard even though I love to listen to pianists and have been influenced by them. I'm trying to get a kind of rawness that you simply can't get from the piano which has a perfect, civilized sound. Rather, I want to get a sharp, cutting edge that is closer to the sound of nature."[128] One critic described the record as "a long, largely polyphonic musical dialogue, using parts of the theme throughout the performance."[129]

"What can be heard on *Saga of the Outlaws* are gangs—hornmen vs. bassmen, with a drummer switching sides or trying to stay independent—getting into position for a final shootout," the critic Norman Weinstein noted.

> It is a sonic transformation of the western gunfight which reflects that uncanny mix of orderliness and anarchy implicit in such a confrontation. Each player has his own song—but is influenced by what is going on around him. Each outlaw has only himself to count on—yet his fellow gang members are beside him, ready to draw. It is not a large imaginative leap from the Beat generation's image of the jazzman as an existential outlaw to the jazzman as western outlaw. Playing "with an edge," a sense of existential urgency takes on a new dimension of meaning when the player is also playing on the edge of a continent, or playing around the edges of prevailing myths about a continent's edges.[130]

The band was featured at a ten-day festival at Studio Rivbea in July 1976 and continued to play the music at other venues over the few years that followed, experimenting with lineups to create new versions of the sound.

BOOKING HIS OWN LOFT: THE BROOK

By August 1976, Tyler had found a new home for his music: a loft called the Brook, located at 40 West Seventeenth Street, just a block and a half west from Union Square.[131] The Brook opened in June 1975 in a building that had formerly been a garment shop and had since functioned as a space for classical avant-garde music.[132] The pianist Frank Ferrucci had taken over the space and was soon joined by the choreographer, dancer, and actor Harry Streep III in May 1976.[133] The dancer Janice Geller joined them about a year later. Their aim was to run a loft that catered to modern dance, music, poetry readings, and theater, all with significant improvisational elements, and they were regularly booking music there by mid-1976.[134] Many interdisciplinary performances also occurred, such as the collaborations between Janice Geller and the drummer Jackson Krall.[135] The Brook hosted many events in this vein, as well as talks by artists and critics, though it initially struggled to draw Black performers or audience.[136] A good audience there numbered around sixty people.

Tyler approached them in the summer of 1976 to see if they would be interested in a jazz series, and they readily agreed to have him book events in the space. "Charles was incredibly generous and open to creative ideas," Ferrucci recalled. "He was connected to the Chicago scene and when the AACM people came, he was able to work with them. Most Black musicians at the time were hesitant to be associated with white musicians, rightly so, and Charles was the bridge. When Charles got involved, he brought the jazz scene to the Brook and it became a space for Black music."[137] Figures such as Arthur Blythe, Julius Hemphill, Phillip Wilson, Steve Reid, Chico Freeman, Ken Simon, Oliver Lake, Jerome Cooper, Wadada Leo Smith, Mark Whitecage, and Ronald Shannon Jackson all led bands at the Brook during its years of operation.[138]

Ferrucci, Geller, and Streep lived in one-third of the space at the Brook, and the remainder was the event space, "with polished floors, large windows, the floors were impeccable because we were having dance in there. Five thousand square feet for very little money," Ferrucci explained. "It had a piano, drums, and several amplifiers that made it easy to host events. The audience would sit in folding chairs or on big pillows right on the floor. There were people from all over the world who came during those years, especially from Europe and Japan who had an advanced understanding of the music. People could bring in drinks if they wanted."[139] William Parker remarked, "It was a really clean place, nothing funky, it was different than the other lofts that way."[140]

By 1976–1977, the jazz lofts were proliferating. The early spaces such as Studio We, Studio Rivbea, the Ladies' Fort, and Ali's Alley were now joined by Environ, Jazzmania, Soundscape, University of the Streets, and the Brook.[141] Tyler organized a loft jazz coalition together with musicians running other spaces. They also garnered interest from critics such as Gary Giddens and Robert Palmer who helped draw attention to the loft shows. "There was an audience for loft jazz at that time, and a lot of musicians wanted to perform at the Brook," Ferrucci recalled. "We paid them with whatever money we collected at the door."[142]

Tyler often used the Brook as a launch pad for original music he was writing or for new ensembles he had organized. When Boykins was unable to join the band for a performance in Philadelphia in the summer of 1976, the group first performed as a trio, and liking that formation, the smaller group became a recurring entity. The group played two nights in September at the Brook. One observer described the evening:

> Mr. Tyler interjected several novel improvisational ideas, including timbre changes and a bagpipe-like drone effect, which kept the group's colors changing. His solos were steaming rhythmic workouts with each note and phrase out

clearly, and the melodic ideas were fresh and well organized. Mr. Cross's lines were prickly, his sound brassy, and his rapport with Mr. Tyler admirable. Mr. Reid was a one-man rhythm section. He uses a relatively small, simple drum kit and favors boldly delineated sounds. At times his insistence is reminiscent of rock drumming, but then he complicates matters with an overlay of secondary rhythms or a spattering series of raps and rolls.[143]

Tyler also continued to pursue education whenever possible while in New York. In the fall of 1976, he enrolled at Columbia University to study composition. During his time there, he was invited to present new, original pieces, and he obtained grants to organize a big band performance, the only known large ensemble of his career. He drew upon the workshops he had led at Grove Street College, his experience playing with Cecil Taylor and Ted Daniel, and what he had witnessed of Sun Ra. Taylor's referred to his big band music as "a powerful force" and added, "The big band seems to be becoming more popular in the 1970s than it was in the 1960s. These are different kinds of big bands but based on the same idea as the ones that were active in the 1930s and 1940s."[144]

Yet economics placed limits on what was possible. "Even if it is possible to bring together about fifteen musicians for one evening," Tyler noted, "I would need a subsidy to keep them together for the time necessary to develop a repertoire, a sound, and a cohesion."[145] With the support of two grants, he assembled a group that included many longtime collaborators, such as Blythe and Murray; his New York associates Boykins, Cross, Ore, and Reid; and new encounters with a range of people including Ahmed Abdullah, Richard Schatzberg, and Julius Hemphill. Though Tyler was not able to sustain the project because of the financial demands of a large ensemble, many of the musicians who took part would continue to be central to the music he made for the remainder of the decade.[146]

Abdullah, Blythe, and Hemphill joined Tyler and a host of others, including Hamiet Bluiett, Chico Freeman, Oliver Lake, Frank Lowe, Sunny Murray, Don Pullen, and Wadada Leo Smith at Environ the following weekend for a three-day festival in celebration of Black creativity.[147] It was through this event that Tyler became friends with the pianist John Fischer, who ran the space. Fischer subsequently hired him for the group INTERface, which was active at Environ and recorded in 1977 and 1978.[148] The critic Robert Palmer referred to the group as "one of a very few racially integrated groups working regularly in the city's jazz lofts."[149] He further described Tyler as "a formidably fluent alto and baritone saxophonist."[150] Another critic stated of Tyler's work in the group, "for some unknown reason [Tyler] still remains the avant-garde's longest best-kept secret."[151] Fischer and Tyler continued to work together, later recording two duo tracks together as well as other brief encounters.[152] Tyler returned to the Brook in February 1977, playing saxophone duets with Arthur Blythe.[153]

Around the same time, through their mutual friend Fischer, Tyler and the poet Barry Wallenstein first met. They began working regularly in various formations, most often as a duo, and at times with other figures including the trumpeter Don Cherry, bassist Cecil McBee, poet Jayne Cortez, and a variety of others. Wallenstein had originally studied with the poet and critic M. L. Rosenthal at New York University and had worked out his approach to jazz poetry with McBee and the pianist Stanley Cowell.[154] "It was with Charles that I really figured out how to collaborate with jazz players as a poet," Wallenstein explained. "He was very open and very funny. He liked working with my voice. I would give him a copy of what I was going to read and we would rehearse. He was a great listener. We really learned how to listen to each other as we played."[155] One of their favorite pieces to perform together was titled "To My Love," with Tyler playing melodically:

> Ever I've Known Her
> she's been moderate in his inhalations
> a slow smoker,
> and she's a person of serious degree.
> The men in her eyes melt
> this way and that way
> and she listens to what
> each one has to say.
> No cloud shape, no catch phrase
> will trip her.
> Lying back, as if to model comfort
> she rides into the night,
> rises with delight.
> Those tickets she holds
> appeared from a friend
> and if lost,
> others with the same allowances
> will appear—
> one-way tickets—
> we'll get on the bus
> one way where we're headed
> One way/ clear ride/
> my desire.

They began working steadily and soon set up a gig once every month or two, which lasted from 1976 until 1984. They performed primarily in lofts at the time such as Soundscape and the Brook, as well as clubs like Cornelia Street Café, and at Rutgers University, Delaware State University, and City College in New York.[156] They performed several times in New York City high schools via a program called "Poets Into the Schools" sponsored by the Department of Education. At the time, Wallenstein stated, "What we are trying to do is to remove poetry from its lofty plain and to bring it closer to the people. I decided to work with jazz rather than with some other form of music because jazz calls for a lot of improvisation, and I can modulate my poetry reading in accordance with whatever rhythms are being played. The whole pace and style of jazz lends itself to the inner-city audience that I am reaching."[157]

They also played numerous concerts at Day Top villages, which were drug rehabilitation centers located in the city and in upstate New York, where they almost always encountered a welcoming and engaged audience. "He was a free jazz screamer," Wallenstein observed, "but not only that. He recorded many beautiful takes of 'To My Love' which showed another side of him. He was a complex person. He was funny, very lovable. But underneath, there was a simmering anger. He was beleaguered by society, by racism, but also because he did not consider himself to be successful. He was haunted by people he played with who overshadowed him."[158] The result of their collaboration was documented on *Taking Off*, which they released on AK-BA Records.[159] Their best-attended concerts were staged in the Great Hall at Cooper Union, where they played annually in the period from 1978 to 1984.[160] In 1981–1982, they did a month-and-a-half tour in theaters, churches, and universities in France.

Tyler often led weekly practice sessions at the Brook, where he played for contact-improvising dancers. Upon hearing about this, the guitarist Eugene Chadbourne went to the loft and introduced himself to Tyler. Years later, Chadbourne remarked that unlike most of the musicians that he knew in New York at that time, Tyler "wasn't into all the heavy drugs . . . at least not with me."[161] The two hit it off immediately and began collaborating on sessions once or twice a week for about a year, from late 1976 through 1977. They eventually did one public concert with the troupe, of which there is no documentation, but Tyler and Chadbourne did record a duo record in September of that year, which was taken from their sole live performance, titled *Ghost Legends*. It was one of Tyler's most minimalist, subdued recordings as the two danced around one another sonically.[162] The music was drawn from Albert Ayler's piece "Ghosts" and from Tyler's piece "Legend of the Lawmen," the latter of which Chadbourne described as "one of his funny tunes about the frontier."[163] The saxophonist John Zorn recorded the concert on a Sony four-track reel-to-reel recorder, and according to Chadbourne, Zorn loved Tyler's playing, "especially on baritone!"[164]

The Charles Tyler Quartet with Cross, Boykins, and Reid went back to Europe in May 1977. They played extensively in the Netherlands and Germany, with an appearance at the Moers Festival as the apex.[165] There they were quite favorably received, and critics at the time considered the group one of the festival's greatest successes.[166] This was a personal high point for Tyler, stating at the time that the group "expresses myself completely and represents me completely. This music is the blossoming of a whole stage of my evolution. I have about forty compositions in reserve that I want to work on, projects that I would like to see come to fruition. There are also compositions by Earl Cross and Ronnie Boykins. We have enough material to work for four or five years. I make music for the people who listen to it."[167]

In a particularly cogent interview during the tour, Tyler spoke openly about the social and political situation in the United States. "I don't think you can really understand what the racial situation is here. Just know that mixed marriages are still exceptions and most often failures . . . it becomes a challenge when you try it against the weight and taboos of an entire society. Having a white wife is another way of asserting oneself as an equal. And being a musician is a way to enter a somewhat marginal artistic environment where taboos are supposed to be nonexistent. Going to Europe is one way to escape the stress that afflicts us here."[168] Tyler elaborated further, "But I think it is a bad way to make music, to see it as a means for social advancement. I make music because for me it is a vital need. It is an end in itself and not a means of making myself better. But even the sincerest musicians need the minimum of respect. This turmoil that surrounds jazz musicians ends up destroying even the best. I can't count the number of musicians who drink or take drugs. Even I am sometimes demoralized and tempted." Despite the discouragement that he faced, he added, "You can be a musician without destroying yourself, while living in balance, fully and for a long time."[169] Later that year, the band returned to Europe and played at the Fest d'Sutomne in Paris.[170] Back in New York, Tyler guest hosted a radio show on Columbia University's WKCR radio station.[171]

But Tyler was getting restless and wanted to try something new. In February 1978, he debuted a new group at the Brook, with the electric bassist Richard Williams, retaining Reid, and calling back Joel Freedman from Tyler's earliest days as a bandleader.[172] By June 1978, Tyler was leading an expanded ensemble that included the soprano saxophonist Akruma and tenor saxophonist Mustafa Abdul Rahim, along with Freedman, Williams, and Reid.[173] John Ore was sometimes added as a second bassist, while guests such as Tyler's former student

Roland P. Young and Barry Wallenstein were sometimes invited to join the group, for example, for the band that Tyler led for a three-week residency at Ali's Alley in October 1978.[174] Of those performances, Young remarked, "He was an introspective player, taking things from other musicians that he played with. He could take a very simple phrase and make it very complex. He talked about Albert Ayler more than anything and the influence he had on him."[175] The group followed with a concert at New York University in December.[176]

The year of experiments culminated with a performance of the music from *Saga of the Outlaws* at the Public Theater on February 17, 1979. The vibraphonist Walt Dickerson opened the night with a solo set, and then Tyler took the stage with his old friend David Baker on cello, Ore on acoustic bass, Williams on electric bass, and Reid on drums. As the critic Robert Palmer characterized Tyler's development, "In [the 1960s] he was a powerful but somewhat monochromatic soloist, given to either rich midrange lyricism or high-register whistling. Now he ranges all over his alto and baritone saxophones, projecting in all registers, balancing melodious fanfares with machine-gun bursts and high, singing melodies with basement rumblings."[177]

Of a performance at the Public Theater in February 1979, Robert Palmer added, "The music was inspired by characters from westerns, but the themes sounded Middle Eastern early on and close to the European Baroque later. Most of the playing was improvised, though, with Mr. Tyler taking encyclopedic solos on both his horns, backed by the crisply layered drumming of Steve Reid. The group's instrumentation was unusual, with John Ore and Richard Williams on acoustic and electric basses and David Baker on cello. The music's range was dark and thick, in keeping with the subject matter."[178] Tyler noted that he thought alto and baritone saxophones both had a resonance with cello, "the combination of a brass [instrument] in E flat and the cello ... it works."[179] The coupling of electric and acoustic bass along with cello was both innovative but also challenging in terms of articulation. But this seemed to hark back to some of the visionary experiments he'd begun with *Eastern Man Alone*.

In this period of experimentation, Tyler also began to develop his solo performance, especially on baritone. He debuted a solo set at Environ, April 21, 1978, and he continued to work on this aspect of his playing into 1979.[180] Surviving unreleased tapes reveal the earliest known version of "Sixty-Minute Man" and other pieces that he was then developing.[181] On May 5, 1979, a live broadcast on WBAI was recorded and released the following year on Adelphia Records as *Sixty Minute Man*. The record documents Tyler in some of his most intense playing, at times lyrical, but often in high-energy ruminations that intermittently returned to themes that he introduced throughout the recording. Among other things, the record debuted the piece "Mid-Western Drifter," which would be the title of a subsequent record all its own. The piece was autobiographical and seemed to tell something of Tyler's travels, scattered family connections, and the uprootedness that he felt throughout his life.

In September 1979, Tyler was supposed to join David Wertman, Frank Lowe, and Steve Reid at the first annual WCUW Music Fair, in Shrewsbury, Massachusetts. Rain caused the outdoor aspects of the festival to be canceled, and a power outage seemed to doom the rest. But Tyler and Reid assembled on stage regardless. "During the power failure, and in near complete darkness, Tyler and Reid gave a blistering performance, continuing until the power was restored," one of the festival organizers recalled. "Words fail in describing the otherworldly music that emanated from the dark hall that afternoon."[182]

That same month, Tyler began a new association that would again be innovative, this time with the French hornist Richard Dunbar.[183] The two would work regularly together over the following three years. They began playing in a trio with David Baker and also sometimes invited the poet Barry Wallenstein to add words to their live performances, in a group they called Composition.[184] The group evolved further when Tyler added his old friend Wilber Morris as well as John Ore on basses and Reid on drums as they prepared for the April 13, 1980, recording date of *Folk and Mystery Stories* and a residency at the Brook in the days following.[185] It was one of Tyler's most direct forays into unfettered lyricism, with clearly defined themes that pervaded the record springing again from folk melodies. Tyler noted of his music, "My music is profane, it comes from the blues, from the street, it swings."[186]

Baker admitted, "I had some serious doubts about what [Tyler] was doing, until one day we were rehearsing . . . we were going to do one of the loft gigs. Then all of a sudden the band just caught on fire and was swinging so hard. Charles stopped and said, 'No. Don't lock it into a groove because you can't move if it's locked in.' It's the first time I realized that Charles really had a different kind of thought, but it was a vision. He knew what he wanted. He said, 'Once we've chosen a tune, don't practice it, because when we practice it, then we'll start to recreate things that work, and it's no longer spontaneous.' My respect jumped 100%."[187] The group continued to evolve and returned to the Brook in December, with Otis Harris returning to the Tyler orbit, the bassist Kevin Ross sitting in, and Dunbar and Reid holding things down.[188]

The loft movement began to fade around 1978, but the Brook continued to host events until the end of 1980. Landlords were renovating such spaces and trying to convert them to residential apartments, facing fights from artists, especially in SoHo. But in the case of the Brook, the landlord successfully argued in court that the space had been used for commercial purposes—concerts and performances—and so ultimately Ferrucci and Streep were evicted. Tyler's series at the Brook came to an end to make way for new condos.[189] Nevertheless, hundreds of concerts occurred at the Brook during its nearly five years of existence, including a festival, and some records were also recorded there.[190]

NEW YORK AFTER THE LOFT ERA

After the closing of the Brook, Tyler moved quickly into a new association, this time with the violinist Billy Bang. By February 1981, they began playing together in a quintet that also included the pianist Michelle Rosewoman, bassist Wilber Morris, and drummer Denis Charles.[191] The following month, Bang and Tyler made a duo record during a live performance at Green Space.[192] Tyler employed harmonica and bells in addition to his saxophones; the two explored their sonic relationship through three compositions by Bang, one by Tyler, and one traditional piece. Tyler's "Legend of the Lawmen" was an extension of material that he had been developing since *Saga of the Outlaws*. Bang's piece "Alabama Africa," containing autobiographical references, is the most extensive example of Tyler's improvising on harmonica on record, with Bang moving from mbira to bells to violin in an innovative piece that explores timbre with touches of Blues elements. Tyler went on to record three subsequent records under Bang's leadership and played extensively with him in 1981 and 1982.

In 1981, Tyler reunited with the trumpeter Earl Cross, with Ross and Reid rounding out the quartet. He took the band to Europe and again found his most ready audience in Sweden. The group developed another autobiographical piece, "Cadiz, of the West Kentucky Woods," as well as numerous other compositions, alongside two pieces by Cross. These were all recorded live at Jazz Club Fasching in Stockholm, on October 20–21, 1981.[193] At an earlier performance in December 1980, in what was Tyler's last public concert at the Brook, he had debuted some of the pieces that were eventually recorded at the session in Stockholm. He featured there an early version of "The Mysteries of the Dark Blue Depths of the Pale Blue Planet." Of the performance, one critic penned, "The saxophonist improvised with his customary wit, discipline and presence, and Steve Reid served notice that he has become one of the most inventively incendiary drummers in contemporary jazz. The . . . pastoral sound [of Richard Dunbar] was particularly attractive in the context of the group's turbulent ensemble improvisations."[194] The reunion with Cross seems to have been short-lived, for Dunbar was with the band through 1982, filling the role of second horn and pairing with Tyler harmonically in the front line.[195]

Around 1982, however, Tyler began to slow down a bit as a bandleader. This was likely financial, as the lofts had closed, the club scene in New York was not supportive of the music, and most American labels abandoned the musicians. Still, Tyler's talent opened opportunities for him to work as a sideperson in some of the great bands of that era. Most prominently he was invited to play with the Cecil Taylor Expanded Unit for what are now considered to be historic performances at Lush Life in March and April 1982, together with figures such as the trumpeters Raphe Malik and Butch Morris; saxophonists Jimmy Lyons, Daniel Carter, Glenn Spearman, David Murray, and Ken Simon; flutist James Newton; bassoonist Karen Borca; trombonist Craig Harris; cellist Muneer Abdul Fataah; bassist William Parker; and drummers Rashid Bakr and Andre Martinez. One critic at the time wrote of Tyler's "astonishing range on baritone saxophone."[196] It was Tyler's only sustained work with Taylor, but it came at a crucial new embarkation point for the pianist's big band work of the mid-1980s.[197]

At the Kool Jazz Festival in July 1983, Tyler brought a one-time quintet that included the aspiring trumpeter Roy Campbell Jr., in their only known performance together, along with the pianist Curtis Clark. As the critic Jon Pareles noted of the performance:

> Tyler led a quintet with his own pieces, most of which merged open-ended harmonies with hard-swinging rhythms. He gets a bright, edgy tone on alto saxophone and a hefty sound on baritone, and even in pieces with complex harmonies he retains a bluesy cry. He showed his connection to the blues most clearly in a swaggering vamp piece dedicated to John Coltrane and Lewis Jordan. Tyler's quintet picked up all of his rhythmic initiatives in the best free-bop tradition, with darting, dramatic solos by the trumpeter Roy Campbell and the pianist Curtis Clark underlining the tunes' angularities with sparse handfuls of notes.[198]

The new lineup for Tyler's ensemble emerged out of the band he presented at the Kool Jazz Festival. Dunbar and Wilber Morris were in the group, and the drummer John Betsch entered the milieu for the first time. The following March they played a live set at Sweet Basil, which happened to be recorded and was released two decades later.[199] The group also performed at the historic Sound Unity Festival, which brought together disparate parts of the Lower East Side free jazz scene, as well as German figures like Peter Brötzmann and Peter Kowald, into community with one other, foreshadowing later developments such as the Vision Festival.[200]

Of his work in New York, Tyler noted: "The period from *Voyage from Jericho* to the end of 1984 was a milestone in my life. The record *Definite* [2 vols.] marks for me the end of an era."[201] Tyler had established himself in New York, released a series of innovative records, managed a loft, and fronted a band with considerable longevity through a turbulent period in the New York scene. But when that came to an end, he was eager to try something new: France.

TO FRANCE

Tyler's last sojourn took him to France. Back in 1979, Tyler had stated, "I want people to hear me. I don't want to be a big star, but simply earn a decent living from my art."[202] But the decline of the club scene through the 1970s and the defunding of the arts that came with the policies of the Reagan administration meant that by the early 1980s, the financial well-being of most jazz artists was quite bleak. After the loft jazz scene dwindled, Tyler did what many musicians at the time were forced to do: seek out opportunities abroad. Just a few years earlier, Tyler had stated, "Europeans are much more advanced in the promotion of the arts [than the United States]. They support art for art's sake, not to make money. They have been supporting our underground music in Europe more and more, I mean our Black music. A number of our musicians have moved to Europe and they live quite well there."[203] The economics of music making was better in Europe, and so he moved to Paris. As his former collaborator from the Brook Frank Ferrucci stated, "Charles had a big name in Europe, but less so in the U.S. It was the same for a lot of musicians."[204]

In July and August 1984, Tyler was a part of some of the dates on the Sun Ra Arkestra tour through France and West Germany. This association got him invited to play a few domestic dates as well, first at the Chicago Jazz Festival in early September and then back in the Windy City for a jazz showcase in early October for a two-week residency.[205] The Arkestra, with Tyler joining them again, did a subsequent European tour through Sweden, France, and West Germany again from July to October 1985.[206]

Touring with Sun Ra convinced Tyler to finally move on from New York. "When I came to Europe with Sun Ra, I decided to settle there for a while. The dollar was rising, many tours had been canceled, and the best way to play there was to live there." Tyler began to forge new collaborations. "In Paris, I often play with Chris Henderson, Bobby Few, and Jack Gregg. I also work in Denmark with Johnny Dyani, with William Little and William Breuker in Amsterdam."[207] Tyler also played with Alan Silva's Celestial Communications Orchestra during the same period.[208]

Tyler was never as prolific in Europe as he had been in New York, but he did forge some important connections over the final seven years of his life. He was featured with the Steve Lacy Quartet in 1986 and recorded with Swedish players in Stockholm in 1988.[209] Wilber Morris and the drummer Denis Charles played with Tyler in France when they were in Europe. Tyler experimented with playing tenor saxophone, piano, and even singing.[210] "My music is a little less rigid, more entertaining," he commented. "I incorporate both the feeling I had in my rock band and things that came to me from new music."[211] His last recordings appeared on the record label Bleu Regard, run by his wife, Marie Cosenza, and he included the pianist Curtis Clark and bassist Didier Levallet in the trio. Levallet in particular was a regular collaborator during these final years. Tyler's final session at Studio Aid in Pernes-les-Fontaines, March 30–31, 1992, was pressed for a disc appropriately titled *Mid Western Drifter*. Tyler's vocals displayed his admiration for Bob Dylan. The title piece from his final record was one of his most autobiographical pieces, bearing these lyrics:

> It was a return to the east
> as in the children's music march
> like in the flight of the Surf ravin
> on a Voyage from Jericho
> they were happy sad hip folks
> who knew of Cadiz of the west Kentucky woods
> they knew not, of the dark blue depths,
> pale blue planet
> lucifer got uptight
> as he gazed upon the wasteland
> of uptown manhattan puerto-rico
> he came as a space traveller
> to play his role in the warlock mystery drama
> little did he know that the adventures of the ode to lady
> day stand so strong.
> It was saga of the outlaws
> verses The legend of the lawman
> you see
> I was only a mid western drifter
> in search of the route
> from saint-louis to Kansas-city by

> way of Chicago
> as told in the tale of bari reed
> a man alone
> who could twing twang twiddle all night long
> with a song, A tale of bari reed
> I was just a mid western drifter

Tyler became quite sick and spent the last six months of his life in and out of the hospital in Marseille. His youngest child, Akbar Tyler, came to France from Cleveland to take care of his father in his final months. Akbar helped produce his final concerts, making posters and helping set things up. These final concerts were by a group that included the violinist Christian Zagaria, guitarist Remy Charmasson, bassist Bernard Santacruz, and drummer Jean-Pierre Jullian, but Tyler was too sick to perform, and the band played without him.[212] Tyler called his old friend Barry Wallenstein and said to him, "Nobody gets out of here alive."[213] Tyler's death in Toulon on June 27, 1992, left a significant artistic legacy that seemed in many ways unfinished.[214]

Tyler was quite haunted by his lack of financial success and his inability to provide more for his family.[215] Tyler once stated, "I sometimes imagine myself being 112 years old with great-great-great grandchildren. It's a wonderful dream and I think it would be beautiful to live, it would be an extraordinary chance to be able to witness, participate in the evolution of the world for a century. I believe the one and only way to pay homage to God . . . is to love life, to want it to be long and beautiful." But then he added, as if braced with reality, "Life is really too short to waste time faking. This is why I take everything I do seriously. If you treat your art seriously, eventually it will pay off and your music will give you back the pain you put into it."[216] Reflecting on his own legacy, Tyler said, "I feel I will leave something of value. Since our lives are short and petty in the larger scheme of things, it's important for me to feel that we will all improve as people. If this happens, then my musical contributions are worthwhile."[217]

CHAPTER 10

ARTISTIC LIBERATION ABROAD

Frank Wright, Bobby Few, Muhammad Ali, and Alan Silva in New York and Paris

> *France was ready to hear free jazz.*
>
> —Simone Few

The saxophonist Frank Wright and pianist Bobby Few were two important Cleveland musicians whose influence was primarily felt outside of the United States.[1] With John Coltrane leading the way, Frank Wright was part of a generation of figures, including Pharoah Sanders and Dewey Redman, that would further the exploration of overtones and harmonics on the saxophone.[2] Albert Ayler was also a clear influence on Wright in his early stages of development, but the latter managed to distinguish his own unique approach even by the time of his first recording in 1965. Bobby Few was a pianist with one foot in bebop but who developed his own vocabulary and approach to free playing. Wright and Few intersected through their careers as they also encountered other key players in their journeys to New York and Paris.

MOVING TO NEW YORK

Having heard about Ayler's contract with ESP Records, Wright left Cleveland for New York in 1965.[3] He spent the following year between Cleveland and New York, assembling a band of fellow Clevelanders that included Few and the bassist Cevera Jeffries Jr.[4] Wright also regularly attended Coltrane's performances in a circle that included Archie Shepp, Marion Brown, John Tchicai, and Carlos Ward, as part of the emerging generation of saxophonist innovators. Coltrane clearly took notice and invited Wright to sit in with him for a concert at the Village Gate. Bernard Stollman, who had just started ESP, attended the show and approached him as he came off the stage, inviting him to record for the label.

On November 11, Wright went into the studio and recorded the self-titled *Frank Wright Trio* with the bassist Henry Grimes and drummer Tom Price. The record opens with a blues-infused solo by Wright on "The Earth," before the other two musicians join and the music begins to gain momentum. Wright often stays in the lower register of the tenor, with thick brush strokes of sound, while occasionally tipping the crests with momentary white-hot surges. Grimes, in particular, matches the aesthetic, giving it a grounded quality. The piece was unique at the time, as Wright's approach to tenor had a more contemplative and mournful quality than either Coltrane or Ayler in that period.

The other two pieces displayed movement and longing. "Jerry" was more of a burning improvisation that reached higher, built on preacher-like arcs and enunciations. Price maintains a propulsive, if a bit mundane, rhythm, with Grimes nimbly navigating the momentary passageways that open up. Wright's lines are brighter but still colored by occasional melancholic undercurrents. "The Moon" is the culmination of the ideas that emerged in the other tracks, though Wright pushes further into the upper register in brief moments; it is the most fully formed piece on the record.

Recording his first record with the endorsement of ESP changed Wright's entire perspective. He realized that he could strike out on his own and that it was possible to pursue his own musical vision. Finding opportunities to play would take patience, but it set him on a new path as he explored his developing sound. Wright was self-taught, but as his future bandmate Kamal Abdul Alim noted, "He had direction and vision. He had a definite sense of expression, just like abstract painters of that era. Frank was very much like that."[5] All of that compelled him to settle for a few years in New York.

On Easter Sunday 1967, Wright recorded a second record for ESP, *Your Prayer*, with a three-horn front line that included a fellow Clevelander, the alto saxophonist Arthur Jones, and the trumpeter Jacques Coursil, as well as the bassist Steve Tintweiss and drummer Muhammad Ali.[6] Jones and Coursil would work together a couple of years later in Paris. Ali was the younger brother of the drummer Rashied Ali, who was playing with Coltrane at that time, and the younger

Ali considered his brother to be one of his primary teachers and the person "who opened my eyes to jazz. He was my beginning."[7]

Muhammad Ali's other major breakthrough with the music was through a childhood friend, the drummer Sunny Murray, who introduced Ali to the free jazz concepts that he had developed playing with Cecil Taylor in the period from 1959 to 1965. Murray said, "With Cecil, I had to originate a completely new direction on drums."[8] Ali described the moment of witnessing Murray play like that for the first time: "Murray sat at the drums and started playing. It was like a volcano erupting from a whole area of mountains. That was it! It took me on a journey. He and Cecil were really the first ones doing those kinds of rhythms, even before Trane came over to it. I put aside everything I had been doing and began working on that to get in on it. It was magnificent new music."[9]

Ali moved from Philadelphia to New York in 1966, initially picking up gigs that his older brother Rashied could not take because he was committed to Coltrane's band, but soon the younger Ali was establishing himself with the alto saxophonist Noah Howard and a number of other groups. Muhammad Ali had played with Coltrane in Philadelphia, and so Coltrane recommended Ali to Wright in 1967. The latter two quickly began working together with regularity.[10] "Bebop is in my soul. I didn't want to sound like Sunny and I didn't want to sound like Rashied," Ali stated. "I wanted to develop my own style. I didn't want to lose the jazz method of drumming and I wanted to swing. But I also wanted to play this new music and figure out how to accompany other musicians with improvisation. So, I developed my own style with multi-directional drumming that also swings."[11]

"Wright was a very emotional and opinionated guy and that came through his music," Tintweiss observed. "He had a lot of rhythm and blues influence and then he was pretty influenced by Albert [Ayler] in Cleveland and began to pick up the mantle in developing further the free form tenor saxophone style. Sometimes he would growl along with the music when he was playing in the lower register."[12] The record also represents the first encounter between Wright and Ali, who continued to work together for nearly a decade.

Your Prayer exhibited a clear influence from gospel and blues through four improvisations under Wright's leadership, as well as showcasing a piece by Jones.[13] Jones's piece, "The Lady," had a sacred quality, produced by the three-horn lineup, Ali's using heavy amounts of cymbal, and Tintweiss elevating everything with the bass undercurrent. Opening unison voices give way to individual solos with a return to unison in a choir-like coalescence. "Train Stop" is a burning improvisation where Wright again explores the lower register of the horn with occasional explosive crests, building toward the final sections, which display minimalist horns and bells evaporating into ethereal transcendence. "No End" begins with a marching theme before each of the horn players takes a solo in turn, including Coursil's first great statements on record.

The final two pieces were where the true power of the recording became manifest. "Fire of Spirits" begins with flickering flames and then, as its title suggests, follows with a high-energy flurry of imagery based on intersecting horns and constant narrative tension from the rhythms beneath them. For several minutes the band maintains this high energy before the horns all recede without much warning in a remarkable moment of tension and release, leaving drums, bass, and bells to project light across the vast openness left in their wake. Finally, the horns return, but with a staunch vocal quality. This piece was one of Wright's most remarkable statements on record. "Your Prayer" forms a more traditional narrative of rhythms with a succession of solos still saturated in symbolism, including one of Arthur Jones's first significant statements on record. To push the overall effect even further, the horns stop playing, and the band members create a chorus of moans and cries that give the prayer aspect of the piece its fullest expression. It cuts off unexpectedly, hinting at the eternity of this prayer.

By the spring of 1966, Wright was steadily getting notice from other figures on the scene. Some of his first work came with Ayler, when the latter returned to Cleveland to play at the La Cave, in April. But Wright was also moving beyond the Cleveland orbit. The pianist Cecil Taylor, for instance, asked him to join his quintet that spring, and he continued to be affiliated with Taylor, getting his greatest exposure yet during a West Coast tour, where they held a two-week residency at Stanford University, played the Berkeley Jazz Festival, and then opened for the psychedelic rock band the Yardbirds in front of about three thousand people at the Fillmore West. Silva referred to Wright as "one of the most fantastic saxophone players of my generation. [He] could really bring it off."[14]

The music critic Jerry Fogel, writing contemporaneously, captured the moment and its importance:

> Music in the hands of genius can be a pure, unbridled expression of thoughts and emotions. Too often it is not: conventions and accepted standards inhibit even the finest artists. The "daring" and the "experimental" are at once praised and condemned by the "open-minded" public. But what is "daring" or "experimental" about elevating an art form to its highest degree of perfection—that point at which form seems to disappear and the artist is communicating directly with his listener? Why should musicians whose creativity and inspiration enables

them to shatter the barriers which have limited their predecessors be relegated to the realm of the "far-out" and "interesting"?[15]

Fogel further complimented the band:

> Each of the six performers is blessed with superb instrumental skill. Cecil Taylor has what Ralph Gleason has called "a frightening command" of the piano; his fingers move with seemingly impossible rapidity. Drummer Andrew Cyrille has both the fluid motion and sense of rhythmic anticipation which make a great percussionist. Sax players Jimmy Lyons (alto) and Frank Wright (tenor) each have their own message, but both have complete mastery of their instrument. The string bass in the hands of Alan Silva becomes as expressive as a cello or violin while providing, along with the drums, the rhythmic backbone of the group's music.[16]

Silva, for his part, remarked, "We did an hour-and-a-half show. Even the guy from the Fillmore came up to us and said, 'This is fantastic, better than Aretha Franklin.' So I knew that the public was ready. I heard Jimi Hendrix, and I knew that we could capture this market too. To most of the kids in this particular period, *sound* was interesting, as long as you could keep it moving. 1968 was a crucial point for free music."[17] The group also got offered a record deal out of the experience, supposedly a single that was to have Taylor's group on one side and the rock band the Doors on the other side, but ultimately Taylor turned it down.[18]

The drummer Andrew Cyrille, who played with Taylor's groups of the time and who much later was hired for Wright's quartet in 1986, spoke of the saxophonist:

> Frank Wright was a soul brother, from Mississippi, who had a feeling about playing improvised music. He was very sincere about it, he had found ways of playing the saxophone that expressed what he wanted. I remember Frank Wright calling on the phone one day and he was depressed and he was crying. And he started playing the saxophone while he was crying and talking. I'd never heard anything like this before. And I'd wished I had some way to record that because . . . that was a true, real work of art. . . . He was distraught but at the same time he was using the instrument in order to relate to me also, and it was something that was a part of him. Frank was talking to me.[19]

The pianist Bobby Few also came to New York but kept a lower profile. Albert Ayler convinced Few to move, and the pianist relocated there by 1967. He moved into an apartment on the Lower East Side with Wright that coincidentally was also the building where the pianist Randy Weston and saxophonist Booker Ervin also lived. Ervin overheard Few practicing in his apartment and hired him for his first gigs in New York. Pleased with Few's contributions, he invited the pianist to a session in January 1968 that resulted in *The In Between*, which was Few's first appearance on record.[20] One critic at the time described the work: "Ervin's assertive, imaginative tenor sax breaks loose on this first-rate modern jazz excursion ... this is an intriguing, varied venture that runs the gamut from free form playing ... to straight-ahead swinging. Ervin is the star, but his sidemen ... have a lot to say, too."[21] Few's playing is agile and added light accompaniment for Ervin's robust tenor sound. After a stint back in Cleveland in early 1969 and then recording *Music Is the Healing Force of the Universe* under Albert Ayler's leadership in August of that year, Few turned his attention to Paris.[22]

GETTING TO PARIS

By 1967 or 1968, Wright was playing with the drummer Sunny Murray in a group that also included the saxophonist and flutist Byard Lancaster and bassist Alan Silva. Murray then recommended Silva to Shepp, whom he joined for the Pan-African Cultural Festival in Algiers in July 1969, before landing in Paris.[23] The French label BYG had made it possible for some of the free jazz players to come to Algiers, with the caveat that they subsequently go to Paris to record.[24] Underlying this migration of artists to Paris was the downturn in the jazz economy in the United States; the rise of the repressive Nixon administration, especially in relation to the Black community; and the image of France as a historic "haven" for Black American artists.[25] By the summer of 1969, many other musicians were heading to Paris on the promise of BYG's recording contracts. The label was entirely focused on recruiting American artists to record.

In many ways, as the journalist Pierre Crepon has argued, this movement of free jazz artists to Paris began with Sunny Murray playing at the Paris Jazz Festival in November 1968. He subsequently remained there for three months and was heralded as "the musician responsible for the most important breakthrough in drumming since John Coltrane Quartet member Elvin Jones."[26] During Murray's tenure in Paris, he assembled a band at the Vielle Grille, a small café-theater, that included three French players: the pianist François Tusques, trumpeter Bernard Vitet, and bassist Beb Guérin, as well as the Jamaican tenor saxophonist Kenneth Terroade and South African alto saxophonist Ronnie Beer.

The bassist Alan Silva and flutist Becky Friend joined in December, and upon Murray's departure in February, Silva retained the band and expanded it into the Celestial Communications Orchestra.[27] Explaining the group's process, Silva stated, "We had no scores, no themes, no variations. Inside the circle... where the musicians are placed, they can play a music that begins and finishes elsewhere; it is in a way a trip that ends only when the energy dies out.... I think that this collective music-making experience demands some adaptation because one must absolutely let go of what one has been accustomed to. I don't mean to say that jazz has never been collective, but it has always been driven by individual forces."[28]

The nearly two dozen sessions recorded under BYG's Actuel imprint from June to September constitute an "unprecedented" assemblage of free jazz musicians and the most concentrated documentation in the entire history of the music.[29] The sessions included a whole generation of players, including the trumpeters Don Cherry, Clifford Thornton, and Lester Bowie; reed and woodwind players Anthony Braxton, Arthur Jones, Archie Shepp, Joseph Jarman, Roscoe Mitchell, Kenneth Terroade, and Hank Mobley; trombonist Grachan Moncur III; harmonica players Chicago Beau and Julio Finn, pianists Dave Burrell and Burton Greene; violinist Leroy Jenkins; bassists Malachi Favors, Alan Silva, and Earl Freeman; drummers Sunny Murray, Andrew Cyrille, Steve McCall, Ed Blackwell, and "Philly" Joe Jones; and vocalist Jeanne Lee, not to mention a couple of European musicians who joined them on a few sessions. "[BYG] wanted to put free jazz on the market," Silva observed, "and the artistic control was by the artists. A whole bunch of artists began working with European labels because none of the American labels were interested. So, you could say this was a revolutionary aspect."[30]

Silva had developed an interest in how people created musical instruments and learned to play them during his study with Alan Lomax in the early 1960s. "I felt that improvisation was the key element in the human transfer of music, from the human being to the instrument. The human voice is the first instrument and language is the first improvisational tool. So, improvisation became the basis for my philosophical outlook on art."[31]

Silva had brought these ideas to the Freeform Improvisation Ensemble in 1964–1965 within the musical milieu that emerged out of the October Revolution and solidified around the Jazz Composers Guild. But Silva had also been deeply interested in big bands. "I thought that the orchestra was the greatest thing Europeans created. A one-hundred piece orchestra was an incredible human development. I also read about an African ritual performance of twenty-five drummers playing where they played for three days without stopping and without one single note written. People were putting a lot of emphasis on the composer, though, and I felt that the players were more important than the composer. I might write something down, but how is a musician going to play it?"

Silva thought of Celestial Communications Orchestra purely as a recording project and also put on concerts that were broadcast via radio. It was too large of an ensemble with which to tour or play regularly, given the economics of music at the time. *Luna Surface*, which came out of the August 1969 sessions, solidified the concept. *Seasons*, which was recorded in December 1970, is one of the brilliant masterpieces of that era and a landmark in big band music.[32]

The music of the group possessed really strong, colorful imagery that manifested like the painting of a picture for the sonic senses. There are flashes of light; all the colors that exist come out in waves at the listener. "I could not have done *Seasons* without LSD. I knew Timothy Leary when I lived in New York, and he turned me onto arts processing and creativity," Silva stated.[33] Silva's music was also filled with life, birth, and death; there are beings alive within the music. "I wanted human beings making that music at a time when a lot of music was going in another direction. I call them light beings. People creating this out of their own minds, a high level of vision and emotion. We call that musical intelligence. I was interested in human intelligence. But the music wasn't for that moment, it was for the future."[34] As Silva stated closer to the time about the role of the artist in society: "The musician is in advance of the culture, in advance of the emotions. He's the cat that will move the future people. He can make people think differently about what they hear, see or understand. He is like an encouragement to lift one's consciousness."[35]

For many of the artists at the time, the recordings were their first to appear on wax or were the most exploratory sounds they had yet documented. Though Wright and Few were not fortunate enough to be among the sessions, when they arrived in the wake of it and began to form their own groups there in the years that followed, it was in a musical landscape that had experienced a seismic shift toward these new sounds, and with ears eager for more.[36]

PARIS AFTER MAY 1968

The political atmosphere in Paris after the May 1968 uprising made it particularly conducive to a free jazz scene. The French leftist uprising was the culmination of a student movement and the resurgence of worker organizing that coalesced into full-fledged revolt against the political, educational, and cultural establishment. Inspired by protest movements elsewhere, such as the American student movements dating back to about 1963, the French took inspiration from figures such as Mario Savio, one of the leading figures in the movement at University of California–Berkeley, who stated, "There is a time when the operation of the machine becomes so odious, makes you sick at heart that you can't take part; you can't even tacitly take part, and you've got to put your bodies on the gears and upon the wheels, upon the levers, upon all the apparatus, and you've got to make it stop. And you've got to indicate to the people who run it, to the people who own it, that unless you're free, the machine will be prevented from working at all."[37] The French student movement also drew inspiration from related movements in West Germany, Italy, and Poland.[38]

The student and worker movements which had been building for months found a catalyst with the closing of the Sorbonne on May 2, 1968. The following day students entered into open revolt and were soon joined by labor unions and high school students, forging a coalition of organizations that grew over the following weeks.[39] These forces reached a climax on May 27, when fifty thousand people gathered at the Charléty stadium, and three days later, when approximately a half million people swelled into the streets of Paris celebrating the president fleeing the capital the day before. The journalist and poet Angelo Quattrocchi wrote of his first-hand experience in the streets:

> Paris, lend your ears and hear the screaming of your troops advancing.
> Hear the shouting of your masked men running through their gases shooting at your kids, your hopes, your tenderness, your reason.
> Blackness advances in a halo of fire.
> The air is blue: thickness.
> Acid is yellow. Flames burst and devour. The first position untenable.
> "Don't panic comrades—they can only take our lives—get away before you faint—don't get in the way of those throwing *pavés* . . ."
> One barricade. Behind, another. Between them: bodies.
> "Don't leave your friends behind, comrades."
> The next barricade.
> Dry lungs and tears and blood.
> Behind closed doors Paris waits for murder to be done, so its cars can circulate again.
> In Saint Michel the first barricade is on fire. A red flag is burning.
> In Guy Lussac hell is advancing slowly.
> People throw water from windows, broken water pipes flood the streets, people scream from windows, shout frightened obscenities at the advancing live tentacles. *Flics* shoot grenades through windows.

> Do not stay behind, nobody stays behind when we abandon a barricade.[40]

Counterprotests, police suppression of protests, and the calling of a new parliamentary election gradually defused the revolt through June.

Central to the uprising was a youth revolt against prevailing institutions, social control, political structures, and cultural stagnation. As Simone Few, the future wife of Bobby Few, stated as a French citizen of the time, "The 1968 revolution changed everything, the social aspects of life. Freedom. Freedom of everything, freedom of body, freedom of politics, it was really a freedom revolution."[41] The multi-instrumentalist Daniel Carter, who had been stationed in Italy in the US Army but happened to be in Paris in May 1968 looking to buy a saxophone, witnessed clashes between paramilitary personnel and French youth.[42] It was an open rebellion that crossed political and cultural lines as people embraced new ideas for the sake of rejecting the old.

For some American musicians in Paris in the wake of the 1968 uprising, it was a moment for their own political evolution. Frank Wright initially stated, "We play the music we love, and we don't have anything to do with the people who protest, we don't even read the newspapers. The only thing that interests us is music."[43] However, he gradually became more politically aware, noting "police patrolling the streets and asking for identification, stopping mostly Algerians and Africans." He also witnessed the economic marginalization of African immigrants, epitomized by the African *balayeur* (street sweeper), and the violence that Algerians faced in France, which "called to mind conditions that [he had] left behind in the United States."[44]

The uprising opened spaces for radical new conceptions of culture in France after May 1968. The American Center in Paris was at the center of much of the vanguard culture at the time. "Music was happening there night and day; it was *the* place," one French student from the time observed.[45] Many Black Americans were leaving the United States because of the Nixon administration's violent and repressive policies, finding Paris to be something of a haven for left-wing, progressive, and avant-garde ideas, writings, poetry, art, dance, and music. But as the journalist Valerie Wilmer noted, "To the French youth, the Black musicians and their angry music represented the revolution taking place in America, and their arrival so soon after the Left Bank student revolts consolidated their heroic position. Black expatriates were cast in a . . . role by the French, that of nationalists and ghetto heroes."[46]

"The American Center was the ideal place for the blossoming of the music. Sometimes it was a bit like who could blow the strongest, but we learned to hang on, to hold on and we played until we were exhausted. Coming out of there, we had music in our ears for a long while," the French musician, producer, and writer Serge Loupien observed.[47] "People felt more comfortable here than in the States. France was ready to hear free jazz," recalled Simone Few, who had been listening to jazz since her mid-teens. "It was a struggle still, for many, and some musicians who came slept on the streets, but there was at least an audience here. A lot of people were listening."[48]

FESTIVAL ACTUEL

Festival Actuel was the catalyst for much of the scene that occurred in Paris in the early 1970s. Sunny Murray's quartet played at Festival Actuel, sponsored by the label, in Amougies, Belgium, in October, where they held the stage between performances by bands such as Pink Floyd and Soft Machine, and were joined by free jazz figures such as Don Cherry, Archie Shepp, and the Art Ensemble of Chicago. Of Murray's group, one writer characterized it as "a long, furious scream . . . the palpable exertions of Murray, Frank Wright, Alan Silva, and Byard Lancaster more than matched the sonic force that the rock acts obtained by means of amplification. Immediacy . . . was a matter of physical intensity."[49] As the journalist Valerie Wilmer observed, "the 75,000 who were drawn to the five days of concerts by the heavy rock names on the bill, went home entranced by the music of people like Howard and Wright, Murray. . . . The festival had been conceived courageously."[50] For the American free jazz musicians involved, it forever altered the trajectory of their careers. As Noah Howard commented, "In three days in Europe, I got more publicity than I had in five years in New York."[51]

Regular demonstrations were still going on in the streets in Paris in 1969. In the midst of that one day while they were there, Wright and Few ducked into a club to avoid the street confrontations and found themselves in Le Chat qui Peche, where the saxophonist Dexter Gordon was playing. During Gordon's break from the stage, he invited them to play there, and from that short episode, they were invited back to play again.[52] Few met his future wife, Simone, at the club, and they married soon after.

Bobby Few and Frank Wright also played Festival Actuel as part of the alto saxophonist Noah Howard's group with the drummer Muhammad Ali. "The idea was," Howard later recalled, "that we were going to play at the festival, and afterward, we would go into town and do some work in Paris. We played there for two or three weeks at a club called Le Chat qui Peche, where Eric Dolphy,

FIGURE 10.1 Muhammad Ali (b. 1936), drummer, and the saxophonists Frank Wright (1935–1990) and Noah Howard (1943–2010), at Festival Amougies, Belgium, 1969.

Source: Courtesy Suong Gras.

Jackie McLean, everybody you could think of who had passed through Paris had played there." BYG had the strategy of inviting bands for the festival, arranging sustained local gigs to give the bands practice time, and then recording them before they left. "They were recording everybody in our kind of music, Alan Silva, Archie Shepp, Frank Wright," Howard stated, "just about everybody who was on the music scene at that time."[53]

Howard, in explaining his background, stated, "My family was not so much musical as they were very religious. So, by being religious, that inferred a musical influence, because everybody in the family sang in the Baptist church. So, it was gospel oriented. My first music lessons were vocal training in the church choir. Later, when I started playing alto, I was influenced by Sonny Simmons, Dewey Redman, Byron Allen."[54] Howard was also interested in developing a tone like Charlie Parker, Ornette Coleman, and Jackie McLean, because "once you're into that, you can hold people's attention from the start. But tone in itself is not the important thing. I hear a lot of people imitate Bird, but they don't have his sound. There's something unique about the great people that can't be imitated. The thing I don't like about bebop are the imitators."[55] Howard was certainly a more melodic player than Wright, and the two presented a contrast in the music that they made together.

Howard first emerged in Los Angeles, where he first met Allen, and then moved to New York in 1963, where he played with Sun Ra; he did his first recordings with ESP in January 1966.[56] From that point on, he generally worked in quartet formations as a leader. Howard recorded the quartet in 1970 with Wright, Few, and Ali and Art Taylor alternating on drums on each track.[57] Howard's music for the group was infused with melancholy, more obvious melodic lyricism, and it tended to use space to accentuate the individual sounds. In many ways, Howard exhibited an interest in applying layer after layer to his music and in his compositions, often comparing his own work to that of a painter.[58]

FRANK WRIGHT QUARTET

What was originally Howard's group quickly became a quartet led by Wright that stayed together for a few years with the same personnel (with Ali on drums). Bobby Few played a crucial role in the group: He would often "write out Wright's ideas on charts and give them structure," since Wright only composed aurally.[59] Howard stated of Wright's playing at that time as "one of the young disciples of Coltrane from the last level, from when Coltrane was going further and further out. He understood Coltrane from that perspective, and he was . . . very pure with it. But then he added his own personality into it. He was from Mississippi, a very rural Black man, trying to express the soul of rural Black people. That's a funny thing about free jazz; a lot of people think it's really weird—but I always associate it with the shouts of the farmhands in the fields, people screaming in the gospel church. . . . It's an expression of the joyousness of human feeling, of human experience."[60]

The group remained in Paris through the fall of 1969 and recorded *One for John* on BYG in early December, dedicated to John Coltrane. The title piece illustrates Wright's clearest Coltrane influence on record, both in terms of tenor sound as well as the orchestration of the ensemble interplay. Few and Ali create an entire environment that serves as a kind of sonic buoy of energy raising everything else up. From there, the horns climb and climb in Coltrane-esque fashion. Few's work on the record constitutes his most distinct improvisations among his early recorded work. One writer stated that Wright's "solos are powerful and fairly disciplined" on the record. The other piece, "China," was composed by Few with contributions from Wright and bears some East Asian elements in the initial sound and rhythms. It is a much more structured piece that seems to constrict the solos.[61] "It was a piece that was a perception of another part of the world, going beyond the European idea of music, and the relationship people had with the spirit. Many of Wright's musical ideas came to him in dreams. He was playing the blues but with these other ideas pushing him in particular directions," Ali explained.[62] The band all shaped the piece as they worked through it as a collective.

Muhammad Ali noted that "with everyone going to Paris around that time, the music started getting really strong in Paris into the early 1970s. We went back and forth for a little while and then we decided to just stay there and be a part of it. The music was flourishing there with many international festivals and concerts, often with all kinds of music on the same bill. We did a lot of those all over Europe."[63]

After a series of additional European performances in Paris, Amsterdam, and elsewhere, the group recorded their best-known record, *Church Number Nine*, in March 1970.[64] This recording is Wright at his most ecstatic. In many ways, the record is an example of free jazz tenor from that time period, with overblowing and group improvisation. But Wright shapes the music in his own way, occasionally using tenor for rhythm or to send signals to direct the action in certain ways. Howard often seems to extend the energy further upward, while Few and Ali create curtains of energy that surge and recede throughout the record. Few has some poignant moments where he shapes the sonic waves and transitions from one trajectory to another. Ali's cymbal work heightens the ecstatic feeling of the music as the group searches for spiritual expression.

Another record, *Uhuru na Umoja*, followed shortly after. The opening piece, "Oriental Mood," seemed to further explore some of the ideas present in "China," including solo chanting, but opens with a repeated hymn-like line that also tethers the music to the musicians' own backgrounds and experiences. It is a work of imaginative cultural fusion. "Aurora Borealis," composed by Howard, is filled with rippling arpeggios from Few and flowing saxophones that one writer described as a "vast landscape of red and gold."[65] The other tracks cut up the sonic ideas introduced in the earlier sections into smaller bits and work through them a bit more systematically. Wright and other members of the band have been heralded as having a transformative place in the Paris music scene in those years generally and are considered a transformative presence in the jazz of that era.[66] In 1970 and 1971, the band occasionally visited New York. Howard was sometimes underutilized in the band, and Wright and Howard had some disagreements. Eventually Howard withdrew from the band.[67]

CENTER OF THE WORLD

The Frank Wright Quartet evolved into Center of the World when Noah Howard departed and they brought in the bassist Alan Silva. Silva had begun playing in the pianist Cecil Taylor's band in 1965 and had met Wright the following year, when the latter first played with the group. Wright became a regular member of Taylor's group in 1968, and he and Silva had gained respect for each other during their residency at Stanford University. More immediately, Wright and Silva had come to Europe with Sunny Murray, and had both decided to stay in Paris.

In 1970, Wright asked Silva to join his band and Silva countered by offering him a spot in a big band he directed in Paris. After a few gigs, Wright asked him again to join the quartet, but Silva "did not abide" with the idea of bands being named for the leader because "free jazz was a group concept if it was not using compositions," and he pushed the band to be a collective, Center of the World.[68] Ultimately, "Bobby was a writer [of music] and Frank had some songs, they both contributed to the compositions, but we all played and shaped them," Silva explained.[69]

"We chose the name because what we were doing came from the center of the world, playing this particular type of music," Ali stated. "And we were trying to establish something that was as new as we could so that we wouldn't just be labeled free jazz. We were doing a futuristic thing. Given how many of the visionaries died in their twenties or thirties, at that time, we felt like we didn't have a lot of time and we were trying to push forward as hard as we could."[70]

On March 26, 1972, Center of the World was invited to Rotterdam, Netherlands, to do a live broadcast for a radio station, which resulted in a high-quality recording. That tape was the basis for their first record, a self-titled foray of extended free improvisations.[71] As one writer at the time noted, the music began with a basic theme, and Wright's "playing, filled with joy and passion ... comes out of the heyday of the free scene in New York in the sixties."[72]

But when the record was reissued on Fractal Records in 1999, writers showed more obvious appreciation of the record's historical importance. The critic Derek Taylor argued that the record and the later *Last Polka in Nancy?* provided "undeniable evidence of the Reverend Frank Wright's rightful place in the pantheon of early free jazz forefathers." Then, comparing him to Ayler, he concluded that Wright's work "is an even darker and sacrosanct music."[73]

The music itself is expressive and cathartic. Taylor described the sounds: "Tenor and echoing chimes [are] almost amplified in their spaciousness. Few's incandescent piano and Ali's torrential drums soon enter.... Minutes into the performance, Wright really starts gaining steam.... The unrelenting turbulence is eventually tempered by the tide of Few's bright tone clusters which are almost tender by comparison to [Wright's] raw, hoary screams."[74] Few was the ideal aesthetic counter to Wright, with Few enveloping Wright's ardent sounds with rippling sonic curtains that seem to move out from the center in all directions at once.

Taylor adds, "It's only when [Silva] brandishes his bow and starts hacking off huge shards of sound from his strings that he's clearly heard above Wright's inexorable squeal."[75] The energy of the rhythm section elevated the entire group sound, which rather quickly melded to give the feeling of an interconnected sonic ecosystem held in balance by its contributors. "At the close of the first part, Silva and Ali engage in a duet [and] Silva creates an almost dirge-like pizzicato cyclone across the blanket of Ali's bells and small percussion which carries the group over into 'Part 2' where Wright switches to soprano. A surprisingly 'inside' drum solo by Ali follows before Few again takes charge with a brief interlude of his own. Wright later alternates from flute to bass clarinet over a boiling ocean of percussion before the lengthy piece [comes] to a close."[76]

The later sections of the piece contained the most exploratory and unexpected material, including chants, bells, and short declarative statements from Wright, which all together made the music rise to the level of the visionary, while the spiritual elements became more visible. The chants allowed the music to connect with some greater human narratives along mystical lines. One writer argued that the recording was an inspiration for the Japanese pianist Yosuke Yamashita to record *Ghosts by Albert Ayler* live at Jazz in West Berlin in 1977.[77]

The reissue of the record made available two tracks that the group played at the performance, drawn from the corpus that Wright had developed with his earlier quartet, that were not included on the original release. Both exhibited gospel- and blues-influenced improvisations. "'No End,'" Taylor stated, "begins with a declamatory ... melody by Wright on tenor. Few creates a gospel urgency that paves the way for a lengthy improvisation from Silva before Wright barrels forth again. The quartet follows a similar direction on 'Church Number 9' and centers their lengthy improvisations on another gospel-tinged vamp. Wright erupts in another rapturous tenor solo.... Few also shines in an up-tempo solo that juggles and twists the opening vamp into a myriad of melodic permutations."[78] Silva observed, "Frank Wright was always playing the blues. That's what I loved about him. He was very emotional and spiritual. The roots of African American music were present in everything he did. He was a real folk artist."[79]

The trumpeter Raphe Malik was in Paris when Center of the World was playing and witnessed their creative power, stating that they "played so much music, had so much presence, so much authority. The reason I admired Frank is because he had a spiritual point of view. He'd tell me, 'We don't determine what's going to happen so why worry about it? I don't know where I am going from moment to moment. I let God direct my feet.' They called him the Rev because he was so involved in that kind of thinking. If you let his message reach you, it was really great. The guy was like a prophet.... He'd say 'You're in outer space. You know what your problem is, you still have a parachute. Why don't you get rid of your parachute? You don't need a parachute in outer space.' It made a big difference to me."[80]

Muhammad Ali noted, "Frank always spoke of the creator. He made a point that everything he was doing musically was filled with spiritual vibrations. He and Albert [Ayler] had a similar thinking in that way. Frank felt he had been put here for that purpose, so that's why we started calling him the Reverend. We all felt some of that—it was music that came from the spirit. It gave us that type of feeling."[81]

"Bobby's playing was a great mix of classical training and improvisation coming out of the African American musical tradition," Alan Silva observed. "Outside of Cecil Taylor, Bobby was one of two or three pianists who really transformed the American piano-bass-drums concept at that time and how to play behind a horn player. Few had a harp concept, using the overtones of his glissando-type playing, but not abstract, purely harmonic. But people haven't given him credit."[82]

"Muhammad Ali was an autodidactic drummer from my perspective," Silva stated. "He was very methodological. A whole generation preceded him that was influenced by Max Roach. But this new generation of Ali, his older brother Rashied Ali, and Sunny Murray were taking things in a new direction. Muhammad Ali was meticulous in developing his fundamentals. His work on the cymbal and the snare drum was particularly interesting. He had a unique sound on the ride cymbal."[83] Ali explained it further: "I'd play freedom on the ride, a changing cymbal beat. And for that to be in line with what was happening with the tune, I needed some bottom that would be different from what the bass was doing. And then get in sync with the rest of the rhythm section and add coloring. It's like painting on a canvas."[84]

They originally pressed three thousand copies of the record for less than $100, and rather than work through a distributor, they "sold records directly to the people" at live performances.[85] Silva had previously worked in the office of the record label ESP-Disk and brought that experience to the role of business manager for the band. "Because we recorded the band with our company, we owned the music," Silva explained. "For all of us, that was the first time we really owned our own music. Not some label paying us for tapes of our music that they then owned, we owned this music." The members of the band had to front the money to make the pressings, but then they took the profits and reinvested them back into the company. "I didn't think of the records as commercial products. I thought of them as real artifacts," Silva explained.[86] Center of the World was in the vanguard of a broader push for self-determination and self-production among musicians at the time within the free jazz movement.

The band began to record every gig that they played—about fifty concerts per year—with a tape recorder and two microphones, amassing a large number of tapes, a few of which they released in the period from 1973 through 1975.[87] Many of these occurred at the American Center for Students and Artists in Paris. The saxophonist Glenn Spearman, who attended the concerts, regularly stated, "I'd see them play in Paris and would almost blank out. They would reach such heights, they'd have six—seven hundred people packed in the American Center every other Friday. There was no comparison."[88]

Paris was a training ground for a lot of American expatriates who were there making music, and Wright was at the focal point. Spearman had sought Wright out as a mentor. "I had been told by [the saxophonist and clarinetist] Donald Garrett that I sound like this guy named Frank Wright," Spearman stated. "I had never heard Frank Wright. I checked some records, saw they were made in France, on BYG and on that hunch I borrowed some money and bought a one-way ticket and went to Paris. Two days after I was in Paris I ran into Frank Wright. I introduced myself to him . . . and then he heard me play and he was like my mentor. He just believed in me, told me to keep on doing what I was doing."[89] The trumpeter Raphe Malik was another young, impressionable figure there, and he referred to Wright as "a very seminal person for me. . . . When Frank heard me, he took me under his wing. He was a very reassuring person."[90]

Center of the World made a rare appearance in New York in the summer of 1973 at the New York Musicians' Festival, which was sponsored by the radio station WKCR. Because Ali was unable to make the trip, the drummer Harold E. Smith sat in with the band. Over an hour and a half, the band was able to stretch out their concepts and solos.

Their next significant performance was in Nancy, France, for the Jazz Pulsations Festival, which resulted in the band's second record, *Last Polka in Nancy?*[91] The critic Derek Taylor described the record: "Bellowing tenor and collective chanting blend an incantatory invocation on Few's 'Winter Echoes.' Ali is a flurry of drums and cymbals, a constant source of tension and release. Silva's 'Guanna Dance' begins with Wright on bass clarinet in a much more sedate mood and with a greater interest on shading and enunciation. 'Part 2' . . . features an extended arco solo by Silva replete with agile pizzicato flourishes. 'Thinking of Monk' is only a fragment, but features Wright playing at his most lyrical, accompanied by Few."[92] Another critic noted, "Ali's roaring, cymbal-dominated style has the intensity so vital to Wright's headlong linear outbursts. Ali accents his line strongly and in so doing provides just the right amount of vertical time keeping."[93]

Wright often employed "blue notes" in his playing and in his abrupt delivery, and some critics detected the rhythm-and-blues influence of his Memphis years. The critic Barry McRae observed, "Wright's improvisational process is based on building away from the theme. He returns to the original statement only rarely in the course of a solo and then refers to it more sparingly than most. He seems happier to construct tiers of ideas, each given reason by its predecessor. He has a Monk-like ability to distort but not destroy a melody statement."[94]

The record revealed an evolved and advanced group sound that they had achieved through a year of playing and practicing together. In fact, by this stage, the group sound took precedence over individual narratives, weaving sounds together that made it feel like one sonic organism. The band was remarkable in that each player had a big sound, but they could swell or diminish to allow for each of the voices to be heard consequentially as the music moved and flowed.

Another session from mid-1974, including the full band, documented their appearance at the Moers Festival in Germany.[95] As one critic noted of the recording, released many years later on ESP-Disk:

> From the moment Ali introduces the piece with heavy cymbal accentuations, clanging metallic percussion and the thunderous bass drum thudding he's known for, the intensity and momentum never stop. Wright quickly swoops in with a ... fierce marching-band theme, constantly developing it. Few ... colors the performance with a chromatic torrent of notes and jarring block chords, occasionally quoting the Chinese pentatonic scale, reminiscent of his composition "China." Silva provides a steady foundation while also contributing texture with his exceptional arco playing. The ensemble communicates with the effortless interaction of four men who have been playing together for years, with each instrument naturally weaving in and out of the mix. The solos even reflect this unbound energy.[96]

The band played at the Willisau Jazz Festival one week later and was back in Willisau, Switzerland, in October in trio formation without Few.[97] This opened the possibility of recording smaller group sessions in 1974 and 1975, in different formations. For example, *More or Less Few* was a trio without Wright, and *Adieu Little Man* featured Wright and Ali as a duo. *Inner Song* was a solo record by Silva, and then two volumes titled *Solo & Duets* featured Wright, Few, and Silva in such formations. These were recorded at the American Center for Students and

Artists in Paris, where Silva taught, and revealed sparse, more open sounds with extended solos and duets in more revealing contexts.[98]

Spring 1975 recordings in Paris and Massy, France, had Wright, Few, and Silva appearing in solo and duet formations. A clear favorite at Willisau, they returned to play the festival again in August of that year in quartet formation. Their final recordings came as solos and duets in November at Palm Studio in Paris and at the jazz festival in Reims.

One of the key tracks on these late recordings by the group was the autobiographical "Grenada," appropriately opening with a solo by Wright. "It soon moves into highly dramatic short bars of free tenor shouts; Wright punctuates between the short tenor statements with breathy screams and gasps—it's effective. Again, raw energy dominates as Mr. Wright moves from low register . . . themes to . . . a field [shout]-like call and response chant with the audience."[99] Center of the World was central to sparking the French free jazz scene. One writer noted, "Thanks to these people we felt that there really was something to do in free jazz and that we should not hesitate to get into it."[100] The big band Operation Rhino, for instance, became a focal point of the Paris scene, taking inspiration also from Silva's Celestial Communications Orchestra, from 1975 onward.

Wright always wanted to bring the band back to the United States, but Silva, in particular, resisted, feeling that they would not be able to maintain their concept there. "In Europe we produced a lot of concerts ourselves. We had our own bus packed with our records. We could go anywhere in Europe that we wanted. We played a lot in France and Germany especially. We were keeping busy there, so I didn't think we could do all of that back in the U.S."[101] Silva further stated, "When you come over to Europe, which has a tradition of supporting avant-garde ideas, it's *easy* to be avant-garde—because you are *not* avant-garde, you're just contemporary."[102]

As the French saxophonist Richard Raux, who was deeply influenced by Frank Wright and Sunny Murray, said plainly, "Playing free is a proof of intelligence. It's another way of thinking, nothing is pre-established. We invent ourselves as we go, we explore territories to which we would have never gone by playing in an academic way; it un-inhibits and sometimes clears the head."[103] The saxophonist Peter Brötzmann observed, "I can understand why people like Frank Wright, Muhammad Ali, Alan Silva, live [in Paris]—they don't suffer the pressures that they would in the States."[104] Ali, in particular, felt that distribution of the records was made difficult through the process of self-production.[105] Ultimately some members of the band wanted to break up the record company, and that led to the end of the band.

AFTER CENTER OF THE WORLD

After the band split up, Wright remained in Europe but frequently spent time in New York when possible. Even before the end of Center of the World, Wright was already exploring other possibilities. In the New York lofts, which had proliferated through the middle part of the 1970s, he found an audience. Ali's Alley was the place he played most, thanks to his work with its founder, the drummer Rashied Ali. One of those concerts, in July 1974, featured Wright playing flute and bass clarinet in addition to tenor with a quartet that included the baritone saxophonist Benny Wilson, guitarist James Blood Ulmer, and Ali. The session was recorded and was released many years later on ESP-Disk under the title *Blues for Albert Ayler*, a belated memorial to the late saxophonist.[106] The work reveals more directly Wright's blues roots, reinforced by Ulmer, though Ali kept the rhythms complex and constantly moving.

In January 1977, Wright brought a trio to the space that included Ulmer and Ali. One critic at the time observed:

> The jazz [Wright] plays was sometimes referred to as "energy music" during the 1960s, and although the term is vague . . . it is appropriate in Mr. Wright's case. The saxophonist sometimes seems to get so caught up in the physicality of his playing that he breaks into little dance steps in the middle of a solo. Although Mr. Wright has remained faithful to the rowdy, celebratory essence of what might be called the Cleveland style, his music has continued to grow. Most of that growth occurred in Europe, where he lives, and in the context of the cooler, more deliberate New York avant-garde of the 70s the combination of maturity and power in his playing comes as something of a shock. [This group] includes the fiercely melodic drummer Rashied Ali and the most original and inventive of the younger jazz guitarists, James (Blood) Ulmer. The sheer force of the music makes it well worth hearing.[107]

The band eventually evolved into a quartet called Aboriginal Society, adding the bassist Amin Akbar, and returned to Ali's Alley in March 1979.[108]

The vibraphonist Khan Jamal (1946–2022) played a few gigs with Wright at the Tin Palace in New York around 1975 or 1976. He stated of their friendship:

> We used to just hang. I'd go over to his house and play, he'd come over to my house and play. We were good friends. . . . We'd put our money together and go get us a steak, some peas, and some fruit, some vegetables and go cook a meal. This was a cat who let out his emotions very strongly, and at the same time, a

very generous, giving person. He came out of the blues, gospel, the African-American experience, and no matter how wild he may have seemed, it was there. Frank wasn't coming out of a European kind of thing, he was coming out of *his* groove, as opposed to trying to come out of some Bartok, or Stockhausen; he was coming out of his southern roots. Because we all have them, we all have our Baptist roots, our African Episcopal roots, our Pentecostal roots, our roots of slavery.[109]

Wright's most sustained music in the late 1970s came through new encounters with the pianist Georges Arvanitas and trumpeter Kamal Abdul Alim. Wright and Arvanitas co-led a quartet session in December 1977 entitled *Shouting the Blues*, which signaled the direction that Wright would pursue in the late 1970s and early 1980s.[110] The saxophonist Glenn Spearman observed, "[Wright] was trying to get off as Blues singer with saxophone accompaniment. That's really what he wanted to do, get over as a Blues shouter. When he came back to New York he really had intentions of settling into the Blues shout tenor groove and expecting to get radio play. He never did. He was always a real Bluesman who played avant garde."[111]

Wright had returned to New York in 1976 and hired the trumpeter Kamal Abdul Alim as his new musical director. Much of Wright's late 1970s work came as a result of having Abdul Alim help arrange ideas for the ensembles that he led. "He was a beautiful person," Alim remarked, "but to understand his music, I had to spend some time around him, really get to know him deeply because it was the kind of thing that took a while. He had a mode of expression and a spiritual commitment and that was the basis of his music."[112]

When Wright recounted his childhood experiences, he would hold his hands up and declare, "These hands used to plow the fields in Mississippi!" Abdul Alim observed:

All of that was in his music, all of what he and his family experienced in Mississippi. You can hear the pain, the agony, he would communicate howls and screams through his instrument, but also love, too, because his music was so raw. He carried all of that with him. He had the ability to focus all of that raw emotion into his music, that is what was profound about him. Sometimes he would lie on the floor and play his horn and almost be crying. He had chains he would drag across the floor like they were chains from Mississippi. It was some kind of catharsis for him. All of that was central to the music he made.[113]

The French writer Serge Loupien later stated that Wright's "exploits were really causing a stir, literally as well as figuratively. The way in which the reverend had the habit of hitting the stage with chains in the middle of his concerts earned him the unconditional support of all the leftist groups, who saw in this sudden frenzy a highly symbolic anti-imperialist gesture."[114]

So Wright organized a session in New York in October 1978 that resulted in the record *Kevin, My Dear Son*. In some ways, it was a conventional turn, with the trumpeter Kamal Abdul Alim arranging some of the pieces, and the record featured the vocalist and lyricist Eddie Jefferson as part of a septet. The rhythm section was tight, with the bassist Reggie Workman and drummer "Philly" Joe Jones keeping a groove at the center as the other players improvised over the top. The record did receive some attention because of the personnel, but it did not give Wright exposure on the radio as he desired.

Wright returned to Germany and recorded a sextet at the Loft in Munich in May 1979 that further displayed his intentions, but despite it showing some development from the previous two records, it never got any traction.[115] Alim noted, "Europe appreciated free jazz and seemed to understand what the musicians were doing. America never really did. But to be able to harness his emotional energy and document that over a long period of years, Wright's work was really extraordinary."[116] Wright's collaborations with three South African players from the groundbreaking band the Blue Notes, the alto saxophonist Dudu Pukwana, bassist Johnny Dyani, and drummer Louis Moholo, at a live concert in Eindhoven, the Netherlands, contained some of Wright's more exploratory work from the period, but they did not continue to work together.[117]

In the early 1980s, Wright played with different quintet lineups that harked back to his original quartet. These groups included Few, Muhammad Ali, and several different bassists, while reuniting with Noah Howard at the Willisau Jazz Festival and including the Clevelander Arthur Jones at the Moers Jazz Festival. Wright also began to play more in the Netherlands and also in Germany, where he recorded with one of Peter Brötzmann's groups for the record *Alarm*.[118] Silva observed, "All the European players had to deal with what Frank Wright did on saxophone. Peter Brötzmann and many others of that generation were strongly influenced by him."[119] The tenor saxophonist Thomas Borgmann referred to Wright as his favorite tenor player and said that he had learned a considerable amount from listening to him on record.[120] Glenn Spearman added, "[The German scene] loved Frank Wright, they knew Frank really had the power."[121] For his part, Brötzmann referred to "the group around Frank Wright" as "very close friends of mine."[122] Wright joined him in New York for the Sound Unity

Festival in 1984 as a part of the ALARM ensemble. A renewed association with Cecil Taylor soon followed for his involvement in the Orchestra of Two Continents in 1984 and for smaller unit work from 1984 to 1986.[123] His connections to the German scene allowed Wright to also maintain sustained associations with the guitarist Frank Wollny, multi-instrumentalist and visual artist A. R. Penck, bassist Peter Kowald, and others.

In observing the European avant-garde scene in relation to the American free jazz scene, Glenn Spearman noted, "I saw it as a different spiritual root. They didn't have the same experience. They had coopted a lot of the energy and feeling associated with the Black American experience. But I saw finally that they had a different history and because the history was different the music was different.... What I admired was their business sense, the way they could stick together, supported each other as an art group, the way they were funded. When I worked ... we were paid. You could expose the music to a much wider audience as a result of the subsidies."[124]

Wright played his last concerts in New York at the Pyramid Club in mid-1989 in a duo format with Andrew Cyrille. A few years later, Cyrille remarked on the concerts, "It was extraordinary, as far as the music that came out, the improvisation, the spontaneity, the feeling, the reaction of the audience. I don't think he lived a year after that. The problem was Frank just had a problem doing business with what he did. Frank also had some insecurities. Frank had difficulty surviving in a place like New York only because of the way that he thought."[125]

Even before his early death at age fifty-four, Wright already was garnering tributes, such as the saxophonist Roscoe Mitchell's piece "The Reverend Frank Wright," which forms the centerpiece of his record *Live at the Knitting Factory* from a performance at the New York club in 1987. Memorial tributes proliferated in the 1990s and early 2000s, from a range of figures such as Glenn Spearman, Noah Howard, Bobby Few, the drummer Paul Murphy, bassist William Parker, and multi-instrumentalist Zusaan Kali Fasteau.[126] The trumpeter Roy Campbell Jr. also considered Frank Wright, among others, to have been an early influence on his musical thinking.[127]

For several years after the end of Center of the World, Few played with a trio in Paris. The lineups varied but often featured the bassist Tom McKenzie and drummer Noel McGhie. He also recorded two solo records, *Few Coming Thru* (1977) and *Continental Jazz Express* (1979).[128] These displayed Few's brilliance in a more open setting, often with incredibly fast playing that produced shimmering curtains of sound, thick sonic shapes that suggested a larger ensemble in its energy and intensity. In 1981, Few got hired by Steve Lacy, or as the pianist Michael Smith (b 1938) observed, "[Lacy] kept writing for [piano] but he couldn't find a piano player who was interesting at all. And then, Frank Wright's group broke up ... so that Bobby was suddenly available and started working with Lacy."[129] Few was an integral figure in Lacy's band until 1994.

Silva continued his work with the Celestial Communications Orchestra in Paris with constantly evolving lineups of musicians, by then mostly with French players, though also with African diaspora figures such as the saxophonist Jo Maka from Guinea and Adolf Winkler from Togo. He also worked with Japanese musicians such as the trumpeter Itaru Oki, as well as occasional American players such as Muhammad Ali, the saxophonist Arthur Doyle, and the flutist and saxophonist Becky Friend.[130]

Silva also developed connections to the Dutch improvisation scene beginning in the late 1970s. For instance, he began working with the Instant Composers Pool in Amsterdam in 1977, where he first met the Dutch drummer Han Bennink and pianist Misha Mengelberg and the German saxophonist Peter Brötzmann, among others.[131] Silva also developed connections to the German scene centered in Berlin, playing with Alexander von Schlippenbach's quartet in 1981 and 1982, who subsequently invited him to play with the Globe Unity Orchestra in the period from 1983 to 1986.[132] Silva enjoyed playing in the smaller unit but was turned off by the chaos he sensed in the Globe Unity Orchestra, or what followed, which he described as "contrived." People would take solos that were quite similar each time they played and he felt they never had enough regular gigs or sessions to really work out their collective craft.[133] So Silva left the band. He did manage to maintain some older affiliations, such as with Sunny Murray and with the pianists Burton Greene and Andrew Hill in their respective groups in the late 1970s and early 1980s.[134] In the 1980s and 1990s, one of his most productive connections was with the British drummer Roger Turner.

Silva got more involved in education, initially at the American Center in Paris, where he drew students from the United States. But after it closed in 1973, he cofounded the Institute for Art, Culture and Perception in central Paris in 1974, a music school meant to fashion a jazz conservatory upon European models.[135] It was one of the first jazz schools in France, and Silva led it as its artistic director for nearly twenty-five years, working with hundreds of students over the years. Silva was particularly interested in connections between audio and visual perception and was influenced by phenomenology, a philosophical school of thought that produced theories about consciousness and described how reality, and specifically artistic reality, was perceived. He considered art to be "abstract rhythms and time."[136] These interests led him to study the impact of psychedelics, including LSD and marijuana, on visual perception, which in turn led him into the field of art therapy.[137] He watched many abstract, silent avant-garde films in that era, thinking about what kind of music would go with them. Some of Silva's students eventually worked in his Celestial Communications Orchestra. Silva had a renewed surge of recordings and various musical involvements from the mid-1990s as he began to step back from his work at the institute, and he remains active up to the present time.

Ali played sporadically as a part of other groups in the 1970s and 1980s. He toured with the Archie Shepp Quintet in Yugoslavia and other parts of Europe in 1973.[138] While in Paris, he played with the Saheb Sarbib Quartet in the mid-1970s.[139] After the breakup of Center of the World, Ali's musical involvements became less sustained. He took part in a European tour with a fiery free jazz group consisting of the trumpeter Earl Cross, saxophonist Idris Ackamoor, and bassist Rashied Al Akbar in 1980.[140] Ali also played with the Michel Pilz Quartet in Germany in the early 1980s.[141] He was deported back to the United States on a minor marijuana possession charge around 1984 or 1985.[142] After his return, he spent over a decade homeless in New York City before eventually moving back to Philadelphia and seeing a rebirth of his career in the 2000s, primarily in the saxophonist David S. Ware's last groups in the early 2010s.[143]

The Paris branch of the Cleveland community, together with so many musicians from other parts of the United States and Europe, was to have a profound effect on the French and European free jazz scenes. For one, it created a permanent diaspora of musicians who worked in and out of Paris and later in Germany, the Netherlands, Belgium, and other parts of Europe, influencing those communities to the present time. And the European scenes absorbed much of their sound, evolving it in other directions and as their own players confronted those concepts as they developed styles of their own.

CONCLUSION

LEGACIES OF FREEDOM IN SOUND

Black creative music that emerged in the greater Ohio Valley and was carried by its practitioners around the United States and the world formulated an aesthetic of freedom in sound. Though in its immediate circumstances the music moved beyond bebop, it made far more profound demands as cultural critique. Drawn from a multigenerational repository of communal memory, the aesthetics of the music were revolutionary in their orchestration but were drawn from a deep history and tradition. This reservoir provided musicians with vast resources to create spontaneous music in the present that gave voice to that history through searing critique.

The narrative I have outlined here is one that delves into social history—the history of human connections, power structures, and conflict—to understand the invention and reception of free jazz as an art form. Pushing against simple narratives that have reduced this arts movement to immediate circumstances or those that attacked its legitimacy, I have argued that free jazz was the result of a century of intergenerational struggle, mobility, and reservoirs of memory and constituted a synthesis of a broad range of cultural matter alongside a series of sonic revolutions.

Histories of jazz, and other music and art forms, have much to gain from close attention to the practitioners, their origins, and the cultural flows represented in their communities and their myriad mobilities. We have only just begun to understand the profound impact that the Great Migration had on the social and cultural fabric of the United States, and we must continue to push through the fog of how it has been represented in historiography. There was a logic and a pattern to migrations. People maintained and expanded social networks while they moved from one place to another, and in these links we find the engines of cultural inheritance and invention over time. More work is needed to further elaborate how the Great Migration set the stage for the outpouring of American music throughout the twentieth century. I founded the Music and Migration Lab at the Pratt Institute to engage with these debates as I work to build international collaborative partners while looking locally, regionally, and globally.

Of the two sites examined in this book, Detroit was most resilient in nurturing successive generations of creative musicians who primarily practiced their craft there. Indeed, to the present, the city has maintained a living tradition through the work of A. Spencer Barefield, Jaribu Shahid, and Wendell Harrison, and a new generation led by Michael Malis and Marcus Elliot has carried this forward to the present. Though Cleveland's great wave of musicians had largely departed by the late 1960s, a successive generation led by Bill DeArango in the early 1970s sparked forward movement through collaborations with Joe Lovano, Frank Doblekar, Phil Raskin, Skip Hadden, and others.

Much of the music that emerged from the greater Ohio Valley, born out of the Great Migration, spawned additional journeys. These mobilities brought the aesthetic of these sounds across the country to Los Angeles and Oakland, to Chicago, New York, and innumerable places in between where musicians disseminated their ideas to audiences and to aspiring musicians of successive generations, who continued to formulate innovative forms of sonic expression. The music has been a sustained tradition that has made its imprint upon national and global music cultures.

The rise and proliferation of free jazz was one of the United States' most profound artistic accomplishments, despite hostility from the cultural establishment, capitalist forces embodied in record companies and music criticism, and a general lack of institutional support. In a country that often declares itself a beacon of freedom, the music came as a sharp critique of the reality of economic inequality, political repression, and cultural conservatism. Free jazz in these times was one of the foremost sonic embodiments of freedom, like Moten's theory of the scream to disrupt the perverse calm, giving voice to the ongoing struggle.

Many musicians found the reality of that freedom in sound and spirit, if even such freedom was not realized in other aspects of their lives. To repeat what the bassist Clyde Shy stated when he listened to Ornette Coleman for the first time: "I heard freedom." In these words, he insisted that the music was the fullest manifestation of freedom as one could sonically articulate in the 1960s. To this, he added, musicians in this pursuit with "their old feelings uncaged, they unbridled their instruments and used them in a different manner to help the world remember."[1]

ACKNOWLEDGMENTS

This book was an immense effort, and there are innumerable people that I must thank for helping bring it into being. First and foremost, I wish to thank Imam Mutawaf Shaheed, who believed in this project from the beginning and offered me numerous suggestions throughout the process and put me in touch with many other people whose input was invaluable. As a participant in this history himself, his counsel was a steadying force throughout the research and writing phases. I cannot express my thanks enough for his wisdom and insights. I also wish to thank my colleague and true brother, Gabriel Vanlandingham-Dunn, for a decade of dialogue and fellowship. Our conversations have no doubt influenced my thinking in all kinds of ways, and I am fortunate that we never stop talking about the music for which we both share a deep love.

In Cleveland, I was blessed to befriend Kamal Abdul Alim during my first research trip to the city. His generous tour of the city transformed my understanding of Cleveland's geography and cultural history. Kamal's thoughtfulness and kindness made indelible marks on this book. I also wish to thank the great Don Freeman, whose lifelong commitment to pursuing justice serves as an inspiration. Hasan Shahid and Yusuf Mumin also were instrumental in understanding the the Cleveland scene in the late 1960s. Thanks are also owed to Larry Hancock, Brent McKesson, and Akbar Tyler.

In my first research visits to Detroit, conducting interviews with Wendell Harrison and Jaribu Shahid were foundational in understanding the development of the music and the community there. I owe a great deal of gratitude to Wendell for granting me access to his unparalleled archive on the Tribe label. I also wish to acknowledge the incredible support of John Sinclair, Leni Sinclair, Robin

Eichele, Ron English, Bill Harris, and George Tysh, who spoke with such conviction about the movement that they led there in the 1960s. Additional appreciation must be given to John and Leni Sinclair for maintaining and preserving their unparalleled archive on free jazz, which they bequeathed to the Bentley Historical Library at the University of Michigan. I also wish to thank Bill Harris for his warm reception and mentorship in relation to the Detroit cultural sphere. Joel Peterson provided me with invaluable suggestions and contacts during my numerous visits to Detroit. Conversations with Phil Ranelin, Sadiq Muhammad Bey, Elreta Dodds, Kafi Patrice Nassoma, Tani Tabbal, David McMurray, M. L. Liebler, Kim Heron, Beverly Ealy, Kathleen Beaufait, Ralph "Buzzy" Jones, Marcus Elliot, and Michael Malis were all crucial to understanding the complexity of Detroit. Thanks also to Michael and Kim for loaning me vital, hard-to-find books from their private collections. Many thanks to M. L. Liebler for also helping me navigate many issues of artist rights in Detroit. Finn Horn worked with me as a student research assistant, especially for the Sinclair archive materials, and though just a freshman at the time, was doing graduate-level work.

The Pratt Institute provided me with vital support to conduct research in all of the sites that I visited as I worked on this book. In addition to those mentioned above, I am indebted to Alan Silva, Muhammadi Ali, Barry Wallenstein, Ted Daniel, William Parker, Steve Tintweiss, Simone Few, Lieve Fransen, and Daniel Carter for interviews on the music. Andreas Vingaard's willingness to share crucial interviews on Charles Tyler from his private archive was invaluable to drawing a fuller picture of the latter's work and career. Barry was also gracious in allowing me access to the recording of Tyler's memorial from his personal collection. I also wish to thank Ras Moshe Burnett for access to numerous recordings from his private archive and Clifford Allen for access to unpublished portions of the interview he conducted with Sunny Murray. I also appreciate Thomas Gauffroy-Naudin's helping me access materials in the Willisau Jazz Archive.

The extensive archival research that I conducted was made far easier by a number of dedicated archivists at a range of institutions: Carlie Burkett and Courtney Pinkard at the Alabama Department of Archives and History, Orville Ifill at the Alabama Jazz Hall of Fame, the reference staff at Birmingham Public Library, Caitlin Moriarty at the Bentley Historical Library at the University of Michigan, Rachel Minetti at the Georgia Historical Society, Michelle Leasure at the George State University archives, Serena McCracken at the Kenan Research Center, Muriel M. Jackson and Lee Shoemaker at the Middle George Regional Library, Louisa Hoffman at the Oberlin College archives, Kaila Jones at the Upson Historical Society, and Ann K. Sindelar at Western Reserve Historical Society.

ACKNOWLEDGMENTS

I have had many conversations with colleagues and friends over the years that undoubtedly influenced my thinking on this book. While I cannot mention them all, I wish, in particular, to thank Prof. Fred Moten, Prof. Leila Adu-Gilmore, and Prof. Kwami Coleman at New York University; Prof. Carl Zimring at the Pratt Institute; Prof. Scott Currie at the University of Minnesota; Paul Harding; Ras Moshe Burnett; Anne Waldman; and James Brandon Lewis. During the bulk of the period during which I wrote this book, I lived near Anne, and her poetic energies were constantly inspiring and uplifting. I also wish to thank Alice Viggiani for her work on the maps.

Finally, I wish to thank my family. My wife, Jennie, has been a constant source of strength and resolve throughout the process of writing this book. I also wish to thank my parents for their years of support. My uncle Nick Remple has been an intellectual guide since childhood. And I wish to thank my two amazing children, Nick and Raine, for reminding me of life's true spirit.

NOTES

INTRODUCTION: BLACK GEOGRAPHIES, NETWORKS, AND MOBILITIES

1. Larry Neal, "New Grass/Albert Ayler," *Cricket* 3 (1969): 37; Leroi Jones, "The Changing Same (R&B and New Black Music)," in *The Black Aesthetic*, ed. Addison Gayle Jr. (Doubleday, 1971), 130; Salim Washington, "'All the Things You Could Be by Now': Charles Mingus Presents Charles Mingus and the Limits of Avant-Garde Jazz," in *Uptown Conversation: The New Jazz Studies*, ed. Robert G. O'Meally et al., (Columbia University Press, 2004), 29.
2. Fred Moten, *Black and Blur* (Duke University Press, 2017), vii; Fred Moten, *In the Break: The Aesthetics of the Black Radical Tradition* (University of Minnesota Press, 2003), 1, 6.
3. Moten, *Black and Blur*, x.
4. Moten, *In the Break*, 255.
5. John R. Logan et al., "Creating the Black Ghetto: Black Residential Patterns Before and During the Great Migration," in "Residential Inequality in American Neighborhoods and Communities," special issue, *Annals of the American Academy of Political and Social Science* 660 (July 2015): 18–35.
6. Steven Hahn, *A Nation Under Our Feet: Black Political Struggles in the Rural South from Slavery to the Great Migration* (Belknap Press of Harvard University Press, 2003), 62–115; Stephanie M. H. Camp, *Closer to Freedom: Enslaved Women and Everyday Resistance in the Plantation South* (University of North Carolina Press, 2004), 12–34.
7. Camp, *Closer to Freedom*, 7.
8. Joe William Trotter Jr., *River Jordan: African American Urban Life in the Ohio Valley* (University Press of Kentucky, 1998).
9. Keith P. Griffler, *Front Line of Freedom: African Americans and the Forging of the Underground Railroad in the Ohio Valley* (University Press of Kentucky, 2004).
10. Cheryl Janifer LaRoche, *Free Black Communities and the Underground Railroad: The Geography of Resistance* (University of Illinois Press, 2014).
11. Darrel E. Bigham, *On Jordan's Banks: Emancipation and Its Aftermath in the Ohio River Valley* (University Press of Kentucky, 2006), 247–70.
12. Quoted in David Evans, "Charley Patton: The Conscience of the Delta," in *Charley Patton: Voice of the Mississippi Delta*, ed. Robert Sacré (University Press of Mississippi, 2018), 56.

13. Robin D. G. Kelley, *Freedom Dreams: The Black Radical Imagination*, revised ed. (Beacon, 2022), 191.
14. Neal, "New Grass/Albert Ayler," 39.
15. John Sinclair, "The Midwestern Jazz Scene," unpublished manuscript, Box 8, Folder 54, John and Leni Sinclair Collection, Bentley Historical Library, University of Michigan, Ann Arbor, MI.
16. Albert Ayler, *The First Recordings*, 2 vols. (Bird Notes, 1962).
17. Albert Ayler Trio, *Spiritual Unity* (ESP-Disk, 1965); Albert Ayler, *Spirits* (Debut Recordings, 1964); Albert Ayler, *Bells* (ESP-Disk, 1965).
18. Center of the World, *Center of the World*, vol. 1 (Center of the World, 1972); Center of the World, *Last Polka in Nancy?*, vol. 2 (Center of the World, 1973); Center of the World, *More or Less Few*, vol. 3 (Center of the World, 1973); Center of the World, *Adieu Little Man* (Center of the World, 1974).
19. Frank Wright Trio, *Frank Wright Trio* (ESP-Disk, 1966); Frank Wright Quintet, *Your Prayer* (ESP-Disk, 1967); Frank Wright Quartet, *Uhuru Na Umoja* (America Records, 1970); Frank Wright Quartet, *Church Number Nine* (Odeon, 1971).
20. Charles Tyler Ensemble, *Charles Tyler Ensemble* (ESP-Disk, 1966); Charles Tyler, *Eastern Man Alone* (ESP-Disk, 1967).
21. Billy Bang Quintet, *Rainbow Gladiator* (Soul Note, 1981); Billy Bang Quintet, *Invitation* (Soul Note, 1982).
22. Norman Howard, *Burn, Baby, Burn* (Homeboy Music, 1993).
23. Claude Delcloo and Arthur Jones, *Africanasia* (BYG Records, 1969); Arthur Jones, *Scorpio* (BYG Records, 1971); Jacques Coursil Unit, *Way Head* (BYG Records, 1969).
24. Black Unity Trio, *Al-Fatihah* (Salaam Records, 1969).
25. Griot Galaxy, *Kins* (Black and White Records, 1982); Griot Galaxy, *Opus Krampus* (Sound Aspects Records, 1985).
26. Wendell Harrison and Phillip Ranelin, *Message from the Tribe* (Tribe Records, 1972); Wendell Harrison, *An Evening with the Devil* (Tribe Records, 1972); Marcus Belgrave, *Gemini II* (Tribe Records, 1974); Phil Ranelin, *The Time Is Now!* (Tribe Records, 1974); Wendell Harrison and the Tribe, *Farewell to the Welfare* (Tribe Records, 1975); Phil Ranelin, *Vibes from the Tribe* (Tribe Records, 1976).
27. James N. Gregory, *The Southern Diaspora: How the Great Migrations of Black and White Southerners Transformed America* (University of North Carolina Press, 2005).
28. James R. Grossman, *Land of Hope: Chicago, Black Southerners, and the Great Migration* (University of Chicago Press, 2017). See also Stanley Stewart E. Tolnay, "The African American 'Great Migration' and Beyond," *Annual Review of Sociology* 29 (2003): 209–32; Townsand Price-Spratlen, "Urban Destination Selection Among African Americans During the 1950s Great Migration," *Social Science History* 32, no. 3 (2008): 437–69; Jeffrey Helgeson, "Politics in the Promised Land: How the Great Migration Shaped the American Midwest," in *Finding a New Midwestern History*, ed. Jon K. Lauck et al. (University of Nebraska Press, 2020), 111–26.
29. Robert H. Zieger, *For Jobs and Freedom: Race and Labor in America Since 1865*, Civil Rights and the Struggle for Black Equality in the Twentieth Century (University Press of Kentucky, 2007). See also J. Trent Alexander et al., "Second-Generation Outcomes of the Great Migration," *Demography* 54, no. 6 (December 2017): 2249–71.
30. Isabel Wilkerson, *The Warmth of Other Suns: The Epic Story of America's Great Migration* (Vintage, 2010).
31. Kwami Coleman, "*Free Jazz* and the 'New Thing': Aesthetics, Identity, and Texture, 1960–1966," *Journal of Musicology* 38, no. 3 (2021): 264.
32. LeRoi Jones, "Don Cherry: Making It the Hard Way," *Down Beat* 30, no. 30 (November 21, 1963): 16.

33. There are innumerable examples. Jeffrey Barr, "Chords and Discords: A Question of Validity," *Down Beat* 31, no. 1 (January 2, 1964): 9.
34. Taylor Castell, "Some Thoughts on Publishing, or ... Yes, LeRoi, There Is a White Power Structure," *Sound & Fury* 2, no. 2 (April 1966): 1.
35. Jerry Guild, "Shepp, Jones, and White America," *Down Beat* 32, no. 5 (February 25, 1965): 10.
36. Coleman, "*Free Jazz* and the 'New Thing,'" 269.
37. *San Francisco Examiner*, November 17, 1968.
38. *Vancouver Sun*, January 3, 1969.
39. *Courier-Post* (Camden, NJ), May 31, 1969.
40. *Baltimore Sun*, September 17, 1969.
41. Ishmael Reed, "The Tragedy of Stanley Crouch," *Counterpunch.org*, October 16, 2020.
42. There are too many to note, but take, for example, Ronald Atkin's article in the *Guardian*, January 23, 1967, and numerous articles in the *Sydney Morning Herald* (Australia).
43. Dixon quoted in *Oakland Tribune*, January 7, 1968.
44. *Indianapolis News*, February 9, 1967.
45. Michael C. Heller, *Loft Jazz: Improvising New York in the 1970s* (University of California Press, 2016).
46. Ben Young, *Dixonia: A Bio-Discography of Bill Dixon* (Greenwood, 1998); Cisco Bradley, *Universal Tonality: The Life and Music of William Parker* (Duke University Press, 2021); Ahmed Abdullah, *A Strange Celestial Road: My Time with the Sun Ra Arkestra* (Blank Forms Editions, 2023); Henry Threadgill and Brent Hayes Edwards, *Easily Slip Into Another World: A Life in Music* (Knopf, 2023).
47. George E. Lewis, *A Power Stronger Than Itself: The AACM and American Experimental Music* (University of Chicago Press, 2009). See also Charles Lester, "'You Can't Keep the Music Unless You Move with It': The Great Migration and the Black Cultural Politics of Jazz in New Orleans and Chicago," in *Escape from New York: The New Negro Renaissance Beyond Harlem*, ed. Davarian L. Baldwin and Minkah Makalani (Minneapolis: University of Minnesota Press, 2013), 313–34.
48. Benjamin Looker, *Point from Which Creation Begins: The Black Artists' Group of St. Louis* (Missouri Historical Society Press, 2004).
49. Steven L. Isoardi, *The Dark Tree: Jazz and Community Arts in Los Angeles* (University of California Press, 2006).
50. Valerie Wilmer, *As Serious as Your Life: The Story of the New Jazz* (Lawrence Hill, 1977).
51. Amy Abugo Ongiri, *Spectacular Blackness: The Cultural Politics of the Black Power Movement and the Search for a Black Aesthetic* (University of Virginia Press, 2010).
52. Philippe Carles and Jean-Louis Comolli, *Free Jazz/Black Power* (Edition Champs Libre, 1971); Ekkehard Jost, *Free Jazz* (Universal Editions, 1975).
53. M. L. Liebler, ed., *Heaven Was Detroit: From Jazz to Hip-Hop and Beyond* (Wayne State University Press, 2016); Mark Stryker, *Jazz from Detroit* (University of Michigan Press, 2019).
54. Beth Tompkins Bates, *The Making of Black Detroit in the Age of Henry Ford* (University of North Carolina Press, 2012).
55. Kimberly L. Phillips, *AlabamaNorth: African-American Migrants, Community, and Working Class Activism in Cleveland, 1915–1945*, The Working Class in American History (University of Illinois Press, 1999).
56. Salim Washington has critiqued this approach. Salim Washington, "'All the Things You Could Be by Now': Charles Mingus Presents Charles Mingus and the Limits of Avant-Garde Jazz," in *Uptown Conversation: The New Jazz Studies*, ed. Robert G. O'Meally et al. (Columbia University Press, 2004), 29.

1. THE UNDERGROUND RAILROAD, FREE BLACK COMMUNITIES, AND THE EARLIEST CULTURAL SPACES IN THE GREATER OHIO VALLEY

1. Leland D. Baldwin, *Pittsburgh: The Story of a City, 1750–1865* (University of Pittsburgh Press, 1981), 159.
2. Richard Wade, "The Negro in Cincinnati, 1800–1830," *Journal of Negro History* 39 (January 1954): 43–57; Darrel E. Bigham, *We Ask Only a Fair Trial: A History of the Black Community of Evansville, Indiana* (Indiana University Press, 1987), 1–7.
3. Joe William Trotter Jr., *River Jordan: African American Urban Life in the Ohio Valley*, Ohio River Valley Series, ed. Rita Kohn and William Lynwood Montell (University Press of Kentucky, 1998), 11.
4. Trotter, *River Jordan*, 14.
5. J. Randolph Kean, "The Development of the 'Valley Line' of the Baltimore and Ohio Railroad," *Virginia Magazine of History and Biography* 60, no. 4 (October 1952): 537–50; Trotter, *River Jordan*, 14.
6. Richard Wade, *Urban Frontier: Pioneer Life in Early Pittsburgh, Cincinnati, Lexington, Louisville, and St. Louis* (University of Chicago Press, 1959): 64–66; Allen J. Share, *Cities in the Commonwealth: Two Centuries of Urban Life in Kentucky* (University Press of Kentucky, 1982), 33–43; Darrel E. Bigham, "River of Opportunity: Economic Consequences of the Ohio," in *Always a River: The Ohio River and the American Experience*, ed. Robert L. Reid (Indiana University Press, 1991), 144.
7. Frank F. Mathias, "John Randolph's Freedmen: The Thwarting of a Will," *Journal of Southern History* 39, no. 2 (May 1973): 265.
8. Cheryl Janifer LaRoche, *Free Black Communities and the Underground Railroad: The Geography of Resistance* (University of Illinois Press, 2014), 72–73.
9. Lewis Frederick Woodson, quoted in *Colored American*, July 28, 1838.
10. Debates and Proceedings, 14th Congress, first session (March 1, 1816), 1115–17; Jesse Torrey to John Randolph, April 29, 1816, Papers of the Select Committee to Inquire Into the Existence of an Inhuman and Illegal Traffic in Slaves in the District of Columbia, HR 14A-C.17.4, National Archives, Washington, DC; Deposition of Francis Scott Key, April 22, 1816, Papers of the Select Committee to Inquire Into the Existence of an Inhuman and Illegal Traffic in Slaves in the District of Columbia, HR 14A-C.17.4, National Archives, Washington, DC; Sworn Statement of Samuel Booker, March 7, 1816, all in Papers of the Select Committee to Inquire Into the Existence of an Inhuman and Illegal Traffic in Slaves in the District of Columbia, HR 14A-C.17.4, National Archives, Washington, DC; *Washington National Intelligencer*, March 2, 1816; *Niles' Weekly Register*, March 9, 1816, 30; Russell Kirk, *John Randolph of Roanoke: A Study in American Politics, with Selected Speeches and Letters* (Regnery, 1964), 131–39; Nicholas Wood, "John Randolph of Roanoke and the Politics of Slavery in the Early Republic," *Virginia Magazine of History and Biography* 120, no. 2 (2012): 115.
11. There are a few parallel cases of manumitted communities moving north to Ohio and Illinois. William H. Pease and Jane H. Pease, "Organized Negro Communities: A North American Experiment," *Journal of Negro History* 47, no. 1 (January 1962): 19.
12. "John Randolph's Slaves," *Wyandotte Gazette* (Wyandotte, KS), June 21, 1878.
13. Members of Randolph's family had previously tied the case up in court in an attempt to "break the will," but all attempts to thwart his wishes failed. The original bequest included eight thousand dollars in cash, with the rest of the value tied up in real estate that was eventually sold. "John Randolph's Slaves," *Middlebury Register* (Middlebury, VT), September 30, 1845; "John Randolph's Slaves," *The Liberator* (Boston), October 3, 1845; "John Randolph's Slaves," *Vermont Chronicle*

1. THE EARLIEST CULTURAL SPACES   ❧   365

     (Bellows Falls, VT), July 22, 1846; *Moton v. Kessens*, Plaintiff's Brief, 19, National Archives, Washington, DC.
14. "Randolph's Slaves," *Anti-Slavery Bugle* (Lisbon, OH), January 9, 1846.
15. *Dayton Journal and Advertiser* (Dayton, OH), July 7, 1846; "John Randolph's Slaves," *Vermont Chronicle* (Bellows Falls, VT), July 22, 1846; "John Randolph's Slaves," *Wyandotte Gazette* (Wyandotte, KS), June 21, 1878; Fountain Randolph, quoted in "Former Slave of J. Randolph Dies in Piqua," *Daily News-Tribune* (Greenville, OH), July 28, 1924.
16. "John Randolph's Slaves," *Vermont Chronicle* (Bellows Falls, VT), July 22, 1846.
17. *Moton v. Kessens*, Plaintiff's Brief, 16–17.
18. The school was founded on twenty thousand dollars left for the purpose in the will of Samuel Emlen, a Quaker from New Jersey. The school survived until 1857, when it was sold, though its primary operator, Augustus Wattles, left in 1848, because of constant threats of tarring and feathering. Edmund L. Binsfield, "The Negro Cemetery at Carthagena," *Northwest Ohio Quarterly* 32 (1959–1960): 30; Henry Howe, *Historical Collections of Ohio: Containing a Collection of the Most Interesting Facts, Traditions, Biographical Sketches, Anecdotes, etc., Relating to Its General and Local History; with Descriptions of Its Counties, Principal Towns, and Villages* (Cincinnati: Derby and Bradley, 1847), 504; "The Emlen Institution for the Benefit of Children of African and Indian Descent," *The Friend* 48 (March 10, 1875): 271; C. A. Powell et al., "Transplanting Free Negroes to Ohio from 1815 to 1858," *Journal of Negro History* 1, no. 3 (June 1916): 308; Dwight L. Dumond, ed., *Letters of James Gillespie Birney, 1831–1857* (D. Appleton-Century, 1938), 2:628–29; Ulrich F. Mueller, *Red, Black, and White: A History of Carthagena, Mercer County, Ohio* (n.p., 1934), 51; Keith P. Griffler, *Front Line of Freedom: African Americans and the Forging of the Underground Railroad in the Ohio Valley* (University Press of Kentucky, 2004), 34.
19. Quote from "Randolph's Slaves," *Sandusky Clarion* (Sandusky, OH), July 28, 1846.
20. *African Repository and Colonial Journal* 23 (March 1847): 70; Woodson, *Century of Negro Migration*, 56.
21. Quote from "Randolph's Slaves," *Sandusky Clarion* (Sandusky, OH), July 28, 1846; "John Randolph's Slaves," *North Star* (Danville, VT), July 6, 1846.
22. "Former Slave of J. Randolph Dies in Piqua," *Daily News-Tribune* (Greenville, OH), July 28, 1924.
23. "John Randolph's Slaves," *Tarboro Press* (Tarboro, NC), September 2, 1846.
24. "Randolph's Slaves," *The Liberator* (Boston), August 7, 1846.
25. "Randolph's Manumitted Slaves," *Anti-Slavery Bugle* (Lisbon, OH), July 17, 1846.
26. John A. Rayner, *The First Century of Piqua, Ohio* (Magee Brothers, 1916), 206.
27. First quote from "John Randolph's Slaves," *Wyandotte Gazette* (Wyandotte, KS), June 21, 1878; second passage taken from Fountain Randolph, quoted in "Former Slave of J. Randolph Dies in Piqua," *Daily News-Tribune* (Greenville, OH), July 28, 1924.
28. "Correspondence of the Morning Herald," *Anti-Slavery Bugle* (Lisbon, OH), August 21, 1846.
29. Quote from A. H. Gerrard, "Correspondence of the Morning Herald," *Anti-Slavery Bugle* (Lisbon, OH), August 21, 1846. Randolph had explicitly requested that they not be sent to Liberia. "John Randolph's Slaves," *The Liberator* (Boston), October 3, 1845; "John Randolph's Slaves," *Middlebury Register* (Middlebury, VT), August 11, 1846; Rayner, *The First Century of Piqua, Ohio*, 206.
30. "John Randolph's Slaves," *Wyandotte Gazette* (Wyandotte, KS), June 21, 1878.
31. "Miami co. Story: Of Baking, Slaves," *Dayton Daily News* (Dayton, OH), June 25, 1953.
32. Church services were held in one of the founders' homes until the Second Baptist Church was erected in Rossville in 1869. The cemetery was later renamed the Jackson Cemetery. Rayner, *The First Century of Piqua, Ohio*, 181; *The History of the John Randolph Freed Slaves of Roanoke, Virginia Who Settled in Miami and Shelby Counties* (Piqua, OH: Rossville-Springcreek Historical Society, n.d.), 11; David Meyers and Elise Meyers Walker, *Historic Black Settlements of Ohio* (History Press, 2020), 125.

33. Vernon R. Vaughn, *Vaughn History* (private pub., 1964), 21, 39; James C. Oda, *An Encyclopedia of Piqua, Ohio* (M. T. Publishing Co., 2007), 8, 69, 101, 104, 162.
34. Oda, *An Encyclopedia of Piqua, Ohio*, 8.
35. "John Randolph's Slaves," *Wyandotte Gazette* (Wyandotte, KS), June 21, 1878.
36. "The Randolph Slaves," *Scientific American*, December 26, 1846, 109.
37. "John Randolph's Slaves," *Wyandotte Gazette* (Wyandotte, KS), June 21, 1878.
38. "John Randolph's Slaves," *Wyandotte Gazette* (Wyandotte, KS), June 21, 1878.
39. "John Randolph's Slaves," *Wyandotte Gazette* (Wyandotte, KS), June 21, 1878.
40. This is representative of a broader trend. 1860 US Census, Miami County, Ohio, population schedule, Union Township, p. 37, dwelling 257, family 249, Geter Moton (NARA microfilm publication M653, roll 365); 1850 US Census, Miami County, Ohio, population schedule, Newton Township, p. 186B (printed, 372 handwritten), dwelling 2632, family 2635, Lott Hill (NARA microfilm publication M432, roll 629); 1850 US Census, Miami County, Ohio, population schedule, Union Township, p. 164A (printed, 327 handwritten), dwelling 2308, family 2312, Philip White (NARA microfilm publication M432, roll 711).
41. 1880 US Census, Miami County, Ohio, agricultural schedule, township of Union, p. 13, enumeration district 145, Geter Moten (NARA microfilm publication T1159, roll 78).
42. Mercer County, Ohio, Common Pleas Record, vol. 27, 105; Lawyer's Brief of John G. Romer, counsel for the defendants, *Moton v. Kessens*, 7 (Clerk of Courts Office, Mercer County Courthouse).
43. "Randolph Slave Case Won by Descendants," *Troy Daily News* (Troy, OH), July 13, 1916; Anita Lunsford, *The Conspiracy of John Randolph's Slaves* (private pub., 2006): 67–69.
44. Goodrich Giles, a figure in the community at Piqua who ran for city council three times in the 1880s, later moved to Dayton, where he opened the Anderson-Giles Classic Theater. It was the site of many performances of figures including Count Basie and Ella Fitzgerald before closing in 1959. Lunsford, *Conspiracy of John Randolph's Slaves*, 55, 59; Oda, *Encyclopedia of Piqua*, 147.
45. 1900 US Census, village of Pleasant Hill, township of Newton, Miami County, Ohio, population schedule, sheet 15, enumeration district 83, dwelling 326, family 331, Albert Hill (NARA microfilm publication T623, roll 305); 1910 US Census, township of Newton, Miami County, Ohio, population schedule, enumeration district 118, sheet 2B, dwelling 32, family 32, Albert Hill (NARA microfilm publication T624, roll 1215).
46. 1930 US Census, Miami County, Ohio, population schedule, city of Troy, enumeration district, 55–56, sheet 11A, dwelling 266, family 329, Albert Hill (NARA microfilm publication T626, roll 583); 1940 US Census, Miami County, Ohio, population schedule, city of Troy, enumeration district 55–57, sheet 11A, household 244, Albert A. Hill (NARA microfilm publication T627, roll 3115).
47. The family of Harvey Call Cobbs Sr. also traced its roots to a similar part of south-central Virginia, Bedford County and the northwestern part of Charlotte County, where the free people of Roanoke had been enslaved. By 1930, they owned a home worth approximately $2,500, clearly indicating that they were part of the Black middle class of Middletown. 1870 US Census, Bedford County, Virginia, agricultural schedule, township of Otter, p. 3, Call Cobbs (NARA microfilm publication T1132, roll 11); 1920 US Census, Butler County, Ohio, population schedule, city of Middletown, enumeration district 47, sheet 8A, dwelling 152, family 175, Harvey C. Cobbs (NARA microfilm publication T625, roll 1352); 1930 US Census, Butler County, Ohio, population schedule, city of Middletown, enumeration district, 9–32, sheet 6A, dwelling 134, family 146, Harvey Cobbs (NARA microfilm publication T626, roll 488); 1940 US Census, Butler County, Ohio, population schedule, city of Middletown, enumeration district 9–57, sheet 11B, household 215, Harvey Call Cobbs (NARA microfilm publication T627, roll 3034).
48. Petition of William Cassels to the Virginia General Assembly, December 17, 1817, Amelia County, Virginia State Archives, Richmond.

1. THE EARLIEST CULTURAL SPACES

49. Cassels appears in Virginia state records in the 1810s, attempting to recover an enslaved person, Hannibal, who had escaped his plantation. William Cassels Petition, December 12, 1817, Legislative Petitions of the General Assembly, 1776–1865, Accession Number 36121, Box 9, Folder 76, Virginia State Archives, Richmond.
50. Amelia County (Va.) Free Negro Register and Register of Estrays, 1791–1835, no. 191, Library of Virginia, Richmond, VA.
51. Amelia County (Va.) Free Negro Register and Register of Estrays, 1791–1835, nos. 192–8, Library of Virginia, Richmond, VA.
52. Ohio Tax Records, Jackson County, Milton Township, 1832–1834, 1836–1838; Ohio Tax Records, Jackson County, Washington Township, 1832–1837.
53. 1860 US Census, Jackson County, Ohio, population schedule, township of Milton, p. 22, dwelling 153, family 138, Rachel Cassel (NARA microfilm publication M653, roll 438); 1870 US Census, Jackson County, Ohio, population schedule, township of Milton, p. 38, dwelling 286, family 281, William Cassel (NARA microfilm publication M593, roll 1226).
54. *Colored American*, October 31, 1840; Judith P. Justus, *Down from the Mountain: The Oral History of the Hemings Family* (Juskurtara, 1990); Byron Woodson, *A President in the Family: Thomas Jefferson, Sally Hemings, and Thomas Woodson* (Praeger, 2001), 1.
55. Charles Spencer Smith, *A History of the African Methodist Episcopal Church* (D. M. Baxter, 1922), 16; Meyers and Walker, *Historic Black Settlements of Ohio*, 80.
56. Griffler, *Front Line of Freedom*, 33.
57. LaRoche, *Free Black Communities*, 80.
58. "Life Among the Lowly: Number II," *Pike County Republican* (Waverly, OH), November 20, 1873; Justus, *Down from the Mountain*; Griffler, *Front Line of Freedom*, 35; LaRoche, *Free Black Communities*, 80–81.
59. Griffler, *Front Line of Freedom*, 33.
60. Augustus Wattles, quoted in *Colored American*, October 31, 1840.
61. *Colored American*, October 31, 1840.
62. LaRoche, *Free Black Communities*, 79.
63. 1850 US Census, Jackson County, Ohio, population schedule, township of Milton, p. 315 printed, 629 handwritten), dwelling 1171, family 1171, Frances Dyers (NARA microfilm publication M432, roll 698).
64. *Gallipolis Journal*, May 1, 1884.
65. 1850 US Census, Gallia County, Ohio, population schedule, township of Addison, p. 470B printed, 940 handwritten), dwelling 1173, family 1183, Jane Tuck (NARA microfilm publication M432, roll 681); 1860 US Census, Gallia County, Ohio, agricultural schedule, township of Addison, p. 43, Jane Tuck (NARA microfilm publication T1159, roll 19).
66. Henson C. Tuck information sheet for Seventy-Fifth Anniversary General Catalogue of Former Students, Alumni and Development Records, Former Student File, Box 257, Henson C. Tuck Folder, Oberlin College Archives.
67. *Oberlin News-Tribune*, October 27, 1955; October 29, 1956.
68. *Oberlin News-Tribune*, October 29, 1956.
69. Members of the Berlin Crossroads community, including women, attended Oberlin College as early as 1852. Meyers and Walker, *Historic Black Settlements of Ohio*, 82.
70. One of her younger brothers attended concurrently with her, and a younger sister attended a few years later. *General Catalogue of Oberlin College, 1833–1908, Including an Account of the Principal Events in the History of the College, with Illustrations of the College Buildings* (Oberlin College, 1909), 992.
71. Samantha Cordelia Tuck information sheet for Seventy-Fifth Anniversary General Catalogue of Former Students, Alumni and Development Records, Former Student File, Box 261, Mrs. Alexander Vivian Folder, Oberlin College Archives.

72. 1920 US Census, Butler County, Ohio, population schedule, city of Middletown, enumeration district 54, sheet 6A, dwelling 120, family 126, John H. Washington (NARA microfilm publication T625, roll 1352).
73. John O. Holzhueter, "Ezekiel Gillespie, Lost and Found," *Wisconsin Magazine of History* 60, no. 3 (1977): 180.
74. 1840 US Census, Madison County, Mississippi, population schedule, p. 18, James Gillespie (NARA microfilm publication M432, roll 216); James Gillespie, Will, August 13, 1842, Madison County Chancery Clerk, Madison County Court, Mississippi; *Evening Wisconsin*, March 31, 1892.
75. 1850 US Census, Vanderburgh County, Indiana, population schedule, p. 403A printed, 877 handwritten), dwelling 552, family 571, Ezekiel Gillespie (NARA microfilm publication M432, roll 176); Holzhueter, "Ezekiel Gillespie, Lost and Found," 180; Jennifer R. Harbour, *Organizing Freedom: Black Emancipation Activism in the Civil War Midwest* (Southern Illinois University Press, 2020), 14.
76. Gillespie regularly advertised in the *Wisconsin Free Democrat* (Milwaukee), which was edited by Sherman Booth, and the two soon became acquaintances and associates. It is thought that Gillespie learned German to facilitate his business in Milwaukee, then prominently peopled by German immigrants. Emma Thornbrough, *The Negro in Indiana: A Study of a Minority*, Indiana Historical Collections 37 (Indiana Historical Bureau, 1957), 40, 53; Holzhueter, "Ezekiel Gillespie, Lost and Found," 180–81.
77. 1860 US Census, Milwaukee County, Wisconsin, population schedule, City of Milwaukee, p. 837, dwelling 357, family 385, Ezekiel Gillespie (NARA microfilm publication M653, roll 421); Holzhueter, "Ezekiel Gillespie, Lost and Found," 181; Diane S. Butler, "The Public Life and Private Affairs of Sherman M. Booth," *Wisconsin Magazine of History* 82, no. 3 (1999): 194.
78. Holzhueter, "Ezekiel Gillespie, Lost and Found," 179.
79. Leslie H. Fishel Jr., "Wisconsin and Negro Suffrage," *Wisconsin Magazine of History* 46, no. 3 (1963): 194–96; Holzhueter, "Ezekiel Gillespie, Lost and Found," 182; Richard N. Current, "The Politics of Reconstruction in Wisconsin, 1865–1873," *Wisconsin Magazine of History* 60, no. 2 (1976–1977): 88–89.
80. "Life Among the Lowly: Number II," *Pike County Republican* (Waverly, OH), November 20, 1873.
81. Emily Foster, *The Ohio Frontier: An Anthology of Early Writings* (University Press of Kentucky, 1996), 79.
82. Andrew Feight, "'Black Friday': Enforcing Ohio's Black Laws in Portsmouth, Ohio," *Scioto Historical Society*, http://www.sciotohistorical.org.
83. LaRoche, *Free Black Communities*, 75.
84. 1820 US Census, Pike County, Ohio, population schedule, p. 386, Zachariah Lucas (NARA microfilm publication M33, roll 89); 1830 US Census, Pike County, Ohio, population schedule, p. 152, Zachariah Lucas (NARA microfilm publication M19, roll 138); US Bureau of Land Management, *Ohio Pre-1908 Homestead & Cash Entry Patent and Cadastral Survey Plot Index* (General Land Office Automated Records Project, 1996), Patent nos. 2500, 2501, 6867, 8182; 1840 US Census, Pike County, Ohio, population schedule, p. 37, Zachariah Lucas (NARA microfilm publication M432, roll 421).
85. Paul Mendel Schrader, "Historical Study of the Negro in Jackson Township, Pike County Ohio Located Just East of Waverly," *Waverly News* (Waverly, OH), July 1, 1959.
86. Saponi territory was rooted in the Virginia and North Carolina piedmont, but in the eighteenth century they were forced to migrate northwestward into what became New York and Pennsylvania. In the sixteenth and seventeenth centuries, the Catawba were one of the most powerful tribes of the Carolinas, often forming strategic alliances with European settlers, and they controlled extensive territory, but through a series of conflicts with other tribes they diminished in the

eighteenth century. "Pike County, OH: As Black as We Wish to Be," *State of the Re:Union*, http://www.stateofthereunion.com.
87. Meyers and Walker, *Historic Black Settlements of Ohio*, 146.
88. Jill E. Rowe, "Mixing It Up: Early African American Settlements in Northwestern Ohio," *Journal of Black Studies* 39, no. 6 (July 2000): 924.
89. Jill E. Rowe, *Invisible in Plain Sight* (Peter Lang, 2017), 53.
90. Howe, *Historical Collections of Ohio*, 465–66.
91. 1850 US Census, Shelby County, Ohio, non-population schedule, Van Buren Township, p. 37, line 18, Zachariah Lucas (NARA microfilm publication T1137, roll 9); "The Colored Farmers of Ohio," *Highland Weekly News* (Highland Co., OH), August 22, 1867; Holzhueter, "Ezekiel Gillespie, Lost and Found," 181.
92. Meyers and Walker, *Historic Black Settlements of Ohio*, 160.
93. Holzhueter, "Ezekiel Gillespie, Lost and Found," 183.
94. 1860 US Census, Seneca County, Ohio, population schedule, District of Tiffin, p. 314, dwelling 1311, family 1269, James McQueen (NARA microfilm publication M653, roll 35).
95. 1900 US Census, Seneca County, Ohio, population schedule, city of Tiffin, enumeration district 103, sheet 20, dwelling 452, family 484, William McQueen (NARA microfilm publication T623, roll 320); 1910 US Census, Seneca County, Ohio, population schedule, city of Tiffin, enumeration district 151, sheet 5A, dwelling 95, family 98, William C. McQueen (NARA microfilm publication T624, roll 1229); 1920 US Census, Seneca County, Ohio, population schedule, city of Tiffin, enumeration district 119, sheet 7A, dwelling 186, family 202, William McQueen (NARA microfilm publication T625, roll 1431); 1930 US Census, Seneca County, Ohio, population schedule, city of Tiffin, enumeration district 16, sheet 6A, dwelling 145, family 169, William C. McQueen (NARA microfilm publication T626, roll 1602).
96. David A. Hall, interview, August 16, 1937, in Federal Writers' Project, *Slave Narratives: A Folk History of Slavery in the United States from Interviews with Former Slaves*, vol. 12: *Ohio Narratives* (Works Progress Administration, 1941), 40–41.
97. 1890 US Census, Seneca County, Ohio, veterans schedule, District of Tiffin, n.p., James S. McQueen (NARA microfilm publication M123, group 15); Bobby L. Lovett, "Memphis Riots: White Reaction to Blacks in Memphis, May 1865–July 1866," *Tennessee Historical Quarterly* 38, no. 1 (1979): 20.
98. Lovett, "Memphis Riots," 21–27.

2. POST-EMANCIPATION MOBILITIES: RECONSTRUCTION, SURVIVAL, AND THE GREAT MIGRATION

1. Anthony E. Kaye, *Joining Places: Slave Neighborhoods in the Old South* (University of North Carolina Press, 2007), 4.
2. Stephanie M. H. Camp, *Closer to Freedom: Enslaved Women and Everyday Resistance in the Plantation South* (University of North Carolina Press, 2004), 1, 4, 6–8.
3. Saidiya Hartman, *Scenes of Subjection: Terror, Slavery, and Self-Making in Nineteenth-Century America*, rev. ed. (Norton, 2022), 221.
4. Thulani Davis, *The Emancipation Circuit: Black Activism Forging a Culture of Freedom* (Duke University Press, 2022), 1–4.
5. Stephanie M. H. Camp, *Closer to Freedom: Enslaved Women and Everyday Resistance in the Plantation South* (University of North Carolina Press, 2004), 7.
6. Davis, *Emancipation Circuit*, 4.

7. Davis, *Emancipation Circuit*, 4.
8. James W. Guthrie and Gary Peevely, "King Cotton's Lasting Legacy of Poverty and Southern Region Contemporary Conditions," *Peabody Journal of Education* 85, no. 1 (2010): 6–7.
9. W. E. B. Du Bois, *Black Reconstruction in America* [1935] (Free Press, 1998), 432.
10. Pete Daniel, "The Metamorphosis of Slavery, 1865–1900," *Journal of American History* 66, no. 1 (June 1979): 89; Alex Lichtenstein, "Was the Emancipated Slave a Proletarian?," *Reviews in American History* 26 (March 1998): 124–48.
11. Steven Hahn, *A Nation Under Our Feet: Black Political Struggles in the Rural South from Slavery to the Great Migration* (Belknap Press of Harvard University Press, 2003), 265–313.
12. Noxubee was derived from the Choctaw word *nakshobi*, to stink. Noxubee County was founded in 1834 and quickly became a significant producer of cotton in the region. In 1850, there were 11,323 enslaved people in the county, and it was noted for its particularly harsh conditions. During the Civil War, cultivation temporarily switched to maize, for which it was well suited, to stock the Confederate army. *Weekly Mississippian*, January 24, 1834; *Cincinnati Enquirer*, July 13, 1865; *Daily Mississippian*, August 13, 1865; Bob Eagle, "Directory of African-Appalachian Musicians," *Black Music Research Journal* 24, no. 1 (2004): 25; Malcolm J. Rohrbough, *Trans-Appalachian Frontier: People, Societies, and Institutions, 1775–1850*, 3rd ed. (Indiana University Press, 2008), 451.
13. 1870 US Census, Noxubee County, Mississippi, population schedule, township 15, p. 112B, dwelling 133, family 136, Suthey Ayler (NARA microfilm publication M593, roll 743); 1880 US Census, Noxubee County, Mississippi, population schedule, enumeration district 30, p. 151A, dwelling 285, family 311, Sully Aler (NARA microfilm publication T9, roll 660); Dan T. Carter, "The Anatomy of Fear: The Christmas Day Insurrection Scare of 1865," *Journal of Southern History* 42, no. 3 (August 1976): 348–49; Elaine Frantz Parsons, *Ku-Klux: The Birth of the Klan During Reconstruction* (University of North Carolina Press, 2015), 86.
14. Julius E. Thompson, *Lynchings in Mississippi: A History, 1865–1965* (McFarland, 2001), 7, 12, 65, 84.
15. Federal Writers' Project, *Mississippi: The WPA Guide to the Magnolia State* (Viking, 1938; University Press of Mississippi, 1988), 228.
16. Sarah Snow, interview, n.d., Federal Writers' Project, *Slave Narratives: A Folk History of Slavery in the United States from Interviews with Former Slaves*, vol. 9: *Mississippi Narratives* (Works Progress Administration, 1941), 138.
17. 1870 US Census, Lauderdale County, Mississippi, population schedule, township 6, p. 91, dwelling 711, family 711, Robert Hunter (NARA microfilm publication M593, roll 735); 1880 US Census, Lauderdale County, Mississippi, population schedule, Hurricane Creek, enumeration district 97, p. 36, dwelling 309, family 310, Robert Hunter (NARA microfilm publication T9, roll 653); Luis-Alejandro Dinnella-Borrego, *The Risen Phoenix: Black Politics in the Post–Civil War South* (University of Virginia Press, 2016), 48.
18. Henry W. Warren, *Reminiscences of a Mississippi Carpet-Bagger* (Holden, Mass.: n.p., 1914), 58; Nettie Henry, interview, n.d., Federal Writers' Project, *Slave Narratives: A Folk History of Slavery in the United States from Interviews with Former Slaves*, vol. 9: *Mississippi Narratives*, 61–7 (Washington: Works Progress Administration, 1941): 65; Sam McAllum, interview, n.d., Federal Writers' Project, *Slave Narratives: A Folk History of Slavery in the United States from Interviews with Former Slaves*, vol. 9: *Mississippi Narratives*, 100–12 (Washington: Works Progress Administration, 1941): 104, 106; Sarah Snow, interview, n.d., Federal Writers' Project, *Slave Narratives: A Folk History of Slavery in the United States from Interviews with Former Slaves*, vol. 9: *Mississippi Narratives*, 135–42 (Washington: Works Progress Administration, 1941): 140.
19. Nettie Henry, interview, n.d., Federal Writers' Project, *Slave Narratives*, vol. 9: *Mississippi Narratives*, 63–64.
20. Nettie Henry, interview, 64.

21. Many reports state the number of killed to be approximately thirty, but a more detailed analysis suggests a much higher number. The data before the 1890s is scarce and fragmentary, but we know that neighboring Kemper County witnessed thirty-five lynchings in 1869 alone and "dozens" more in 1870–1. J. S. Hamm to Gov. James L. Alcorn, Meridian, Mississippi, March 27, 1871, State Government Records, Correspondence and Papers, 1869–1871, Mississippi Governor (1870–1871: Alcorn), Series 786, Box 972, Mississippi Department of Archives and History, Jackson, MS; J. S. McNeilly, "The Enforcement Act of 1871 and the Ku Klux Klan in Mississippi," ed. Franklin L. Riley, *Publications of the Mississippi Historical Society* 9 (1906): 109–71; Thompson, *Lynchings in Mississippi*, 12; Hannah Rosen, *Terror in the Heart of Freedom: Citizenship, Sexual Violence, and the Meaning of Race in the Postemancipation South*, Gender and American Culture series (University of North Carolina Press, 2009), 226–28; Dinnella-Borrego, *Risen Phoenix*, 197.
22. It is interesting to note that the one oral account told years later by a freedwoman who witnessed some of these events hinged on the position that the Reconstruction officials set up the Black residents in this show of force and then did not come to their aid when vigilante white forces counterattacked. Nettie Henry, interview, 66.
23. Loyal, "Letter from Mississippi," *New National Era*, March 14, 1872.
24. W. Silas Vance, "The Marion Riot," *Mississippi Quarterly* 27, no. 4 (1974): 447–48.
25. The Enforcement Act of 1871 empowered the president to employ federal troops instead of state militias to enforce the law and to suspend the writ of habeas corpus to prosecute members of the KKK. Dinnella-Borrego, *Risen Phoenix*, 70.
26. Berry Smith, interview, n.d., Federal Writers' Project, *Slave Narratives*, vol. 9: *Mississippi Narratives*, 132.
27. Thompson, *Lynchings in Mississippi*, 36, 49, 65, 84.
28. Nettie Henry, interview, 67.
29. Meridian had been founded in 1831 on land seized from the Choctaw tribe. It became more populous after the M&O Railroad was built through the town in 1853. The city rose with the railroad boom, ultimately positioned at the junction of M&O Railroad, New Orleans and Northeastern Railroad, Alabama and Vicksburg Railroad, Alabama Great Southern Railroad, and Kansas City, Memphis, and Birmingham Railroad. Federal Writers' Project, *Mississippi: The WPA Guide*, 228–30.
30. Meridian Garment Factory and Hamm Lumber Mill were two significant companies founded in the 1910s. Federal Writers' Project, *Mississippi: The WPA Guide*, 232.
31. Berry Smith, interview, 131.
32. 1900 US Census, Lauderdale County, Mississippi, population schedule, town of Meridian, enumeration district 19, sheet 1, dwelling 23, family 24, Wallace Hunter (NARA microfilm publication T623, roll 815).
33. 1900 US Census, Lauderdale County, Mississippi, population schedule, enumeration district 19, sheet 1, dwelling 23, family 24, Wallace Hunter (NARA microfilm publication T623, roll 815); Eric Arnesen, *Brotherhoods of Color: Black Railroad Workers and the Struggle for Equality* (Harvard University Press, 2001), 24–25.
34. Federal Writers' Project, *Mississippi: The WPA Guide*, 230.
35. A fireman was tasked with shoveling coal into the steam engine's firebox. The job involved difficult physical labor, but it paid better than common labor positions with the railroad. 1920 US Census, Jefferson County, Alabama, population schedule, enumeration district 55, sheet 11B, dwelling 190, family 246, Will Hunter (NARA microfilm publication T625, roll 24); Glenn N. Sisk, "Negro Migration in the Alabama Black Belt, 1875–1917," *Negro History Bulletin* 17, no. 2 (November 1953): 32; Kimberly L. Phillips, *AlabamaNorth: African-American Migrants, Community, and Working Class Activism in Cleveland, 1915–1945*, The Working Class in American History (University of Illinois Press, 1999), 17–18; J. Parker Lamb, *Railroads of Meridian* (Indiana University Press, 2012): 24.

36. 1880 US Census, Newton County, Alabama, population schedule, enumeration district 88, p. 57A, dwelling 527, family 527, Wesley Watts (NARA microfilm publication T9, roll 153); 1900 US Census, Newton County, Alabama, population schedule, enumeration district 53, sheet 17, dwelling 332, family 332, Milton Watts (NARA microfilm publication T623, roll 206).
37. 1920 US Census, Wayne County, Michigan, population schedule, city of Detroit, enumeration district 164, sheet 15A, dwelling 151, family 269, Milton Watts (NARA microfilm publication T625, roll 599).
38. Sketches of the Early History of Greene County, Ala., SG-6862, Folder 10, p. 1–3, Public Information Files: County collection, Greene and Hale counties, Alabama Department of Archives and History, Montgomery, AL; *Historic Preservation* (West Alabama Planning and Development Council, 1971), 9.
39. *Historic Preservation* (West Alabama Planning and Development Council, 1971), 2; *Montgomery Advertiser*, November 5, 1961.
40. Dock Reed and Vera Hall Ward, *Negro Folk Music of Alabama*, vol. 5: *Spirituals* (Ethnic Folkways Library, 1960).
41. *Afro-American Blues and Game Songs* (Library of Congress, 1976); *Negro Folk Music of Alabama: Religious* (Folkways Records, 1956).
42. 1870 US Census, Hale County, Alabama, population schedule, p. 29, dwelling 304, family 304, Henry Burrell (NARA microfilm publication M593, roll 735).
43. Henry Watson to James Dixon, December 20, 1867, Henry Watson Papers, William R. Perkins Library, Duke University, Durham, NC; Michael W. Fitzgerald, "'To Give Our Votes to the Party': Black Political Agitation and Agricultural Change in Alabama, 1865–1870," *Journal of American History* 76, no. 2 (September 1989): 492.
44. The murderer, John Orrick, was soon after allowed to escape by the local authorities. *Mobile Nationalist*, May 10, 1866; Dorman to Wager Swayne, June 14, 1867, Swayne Papers, Alabama Department of Archives and History, Montgomery, AL; J. Parrish to Henry Watson, June 20, 1867, Henry Watson Papers, William R. Perkins Library, Duke University, Durham, NC.
45. Thomas J. Smith to Ben Wade, March 26, 1868, Benjamin Wade Papers, Library of Congress, Washington, DC; W. O'Berry to Paul Cameron, November 26, 1868, Cameron Family Papers, William R. Perkins Library, Duke University, Durham, NC; Fitzgerald, "'To Give Our Votes to the Party'," 495; Simon Phillips, interview, n.d., Federal Writers' Project, *Slave Narratives: A Folk History of Slavery in the United States from Interviews with Former Slaves*, vol. 1: *Alabama Narratives* (Works Progress Administration, 1941), 314–15; Michael W. Fitzgerald, "The Ku Klux Klan: Property Crime and the Plantation System in Reconstruction Alabama," *Agricultural History* 71, no. 2 (1997): 191.
46. L. L. Singleton to P. B. Cabell, May 2, 1868, Cabell Family Papers, Manuscripts Department and University Archives, Alderman Library, University of Virginia, Charlottesville, VA; Fitzgerald, "Ku Klux Klan," 191, 199–200, 204.
47. *Mobile Register*, May 30, 1869.
48. The Burrell family lived in Goosey, Yazoo County, Mississippi, in 1880 and in Vicksburg, Mississippi, in 1900. 1880 US Census, Yazoo County, Mississippi, population schedule, enumeration district 124, p. 45A, dwelling 475, family 488, Henry Burrell (NARA microfilm publication T9, roll 15); 1900 US Census, Warren County, Mississippi, population schedule, city of Vicksburg, district 123, sheet 15, dwelling 371, family 321, Henry Burrell (NARA microfilm publication T623, roll 20); Sisk, "Negro Migration in the Alabama Black Belt," 32.
49. Pamela E. Brooks, *Boycotts, Buses, and Passes: Black Women's Resistance in the U.S. South and South Africa* (University of Massachusetts Press, 2008), 62.
50. The earliest figure in the family, Ferdinand Pryor (c. 1832–1915), appears on Reconstruction voter lists for Hale County, Alabama, in 1867. The county had been created out of Greene County in

that year by the Reconstruction legislature, though named for a Confederate officer. Alabama 1867 Voter Registration Records Database, Alabama Department of Archives and History, Montgomery, AL; 1870 US Census, Hale County, Alabama, population schedule, p. 45, dwelling 429, family 429, Ferdinand Prior (NARA microfilm publication M593, roll 735); 1880 US Census, Hale County, Alabama, population schedule, enumeration district 62, p. 458D, dwelling 503, family 548, Ferdinand Prior (NARA microfilm publication T9, roll 15); 1900 US Census, Jefferson County, Alabama, population schedule, village of Smithfield, district 93, sheet 9, dwelling 192, family 203, Lula Prior (NARA microfilm publication T623, roll 20); 1910 US Census, Jefferson County, Alabama, population schedule, city of Birmingham, enumeration district 51, sheet 36B, dwelling 724, family 885, Lula Pryor (NARA microfilm publication T624, roll 18); 1920 US Census, Jefferson County, Alabama, population schedule, city of Birmingham, enumeration district 55, sheet 11B, dwelling 191, family 247, Lula Pryor (NARA microfilm publication T625, roll 24); Sisk, "Negro Migration in the Alabama Black Belt," 33.

51. 1880 US Census, Greene County, Alabama, population schedule, town of Forkland, enumeration district 81, p. 50D, dwelling 571, family 590, Joseph Gales (NARA microfilm publication T9, roll 153); *Birmingham News*, November 6, 1931; *Historic Preservation* (West Alabama Planning and Development Council, 1971), 10.

52. Typescript description of Greene County, undated, SDG-6862, Folder 10, Public Information Files: County collection, Greene and Hale counties, Alabama Department of Archives and History, Montgomery, AL.

53. Other farmers in the area grew cotton, a range of vegetables such as cabbages, onions, and turnips, or raised chickens. 1870 US Census, Greene County, Alabama, population schedule, town of Forkland, p. 13, dwelling 140, family 140, Jos Gales (NARA microfilm publication M593, roll 1165); 1880 US Census, Greene County, Alabama, population schedule, town of Forkland, enumeration district 81, p. 50D, dwelling 571, family 590, Joseph Gales (NARA microfilm publication T9, roll 153); *Forkland Progress*, May 31, 1890; July 5, 1890.

54. The town of Erie was not long inhabited given the town's "not being centrally located" and "its muddy situation and poor water supply," which brought about a gradual abandonment. Flooding and yellow fever may have also played a role. At its peak, Erie was home to 1,500 people. Typescript description of Erie with handwritten notes, undated, SG-6862, Folder 6, Public Information Files: County collection, Greene and Hale counties, Alabama Department of Archives and History, Montgomery, AL; *Montgomery Advertiser*, March 9, 1941; December 25, 1960; *Greensboro Watchman*, October 27, 1966.

55. *Greensboro Watchman*, October 27, 1966.

56. *Alabama Beacon*, September 23, 1871; *Marengo News-Journal*, September 6, 1873; November 28, 1874; *Eutaw Whig and Observer*, December 31, 1874; October 28, 1875; Mary Ellen Curtin, "'Negro Thieves' or Enterprising Farmers?: Markets, the Law, and African American Community Regulation in Alabama, 1866–1877," *Agricultural History* 74, no. 1 (2000): 29–30.

57. *Forkland Progress*, March 21, 1891; *Union Springs Herald*, December 18, 1909; Glenn N. Sisk, "The Wholesale Commission Business in the Alabama Black Belt, 1875–1917," *Journal of Farm Economics* 38, no. 3 (August 1956): 802.

58. George Dillard, interview, n.d., Federal Writers' Project, *Slave Narratives*, vol. 1: *Alabama Narratives*, 111.

59. Charles A. Brown, "Lloyd Leftwich, Alabama State Senator," *Negro History Bulletin* 26, no. 5 (February 1963): 161–62.

60. A renovation of the church was announced in October 1890, suggesting it had been there for some time by then. *Forkland Progress*, October 11, 1890.

61. *Forkland Progress*, August 16, 1890.

62. Shelly O'Foran, *Little Zion: A Church Baptized by Fire* (University of North Carolina Press, 2006), 210–11.

63. *Forkland Progress*, December 20, 1890.
64. 1910 US Census, Greene County, Alabama, population schedule, enumeration district 22, sheet 9B, dwelling 213, family 215, Edward Gales (NARA microfilm publication T624, roll 1129); 1920 US Census, Greene County, Alabama, population schedule, enumeration district 22, sheet 5B, dwelling 141, family 142, Edd Gales (NARA microfilm publication T625, roll 1319); 1930 US Census, Greene County, Alabama, population schedule, town of Forkland, enumeration district, 32–3, sheet 3A, dwelling 54, family 55, Eddie Gayles (NARA microfilm publication T626, roll 2341).
65. William Barlow, *Looking Up at Down: The Emergence of Blues Culture* (Temple University Press, 1989), 285–86; Bill Greensmith et al., eds., *Blues Unlimited: Essential Interviews from the Original Blues Magazine* (University of Illinois Press, 2015), 179–80.
66. 1940 US Census, Wayne County, Michigan, population schedule, City of Detroit, enumeration district 84–784, sheet 5B, household 82, Jesse Davis (NARA microfilm publication T627, roll 1863); *Draft Registration Cards for Michigan, 10/16/1940–03/31/1947*, Record Group: Records of the Selective Service System, 147, Box 270, National Archives at St. Louis, St. Louis, MO.
67. W. C. Handy, *Father of the Blues: An Autobiography* (Macmillan, 1941), 1–2.
68. Handy, *Father of the Blues*, 5.
69. 1870 US Census, Hinds County, Mississippi, population schedule, township 4, p. 20, dwelling 156, family 157, Morgan McGowen (NARA microfilm publication M593, roll 730); 1910 US Census, Tallahatchie County, Mississippi, population schedule, enumeration district 77, sheet 20A, dwelling 416, family 419, Bracy Moore (NARA microfilm publication T624, roll 760); 1920 US Census, Colbert County, Alabama, population schedule, enumeration district 4, sheet 11A, dwelling 223, family 320, Bracey Moore (NARA microfilm publication T625, roll 9); Beverly Ealy, interview by author, digital recording, January 31, 2023.
70. 1880 US Census, Lauderdale County, Alabama, population schedule, enumeration district 145, p. 8, dwelling 64, family 64, Fanny Armstead (NARA microfilm publication T9, roll 17); 1900 US Census, Lauderdale County, Alabama, population schedule, village of Woodland, district 8, sheet 6, dwelling 101, family 107, Charles Armstead (NARA microfilm publication T623, roll 24); 1920 US Census, Lauderdale County, Alabama, population schedule, enumeration district 70, sheet 3A, dwelling 45, family 45, Charles Armstead (NARA microfilm publication T625, roll 27); Alabama Department of Corrections and Institutions, State Convict Records, 1889–1952, box 17: 1933–34, Alabama Department of Archives and History, Montgomery, AL.
71. Beverly Ealy, interview.
72. Beverly Ealy, interview.
73. Beverly Ealy, interview.
74. Kathleen Beaufait, interview by author, December 20, 2022; Beverly Ealy, interview.
75. Kathleen Beaufait, interview.
76. Beverly Ealy, interview.
77. He was born with the name Amos Gordon Jr. and in the late 1960s was known as Hasan al-Hut. 1870 US Census, Lowndes County, Alabama, population schedule, p. 41, dwelling 305, family 328, James Brown (NARA microfilm publication M593, roll 179); 1900 US Census, Autauga County, Alabama, population schedule, enumeration district 3, Washington District, sheet 7, dwelling 128, family 144, Tilden May (NARA microfilm publication T623, roll 226); Ned T. Jenkins, *Mapping the Mississippian Shatter Zone: The Colonial Indian Slave Trade and Regional Instability in the American South* (University of Nebraska Press, 2009), 195–236.
78. Christopher D. Haveman, *Bending Their Way Onward: Creek Indian Removal in Documents* (University of Nebraska Press, 2018), 155; Christopher D. Haveman, *Rivers of Sand: Creek Indian Emigration, Relocation, and Ethnic Cleansing in the American South*, Indians of the Southeast series (University of Nebraska Press, 2020), 140–41.

79. Martin Ruef, *Between Slavery and Capitalism: The Legacy of Emancipation in the American South* (Princeton University Press, 2014), 167.
80. Ruef, *Between Slavery and Capitalism*, 162.
81. 1910 US Census, Autauga County, Alabama, population schedule, enumeration district 2, sheet 20A, family 349, Tilton May (NARA microfilm publication T624, roll 501); 1920 US Census, Autauga County, Alabama, population schedule, enumeration district 2, sheet 16B, family 328, Tilton May (NARA microfilm publication T625, roll 599).
82. *Prattville Progress*, January 11, 1917; January 23, 1919; January 15, 1920.
83. The earliest enslaved people were brought to Upson County in the 1820s when it was first being systematically settled. Susie Johnson, interview, September 4, 1936; Federal Writers' Project, *Slave Narratives: A Folk History of Slavery in the United States from Interviews with Former Slaves*, vol. 4: *Georgia Narratives* (Works Progress Administration, 1941), 343; Henry Nix, interview, September 24, 1936, Federal Writers' Project, *Slave Narratives*, vol. 4: *Georgia Narratives*, 143; David F. Weiman, "Peopling the Land by Lottery? The Market in Public Lands and the Regional Differentiation of Territory on the Georgia Frontier," *Journal of Economic History* 51, no. 4 (December 1991): 840.
84. Shade Richards, interview, n.d., Federal Writers' Project, *Slave Narratives*, vol. 4: *Georgia Narratives*, 201.
85. James McGill, *The First One-Hundred Years of Upson County Negro History* (AuthorHouse, 2017), 1, 5.
86. David E. Paterson, "Slavery, Slaves, and Cash in a Georgia Village, 1825–1865," *Journal of Southern History* 75, no. 4 (November 2009): 879; McGill, *First One-Hundred Years*, 3–4.
87. Freedmen's Bureau Acting Subassistant Commissioner at Griffin, Georgia, to the Headquarters of the Georgia Freedman's Bureau Assistant Commissioner, December 17, 1866, reprinted in René Hayden et al., eds., *Freedom: A Documentary History of Emancipation, 1861–1867*, ser. 3, vol. 2: *Land and Labor, 1866–1867* (University of North Carolina Press, 2013), 854.
88. Freedmen's Bureau Acting Subassistant Commissioner at Griffin, Georgia, to the Headquarters of the Georgia Freedman's Bureau Assistant Commissioner, Jan 4, 1867, reprinted in Hayden et al., eds., *Freedom*, ser. 3, vol. 2: *Land and Labor, 1866–1867*, 854–55; W. E. B. Du Bois, *Black Reconstruction in America* [1935] (Free Press, 1998), 495.
89. 1870 US Census, Upson County, Georgia, population schedule, p. 137, dwelling 1091, family 1091, James Few (NARA microfilm publication M593, roll 179); 1880 US Census, Upson County, Georgia, population schedule, enumeration district 140, Union Hill District, p. 35, dwelling 300, family 311, James Few (NARA microfilm publication T9, roll 169).
90. The consensus now points to the term's derivation from the Ki-kongo verb *zuba*, to slap. Related variants of patting juba have been observed in Bahia, Brazil; Lima, Peru; and throughout the Caribbean. Some iterations in the US performance practice is called hambone. Emily Mays, interview, n.d., Federal Writers' Project, *Slave Narratives*, vol. 4: *Georgia Narratives*, 119; Elizabeth C. Fine, *Soulstepping: African American Step Shows* (University of Illinois Press, 2003), 81; Julian Gerstin, "Tangled Roots: Kalenda and Other Neo-African Dances in the Circum-Caribbean," *NWIG: New West Indian Guide* 78, no. 1/2 (2004): 16; Roger D. Abrahams et al., *Blues for New Orleans: Mardi Gras and America's Creole Soul*, The City in the Twenty-First Century series (University of Pennsylvania Press, 2006), 46, 48.
91. Lewis W. Paine, *Six Years in a Georgia Prison: Narrative of Lewis W. Paine, Who Suffered Imprisonment Six Years in Georgia, for the Crime of Aiding the Escape of a Fellowman from That State, After He Fled from Slavery* (New York, 1851), 179.
92. Solomon Northup, *Twelve Years a Slave: The Narrative of Solomon Northup, a Citizen of New-York, Kidnapped in Washington City in 1841 and Rescued in 1853, from a Cotton Plantation Near the Red River in Louisiana* (Auburn, NY: Derby and Miller, 1853), 219.

93. Berndt Ostendorf, "Celebration or Pathology? Commodity or Art? The Dilemma of African-American Expressive Culture," *Black Music Research Journal* 20, no. 2 (2000): 221.
94. With the relocation of enslaved peoples, the practice of patting juba spread widely before Emancipation. By the 1870s, the practice existed from Georgia and Kentucky to Cincinnati and the Mississippi River. Some have claimed that it spread from Kongo Square in New Orleans up the river from the early nineteenth century, but others have traced contemporaneous instances of the practice in Georgia and the Carolinas. Robert Anderson, *From Slavery to Affluence: Memoirs of Robert Anderson, Ex-slave* (Hemingford, NE, 1927), 30–31; Lafcadio Hearn, *Children of the Levee*, ed. O. W. Frost (University of Kentucky Press, 1957), 61–62, 77; Sterling Stuckey, *Slave Culture: Nationalist Theory and the Foundations of Black America* (Oxford University Press, 1994), 11; Gerstin, "Tangled Roots," 16; Abrahams et al., *Blues for New Orleans*, 46, 48; Phil Jamison, *Hoedowns, Reels, and Frolics: Roots and Branches of Southern Appalachian Dance*, Music in American Life (University of Illinois Press, 2015), 41–42, 68, 131.
95. Gladys-Marie Fry, *Night Riders in Black Folk History* (University of North Carolina Press, 2001), 94–95.
96. Paine, *Six Years in a Georgia Prison*, 179–80.
97. Anderson, *From Slavery to Affluence*, 30.
98. Marion Brown Septet, *Juba-Lee* (Fontana, 1967).
99. There were disproportionate numbers of people escaping slavery compared to other parts of Georgia during the same time period at least in part because Upson County lacked policing and patrols that were commonly developed elsewhere to control and monitor the enslaved population. *Southern Recorder*, February 25, 1840; *Columbus Enquirer*, February 28, 1840; Upson County Record Book (Minutes of Superior Court Grand Jury Presentments), vol. A: 1825–35: 144, 312; vol. B: 1835–44: 66, DOC-2486, Georgia Archives, Morrow, GA.
100. *National Observer*, April 2, 1977.
101. *Upson Pilot*, April 7, 1859.
102. Shade Richards, interview, 202.
103. Susie Johnson, interview, 344.
104. *Upson Pilot*, March 31, 1859.
105. Bobby Few's paternal grandmother's family, the Colliers, had been enslaved on the plantation of Robert Stephens in Upson County. 1870 US Census, Upson County, Georgia, population schedule, p. 75A, dwelling 5, family 5, Martha Collier (NARA microfilm publication M593, roll 179); 1900 US Census, Upson County, Georgia, population schedule, enumeration district 140, Union Hill District, sheet 7, dwelling 128, family 132, Cam Few (NARA microfilm publication T623, roll 226); 1900 US Census, Upson County, Georgia, population schedule, enumeration district 104, The Rock, sheet 17, dwelling 288, family 298, Calvin Collier (NARA microfilm publication T623, roll 226).
106. Upson County Record Book (Minutes of Superior Court Grand Jury Presentments), vol. J: 1890–93: 415, DOC-2486, Georgia Archives, Morrow, GA.
107. 1910 US Census, Upson County, Georgia, population schedule, enumeration district 136, The Rock, sheet 6B, dwelling 108, family 108, Camp Few (NARA microfilm publication T624, roll 218); 1910 US Census, Upson County, Georgia, population schedule, enumeration district 136, The Rock, sheet 8B, dwelling 138, family 138, Calvin Collier (NARA microfilm publication T624, roll 218).
108. Upson County Record Book (Minutes of Superior Court Grand Jury Presentments), vol. O: 1904–08: 415; vol. P: 1909–13: 297, 364, 413, 473, 528; vol. Q: 1913–20: 21, 68, 114, 148, 449, 502, 540; vol. R: 1920–25: 16, 74, 144, 283, 375, 429, 549; vol. S: 1925–34: 7, 80, 125, 203, 240, 334, 368, 455; vol. T: 1929–35: 81, 106, 130, 210, 235, 292, 369, 392, DOC-2486, Georgia Archives, Morrow, GA.
109. Douglass Theater was the only Black-owned theater in Georgia in the 1910s.

2. POST-EMANCIPATION MOBILITIES   ❧   377

110. Lloyd Pinckney to Douglass, April 3, 1924, Douglass Business Records, 1906–67, Theater Records, Performing Artist Records, Correspondence, 1924, Middle Georgia Regional Library, Macon, GA; S. H. Gray to Douglass, January 23, 1925, Douglass Business Records, 1906–67, Theater Records, Performing Artist Records, Correspondence, 1925, Middle Georgia Regional Library, Macon, GA; Sam E. Reevis to Douglass, January 2, 1925, Douglass Business Records, 1906–67, Theater Records, Performing Artist Records, Correspondence (TOBA), Jan–Jun 1925, Middle Georgia Regional Library, Macon, GA; Sam E. Reevis to Douglass, January 21, 1925, Douglass Business Records, 1906–67, Theater Records, Performing Artist Records, Correspondence (TOBA), Jan–Jun 1925, Middle Georgia Regional Library, Macon, GA; Sam E. Reevis to William Smith, February 4, 1925, Douglass Business Records, 1906–67, Theater Records, Performing Artist Records, Correspondence (TOBA), Jan–Jun 1925, Middle Georgia Regional Library, Macon, GA; Sam E. Reevis to Douglass, April 11, 1925, Douglass Business Records, 1906–67, Theater Records, Performing Artist Records, Correspondence (TOBA), Jan–Jun 1925, Middle Georgia Regional Library, Macon, GA; Sam E. Reevis to Douglass, May 5, 1925, Douglass Business Records, 1906–67, Theater Records, Performing Artist Records, Correspondence (TOBA), Jan–Jun 1925, Middle Georgia Regional Library, Macon, GA; Sam E. Reevis to Douglass, May 27, 1925, Douglass Business Records, 1906–67, Theater Records, Performing Artist Records, Correspondence (TOBA), Jan–Jun 1925, Middle Georgia Regional Library, Macon, GA; Sam E. Reevis to Douglass, June 8, 1925, Douglass Business Records, 1906–67, Theater Records, Performing Artist Records, Correspondence (TOBA), Jan–Jun 1925, Middle Georgia Regional Library, Macon, GA; Sam E. Reevis to Douglass, June 20, 1925, Douglass Business Records, 1906–67, Theater Records, Performing Artist Records, Correspondence (TOBA), Jan–Jun 1925, Middle Georgia Regional Library, Macon, GA; Sam E. Reevis to Douglass, July 29, 1925, Douglass Business Records, 1906–67, Theater Records, Performing Artist Records, Correspondence (TOBA), Jul–Dec 1925, Middle Georgia Regional Library, Macon, GA; Sam E. Reevis to Douglass, November 18, 1925, Douglass Business Records, 1906–67, Theater Records, Performing Artist Records, Correspondence (TOBA), Jul–Dec 1925, Middle Georgia Regional Library, Macon, GA; Sam E. Reevis to Douglass, December 3, 1925, Douglass Business Records, 1906–67, Theater Records, Performing Artist Records, Correspondence (TOBA), Jul–Dec 1925, Middle Georgia Regional Library, Macon, GA.
111. Sandra R. Lieb, *Mother of the Blues: A Study of Ma Rainey* (University of Massachusetts Press, 1982), 26–27.
112. *Macon Telegraph*, August 24, 1923; August 25, 1923.
113. The Allman Brothers learned some of their slide-guitar techniques from Brown. Testifyin': A Narrative Submitted by Bob Young, Rev. Pearly Brown, biography/obituary files, Middle Georgia Regional Library, Macon, GA.
114. Hugh Dorsey, *A Statement from Governor Hugh M. Dorsey as to the Negro in Georgia* [n.p., 1921]: [10]–[21].
115. Dorsey, *Statement from Governor Hugh M. Dorsey*, [16]–[18]; *New York Herald*, May 12, 1921; Timothy J. Pitts, "Hugh M. Dorsey and 'The Negro in Georgia,'" *Georgia Historical Quarterly* 89, no. 2 (2005): 198–200.
116. Caleb A. Ridley et al., *The 'Negro in Georgia': Another 'Pamphlet' Called Forth by Governor Hugh M. Dorsey's Slanderous Document, Scattered Broadcast Over the Country, and in Which He Purported to Set Forth the Brutal Treatment Accorded the Negro by White Citizens of Georgia, the 'American Belgian Congo'* (Dixie Defense Committee, Georgia Division, [1921]), 6; *Jackson Progress-Argus*, May 13, 1921; Pitts, "Hugh M. Dorsey and 'The Negro in Georgia,'" 198–201.
117. *Thomaston Times*, March 4, 1892.
118. *Thomaston Times*, January 13, 1922.
119. Georgia, Office of the Governor, Returns of qualified voters under the Reconstruction Act, 1867, Georgia Archives, Morrow, GA; Georgia, Office of the Governor, Reconstruction registration oath

books, 1867, Georgia Archives, Morrow, GA; Georgia Tax Digests [1869, 1882, 1887], 140 vols., Georgia Archives, Morrow, GA; 1870 US Census, Pike County, Georgia, population schedule, p. 195, dwelling 1416, family 1428, Nathan Willis (NARA microfilm publication M593, roll 159).

120. 1880 US Census, Upson County, Georgia, population schedule, Union Hill District, enumeration district 140, p. 39C, dwelling 335, family 347, Nathan Willis (NARA microfilm publication T9, roll 153).

121. 1870 US Census, Jasper County, Georgia, population schedule, Wyatt District, p. 456A, dwelling 626, family 658, Susan Shy (NARA microfilm publication M593, roll 159).

122. Cotton was the primary crop of the entire region, but some plantations also had herds of cattle or grew vegetables. Benjamin Henderson, interview, January 22, 1937, Federal Writers' Project, *Slave Narratives*, vol. 4: *Georgia Narratives*, 173.

123. 1870 US Census, Jasper County, Georgia, population schedule, Lane and Fears District, p. 424A, dwelling 1626, family 1674, Paschal Showers (NARA microfilm publication M593, roll 159); 1880 US Census, Jasper County, Georgia, population schedule, Wyatt District, enumeration district 71, p. 22C, dwelling 21, family 26, Peter Shy (NARA microfilm publication T9, roll 153); 1900 US Census, Jasper County, Georgia, population schedule, Monticello District, enumeration district 59, sheet 18, dwelling 357, family 360, Freeman Shy (NARA microfilm publication T623, roll 206); Benjamin Henderson, interview, January 22, 1937, Federal Writers' Project, *Slave Narratives*, vol. 4: *Georgia Narratives*, 176–77.

124. Rev. Showers and other relations appear on the Reconstruction-era Black voter rolls in Jasper County in 1867. Georgia 1867 Voter Rolls, Georgia, Office of the Governor, Georgia Archives, Morrow, GA; *Atlanta Constitution*, January 21, 1871.

125. Spencer Jordan owned land there worth $600 at the time. 1880 US Census, Jasper County, Georgia, non-population schedule, District 295, p. 21, line 5, Spencer Jordan (NARA microfilm publication T1137, roll 15).

126. 1900 US Census, Bibb County, Georgia, population schedule, city of Macon, enumeration district 28, sheet 17, dwelling 299, family 357, Lott Jordan (NARA microfilm publication T623, roll 181).

127. 1870 US Census, Stewart County, Georgia, population schedule, p. 211, dwelling 1790, family 1779, Lemon Moses (NARA microfilm publication M593, roll 159); 1900 US Census, Stewart County, Georgia, population schedule, Antioch District, enumeration district 50, sheet 11, dwelling 205, family 213, Lemon Moses (NARA microfilm publication T623, roll 552); 1910 US Census, Stewart County, Georgia, population schedule, enumeration district 93, sheet 3A, dwelling 33, family 33, Lemon Moses (NARA microfilm publication T624, roll 501).

128. Rhodus Walton, interview, n.d., Federal Writers' Project, *Slave Narratives*, vol. 4: *Georgia Narratives*, 124.

129. Rhodus Walton, interview, 124.

130. 1880 US Census, Madison County, Florida, population schedule, enumeration district 87, p. 20, dwelling 115, family 164, Ishmael McKinney (NARA microfilm publication T9, roll 660); Erin Stewart Mauldin, "Freedom, Economic Autonomy, and Ecological Change in the Cotton South, 1865–1880," *Journal of the Civil War Era* 7, no. 3 (September 2017): 414.

131. Edward C. Williamson, "Black Belt Political Crisis: The Savage-James Lynching, 1882," *Florida Historical Quarterly* 45, no. 4 (April 1967): 402.

132. "Ancestry," *Ashanti Drum*, https://theashantidrum.com/about/our-ancestry/.

133. 1900 US Census, Suwannee County, Florida, population schedule, enumeration district 110, sheet 2, dwelling 33, family 37, George McKiney (NARA microfilm publication T623, roll 552); 1910 US Census, Suwannee County, Florida, population schedule, enumeration district 147, sheet 7A, dwelling 148, family 151, Rev. Geo P. McKinny (NARA microfilm publication T624, roll 501); 1920 US Census, Suwannee County, Florida, population schedule, city of Live Oak, enumeration district

148, sheet 13B, dwelling 200, family 220, George P. McKinney (NARA microfilm publication T625, roll 599); "Ancestry," *Ashanti Drum*.

134. Clifton Paisley, "Madison County's Sea Island Cotton Industry, 1870–1916," *Florida Historical Quarterly* 54, no. 3 (January 1976): 285.

135. Paisley, "Madison County's Sea Island Cotton Industry," 301–4.

136. 1930 US Census, Wayne County, Michigan, population schedule, city of Detroit, enumeration district 82–131, sheet 3A, dwelling 15A, family 54, Clarence McKinney (NARA microfilm publication T626, roll 513).

137. This type of tobacco was unique to the region and a few areas of Virginia. Charles S. Guthrie, "Tobacco: Cash Crop of the Cumberland Valley," *Kentucky Folklore Record* 14 (1968): 38–43; Suzanne M. Hall, "Working the Black Patch: Tobacco Farming Traditions, 1890–1930," *Register of the Kentucky Historical Society* 89, no. 3 (1991): 266, 270.

138. Suzanne Marshall, *Violence in the Black Patch of Kentucky and Tennessee* (University of Missouri Press, 1994), 3–4; Marion B. Lucas, *A History of Blacks in Kentucky: From Slavery to Segregation, 1760–1891* (University of Kentucky Press, 2003), xix.

139. Victor B. Howard, *Black Liberation in Kentucky: Emancipation and Freedom* (University of Kentucky Press, 1983), 94; Lucas, *History of Blacks in Kentucky*, 61.

140. W. F. Axton, *Tobacco and Kentucky* (University of Kentucky Press, 1975), 28–30, 43, 46–49; Marshall, *Violence in the Black Patch*, 16–17; Lucas, *History of Blacks in Kentucky*, 5; Charles L. Davis, "Racial Politics in Central Kentucky During the Post-Reconstruction Era: Bourbon County, 1877–1899," *Register of the Kentucky Historical Society* 108, no. 4 (2010): 348–49; Aaron Astor, "The Crouching Lion's Fate: Slave Politics and Conservative Unionism in Kentucky," *Register of the Kentucky Historical Society* 110, no. 3/4 (2012): 296–97.

141. Frederic Bancroft, *Slave-Trading in the Old South* (J. H. Furst, 1931), 130; Amy Elizabeth Patterson, interview, n.d., Federal Writers' Project, *Slave Narratives: A Folk History of Slavery in the United States from Interviews with Former Slaves*, vol. 5: *Indiana Narratives* (Works Progress Administration, 1941), 150–51; Hall, "Working the Black Patch," 266; Lucas, *History of Blacks in Kentucky*, 93.

142. Lucas, *History of Blacks in Kentucky*, 267.

143. Charles B. Dew, "Black Ironworkers and the Slave Insurrection Panic of 1856," *Journal of Southern History* 41 (1975): 332; Lowell H. Harrison, *The Antislavery Movement in Kentucky* (University of Kentucky Press, 1978), 84; Richard L. Troutman, ed., *The Heavens Are Weeping: The Diaries of George Richard Browder, 1852–1886* (Zondervan, 1987), 94; Lucas, *History of Blacks in Kentucky*, 59–60.

144. *Louisville Daily Journal*, September 5, 1861; Howard, *Black Liberation in Kentucky*, 88; Barry Craig, *Kentucky Confederates: Secession, Civil War, and the Jackson Purchase* (University of Kentucky Press, 2014), 125–26, 168.

145. *Compiled Military Service Records of Volunteer Union Soldiers Who Served with the United States Colored Troops: Artillery Organizations*, Microfilm Serial M1818, roll 260, National Archives, Washington, DC; Howard, *Black Liberation in Kentucky*, 47–48, 51–52, 66; Lucas, *History of Blacks in Kentucky*, 155.

146. George C. Wright, *Racial Violence in Kentucky, 1865–1940: Lynching, Mob Rule, and "Legal Lynchings"* (Louisiana State University Press, 1990), 20; Lucas, *History of Blacks in Kentucky*, 206.

147. Wright, *Racial Violence in Kentucky*, 307–11; Lucas, *History of Blacks in Kentucky*, 293; Anne E. Marshall, *Creating a Confederate Kentucky: The Lost Cause and Civil War Memory in a Border State* (University of North Carolina Press, 2013), 57.

148. Lucas, *History of Blacks in Kentucky*, 188.

149. Wright, *Racial Violence in Kentucky*, 73–74, 307–23; George C. Wright, *A History of Blacks in Kentucky*, vol. 2: *In Pursuit of Equality, 1890–1980* (Kentucky Historical Society, 1992), 79–80.

150. Lucas, *History of Blacks in Kentucky*, xxi.
151. Mary Wright, interview, n.d., Federal Writers' Project, *Slave Narratives: A Folk History of Slavery in the United States from Interviews with Former Slaves*, vol. 7: *Kentucky Narratives* (Works Progress Administration, 1941), 62.
152. J. H. Spencer, *A History of Kentucky Baptists from 1769 to 1855* (Cincinnati: J. R. Baumes, 1885), 1:653; Christopher Beckham, "The Paradox of Religious Segregation: White and Black Baptists in Western Kentucky, 1855–1900," *Register of the Kentucky Historical Society* 97, no. 3 (1999): 309.
153. William Warfield, interview, n.d., Federal Writers' Project, *Slave Narratives*, vol. 7: *Kentucky Narratives*, 103.
154. Lucas, *History of Blacks in Kentucky*, 8.
155. The firm D. Hillman & Sons operated two ironworks factories in the area. Major Jonathan H. Donovan to Brevet Brigadier General John Ely, June 30, 1866, reprinted in René Hayden et al., eds., *Freedom: A Documentary History of Emancipation, 1861–1867*, ser. 3, vol. 2: *Land and Labor, 1866–1867* (University of North Carolina Press, 2013), 509–10.
156. 1870 US Census, Trigg County, Kentucky, population schedule, Cadiz Precinct, p. 20A, dwelling 245, family 245, Dick Taylor (NARA microfilm publication M593, roll 501); 1880 US Census, Trigg County, Kentucky, population schedule, Montgomery District, enumeration district 147, p. 315D, dwelling 99, family 101, Margaret Tyler (NARA microfilm publication T9, roll 660); 1900 US Census, Trigg County, Kentucky, population schedule, North Cadiz Precinct, enumeration district 81, sheet 16, dwelling 297, family 297, Granvil Tyler (NARA microfilm publication T623, roll 552).
157. 1910 US Census, Trigg County, Kentucky, population schedule, enumeration district 150, sheet 12A, dwelling 220, family 223, Granvil Tyler (NARA microfilm publication T624, roll 501); 1920 US Census, Trigg County, Kentucky, population schedule, North Cadiz District, enumeration district 175, sheet 1B, dwelling 12, family 13, Granville Tyler (NARA microfilm publication T625, roll 599); 1930 US Census, Trigg County, Kentucky, population schedule, North Cadiz Precinct, enumeration district 5, sheet 7A, dwelling 2, family 2, Margaret Tyler (NARA microfilm publication T626, roll 513).
158. Hall, "Working the Black Patch," 268.
159. David Leander Williams, *Indianapolis Jazz: The Masters, Legends, and Legacy of Indiana Avenue* (History Press, 2014), 57–59.
160. Kazuko Uchimura, "Coal Operators and Market Competition: The Case of West Virginia's Smokeless Coalfields and the Fairmont Field, 1853–1933," *West Virginia History* 4, no. 2 (2010): 59–86.
161. Donald A. Clark, "'If Just One of the Boats Had Remained': The 1862 Battle of Augusta and Its Aftermath," *Register of the Kentucky Historical Society* 114, no. 1 (2016): 50–51, 53, 66; William A. Penn, *Kentucky Rebel Town: The Civil War Battles of Cynthiana and Harrison County* (University Press of Kentucky, 2016).
162. 1870 US Census, Pendleton County, Kentucky, population schedule, p. 362B, dwelling 78, family 78, Lucy Duncan (NARA microfilm publication M593, roll 723).
163. 1870 US Census, Pendleton County, Kentucky, population schedule, p. 436B, dwelling 228, family 224, Jack Brodus (NARA microfilm publication M593, roll 723).
164. 1880 US Census, Pendleton County, Kentucky, veterans schedule, Falmouth Precinct, p. 2, line 2, Aaron Broadus (NARA microfilm publication T1137, roll 15).
165. 1910 US Census, Pendleton County, Kentucky, population schedule, town of Falmouth, enumeration district 138, sheet 9B, dwelling 174, family 185, Aaron Broadus (NARA microfilm publication T624, roll 18); 1920 US Census, Pendleton County, Kentucky, population schedule, town of Falmouth, enumeration district 146, sheet 14A, dwelling 345, family 369, Aaron Broadus (NARA microfilm publication T625, roll 24).

166. 1920 US Census, Franklin County, Ohio, population schedule, town of Columbus, enumeration district 167, sheet 1A, dwelling 1, family 1, Orlando Broadus (NARA microfilm publication T625, roll 24).
167. Lucas, *History of Blacks in Kentucky*, 8.
168. Quoted in Wright, *Racial Violence in Kentucky*, 39.
169. Quoted in Lucas, *History of Blacks in Kentucky*, 196.
170. Wright, *History of Blacks in Kentucky*, 11; Lucas, *History of Blacks in Kentucky*, 195; Bigham, *On Jordan's Banks*, 205–6.
171. Wright, *History of Blacks in Kentucky*, 109–11; Lucas, *History of Blacks in Kentucky*, 241–22.
172. Bigham, *On Jordan's Banks*, 117.
173. 1930 US Census, Jefferson County, Kentucky, population schedule, city of Steubenville, enumeration district 41–34, sheet 15B, dwelling 310, family 322, Marion Randline (NARA microfilm publication T626, roll 2341).
174. 1900 US Census, Mason County, Kentucky, population schedule, town of Mays Lick, enumeration district 96, sheet 17, dwelling 312, family 322, Charles Washington (NARA microfilm publication T623, roll 552); 1920 US Census, Mason County, Ohio, population schedule, town of Mays Lick, enumeration district 169, sheet 6A, dwelling 4, family 4, Charles Washington (NARA microfilm publication T625, roll 24).
175. 1810 US Census, Woodford County, Kentucky, population schedule, p. 396, Winny Demar (NARA microfilm publication 252, roll 8).
176. 1830 US Census, Franklin County, Kentucky, population schedule, p. 131, Winny Demar (NARA microfilm publication M19, roll 36); 1840 US Census, Franklin County, Kentucky, population schedule, p. 316A, Haydon Demar (NARA microfilm publication M825, roll 110).
177. Loren Schweninger, "Prosperous Blacks in the South, 1790–1880," *American Historical Review* 95, no. 1 (February 1990): 43.
178. John G. Fee, *Autobiography of John G. Fee, Berea, Kentucky* (Chicago: National Christian Association, 1891), 143; E. E. Underwood, *A Brief History of the Colored Churches of Frankfort, Kentucky* (Bugle Pub. Co., 1906), 4.
179. Lucas, *History of Blacks in Kentucky*, 211.
180. Lucas, *History of Blacks in Kentucky*, 141, 144.
181. Lucas, *History of Blacks in Kentucky*, 110.
182. The meeting was then known as the "Convention of the Friends of Emancipation in Kentucky." James A. Ramage and Andrea S. Watkins, *Kentucky Rising: Democracy, Slavery, and Culture from the Early Republic to the Civil War* (University Press of Kentucky, 2011), 271; Bridget Ford, "Black Spiritual Defiance and the Politics of Slavery in Antebellum Louisville," *Journal of Southern History* 78, no. 1 (February 2012): 86.
183. Orlando Brown to "My Dear Son," September 23, 1856, Orlando Brown Papers, Manuscript Division, Filson Club, Louisville, KY.
184. 1860 US Census, Franklin County, Kentucky, population schedule, p. 68, dwelling 462, family 459, Hayan Demar (NARA microfilm publication M653, roll 338).
185. Wright, *Racial Violence in Kentucky*, 38.
186. 1870 US Census, Franklin County, Kentucky, population schedule, p. 2, dwelling 11, family 10, Haydon Demars (NARA microfilm publication M593, roll 723).
187. *Compiled Military Service Records of Volunteer Union Soldiers Who Served with the United States Colored Troops: 1st through 5th United States Colored Cavalry, 5th Massachusetts Cavalry (Colored), 6th United States Colored Cavalry*, Microfilm Serial: M1817, Microfilm Roll: 97, National Archives, Washington, DC; *U.S. Colored Troops Military Service Records, 1861–1865*, Microfilm Serial: M1817, Microfilm roll: 63, National Archives, Washington, DC.

188. Official Records, 3rd ser., 5:122; "Regimental Personal Descriptions, Orders, Letters, Guard Reports, Council of Administration, Funds accounts, Telegrams, and Clothing Accounts of Noncommissioned Staff," vol. 1: "5th United States Colored Cavalry," Record Group 94, National Archives, Washington, D.C.
189. *U.S. Colored Troops Military Service Records, 1861–1865*, Microfilm Serial: M1817, Microfilm roll: 63, National Archives, Washington, DC.
190. *U.S. Colored Troops Military Service Records, 1861–1865*, Microfilm Serial: M1817, Microfilm roll: 63, National Archives, Washington, DC.
191. *U.S. Colored Troops Military Service Records, 1861–1865*, Microfilm Serial: M1817, Microfilm roll: 63, National Archives, Washington, DC.
192. *U.S. Colored Troops Military Service Records, 1861–1865*, Microfilm Serial: M1817, Microfilm roll: 63, National Archives, Washington, DC.
193. Brian K. Robertson, "'Will They Fight? Ask the Enemy': United States Colored Troops at Big Creek, Arkansas, July 26, 1864," *Arkansas Historical Quarterly* 66, no. 3 (2007): 323.
194. 1870 US Census, Phillips County, Arkansas, population schedule, Richland, p. 43, dwelling 393, family 390, Washington DeMar (NARA microfilm publication M593, roll 743).
195. 1910 US Census, Lee County, Arkansas, population schedule, town of Marianna, enumeration district 73, sheet 37B, dwelling 785, family 795, Neza Walton (NARA microfilm publication T624, roll 18).
196. 1920 US Census, Lee County, Arkansas, population schedule, town of Marianna, enumeration district 121, sheet 1A, dwelling 8, family 9, Emma Walton (NARA microfilm publication T625, roll 24).
197. Philip R. Ratcliffe, *Mississippi John Hurt: His Life, His Times, His Blues* (University Press of Mississippi, 2011), 78–79.
198. Irene Robertson, interview, n.d., Federal Writers' Project, *Slave Narratives: A Folk History of Slavery in the United States from Interviews with Former Slaves*, vol. 2: *Arkansas Narratives* (Works Progress Administration, 1941), 208.
199. Sarah Gary had been sold off of the plantation where her parents and siblings lived in nearby Carroll County in the final years of slavery but reunited with them after Emancipation. 1870 US Census, Carroll County, Mississippi, population schedule, township 18, p. 562B, dwelling 81, family 81, Ned Gary (NARA microfilm publication M593, roll 723); 1900 US Census, Grenada County, Mississippi, population schedule, enumeration district 34, sheet 15, dwelling 259, family 259, Sarah Gary (NARA microfilm publication T623, roll 808).
200. 1910 US Census, Grenada County, Mississippi, population schedule, enumeration district 74, sheet 14B, dwelling 293, family 310, Sarah Gary (NARA microfilm publication T624, roll 740).
201. Ratcliffe, *Mississippi John Hurt*, 5.
202. The blues musician Mississippi John Hurt's father, Isom Hurt, was a trustee of Mitchell Springs School in Teoc in the 1870s. Schools Superintendents Record for Carroll County, 1880, Old Records Room of the Courthouse, Carrollton, MS; Ratcliffe, *Mississippi John Hurt*, 7.
203. Austin Pen Parnell, interview, n.d., Federal Writers' Project, *Slave Narratives*, vol. 2: *Arkansas Narratives*, 268. Other versions of this song were known to exist in the delta. See William Francis Allen et al., eds., *Slave Songs of the United States* (New York: A. Simpson, 1867), 89.
204. Ratcliffe, *Mississippi John Hurt*, 10, 42.
205. Lynn Abbott and Doug Seroff, *Ragged but Right: Black Traveling Shows, "Coon Songs," and the Dark Pathway to Blues and Jazz* (University Press of Mississippi, 2007), 89; Ratcliffe, *Mississippi John Hurt*, 21.
206. Ratcliffe, *Mississippi John Hurt*, 53, 57, 75.
207. John Hurt, quoted in Ratcliffe, *Mississippi John Hurt*, 53.

208. Bea Anderson (fiddle, mandolin) and George Hanks (fiddle) arrived in the area around 1930. Ratcliffe, *Mississippi John Hurt*, 74.
209. Ratcliffe, *Mississippi John Hurt*, 77.
210. Austin Pen Parnell, interview, n.d., Federal Writers' Project, *Slave Narratives*, vol. 2: *Arkansas Narratives*, 267–68.
211. "Southern Gleanings," *Magnolia Gazette*, July 17, 1885; Thompson, *Lynchings in Mississippi*, 25, 36.
212. *New York Times*, August 2, 1901; *New York Times*, August 4, 1901.
213. Michael Hamlin, *A Black Revolutionary's Life in Labor: Black Workers Power in Detroit* (Against the Tide Books, 2012), 2.
214. Ratcliffe, *Mississippi John Hurt*, 11.
215. Clyde Woods, *Development Arrested: The Blues and Plantation Power in the Mississippi Delta*, new ed. (Verso, 2017), 84.
216. Austin Pen Parnell, interview, 270.
217. Austin Pen Parnell, interview, 270. A variant of the song appeared in a collection of songs published immediately after the end of the Civil War. Allen et al., eds., *Slave Songs of the United States*, 84.
218. Sarah Snow, interview, 139.
219. Molly Caldwell Crosby, *The American Plague: The Untold Story of Yellow Fever, the Epidemic That Shaped Our History* (Berkeley, 2006), 74; Eudora Welty, "Cindy and the Joyful Noise," *Eudora Welty Review* 5 (2013): 20.
220. Elmo Howell, *Mississippi Backroads: Notes on Literature and History* (Langford, 1998), 63.
221. She may be the Cintha Mitchell who appears in neighboring Lafayette County in 1870, where the record indicates that she and her husband ran a farm. 1870 US Census, Lafayette County, Mississippi, population schedule, p. 511B, dwelling 435, family 435, Cintha Mitchell (NARA microfilm publication M593, roll 734); James S. Evans Jr. "A New Religion in Mississippi," *Daily Picayune* (New Orleans), September 18, 1887.
222. Evans, "A New Religion in Mississippi"; Cindy Mitchell, quoted in Eudora Welty, "Cindy and the Joyful Noise," *Eudora Welty Review* 5 (2013): 22.
223. Evans, "A New Religion in Mississippi."
224. Welty, "Cindy and the Joyful Noise," 22.
225. Evans, "A New Religion in Mississippi."
226. The photographer, journalist, and writer Eudora Welty visited John and Ellen Goodall, who still lived in the area of Grenada where Mitchell had been in the 1930s. Welty, "Cindy and the Joyful Noise," 20–21.
227. Evans, "A New Religion in Mississippi."
228. Evans, "A New Religion in Mississippi."
229. Randy J. Sparks, *On Jordan's Stormy Banks: Evangelicalism in Mississippi, 1773–1876* (University of Georgia Press, 1994), 197.
230. Evans, "A New Religion in Mississippi."
231. Mitchell, quoted in Welty, "Cindy and the Joyful Noise," 22.
232. Mitchell, quoted in Welty, "Cindy and the Joyful Noise," 21–22.
233. Mitchell, quoted in Welty, "Cindy and the Joyful Noise," 22.
234. Welty, "Cindy and the Joyful Noise," 22.
235. Evans, "A New Religion in Mississippi."
236. Some of the details are corroborated in Federal Writers' Project, *Mississippi: The WPA Guide*, 24–26; Evans, "A New Religion in Mississippi."
237. Welty, "Cindy and the Joyful Noise," 22.

3. URBANIZATION, LABOR STRUGGLES, THE BLUES, AND THE GREAT MIGRATION: INDUSTRIALIZATION AND CULTURAL SPACE IN THE EARLY TWENTIETH CENTURY

1. "The Early Labor Movement in Alabama," [1–2], unpublished manuscript, Alabama Department of Archives and History, Montgomery, AL.
2. 1900 US Census, Noxubee County, Mississippi, population schedule, town of Brooksville, enumeration district 58, sheet 6, dwelling 68, family 72, Suller Aler (NARA microfilm publication T623, roll 822); 1910 US Census, Mobile County, Alabama, population schedule, enumeration district 68, sheet 8A, dwelling 150, family 153, Suzzie Ayler (NARA microfilm publication T624, roll 39).
3. Michael W. Fitzgerald, *Urban Emancipation: Popular Politics in Reconstruction Mobile 1860–1890* (Louisiana State University Press, 2002), 89.
4. Before the Civil War, large quantities of cotton produced in the Black Belt by enslaved laborers were transported south, primarily along the Tombigbee River, to Mobile. The city never fully regained its position as a cotton exporter after the war, though it was one of the chief ports of the Gulf Coast at the turn of the century, with other regular trade and passenger ships going to and from Huasacualco, Matamoras, Tampico, and Vera Cruz, in Mexico; Chagres, Panama; Belize; and Havana, Cuba; not to mention via the Panama Canal to California and via trans-Atlantic routes to Europe. *Skeleton Map Showing the Route of the Mobile and Ohio Railroad and the Distances from Various Ports of the Gulf to Mobile* (James & Newman, n.d.); *Poor's Manual of the Railroads of the United States* (American Bank Note Co., 1903), 267; Pet Franks, interview, n.d., in Federal Writers' Project, *Slave Narratives: A Folk History of Slavery in the United States from Interviews with Former Slaves*, vol. 9: *Mississippi Narratives*, 56–60 (Works Progress Administration, 1941), 57–58; Fitzgerald, *Urban Emancipation*, 65–66, 136.
5. There was already anticipation of the building of a canal to link the Atlantic and Pacific by the 1840s, comparing its potential to that of the Erie Canal. *Hunt's Merchants' Magazine and Commercial Review*, December 1848, 580–83.
6. M&O managed to survive economic difficulty, including a full default on their mortgage bonds in 1875. M&O Railroad was partially merged with Southern Railway in 1902. In 1940, it was further merged to form the Gulf, Mobile and Ohio Railroad. *27th Annual Report of the Mobile & Ohio R. R. Co. for the Year Ending December 31, 1875* (New York: Evening Post Stream Presses, 1876), 3, 16–31; *32nd Annual Report of the Mobile and Ohio R. R. Co. 1879–80* (New York: Douglas Taylor, 1880), 12–13; *Thirty-Third Annual Report of the Mobile & Ohio R. R. Co. 1880–1* (New York: Douglas Taylor, 1881), 9–10; *Fifty-Second Annual Report of the Mobile and Ohio Railroad Co. 1899–1900* (New York: Evening Post Job Printing House, 1900), 8–9; Williamson Murray and Wayne Wei-siang Hsieh, *A Savage War: A Military History of the Civil War* (Princeton University Press, 2018), 308–9.
7. *Hunt's Merchants' Magazine and Commercial Review*, December 1848, 579; *Thirty-Seventh Annual Report of the Mobile and Ohio R. R. Co. 1884–5* (New York: Douglas Taylor, 1885), 9–11; *Forty-Eighth Annual Report of the Mobile and Ohio R. R. Co. 1895–96* (New York: Evening Post Job Printing House, 1896), 10; *Sixtieth Annual Report of the Mobile and Ohio Railroad Company, Year Ended June 30, 1908* (New York, 1908), 8.
8. J. Parker Lamb, *Railroads of Meridian* (Indiana University Press, 2012), 23.
9. "Coaches of Splendor," *Meridian Evening Star*, January 8, 1898.
10. *Mobile Daily Register*, October 18, 1870; October 19, 1870; October 21, 1870; December 3, 1870; *Mobile Republican*, October 20, 1870; Philip S. Foner and Ronald L. Lewis, eds., *The Black Worker*, vol. 2: *The Black Worker During the Era of the National Labor Union* (Temple University Press, 1978), 140–44; Fitzgerald, *Urban Emancipation*, 88–93, 152.

3. URBANIZATION, LABOR STRUGGLES, THE BLUES 385

11. "The Early Labor Movement in Alabama," [11].
12. Holman Head, "The Development of the Labor Movement in Alabama Prior to 1900," an unpublished manuscript in the School of Commerce and Business Administration, University of Alabama.
13. Black leadership positions within the unions were rare in the case of integrated unions, though some were elected, such as in one chapter of the Knights of Labor in 1902. "The Early Labor Movement in Alabama," [41–42].
14. Fitzgerald, *Urban Emancipation*, 240–41.
15. Robert H. Woodrum, "Race, Unionism, and the Open-Shop Movement Along the Waterfront in Mobile, Alabama," in *Against Labor: How U.S. Employers Organized to Defeat Union Activism*, ed. Rosemary Feurer and Chad Pearson (University of Illinois Press, 2017), 104–5.
16. Woodrum, "Race, Unionism, and the Open-Shop Movement," 104–5.
17. Philip S. Foner and Ronald L. Lewis, *The Black Worker*, vol. 5: *The Black Worker from 1900 to 1919* (Temple University Press, 1980), 478.
18. The freedmen of Prichard came from neighboring parts of Alabama and Mississippi. Henry Barnes, interview, June 11, 1937, in Federal Writers' Project, *Slave Narratives: A Folk History of Slavery in the United States from Interviews with Former Slaves*, vol. 1: *Alabama Narratives* (Works Progress Administration, 1941), 20.
19. Zora Neale Hurston, *Barracoon: The Story of the Last "Black Cargo"* (Amistad, 2018), 43–57.
20. Sylviane A. Diouf, *Dreams of Africa in Alabama: The Slave Ship* Clotilda *and the Story of the Last Africans Brought to America* (Oxford University Press, 2007), 156–57.
21. Hurston, *Barracoon*, 68.
22. The most visible remnants of Africatown are a cemetery and a small museum adjacent that holds a number of instruments constructed by members of the community. John S. Sledge, *The Mobile River* (University of South Carolina Press, 2015), 269.
23. Terence McArdle, "Lil Greenwood Dies; Singer Toured with Duke Ellington," *Washington Post*, July 25, 2011.
24. Ethel Ayler's work is extensive. She debuted off-Broadway in a performance of Langston Hughes's musical *Simply Heavenly* in 1957. She debuted later that year in *Jamaica*, mentored by Lena Horne. She got extensive experience and exposure in Jean Genet's play *The Blacks: A Clown Show*, which had a run of over 1,400 performances, with her fellow cast members James Earl Jones, Cicely Tyson, and Louis Gossett Jr. She worked regularly with the Negro Ensemble Company. Her most noted stage performances were in *The First Breeze of Summer* (1975), *Eden* (1976), *Nevis Mountain Dew* (1978), and *Weep Not for Me* (1981). She was nominated for an Independent Spirit Award for her performance in the film *To Sleep with Anger* (1990). Thomas S. Hischak, *Enter the Players: New York Stage Actors in the Twentieth Century* (Scarecrow, 2003), 16; Mary Ellison, "Echoes of Africa in 'To Sleep with Anger' and 'Eve's Bayou,'" *African American Review* 39, no. 1/2 (2005): 223, 226.
25. 1910 US Census, Mobile County, Alabama, population schedule, enumeration district 68, sheet 8A, dwelling 150, family 153, Albert Ayler (NARA microfilm publication T624, roll 39).
26. WWI Soldiers' Draftees, by County, 1918–1919, SG017111-3, sheet 5, Alabama Department of Archives and History, Montgomery, AL.
27. 1920 US Census, Mobile County, Alabama, population schedule, enumeration district 81, sheet 42A, dwelling 8, family 8, Albert Ailer (NARA microfilm publication T625, roll 34).
28. James E. Lewis was lynched in Prichard, June 6, 1919. CSDE Lynching Database, http://lynching.csde.washington.edu/#/search/AL1919060601.
29. *Negro World*, December 1, 1923; *Negro World*, August 14, 1926; *Negro World*, June 4, 1927; Robert Hill, ed., *The Marcus Garvey and Universal Negro Improvement Association Papers* (University of California Press, 1985), 4:667; Robin D. G. Kelley, *Hammer and Hoe: Alabama Communists During the Great Depression* (University of North Carolina Press, 2015), 8.

30. 1910 US Census, Mobile County, Alabama, population schedule, precinct 10, enumeration district 70, sheet 24A, dwelling 478, family 490, Augusta Thomas (NARA microfilm publication T624, roll 18).
31. Augusta Thomas's parents were married in Mobile in 1871. 1880 US Census, Mobile County, Alabama, population schedule, Albrittons precinct, enumeration district 114, p. 63B, dwelling 58, family 58, Nelson Thomas (NARA microfilm publication T9, roll 24); 1900 US Census, Mobile County, Alabama, population schedule, district of Mobile, enumeration district 94, sheet 11B, dwelling 203, family 227, Nelson Thomas (NARA microfilm publication T623, roll 31); Charlie Aarons, interview, August 6, 1937, Federal Writers' Project, *Slave Narratives*, vol. 1: *Alabama Narratives*, 4.
32. Edward Ayler does not appear in his father's household in 1920, nor does he appear in any other census record in 1920 or 1930.
33. "The Early Labor Movement in Alabama," [7].
34. These strikes constituted half of the overall strikes in all industries across Alabama in the period, thus illustrating that coal mining was the most intense foci of the labor movement at the time. "Labor Organization in the Alabama Coal Fields," 3, unpublished manuscript, Birmingham Public Library, Birmingham, AL.
35. C. H. Nesbitt, *Annual Report of Coal Mines, State of Alabama, 1913* (Birmingham Public Library Archive), 37.
36. Roughly six in ten of Shahid's ancestors came from what is now Ghana. 1870 US Census, Lee County, Alabama, population schedule, Opelika Precinct, p. 257B, dwelling 425, family 425, E. Gordon (NARA microfilm publication M593, roll 23); 1880 US Census, Lee County, Alabama, population schedule, Opelika Precinct, enumeration district 89, p. 28C, dwelling 246, family 303, Eliza Gordon (NARA microfilm publication T9, roll 19). Hasan Shahid, interview by author, digital recording, August 24, 2020.
37. F. L. Cherry, *A History of Opelika and Her Agricultural Tributary Territory* (Genealogical Society of East Alabama, 1996), 255–63.
38. Willie Collins, "The Moan-and-Prayer Event in African-American Worship," in *In the Spirit: Alabama's Sacred Music Traditions*, ed. Henry Willett (Black Belt, 1995), 22.
39. Collins, "Moan-and-Prayer Event," 23.
40. Rev. Anson West, quoted in Willie Collins, "Moan-and-Prayer Event," 25.
41. Mary Francis Crawford, quoted in Willie Collins, "Moan-and-Prayer Event," 26.
42. Willie Collins, "Moan-and-Prayer Event," 22.
43. Willie Collins, "Moan-and-Prayer Event," 23.
44. 1900 US Census, Jefferson County, Alabama, population schedule, Precinct 29, enumeration district 112, sheet 6, dwelling 129, family 135, Gustaras Gordon (NARA microfilm publication T623, roll 21).
45. In 1900, for instance, an estimated ten thousand Black convict laborers worked in the Pratt Mines. Melanie S. Morrison, *Murder on Shades Mountain: The Legal Lynching of Willie Peterson and the Struggle for Justice in Jim Crow Birmingham* (Duke University Press, 2018), 26.
46. Bobby M. Wilson, *America's Johannesburg: Industrialization and Racial Transformation in Birmingham*, new ed., Geographies of Justice and Social Transformation (University of Georgia Press, 2019), 114.
47. Wilson, *America's Johannesburg*, 114.
48. Wilson, *America's Johannesburg*, 117.
49. Alexander C. Lichtenstein, *Twice the Work of Free Labor: The Political Economy of Convict Labor in the New South* (Verso, 1996), 9.
50. 1910 US Census, Jefferson County, Alabama, population schedule, enumeration district 91, sheet 7A, dwelling 149, family 171, Augustus J. Gordon (NARA microfilm publication T624, roll 33).

51. Douglas A. Blackmon, "From Alabama's Past, Capitalism Teamed with Racism to Create Cruel Partnership," *Wall Street Journal*, July 16, 2001.
52. Joseph W. Winston et al., *First Biennial Report of the Inspectors of Convicts* (1886), 336–8, 340–41, Birmingham Public Library, Birmingham, AL; Wilson, *America's Johannesburg*, 118.
53. Blackmon, "From Alabama's Past."
54. Quarterly report, *First Biennial Report of the Inspectors of Convicts* (1886): 36, 236–37, 244, 255–60, Birmingham Public Library, Birmingham, AL; "Labor Organization in the Alabama Coal Fields," 3.
55. Marlene Hunt Rikard, *The Black Industrial Experience in Early Twentieth Century Birmingham* (Alabama Center for Higher Education, 1979).
56. Blackmon, "From Alabama's Past."
57. William H. Worger, "Convict Labour, Industrialists and the State in the US South and South Africa, 1870–1930," *Journal of Southern African Studies* 30, no. 1 (March 2004): 75, 77; Alexander C. Lichtenstein, *Twice the Work of Free Labor: The Political Economy of Convict Labor in the New South* (Verso, 1996), 94, 221.
58. Wilson, *America's Johannesburg*, 172.
59. "Labor Organization in the Alabama Coal Fields," 8.
60. Alabama Coal Operator's Association/Mining Institute, AR 916, Folder 3, Description of the 1894 Strike, Birmingham Public Library, Birmingham, AL.
61. *Iron Age* (Birmingham), May 11, 1882; *Alabama Sentinel*, May 28, 1887; June 4, 1887; *United Mine Workers' Journal*, September 14, 1893; July 5, 1894; Daniel Letwin, "Interracial Unionism, Gender, and 'Social Equality' in the Alabama Coalfields, 1878–1908," *Journal of Southern History* 61, no. 3 (August 1995): 532.
62. Martha Mitchell, "Birmingham: A Biography of a City of the New South," PhD diss., University of Chicago, 1946, 124; Holman Head, "The Development of the Labor Movement in Alabama Prior to 1900," MA thesis, University of Alabama, 1955, 168–69; Chris Evans, *The Histories of the United Mine Workers of America*, vol. 2: *1890–1900*, microfiche (Library Resources, 1970), 586–96.
63. Ronald L. Lewis, *Black Coal Miners in America: Race, Class, and Community Conflict, 1780–1980* (University Press of Kentucky, 1987), 41.
64. Frank V. Evans, Coal Miners' Strike in the Alabama Coal District in the Year 1908, AR 916, Folder 3, Birmingham Public Library, Birmingham, AL.
65. *Birmingham Age-Herald*, August 8, 1908; *Labor Advocate*, October 29, 1909; "Labor Organization in the Alabama Coal Fields," 26.
66. *New York Times*, July 18, 1908; Frank V. Evans, Coal Miners' Strike in the Alabama Coal District in the Year 1908, AR 916, Folder 3, Birmingham Public Library, Birmingham, AL.
67. *Birmingham Age-Herald*, July 8, 1908; July 18, 1908; July 30, 1908; August 4, 1908; August 18, 1908; August 20, 1908; *New York Times*, July 18, 1908.
68. *Birmingham Age-Herald*, July 18, 1908.
69. *New York Times*, July 18, 1908.
70. *Birmingham Age-Herald*, July 30, 1908; August 20, 1908; August 22, 1908.
71. Hasan Shahid, interview by author, digital recording, August 24, 2020.
72. B. B. Comer, quoted in "Labor Organization in the Alabama Coal Fields," 29.
73. Wilson, *America's Johannesburg*, 115.
74. *Labor Advocate*, September 8, 1908.
75. *Proceedings of the Tenth Annual Convention of the Alabama State Federation of Labor* (1910), 57–58, Birmingham Public Library, Birmingham, AL.
76. Hasan Shahid, interview by author, December 3, 2021.
77. Hasan Shahid, interview by author, digital recording, August 24, 2020.

78. The visual artist and author Dr. Lorenzo Pace also had roots in the mining camps of Pratt City.
79. Hasan Shahid, interview by author, digital recording, August 24, 2020.
80. *Down Beat*, July 1, 1944, 13.
81. *Down Beat*, March 24, 1948, 23b; *Down Beat*, July 14, 1950, 3.
82. Foner and Lewis, eds., *The Black Worker*, 5:107–29; Peter J. Albert and Grace Palladino, eds., *The Samuel Gompers Papers*, vol. 8: *Progress and Reaction in the Age of Reform, 1909–13* (University of Illinois Press, 2001), 244.
83. David Montgomery, *Workers' Control in America: Studies in the History of Work, Technology, and Labor Struggles* (Cambridge University Press, 1979), 96; Joseph A. McCartin, *Labor's Great War: The Struggle for Industrial Democracy and the Origins of Modern American Labor Relations, 1912–1921* (Duke University Press, 1997), 39; Eric Arnesen, *Brotherhoods of Color: Black Railroad Workers and the Struggle for Equality* (Harvard University Press, 2001), 50–51.
84. *Twenty-Second Annual Report of the Southern Railway Company, Year Ended June 30, 1916* (New York, 1916), 6–12; *Twenty-Third Annual Report of the Southern Railway Company, for the Year Ended June 30, 1917* (New York, 1917), 3–6.
85. *Twenty-Second Annual Report of the Southern Railway Company*, 4.
86. Joseph Kelly, "Showing Agency on the Margins: African American Railway Workers in the South and Their Unions, 1917–1930," *Labour/Le Travail* 71 (2013): 127.
87. Arnesen, *Brotherhoods of Color*, 53–54, 66.
88. Kelly, "Showing Agency on the Margins," 130–33.
89. *Camp Hill Star*, November 14, 1930.
90. *Camp Hill Star*, June 21, 1929.
91. R. C. Kennedy, quoted in John Beecher, "The Share Croppers' Union in Alabama," *Social Forces* 13, no. 1 (October 1934–May 1935): 125.
92. *Birmingham Age-Herald*, July 18, 1931; Beecher, "The Share Croppers' Union in Alabama," 125.
93. Kelley, *Hammer and Hoe*, 38.
94. *Southern Worker*, August 16, 1930.
95. *Southern Worker*, August 16, 1930.
96. *Southern Worker*, March 14, 1931.
97. In 1930 alone, the paper documented thirty-seven lynchings in the south but also sometimes reported similar violence in the north.
98. *Southern Worker*, October 11, 1930; *Southern Worker*, January 24, 1931.
99. *Southern Worker*, November 29, 1930.
100. *Southern Worker*, March 14, 1931.
101. Elizabeth Lawson, "The Jobless Negro," in *The Black Worker*, vol. 6: *The Era of Post-War Prosperity and the Great Depression, 1920–1936*, ed. Philip S. Foner and Ronald L. Lewis (Temple University Press, 1981), 487; Walter T. Howard, *We Shall Be Free! Black Communist Protests in Seven Voices* (Temple University Press, 2013), 26–27.
102. Kelley, *Hammer and Hoe*, 40.
103. *Southern Worker*, February 14, 1931.
104. *Southern Worker*, March 13, 1931.
105. The Camp Hill massacre was one of the major violent reactions to rural labor organizing in the period, and one that had national implications. *Draft Registration Cards for Ohio, 10/16/1940–03/31/1947*, Record Group: *Records of the Selective Service System, 147*, Box: 616, National Archives at St. Louis, St. Louis, Missouri; Hosea Hudson, *Black Workers in the Deep South: A Personal Record* (International Publishers, 1972), 35–36.
106. Allison Dorsey, *To Build Our Lives Together: Community Formation in Black Atlanta, 1875–1906* (University of Georgia Press, 2004), 150.

3. URBANIZATION, LABOR STRUGGLES, THE BLUES

107. 1900 US Census, Fulton County, Georgia, population schedule, Atlanta Ward 2, enumeration district 50, sheet 9, dwelling 129, family 141, Force Gresham (NARA microfilm publication T623, roll 198).
108. 1910 US Census, Fulton County, Georgia, population schedule, enumeration district 42, sheet 15A, dwelling 383, family 388, Force Gresham (NARA microfilm publication T624, roll 190).
109. H. Paul Thompson, *A Most Stirring and Significant Episode: Religion and the Rise and Fall of Prohibition in Black Atlanta, 1865–1887* (Cornell University Press, 2013), 150.
110. Bartow Elmore, "Hydrology and Residential Segregation in the Postwar South: An Environmental History of Atlanta, 1865–1895," *Georgia Historical Quarterly* 94, no. 1 (2010): 35.
111. As early as the Reconstruction period, Black draymen had encountered financial success working in the city. 1910 US Census, Fulton County, Georgia, population schedule, enumeration district 45, sheet 7A, dwelling 144, family 173, Force Gresham (NARA microfilm publication T624, roll 250). John N. Ingham, "Building Businesses, Creating Communities: Residential Segregation and the Growth of African American Business in Southern Cities, 1880–1915," *Business History Review* 77, no. 4 (2003): 656; Dorsey, *To Build Our Lives Together*, 29.
112. Bruce Bastin, *Red River Blues: The Blues Tradition in the Southeast* (University of Illinois Press, 1986), 101–2.
113. Howell bore influence upon literary figures such as Langston Hughes. Peg Leg Howell, *Vol. 1 (1926–27): Complete Recordings in Chronological Order* (Matchbox Records, 1986); Steven C. Tracy, "To the Tune of Those Weary Blues: The Influence of the Blues Tradition in Langston Hughes's Blues Poems," *MELUS* 8, no. 3 (1981): 82; William Barlow, *Looking Up at Down: The Emergence of Blues Culture* (Temple University Press, 1989), 133.
114. Bastin, *Red River Blues*, 39.
115. Peter J. Welding, "I'm Peg Leg Howell," in *Nothing but the Blues*, ed. Mike Leadbitter (Michael Joseph, 1960), 258.
116. Beaver Slide was replaced by the University Homes public housing project initiated by faculty at Morehouse College and Atlanta University. 1930 US Census, DeKalb County, Georgia, population schedule, enumeration district 24, sheet 23A; dwelling 435, family 453, Fred McMullen (NARA microfilm publication T626, roll 86); Curley Weaver and Fred McMullen, *Leg Iron Blues/DeKalb Chain Gang* (Perfect, 1933).
117. Bastin, *Red River Blues*, 106, 112.
118. Barbecue Bob and Laughing Charley, *It Won't Be Long Now* (Columbia, 1927); Paul Oliver, "Mining 'The True Folk Vein': Some Directions for Research in Black Music," *Black Music Research Journal* 5 (1985): 28; Barlow, *Looking Up at Down*, 196–97.
119. Bastin, *Red River Blues*, 106.
120. Willie Mae Jackson was Robert Hicks's sister. Willie Mae Jackson, interview by Bernard West, written transcript, February 10, 1979, 2–4, Folder 15, Box 37, MSS 637: Living Atlanta, Kenan Research Center, Atlanta History Center, Atlanta, GA.
121. Barbecue Bob, *Atlanta Moan/Doin' the Scraunch* (Columbia, 1931).
122. Georgia Cotton Pickers, *Diddle-da-Diddle/She's Coming Back Some Cold Rainy Day* (Columbia, 1931); Georgia Cotton Pickers, *I'm on My Way Home/She Looks So Good* (Columbia, 1931).
123. Bruce Bastin, "From the Medicine Show to the Stage: Some Influences Upon the Development of a Blues Tradition in the Southeastern United States," *American Music* 2, no. 1 (1984): 31–32; Barlow, *Looking Up at Down*, 85; Jas Obrecht, *Early Blues: The First Stars of Blues Guitar* (University of Minnesota Press, 2015), 87, 94–95.
124. Bastin, *Red River Blues*, 106, 113.
125. Kate McTell (Ruth Seabrooks), interview by Bernard West, written transcript, February 3, 1979, 2, Folder 12, Box 38, MSS 637: Living Atlanta, Kenan Research Center.

126. McTell picked up the songs of Blind Lemon Jefferson, Buddy Moss, and Blind Blake, among others. He also supposedly could play some classical music, spirituals, and hillbilly music, too, though he did not perform them live. Kate McTell, interview.
127. Kate McTell, interview.
128. Obrecht, *Early Blues*, 87–109.
129. A white jazz scene existed around the Roslyn Ballroom on Peachtree Street and at the City Auditorium, but the two scenes were segregated and did not directly interact. Buddy Moss, interview by Bernard West, written transcript, February 23, 1979, 6, Folder 18, Box 38, MSS 637: Living Atlanta, Kenan Research Center; Jack Cathcart, interview by Cliff Kuhn, written transcript, August 21, 1979: 1, Folder 1, 14–15, Box 36, MSS 637: Living Atlanta, Kenan Research Center.
130. C. C. Hart, quoted in C. C. and Phoebe Hart, interview by Bernard West, written transcript, July 18, 1979, 2–3, Folder 5, Box 37, MSS 637: Living Atlanta, Kenan Research Center; Horace Sinclair, interview by Bernard West, written transcript, July 18, 1979: 2–4, Folder 14, Box 39, MSS 637: Living Atlanta, Kenan Research Center.
131. The Silver Slipper was another important venue of that era. Willis recorded for ARC in Atlanta in 1931, and she recorded with Weaver and McMullen in New York two years later. Curly Weaver et al., *Some Cold Rainy Day/Just Can't Stand It* (Perfect, 1933); Kate McTell, interview; Willie Mae Jackson, interview by Bernard West, written transcript, February 10, 1979: 5, Folder 15, Box 37, MSS 637: Living Atlanta, Kenan Research Center; Horace Sinclair, interview.
132. Like many other Black cultural districts, it was demolished in the 1950s and 1960s to make way for the building of interstate highways, public housing projects, and other urban redevelopment schemes. Kate McTell, interview.
133. Kate McTell, interview.
134. Weaver's death came just three weeks after tuberculosis claimed the life of Robert Hicks. Roger S. Brown, "Atlanta Odds and Ends," *Living Blues* 14 (1973): 29.
135. Kate McTell, interview; Willie Mae Jackson, interview; Buddy Moss, interview; Bastin, *Red River Blues*, 107–8.
136. Dunn credited street teachers such as Jonas Brown, Paul McGiddings, Cliff Lee, and someone called Bo Weevil, who are otherwise unknown. Dunn was under-recorded, with his most substantial documentation not coming until the early 1970s. Roy Dunn, *Know'd Them All* (Trix, 1975); Kate McTell, interview.
137. Janice L. Sumler-Edmond, "Free Black Life in Savannah"; Dawn Herd-Clark, "Jane Deveaux and Her Secret School," both in *Slavery and Freedom in Savannah*, ed. Leslie M. Harris and Daina Ramey Berry (University of Georgia Press, 2014), 125–26, 134–35.
138. Jonathan M. Bryant, "'We Defy You': Politics and Violence in Reconstruction Savannah," in *Slavery and Freedom in Savannah*, ed. Leslie M. Harris and Daina Ramey Berry (University of Georgia Press, 2014), 167.
139. Bryant, "'We Defy You,'" 183.
140. First African Baptist Church (Saint Catherine's Island), GA, records, MS 1763, Georgia Historical Society, Savannah, GA.
141. 1880 US Census, Wilkes County, Georgia, population schedule, District 178, enumeration district 131, p. 219C, dwelling 411, family 445, George Sutton (NARA microfilm publication T9, roll 172); 1910 US Census, Chatham County, Georgia, population schedule, enumeration district 46, sheet 6A, dwelling 145, family 151, Richard V. Sutton (NARA microfilm publication T624, roll 177).
142. Bobby J. Donaldson, "'The Fighting Has Not Been in Vain': African American Intellectuals in Jim Crow Savannah," in *Slavery and Freedom in Savannah*, ed. Leslie M. Harris and Daina Ramey Berry (University of Georgia Press, 2014), 206–9.
143. 1910 US Census, Stewart County, Georgia, population schedule, enumeration district 92, sheet 3A, dwelling 33, family 33, Lemon Moses (NARA microfilm publication T624, roll 209).

3. URBANIZATION, LABOR STRUGGLES, THE BLUES 🍀 391

144. 1900 US Census, Hancock County, Georgia, population schedule, Militia District 117, enumeration district 19, sheet 11, dwelling 203, family 203, Ellick Washington (NARA microfilm publication T623, roll 203); 1920 US Census, Washington County, Georgia, population schedule, Deepstep, enumeration district 144, sheet 4A, dwelling 62, family 62, Dolfus Washington (NARA microfilm publication T625, roll 284); 1930 US Census, Chatham County, Georgia, population schedule, enumeration district 12, sheet 27A; dwelling 615, family 706, Dolphus Washington (NARA microfilm publication T626, roll 79).
145. Bastin, *Red River Blues*, 42–43.
146. Margaret Johnson, *When a 'Gator Holler, Folks Say It's a Sign of Rain/Graysom Street Blues* (Victor, 1926); Bastin, *Red River Blues*, 93.
147. Bastin, *Red River Blues*, 158–59.
148. *New York Times*, December 26, 1926.
149. Arthur Gibbs and His Gang, *Louisville Lou/Beale Street Mamma* (Victor, 1923); Arthur Gibbs and His Gang, *Old Fashioned Love/Charleston Medley* (Victor, 1923).
150. Julius Hornstein, *Sites and Sounds of Savannah Jazz* (Gaston Street, 1994), 26.
151. Shannon M. Smith, "'They Met Force with Force': African American Protests and Social Status in Louisville's 1877 Strike," *Register of the Kentucky Historical Society* 115, no. 1 (2017): 2.
152. *Louisville Courier-Journal*, July 25, 1877.
153. Smith, "'They Met Force with Force,'" 21.
154. George C. Wright, *Life Behind a Veil: Blacks in Louisville, Kentucky, 1865–1930* (Louisiana State University Press, 1985), 86.
155. 1910 US Census, Jefferson County, Kentucky, population schedule, enumeration district 106, sheet 14A, dwelling 213, family 317, Nathaniel Allen (NARA microfilm publication T624, roll 485).
156. Wright, *Life Behind a Veil*, 86–87.
157. Herbert Finch, "Organized Labor in Louisville, Kentucky 1865–1914," PhD diss., University of Louisville, 1965, 75.
158. 1870 US Census, Trigg County, Kentucky, population schedule, Cadiz Precinct, p. 21B, dwelling 271, family 271, Harriett White (NARA microfilm publication M593, roll 501); 1880 US Census, Trigg County, Kentucky, population schedule, Roaring Spring Precinct, enumeration district 149, p. 342B, dwelling n.n., family n.n., William Tinsley (NARA microfilm publication T9, roll 443); 1900 US Census, Trigg County, Kentucky, population schedule, Roaring Spring Precinct, enumeration district 85, sheet 18, dwelling 350, family 350, William Tinsley (NARA microfilm publication T623, roll 552); 1920 US Census, Trigg County, Kentucky, population schedule, Roaring Spring Precinct, enumeration district 179, sheet 12A, dwelling 37, family 37, William Tinsley (NARA microfilm publication T625, roll 599); 1930 US Census, Trigg County, Kentucky, population schedule, enumeration district 6, sheet 1B, dwelling 11, family 11, Ed Tinsley (NARA microfilm publication T626, roll 513); 1940 US Census, Trigg County, Kentucky, population schedule, City of Cadiz, enumeration district 111–4, sheet 15A, household 325, Ed Tinsley (NARA microfilm publication T627, roll 1358).
159. George C. Wright, *Racial Violence in Kentucky, 1865–1940: Lynching, Mob Rule, and "Legal Lynchings"* (Louisiana State University Press, 1990), 134; Suzanne Marshall, *Violence in the Black Patch of Kentucky and Tennessee* (University of Missouri Press, 1994), 113–14.
160. Suppression of Black labor organizations went beyond agricultural work, and Black ministers who voiced support for labor groups or individuals were threatened with lynching. Unions were segregated in the area. Christopher Waldrep, "Planters and the Planters' Protective Association in Kentucky and Tennessee," *Journal of Southern History* 52, no. 4 (November 1986): 573–74, 581–82, 587; Marshall, *Violence in the Black Patch*, 129; Marion B. Lucas, *A History of Blacks in Kentucky: From Slavery to Segregation, 1760–1891* (University of Kentucky Press, 2003), 5, 285.
161. Tracy Campbell, *The Politics of Despair: Power and Resistance in the Tobacco Wars* (University Press of Kentucky, 1993), 90–93.

162. Marshall, *Violence in the Black Patch*, 122.
163. *Hopkinsville Daily Kentucky New Era*, January 1, 1908; James O. Nall, *The Tobacco Night Riders of Kentucky and Tennessee, 1905–1909* (Standard Press, 1939), 116.
164. *Hopkinsville Daily Kentucky New Era*, January 16, 1908; *Cadiz Record*, November 15, 1908.
165. George C. Wright, *A History of Blacks in Kentucky: In Pursuit of Equality, 1890–1980* (University Press of Kentucky, 1992), 5–6.
166. *New York Times*, May 14, 1908; John G. Miller, *The Black Patch War* (University of North Carolina Press, 1936), 25–36, 62–72; Nall, *Tobacco Night Riders*, 165–68; Wright, *Racial Violence in Kentucky*, 135.
167. *Hopkinsville Daily Kentucky New Era*, February 17, 1908; *Cadiz Record*, February 20, 1908; Nall, *Tobacco Night Riders*, 108–10; Campbell, *Politics of Despair*, 78; Marshall, *Violence in the Black Patch*, 132–33, 142.
168. Hugh D. Palmer, interview by Terry Birdwhistell and George Wright, August 21, 1985, Oral History Collection, Special Collections, University of Kentucky, Lexington, KY; Harry Harrison Kroll, *Riders in the Night* (University of Pennsylvania Press, 1965), 144.
169. Quoted in Wright, *Racial Violence in Kentucky*, 135.
170. *Kentuckian* (Hopkinsville), April 10, April 13, 1909; *Louisville Courier-Journal*, April 10, August 10, 1909.
171. *Louisville News*, March 3, 1923; *Kentucky Irish-American*, June 25, July 9, August 13, August 20, 1927; Wright, *History of Blacks in Kentucky*, 85.
172. Phil Ranelin, interview by author, digital recording, September 1, 2021.
173. Phil Ranelin, interview by author, digital recording, September 1, 2021.
174. The homes included buildings at 2418, 2428, and 2435 North Oxford Street.
175. 1880 US Census, Marion County, Indiana, population schedule, Center Township north, enumeration district 105, p. 597C, dwelling 140, family 140, Isaac Kimbrough (NARA microfilm publication T9, roll 294).
176. *Indianapolis, Indiana, City Directory, 1886*.
177. Today the church is named the Good Hope Baptist Church.
178. Will of Isaac Kimbrough, *Record of Wills, 1824–1939*, Marion County (Indiana), Circuit Court Clerk, Marion Co., IN; Phil Ranelin, interview by author, digital recording, September 1, 2021.
179. 1910 US Census, Marion County, Indiana, population schedule, enumeration district 33, sheet 6B, dwelling 131, family 132, Arthur Kimbrough (NARA microfilm publication T624, roll 366).
180. Phil Ranelin, interview by author, digital recording, September 1, 2021.
181. 1910 US Census, Marion County, Indiana, population schedule, enumeration district 143, sheet 12A, dwelling 202, family 265, Fernie Hayes (NARA microfilm publication T624, roll 39).
182. Ranelin's father owned Ranelin & Son, one of two Black-owned cement companies in Indianapolis, and young Ranelin assisted his father as a dispatcher. Phil Ranelin, interview by author, digital recording, September 1, 2021.
183. Phil Ranelin, interview by author, digital recording, September 1, 2021.
184. 1950 US Census, Indianapolis, Marion County, Indiana, population schedule, enumeration district 98-388B, sheet 82, social unit 223, Lacy H. Tyler (Record Group Number 29, roll 2630); Fannie Dickerson, interview by Andreas Vingaard, digital recording, March 31, 2020.
185. David Williams, interview by Andreas Vingaard, digital recording, May 15, 2020.
186. David Williams, interview.
187. Fannie Dickerson, interview.
188. David Williams, interview.
189. Translated from the French by author. Charles Tyler quoted in Chris Flicker, "Charles Tyler," *Jazz Magazine*, June 1977, 18.
190. Akbar Tyler, interview by author, digital recording, February 3, 2023.

191. Charles Tyler, interview on WKCR-FM, audio recording, Ras Moshe Burnett private collection, July 26, 1974.
192. Barry Wallenstein, Charles Tyler memorial concert at St. Peters, New York, digital recording, n.d., Barry Wallenstein private collection.
193. Charles Tyler, resumé, 1967, Clifford Allen private collection; Fannie Dickerson, interview; David Williams, interview.
194. David Leander Williams, *Indianapolis Jazz: The Masters, Legends, and Legacy of Indiana Avenue* (History Press, 2014), 60–102.
195. Flicker, "Charles Tyler," 19.
196. Charles Tyler, interview on WKCR-FM, audio recording, Ras Moshe Burnett private collection, July 26, 1974.
197. Fannie Dickerson, interview.
198. Charles Keil, *Urban Blues* (University of Chicago Press, 1966), 65–68.
199. Louis Cantor, *Wheelin' on Beale* (Pharos, 1992), 21.
200. Nick Tosches, *Unsung Heroes of Rock 'n' Roll* (Charles Scribner's Sons, 1984), 133.
201. James M. Salem, "Death and the Rhythm-and-Bluesmen: The Life and Recordings of Johnny Ace," *American Music* 11, no. 3 (1993): 321.
202. Roscoe Gordon, *Booted/Love You 'Til the Day I Die* (Chess, 1951); Paul Kauppila, "'From Memphis to Kingston': An Investigation Into the Origin of Jamaican Ska," *Social and Economic Studies* 55, no. 1/2 (March/June 2006): 82, 86; Albin J. Zak, *I Don't Sound Like Nobody: Remaking Music in 1950s America* (University of Michigan Press, 2010), 98.
203. Kauppila, "'From Memphis to Kingston,'" 76.
204. Bobby Bland, *Sometime Tomorrow/Farther Up the Road* (Duke, 1957); Bobby Bland, *Little Boy Blue/Last Night* (Duke, 1958).
205. David Whiteis, *Southern Soul-Blues* (University of Illinois Press, 2013), 16.
206. Larry Hancock, interview by author, digital recording, October 14, 2021.

4. CLEVELAND: JAZZ, SEGREGATION, AND WORKING-CLASS AESTHETICS

1. Kimberley L. Phillips, *AlabamaNorth: African-American Migrants, Community, and Working-Class Activism in Cleveland, 1915–45*, The Working Class in American History (University of Illinois Press, 1999), 46.
2. Kenneth L. Kusmer, *A Ghetto Takes Shape: Black Cleveland, 1870–1930* (University of Illinois Press, 1976), 159–60.
3. Kusmer, *A Ghetto Takes Shape*, 162–66.
4. Kamal Abdul Alim, interview by author, digital recording, June 12, 2021.
5. Kamal Abdul Alim, interview, June 12, 2021.
6. Edward L. Pucel, *City of Cleveland Housing Report for the Year 1945* (Cleveland City Council, 1945), 12, 15–8, 74; Daniel Kerr, "'The Reign of Wickedness': The Changing Structures of Prostitution, Gambling, and Political Protection in Cleveland from the Progressive Era to the Great Depression," MA thesis, Case Western Reserve University, 1998, 11–23; Daniel R. Kerr, *Derelict Paradise: Homelessness and Urban Development in Cleveland, Ohio* (University of Massachusetts Press, 2011), 68, 92–93.
7. *Cleveland Plain-Dealer*, March 19, 1930; October 6, 1931; October 7, 1931; July 14, 1934; *Cleveland Press*, October 6, 1931.
8. Quoted in Kerr, *Derelict Paradise*, 90.

9. Kamal Abdul Alim, interview, June 12, 2021.
10. Kerr, *Derelict Paradise*, 131–32.
11. Yusuf Mumin, interview by author, email transcript, January 19–September 17, 2021.
12. Kerr, *Derelict Paradise*, 68.
13. *Cleveland Plain-Dealer*, December 16, 1934; *Cleveland Press*, May 11, 1937; Pucel, *City of Cleveland Housing Report*, 11; Kerr, *Derelict Paradise*, 52, 103–4.
14. Kerr, *Derelict Paradise*, 68–70.
15. Kamal Abdul Alim, interview, June 12, 2021.
16. *Cleveland Press*, January 22, 1935; Christopher G. Wye, "The New Deal and the Negro Community: Toward a Broader Conceptualization," *Journal of American History* 59 (December 1972): 623–26; Kerr, *Derelict Paradise*, 101–2.
17. *Cleveland Press*, August 20, 1937.
18. Kamal Abdul Alim, interview, June 12, 2021.
19. Alim and his brother were also able to go to a jazz club their cousin managed called the Loop Lounge, well before they were of legal age. Other owners would admit them to the Cotton Club. They saw Miles Davis, John Coltrane, Thelonious Monk, Bud Powell, Lester Young, and many others as teenagers. Don Freeman, interview by author, digital recording, June 13, 2021.
20. Kamal Abdul Alim, interview, June 12, 2021.
21. Kamal Abdul Alim, interview, June 12, 2021.
22. Kusmer, *A Ghetto Takes Shape*, 207.
23. Kusmer, *A Ghetto Takes Shape*, 228.
24. Kamal Abdul Alim, interview, June 12, 2021.
25. Hawkins was born in Birmingham, Alabama, and followed a similar migratory route to Cleveland as many of the free jazz figures. W. Allen Taylor, "In Search of My Father: Walkin' Talkin' Bill Hawkins," *Walkintalkin.com*, 2007, http://www.walkintalkin.com/bios2.html.
26. Mutawaf Shaheed, interview by author, digital recording, June 11, 2021.
27. Kamal Abdul Alim, interview, June 12, 2021; Don Freeman, interview.
28. *Cleveland Press*, April 24, 1957; April 26, 1957; Kerr, *Derelict Paradise*, 151–52, 157.
29. Judson L. Jeffries, *Comrades: A Local History of the Black Panther Party* (Indiana University Press, 2007), 93–101.
30. James Robenalt, *Ballots and Bullets: Black Power Politics and Urban Guerilla Warfare in 1968 Cleveland* (Lawrence Hill, 2018), 32.
31. Malcolm X, live speech, audio transcript, https://www.youtube.com/watch?v=F36JIofhiE4; Robenalt, *Ballots and Bullets*, 44–45.
32. Don Freeman, *Reflections of a Resolute Radical* (Monroe, IL: self-published, 2017).
33. Don Freeman, interview.
34. Don Freeman, interview.
35. Mutawaf Shaheed, interview by Andreas Vingaard, digital recording, March 25, 2020.
36. Don Freeman, interview.
37. One of his earlier essays published in late 1963 calls for a Black political party. Donald Freeman, "The Politics of Black Liberation," *Black America* 1, no. 7/8 (November–December 1963): 6, 18.
38. Harold Cruse, "On Domestic Colonialism," *Black America* 2, no. 2 (Fall 1964): 10.
39. For the intellectual evolution of the organization, see their publication *Black America*, which was published in approximately ten issues from 1963 to 1965.
40. Maxwell C. Stanford, "Revolutionary Action Movement (RAM): A Case Study of an Urban Revolutionary Movement in Western Capitalist Society," MA thesis, Atlanta University, 1986; Robin D. G. Kelley, *Freedom Dreams: The Black Radical Imagination*, rev. ed. (Beacon, 2022), 72, 77.
41. Don Freeman, interview.

4. CLEVELAND   395

42. Don Freeman, "Black Youth and Afro-American Liberation," *Black America* 2, no. 2 (1964): 15.
43. Williams had been a leader of the NAACP and started a chapter of the National Rifle Association to defend the Black community in Monroe, North Carolina. After he faced false charges created by police in 1961, he fled to Cuba. Some people within RAM's emerging network at the time were invited to Cuba in the summer of 1964 to meet with the revolutionary leader Che Guevara. Don Freeman, interview.
44. Don Freeman, interview.
45. William Worthy, "The Red Chinese American Negro," *Esquire*, October 1964, 23; Don Freeman, interview.
46. Don Freeman, interview.
47. Freeman, *Reflections of a Resolute Radical*, 92–94; Robenalt, *Ballots and Bullets*, 70.
48. Robenalt, *Ballots and Bullets*, 64; Don Freeman, interview.
49. Freeman, *Reflections of a Resolute Radical*, 329–30.
50. *Cleveland Call and Post*, July 23, 1966. Stanford later took the name Muhammad Ahmad. Much later, he clarified RAM's direct role via a system of lieutenants who coordinated some of the actions taken during the Hough uprising. Stanford, *Revolutionary Action Movement*, 67.
51. Robenalt, *Ballots and Bullets*, 125.
52. Edward E. Curtis IV, "Islamism and Its African American Muslim Critics: Black Muslims in the Era of the Arab Cold War," *American Quarterly* 59, no. 3 (September 2007): 684.
53. Aminah Beverly McCloud, *African American Islam* (Routledge, 1995), 24–27.
54. Mutawaf Shaheed, interview by author, digital recording, September 13, 2022.
55. Mutawaf Shaheed, interview, September 13, 2022.
56. Mutawaf Shaheed, interview, September 13, 2022.
57. Mutawaf Shaheed, interview by author, digital recording, December 27, 2020.
58. Because of the alliance between the United States and Saudi Arabia in the 1960s, there was a concerted effort by the US government to displace the Indian influence on American Islam and replace it with Saudi influence, which ultimately manifested in the formation of the Council of the Islamic Organizations of America in 1972. Mutawaf Shaheed, interview, September 13, 2022.
59. Yusuf Mumin, interview.
60. 1930 US Census, Cuyahoga County, Ohio, population schedule, enumeration district 330, sheet 20A; dwelling 24, family 66, Augusta Ceaser (NARA microfilm publication T626, roll 507).
61. Phillips, *AlabamaNorth*, 49.
62. 1930 US Census, Cuyahoga County, Ohio, population schedule, city of Cleveland, enumeration district 325, sheet 5A, dwelling 62, family 108, Lula M. Hunter (NARA microfilm publication T626, roll 507).
63. Thompson Products is now famous for developing local company unions to foster better labor relations and to fend off national labor organizations. It had originally manufactured parts for automobiles but had switched to airplane engines during World War II, which allowed it to expand its operations. It was merged with another company to form TRW, Inc., in 1958. 1940 US Census, Cuyahoga County, Ohio, population schedule, City of Cleveland, enumeration district 92–443, sheet 3A, household 41, Edward Aylar (NARA microfilm publication T627, roll 3220); Sanford M. Jacoby, *Modern Manors: Welfare Capitalism Since the New Deal* (Princeton University Press, 1997), 143–46.
64. Nat Hentoff, "Albert Ayler—the Truth Is Marching In," *Down Beat*, November 17, 1966, 16.
65. "Goodbye Cleveland—Hello Sweden," *Cleveland Call and Post*, April 21, 1962.
66. Albert Ayler, quoted in Daniel Caux, "My Name Is . . . Albert Ayler," *Chroniques de l'Art Avant Vivant* 17 (February 1971): 24.
67. 1920 US Census, Upson County, Georgia, population schedule, enumeration district 188, sheet 6B, dwelling 121, family 121, Simon Few (NARA microfilm publication T625, roll 282).

68. 1930 US Census, Cuyahoga County, Ohio, population schedule, enumeration district 330, sheet 17A; dwelling 19, family 28, Simon Few (NARA microfilm publication T626, roll 507).
69. 1940 US Census, Cuyahoga County, Ohio, population schedule, City of Cleveland, enumeration district 92–461, sheet 7A, household 139, Robert Few (NARA microfilm publication T627, roll 3221); Simone Few, interview by author, digital recording, March 22, 2022.
70. 1930 US Census, Cuyahoga County, Ohio, population schedule, city of Cleveland, enumeration district 188, sheet 7B, dwelling 5, family 14, Jesse Lee Henderson (NARA microfilm publication T626, roll 503); Kerr, *Derelict Paradise*, 94.
71. George was classified as white in 1900 and 1920, Black in 1880, 1910, 1930, and 1940, and mulatto in 1870, proving the arbitrary nature of racial classifications. 1870 US Census, Cuyahoga County, Ohio, population schedule, Cleveland Precinct, p. 84B, dwelling 1276, family 1383, John Fairfax (NARA microfilm publication M593, roll 1190); 1880 US Census, Cuyahoga County, Ohio, population schedule, Cleveland Precinct, enumeration district 18, p. 42B, dwelling 202, family 231, John Fairfax (NARA microfilm publication T9, roll 1006); 1900 US Census, Cuyahoga County, Ohio, population schedule, Cleveland Precinct, enumeration district 42, sheet 4, dwelling 68, family 90, Geo. Fairfax (NARA microfilm publication T623, roll 253); 1910 US Census, Cuyahoga County, Ohio, population schedule, enumeration district 207, sheet 7A, dwelling 76, family 123, George Fairfax (NARA microfilm publication T624, roll 1170); 1920 US Census, Cuyahoga County, Ohio, population schedule, Cleveland Precinct, enumeration district 232, sheet 9B, dwelling 94, family 188, George Fairfax (NARA microfilm publication T625, roll 1364); 1930 US Census, Cuyahoga County, Ohio, population schedule, enumeration district 188, sheet 3B, dwelling 22, family 43, George Fairfax (NARA microfilm publication T626, roll 503); 1940 US Census, Cuyahoga County, Ohio, population schedule, City of Cleveland, enumeration district 92–299, sheet 2B, household 55, George Fairfax (NARA microfilm publication T627, roll 3215).
72. 1870 US Census, Lowndes County, Alabama, population schedule, p. 6, dwelling 47, family 49, Sabray Gordon (NARA microfilm publication M593, roll 25); 1880 US Census, Dallas County, Alabama, population schedule, Old Town Precinct, enumeration district 52, p. 17, dwelling 7, family 7, Jerre Gordon (NARA microfilm publication T9, roll 1006); 1900 US Census, Dallas County, Alabama, population schedule, Oldtown Precinct, enumeration district 22, sheet 12, dwelling 266, family 267, Jerry Gordon (NARA microfilm publication T623, roll 13); 1910 US Census, Dallas County, Alabama, population schedule, Old Town Precinct, enumeration district 74, sheet 8A, dwelling 131, family 131, Tim Gordon (NARA microfilm publication T624, roll 11); 1920 US Census, Dallas County, Alabama, population schedule, Oldtown Precinct, enumeration district 79, sheet 9B, dwelling 202, family 214, Tim Gordon (NARA microfilm publication T625, roll 13); 1930 US Census, Dallas County, Alabama, population schedule, Oldtown precinct, enumeration district 24–13, sheet 21A, dwelling 464, family 465-0, Tim Gordon (NARA microfilm publication T626, roll 749).
73. 1940 US Census, Cuyahoga County, Ohio, population schedule, City of Cleveland, enumeration district 92–297, sheet 3B, household 70, James Jones (NARA microfilm publication T627, roll 3215).
74. Don Freeman, interview.
75. Booker T. Washington to Milton Smith, February 1, 1912, Booker T. Washington Papers, Manuscript Division, Library of Congress; George C. Wright, *A History of Blacks in Kentucky*, vol. 2: *In Pursuit of Equality, 1890–1980* (Kentucky Historical Society, 1992), 58, 74–76, 78–79.
76. 1920 US Census, Christian County, Kentucky, population schedule, Township of Pembroke, enumeration district 8, sheet 6A, dwelling 124, family 129, David Sebree (NARA microfilm publication T625, roll 565); 1940 US Census, Cuyahoga County, Ohio, population schedule, City of Cleveland, enumeration district 92–279, sheet 3B, household 60, David Sebree (NARA microfilm publication T627, roll 3214).

77. 1900 US Census, Jasper County, Georgia, population schedule, district of Henderson and Crook, enumeration district 62, sheet 5, dwelling 77, family 79, Peter Shy (NARA microfilm publication T623, roll 206); 1910 US Census, Cuyahoga County, Ohio, population schedule, enumeration district 406, sheet 3A, dwelling 43, family 55, Peter Shy (NARA microfilm publication T624, roll 1176).
78. Kerr, *Derelict Paradise*, 150.
79. Simone Few, interview.
80. "Monday Morning Party: Tia Juana Features Bermuda Shorts Hop," *Cleveland Call and Post*, September 18, 1954.
81. *Cleveland Call and Post*, October 30, 1954; March 5, 1955; March 17, 1956.
82. *Cleveland Call and Post*, December 22, 1956; January 12, 1957.
83. *Cleveland Call and Post*, October 30, 1954; Simone Few, interview.
84. Simone Few, interview.
85. *Cleveland Call and Post*, February 7, 1959; March 14, 1959; April 11, 1959; April 25, 1959; May 2, 1959; May 16, 1959; November 7, 1959.
86. *Cleveland Call and Post*, August 6, 1960; April 15, 1961; *Down Beat* 24 (November 24, 1960): 48.
87. Yusuf Mumin, interview.
88. *Simply Heavenly* debuted at Karamu House, May 1, 1959, but was in demand and returned later that same year. The 1961 performance was its third run at the theater in as many years. Handbill, *Simply Heavenly* by Langston Hughes, Karamu Theatre, September 19, 1961, Western Reserve Historical Society, Case Western Reserve University.
89. The bassist Earl Sparks sometimes played in place of Jeffries. David Durrah, interview by Andreas Vingaard, digital recording, April 17, 2020.
90. "East Jazz Trio on Cultural Arts Series," *Cleveland Call and Post*, March 23, 1963.
91. "East Jazz Trio on Cultural Arts Series," *Cleveland Call and Post*, March 23, 1963. Jeffries had previously worked with Betty Carter and Rahsaan Roland Kirk, and Farris had worked with Bill Hardman and Stan Getz.
92. "East Jazz Trio on Cultural Arts Series," *Cleveland Call and Post*, March 23, 1963.
93. *Cleveland Call and Post*, May 25, 1963; February 1, 1964; February 22, 1964; May 13, 1967; March 1, 1969; March 15, 1969; April 12, 1969; January 17, 1970; January 24, 1970; February 7, 1970; March 20, 1971; January 8, 1972; January 29, 1972.
94. Simone Few, interview.
95. *Cleveland Call and Post*, February 9, 1963; March 23, 1963; March 30, 1963; April 6, 1963; August 1, 1964; November 21, 1964; December 5, 1964; January 2, 1965; July 3, 1965.
96. *Cleveland Call and Post*, July 3, 1965.
97. Two biographies have appeared for Ayler. Peter Niklas Wilson, *Spirits Rejoice! Albert Ayler and His Message*, trans. Jane White (Wolke Verlag Hofheim, 1996); Richard Koloda, *Holy Ghost: The Life and Death of Free Jazz Pioneer Albert Ayler* (Jawbone, 2022).
98. Albert Ayler, quoted in Caux, "My Name Is . . . Albert Ayler," 24.
99. Albert Ayler, quoted in Caux, "My Name Is . . . Albert Ayler," 24.
100. Kiyoshi Koyama, "Albert Ayler Interview," *Swing Journal*, recorded July 25, 1970, https://www.youtube.com/watch?v=uxYKj1CLUKo.
101. Koyama, "Albert Ayler Interview."
102. Ayler, quoted in Valerie Wilmer, "Ayler: Mystic Tenor with a Direct Hot Line to Heaven?," *Melody Maker*, October 15, 1966.
103. Albert Ayler, quoted in Caux, "My Name Is . . . Albert Ayler," 24.
104. Koyama, "Albert Ayler Interview."
105. Ayler, quoted in Hentoff, "Albert Ayler," 17.

4. CLEVELAND

106. Beaver Harris, quoted in Elliott Bratton, interview with Beaver Harris, WKCR-FM broadcast, July 13, 1987.
107. Jon Goldman and Martin Davidson, "Albert Ayler: Life and Recordings," *Cadence* 1, no. 4 (April 1976): 8.
108. Ayler went to John Adams High School, as did his brother Donald and Clyde Shy.
109. Ayler, quoted in Hentoff, "Albert Ayler," 16.
110. Mutawaf Shaheed, interview by author, digital recording, December 4, 2020.
111. Mutawaf Shaheed, interview, December 4, 2020.
112. Ayler, quoted in Caux, "My Name Is . . . Albert Ayler," 24.
113. Lloyd Pearson, quoted in Val Wilmer, "Spiritual Unity," in Albert Ayler, *Holy Ghost* (Revenant, 2004), 13.
114. Ayler, quoted in Caux, "My Name Is . . . Albert Ayler," 24.
115. Ayler, quoted in Wilmer, "Ayler: Mystic Tenor."
116. Koyama, "Albert Ayler Interview."
117. Mutawaf Shaheed, interview, December 27, 2020.
118. Goldman and Davidson, "Albert Ayler: Life and Recordings," 8.
119. Ayler, quoted in Hentoff, "Albert Ayler," 16.
120. Koyama, "Albert Ayler Interview."
121. Harold Budd, "The Harold Budd Interview #1," March 23, 1987, http://gaffa.org/archives/1987-06/msg00075.html.
122. Beaver Harris, quoted in Elliott Bratton, interview with Beaver Harris, WKCR-FM broadcast, July 13, 1987.
123. Chalmer Adams, quoted in Marc Chaloin, "Albert Ayler in Europe: 1959–62," in Albert Ayler, *Holy Ghost* (Revenant, 2004), 68.
124. Ayler, quoted in Hentoff, "Albert Ayler," 17.
125. Lewis Worrell, quoted in Chaloin, "Albert Ayler in Europe," 77.
126. Perry Robinson, quoted in Ben Young, "Witnesses," in Albert Ayler, *Holy Ghost* (Revenant, 2004), 111.
127. Ayler, quoted in Chaloin, "Albert Ayler in Europe," 79.
128. Jørgen Frigård, quoted in Chaloin, "Albert Ayler in Europe," 78.
129. Anders Lindskog, quoted in Chaloin, "Albert Ayler in Europe," 79.
130. Ayler, quoted in Caux, "My Name Is . . . Albert Ayler," 24.
131. Lloyd Pearson, quoted in Wilmer, "Spiritual Unity," 18.
132. Goldman and Davidson, "Albert Ayler: Life and Recordings," 8.
133. The trumpeter Kamal Abdul Alim, then Gerald Freeman, and younger brother of the prominent Black nationalist Don Freeman, also attended high school in that circle. The pianist David Durrah's older brother was also their age, so Durrah was connected loosely to that circle as well. Strickland was born in Birmingham, Alabama, and his parents migrated north to Cleveland when he was very young, thus following a similar route as the Ayler and Freeman families. David Durrah, interview by Andreas Vingaard, digital recording, April 17, 2020.
134. Mutawaf Shaheed, interview by Andreas Vingaard.
135. Mutawaf Shaheed, interview, December 27, 2020.
136. Mutawaf Shaheed, interview by Andreas Vingaard.
137. Mutawaf Shaheed, interview by author, digital recording, October 4, 2022.
138. Mutawaf Shaheed, interview, December 4, 2020.
139. Translated from French by author. Charles Tyler, quoted in Christian Gauffre, "Charles Tyler," *Jazz Magazine*, November 1985, 27.
140. Fannie Dickerson, interview by Andreas Vingaard, digital recording, March 31, 2020; Mutawaf Shaheed, interview, December 4, 2020.

141. Clifford Jay Safane, "Charles Tyler: The Saga of a Saxophonist," *Music Journal*, September 1979, 18.
142. Tyler, quoted in Safane, "Charles Tyler: The Saga of a Saxophonist," 18.
143. Hancock also recalled playing free with the pianist Tony Smith. Larry Hancock, interview by author, digital recording, October 14, 2021.
144. Translated from French by author. Charles Tyler, quoted in Chris Flicker, "Charles Tyler," *Jazz Magazine*, June 1977, 18.
145. Hancock had an eclectic career, playing with a wide range of people, including John Handy, Barry Harris, Mary Lou Williams, Archie Shepp, Lonnie Smith, John Patton, Steve Cohn, and Bobby Hutcherson, among others. Larry Hancock, interview.
146. "Lamont's Lament" was named for Tyler's oldest son. Neither of the pieces was ever recorded. Mutawaf Shaheed, interview by Andreas Vingaard.
147. Kamal Abdul Alim, interview by author, digital recording, January 31, 2021.
148. David Durrah, interview by Andreas Vingaard.
149. Mutawaf Shaheed, interview, August 30, 2020.
150. Mutawaf Shaheed, interview by Andreas Vingaard.
151. Larry Hancock, interview.
152. The early phase of the club was less avant-garde oriented. Durrah's group would play pieces by Randy Weston, early John Coltrane, and Cannonball Adderley. Durrah, who had a brief career in the mid-1970s in fusion, played free jazz gigs there in the mid-1960s. The drummer Larry Hancock, who played primarily on the West Coast as a post-bop drummer with figures such as Bobby Hutcherson, Steve Cohn, and Freddy Redd, also played early free sessions there. Strickland later changed his name to Mustafa Abdul Rahman after converting to Islam. He died in Turkey. Otis Harris had a brief career playing with Ted Daniel in New York around 1970. David Durrah, interview by Andreas Vingaard, digital recording, April 17, 2020; Mutawaf Shaheed, interview, August 30, 2020; Mutawaf Shaheed, interview, December 27, 2020; Larry Hancock, interview.
153. Larry Hancock, interview.
154. Mutawaf Shaheed, interview, August 30, 2020.
155. Mutawaf Shaheed, interview by Andreas Vingaard.
156. "Purdue Professor Declares Race Tensions to Continue in Music," *Cleveland Call and Post*, May 6, 1967.
157. Mutawaf Shaheed, interview by author, December 4, 2020.
158. Yusuf Mumin, interview; Abdul Wadud, interview by Ben Young, WKCR-FM, May 2, 2004, Ras Moshe Burnett collection. Leo's began as a bar but expanded into a jazz room, featuring musicians such as Dizzy Gillespie and Cannonball Adderley. The Majestic Hotel hosted figures such as Tadd Dameron and lesser-known local acts like Herman "Duke" Jenkins. Grant Segall, "Herman 'Duke' Jenkins, Played Jazz Clubs for Decades," *Cleveland.com*, November 17, 2009, https://www.cleveland.com/obituaries/2009/11/herman_duke_jenkins_played_jaz.html.
159. Yusuf Mumin, interview. Many years later, Mumin recorded the piece "Kingsbury Run" as a memory of these early experiences. Yusuf Mumin, *Sketches of the Invisible* (self-released, 2021). The bridge was set on fire during the Hough uprising of 1965, supposedly by white people on the other side who wanted to prevent the riot from spreading into their neighborhood. The bridge was never repaired.
160. Yusuf Mumin, interview. Jean Murrell Capers (1913–2017), who was the first Black member of the Cleveland city council and a successful judge, lived in the same neighborhood, and her family had migrated north form the same region of central Kentucky from which Mumin's family originated.
161. His family came from Sylvester, Georgia, where peanut farming was the staple crop. Draft Registration Cards for Ohio, October 16, 1940–March 31, 1947, Records of the Selective Service System 147, box 346, National Archives at St. Louis, St. Louis, Missouri.

162. 1930 US Census, Cuyahoga County, Ohio, population schedule, enumeration district 338, sheet 52A; dwelling 17, family 26, Edward DeVaughn (NARA microfilm publication T626, roll 507); 1940 US Census, Cuyahoga County, Ohio, population schedule, City of Cleveland, enumeration district 92–422, sheet 3A, household 64, Edward DeVaughn (NARA microfilm publication T627, roll 3220); 1950 US Census, Cuyahoga County, Ohio, population schedule, City of Cleveland, enumeration district 92–451, sheet 40, household 2356, Edward M. DeVaughn (NARA microfilm publication T627, roll 3744).
163. Yusuf Mumin, quoted in Pierre Crepon, "Cleveland Memories of Abdul Wadud," *The Wire*, August 2022, https://www.thewire.co.uk/in-writing/essays/cleveland-memories-of-abdul-wadud.
164. Abdul Wadud, interview by Ben Young.
165. Yusuf Mumin, quoted in Crepon, "Cleveland Memories of Abdul Wadud."
166. Abdul Wadud, interview by Ben Young.
167. Yusuf Mumin, interview.
168. Mumin called his exploration of old pianos "before birth music." Yusef Lateef, *Jazz and the Sounds of Nature* (Savoy Records, 1958); Yusuf Mumin, interview. Another early inspiration was Modern Jazz Quartet, *Music from "Odds Against Tomorrow"* (United Artists Records, 1959); Pierre Crepon, "*Wire* Playlist: Yusuf Mumin and the Black Unity Trio," *The Wire*, November 2020, https://www.thewire.co.uk/audio/tracks/wire-playlist-yusuf-mumin-and-the-black-unity-trio.
169. Yusuf Mumin, interview.
170. Cosmic Music was located near 124th Street and Superior Avenue. Pierre Crepon, "Avant Garde Jazz and Black Rights Activism in 1960s Cleveland, Ohio: An Interview with Mutawaf A. Shaheed," *The Wire*, March 2019, https://www.thewire.co.uk/in-writing/interviews/avant-garde-jazz-cleveland-interview-with-mutawaf-a-shaheed; Yusuf Mumin, interview.
171. Yusuf Mumin, interview.
172. Patty Waters's piece "Black Is the Color of My True Love's Hair" was particularly popular at the time. Patty Waters, *Sings* (ESP-Disk, 1966).
173. Hasan Abdur-Razzaq, "Creative Urban Momentum: Witnessing the Black Unity Trio," *Chimurenga*, November 17, 2020, https://chimurengachronic.co.za/creative-urban-momentum-witnessing-the-black-unity-trio/.
174. Dianne McIntyre, interview by author, digital recording, August 17, 2020.
175. Various, *The New Wave in Jazz* (Impulse!, 1966); Albert Ayler, *Live in Greenwich Village* (Impulse!, 1967); Andreas Vingaard, email to author, June 30, 2022.
176. Abdul Wadud, quoted in Joel Wanek and Tomeka Reid, "By Myself: An Interview with Abdul Wadud," *PointofDeparture.org*, November 2014, https://www.pointofdeparture.org/PoD57/PoD57Wadud.html.
177. Crepon, "*Wire* Playlist."
178. Wadud credits his classical training as "furthering my avant-garde ventures tremendously." Oliver Jackson, a professor of Black history at Oberlin, knew about the Black Artists Group and invited Hemphill to play at Oberlin. Abdul Wadud, quoted in Wanek and Reid, "By Myself."
179. Abdul Wadud, interview by Ben Young.
180. Wilson grew up in St. Louis and knew members of the Black Artists Group there. He attended Washington University (1959) for his undergraduate education, the University of Illinois (1960) for his master's degree, and received his PhD from the University of Iowa in 1964. He first taught at Florida Agricultural and Mechanical University before getting a position at Oberlin from 1965 to 1970. He then taught at the University of California–Berkeley from 1970 until he retired in 2002, where he happened to have Charles Tyler as a student (see chapter 9). Crepon, "Cleveland Memories."
181. Around that time, the enrollment of Black students at Oberlin began to increase. Abdul Wadud, quoted in Wanek and Reid, "By Myself."

182. Wanek and Reid, "By Myself"; Crepon, "Cleveland Memories."
183. David Lee, "Knocking Down Barriers: An Interview with Abdul Wadud, 1980," originally published in *Coda*, 1980; reprinted in *PointofDeparture.org*, 2021, https://pointofdeparture.org/PoD73/PoD73Wadud.html.
184. This music remained unreleased until 2007, though Mumin claims it was unauthorized. Norman Howard and Joseph Phillips, *Burn, Baby, Burn* (ESP-Disk, 2007). A more recent release of "Sad Miss Holiday" included Howard's lyrics for the first time. Mumin, *Sketches of the Invisible*.
185. Yusuf Mumin, email to author, February 7, 2022.
186. Yusuf Mumin, email, February 7, 2022.
187. Little Brenda Duff, *The Army's Got Me Crying/Tell Me Where'er You Going* (Downbeat, n.d.).
188. Hasan Shahid, quoted in Pierre Crepon, "The Blistering Cosmic Music of the Black Unity Trio," *The Wire*, March 2020, https://www.thewire.co.uk/in-writing/interviews/the-black-unity-trio-cleveland-ohio-1968-1969-interviews-hasan-shahid-pierre-crepon.
189. Hasan Shahid, quoted in Crepon, "Blistering Cosmic Music."
190. Hasan Shahid, interview by author, digital recording, August 24, 2020.
191. Hasan Shahid, interview.
192. Crepon, "*Wire* Playlist."
193. Hasan Shahid, interview.
194. Yusuf Mumin, interview.
195. Hasan Shahid, interview.
196. Abdur-Razzaq, "Creative Urban Momentum."
197. Abdul Wadud, quoted in Wanek and Reid, "By Myself." Hasan Shahid thought that Wadud had a similarity in sound to the Spanish guitarist Andrés Segovia. Hasan Shahid, interview.
198. Hasan Shahid, interview.
199. Hasan Shahid, quoted in Crepon, "Blistering Cosmic Music."
200. Hasan Shahid, interview.
201. Hasan Shahid, interview.
202. Occasionally they would add special guests to the band, such as the bass clarinetist Mustafa Abdul Rahim at Antioch. Hasan Shahid, quoted in Crepon, "Blistering Cosmic Music"; Hasan Shahid, interview; Abdur-Razzaq, "Creative Urban Momentum."
203. The passage is a quote from the Qur'an, 6:162. Hasan Shahid, interview.
204. Lee, "Knocking Down Barriers."
205. Yusuf Mumin, email to author, August 12, 2022.
206. Hasan Shahid, quoted in Crepon, "Blistering Cosmic Music."
207. The band existed briefly as a quartet with Wadud's bass teacher at Oberlin, Ollie Jackson, also playing with the band. Yusuf Mumin, interview.
208. Yusuf Mumin, interview.
209. Yusuf Mumin, interview.
210. Hasan Shahid, interview.
211. At least one other session was also recorded at a small studio in Cleveland run by Thomas Boddie, but those tapes have also been lost. That session included an expanded unit including the bassist Mutawaf Shahid and flutist Jacques Roulette (who later changed his name to Abdul Lateef). This lineup also played at the University of Toledo and at an unspecified university in Cleveland. Hasan Shahid, quoted in Crepon, "Blistering Cosmic Music"; Abdur-Razzaq, "Creative Urban Momentum."
212. Hasan Shahid, interview.
213. Hasan Shahid, quoted in Crepon, "Blistering Cosmic Music."
214. Yusuf Mumin, interview.
215. Lee, "Knocking Down Barriers."

216. Hasan Shahid, quoted in Crepon, "Blistering Cosmic Music."
217. Mutawaf Shaheed, interview by author, digital recording, September 7, 2022.
218. Hasan Shahid, interview.
219. Other musicians that Mumin collaborated with include Nathaniel Morgan (piano), Linda Hill (piano), Raymond King (piano), Woody Theus (drums), and Tylon Barea (drums). Unreleased tapes of Mumin in various sessions are contained in the Horace Tapscott Jazz Collection at University of California–Los Angeles. Yusuf Mumin, interview.
220. Hasan Shahid, interview.
221. *Cleveland Call and Post*, February 8, 1969; June 14, 1969; April 11, 1970; May 16, 1970; April 29, 1972; Mutawaf Shaheed, interview by author, digital recording, June 3, 2021.
222. Mutawaf Shaheed, interview, June 3, 2021.
223. Mutawaf Shaheed, interview, June 3, 2021.
224. Mutawaf Shaheed, interview by author, digital recording, August 30, 2020.
225. Crepon, "Avant Garde Jazz and Black Rights Activism."

5. SOLIDARITY AND CRISIS IN DETROIT: THE DETROIT ARTISTS' WORKSHOP AND THE FORGING OF RADICAL CULTURE

1. Veta Smith Tucker, "Uncertain Freedom in Frontier Detroit," in *A Fluid Frontier: Slavery, Resistance, and the Underground Railroad in the Detroit River Borderland*, ed. Karolyn Smardz Frost and Veta Smith Tucker (Wayne State University Press, 2016), 29–30; Karolyn Smardz Frost, "Forging Transnational Networks for Freedom: From the War of 1812 to the Blackburn Riots of 1833," in Frost and Tucker, eds., *Fluid Frontier*, 44–46.
2. Barbara Hughes Smith, "Worship Waystations in Detroit," in Frost and Tucker, eds., *Fluid Frontier*, 103–4; Herb Boyd, *Black Detroit: A People's History of Self-Determination* (Amistad, 2017), 49–51.
3. Roy Finkenbine, "A Community Militant and Organized: The Colored Vigilant Committee of Detroit," in Frost and Tucker, eds., *Fluid Frontier*, 154.
4. Boyd, *Black Detroit*, 57–67.
5. Mark Jay and Virginia Leavell, "Material Conditions of Detroit's Great Rebellion," *Social Justice* 44, no. 4 (2017): 28.
6. Michael Hamlin, *A Black Revolutionary's Life in Labor: Black Workers Power in Detroit* (Against the Tide Books, 2012), 6.
7. Charles S. Johnson, *Negro Housing: Report of the Committee on Negro Housing* [1932] (Negro Universities Press, 1969), 42; Douglas S. Massey and Nancy A. Denton, *American Apartheid: Segregation and the Making of the Underclass* (Harvard University Press, 1993), 188.
8. Beth Tompkins Bates, *The Making of Black Detroit in the Age of Henry Ford* (University of North Carolina Press, 2012), 105.
9. Thomas James Ticknor, "Motor City: The Impact of the Automobile Industry Upon Detroit, 1900–1975," PhD diss., University of Michigan, 1978, 168, 171, 173; Joyce Shaw Peterson, "Black Automobile Workers in Detroit, 1910–1930," *Journal of Negro History* 64, no. 3 (1979): 177; Elizabeth Anne Martin, *Detroit and the Great Migration, 1916–1929*, Bulletin no. 40 (Bentley Historical Library, University of Michigan, 1993), 1, 4; Bates, *Making of Black Detroit*, 16–17.
10. Bill Harris, interview by author, digital recording, December 15, 2022; Bill Harris, interview by author, digital recording, November 21, 2022.
11. Elreta Dodds, interview by author, digital recording, February 15, 2023.
12. Marcus Elliot, interview by author, digital recording, December 16, 2022.

13. The term was originally coined by the pianist Harold McKinney but was popularized by Beans Bowles. Dennis Bowles, *Dr. Beans Bowles "Fingertips": The Untold Story* (Sho-nuff Productions, 2003), 33; Lars Bjorn and Jim Gallert, "Teddy Harris: A Jazz Man in Motown," in *Heaven Was Detroit: From Jazz to Hip-Hop and Beyond*, ed. M. L. Liebler (Wayne State University Press, 2016), 20; Bill Harris, interview, December 15, 2022; Marcus Elliot, interview.
14. Wendell Harrison, interview by author, digital recording, August 5, 2021.
15. Terri Laws and Kimberly R. Enard, "'I AM What I AM': The Religion of White Rage, Great Migration Detroit, and the Ford Motor Company," in *The Religion of White Rage: Religious Fervor, White Workers, and the Myth of Black Racial Progress*, ed. Stephen C. Finley et al. (Edinburgh University Press, 2020), 58–72.
16. Melba Joyce Boyd, "The Problem Was the Police," in *Detroit 1967: Origins, Impacts, Legacies*, ed. Joel Stone (Wayne State University Press, 2017), 165–72. Mark Jay and Philip Conklin, *A People's History of Detroit* (Duke University Press, 2020): 83–86.
17. Steve Babson et al., *Working Detroit: The Making of a Union Town* (Adama Books, 1984), 79–81.
18. Stephen M. Ward, ed., *Pages from a Black Radical's Notebook: A James Bogg Reader* (Wayne State University Press, 2011), 96–107.
19. *Finally Got the News* (Black Star Productions, 1970), film directed by John Watson; Hamlin, *Black Revolutionary's Life in Labor*, 36–37, 63.
20. Stephen M. Ward, *In Love and Struggle* (University of North Carolina Press, 2016), 238; Jay and Conklin, *People's History of Detroit*, 114.
21. Jeremy Peters, "Cultural and Social Mecca: Entrepreneurial Action and Venue Agglomeration in Detroit's Paradise Valley and Black Bottom Neighborhoods," *Artivate* 9, no. 1 (2020): 20–41.
22. Larry Gabriel, "Rebirth of Tribe," in Liebler, ed., *Heaven Was Detroit*, 28.
23. Robert Hayden, *Collected Prose* (University of Michigan Press, 1984), 141.
24. Peters, "Cultural and Social Mecca," 22–24.
25. Bill Harris, interview, November 21, 2022.
26. In one incident in July 1966, "neighbors" of the Workshop shouted racist epithets at members of the organization and physically attacked them. They faced regular intimidation and surveillance from local police as well as the FBI. Newsletter 8, Artists' Workshop Society, July 25, 1966, Box 7, Folder 27, John and Leni Sinclair Collection (JLSC), Bentley Historical Library, University of Michigan, Ann Arbor.
27. Bill Harris, interview, November 21, 2022.
28. Monteith College Archives Collection Papers 1958–1972, Accession no. 453, Monteith College Archives, Wayne State University, Ann Arbor, MI.
29. Melba Joyce Boyd and M. L. Liebler, eds., *Abandon Automobile: Detroit City Poetry 2001* (Wayne State University Press, 2001), 24–27; Melba Joyce Boyd, *Wrestling with the Muse: Dudley Randall and the Broadside Press* (Columbia University Press, 2003), 35–39.
30. John Sinclair, interview by author, digital recording, January 9, 2023.
31. George Tysh, interview by author, digital recording, November 4, 2022.
32. Ron English to John Sinclair, Jan 17, 1965, Box 1, Folder 18, JLSC.
33. George Tysh, interview.
34. Harold McKinney, quoted in You!!, Part 2, Box 7, Folder 32, JLSC.
35. Michael J. Kramer, "'Can't Forget the Motor City': *Creem* Magazine, Rock Music, Detroit Identity, Mass Consumerism, and the Counterculture," *Michigan Historical Review* 28, no. 2 (2002): 49.
36. Ovell Arnold to John Sinclair, September 29, 1965, Box 1, Folder 26, JLSC.
37. Charles Moore to R. M. Buszek, November 5, 1965, Box 1, Folder 29, JLSC.
38. Ron English and Robin Eichele, interview by author, digital recording, December 18, 2022.
39. Kathleen Beaufait, interview by author, digital recording, December 20, 2022.

40. "Monteith College: Roots of the Workshop," https://www.detroitartistsworkshop.com/monteith-college-roots-of-the-workshop/; Robin Eichele, interview by author, digital recording, October 14, 2022.
41. English and Eichele, interview.
42. Ron English, interview by author, digital recording, May 18, 2022.
43. Sinclair was the son of a General Motors executive. English and Eichele, interview.
44. John Sinclair, interview, January 9, 2023.
45. Leni Sinclair, *Motor City Underground: Photographs 1963–1978* (Museum of Contemporary Art Detroit, 2021); Leni Sinclair, *Participant Observer: Fotografien von 1960 bis 2000* (Mitteldeutscher Verlag, 2021).
46. "Monteith College: Roots of the Workshop."
47. Leni Sinclair, interview by author, digital recording, February 7, 2022; Joseph DeLeon, "'A Vital Human Place' for the Counterculture: Fifth Estate and Amateur Film Culture in Detroit, 1965–1967," in *Global Perspectives on Amateur Film Histories and Cultures*, ed. Masha Salazkina and Enrique Fibla-Gutierrez (Indiana University Press, 2020), 229.
48. John Sinclair, "The Local Scene," *Arts and Artists* 4, no. 4 (October–November 1964): 6; Robin Eichele and John Sinclair, "Getting Out from Under," *New University Thought* 4, no. 2 (1965): 22; George Tysh, interview.
49. Jazz around Detroit, n.d., Box 7, Folder 20, JLSC.
50. Leni Sinclair, interview.
51. John Sinclair, interview, January 9, 2023.
52. John Sinclair, interview by author, digital recording, September 1, 2021.
53. Leni Sinclair, interview.
54. John Sinclair, "Detroit Downtown," *Arts and Artists* 4, no 4 (October–November 1964): 4.
55. John Sinclair, "This Is Our Music," in *Free Poems/Among Friends*, vol. 2, ed. John Sinclair and Magdalene Sinclair (1966), [12].
56. John Sinclair to Leroi Jones, October 2, 1964, Box 1, Folder 14, JLSC.
57. John Sinclair to Pauline Rivelli, October 4, 1964, Box 1, Folder 14, JLSC.
58. The Detroit Contemporary 5 and the Pierre Rochon Workshop Arts Quintet held daily rehearsals at the space for periods in 1965. John Sinclair to Pauline Rivelli, January 24, 1965, Box 1, Folder 18, JLSC.
59. Robin Eichele, interview.
60. Harold McKinney petitioned *Down Beat* for Sinclair to be the correspondent because previous writers had not paid enough attention to Black artists in Detroit. Pauline Rivelli to John Sinclair, July 22, 1964, Box 1, Folder 13, JLSC; Don DeMichael to John Sinclair, July 28, 1964, Box 1, Folder 13, JLSC; Pauline Rivelli to John Sinclair, August 20, 1964, Box 1, Folder 13, JLSC; Pauline Rivelli to John Sinclair, August 21, 1964, Box 1, Folder 13, JLSC; Pauline Rivelli to John Sinclair, August 27, 1964, Box 1, Folder 13, JLSC; Don DeMichael to John Sinclair, October 1, 1964, Box 1, Folder 14, JLSC; John Sinclair to Don DeMichael, October 6, 1964, Box 1, Folder 14, JLSC; John Sinclair, interview by author, digital recording, December 17, 2022.
61. John Norris to John Sinclair, January 13, 1965, Box 1, Folder 18, JLSC; John Sinclair to George Tysh, January 28, 1965, Box 1, Folder 18, JLSC; John Norris to John Sinclair, March 14, 1965, Box 1, Folder 20, JLSC; Charles Fero to John Sinclair, August 30, 1965, Box 1, Folder 25, JLSC.
62. John Sinclair to Don DeMichael, November 2, 1964, Box 1, Folder 15, JLSC; John Sinclair to Ken Schooner, June 26, 1965, Box 1, Folder 23, JLSC; John Sinclair to Barry G. Parsons, November 6, 1965, Box 1, Folder 27, JLSC; John Sinclair, interview, December 17, 2022.
63. John Sinclair to Barney Rosset, October 12, 1964, Box 1, Folder 14, JLSC; John Sinclair to Jonathon Williams, October 13, 1964, Box 1, Folder 14, JLSC; John Sinclair to Bart deMalignon, October 15, 1964, Box 1, Folder 14, JLSC; John Sinclair to Lita Hornick, October 15, 1964, Box 1, Folder

5. SOLIDARITY AND CRISIS IN DETROIT ❦ 405

14, JLSC; Lita Hornick to John Sinclair, October 25, 1964, Box 1, Folder 14, JLSC; John Sinclair to Lita Hornick, October 30, 1964, Box 1, Folder 14, JLSC; John Sinclair to Rick Ward, December 4, 1964, Box 1, Folder 15, JLSC.
64. Eichele and Sinclair, "Getting Out from Under," 22.
65. Untitled manifesto, Detroit Artists' Workshop, undated, Box 7, Folder 11, JLSC.
66. John Sinclair, interview, September 1, 2021.
67. John Sinclair, interview, January 9, 2023.
68. John Sinclair to Tam Fiofori, December 22, 1965, Box 1, Folder 33, JLSC.
69. Eichele and Sinclair, "Getting Out from Under," 23–4.
70. John Sinclair to Nat Hentoff, February 28, 1965, Box 1, Folder 19, JLSC.
71. Untitled manifesto, Detroit Artists' Workshop, undated, Box 7, Folder 11, JLSC.
72. Eichele and Sinclair, "Getting Out from Under," 22; Leni Sinclair, interview.
73. Program 2, Artists' Workshop Press, November 8, 1964, Box 7, Folder 29, JLSC.
74. John Sinclair to Pauline Rivelli, November 6, 1964, Box 1, Folder 15, JLSC.
75. John Sinclair to Leroi Jones, November 10, 1964, Box 1, Folder 15, JLSC.
76. John Sinclair to Pauline Rivelli, November 6, 1964, Box 1, Folder 15, JLSC.
77. Program 2, Artists' Workshop Press, November 8, 1964, Box 7, Folder 29, JLSC.
78. John Sinclair, interview, September 1, 2021.
79. John Sinclair to Leroi Jones, October 2, 1964, Box 1, Folder 14, JLSC.
80. John Sinclair to Don DeMichael, October 21, 1964, Box 1, Folder 14, JLSC; John Sinclair to Jimmy Garrison, October 21, 1964, Box 1, Folder 14, JLSC.
81. John Sinclair to Pauline Rivelli, October 5, 1964, Box 1, Folder 14, JLSC.
82. George Tysh, interview.
83. David Sinclair to John Sinclair, November 6, 1964, Box 1, Folder 15, JLSC.
84. Rochon was originally from Montreal, had relocated to Windsor, and then came to study music theory and composition at Wayne State. Brent Majors also studied at Wayne State and played a range of reeds. John Sinclair to Pauline Rivelli, November 6, 1964, Box 1, Folder 15, JLSC.
85. John Sinclair to Pauline Rivelli, November 6, 1964, Box 1, Folder 15, JLSC; John Sinclair to Pauline Rivelli, November 10, 1964, Box 1, Folder 15, JLSC. John Sinclair to David Sinclair, November 10, 1964, Box 1, Folder 15, JLSC; John Sinclair to Alex Trocchi, November 13, 1964, Box 1, Folder 15, JLSC; Program 4, Artists' Workshop Press, November 22, 1964, Box 7, Folder 29, JLSC.
86. Eichele and Sinclair, "Getting Out from Under," 24.
87. Bill Harris, "prismatic & allhearing," unpublished manuscript, Box 8, Folder 18, JLSC.
88. Bill Harris, interview, December 15, 2022.
89. John Sinclair to Leroi Jones, October 2, 1964, Box 1, Folder 14, JLSC; John Sinclair to Pauline Rivelli, October 4, 1964, Box 1, Folder 14, JLSC; John Sinclair to Jimmy Garrison, October 21, 1964, Box 1, Folder 14, JLSC; John Sinclair to Pauline Rivelli, November 6, 1964, Box 1, Folder 15, JLSC; Pauline Rivelli to John Sinclair, November 11, 1964, Box 1, Folder 15, JLSC; Leroi Jones to John Sinclair, November 30, 1964, Box 1, Folder 15, JLSC.
90. John Sinclair to Archie Shepp, December 14, 1964, Box 1, Folder 16, JLSC.
91. John Sinclair to Charles Mingus, December 14, 1964, Box 1, Folder 16, JLSC; John Sinclair to John Tchicai, December 14, 1964, Box 1, Folder 16, JLSC.
92. Judith Mingus to John Sinclair, January 28, 1965, Box 1, Folder 18, JLSC; John Sinclair to Judith Mingus, February 4, 1965, Box 1, Folder 19, JLSC.
93. John Sinclair to George Tysh, January 28, 1965, Box 1, Folder 18, JLSC.
94. John Sinclair, interview, January 9, 2023.
95. John Sinclair to George Tysh, January 28, 1965, Box 1, Folder 18, JLSC.
96. John Sinclair to Danny Spencer, January 29, 1965, Box 1, Folder 18, JLSC; Workshop Organization, undated, Box 7, Folder 11, JLSC.

97. Artists' Workshop Membership Announcement, [2], Box 7, Folder 11, JLSC.
98. Leni Sinclair, interview.
99. The mimeograph was revolutionary in that it made it possible for small publishers to produce magazines cheaper and more easily. Ed Sanders's avant-garde journal *Fuck You/A Magazine of the Arts* was a prime inspiration for the Workshop press publications. Program 17, Artists' Workshop Press, February 28, 1965, Box 7, Folder 29, JLSC; *Daily Collegian*, March 9, 1965; "Monteith College: Roots of the Workshop."
100. Leni Sinclair, interview.
101. Artists' Workshop Society Membership, November 18, 1964, Box 7, Folder 26, JLSC; Membership List, March 18, 1965, Box 7, Folder 26, JLSC.
102. Bill Harris, interview, November 21, 2022.
103. John Sinclair to the Collegian, February 17, 1965, Box 1, Folder 19, JLSC.
104. Eichele and Sinclair, "Getting Out from Under," 23–24; Free University of Detroit Catalog, Winter–Spring term 1966, Free University of Detroit, Box 7, Folder 24, JLSC; *Detroit Free Press*, April 1, 1966.
105. John Sinclair, quoted in *Daily Collegian*, January 24, 1966.
106. Ron English, quoted in Eichele and Sinclair, "Getting Out from Under," 25–26.
107. Eichele and Sinclair, "Getting Out from Under," 26.
108. Jazz Club Proposal, January 26, 1965, Box 7, Folder 11, JLSC; John Sinclair to Danny Spencer, January 29, 1965, Box 1, Folder 18, JLSC.
109. *Daily Collegian*, November 17, 1965.
110. Sinclair, "Local Scene," 6.
111. Kathleen Beaufait, interview.
112. George Tysh, interview.
113. Concert Flyer, Artists' Workshop Press, December 18, 1964, Box 7, Folder 13, JLSC; Concert Program, Artists' Workshop Press, June 29, 1965, Box 7, Folder 11, JLSC; John Sinclair, "The Detroit Contemporary 5," unpublished manuscript, n.d., Box 8, Folder 54, JLSC.
114. Kathleen Beaufait, interview.
115. Ron English, interview by author, digital recording, May 13, 2022.
116. Leni Sinclair, interview.
117. John Sinclair, "Adolescence: A Musical Reality for Cornet, Saxophone, and Rhythm," January 3, 1965, Box 8, Folder 51, JLSC.
118. Sinclair, "Adolescence: A Musical Reality."
119. Concert Program, Artists' Workshop Press, March 28, 1965, Box 7, Folder 13, JLSC.
120. The Workshop artists could not afford to rent a recording studio, and no label was covering the music in Detroit at the time. John Sinclair, interview, January 9, 2023.
121. Various, *Detroit Artists Workshop: Community, Jazz and Art in the Motor City 1965–1981* (Art Yard, 2022).
122. The Detroit Jazz Scene 1965: A Discussion, analog recording transcript, Box 7, Folder 19, JLSC.
123. The Detroit Jazz Scene 1965.
124. Lawrence Ballen to Leni Sinclair, July 5, 1966, Box 2, Folder 7, JLSC; Magdalene Sinclair, "Untitled," *Change* 2 (1966): 33; A Proposal to the People of Detroit, undated, Box 7, Folder 11, JLSC.
125. Concert Flyer, Artists' Workshop Press, March 28, 1965, Box 7, Folder 13, JLSC; Concert Program, Artists' Workshop Press, April 25, 1965, Box 7, Folder 13, JLSC; Concert Poster, Artists' Workshop Press, June 1, 1965, Box 7, Folder 13, JLSC; Concert Poster, Artists' Workshop Press, June 29, 1965, Box 7, Folder 13, JLSC.
126. Bud Spangler to John Sinclair, September 28, 1965, Box 1, Folder 26, JLSC.

5. SOLIDARITY AND CRISIS IN DETROIT 407

127. Charles Moore quoted in Concert Program, Artists' Workshop Press, October 14, 1965, Box 7, Folder 13, JLSC. Moore first publicly expressed these ideas at the Detroit Jazz Scene 1965 event in April 1965.
128. Concert Poster, Artists' Workshop Press, October 14, 1965, Box 7, Folder 13, JLSC.
129. John Sinclair to David Franks, November 1, 1965, Box 1, Folder 30, JLSC; John Sinclair to Tam Fiofori, November 13, 1965, Box 1, Folder 30, JLSC; Untitled Transcript, n.d., Box 7, Folder 41, JLSC.
130. John Sinclair, "The Destruction of America," in *This Is Our Music*, Workshop Books 3 (Artists' Workshop Press, 1965), [30–31].
131. John Sinclair to David Sinclair, November 6, 1965, Box 1, Folder 30, JLSC; John Sinclair to Clark Coolidge, November 6, 1965, Box 1, Folder 29, JLSC; John Sinclair to George Tysh, November 14, 1965, Box 1, Folder 30, JLSC.
132. John Sinclair to Tam Fiofori, November 24, 1965, Box 1, Folder 30, JLSC.
133. John Sinclair to Marion Brown, November 10, 1965, Box 1, Folder 30, JLSC.
134. John Sinclair to Don Heckman, January 31, 1965, Box 1, Folder 32, JLSC.
135. John Sinclair, "The Home Front," *Change* 2 (1966): 27.
136. Stuart Broomer to John Sinclair, November 14, 1965, Box 1, Folder 30, JLSC; John Sinclair to Ron Caplan, December 22, 1965, Box 1, Folder 33, JLSC; John Sinclair to Clark Coolidge, December 22, 1965, Box 1, Folder 33, JLSC; John Sinclair to Ron Caplan, December 22, 1965, Box 1, Folder 33, JLSC; John Sinclair to Clark Coolidge, December 22, 1965, Box 1, Folder 33, JLSC; John Sinclair to Don Heckman, December 31, 1965, Box 1, Folder 32, JLSC; Concert Program, Artists' Workshop Press, January 21, 1966, Box 7, Folder 13, JLSC; Concert Poster, Artists' Workshop Press, February 1, 1966, Box 7, Folder 13, JLSC; John Sinclair, "The Home Front," 27.
137. Concert Program, Artists' Workshop Press, January 21, 1966, Box 7, Folder 13, JLSC.
138. Marion Brown, "Wordsong," unpublished manuscript, Box 8, Folder 5, JLSC.
139. Sinclair's poem later appeared in a larger collection titled *Fire Music*. John Sinclair and Magdalene Sinclair, eds., *Free Poems/Among Friends*, vol. 2 (Artists' Workshop Press, 1966), [3]. This edited volume gathered poems that Workshop members had distributed on the Wayne State University campus and at other locations in Detroit as part of a movement to engage the student body and broader youth public.
140. Concert Program, Artists' Workshop Press, March 1, 1966, Box 7, Folder 13, JLSC.
141. John Sinclair, "Tribute to the Hard Core," unpublished manuscript, December 29, 1966, Box 8, Folder 47, JLSC; Concert Program, Artists' Workshop Press, October 1, 1966, Box 7, Folder 13, JLSC.
142. English and Eichele, interview.
143. Magdalene Sinclair, "Untitled," 32.
144. Joseph Jarman, "On Hearing Detroit Contemporary 4 Singing," unpublished manuscript, Box 7, Folder 41, JLSC.
145. Concert Poster, Artists' Workshop Press, February 1, 1966, Box 7, Folder 13, JLSC, Ann Arbor, MI; Concert Program, Artists' Workshop Press, February 1, 1966, Box 7, Folder 13, JLSC, Ann Arbor, MI; Concert Program, Artists' Workshop Press, March 1, 1966, Box 7, Folder 13, JLSC, Ann Arbor, MI; Leni Sinclair to John Sinclair, June 1, 1966, Box 2, Folder 4, JLSC; Keith Shuert to Leni Sinclair, June 3, 1966, Box 2, Folder 4, JLSC; James Kane to Leni Sinclair, June 6, 1966, Box 2, Folder 4, JLSC; Leni Sinclair to John Sinclair, July 8, 1966, Box 2, Folder 9, JLSC.
146. Leni Sinclair to John Sinclair, July 8, 1966, Box 2, Folder 9, JLSC.
147. Concert Program, Cranbrook Jazz Society, January 6, 1967, Box 7, Folder 13, JLSC; Concert Program, Cranbrook Jazz Society, April 28, 1967, Box 7, Folder 13, JLSC.
148. Charles Moore quoted in Leni Sinclair to John Sinclair, March 28, 1966, Box 1, Folder 43, JLSC.
149. Concert Program, Artists' Workshop Press, June 29, 1965, Box 7, Folder 11, JLSC.

150. George Garnett was tragically killed in an accident in late 1965. John Sinclair to Drew and Terri, December 31, 1965, Box 1, Folder 32, JLSC.
151. Concert Program, Artists' Workshop Press, March 28, 1965, Box 7, Folder 13, JLSC; Program 23, Artists' Workshop Press, April 18, 1965, Box 7, Folder 29, JLSC; Program 25, Artists' Workshop Press, May 2, 1965, Box 7, Folder 29, JLSC; Concert Poster, Artists' Workshop Press, June 29, 1965, Box 7, Folder 13, JLSC.
152. Concert Poster, Artists' Workshop Press, November 18, 1965, Box 7, Folder 13, JLSC; Press Release, Artists' Workshop Press, Box 1, Folder 29, JLSC.
153. Jim Semark, "The Mechanics of Social Exploitation: From the Concerto for Charles Moore," *Artists' Worksheet* 6, Artists' Workshop Press, March 28, 1965, Box 7, Folder 14, JLSC.
154. "Concerto for Charles Moore," Concert Flyer, Artists' Workshop Press, undated, Box 7, Folder 11, JLSC.
155. "Black Music: The New Wave," in "Concerto for Charles Moore," Concert Flyer, Artists' Workshop Press, undated, Box 7, Folder 11, JLSC.
156. "Black Music: The New Wave," in "Concerto for Charles Moore," Concert Flyer, Artists' Workshop Press, undated, Box 7, Folder 11, JLSC.
157. John Sinclair to Leni Sinclair, April 3, 1966, Box 1, Folder 45, JLSC; Concert Program, Artists' Workshop Press, August 7, 1966, Box 7, Folder 13, JLSC.
158. Jim Semark, "Jack and Jill in Heaven Town. Part 2: The World/King of Heaven Town," unpublished manuscript, Box 8, Folder 44, JLSC.
159. Concert Poster, June 1, 1965, Box 7, Folder 19, JLSC; Concert Poster, June 29, 1965, Box 7, Folder 13, JLSC.
160. John Sinclair, interview by author, digital recording, April 7, 2023.
161. John Sinclair, interview, September 1, 2021.
162. Concert Poster, October 14, 1965, Box 7, Folder 13, JLSC; Concert Poster, November 18, 1965, Box 7, Folder 13, JLSC.
163. John Sinclair quoted in Concert Program, February 1, 1966, Box 7, Folder 13, JLSC; Concert Poster, March 1, 1966, Box 7, Folder 13, JLSC.
164. English and Eichele, interview.
165. Concert Program, August 7, 1966, Box 7, Folder 13, JLSC.
166. Concert Program, October 1, 1966, Box 7, Folder 13, JLSC; Concert Program, Jan 1, 1967, Box 7, Folder 13, JLSC.
167. Lyman Woodard Organization, *Saturday Night Special* (Strata Records, 1975).
168. Mailing List, Artists' Workshop Society, January 20, 1965, Box 7, Folder 26, JLSC; Mailing List, Artists' Workshop Society, February 1, 1965, Box 7, Folder 26, JLSC; Mailing List, Artists' Workshop Society, March 18, 1965, Box 7, Folder 26, JLSC; Mailing List, Artists' Workshop Society, February 6, 1966, Box 7, Folder 26, JLSC.
169. John Sinclair, interview, September 1, 2021.
170. John Sinclair to Jamey Aebersold, December 18, 1965, Box 1, Folder 33, JLSC.
171. John Sinclair, interview, January 9, 2023.
172. The Workshop was most interested in inviting Archie Shepp, Marion Brown, and Cecil Taylor for performances, but Sinclair cited lack of funds as the main impediment. John Sinclair to Bernard Stollman, October 3, 1965, Box 1, Folder 27, JLSC.
173. Ultimately Ayler, as well as Cecil Taylor, requested payment higher than that to which Wayne State University or the University of Michigan would agree. A second attempt was made for May 1966, but that, too, failed to materialize. The historian Frank Kofsky, at the University of Pittsburgh, suggested that the Artists' Workshop split travel costs to bring musicians from New York, and Sinclair suggested they try to create tours through Pittsburgh, Detroit, Buffalo, and Toronto, but they never materialized. Bernard Stollman to John Sinclair, November 12, 1965, Box 1, Folder 30,

5. SOLIDARITY AND CRISIS IN DETROIT ❧ 409

JLSC; John Sinclair to Bernard Stollman, November 15, 1965, Box 1, Folder 30, JLSC; Dave Lundin to John Sinclair, November 17, 1965, Box 1, Folder 30, JLSC; John Sinclair to Dave Sinclair, November 17, 1965, Box 1, Folder 30, JLSC; George Tysh to John Sinclair, November 27, 1965, Box 1, Folder 30, JLSC; John Sinclair to George Tysh, November 30, 1965, Box 1, Folder 30, JLSC; Dave Lundin to John Sinclair, December 5, 1965, Box 1, Folder 33, JLSC; Leni Sinclair to John Sinclair, April 19, 1966, Box 1, Folder 48, JLSC; Frank Kofsky to Leni Sinclair, May 29, 1966, Box 2, Folder 1, JLSC; Frank Kofsky to Leni Sinclair, Box 2, Folder 7, JLSC; John Sinclair to Leni Sinclair, July 10, 1966, Box 2, Folder 7, JLSC.

174. Dave Lundin to John Sinclair, December 5, 1965, Box 1, Folder 33, JLSC; J. B. Figi to John Sinclair, December 24, 1965, Box 1, Folder 32, JLSC.

175. J. B. Figi to Leni Sinclair, March 26, 1966, Box 1, Folder 43, JLSC; Kathy Casement to John Sinclair, April 2, 1966, Box 1, Folder 46, JLSC; Joseph Jarman to Leni Sinclair, April 4, 1966, Box 1, Folder 46, JLSC; John Sinclair to Leni Sinclair, April 16, 1966, Box 1, Folder 48, JLSC; Joseph Jarman to Leni Sinclair, April 24, 1966, Box 1, Folder 48, JLSC; Leni Sinclair to John Sinclair, April 27, 1966, Box 2, Folder 1, JLSC; Leni Sinclair to John Sinclair, April 28, 1966, Box 2, Folder 3, JLSC; Joseph Jarman to Leni Sinclair, May 1966, Box 2, Folder 1, JLSC; J.B. Figi to Leni Sinclair, June 25, 1966, Box 2, Folder 5, JLSC; Leni Sinclair to John Sinclair, June 28, 1966, Box 2, Folder 7, JLSC; John Sinclair to Leni Sinclair, July 14, 1966, Box 2, Folder 7, JLSC.

176. Joseph Jarman, Concert Flyer, Artists' Workshop Press, March 18, 1966, Box 7, Folder 11, JLSC; John Sinclair to Leni Sinclair, May 9, 1966, Box 2, Folder 1, JLSC.

177. Concert Poster, Artists' Workshop Press, June 3, 1966, Box 7, Folder 13, JLSC; Leni Sinclair to John Sinclair, June 6, 1966, Box 2, Folder 5, JLSC.

178. Joseph Jarman, *Song For* (Delmark Records, 1967).

179. Concert Program, Artists' Workshop Press, August 7, 1966, Box 7, Folder 13, JLSC.

180. The MC5 admired John Coltrane and were influenced by free jazz. Their lead singer, Rob Tyner, born with the surname Derminer, changed his name in honor of the pianist McCoy Tyner. Concert Program, Artists' Workshop Press, October 1, 1966, Box 7, Folder 13, JLSC; Concert Program, Artists' Workshop Press, January 1, 1967, Box 7, Folder 13, JLSC; Concert Poster, Cranbrook Jazz Society, April 28, 1967, Box 7, Folder 13, JLSC; John Sinclair, interview, December 17, 2022.

181. Concert Poster, Bohemian Embassy, Box 7, Folder 32, JLSC.

182. John Sinclair to Tam Fiofori, December 10, 1965, Box 1, Folder 33, JLSC.

183. Concert Program, Artists' Workshop Press, February 1, 1966, Box 7, Folder 13, JLSC.

184. Marion Brown to John Sinclair, October 15, 1965, Box 1, Folder 27, JLSC; Marion Brown to John Sinclair, October 24, 1965, Box 1, Folder 27, JLSC; John Sinclair to Victor Coleman, November 6, 1965, Box 1, Folder 30, JLSC; Concert Program, Creative Arts Festival, undated, Box 7, Folder 13, JLSC; Newsletter 5, Artists' Workshop Society, March 29, 1966, Box 7, Folder 27, JLSC.

185. Concert Poster, November 17, 1966, Box 7, Folder 13, JLSC.

186. Burton Greene, liner notes, *The Burton Greene Quartet* (ESP-Disk, 1966).

187. John Sinclair to Victor Coleman, February 28, 1965, reprinted in Artists' Worksheet 8, Artists' Workshop Press, April 11, 1965, Box 7, Folder 15, JLSC.

188. John Sinclair, "The Whip," Artists' Worksheet 8, April 11, 1965, Box 7, Folder 15, JLSC.

189. John Sinclair, "The Detroit Jazz Scene 1965: A Discussion," analog recording transcript, Box 7, Folder 19, JLSC.

190. Charles Moore, "The Detroit Jazz Scene 1965: A Discussion," analog recording transcript, Box 7, Folder 19, JLSC.

191. Conference Program, April 1965, Box 7, Folder 11, JLSC.

192. Concert Program, Artists' Workshop Press, April 1965, Box 7, Folder 13, JLSC.

193. John Sinclair to Robert Kelly, November 22, 1965, Box 1, Folder 30, JLSC.

194. John Sinclair to Jamey Aebersold, December 18, 1965, Box 1, Folder 33, JLSC.

195. John Sinclair, quoted in Untitled Transcript, n.d., Box 7, Folder 41, JLSC.
196. Charles Moore to Editor of *Jazz*, December 20, 1965, Box 1, Folder 32, JLSC.
197. Some of the editors and writers involved saw *Change* as filling a vital gap that was created when *Kulchur* stopped published reviews by Leroi Jones, A. B. Spellman, and others. Lita Hornick to John Sinclair, October 25, 1964, Box 1, Folder 14, JLSC; John Sinclair to Lita Hornick, October 30, 1964, Box 1, Folder 14, JLSC; John Sinclair to Rick Ward, December 4, 1964, Box 1, Folder 15, JLSC; Tam Fiofori to John Sinclair, October 25, 1965, Box 1, Folder 27, JLSC.
198. Marion Brown was their chief contact in New York and helped them make contact with musicians there. Fiofori and Sinclair developed a friendship via their letters and shared enthusiasm about the music. John Sinclair to Andrew Crozier, November 10, 1965, Box 1, Folder 29, JLSC; John Sinclair, interview, January 9, 2023.
199. *Change* was also advertised in *Down Beat*. George Fox to John Sinclair, October 11, 1965, Box 1, Folder 28, JLSC; Frank Kofsky to John Sinclair, October 12, 1965, Box 1, Folder 28, JLSC.
200. Bernard Stollman attempted to set up concerts for ESP label artists in Michigan. Bernard Stollman to WKAR-FM, September 2, 1965, Box 1, Folder 27, JLSC; Bud Spangler to Bernard Stollman, September 16, 1965, Box 1, Folder 27, JLSC; John Sinclair to Bernard Stollman, October 3, 1965, Box 1, Folder 27, JLSC; Bernard Stollman to John Sinclair, October 9, 1965, Box 1, Folder 27, JLSC; Marion Brown to John Sinclair, October 24, 1965, Box 1, Folder 27, JLSC; Rick Ward to John Sinclair, October 28, 1965, Box 1, Folder 27, JLSC; John Sinclair to Tam Fiofori, November 13, 1965, Box 1, Folder 30, JLSC.
201. John Sinclair, "Untitled," *Change* 1 (1965): iii, v.
202. Gary J. to Charles Moore, September 14, 1965, Box 1, Folder 26, JLSC.
203. *Detroit News*, August 17, 1965; August 18, 1965.
204. English and Eichele, interview.
205. An Appeal to the Friends of John Sinclair, undated, Box 7, Folder 11, JLSC.
206. *Daily Collegian*, February 25, 1966.
207. Burton Greene to Leni Sinclair, March 1966, Box 1, Folder 43, JLSC.
208. Leni Sinclair, "Emergency Meeting," March 7, 1966, Box 7, Folder 18, JLSC.
209. Leni Sinclair, Newsletter, March 29, 1966, Box 7, Folder 18, JLSC.
210. That summer, Spencer also went on tour with Stanley Cowell's group in Europe. Leni Sinclair to John Sinclair, May 22, 1966, Box 2, Folder 3, JLSC.
211. John Sinclair to Charles Moore, June 29, 1966, Box 2, Folder 5, JLSC.
212. Leni Sinclair to John Sinclair, July 1, 1966, Box 2, Folder 10, JLSC; Leni Sinclair to John Sinclair, July 27, 1966, Box 2, Folder 9, JLSC; John Sinclair to Charles Moore, July 29, 1966, Box 2, Folder 9, JLSC.
213. Leni Sinclair to John Sinclair, July 5, 1966, Box 2, Folder 9, JLSC.
214. Leni Sinclair to John Sinclair, May 18, 1966, Box 2, Folder 3, JLSC; Leni Sinclair to John Sinclair, June 28, 1966, Box 2, Folder 7, JLSC.
215. A Questionnaire for a Bunch of Questionable People, July 19, 1966, Box 7, Folder 14, JLSC.
216. John Sinclair, Newsletter, November 15, 1966, Box 7, Folder 18, JLSC.
217. Leni Sinclair, interview.
218. *Detroit News*, January 25, 1967, January 26, 1967; *Daily Collegian*, January 27, 1967; *The Fifth Estate*, February 1–15, 1967.
219. *Detroit News*, January 25, 1967.
220. Heads of State Defense Committee to Membership, undated, Box 7, Folder 11, JLSC.
221. *Detroit News*, January 25, 1967.
222. John Sinclair, interview, September 1, 2021.
223. Kathleen Beaufait, interview; Kathleen Beaufait and Ralph "Buzzy" Jones, interview by author, digital recording, December 20, 2022.

224. Kathleen Beaufait, interview.
225. Kathleen Beaufait, interview.
226. Leni Sinclair, interview.
227. John Sinclair, interview, December 17, 2022.

6. "MY MIND AND MY SPIRIT WERE LIBERATED DURING THE RIOT": FARUQ Z. BEY AND GRIOT GALAXY IN DETROIT

1. Epigraph: Faruq Z. Bey, quoted in Kofi Natambu, "Faruq Z. Bey at the Belcrest Hotel, Detroit, Michigan," in *Solid Ground: A New World Journal* 1, no. 3/4 (1983): 66.
2. Thomas J. Sugrue, "'Forget About Your Inalienable Right to Work': Deindustrialization and Its Discontents at Ford, 1950–1953," *International Labor and Working-Class History* 48 (1995): 112–30; Thomas A. Klug, "The Deindustrialization of Detroit," in *Detroit 1967: Origins, Impacts, Legacies*, ed. Joel Stone (Wayne State University Press, 2017), 65–66.
3. Stephen M. Ward, ed., *Pages from a Black Radical's Notebook: A James Boggs Reader* (Wayne State University Press, 2011), 72; Mark Jay and Virginia Leavell, "Material Conditions of Detroit's Great Rebellion," *Social Justice* 44, no. 4 (2017): 37.
4. Michele Gibbs, quoted in Michael Hamlin, *A Black Revolutionary's Life in Labor: Black Workers Power in Detroit* (Against the Tide, 2012), 40–41.
5. Mike Johnston, interview by author, digital recording, October 25, 2023.
6. Hamlin, *A Black Revolutionary's Life in Labor*, 24–25; see also Ernest Allen Jr., "The League of Revolutionary Black Workers: An Assessment," in *Workers' Struggles Past and Present: A 'Radical America' Reader*, ed. James Green (Temple University Press, 1983), 288–92; Jack Taylor, "Revolution at the Point of Production: An Interview with Mike Hamlin of DRUM and the League of Revolutionary Black Workers," *Spectrum: A Journal on Black Men* 2, no. 1 (2013): 99–112.
7. Michele Gibbs, quoted in Hamlin, *A Black Revolutionary's Life in Labor*, 33.
8. Alex Elkins, "Liberals and 'Get Tough' Policing in Post-War Detroit," in *Detroit 1967: Origins, Impacts, Legacies*, ed. Joel Stone (Wayne State University Press, 2017), 106, 112.
9. Bill Harris, interview by author, digital recording, November 21, 2022.
10. Hamlin, *A Black Revolutionary's Life in Labor*, 64.
11. Hamlin, *A Black Revolutionary's Life in Labor*, 30, 42; Sandra Hines, "Detroit Coalition Against Police Brutality," in *Why Detroit Matters: Decline, Hope, and Renewal in a Divided City*, ed. Brian Doucet (Bristol University Press, 2017), 283.
12. Jaribu Shahid, interview by author, digital recording, August 5, 2021.
13. Sidney Fine, *Violence in the Model City: The Cavanaugh Administration, Race Relations, and the Detroit Riot of 1967* (Michigan State University Press, 2007), 155–56.
14. William Walter Scott III, *Hurt, Baby, Hurt* (New Ghetto Press, 1970), 103.
15. Scott, *Hurt, Baby, Hurt*, 105.
16. Scott, *Hurt, Baby, Hurt*, 106–7.
17. Blind pigs had existed in Detroit since the early twentieth century and were woven into the social fabric of the city.
18. Scott, *Hurt, Baby, Hurt*, 116.
19. Scott, *Hurt, Baby, Hurt*, 120.
20. Scott, *Hurt, Baby, Hurt*, 126–27.
21. "The 1967 Detroit Rebellion," *Revolutionary Worker* 915 (July 1997); Jordan T. Camp, *Incarcerating the Crisis: Freedom Struggles and the Rise of the Neoliberal State* (University of California Press, 2016), 44; Jay and Leavell, "Material Conditions of Detroit's Great Rebellion," 40.

22. Sadiq Muhammad Bey, interview by author, digital recording, May 24, 2023.
23. Scott, *Hurt, Baby, Hurt*, 132, 135.
24. Dan Georgakas and Marvin Surkin, *Detroit: I Do Mind Dying; A Study in Urban Revolution*, 3rd ed. (Haymarket, 2012), 14; Camp, *Incarcerating the Crisis*, 45–46.
25. *Inner City Voice*, October 1967.
26. Georgakas and Surkin, *Detroit: I Do Mind Dying*, 16.
27. *Inner City Voice*, February 29, 1968.
28. Georgakas and Surkin, *Detroit: I Do Mind Dying*, 17.
29. Imari Abubakari Obadele, "The Struggle of the Republic of New Africa," *The Black Scholar* 5, no. 9 (June 1974): 32–41; Chokwe Lumumba, "Short History of the U.S. War on the R.N.A.," *The Black Scholar* 12, no. 1 (January/February 1981): 72–81.
30. Chris DeVito et al., *The John Coltrane Reference* (Routledge, 2008): 347–48.
31. Faruq Z. Bey, interview by Detroit JazzStage, digital recording, October 19, 2006, https://www.youtube.com/watch?v=rEfockEsBYM.
32. W. Kim Heron, *Detroit Metro Times*, June 25, 2003; Marcus Elliot, interview by author, digital recording, December 16, 2022; Sadiq Muhammad Bey, interview.
33. Joel Peterson, interview by author, digital recording, December 17, 2022.
34. Faruq Z. Bey, interview for Detroit JazzStage.
35. Faruq Z. Bey, quoted in *Lansing State Journal*, February 17, 1979.
36. *Detroit Free Press*, November 27, 1981.
37. Kofi Natambu, "Faruq Z. Bey at the Belcrest Hotel," 66; Joel Peterson, interview, December 17, 2022.
38. Faruq Z. Bey, interview for Detroit JazzStage.
39. Bey, quoted in W. Kim Heron, *Detroit Metro Times*, June 25, 2003.
40. Sadiq Muhammad Bey, quoted in Heron, *Detroit Metro Times*, June 25, 2003.
41. Heron, *Detroit Metro Times*, June 25, 2003; Sadiq Muhammad Bey, interview.
42. Faruq Z. Bey, interview for Detroit JazzStage.
43. Wilbur Mackenzie, "Faruq Z. Bey," *Allaboutjazz.com*, May 23, 2010, https://www.allaboutjazz.com/faruq-z-bey-faruq-z-bey-by-wilbur-mackenzie.
44. Sadiq Muhammad Bey, quoted in W. Kim Heron, "Musician Interrupted: Faruq Z. Bey," in *Heaven Was Detroit: From Jazz to Hip-Hop and Beyond*, ed. M. L. Liebler (Wayne State University, 2016), 50.
45. Sadiq Muhammad Bey, interview.
46. Abdul Jalil Bey came up with the band name. Wilbur Mackenzie, "Faruq Z. Bey"; Sadiq Muhammad Bey, interview.
47. Faruq Z. Bey, quoted in *Lansing State Journal*, February 17, 1979.
48. Gertrude Lowthian Bell, trans., *Poems from the Divan of Hafez* (London: William Heinemann, 1897), 72, 82.
49. Sadiq Muhammad Bey, interview.
50. Sadiq Muhammad Bey developed a majority of their pieces. Sadiq Muhammad Bey, interview.
51. Faruq Z. Bey, quoted in Natambu, "Faruq Z. Bey at the Belcrest Hotel," 66.
52. Faruq Z. Bey, quoted in Natambu, "Faruq Z. Bey at the Belcrest Hotel," 66.
53. Gayle Addison Jr., ed., *The Black Aesthetic* (Doubleday, 1971).
54. *Detroit Free Press*, November 27, 1981.
55. Sadiq Muhammad Bey, interview.
56. Jaribu Shahid, interview, August 5, 2021.
57. Wilbur Mackenzie, "Faruq Z. Bey."
58. Sadiq Muhammad Bey, interview.
59. Jaribu Shahid, interview, August 5, 2021.

60. After leaving the band in 1977, Pierce became more involved in Motown. *Lansing State Journal*, February 17, 1979.
61. Kafi Patrice Nassoma, interview by author, digital recording, April 15, 2023.
62. Jaribu Shahid, interview, August 5, 2021.
63. Dodds grew up in a family that appreciated both jazz and classical music. Elreta Dodds, interview by author, digital recording, February 15, 2023. Allen released her first record as a leader, *Home Grown* (Minor Music), in 1985 and went on to have a prolific career both as a recording artist and as an educator.
64. Elreta Dodds, interview.
65. Nassoma later played with Billy Bang, Joseph Jarman, and Geri Allen and recorded with Pheeroan akLaff on his debut record, *Fits Like a Glove* (Gramavision, 1983); *Detroit Free Press*, August 17, 1984.
66. Kafi Patrice Nassoma, interview.
67. Nassoma, quoted in W. Kim Heron, *Detroit Metro Times*, June 25, 2003; Heron, "Musician Interrupted: Faruq Z. Bey," 51.
68. Kafi Patrice Nassoma, interview; Charlie Parker, *No. 3* (Dial Records, 1949); Ornette Coleman, *Science Fiction* (CBS, 1972).
69. Kofi Natambu, "The Visionary Consciousness of Faruq Z. Bey and the Long Revolution of the Black Creative Music Tradition," *Sound Projections*, https://panopticonreview.blogspot.com/2012/06/faruq-z-bey-1942-2012-visionary-jazz.html.
70. Faruq Z. Bey, quoted in *Detroit Free Press*, February 1, 1984.
71. Faruq Z. Bey, quoted in Natambu, "Faruq Z. Bey at the Belcrest Hotel," 66.
72. Faruq Z. Bey, quoted in Natambu, "Faruq Z. Bey at the Belcrest Hotel," 66.
73. Faruq Z. Bey, quoted in Natambu, "Faruq Z. Bey at the Belcrest Hotel," 66.
74. Faruq Z. Bey, "Mizimu," in *Solid Ground: A New World Journal* 3, no. 2 (1987): 63.
75. Faruq Z. Bey, interview for Detroit JazzStage.
76. Bey, quoted in Heron, *Detroit Metro Times*, June 25, 2003.
77. Faruq Z. Bey, interview for Detroit JazzStage.
78. Elreta Dodds, interview.
79. Dodds bore some compositional influence from the multi-instrumentalist Anthony Braxton, especially his record *Five Pieces 1975* (Arista Records, 1975). None of Griot Galaxy's material from the 1970s was ever released. Elreta Dodds, interview.
80. Faruq Z. Bey, quoted in Natambu, "Faruq Z. Bey at the Belcrest Hotel," 66.
81. Faruq Z. Bey, quoted in *Lansing State Journal*, February 17, 1979.
82. Kofi Natambu, "The Visionary Consciousness of Faruq Z. Bey."
83. The concert was broadcast on WDET-FM. *Detroit Free Press*, March 31, 1976.
84. *Detroit Free Press*, August 19, 1977; April 23, 1978.
85. *Ann Arbor Sun*, September 17, 1976.
86. The band's regular engagement at Cobb's Corner began in the summer of 1977 and continued until one of the owners, Harry Normile, was shot in an altercation in early 1979, after which they sporadically played at the club. *Detroit Free Press*, August 19, 1977; August 21, 1977; August 26, 1977; September 9, 1977; September 23, 1977; September 30, 1977; December 26, 1977; January 23, 1978; April 23, 1978; September 17, 1978; October 14, 1978; May 11, 1979; May 25, 1979; Heron, "Musician Interrupted," 51.
87. Jaribu Shahid, interview, August 5, 2021; *Lansing State Journal*, February 17, 1979.
88. Sadiq Muhammad Bey, quoted in Heron, *Detroit Metro Times*, June 25, 2003.
89. Kofi Natambu, quoted in Heron, *Detroit Metro Times*, June 25, 2003.
90. *Detroit Free Press*, December 26, 1977. The only known video excerpt of the band from this period was broadcast on the *Detroit Black Journal* on Detroit Public Television, May 4, 1978: https://www.youtube.com/watch?v=uU8uJNhdOyI.

6. LIBERATED DURING THE RIOT

91. The Detroit Jazz Renaissance and trumpeter Marcus Belgrave both also appeared at the fundraiser. *Detroit Free Press*, April 27, 1978.
92. *Detroit Free Press*, March 15, 1984; March 16, 1984.
93. *Detroit Free Press*, January 15, 1978; April 27, 1978; May 12, 1978, June 9, 1978; January 21, 1979.
94. *Detroit Free Press*, February 4, 1979.
95. Club Con Brio closed after about a year of operations. *Detroit Free Press*, July 4, 1979; October 10, 1979; October 26, 1979; *Windsor Star*, July 6, 1979; July 13, 1979; Ron English, interview by author, December 18, 2022.
96. One exception was a relatively brief residency at Alvin's Finer Twilight Bar in 1982. Alvin's became the main venue for the music in the 1980s, hosting bands like Sun Ra and the David S. Ware Quartet, as well as local groups like Griot Galaxy. *Detroit Free Press*, September 16, 1982; Joel Peterson, interview by author, December 17, 2022.
97. Michael LeBlanc, quoted in *Lansing State Journal*, February 17, 1979.
98. *Lansing State Journal*, December 1, 1977.
99. Tani Tabbal, interview by author, January 24, 2023.
100. Tani Tabbal, interview by author, January 24, 2023.
101. McMurray was versatile and went on to record with the Rolling Stones and other pop bands as well as lead his own mainstream jazz groups. Barefield left the band to focus his efforts on building Creative Arts Collective, a Detroit-based nonprofit organization that produced concerts at the DIA and other venues. Heron, "Musician Interrupted," 52.
102. *Detroit Free Press*, December 24, 1982.
103. In the 1980s, McMurray fronted a funk band named Midnight Sky. Midnight Sky, *Captain Midnight/So Real* (Skylife Production, 1983).
104. David McMurray, interview by author, February 5, 2023.
105. Faruq Z. Bey, quoted in Heron, *Detroit Metro Times*, June 25, 2003.
106. Jaribu Shahid, interview, August 5, 2021.
107. Geoffrey Jacques, quoted in Heron, *Detroit Metro Times*, June 25, 2003.
108. Tani Tabbal, interview by author, digital recording, January 24, 2023.
109. Jaribu Shahid, interview, August 5, 2021.
110. Sadiq Muhammad, "Mathematics of Melody," repr. in *Solid Ground: A New World Journal* 1, no. 2 (1982): 32. Sadiq Muhammad Bey had left the band a few years earlier to lead a reggae band named Aziz. Heron, "Musician Interrupted," 52.
111. Tani Tabbal, interview.
112. David McMurray, interview by author, digital recording, February 5, 2023.
113. *Detroit Free Press*, August 29, 1982.
114. Muhammad, "Mathematics of Melody," 32.
115. Faruq Z. Bey, quoted in Muhammad, "Mathematics of Melody," 32.
116. Faruq Z. Bey, quoted in Natambu, "Faruq Z. Bey at the Belcrest Hotel," 66.
117. Faruq Z. Bey, quoted in Muhammad, "Mathematics of Melody," 32.
118. Faruq Z. Bey, quoted in *Detroit Free Press*, November 27, 1981.
119. Tani Tabbal, interview.
120. David McMurray, interview.
121. Griot Galaxy, *Kins* (Black & White Records, 1982); Wilbur Mackenzie, "Faruq Z. Bey," *Allaboutjazz.com*, May 23, 2012, https://www.allaboutjazz.com/faruq-z-bey-faruq-z-bey-by-wilbur-mackenzie; Heron, *Detroit Metro Times*, June 25, 2003.
122. David McMurray, interview.
123. *Detroit Free Press*, May 30, 1982.
124. *Detroit Free Press*, November 27, 1981.

6. LIBERATED DURING THE RIOT   ♣   415

125. *Windsor Star*, June 20, 1980; September 3, 1982; September 2, 1983; August 1, 1986; *Detroit Free Press*, September 1, 1980; September 4, 1981; September 6, 1982; September 9, 1983; August 31, 1984; August 30, 1985; August 24, 1986; September 2, 1987.
126. *Detroit Free Press*, March 13, 1981; *Tallahassee Democrat*, July 17, 1981; *Oakland Tribune*, August 21, 1982; *Arizona Daily Star*, September 19, 1982; August 28, 1983; June 24, 1984; *Missoulian*, July 29, 1983; June 1, 1984; July 6, 1984; *Montana Standard*, July 30, 1983; *Indianapolis News*, August 13, 1983; August 14, 1983; *La Crosse Tribune*, August 13, 1983; July 21, 1984; *Berkeley Gazette*, September 27, 1983; *Ithaca Journal*, June 15, 1984; *Berkshire Eagle*, June 26, 1984; *Clarion-Ledger* (Jackson, MS), September 5, 1987; *Boston Globe*, July 16, 1989.
127. Bey, quoted in Jacques Karamanoukian, "Detroit Voices, Part 1: Faruq Z. Bey, Ancient Warrior and Griot," *Agenda*, February 1997, 6.
128. Wilbur Mackenzie, "Faruq Z. Bey," May 23, 2012, *Allaboutjazz.com*, https://www.allaboutjazz.com/faruq-z-bey-faruq-z-bey-by-wilbur-mackenzie.
129. Heron, *Detroit Metro Times*, June 25, 2003.
130. *Windsor Star*, February 2, 1981.
131. *Detroit Free Press*, January 29, 1982.
132. For instance, Bey and Tabbal both played in the band Onyxz. *Detroit Free Press*, February 5, 1983.
133. Ray Waller, "Creative Arts Collective Concert: Holland & Bey Explode the 'Classical Conceit,'" *Solid Ground: A New World Journal* 1, no. 3/4 (1983): 43.
134. Waller, "Creative Arts Collective Concert," 43.
135. Waller, "Creative Arts Collective Concert," 43.
136. Griot Galaxy, *Live at the D.I.A.* (Entropy Stereo Recordings, 2003).
137. *Detroit Metro Times*, June 25, 2003.
138. Jaribu Shahid, interview by author, digital recording, July 3, 2023.
139. *Detroit Metro Times*, June 25, 2003.
140. David McMurray, interview.
141. *Detroit Free Press*, August 2, 1983.
142. *Detroit Free Press*, August 16, 1984; August 24, 1984.
143. Tani Tabbal, interview.
144. Griot Galaxy, *Opus Krampus* (Sound Aspects Records, 1985).
145. *Detroit Free Press*, January 12, 1986.
146. *Lake Geneva Regional News*, April 17, 1986.
147. Bey, quoted in Heron, *Detroit Metro Times*, June 25, 2003.
148. Heron, "Musician Interrupted," 54.
149. Sadiq Muhammad Bey, "Excerpts from the Jesse Davis Medical Fund," in *Nostalgia for the Present: An Anthology of Writings (from Detroit)*, ed. Kofi Natambu (Post Aesthetic, 1985), 108.
150. Heron, *Detroit Metro Times*, June 25, 2003.
151. Kofi Natambu, "We Think We Know You or the Roving Enigma Blues," *Past Tents Press*, 1991, 49–50.
152. Bey, quoted in Heron, *Detroit Metro Times*, June 25, 2003.
153. Faruq Z. Bey, "Untitled," *Solid Ground: A New World Journal* 2, no. 1 (February 1985): 57.
154. David McMurray, interview.
155. Tani Tabbal, interview.
156. Faruq Z. Bey, "Notes on Tonal Physics," *Solid Ground: A New World Journal* 3, no. 2 (1987): 17.
157. Bey, "Notes on Tonal Physics," 17.
158. Bey, "Notes on Tonal Physics," 18.
159. Joel Peterson, interview, December 17, 2022.

7. TRIBE: COLLECTIVITY, SELF-DETERMINATION, AND THE DETROIT VISIONARIES OF THE 1970S

1. Epigraph: Wendell Harrison, interview by author, digital recording, August 5, 2021.
2. Von Battle migrated north from Macon, Georgia, in the 1930s, which meant that he came from the same fertile Black musical zone in the west central Georgia piedmont as the families of the pianist Bobby Few, bassist Clyde Shy, saxophonist Paul Gresham, and drummer J. C. Moses, discussed in chapter 2. Marsha Music, "Joe Von Battle: Requiem for a Record Shop Man," November 2008, https://marshamusic.wordpress.com/page-joe-von-battle-requiem-for-a-record-shop-man/; Shawn Ciavattone, "A Tribute: Joe's Record Shop—a Detroit Legacy," *Vinylwriters.com*, September 30, 2019, https://vinylwriters.com/a-tribute-joes-record-shop-a-detroit-legacy/.
3. Marsha Music, "Joe Von Battle."
4. Jaribu Shahid, interview by author, digital recording, August 5, 2021.
5. Wendell Harrison, quoted in Larry Gabriel, "Rebirth of Tribe," in ed. *Heaven Was Detroit: From Jazz to Hip-Hop and Beyond*, ed. M. L. Liebler (Wayne State University Press, 2016), 28.
6. Gabriel, "Rebirth of Tribe," 29.
7. David Durrah, interview by Andreas Vingaard, digital recording, April 17, 2020.
8. *Detroit Free Press*, November 20, 1970; *Berkeley Gazette*, April 17, 1971.
9. David Durrah, interview.
10. Joel Peterson, interview by author, digital recording, December 17, 2022.
11. Phil Ranelin, interview by author, digital recording, September 5, 2021.
12. Gabriel, "Rebirth of Tribe," 29.
13. *Detroit Free Press*, August 4, 1971.
14. Phil Ranelin, interview, September 5, 2021.
15. Phil Ranelin, interview, September 5, 2021.
16. Wendell Harrison, interview.
17. Wendell Harrison, interview.
18. Wendell Harrison, interview.
19. Wendell Harrison, interview.
20. Wendell Harrison, interview.
21. Phil Ranelin, interview, September 5, 2021.
22. Phil Ranelin, quoted in Gabriel, "Rebirth of Tribe," 28.
23. Wendell Harrison, quoted in Gabriel, "Rebirth of Tribe," 29.
24. Ali Muhammad Jackson and Willie Metcalf, quoted in *Detroit Free Press*, June 26, 1972.
25. Wendell Harrison, interview; Phil Ranelin, interview, September 5, 2021.
26. Wendell Harrison and Phil Ranelin, *Message from the Tribe* (Tribe, 1972); Gabriel, "Rebirth of Tribe," 30.
27. Phil Ranelin, interview by author, September 5, 2021.
28. Wendell Harrison, interview.
29. Grant Martin, "All That Jazz," *Tribe* 3, no. 1 (1975): 30.
30. Wendell Harrison, interview.
31. Grant Martin, "Caught in the Act: The Creative Profiles 'Live and Well' at the Blackhorse," *Tribe* 2, no. 1 (1974): 43.
32. Martin, "All That Jazz," 30.
33. Gabriel, "Rebirth of Tribe," 33.
34. Gabriel, "Rebirth of Tribe," 31.
35. Harrison and Ranelin, *Message from the Tribe*.
36. Jeamel Lee, liner notes, *Message from the Tribe* (Tribe, 1972).
37. Lee, liner notes.

38. Phil Ranelin, interview, September 5, 2021.
39. The sound quality on the debut record, *Message from the Tribe*, was not at the standards for radio at the time, so the label worked to improve it on subsequent recordings that they released. Martin, "All That Jazz," 30; Gabriel, "Rebirth of Tribe," 30.
40. Ranelin, quoted in Gabriel, "Rebirth of Tribe," 31.
41. Gabriel, "Rebirth of Tribe," 30.
42. Phil Ranelin, *Vibes from the Tribe* (Tribe, 1976).
43. Phil Ranelin, quoted in Ed Nelson, "Concert Review," *Tribe* 4, no. 3 (May–June 1976): 23.
44. The Black Messengers were similar to the Last Poets aesthetically but were not recorded. Gabriel, "Rebirth of Tribe," 32.
45. Wendell Harrison, *An Evening with the Devil* (Tribe, 1973).
46. Wendell Harrison, quoted in Grant Martin, "Wendell Harrison and Tribe Present *An Evening with the Devil*," *Tribe* 1, no. 3 (1973): 46.
47. Harrison, quoted in Grant Martin, "Wendell Harrison and Tribe Present," 46.
48. *Detroit Free Press*, August 4, 1972; August 27, 1972; February 9, 1973; June 1, 1973.
49. *Detroit Free Press*, August 4, 1972; August 27, 1972.
50. Gabriel, "Rebirth of Tribe," 28–29.
51. Gabriel, "Rebirth of Tribe," 32.
52. *Detroit Free Press*, May 12, 1974; May 19, 1974; May 19, 1974; May 24, 1974; May 26, 1974; June 2, 1974; June 9, 1974; June 14, 1974, June 16, 1974.
53. Harold McKinney, *Voices and Rhythms from the Creative Profile* (Tribe, 1974).
54. Nelson, "Concert Review," 23.
55. Gabriel, "Rebirth of Tribe," 29.
56. *Detroit Free Press*, October 3, 1973.
57. Live concert recordings in Detroit were rare even in the 1970s. Charles Moore, who was executive president of the independent record label Strata Corporation, was instrumental in orchestrating the record. Martin, "Caught in the Act: The Creative Profiles," 42.
58. Battle had worked with Creative Profile previously before departing for New York. Martin, "Caught in the Act: The Creative Profiles," 45.
59. Martin, "Caught in the Act: The Creative Profiles," 44.
60. Martin, "Caught in the Act: The Creative Profiles," 44.
61. Martin, "Caught in the Act: The Creative Profiles," 45.
62. Doug Hammond and David Durrah, *Reflections in the Sea of Nurnen* (Tribe, 1975).
63. Mixed Bag, *Mixed Bag's First Album* (Tribe, 1976).
64. Herb Boyd, "Of Black Republicans and Others," *Tribe* 1, no. 3 (1973): 11–14.
65. Herb Boyd, "The Year of the Jackal or Down the Revolutionary Path," *Tribe* 2, no. 1 (1974): 27–28; Mulele Gizenga, "Africa: America's Next Vietnam?" *Tribe* 2, no. 1 (1974): 32–33; Mulele Gizenga, "Phony Détente: South Africa Prepares for War," *Tribe* 3, no. 3 (1975): 8.
66. "The African POW Movement and Solidarity Day," *Tribe* 1, no. 3 (1973): 38–41.
67. Geoffrey Jacques, "The Nigger Beaters," *Tribe* 1, no. 3 (1973): 42; "About Our City: Mr. Mayor... Set It Out!" *Tribe* 1, no. 4 (1973): 16–20; Jim Ingram, "Mayor Coleman A. Young's First Year in Office: How Did It Go?" *Tribe* 3, no. 1 (1975): 14–17.
68. Sally Wright, "Black Nation in the Western Hemisphere," *Tribe* 1, no. 4 (1973): 38–40; Charles E. Colding, "Blacks and the Economy," *Tribe* 3, no. 1 (1975): 9; Betty Holloway, "Here's Looking at Unemployment," *Tribe* 3, no. 1 (1975): 11–13; Janet Brooks, "Unemployment and Inflation: Detroiter's Comment," *Tribe* 3, no. 2 (1975): 7–9; Jim Ingram, "The Economy and Detroit," *Tribe* 3, no. 2 (1975): 32–35.
69. "A Rap with Melvin Van Peebles," *Tribe* 1, no. 3 (1973): 15. Grant Martin ran a regular column titled "For My People," which addressed a range of media issues and critiqued mainstream narratives that

418 ❦ 7. TRIBE

either distorted or ignored issues of Black politics and culture. Grant Martin, "For My People," *Tribe* 2, no. 1 (1974): 20–21; Grant Martin, "For My People," *Tribe* 2, no. 2 (1974): 21; Grant Martin, "For My People," *Tribe* 3, no. 1 (1975): 27–33.

70. Demon Smith, "Toward a Black Theatre Quintessence," *Tribe* 2, no. 1 (1974): 37–40; Betty L. Holloway, "Rappin' with Butter," *Tribe* 3, no. 1 (1975): 24–25.
71. "Blacks in Communications," *Tribe* 2, no. 2 (1974): 10–16; Janet Brooks, "Black Women in Broadcasting," *Tribe* 2, no. 1 (1974): 10–16; "Black Women Involved in Broadcast Communications," *Tribe* 2, no. 3 (1974): 15–21.
72. "Detroit Jazz," *Tribe* 1, no. 3 (1973): 20–22; Ron English, "Jazz in Detroit: Strata Concert Gallery 46 Selden," *Tribe* 1, no. 3 (1973): 35–36.
73. Grant Martin, "The Prodigal Son Returns: An Interview with Donald Byrd," *Tribe* 1, no. 3 (1973): 25–34.
74. Geoffrey Jacques, "Kalaparusha: Forces and Feelings," *Tribe* 1, no. 3 (1973): 45; Grant Martin, "The Immortal John Coltrane," *Tribe* 1, no. 4 (1973): 24–30; Grant Martin, "A Profile of Sun Ra," *Tribe* 3, no. 2 (1975): 20–23; *Tribe* 4, no. 1 (January–February 1976): 26.
75. Kenneth L. Cox, "Cultural Colonization and the Self Determination Movement in Music," *Tribe* 2, no. 2 (1974): 26–27, 29–31.
76. Gabriel, "Rebirth of Tribe," 27.
77. Belgrave, quoted in Gabriel, "Rebirth of Tribe," 29.

8. "DON'T BE SCARED TO TELL THEM THE TRUTH": THE MUSIC OF ALBERT AYLER IN NEW YORK AND EUROPE

1. Epigraph: Albert Ayler quoted in Nat Hentoff, "Albert Ayler—the Truth Is Marching In," *Down Beat* (November 17, 1966): 18; "Goodbye Cleveland—Hello Sweden," *Cleveland Call and Post*, April 21, 1962.
2. Albert Ayler, quoted in Caux, "My Name Is . . . Albert Ayler," *Chroniques de l'Art Avant Vivant* 17 (February 1971): 24.
3. Ayler, quoted in Caux, "My Name Is . . . Albert Ayler," 24.
4. Bengt Nordström, quoted in Marc Chaloin, "Albert Ayler in Europe: 1959–62," in liner notes, Albert Ayler, *Holy Ghost* (Revenant, 2004), 83.
5. Nils Edström, quoted in Chaloin, "Albert Ayler in Europe," 88–89.
6. Chaloin, "Albert Ayler in Europe," 88.
7. Ayler quoted in Hentoff, "Albert Ayler—the Truth Is Marching In," *Down Beat*, November 17, 1966, 17–18.
8. Albert Ayler, *Something Different!!!!!!* (Bird Notes, 1963).
9. Harold Jefta, quoted in Chaloin, "Albert Ayler in Europe," 91.
10. Ayler, quoted in Chaloin, "Albert Ayler in Europe," 91.
11. Jefta, quoted in Chaloin, "Albert Ayler in Europe," 91.
12. Ayler, quoted in Val Wilmer, "Spiritual Unity," in liner notes, Albert Ayler, *Holy Ghost* (Revenant, 2004), 19.
13. Ben Young, "Tracks," in liner notes, Albert Ayler, *Holy Ghost* (Revenant, 2004), 140.
14. Albert Ayler, *My Name Is Albert Ayler* (Debut Records, 1964); Amiri Baraka, "You Think This Is About You?," in Albert Ayler, *Holy Ghost* (Revenant, 2004), 38–40.
15. Jon Goldman and Martin Davidson, "Albert Ayler: Life and Recordings," *Cadence* 1, no. 4 (April 1976): 8.
16. *Greensboro Record* (NC), January 15, 1968.

17. David Sandberg to John Sinclair, October 5, 1965, Box 1, Folder 27, John and Leni Sinclair Collection (JLSC), Bentley Historical Library, University of Michigan, Ann Arbor, MI; David Sandberg to John Sinclair, October 15, 1965, Box 1, Folder 27, JLSC.
18. Jefta, quoted in Chaloin, "Albert Ayler in Europe," 92–93.
19. Hentoff, "Albert Ayler—the Truth Is Marching In," 17.
20. "'Free Music'... Discorded Chaos?," *Cleveland Call and Post*, February 9, 1963.
21. Albert Ayler, quoted in "'Free Music'... Discorded Chaos?"
22. Kiyoshi Koyama, "Albert Ayler Interview," *Swing Journal*, recorded Jul 25, 1970, https://www.youtube.com/watch?v=uxYKj1CLUKo.
23. Yusuf Mumin, quoted in Pierre Crepon, "*Wire* Playlist: Yusuf Mumin and the Black Unity Trio," *The Wire*, November 2020, https://www.thewire.co.uk/audio/tracks/wire-playlist-yusuf-mumin-and-the-black-unity-trio.
24. Larry Hancock, interview by author, digital recording, October 14, 2021.
25. Donald Ayler, quoted in Mary Lynn, "Don Ayler Named to Who's Who in World," *Cleveland Call and Post*, May 17, 1975.
26. Albert Ayler, quoted in "'Free Music'... Discorded Chaos?"
27. Ayler, quoted in Caux, "My Name Is... Albert Ayler," 24.
28. In his early days in New York, Ayler had to take whatever work he could get, including performing once for a fashion show. *New York Amsterdam News*, May 9, 1981.
29. Alan Silva, quoted in Larry Nai, "Alan Silva Interview," *Cadence* 24, no. 7 (July 1999): 11.
30. *Cleveland Call and Post*, February 1, 1964.
31. Raphael McAden, quoted in Ben Young, "Witnesses," in Albert Ayler, *Holy Ghost* (Revenant, 2004), 116.
32. Albert Ayler, *Spirits* (Debut Records, 1964).
33. Leroi Jones, quoted in Goldman and Davidson, "Albert Ayler: Life and Recordings," 9.
34. Albert Ayler, *Swing Low Sweet Spiritual* (Osmosis Records, 1971).
35. William Francis Allen et al., eds., *Slave Songs of the United States* (New York: A. Simpson, 1867), 55.
36. Baraka, "You Think This Is About You?," 44.
37. Coltrane, quoted in Baraka, "You Think This Is About You?," 44.
38. Ayler, quoted in Caux, "My Name Is... Albert Ayler," 24.
39. Gary Peacock, quoted in Young, "Witnesses," 119.
40. Goldman and Davidson, "Albert Ayler: Life and Recordings," 10.
41. Ayler, quoted in Wilmer, "Spiritual Unity," 22.
42. Steve Tintweiss, interview by author, digital recording, June 1, 2022.
43. Leroi Jones, quoted in *Buffalo News*, July 15, 1964.
44. Mutawaf Shaheed, interview by author, August 30, 2020.
45. Bernard Stollman, quoted in John Kruth, "Bernard Stollman: The Man from 5D," *Signal to Noise* 34 (2004): 37.
46. Joe Pinelli, "Ayler on Record: Lyrical Rockets," *Change* 2 (1966): 112.
47. Goldman and Davidson, "Albert Ayler: Life and Recordings," 13.
48. Baraka, "You Think This Is About You?," 40.
49. Clark Coolidge to John Sinclair, October 30, 1965, Box 1, Folder 27, JLSC.
50. *Sydney Morning Herald* (Australia), August 6, 1966.
51. *The Province* (Vancouver), January 6, 1967.
52. First quote of Michael Snow quoted in *Austin Chronicle*, September 17, 1999; second quote of Snow in Jason Weiss, *Always in Trouble: An Oral History of ESP-Disk, the Most Outrageous Record Label in America* (Wesleyan University Press, 2012), 142.
53. Don Cherry, interview on Albert Ayler, part 1, https://www.youtube.com/watch?v=fKoBBz1Sbzg.

54. Don Cherry, interview on Albert Ayler, part 1.
55. Rudd, quoted in Ben Young, "Whence," in Albert Ayler, *Holy Ghost* (Revenant, 2004), 55.
56. Archie Shepp, interview, https://www.youtube.com/watch?v=3BUzRl_fFiA.
57. Ayler, quoted in Caux, "My Name Is... Albert Ayler," 24.
58. Don Cherry, quoted in Goldman and Davidson, "Albert Ayler: Life and Recordings," 9.
59. Albert Ayler, *Ghosts* (Debut Records, 1965); Albert Ayler Quartet, *The Hilversum Session* (Osmosis Records, 1980); Albert Ayler, *The Copenhagen Tapes* (Ayler Records, 2002).
60. Ayler, quoted in Hentoff, "Albert Ayler—the Truth Is Marching In," 18.
61. Albert Ayler et al., *New York Eye and Ear Control* (ESP-Disk, 1966).
62. Ayler, quoted in Wilmer, "Ayler: Mystic Tenor with a Direct Hot Line to Heaven?," *Melody Maker*, October 15, 1966.
63. John Coltrane, quoted in Carter Mathes, *Imagine the Sound: Experimental African American Literature After Civil Rights* (University of Minnesota, 2015), 45.
64. Ayler, quoted in Wilmer, "Ayler: Mystic Tenor."
65. Ayler, quoted in Nat Hentoff, "Albert Ayler—the Truth Is Marching In," 18.
66. Ayler, quoted in Caux, "My Name Is... Albert Ayler," 24.
67. Ayler, quoted in Caux, "My Name Is... Albert Ayler," 24.
68. Koyama, "Albert Ayler Interview."
69. Ayler, quoted in Hentoff, "Albert Ayler—the Truth Is Marching In," 40.
70. Various, *The New Wave in Jazz* (Impulse!, 1966).
71. Leroi Jones, liner notes, *The New Wave in Jazz* (Impulse!, 1966).
72. *New York Amsterdam News*, March 27, 1965.
73. Kimberly W. Benston, *Baraka: The Renegade and the Mask* (Yale University Press, 1976), 51–52; Addell Austin, "The Present State of Black Theatre," *TDR* 32, no. 3 (1988): 86; S. E. Wilmer, *Theatre, Society, and the Nation: Staging American Identities* (Cambridge University Press, 2002), 136–37.
74. Daniel Matlin, "'Lift Up Yr Self!': Reinterpreting Amiri Baraka (Leroi Jones), Black Power, and the Uplift Tradition," *Journal of American History* 93, no. 1 (June 2006): 96. See also Austin, "The Present State of Black Theatre," 86; Erik Nielson, "White Surveillance of the Black Arts," *African American Review* 47, no. 1 (2014): 174.
75. Lorenzo Thomas, "The Shadow World: New York's Umbra Workshop & Origins of the Black Arts Movement," *Callaloo* 4 (October 1978): 69.
76. "Jazz Concert to Aid Harlem Repertory School," *New York Amsterdam News*, May 1, 1965.
77. "Jazz Concert to Aid Harlem Repertory School."
78. "Jazz Concert to Aid Harlem Repertory School."
79. Thomas, "The Shadow World," 68.
80. Larry Neal, *Visions of a Liberated Future: Black Arts Movement Writings*, ed. Michael Schwartz (Thunder's Mouth, 1989), 66.
81. "Black Arts Repertory Opens Doors Friday," *New York Amsterdam News*, May 1, 1965; "Jazz Concert to Aid Harlem Repertory School," *New York Amsterdam News*, May 1, 1965.
82. Albert Ayler, *Bells* (ESP-Disk, 1965).
83. Ayler, quoted in Caux, "My Name Is... Albert Ayler," 24.
84. Koyama, "Albert Ayler Interview."
85. Ayler, quoted in Wilmer, "Spiritual Unity," 24.
86. Ayler, quoted in Wilmer, "Ayler: Mystic Tenor."
87. Ayler, quoted in Goldman and Davidson, "Albert Ayler: Life and Recordings," 9.
88. Ayler, quoted in Caux, "My Name Is... Albert Ayler," 24.
89. Donald Ayler, quoted in *The National Observer*, June 7, 1965.
90. Newman Alexander, quoted in Chaloin, "Albert Ayler in Europe," 91.

8. "DON'T BE SCARED TO TELL THEM THE TRUTH"   421

91. Pinelli, "Ayler on Record," 112.
92. David Sandberg, "Bells," *Change* 2 (1966): 113.
93. Ayler's band also did a brief tour in Canada around this time. Charles Tyler, interview on WKCR-FM, July 26, 1974, audio recording, Ras Moshe Burnett private collection, July 26, 1974.
94. E. M. Burrus, "The Sound of . . . Something Different!," *Cleveland Call and Post*, July 24, 1965.
95. Albert Ayler, *Bells*; Burrus, "The Sound of . . . Something Different!"
96. Burrus, "The Sound of . . . Something Different!"
97. Donald Ayler, quoted in Burrus, "The Sound of . . . Something Different!"
98. Albert Ayler, *Spirits Rejoice* (ESP-Disk, 1965).
99. Ayler, quoted in Caux, "My Name Is . . . Albert Ayler," 24.
100. Henry Grimes, quoted in Alyn Shipton, "Interview with Henry Grimes," recorded May 2, 2009, broadcast on BBC Radio 3's Jazz Library program, May 23, 2009.
101. Pinelli, "Ayler on Record," 112.
102. Pinelli, "Ayler on Record," 111–12.
103. Baraka, "You Think This Is About You?," 40.
104. Alan Silva, interview by Ben Young, WKCR-FM, n.d., Ras Moshe Burnett private collection.
105. *Herald Express* (Birmingham, United Kingdom), February 18, 1966; Burrus, "The Sound of . . . Something Different!"
106. Joe Pinelli to Leni Sinclair, March 10, 1966, Box 1, Folder 43, JLSC.
107. *East Village Other*, March 15, 1966.
108. Baraka, "You Think This Is About You?," 40.
109. Leroi Jones, "The Changing Same (R&B and New Black Music)," in *The Black Aesthetic*, ed. Addison Gayle Jr. (Doubleday, 1971), 130.
110. Goldman and Davidson, "Albert Ayler: Life and Recordings," 9.
111. Mutawaf Shaheed, interview by author, digital recording, August 30, 2020; Mutawaf Shaheed, interview by author, digital recording, December 4, 2020.
112. The direct quote from Albert Ayler is: "When music changes, people change, too." Albert Ayler, untitled, *International Times* 10 (March 13–26, 1967): 9, reprinted and translated from Albert Ayler, untitled, *Jazz Magazine* 125 (December 1965): 41; Mutawaf Shaheed, interview, August 30, 2020; Mutawaf Shaheed, interview, December 4, 2020.
113. Bert Vuijsje, "Michel Samson: Ik Probeer Niet Echt Jazz te Spelen," *Jazzwereld*, March 11, 1967.
114. Goldman and Davidson, "Albert Ayler: Life and Recordings," 12.
115. Ayler quoted in Hentoff, "Albert Ayler—the Truth Is Marching In," 18.
116. Koyama, "Albert Ayler Interview."
117. Koyama, "Albert Ayler Interview."
118. *Cleveland Call and Post*, February 4, 1967.
119. Art Williams to Leni Sinclair, April 27, 1966, Box 1, Folder 46, JLSC; Art Williams to Leni Sinclair, May 25, 1966, Box 2, Folder 1, JLSC.
120. Steve Tintweiss, interview, June 1, 2022.
121. Michel Samson quoted in Rudie Kagie, "Avonturen in de New Thing," *Jazz Bulletin* 83 (June 2012): 37.
122. Bill Folwell, interview by Ben Young, WKCR-FM broadcast, Jazz Profiles, July 29, 2007, Ras Moshe Burnett private collection.
123. Beaver Harris, interview by Elliott Bratton, WKCR-FM broadcast, July 13, 1987, Ras Moshe Burnett private collection.
124. *Buffalo News*, November 4, 1966.
125. Daniel Caux, "Apparitions of Albert the Great in Paris and Saint-Paul-de-Vence," in Albert Ayler, *Holy Ghost* (Revenant, 2004), 100.
126. Folwell, interview by Ben Young.

127. *Evening Standard*, November 18, 1966.
128. Ayler quoted in Hentoff, "Albert Ayler—the Truth Is Marching In," 16.
129. Donald Ayler quoted in Hentoff, "Albert Ayler—the Truth Is Marching In," 16.
130. Ayler, quoted in Nat Hentoff, liner notes, Albert Ayler, *In Greenwich Village* (Impulse!, 1967).
131. Samson, quoted in Vuijsje, "Michel Samson."
132. Folwell, interview by Ben Young.
133. Harris, interview by Elliott Bratton.
134. Harris, interview by Elliott Bratton.
135. Ayler, quoted in Wilmer, "Ayler: Mystic Tenor."
136. Albert Ayler, *In Greenwich Village* (Impulse!, 1967); Albert Ayler, *The Village Concerts* (Impulse!, 1978).
137. *The Guardian*, January 23, 1967; Ayler, quoted in Hentoff, "Albert Ayler—the Truth Is Marching In," 18.
138. Ayler, quoted in Hentoff, "Albert Ayler—the Truth Is Marching In," 18.
139. Ayler was brought to the United Kingdom by BBC-2 for an interview and performance, but the recording was never aired. *The Guardian*, January 23, 1967.
140. Nai, "Alan Silva Interview," 11.
141. *New York Times*, February 27, 1967.
142. *Greensboro Record* (NC), January 15, 1968.
143. Ayler, quoted in Caux, "My Name Is . . . Albert Ayler," 24.
144. *Greensboro Record* (NC), January 15, 1968.
145. Derek Van Pelt, "Albert Ayler's Ghost," *Cleveland Magazine* (December 1978): 43.
146. Harris, interview by Elliott Bratton.
147. Samson, quoted in Vuijsje, "Michel Samson."
148. *Oakland Tribune*, December 17, 1967.
149. *Van Nuys News* (CA), January 26, 1968.
150. *Los Angeles Times*, July 3, 1967.
151. *Star-Gazette* (Elmira, NY), July 9, 1967; *Boston Globe*, July 9, 1967.
152. Kagie, "Avonturen in de New Thing," 37.
153. Ayler, quoted in Caux, "My Name Is . . . Albert Ayler," 24.
154. Koyama, "Albert Ayler Interview."
155. Ayler, quoted in Caux, "My Name Is . . . Albert Ayler," 24.
156. *Newsday* (Melville, NY), July 22, 1967.
157. *Orlando Evening Star*, August 10, 1967.
158. Albert Ayler, *Holy Ghost* (Revenant Records, 2004).
159. Harris, interview by Elliott Bratton.
160. Albert Ayler, *Love Cry* (Impulse!, 1968).
161. Silva, quoted in Nai, "Alan Silva Interview," 11–12.
162. Ayler, quoted in Caux, "My Name Is . . . Albert Ayler," 24.
163. Goldman and Davidson, "Albert Ayler: Life and Recordings," 11.
164. Goldman and Davidson, "Albert Ayler: Life and Recordings," 11.
165. *Kansas City Times*, August 4, 1966.
166. *Kingston Whig-Standard* (NY), February 3, 1968; February 22, 1969; July 12, 1969; July 24, 1971; February 24, 1973.
167. *San Francisco Examiner*, January 7, 1969.
168. *Knoxville News-Sentinel*, February 19, 1971; March 12, 1971; *Wisconsin State Journal*, August 15, 1971; *Ottawa Journal*, September 20, 1971; September 21, 1971; *New York Amsterdam News*, December 4, 1971; *Minneapolis Star*, February 26, 1973; *Star Tribune* (Minneapolis), March 4, 1973; *Montreal Star*, June 2, 1973; June 4, 1973.

169. Silva, quoted in Nai, "Alan Silva Interview," 12.
170. Koyama, "Albert Ayler Interview."
171. Alan Silva, interview by Ben Young.
172. Frank Kofsky to Leni Sinclair, May 29, 1966, Box 2, Folder 1, JLSC; Frank Kofsky to Leni Sinclair, Box 2, Folder 7, JLSC; John Sinclair to Leni Sinclair, July 10, 1966, Box 2, Folder 7, JLSC.
173. This effort may have been initially inspired by enthusiasm that followed a concert that Ayler played in San Francisco around 1967, though little information exists about the supposed performance. *Honolulu Star-Bulletin*, October 15, 1967; *Daily Utah Chronicle*, March 1, 1968.
174. Concert announcements appeared in August and December 1967, but there is no other evidence that they ever happened. *Montreal Star*, August 15, 1967; August 16, 1967; August 17, 1967; August 18, 1967; December 2, 1967; December 9, 1967.
175. Koyama, "Albert Ayler Interview."
176. Larry Neal, "New Grass/Albert Ayler," *Cricket* 3 (1969): 37.
177. Neal, "New Grass/Albert Ayler," 37.
178. Jones, "The Changing Same," 130.
179. Jones, "The Changing Same," 131.
180. *Buffalo Courier-Express*, March 10, 1968; *Buffalo News*, March 11, 1968.
181. *Buffalo Courier-Express*, March 10, 1968.
182. First Ayler quote from Koyama, "Albert Ayler Interview"; second quote from Caux, "My Name Is . . . Albert Ayler," 24.
183. Ayler, quoted in Caux, "My Name Is . . . Albert Ayler," 24.
184. Ayler, quoted in Caux, "My Name Is . . . Albert Ayler," 24.
185. *Sunday Sun* (Newcastle-upon-Tyne, UK), April 20, 1969.
186. *Daily Telegraph* (London), October 18, 1969.
187. Nai, "Alan Silva Interview," 12.
188. Alan Silva, interview by Ben Young.
189. Neal, "New Grass/Albert Ayler," 37–38.
190. Neal, "New Grass/Albert Ayler," 38–39.
191. *Columbus Leader*, March 30, 1969.
192. *News and Observer* (Raleigh, NC), March 30, 1969.
193. Ayler, quoted in Wilmer, "Spiritual Unity," 27.
194. Koyama, "Albert Ayler Interview."
195. Ayler, quoted in Caux, "My Name Is . . . Albert Ayler," 24; Koyama, "Albert Ayler Interview."
196. Albert Ayler, "To Mr. Jones—I Had a Vision," *Cricket* 3 (1969): 29–30.
197. Jones, "The Changing Same," 130.
198. Koyama, "Albert Ayler Interview."
199. Muhammad Ali, interview by author, digital recording, October 8, 2020.
200. Muhammad Ali, interview by author, digital recording, October 8, 2020. Two records ultimately emerged from the recording session. Albert Ayler, *Music Is the Healing Force of the Universe* (Impulse!, 1970); Albert Ayler, *The Last Album* (Impulse!, 1971).
201. Event poster, Black Mind, April 4, 1969, Ras Moshe Burnett private collection.
202. Ayler, quoted in Caux, "My Name Is . . . Albert Ayler," 24.
203. Harris, interview by Elliott Bratton.
204. Folwell, interview by Ben Young.
205. Koyama, "Albert Ayler Interview."
206. Robert Rusch, "Two: Ayler, Twice," *Hip* (1970): 17.
207. Ayler, quoted in Caux, "My Name Is . . . Albert Ayler," 24.
208. Koyama, "Albert Ayler Interview."
209. Caux, "Apparitions of Albert the Great," 100.

210. Koyama, "Albert Ayler Interview."
211. Koyama, "Albert Ayler Interview."
212. Wilmer, "Spiritual Unity," 27–28.
213. Steve Tintweiss, interview, June 1, 2022.
214. Steve Tintweiss, interview by author, digital recording, August 2, 2023.
215. Ayler, quoted in Caux, "My Name Is ... Albert Ayler," 24; Caux, "Apparitions of Albert the Great," 100.
216. Steve Tintweiss, interview, June 1, 2022.
217. Albert Ayler, *Holy Ghost* (Revenant, 2004).
218. Ayler, quoted in Caux, "My Name Is ... Albert Ayler," 24.
219. Steve Tintweiss, interview, August 2, 2023.
220. *Cleveland Call and Post*, December 12, 1970.
221. *New York Times*, December 20, 1970.
222. *New York Times*, December 20, 1970.
223. Don Cherry, interview on Albert Ayler.
224. Charles Tyler, quoted in Wilmer, "Spiritual Unity," 29.
225. Edward Ayler, quoted in *New York Times*, December 4, 1970.
226. "Musicians Boost Scholarship Fund," *Cleveland Call and Post*, March 6, 1971. Also see Naomi L. Fell, "Nai's Potpourri," *Cleveland Call and Post*, February 27, 1971; "Karamu Announces New Art Gallery," *Cleveland Call and Post*, March 27, 1971; Naomi L. Fell, "Nai's Potpourri," *Cleveland Call and Post*, April 10, 1971.
227. Fell, "Naomi's Potpourri," April 10, 1971.
228. Faruq Z. Bey, "Albert Ayler: 1936–1970," in *Solid Ground: A New World Journal* 1, no. 1 (1981): 39.
229. Neal, "New Grass/Albert Ayler," 37; Jones, "The Changing Same," 130–31.
230. Ayler, quoted in Caux, "My Name Is ... Albert Ayler," 24.

9. MIDWESTERN DRIFTER: CHARLES TYLER IN CALIFORNIA, NEW YORK, AND FRANCE

1. Epigraph: From French original, translated by author. Charles Tyler, quoted in "Charles Tyler," *Jazz Magazine* 12 (1965): 67.
2. Translated from French original by author. Charles Tyler, quoted in Chris Flicker, "Charles Tyler," *Jazz Magazine*, June 1977, 19.
3. From French original, translated by author. Tyler, quoted in "Charles Tyler," *Jazz Magazine* 12 (1965): 67.
4. Clifford Jay Safane, "Charles Tyler: The Saga of a Saxophonist," *Music Journal*, September 1979, 18.
5. Tyler, quoted in Safane, "Charles Tyler: The Saga of a Saxophonist," 18.
6. Charles Tyler, interview on WKCR-FM, July 26, 1974, audio recording, Ras Moshe Burnett private collection, July 26, 1974.
7. Earle Henderson, quoted in Valerie Wilmer, *As Serious as Your Life: The Story of the New Jazz* (Lawrence Hill, 1977), 104.
8. Barry Wallenstein, Charles Tyler memorial concert at St. Peters, New York, digital recording, n.d., Barry Wallenstein private collection.
9. Translated from French original by author. Tyler, quoted in Flicker, "Charles Tyler," 18.
10. Leroi Jones, *Black Music* (W. Morrow, 1967), 127, 135.
11. Joe Pinelli, "Ayler on Record: Lyrical Rockets," *Change* 2 (1966): 112.

12. K. Leander Williams, "Reissues," *Cadence* 19, no. 2 (February 1993): 19.
13. Translated from French original by author. Tyler, quoted in Flicker, "Charles Tyler," 18.
14. Safane, "Charles Tyler: The Saga of a Saxophonist," 19.
15. Ben Young, "Tracks," in Albert Ayler, *Holy Ghost* (Revenant, 2004), 148.
16. Mutawaf Shaheed, interview by author, digital recording, September 13, 2022.
17. Translated from French by author. Tyler, quoted in Flicker, "Charles Tyler," 18.
18. Moffett had risen to prominence from 1961 in groups led by Ornette Coleman and had previously led a group that included Pharoah Sanders and Carla Bley. Freedman had previously worked with Ayler. Grimes was one of the key free jazz bassists of the mid-1960s, performing with Cecil Taylor, Don Cherry, Steve Lacy, Pharoah Sanders, and many others. It was Ronald Jackson's first appearance on record.
19. Bob Rusch, "Charles Moffett Interview," *Cadence* 23, no. 2 (February 1997): 16.
20. *Coda*, December 1968, 17. *Klangfarbenmelodie* was a concept introduced by Arnold Schoenberg in 1911. It might be further defined as "a common twentieth-century practice in which the timbres of successive tones gain melodic importance comparable to that of pitch." Alfred Cramer, "Schoenberg's *Klangfarbenmelodie*: A Principle of Early Atonal Harmony," *Music Theory Spectrum* 24, no. 1 (2002): 1.
21. Tyler attended one semester at Indiana University, which likely coincided with one of his recording sessions in Indianapolis. Allan Morrison, "A New Surge in the Arts: Younger Generation Enhances Long Tradition of Creative Expression," *Ebony*, August 1967, 136.
22. It was the first appearance of McKesson and Brinkley on record. McKesson went on to record extensively with the Airmen of Note and also with the Tim Eyermann Quartet. Brinkley recorded on many records with Freddie Hubbard, among others. Baker was known primarily as a conductor, composer, and educator.
23. "Jazz Professor," *Ebony*, May 1970, 111.
24. Lloyd Weaver, liner notes, *Eastern Man Alone* (ESP-Disk, 1967).
25. Baker mentored many successful jazz figures over the years, including Randy Brecker, Jamey Aebersold, Freddie Hubbard, and Tyler, among others. Charles Tyler, quoted in Lloyd Weaver, liner notes, *Eastern Man Alone* (ESP-Disk, 1967); "Jazz Professor," 110–11.
26. "Jazz Professor," 110.
27. Brent McKesson, interview by author, digital recording, October 5, 2022.
28. Brent McKesson, interview.
29. David Baker, quoted in "Jazz Professor," 110.
30. Amiri Baraka, quoted in "Jazz Professor," 110.
31. McKesson was from South Bend, Indiana, and was drawn to jazz from an early age through a local community jazz orchestra. His father and sister were saxophone players. The first record that made an impression on him was Miles Davis's *Milestones* (Columbia, 1958), and he also listened to Charles Mingus extensively. Brent McKesson, interview.
32. Brent McKesson, interview.
33. Brent McKesson, interview.
34. Chuck Nessa, interview by Andreas Vingaard, email transcript, April 30–May 5, 2020.
35. Brent McKesson, interview.
36. Brent McKesson, interview.
37. Brent McKesson, interview.
38. Weaver, liner notes, *Eastern Man Alone*.
39. Tyler was involved in the Nation of Islam but never converted to orthodox Sunni Islam, though his wife did, and she raised their children as Muslims after he moved to Los Angeles in 1969. Mutawaf Shaheed, interview by author, digital recording, October 4, 2022; Akbar Tyler, interview by author, digital recording, February 3, 2023.

9. MIDWESTERN DRIFTER

40. Weaver wrote several books and later moved to Nigeria.
41. Weaver, liner notes, *Eastern Man Alone*.
42. Safane, "Charles Tyler: The Saga of a Saxophonist," 18.
43. Elliott Levin Quartet, *The Motion of Emotion*, Spirit Room 48 (CIMP, 1998); *Cadence* 24, no. 7 (July 1998): 121.
44. Tyler, quoted in Morrison, "A New Surge in the Arts," 138.
45. Raoul's birth name was Ralph Hoskins. Mutawaf Shaheed, interview, October 4, 2022.
46. Raoul was also a composer who may have been mentored by Emil Boyd. *Jazz*, April 1967, 18; Mutawaf Shaheed, interview, October 4, 2022.
47. "CORE Wants Negro Holiday on Date of Malcolm X's Death," *Cleveland Plain-Dealer*, February 10, 1968.
48. Wajid is otherwise unknown. Shabazz worked with Alice Coltrane from 1971 to 1973.
49. Translated from French by author. Guy Kopelowicz, "Impressions de New York," *Jazz Hot* 1 (1968): 21.
50. Translated from French by author. Kopelowicz, "Impressions de New York," 21.
51. The trumpeter Ahmed Abdullah's first ever live performance was sitting in with the band. The saxophonist Joe Rigby may have also played with the group. Ahmed Abdullah, interview by Andreas Vingaard, digital recording, May 9, 2020.
52. Ahmed Abdullah, interview by Andreas Vingaard.
53. The band's most popular song was the Beatles tune "Michelle," but they never recorded, and there is little other record of their activities. Translated from French original by author. Tyler quoted in Flicker, "Charles Tyler," 18.
54. Christian Gauffre, "Charles Tyler," *Jazz*, November 1985, 26.
55. Barry Wallenstein, interview by author, digital recording, November 15, 2022.
56. Translated from French by author. Tyler, quoted in Gauffre, "Charles Tyler," 26.
57. Translated from French by author. Tyler, quoted in Flicker, "Charles Tyler," 18.
58. Barry Wallenstein, Charles Tyler memorial concert.
59. Idris Ackamoor, interview by Andreas Vingaard, digital recording, April 25, 2020.
60. Even the musicians' union integrated in the early 1950s. A. B. Spellman, *Four Lives in the Bebop Business* (Limelight, 1966), 104–25; Wilmer, *As Serious as Your Life*, 68–70; John Litweiler, *The Freedom Principle: Jazz After 1958* (Da Capo, 1984), 33–40; Ted Gioia, *West Coast Jazz: Modern Jazz in California, 1945–1960* (Oxford University Press, 1992), 348–59; Horace Tapscott, "Horace Tapscott," in *Central Avenue Sounds: Jazz in Los Angeles*, ed. Clora Bryant et al. (University of California Press, 1998), 299; Horace Tapscott, *Songs of the Unsung: The Musical and Social Journey of Horace Tapscott*, ed. Steven Isoardi (Duke University Press, 2001): 36–37, 42–50; Steve Isoardi, *The Dark Tree: Jazz and Community Arts in Los Angeles* (University of California Press, 2006): 19, 30, 32–40.
61. Charles Sharp, "Seeking John Carter and Bobby Bradford: Free Jazz and Community in Los Angeles," *Black Music Research Journal* 31, no. 1 (2011): 65–81; Tapscott, *Songs of the Unsung*, 101; Isoardi, *Dark Tree*, 113.
62. "Spanish Gathering" is not otherwise known and was not recorded. Idris Ackamoor, interview.
63. Gauffre, "Charles Tyler," 26.
64. *San Francisco Chronicle*, May 28, 1971.
65. *General Catalogue, 1969–1970* (University of California–Berkeley, 1969), 419–22; *General Catalogue, 1970–1971* (University of California–Berkeley, 1970): 434–37; *General Catalogue, 1971–1972* (University of California–Berkeley, 1971), 76, 342–45.
66. *General Catalogue, 1973–1974* (University of California–Berkeley, 1973), 84, 380–83.
67. Miyoshi Smith, "Lawrence 'Butch' Morris Interview," *Cadence* 15, no. 7 (July 1989): 13.

68. David Durrah, interview by Andreas Vingaard, digital recording, April 17, 2020.
69. Safane, "Charles Tyler: The Saga of a Saxophonist," 19.
70. Tyler also played at New Orleans House in Berkeley. *Berkeley Tribe*, May 2–9, 1971; May 7–13, 1971; May 14–21, 1971; May 21–27, 1971; June 11–18, 1971; June 19–26, 1971; October 22–28, 1971.
71. David Durrah, interview by Andreas Vingaard, digital recording, April 17, 2020.
72. The student Roland P. Young claimed that the residency occurred in 1969, though 1970 or 1971 seem more likely. Roland P. Young, interview by Andreas Vingaard, digital recording, April 23, 2020; Idris Ackamoor, interview.
73. Roland P. Young, interview.
74. Roland P. Young, interview
75. Roland P. Young, interview.
76. The college had been previously named Merritt College, but that had moved to the eastern Oakland hills in 1971. The remaining students advocated to have the old college be renamed Grove Street College, but it was soon renamed again as Peralta Community College. Tyler also apparently taught at the Odyssey School in Berkeley.
77. Bobby Seale, "The Black Scholar Interviews: Bobby Seale," *Black Scholar* 4, no. 1 (September 1972): 8.
78. David Durrah, interview.
79. Lewis Jordan, interview by Andreas Vingaard, digital recording, March 20, 2020.
80. Lewis Jordan, interview.
81. Translated from French original by author. Tyler, quoted in Flicker, "Charles Tyler," 19.
82. Durrah taught music theory at Grove. David Durrah, interview; Idris Ackamoor, interview; Michael Wilderman, interview by Andreas Vingaard, digital recording, May 15, 2020.
83. David Murray, interview by Andreas Vingaard, digital recording, April 17, 2020.
84. David Durrah, interview.
85. The production continued to be publicly presented, and Tyler played with the play. "Jazz, Art, Drama to Highlight Black Culture Festival," *Hayward Daily Review*, June 15, 1971; *Berkeley Barb*, October 22, 1971.
86. Tyler's trio with Wilber Morris and Jackie Prentice never recorded.
87. Lewis Jordan, interview.
88. "The Queen" is one of numerous compositions by Charles Tyler that he never recorded. Lewis Jordan, interview.
89. David Durrah, interview.
90. David Murray, interview.
91. Glenn Spearman, quoted in Bob Rusch, "Glenn Spearman Interview," *Cadence* 20, no. 5 (May 1994): 8, 14.
92. Tyler's childhood friend recalled seeing him in Colorado in 1970. Wilmer, *As Serious as Your Life*, 244, 281; David Williams, interview by Andreas Vingaard, digital recording, May 15, 2020.
93. Steve Buchanan, "A Conversation with James Newton," *The Grackle* 1, no. 5 (1979): 16.
94. Mae Tate, "Scan Profile: Stanley Crouch—'Art Is Power' His Belief," *Progress Bulletin* (Pomona, CA), May 1, 1971.
95. Charles Tyler, interview on WKCR-FM.
96. Translated from French original by author. Tyler, quoted in Flicker, "Charles Tyler," 19.
97. *New York Times*, February 26, 1974.
98. Charles Tyler, interview on WKCR-FM.
99. William Parker, interview by Andreas Vingaard, digital recording, May 8, 2020.
100. Charles Tyler, interview on WKCR-FM, audio recording, Ras Moshe Burnett private collection, July 26, 1974.

101. Randy Hutton, review of Rivbea Summer Music Festival, *Coda* 11 (September 1974): 32.
102. Translated from German original by author. Charles Tyler, quoted in Ekkhard Jost, *Jazzmusiker: Materialen zur Soziologie der Afro-Amerikanischen Musik* (Ullstein, 1982), 128.
103. *The Grackle* 1, no. 3 (1976): 43.
104. Charles Tyler, interview on WKCR-FM.
105. Mutawaf Shaheed, interview, October 4, 2022.
106. *The Grackle* 1, no. 3 (1976): 43.
107. *The Grackle* 1, no. 3 (1976): 43.
108. *Cadence* 1, no. 6 (June 1976): 20.
109. Thomas Albright, "A Looping, Soaring Tyler 'Voyage,'" *San Francisco Examiner*, May 30, 1976.
110. Keith Knox, "Earl Cross: Interview," *Cadence* 9, no. 7 (July 1983): 6.
111. William Parker, interview by Andreas Vingaard.
112. *The Grackle* 1, no. 3 (1976): 42.
113. William Parker, interview by Andreas Vingaard.
114. Charles Tyler, interview on WKCR-FM.
115. Jost, *Jazzmusiker*, 128.
116. Translated from German by author. Tyler, quoted in Jost, *Jazzmusiker*, 128.
117. Ted Daniel, interview by Andreas Vingaard, digital recording, April 23, 2020.
118. Ted Daniel, *In the Beginning* (Altura Music, 1997).
119. Charles Tyler, *Live in Europe: Jazz Festival Umea* (AK-BA Records, 1977).
120. *San Francisco Examiner*, June 19, 1977.
121. *San Francisco Examiner*, June 19, 1977.
122. *New York Times*, March 7, 1976; *The Grackle* 1, no. 2 (1976): 42; "Steve Lacy," *The Grackle* 1, no. 3 (1976): 14.
123. Peter Occhiogrosso, "Up from Under," *Soho Weekly News*, March 11, 1976.
124. *Cadence* 1, no. 8 (July 1976): 2; Charles Tyler Ensemble, *Saga of the Outlaws* (Nessa Records, 1978).
125. Charles Tyler Ensemble, *Saga of the Outlaws* (Nessa Records, 1978).
126. Charles Tyler, liner notes, Charles Tyler Ensemble, *Saga of the Outlaws* (Nessa Records, 1978).
127. Translated from French by author. Tyler quoted in Emanuele Pinotti, "Charles Lacy Tyler," *Improjazz* (February 1997): 20.
128. Tyler, quoted in Safane, "Charles Tyler: The Saga of a Saxophonist," 18–19.
129. Safane, "Charles Tyler: The Saga of a Saxophonist," 18.
130. Norman Weinstein, "Charles Tyler's *Saga of the Outlaws*: Jazz at the Threshold of a Shootout," *Noh Quarter* (1987): 43–4.
131. Log Book, The Brook, Frank Ferrucci private collection, n.d., 41.
132. Log Book, The Brook, 25.
133. Ferrucci played with Gato Barbieri among others. *New York Times*, May 5, 1976; May 28, 1976; Janice Geller, interview by Andreas Vingaard, digital recording, May 8, 2020.
134. Log Book, The Brook.
135. Janice Geller, interview.
136. *New York Times*, May 5, 1976; May 28, 1976; June 2, 1976; June 4, 1976; June 19, 1976; November 14, 1976.
137. Frank Ferrucci, interview by Andreas Vingaard, digital recording, April 2, 2020.
138. *New York Times*, September 3, 1976; June 3, 1977; June 4, 1977; Log Book, The Brook, 47–52, 59–63, 71, 143, 172, 174–75, 184, 204, 208, 212, 218, 250, 258–59; William Parker, interview by Andreas Vingaard; Ahmed Abdullah, interview by Andreas Vingaard.
139. Frank Ferrucci, interview.
140. William Parker, interview by Andreas Vingaard.

9. MIDWESTERN DRIFTER   429

141. Stanley Crouch, "Jazz Lofts: A Walk Through the Wild Sounds," *New York Times*, April 17, 1977.
142. Frank Ferrucci, interview by Andreas Vingaard.
143. Robert Palmer, "Music: At Brook," *New York Times*, September 12, 1976.
144. Charles Tyler, interview on WKCR-FM.
145. Translated from French original by author. Tyler, quoted in Flicker, "Charles Tyler," 19.
146. Tyler obtained grants from Jazz/Folk/Ethnic Performance Fellowship Grant from the National Endowment for the Arts and from the Meet the Composer fund. The Cleveland cellist Abdul Wadud also played. Flicker, "Charles Tyler," 18.
147. This concert was sponsored by Creative Energy Center Corporation and Next Stop Productions, November 5–7, 1976. Andreas Vingaard, email to author, June 30, 2022.
148. *New York Times*, March 6, 1977; April 8, 1977; June 5, 1977; INTERface, *Live at Environ* (ReEntry Records, 1977); *Radio Free Jazz* 19, no. 3 (March 1978): 12; INTERface, *Environ Days* (Konnex, 1991).
149. Robert Palmer, "Interface, Jazz Band, Evolves Over a Year," *New York Times*, June 5, 1977.
150. Robert Palmer, "Brubecks Top Weekend of Loft Jazz," *New York Times*, April 8, 1977.
151. *Cadence* 3, no. 10 (February 1978): 39.
152. John Fischer, *6x1=10 Duos for a New Decade* (ReEntry Records, 1980), tracks 8–9.
153. Andreas Vingaard, email.
154. Wallenstein was also influenced by Ezra Pound, William Carlos Williams, and proletarian poets such as Kenneth Fearing and Kenneth Patchen.
155. Barry Wallenstein, interview by author, digital recording, June 16, 2022.
156. The duo also played often in New York City public schools, giving workshops or putting on concerts. Log Book, The Brook, 224–25, 241; *New York Times*, October 16, 1977; *Cadence* 5, no. 11 (November 1979): 43; Andreas Vingaard, email; Barry Wallenstein, interview, June 16, 2022; Barry Wallenstein, interview by author, digital recording, November 15, 2022.
157. Barry Wallenstein, quoted in Joyce White, "Poetry and Jazz Sound a High Note for Students," *Daily News* (New York), December 20, 1977.
158. Barry Wallenstein, interview, November 15, 2022.
159. Barry Wallenstein, *Taking Off* (AK-BA Records, 1982).
160. Barry Wallenstein, interview, November 15, 2022.
161. Eugene Chadbourne, interview by Andreas Vingaard, email transcript, April 19, 2020.
162. Eugene Chadbourne and Charles Tyler, *Ghost Legends* (House of Chadula, n.d.)
163. Eugene Chadbourne, interview.
164. Eugene Chadbourne, interview.
165. *Cadence* 2, no. 12 (July 1977): 16.
166. *Cadence* 3, no. 1 (August 1977): 58.
167. Translated from French original by author. Tyler, quoted in Flicker, "Charles Tyler," 19.
168. Translated from French original by author. Tyler, quoted in Flicker, "Charles Tyler," 18.
169. Translated from French original by author. Tyler, quoted in Flicker, "Charles Tyler," 18–19.
170. *Cadence* 3, no. 7 (December 1977): 64.
171. *Cadence* 3, no. 7 (December 1977): 64.
172. *Cadence* 3, no. 10 (February 1978): 68; Andreas Vingaard, email.
173. *Cadence* 4, no. 4 (July 1978): 75.
174. Roland P. Young, interview; Andreas Vingaard, email.
175. Roland P. Young, interview.
176. *New York Times*, December 14, 1978.
177. Robert Palmer, "Charles Tyler Adds to Range," *New York Times*, February 20, 1979.
178. Palmer, "Charles Tyler Adds to Range."
179. Charles Tyler, liner notes, Charles Tyler Ensemble, *Saga of the Outlaws*.

180. He also played solo at Soundscape, May 5, 1979, which was broadcast on WBAI, hosted by Vera Gillis. Another performance on September 20, 1979, was broadcast live on WKCR. *New York Times*, April 21, 1978; *New York Times*, May 5, 1979; Andreas Vingaard, email.
181. Charles Tyler Solo, Live at Environ, April 21, 1978, analog recording, Ras Moshe Burnett private collection.
182. Bob Jordan, email to Andreas Vingaard, n.d.
183. Tyler also played in Dunbar's bands, and they recorded one duet track together that was released on Dunbar's label. Richard Dunbar, *Running Buddies*, vol. 1 (Jahari, 1983); Andreas Vingaard, email.
184. *Cadence* 5, no. 10 (October 1979): 79; *Cadence* 5, no. 11 (November 1979): 43; Andreas Vingaard, email.
185. Morris later invited Tyler to record with the former's trio, which also included the drummer Denis Charles in 1981. Charles Tyler, *Folk and Mystery Stories* (Sonet, 1981); Wilber Morris Trio, *Collective Improvisations* (Bleu Regard, 1994); Andreas Vingaard, email.
186. Tyler, quoted in Pinotti, "Charles Lacy Tyler," 20.
187. David Baker, interview by Lida Baker, transcript, June 19–21, 2000, Archives Center, National Museum of American History, Smithsonian Institution, Washington.
188. Robert Palmer, "Cabaret: Tyler on Saxophone," *New York Times*, December 9, 1980.
189. Frank Ferrucci, interview by Andreas Vingaard.
190. *New York Times*, May 29, 1977. The saxophonists Arthur Blythe and Arthur Doyle both recorded records there in 1977, for instance. Arthur Blythe, *The Grip* (India Navigation, 1977); Arthur Doyle Plus 4, *Alabama Feeling* (AK-BA Records, 1978).
191. *Cadence* 7, no. 2 (February 1981): 4.
192. Billy Bang and Charles Tyler, *Live at Green Space* (Anima Productions, 1982); Billy Bang Quartet, *Rainbow Gladiator* (Soul Note, 1981); Billy Bang Quintet, *Invitation* (Soul Note, 1982); Billy Bang, *Outline no. 12* (Celluloid, 1983).
193. Charles Tyler Quartet, *Definite*, vol. 1 (Storyville, 1982); Charles Tyler Quartet, *Definite*, vol. 2 (Storyville, 1984).
194. Robert Palmer, "Cabaret: Tyler on Saxophone," *New York Times*, December 9, 1980.
195. *Cadence* 8, no. 1 (January 1982): 95.
196. John S. Wilson, "Jazz: Cecil Taylor and Band at Club," *New York Times*, March 12, 1982.
197. This also likely led Tyler to be involved in the William Parker Centering Big Band performance at the Kool Jazz Festival in June 1984. John S. Wilson, "Kool Festival: A Tribute to Basie, Opens Today," *New York Times*, June 22, 1984.
198. Jon Pareles, "Tyler, Lyons and New Music," *New York Times*, July 5, 1983.
199. Charles Tyler Ensemble, *Live at Sweet Basil*, 2 vols. (Bleu Regard, 2006).
200. *New York Times*, June 1, 1984; *Rising Tones Cross*, film by Ebba Jahn (FilmPals, 1985).
201. Translated from French by author. Tyler quoted in Gauffre, "Charles Tyler," 26.
202. Tyler quoted in Safane, "Charles Tyler: The Saga of a Saxophonist," 19.
203. Translated from German by author. Tyler quoted in Jost, *Jazzmusiker*, 129.
204. Frank Ferrucci, interview by Andreas Vingaard.
205. Charles Doherty to Hartmut Geerken, October 17, 1984, Sun Ra Archives.
206. Robert L. Campbell and Christopher Trent, *The Earthly Recordings of Sun Ra* (Cadence Jazz Books, 1994).
207. Translated from French by author. Tyler, quoted in Gauffre, "Charles Tyler," 27.
208. Pinotti, "Charles Lacy Tyler," 21.
209. Steve Lacy Quartet Featuring Charles Tyler, *One Fell Swoop* (Silkheart, 1987); Charles Tyler/Brus Trio, *Autumn in Paris* (Silkheart, 1988).
210. Gauffre, "Charles Tyler," 27.
211. Translated from French by author. Tyler quoted in Gauffre, "Charles Tyler," 27.

212. Tyler's son, Akbar, conducted extensive interviews with his father, but unfortunately the cassette tapes were later lost. Akbar Tyler, interview.
213. Barry Wallenstein, interview, November 15, 2022.
214. Tyler had been scheduled to play a concert in France with Denis Charles and Bernard Santacruz on July 3. They played with him in absence as the first of a number of memorials in his honor. They played again at the memorial at St. Peter's Cathedral in New York in early 1993. Barry Wallenstein, Charles Tyler memorial concert.
215. Barry Wallenstein, interview, November 15, 2022.
216. Translated from French original by author. Tyler, quoted in Flicker, "Charles Tyler," 19.
217. Tyler, quoted in Safane, "Charles Tyler: The Saga of a Saxophonist," 19.

10. ARTISTIC LIBERATION ABROAD: FRANK WRIGHT, BOBBY FEW, MUHAMMAD ALI, AND ALAN SILVA IN NEW YORK AND PARIS

1. Epigraph: Simone Few, interview by author, digital recording, March 22, 2022.
2. Valerie Wilmer, *As Serious as Your Life: The Story of the New Jazz* (Lawrence Hill, 1977), 25.
3. Kamal Abdul Alim, interview by author, digital recording, January 31, 2021.
4. One of the lesser-known Clevelanders of this generation, Jeffries recorded with the saxophonists Booker Ervin and Marzette Watts in the late 1960s. Booker Ervin, *The In Between* (Blue Note, 1968); Marzette Watts Ensemble, *Marzette Watts Ensemble* (Savoy Records, 1969).
5. Kamal Abdul Alim, interview, January 31, 2021.
6. Frank Wright Quintet, *Your Prayer* (ESP-Disk, 1967).
7. Muhammad Ali, interview by author, digital recording, July 7, 2020.
8. Sunny Murray, quoted in Wilmer, *As Serious as Your Life*, 50.
9. Muhammad Ali, interview, July 7, 2020.
10. Muhammad Ali, interview by author, digital recording, October 8, 2020.
11. Muhammad Ali, interview, July 7, 2020.
12. Steve Tintweiss, interview by author, digital recording, June 1, 2022; Steve Tintweiss, interview by author, digital recording, August 2, 2023.
13. Derek Taylor, review of *Center of the World* (Center of the World, 1972; reissued: Fractal, 1999) and *Last Polka in Nancy?* (Center of the World, 1973, reissued: Fractal, 1999), *Cadence* 25, no. 11 (November 1999): 29.
14. Larry Nai, "Alan Silva Interview," *Cadence* 25, no. 7 (July 1999): 14.
15. *Stanford Daily*, May 1, 1968.
16. *Stanford Daily*, May 1, 1968.
17. Nai, "Alan Silva Interview," 14.
18. Dan Warburton, "Alan Silva: Interviews with Dan Warburton," *Paris Transatlantic*, November 8–22, 2002, http://www.paristransatlantic.com/magazine/interviews/silva.html.
19. Bob Rusch, "Andrew Cyrille Interview, Part Two," *Cadence* 21, no. 2 (February 1995): 27–28.
20. Ervin, *The In Between*.
21. Don Lass, "Record Previews," *Asbury Park Press*, February 1969, 4.
22. *Cleveland Call and Post*, March 1, 1969; March 15, 1969; April 12, 1969; Albert Ayler, *Music Is the Healing Force of the Universe* (Impulse!, 1970); Albert Ayler, *The Last Album* (Impulse!, 1971).
23. Sunny Murray, interview by Clifford Allen, written transcript, Clifford Allen private collection. An abridged version of the interview was published: Clifford Allen, "Interview: Sunny Murray," *All About Jazz—New York* 18 (October 2003): 5, 25.

24. Nai, "Alan Silva Interview," 16–17.
25. Eric Drott, "Free Jazz and the French Critic," *Journal of the American Musicological Society* 61, no. 3 (2008): 542.
26. Pierre Crepon, "The Summer of '69," *Chimurenga: Imagi-nation Nwar*, April 2021, 26.
27. Larry Nai, "Alan Silva Interview," *Cadence* 25, no. 7 (July 1999): 16.
28. Alan Silva quoted in Crepon, "Summer of '69," 28.
29. Wilmer, *As Serious as Your Life*, 229.
30. Nai, "Alan Silva Interview," 17.
31. Alan Silva, interview by author, digital recording, February 25, 2022.
32. Alan Silva and His Celestial Communications Orchestra, *Luna Surface* (BYG Records, 1969); Alan Silva and the Celestial Communications Orchestra, *Seasons* (BYG Records, 1971). The latter recording included Silva (bass, sarangi); Alan Shorter (trumpet); Lester Bowie (trumpet, flugelhorn); Bernard Vitet (trumpet, French horn); Ronnie Beer (tenor and soprano saxophones, flute); Joseph Jarman (saxophone, flute, bassoon); Robin Kenyatta (alto saxophone, flute); Steve Lacy (soprano saxophone); Roscoe Mitchell (saxophone, flute, oboe); Michel Portal (alto saxophone, clarinet); Bobby Few, Dave Burrell, and Joachim Kuhn (piano); Jouk Minor (viola); Irene Aebi (cello, celeste); Kent Carter (cello); Beb Guérin (bass); Malachi Favors (bass, whistle); Jerome Cooper and Don Moye (drums, percussion); Oliver Johnson (timpani, percussion).
33. Alan Silva, interview, February 25, 2022.
34. Alan Silva, interview, February 25, 2022.
35. Silva quoted in Wilmer, *As Serious as Your Life*, 253.
36. Bobby Few was a versatile musician and played in a lot of different circles. In addition to the BYG community and free jazz bands like Wright's quartet, he also played with hard boppers such as the drummer Philly Joe Jones, as well as cocktail jazz music to support himself. He soon began composing himself. Alan Silva, interview by author, digital recording, March 11, 2022.
37. Quoted by S. Stern in M. V. Miller and S. Gilmore, *Revolution at Berkeley* (Laurel, 1965), 232–33; Pierre Vidal-Naquet, "Outline of a Revolution," in *The French Student Uprising November 1967–June 1968: An Analytical Record*, ed. Alain Schapp and Pierre Vidal-Naquet, trans. Maria Jolas (Beacon, 1969), 31–36.
38. Schapp and Vidal-Naquet, *French Student Uprising*, 74–85.
39. Schapp and Vidal-Naquet, *French Student Uprising*, 155–56, 159–62, 189–90.
40. Angelo Quattrocchi, "What Happened," in Angelo Quattrocchi and Tom Nairn, *The Beginning of the End* (Panther Books, 1968; repr. Verso, 1998).
41. Simone Few, interview.
42. Daniel Carter, interview by author, digital recording, January 13, 2021.
43. Frank Wright, quoted in François Postif, "The Noah Howard-Frank Wright Quartet: Une Interview de François Postif," *Jazz Hot* 257 (January 1970): 18–19.
44. Frank Wright, cited in Michel Fibre, *From Harlem to Paris: Black American Writers in France, 1840–1980* (University of Illinois Press, 1991), 260. Also see Drott, "Free Jazz and the French Critic," 572.
45. Simone Few, interview.
46. Wilmer, *As Serious as Your Life*, 251.
47. Translated from French by author. Serge Loupien, *La France underground: Free jazz et rock pop, 1965/1979, le temps des utopies* (Rivages Rouge, 2018), 178.
48. Simone Few, interview.
49. Paul Alessandrini, "Freepop," *Jazz* 173 (December 1969): 28.
50. Wilmer, *As Serious as Your Life*, 251.
51. Noah Howard, quoted in Wilmer, *As Serious as Your Life*, 251.
52. Simone Few, interview.

10. ARTISTIC LIBERATION ABROAD

53. Noah Howard, quoted in Larry Nai, "Noah Howard Interview," *Cadence* 24, no. 1 (January 1998): 6.
54. Howard, quoted in Nai, "Noah Howard Interview," 6. Most of his experience with those players, as well as Ornette Coleman's trumpeter Dewey Johnson, came in after-hours sessions on the West Coast in the early 1960s. See Valerie Wilmer, "Noah: Feeling for His Roots," *Melody Maker*, May 1, 1971, 26.
55. Wilmer, "Noah: Feeling for His Roots," 26.
56. Noah Howard Quartet, *Noah Howard Quartet* (ESP-Disk, 1966).
57. Noah Howard, *Space Dimension* (America Records, 1971).
58. Lieve Fransen, interview by author, digital recording, December 9, 2020.
59. Kamal Abdul Alim, interview, January 31, 2021.
60. Howard quoted in Nai, "Noah Howard Interview," 6–7.
61. Bob Rusch, review of Frank Wright, *One for John* (BYG, 1970), *Cadence* 5, no. 10 (October 1979): 29.
62. Muhammad Ali, interview by author, digital recording, July 22, 2020.
63. Muhammad Ali, interview, July 22, 2020.
64. Frank Wright Quartet, live in Amsterdam, December 1970, archival recording, https://www.youtube.com/watch?v=PeMTENwtCCQ.
65. Guillaume Belhomme, "All Wright: Souvenir de Music in My Soul," in *Free Fight: This Is Our (New) Thing*, ed. Guillaume Belhomme and Philippe Robert (Camion Blanc, 2012), 141.
66. Belhomme, "All Wright," 143.
67. Alan Silva, interview by author, digital recording, March 4, 2022. It also seems that at times Howard was unfairly overshadowed by Wright. The *Uhuru na Umoja* date, for example, was Howard's session, but the record was released under Wright's name. This seems more a product of the record labels than any maneuverings by the musicians themselves. Wilmer, "Noah: Feeling for His Roots," 26.
68. Silva had previously left Cecil Taylor's band on the grounds that it was not named as a collective. Alan Silva, interview, March 4, 2022.
69. Alan Silva, interview, March 4, 2022.
70. Muhammad Ali, interview, July 22, 2022.
71. Center of the World, *Center of the World*, vol. 1 (Center of the World, 1972).
72. Taylor, review of Frank Wright Unit: *Center of the World* (Center of the World, 1972), *Cadence* 4, no. 11 (1978): 46.
73. Taylor, review of *Center of the World*, 29.
74. Taylor, review of *Center of the World*, 29.
75. Taylor, review of *Center of the World*, 29.
76. Taylor, review of *Center of the World*, 29.
77. *Cadence* 17, no. 10 (October 1991): 86; Yosuke Yamashita Trio, *Ghosts by Albert Ayler* (West Wind, 1990).
78. Taylor, review of *Center of the World*, 29.
79. Alan Silva, interview, March 4, 2022.
80. Raphe Malik, quoted in Bob Rusch, "Raphe Malik Interview," *Cadence* 20, no. 11 (November 1994): 9.
81. Muhammad Ali, interview, July 22, 2022.
82. Alan Silva, interview by author, digital recording, March 11, 2022.
83. Alan Silva, interview, March 11, 2022.
84. Muhammad Ali, interview, July 7, 2020.
85. The record ultimately sold approximately ten thousand copies. Nai, "Alan Silva Interview," 7.
86. Alan Silva, interview, Mar 4ch, 2022. Also see Nai, "Alan Silva Interview," 7.
87. Nai, "Alan Silva Interview," 8.

88. Bob Rusch, "Glenn Spearman Interview," *Cadence* 20, no. 5 (May 1994): 10–11.
89. Rusch, "Glenn Spearman Interview," 8.
90. Raphe Malik, quoted in Rusch, "Raphe Malik Interview," 9.
91. Center of the World, *Volume 2: Last Polka in Nancy?* (Center of the World, 1973).
92. Taylor, review of *Center of the World*, 30.
93. Barry McRae, "Avant Courier: Frank Wright—Working on," *Jazz Journal* 28, no. 8 (August 1978): 13.
94. McRae, "Avant Courier: Frank Wright," 13.
95. Frank Wright, *Unity* (ESP-Disk, 2006).
96. Scott Verrastro, "Frank Wright: Unity," *Jazz Times*, April 25, 2019.
97. "1974, June 8," Willisau Jazz Archive, Lucerne University of Applied Arts and Sciences, https://www.willisaujazzarchive.ch/concerts/1974/1094.html; "1974, October 12," Willisau Jazz Archive, Lucerne University of Applied Arts and Sciences, https://www.willisaujazzarchive.ch/concerts/1974/1097.html.
98. Center of the World, *Volume 3: More or Less Few* (Center of the World, n.d.); Center of the World, *Volume 4: Adieu Little Man* (Center of the World, n.d.); Center of the World, *Volume 5: Inner Song* (Center of the World, 1978); Center of the World, *Volume 6: Solos & Duets* (Center of the World, n.d.); Center of the World, *Volume 7: Solos & Duets* (Center of the World, 1975).
99. Bob Rusch, review of Bobby Few, Alan Silva, Frank Wright, *Solo et Duets* (Sun Records, 1975), *Cadence* 2, no. 5 (February 1977): 35–36.
100. Loupien, *La France underground*, 178.
101. Alan Silva, interview, March 4, 2022.
102. Nai, "Alan Silva Interview," 18.
103. Richard Roux, quoted in Loupien, *La France underground*, 179.
104. H. Lukas Lindenmaier, "Peter Brötzmann: Interview," *Cadence* 4, no. 10 (October 1978): 41.
105. Muhammad Ali, interview, July 22, 2022.
106. Frank Wright Quartet, *Blues for Albert Ayler* (ESP-Disk, 2012).
107. Robert Palmer, "Frank Wright's Saxophone Warms Ali's Alley," *New York Times*, January 6, 1977.
108. *New York Magazine*, April 2, 1979.
109. Larry Nai, "Khan Jamal Interview," *Cadence* 24, no. 11 (November 1998): 21.
110. Frank Wright and George Arvanitas, *Shouting the Blues* (Sun Records, 1977).
111. Rusch, "Glenn Spearman Interview," 9.
112. Kamal Abdul Alim, interview, January 31, 2021.
113. Abdul Alim also stated, "Frank would notate his experiences through drawings. They were very crudely drawn. It was like somebody scribbling emotions on paper." Kamal Abdul Alim, interview, January 31, 2021.
114. Translation from French by author. Loupien, *La France underground*, 177.
115. Frank Wright Sextet, *Stove Man, Love Is the Word* (Sandra Music Productions, 1979).
116. Kamal Abdul Alim, interview, January 31, 2021.
117. Louis Moholo-Moholo et al., *Spiritual Knowledge and Grace* (Ogun, 2011).
118. Peter Brötzmann Group, *Alarm* (FMP, 1983).
119. Alan Silva, interview, March 4, 2022.
120. Thomas Borgmann, interview by author, digital recording, June 8, 2023.
121. Rusch, "Glenn Spearman Interview," 9.
122. Lindenmaier, "Peter Brötzmann: Interview," 40.
123. Cisco Bradley, *Universal Tonality: The Life and Music of William Parker* (Duke University Press, 2021), 161–64.
124. Rusch, "Glenn Spearman Interview," 9.
125. Rusch, "Andrew Cyrille Interview, Part 2," 28.

126. Trio Hurricane, *Suite of Winds* (Black Saint, 1994); Zusaan Kali Fasteau et al., *Expatriate Kin* (CIMP, 1997).
127. *Cadence* 25, no. 12 (December 1999): 20.
128. Bobby Few, *Few Coming Thru* (Sun Records, 1977); Bobby Few, *Jazz Continental Express* (Vogue, 1979).
129. Michael Smith, quoted in Milo Fine, "Michael Smith: Interview," *Cadence* 11, no. 9 (September 1985): 11.
130. Alan Silva and the Celestial Communications Orchestra, *The Shout: Portrait for a Small Woman* (Chiaroscuro Records, 1979); Alan Silva and the Celestial Communication Orchestra, *Desert Mirage* (I.A.C.P., 1982).
131. ICP Tentet, *Tetterettet* (Instant Composers Pool, 1977).
132. Schlippenbach Quartet, *Anticlockwise* (FMP, 1983); Schlippenbach Quartett, *Das Hohe Lied* (Po Torch Records, 1991); Globe Unity Orchestra, *Intergalactic Blow* (Japo Records, 1983); Globe Unity Orchestra, *20th Anniversary* (FMP, 1993).
133. Nai, "Alan Silva Interview," 16.
134. Burton Greene, *Firmanence* (Fore, 1980); Andrew Hill Trio, *Strange Serenade* (Soul Note, 1980); Sunny Murray Quintet, *Aigu-Grave* (Marge, 1980); Burton Greene and Alan Silva, *The Ongoing Strings* (Hat Hut Records, 1981).
135. Nai, "Alan Silva Interview," 5.
136. Alan Silva, interview by author, digital recording, February 8, 2023.
137. Alan Silva, interview, February 8, 2023.
138. Archie Shepp Quintet, *Live 1973* (Blu Jazz, n.d.).
139. Saheb Sarbib Quartet, *Live in Europe*, vol. 2 (Marge, 1976).
140. Rashied Al Akbar et al., *Ascent of the Nether Creatures* (NoBusiness Records, 2014).
141. Michel Pilz Quartet, *Jamabiko* (M.P., 1984).
142. Lieve Fransen, interview.
143. David S. Ware et al., *Planetary Unknown* (AUM Fidelity, 2011); David S. Ware et al., *Planetary Unknown: Live at the Jazzfestival Saalfelden 2011* (AUM Fidelity, 2012).

CONCLUSION: LEGACIES OF FREEDOM IN SOUND

1. Mutawaf Shaheed, interview by author, digital recording, December 4, 2020.

BIBLIOGRAPHY

ARCHIVES

Alabama Department of Archives and History. Montgomery, AL.
Alderman Library, University of Virginia. Charlottesville, VA.
Barry Wallenstein private collection. New York, NY.
Bentley Historical Library, University of Michigan. Ann Arbor, MI.
Birmingham Public Library. Birmingham, AL.
Carrollton Courthouse. Carrollton, MS.
Clifford Allen private collection. Kingston, NY.
Filson Club. Louisville, KY.
Frank Ferucci private collection.
Georgia Historical Society. Savannah, GA.
Georgia State University Archives. Atlanta, GA.
GM&O Historical Society Archives. Online.
Kenan Research Center, Atlanta History Center. Atlanta, GA.
Library of Congress. Washington, DC.
Library of Richmond. Richmond, VA.
Madison County Courthouse. Canton, MS.
Marion County Courthouse. Indianapolis, IN.
Middle Georgia Regional Library. Macon, GA.
Mississippi Department of Archives and History. Jackson, MS.
Monteith College Archives, Wayne State University. Detroit, MI.
National Archives. Washington, DC.
National Archives at St. Louis. St. Louis, MO.
National Museum of American History, Smithsonian Institution. Washington, DC.
Oberlin College Archives. Oberlin, OH.
Ras Moshe private collection. New York, NY.
School of Commerce and Business Administration, University of Alabama. Tuscaloosa, AL.
Sun Ra Archives. Philadelphia, PA.
University of Kentucky Library. Lexington, KY.
Upson Historical Society. Thomaston, GA.

Virginia State Archives. Richmond, VA.
Western Reserve Historical Society, Case Western Reserve University. Cleveland, OH.
William R. Perkins Library, Duke University. Durham, NC.
Willisau Jazz Archive, Lucerne University of Applied Arts and Sciences. Lucerne, Switzerland.

ARCHIVAL SOURCES

This study employs numerous census records which are summarized here for the sake of brevity.

1810 US Census

Kentucky: Woodford

1820 US Census

Ohio: Pike

1830 US Census

Kentucky: Franklin
Ohio: Pike

1840 US Census

Kentucky: Franklin
Mississippi: Madison
Ohio: Pike

1850 US Census

Indiana: Vanderburgh
Ohio: Gallia, Jackson, Miami, Shelby

1860 US Census

Kentucky: Franklin
Ohio: Gallia, Jackson, Miami, Seneca
Wisconsin: Milwaukee

1870 US Census

Alabama: Greene, Hale, Lee, Lowndes
Arkansas: Phillips
Georgia: Jasper, Pike, Stewart, Upson
Kentucky: Franklin, Pendleton, Trigg
Mississippi: Carroll, Hinds, Lafayette, Lauderdale, Noxubee
Ohio: Cuyahoga, Jackson
Virginia: Bedford

1880 US Census

Alabama: Dallas, Greene, Hale, Lauderdale, Lee, Mobile, Newton
Florida: Madison
Georgia: Jasper, Upson, Wilkes
Indiana: Marion
Kentucky: Pendleton, Trigg
Mississippi: Lauderdale, Noxubee, Warren, Yazoo
Ohio: Cuyahoga, Miami

1890 US Census

Ohio: Seneca (veterans schedule)

1900 US Census

Alabama: Autauga, Dallas, Jefferson, Lauderdale, Mobile, Newton
Florida: Suwannee
Georgia: Bibb, Fulton, Hancock, Jasper, Stewart, Upson
Kentucky: Mason, Trigg
Mississippi: Grenada, Lauderdale, Noxubee, Warren
Ohio: Cuyahoga, Miami, Seneca

1910 US Census

Alabama: Autauga, Dallas, Greene, Jefferson, Mobile
Arkansas: Lee
Florida: Suwannee
Georgia: Chatham, Fulton, Stewart, Upson
Indiana: Marion
Kentucky: Pendleton, Trigg
Mississippi: Grenada, Tallahatchie
Ohio: Cuyahoga, Miami, Seneca

1920 US Census

Alabama: Autauga, Colbert, Dallas, Greene, Jefferson, Mobile
Arkansas: Lee
Florida: Suwannee
Georgia: Upson, Washington
Kentucky: Christian, Mason, Pendleton, Trigg
Michigan: Wayne
Ohio: Butler, Cuyahoga, Franklin, Seneca

1930 US Census

Alabama: Dallas, Greene
Georgia: Chatham, DeKalb
Kentucky: Jefferson, Trigg

Michigan: Wayne
Ohio: Butler, Cuyahoga, Miami, Seneca

1940 US Census

Kentucky: Trigg
Michigan: Wayne
Ohio: Butler, Cuyahoga, Miami

1950 US Census

Indiana: Marion
Ohio: Cuyahoga

NEWSPAPERS

African Repository and Colonial Journal. Washington, DC.
Alabama Beacon. Greensboro, AL.
Alabama Sentinel. Birmingham, AL.
Ann Arbor Sun. Ann Arbor, MI.
Anti-Slavery Bugle. Lisbon, OH.
Arizona Daily Star. Tucson, AZ.
Asbury Park Press. Asbury Park, NJ.
Austin Chronicle. Austin, TX.
Baltimore Sun. Baltimore, MD.
Berkeley Barb. Berkeley, CA.
Berkeley Gazette. Berkeley, CA.
Berkeley Tribe. Berkeley, CA.
Berkshire Eagle. Pittsfield, MA.
Birmingham Age-Herald. Birmingham, AL.
Boston Globe. Boston, MA.
Cadiz Record. Cadiz, KY.
Camp Hill Star. Camp Hill, AL.
Chicago Defender. Chicago, IL.
Christian Recorder. Nashville, TN.
Cincinnati Enquirer. Cincinnati, OH.
Clarion-Ledger. Jackson, MS.
Cleveland Call and Post. Cleveland, OH.
Cleveland Plain-Dealer. Cleveland, OH.
Cleveland Press. Cleveland, OH.
Colored American. New York, NY.
Columbus Leader. Columbus, OH.
Counterpunch.org. Online.
Courier-Post. Camden, NJ.
Daily Collegian. Detroit, MI.
Daily News. New York, NY.
Daily News-Tribune. Greenville, OH.

Daily Picayune. New Orleans, LA.
Daily Telegraph. London, UK.
Daily Utah Chronicle. Salt Lake City, UT.
Dayton Daily News. Dayton, OH.
Dayton Journal and Advertiser. Dayton, OH.
Detroit Free Press. Detroit, MI.
Detroit Metro Times. Detroit, MI.
Detroit News. Detroit, MI.
East Village Other. New York, NY.
Eutaw Whig and Observer. Eutaw, AL.
Evening Standard. London, UK.
Fifth Estate. Detroit, MI.
Forkland Progress. Forkland, AL.
Gallipolis Journal. Gallipolis, OH.
Greensboro Record. Greensboro, NC.
Greensboro Watchman. Greensboro, AL.
Guardian. London, United Kingdom.
Hayward Daily Review. Hayward, CA.
Herald Express. Birmingham, United Kingdom.
Highland Weekly News. Hillsboro, OH.
Honolulu Star-Bulletin. Honolulu, HI.
Hopkinsville Daily Kentucky New Era. Hopkinsville, KY.
Indianapolis News. Indianapolis, IN.
Inner City Voice. Detroit, MI.
Iron Age. Birmingham, AL.
Ithaca Journal. Ithaca, NY.
Jackson Progress-Argus. Athens, GA.
Jazzwereld. Amsterdam, Netherlands.
Kansas City Times. Kansas City, MO.
Kentuckian. Hopkinsville, KY.
Kentucky Irish-American. Louisville, KY.
Kingston Whig-Standard. Kingston, NY.
Knoxville News-Sentinel. Knoxville, TN.
La Crosse Tribune. La Crosse, WI.
Labor Advocate. Birmingham, AL.
Lake Geneva Regional News. Lake Geneva, WI.
Lansing State Journal. Lansing, MI.
Liberator. Boston, MA.
Los Angeles Times. Los Angeles, CA.
Louisville Courier-Journal. Louisville, KY.
Louisville Daily Journal. Louisville, KY.
Louisville News. Louisville, KY.
Macon Telegraph. Macon, GA.
Magnolia Gazette. Magnolia, MS.
Marengo News-Journal. Demopolis, AL.
Melody Maker. London, United Kingdom.
Meridian Evening Star. Meridian, MS.
Middlebury Register. Middlebury, VT.
Minneapolis Star. Minneapolis, MN.

Missoulian. Missoula, MT.
Mobile Daily Register. Mobile, AL.
Mobile Nationalist. Mobile, AL.
Mobile Register. Mobile, AL.
Mobile Republican. Mobile, AL.
Montana Standard. Butte, MT.
Montgomery Advertiser. Montgomery, AL.
Montreal Star. Montreal, QB, Canada.
National Observer. Washington, DC.
New National Era. Washington, DC.
New York Amsterdam News. New York, NY.
New York Herald. New York, NY.
New York Times. New York, NY.
News and Observer. Raleigh, NC.
Newsday. Melville, NY.
Niles' Weekly Register. Baltimore, MD.
North Star. Danville, VT.
Oakland Tribune. Oakland, CA.
Oberlin News-Tribune. Oberlin, OH.
Orlando Evening Star. Orlando, FL.
Ottawa Journal. Ottawa, ON, Canada.
Palladium of Liberty. Columbus, OH.
Pike County Republican. Waverly, OH.
Prattville Progress. Prattville, AL.
Progress Bulletin. Pomona, CA.
Province. Vancouver, BC, Canada.
Revolutionary Worker. Chicago, IL.
San Francisco Chronicle. San Francisco, CA.
San Francisco Examiner. San Francisco, CA.
Sandusky Clarion. Sandusky, OH.
Scientific American. New York, NY.
Soho Weekly News. New York, NY.
Southern Worker. Birmingham, AL.
Stanford Daily. Stanford, CA.
Star Tribune. Minneapolis, MN.
Star-Gazette. Elmira, NY.
Sunday Sun. Newcastle-upon-Tyne, UK.
Sydney Morning Herald. Sydney, Australia.
Tallahassee Democrat. Tallahassee, FL.
Tarboro Press. Tarboro, NC.
Thomaston Times. Thomaston, GA.
Tonawanda NEWS. Tonawanda, NY.
Troy Daily News. Troy, OH.
Union Springs Herald. Union Springs, AL.
United Mine Workers' Journal. Columbus, OH.
Upson Pilot. Thomaston, GA.
Van Nuys News. Van Nuys, CA.
Vancouver Sun. Vancouver, BC, Canada.

Vermont Chronicle. Bellows Falls VT.
Wall Street Journal. New York, NY.
Washington National Intelligencer. Washington, DC.
Waverly News. Waverly, OH.
Weekly Mississippian. Jackson, MS.
Windsor Star. Windsor, ON, Canada.
Wisconsin Free Democrat. Milwaukee, WI.
Wisconsin State Journal. Madison, WI.
Wyandotte Gazette. Wyandotte, KS.

PUBLISHED PRIMARY SOURCES

Abdur-Razzaq, Hasan. "Creative Urban Momentum: Witnessing the Black Unity Trio." *Chimurenga*, November 17, 2020, https://chimurengachronic.co.za/creative-urban-momentum-witnessing-the-black-unity-trio/.

Albert, Peter J., and Grace Palladino, eds. *The Samuel Gompers Papers*. Vol. 8: *Progress and Reaction in the Age of Reform, 1909–13*. University of Illinois Press, 2001.

Allen, William Francis, et al., eds. *Slave Songs of the United States*. 1867; Dover, 1995.

Anderson, Robert. *From Slavery to Affluence: Memoirs of Robert Anderson, Ex-slave*. Hemingford, Nebraska: n.p., 1927.

Ayler, Albert. "To Mr. Jones—I Had a Vision." *Cricket* 3 (1969): 27–30.

Bey, Faruq Z. "Notes on Tonal Physics." *Solid Ground: A New World Journal* 3, no. 2 (1987): 17.

CDSE Lynching Database. http://lynching.csde.washington.edu/#/home.

Cleveland City Directory 1925. Cleveland Directory Company, 1925.

Donovan, Maj. Jonathan to Brevet Brigadier General John Ely, Jun 30, 1866, reprinted in eds., René Hayden, et al. Freedom: A Documentary History of Emancipation, 1861–1867. Ser. 3, vol. 2: *Land and Labor, 1866–1867*. Chapel Hill, NC: University of North Carolina Press, 2013.

Dorsey, Hugh M. "A Statement by Governor Hugh M. Dorsey as to the Negro in Georgia." n.p., [1921].

Douglass, Frederick. *Narrative of the Life of Frederick Douglass, an American Slave*. Ed. Henry Louis Gates Jr. In *The Classic Slave Narratives*. Mentor, 1987.

Eichele, Robin, and John Sinclair. "Getting Out from Under." *New University Thought* 4, no. 2 (1965): 22–24.

Freeman, Don. "Black Youth and Afro-American Liberation." *Black America* 2, no. 2 (1964): 15.

———. "The Politics of Black Liberation." *Black America* 1, no. 7/8 (November–December 1963): 6–18.

———. *Reflections of a Resolute Radical*. Monroe, IL: self-published, 2017.

Indianapolis, Indiana. *City Directory*, 1886.

Johnson, Charles S. *Negro Housing: Report of the Committee on Negro Housing*. 1932; Negro Universities Press, 1969.

Lee, Jeamel. Liner notes. *Message from the Tribe*. Tribe, 1972.

Mobile & Ohio Railroad. *Fifty Second Annual Report of the Mobile and Ohio Railroad Co. 1899–1900*. New York: Evening Post Job Printing House, 1900.

———. *Forty-Eighth Annual Report of the Mobile and Ohio R. R. Co. 1895–96*. New York: Evening Post Job Printing House, 1896.

———. *27th Annual Report of the Mobile & Ohio R. R. Co. for the Year Ending December 31, 1875*. Evening Post Stream Presses, 1876.

———. *32nd Annual Report of the Mobile & Ohio R. R. Co. 1879–80*. Douglas Taylor, 1880.

———. *Thirty-Third Annual Report of the Mobile Ohio R. R. Co. 1880–1*. Douglas Taylor, 1881.
———. *Thirty-Seventh Annual Report of the Mobile and Ohio R. R. Co. 1884–85*. Douglas Taylor, 1885.
———. *Sixtieth Annual Report of the Mobile and Ohio Railroad Company, Year Ended June 30, 1908*. New York, 1908.
Northup, Solomon. *Twelve Years a Slave: The Narrative of Solomon Northup, a Citizen of New-York, Kidnapped in Washington City in 1841 and Rescued in 1853, from a Cotton Plantation Near the Red River in Louisiana*. Auburn, NY: Derby and Miller, 1853.
Paine, Lewis W. *Six Years in a Georgia Prison: Narrative of Lewis W. Paine, Who Suffered Imprisonment Six Years in Georgia, for the Crime of Aiding the Escape of a Fellowman from that State, After He Fled from Slavery*. New York: n.p., 1851.
Pinelli, Joe. "Ayler on Record: Lyrical Rockets." *Change* 2 (1966): 111–13.
Poor's Manual of the Railroads of the United States. American Bank Note Co., 1903.
Pucel, Edward L. *City of Cleveland Housing Report for the Year 1945*. Cleveland City Council, 1945.
Ridley, Caleb A., et al. *The 'Negro in Georgia': Another 'Pamphlet' Called Forth by Governor Hugh M. Dorsey's Slanderous Document, Scattered Broadcast Over the Country in Which He Purported to Set Forth the Brutal Treatment Accorded the Negro by White Citizens of Georgia, the 'American Belgian Congo.'* Dixie Defense Committee, [1921].
Scott, William Walter, III. *Hurt, Baby, Hurt*. New Ghetto, 1970.
Sinclair, John. "Detroit Downtown." *Arts and Artists* 4, no. 4 (October–November 1964): 4.
———. "The Home Front." *Change* 2 (1966): 27.
———. "The Local Scene." *Arts and Artists* 4, no. 4 (October–November 1964): 6.
———. "Untitled." *Change* 1 (1965): i–v.
Sinclair, Magdalene. "Untitled." *Change* 2 (1966): 32–3.
Southern Railway Company. *Twenty-Second Annual Report of the Southern Railway Company, Year Ended June 30, 1916*. New York, 1916.
———. *Twenty-Third Annual Report of the Southern Railway Company, for the Year Ended June 30, 1917*. New York, 1917.
Stanford, Maxwell C. "Revolutionary Action Movement (RAM): A Case Study of an Urban Revolutionary Movement in Western Capitalist Society." MA thesis, Atlanta University, 1986.
Tapscott, Horace. "Horace Tapscott." In *Central Avenue Sounds: Jazz in Los Angeles*, ed. Clora Bryant et al. University of California Press, 1998.
———. *Songs of the Unsung: The Musical and Social Journey of Horace Tapscott*. Ed. Steven Isoardi. Duke University Press, 2001.
Tyler, Charles. Liner notes. *Saga of the Outlaws*. Nessa Records, 1978.
University of California–Berkeley. *General Catalogue, 1969–1970*. 1969.
———. *General Catalogue, 1970–1971*. 1970.
———. *General Catalogue, 1971–1972*. 1971.
———. *General Catalogue, 1973–1974*. 1973.
Weaver, Lloyd. Liner Notes. *Eastern Man Alone*. ESP Disk, 1967.
West Alabama Planning and Development Council. *Historic Preservation*. 1971.

MAPS

Skeleton Map Showing the Route of the Mobile and Ohio Railroad and the Distances from Various Ports of the Gulf to Mobile. James & Newman, n.d.

INTERVIEWS AND MEMOIRS

Aarons, Charlie. Interview. August 6, 1937. In *Slave Narratives: A Folk History of Slavery in the United States from Interviews with Former Slaves*, vol. 1: *Alabama Narratives*, ed. Federal Writers' Project, 1–5. Works Progress Administration, 1941.

Abdul Alim, Kamal. Interview by author. Digital recording. January 31, 2021.

———. Interview by author. Digital recording. June 12, 2021.

Abdullah, Ahmed. Interview by Andreas Vingaard. Digital recording. May 9, 2020.

Ackamoor, Idris. Interview by Andreas Vingaard. Digital recording. April 25, 2020.

Ali, Muhammad. Interview by author. Digital recording. July 7, 2020.

———. Interview by author. Digital recording. July 22, 2020.

———. Interview by author. Digital recording. October 8, 2020.

Allen, Clifford. "Interview: Sunny Murray." *All About Jazz—New York* 18 (October 2003): 5, 25.

Ayler, Albert. "Untitled." *International Times* 10 (March 13–26, 1967): 9; repr. *Jazz* 125 (December 1965): 41.

Baker, David. Interview by Lida Baker. Transcript. June 19–21, 2000. Archives Center, National Museum of American History, Smithsonian Institution, Washington.

Barnes, Henry. Interview. June 11, 1937. In *Slave Narratives: A Folk History of Slavery in the United States from Interviews with Former Slaves*, vol. 1: *Alabama Narratives*, ed. Federal Writers' Project, 20–24. Works Progress Administration, 1941.

Beaufait, Kathleen. Interview by author. Digital recording. December 20, 2022.

Bey, Faruq Z. Interview by Detroit JazzStage, digital recording, October 19, 2006. https://www.youtube.com/watch?v=rEfockEsBYM.

Bey, Sadiq Muhammad. Interview by author. Digital recording. May 24, 2023.

Borgmann, Thomas. Interview by author. Digital recording. June 8, 2023.

Buchanan, Steve. "A Conversation with James Newton." *The Grackle* 1, no. 5 (1979): 16–19.

Budd, Harold. "Interview #1." *Gaffa.org*, March 23, 1987. http://gaffa.org/archives/1987-06/msg00075.html.

Carter, Daniel. Interview by author. Digital recording. January 13, 2021.

Caux, Daniel. "My Name Is . . . Albert Ayler." *Chroniques de l'Art Avant* 17 (February 1971): 24–25.

Chadbourne, Eugene. Interview by Andreas Vingaard. Email transcript. April 19, 2020.

Cherry, Don. Interview on Albert Ayler. Part 1. https://www.youtube.com/watch?v=fKoBBz1Sbzg.

Crepon, Pierre. "Avant Garde Jazz and Black Rights Activism in 1960s Cleveland, Ohio: An Interview with Mutawaf A. Shaheed." *The Wire*, March 2019, https://www.thewire.co.uk/in-writing/interviews/avant-garde-jazz-cleveland-interview-with-mutawaf-a-shaheed.

———. "Cleveland Memories of Abdul Wadud." *The Wire*, August 2022, https://www.thewire.co.uk/in-writing/essays/cleveland-memories-of-abdul-wadud.

———. "*Wire* Playlist: Yusuf Mumin and the Black Unity Trio." *The Wire*, November 2020, https://www.thewire.co.uk/audio/tracks/wire-playlist-yusuf-mumin-and-the-black-unity-trio.

Daniel, Ted. Interview by Andreas Vingaard. Digital recording. April 23, 2020.

Dickerson, Fannie. Interview by Andreas Vingaard. Digital recording. March 31, 2020.

Dillard, George. Interview. N.d. In *Slave Narratives: A Folk History of Slavery in the United States from Interviews with Former Slaves*, vol. 1: *Alabama Narratives*, ed. Federal Writers' Project, 111–12. Works Progress Administration, 1941.

Dodds, Elreta. Interview by author. Digital recording. February 15, 2023.

Durrah, David. Interview by Andreas Vingaard. Digital recording. April 17, 2020.

Ealy, Beverly. Interview by author. Digital recording. January 31, 2023.

Eichele, Robin. Interview by author. Digital recording. October 14, 2022.

Elliot, Marcus. Interview by author. Digital recording. December 16, 2022.
English, Ron. Interview by author. Digital recording. May 13, 2022.
———. Interview by author. Digital recording. May 18, 2022.
English, Ron, and Robin Eichele. Interview by author. Digital recording. December 18, 2022.
Fee, John G. *Autobiography of John G. Fee, Berea, Kentucky*. Chicago: National Christian Association, 1891.
Ferrucci, Frank. Interview by Andreas Vingaard. Digital recording. April 2, 2020.
Few, Simone. Interview by author. Digital recording. March 22, 2022.
Fine, Milo. "Michael Smith: Interview." *Cadence* 11, no. 9 (September 1985): 11–28.
Flicker, Chris. "Charles Tyler." *Jazz*, June 1977, 18.
Folwell, Bill. Interview by Ben Young. Broadcast on WKCR-FM, Jazz Profiles, July 29, 2007. Cassette recording. Ras Moshe Burnett private collection.
Franks, Pet. Interview. N.d. In *Slave Narratives: A Folk History of Slavery in the United States from Interviews with Former Slaves*, vol. 9: *Mississippi Narratives*, ed. Federal Writers' Project, 56–60. Works Progress Administration, 1941.
Fransen, Lieve. Interview by author. Digital recording. December 9, 2020.
Freeman, Don. Interview by author. Digital recording. June 13, 2021.
Gauffre, Christian. "Charles Tyler." *Jazz*, November 1985, 27.
Geller, Janice. Interview by Andreas Vingaard. Digital recording. May 8, 2020.
Greensmith, Bill, et al., eds. *Blues Unlimited: Essential Interviews from the Original 'Blues Magazine.'* University of Illinois Press, 2015.
Hall, David A. Interview. August 16, 1937. In *Slave Narratives: A Folk History of Slavery in the United States from Interviews with Former Slaves*, vol. 12: *Ohio Narratives*, ed. Federal Writers' Project, 39–41. Works Progress Administration, 1941.
Hancock, Larry. Interview by author. Digital recording. October 14, 2021.
Harris, Beaver. Interview by Elliott Bratton. WKCR-FM broadcast, July 13, 1987. Ras Moshe Burnett private collection.
Harris, Bill. Interview by author. Digital recording. November 21, 2022.
———. Interview by author. Digital recording. December 15, 2022.
Harrison, Wendell. Interview by author. Digital recording. August 5, 2021.
Henderson, Benjamin. Interview. N.d. In *Slave Narratives: A Folk History of Slavery in the United States from Interviews with Former Slaves*, vol. 4: *Georgia Narratives*, ed. Federal Writers' Project, 173–77. Works Progress Administration, 1941.
Henry, Nettie. Interview. N.d. In *Slave Narratives: A Folk History of Slavery in the United States from Interviews with Former Slaves*, vol. 9: *Mississippi Narratives*, ed. Federal Writers' Project, 61–67. Works Progress Administration, 1941.
Johnson, Susie. Interview. September 4, 1936. In *Slave Narratives: A Folk History of Slavery in the United States from Interviews with Former Slaves*, vol. 4: *Georgia Narratives*, ed. Federal Writers' Project, 343–44. Works Progress Administration, 1941.
Johnston, Mike. Interview by author. Digital recording. October 25, 2023.
Jones, Ralph "Buzzy," and Kathleen Beaufait. Interview by author. Digital recording. December 20, 2022.
Jordan, Lewis. Interview by Andreas Vingaard. Digital recording. March 20, 2020.
Karamanoukian, Jacques. "Detroit Voices, Part 1: Faruq Z. Bey, Ancient Warrior and Griot." *Agenda*, February 1997, 6.
Knox, Keith. "Earl Cross: Interview." *Cadence* 9, no. 7 (July 1983): 5–7, 28.
Koyama, Kiyoshi. "Albert Ayler Interview." *Swing Journal*, recorded July 25, 1970. https://www.youtube.com/watch?v=uxYKj1CLUKo.
Kruth, John. "Bernard Stollman: The Man from 5D." *Signal to Noise* 34 (2004): 17.
Lee, David. "Knocking Down Barriers: An Interview with Abdul Wadud, 1980." *Coda*, 1980; repr. *Point of Departure*, 2021, https://pointofdeparture.org/PoD73/PoD73Wadud.html.

Lindenmaier, H. Lukas. "Peter Brötzmann: Interview." *Cadence* 4, no. 10 (October 1978): 3–7, 20.
Mays, Emily. Interview. N.d. In *Slave Narratives: A Folk History of Slavery in the United States from Interviews with Former Slaves*, vol. 4: *Georgia Narratives*, ed. Federal Writers' Project, 118–20. Works Progress Administration, 1941.
McAllum, Sam. Interview. N.d. In *Slave Narratives: A Folk History of Slavery in the United States from Interviews with Former Slaves*, vol. 9: *Mississippi Narratives*, ed. Federal Writers' Project. Works Progress Administration, 1941.
McIntyre, Dianne. Interview by author. Digital recording. August 17, 2020.
McKesson, Brent. Interview by author. Digital recording. October 5, 2022.
McMurray, David. Interview by author. Digital recording. February 5, 2023.
Mumin, Yusuf. Interview by author. Email transcript. January 19–September 17, 2021.
Murray, David. Interview by author. Digital recording. April 17, 2020.
Murray, Sunny. Interview by Clifford Allen. Transcript. N.d. Clifford Allen private collection.
Nai, Larry. "Alan Silva Interview." *Cadence* 25, no. 7 (July 1999): 5–19, 135.
———. "Khan Jamal Interview." *Cadence* 24, no. 11 (November 1998): 18–26.
———. "Noah Howard Interview." *Cadence* 24, no. 1 (January 1998): 5–8, 138.
Nassoma, Kafi Patrice. Interview by author. Digital recording. April 15, 2023.
Natambu, Kofi. "Faruq Z. Bey at the Belcrest Hotel, Detroit, Michigan." *Solid Ground: A New World Journal* 1, no. 3/4 (1986): 64–68.
Nessa, Chuck. Interview by Andreas Vingaard. Email transcript. April 30–May 5, 2020.
Palmer, Hugh D. Interview by Terry Birdwhistell and George Wright, August 21, 1985. Oral History Collection, Special Collections, University of Kentucky, Lexington.
Parker, William. Interview by Andreas Vingaard. Digital recording. May 8, 2020.
Parnell, Austin Pen. Interview. N.d. In *Slave Narratives: A Folk History of Slavery in the United States from Interviews with Former Slaves*, vol. 2: *Arkansas Narratives*, ed. Federal Writers' Project, 262–72. Works Progress Administration, 1941.
Patterson, Amy Elizabeth. Interview. N.d. In *Slave Narratives: A Folk History of Slavery in the United States from Interviews with Former Slaves*, vol. 5: *Indiana Narratives*, ed. Federal Writers' Project, 150–52. Works Progress Administration, 1941.
Peterson, Joel. Interview by author. Digital recording. December 17, 2022.
Phillips, Simon. Interview. N.d. In *Slave Narratives: A Folk History of Slavery in the United States from Interviews with Former Slaves*, vol. 1: *Alabama Narratives*, ed. Federal Writers' Project, 312–15. Works Progress Administration, 1941.
Postif, Francois. "The Noah Howard-Frank Wright Quartet: Une interview de François Postif." *Jazz Hot* 257 (January 1970): 18–19.
Ranelin, Phil. Interview by author. Digital recording. September 1, 2021.
———. Interview by author. Digital recording. September 5, 2021.
Richards, Shade. Interview. N.d. In *Slave Narratives: A Folk History of Slavery in the United States from Interviews with Former Slaves*, vol. 4: *Georgia Narratives*, ed. Federal Writers' Project, 200–5. Works Progress Administration, 1941.
Robertson, Irene. Interview. N.d. In *Slave Narratives: A Folk History of Slavery in the United States from Interviews with Former Slaves*, vol. 2: *Arkansas Narratives*, ed. Federal Writers' Project, 208–11. Works Progress Administration, 1941.
Rusch, Bob. "Andrew Cyrille Interview, Part 2." *Cadence* 21, no. 2 (February 1995): 17–28, 107.
———. "Charles Moffett Interview." *Cadence* 23, no. 2 (February 1997): 5–17.
———. "Glenn Spearman Interview." *Cadence* 20, no. 5 (May 1994): 5–14.
———. "Raphe Malik Interview." *Cadence* 20, no. 11 (November 1994): 5–18.
Seale, Bobby. "The Black Scholar Interviews: Bobby Seale." *Black Scholar* 4, no. 1 (September 1972): 7–16.
Shaheed, Mutawaf. Interview by Andreas Vingaard. Digital recording. March 25, 2020.

———. Interview by author. Digital recording. August 30, 2020.
———. Interview by author. Digital recording. December 4, 2020.
———. Interview by author. Digital recording. December 27, 2020.
———. Interview by author. Digital recording. June 3, 2021.
———. Interview by author. Digital recording. June 11, 2021.
———. Interview by author. Digital recording. September 7, 2022.
———. Interview by author. Digital recording. September 13, 2022.
———. Interview by author. Digital recording. October 4, 2022.
Shahid, Hasan. Interview by author. Digital recording. August 24, 2020.
Shahid, Jaribu. Interview by author. Digital recording. August 5, 2021.
———. Interview by author. Digital recording. July 3, 2023.
Shipton, Alyn. Interview with Henry Grimes. Recorded May 2, 2009. *Jazz Library*, BBC Radio 3, May 23, 2009.
Silva, Alan. Interview by author. Digital recording. February 8, 2023.
———. Interview by author. Digital recording. February 25, 2022.
———. Interview by author. Digital recording. March 4, 2022.
———. Interview by author. Digital recording. March 11, 2022.
———. Interview by Ben Young. WKCR-FM, n.d. Ras Moshe Burnett private collection.
Sinclair, John. Interview by author. Digital recording. December 17, 2022.
———. Interview by author. Digital recording. January 9, 2023.
———. Interview by author. Digital recording. September 1, 2021.
Sinclair, Leni. Interview by author. Digital recording. February 7, 2022.
Smith, Berry. Interview. N.d. In *Slave Narratives: A Folk History of Slavery in the United States from Interviews with Former Slaves*, vol. 12: *Mississippi Narratives*, ed. Federal Writers' Project. Works Progress Administration, 1941.
Smith, Miyoshi. "Lawrence 'Butch' Morris Interview." *Cadence* 15, no. 7 (July 1989): 13–8.
Snow, Sarah. Interview. N.d. In *Slave Narratives: A Folk History of Slavery in the United States from Interviews with Former Slaves*, vol. 9: *Mississippi Narratives*, ed. Federal Writers' Project, 135–42. Works Progress Administration, 1941.
"Steve Lacy." *The Grackle* 1, no. 3 (1976): 14.
Tabbal, Tani. Interview by author. Digital recording. January 24, 2023.
Tintweiss, Steve. Interview by author. Digital recording. June 1, 2022.
Troutman, Richard L., ed. *The Heavens Are Weeping: The Diaries of George Richard Browder, 1852–1886*. Zondervan, 1987.
Tyler, Akbar. Interview by author. Digital recording. February 3, 2023.
Tyler, Charles. Interview on WKCR-FM. July 26, 1974. Cassette recording. Ras Moshe Burnett private collection.
Tysh, George. Interview by author. Digital recording. November 4, 2022.
Wadud, Abdul. Interview by Ben Young. WKCR-FM, May 2, 2004. Ras Moshe Burnett private collection.
Wallenstein, Barry. Interview by author. Digital recording. June 16, 2022.
———. Interview by author. Digital recording. November 15, 2022.
Walton, Rhodus. Interview. N.d. In *Slave Narratives: A Folk History of Slavery in the United States from Interviews with Former Slaves*, vol. 4: *Georgia Narratives*, ed. Federal Writers' Project, 123–27. Works Progress Administration, 1941.
Wanek, Joel, and Tomeka Reid. "By Myself: An Interview with Abdul Wadud." *Point of Departure*, November 2014, https://www.pointofdeparture.org/PoD57/PoD57Wadud.html.
Warburton, Dan. "Alan Silva: Interviews with Dan Warburton." *Paris Transatlantic*, November 8–22, 2002, http://www.paristransatlantic.com/magazine/interviews/silva.html.

Warfield, William. Interview. N.d. *Slave Narratives: A Folk History of Slavery in the United States from Interviews with Former Slaves*, vol. 7: *Kentucky Narratives*, ed. Federal Writers' Project, 102–3. Works Progress Administration, 1941.
Warren, Henry W. *Reminiscences of a Mississippi Carpet-Bagger*. Holden, MA: n.p., 1914.
Wilderman, Michael. Interview by Andreas Vingaard. Digital recording. May 15, 2020.
Williams, David. Interview by Andreas Vingaard. Digital recording. May 15, 2020.
Wright, Mary. Interview. N.d. In *Slave Narratives: A Folk History of Slavery in the United States from Interviews with Former Slaves*, vol. 7: *Kentucky Narratives*, ed. Federal Writers' Project, 61–66. Works Progress Administration, 1941.
Young, Roland P. Interview by Andreas Vingaard. Digital recording. April 23, 2020.

LITERARY SOURCES

Bell, Gertrude Lowthian, trans. *Poems from the Divan of Hafez*. London: William Heinemann, 1897.
Bey, Faruq Z. "Albert Ayler: 1936–1970." *Solid Ground: A New World Journal* 1, no. 1 (1981): 39.
———. "Mizimu." *Solid Ground: A New World Journal* 3, no. 2 (1987): 63.
———. "Untitled." *Solid Ground: A New World Journal* 2, no. 1 (February 1985): 57.
Hayden, Robert. *Collected Prose*. University of Michigan Press, 1984.
Muhammad, Sadiq. "Excerpts from the Jesse Davis Medical Fund." In *Nostalgia for the Present: An Anthology of Writings (from Detroit)*, ed. Kofi Natambu, 107–10, 165. Post Aesthetic, 1985.
Natambu, Kofi. "We Think We Know You or the Roving Enigma Blues." *Past Tents Press*, 1991, 49–50.
Sinclair, John. "The Destruction of America." In *This Is Our Music*. Workshop Books 3. Artists' Workshop, 1965.
———. "This Is Our Music." In *Free Poems/Among Friends*, vol. 2, ed. John Sinclair and Magdalene Sinclair. Artists' Workshop, 1966.
Sinclair, John, and Magdalene Sinclair, eds. *Free Poems/Among Friends*, vol. 2. Artists' Workshop, 1966.

MUSICAL RECORDINGS

Afro-American Blues and Game Songs. Library of Congress, 1976.
Akbar, Rashied Al, et al. *Ascent of the Nether Creatures*. NoBusiness Records, 2014.
akLaff, Pheeroan. *Fits Like a Glove*. Gramavision, 1983.
Alan Silva and His Celestial Communications Orchestra. *Desert Mirage*. I.A.C.P, 1982.
———. *Luna Surface*. BYG Records, 1969.
———. *Seasons*. BYG Records, 1971.
———. *The Shout: Portrait for a Small Woman*. Chiaroscuro Records, 1979.
Albert Ayler Trio. *Spiritual Unity*. ESP-Disk, 1965.
Andrew Hill Trio. *Strange Serenade*. Soul Note, 1980.
Archie Shepp Quintet. *Live 1973*. Blu Jazz, n.d.
Arthur Doyle Plus 4. *Alabama Feeling*. AK-BA Records, 1978.
Arthur Gibbs and His Gang. *Louisville Lou/Beale Street Mamma*. Victor, 1923.
———. *Old Fashioned Love/Charleston Medley*. Victor, 1923.
Ayler, Albert. *Bells*. ESP-Disk, 1965.
———. *The Copenhagen Tapes*. Ayler Records, 2002.

———. *First Recordings*, 2 vols. Bird Notes, 1962.
———. *Ghosts*. Debut Records, 1965.
———. *The Hilversum Session*. Osmosis Records, 1980.
———. *Holy Ghost*. Revenant, 2004.
———. *In Greenwich Village*. Impulse!, 1967.
———. *The Last Album*. Impulse!, 1971.
———. *Live in Greenwich Village*. Impulse!, 1967.
———. *Love Cry!* Impulse!, 1968.
———. *Music Is the Healing Force of the Universe*. Impulse!, 1970.
———. *My Name Is Albert Ayler*. Debut Records, 1964.
———. *Something Different!!!!!!* Bird Notes, 1963.
———. *Spirits*. Debut Records, 1964.
———. *Spirits Rejoice*. ESP-Disk, 1965.
———. *Swing Low Sweet Spiritual*. Osmosis Records, 1971.
———. *The Village Concerts*. Impulse!, 1978.
Ayler, Albert, et al. *New York Eye and Ear Control*. ESP-Disk, 1966.
Bang, Billy. *Outline no. 12*. Celluloid, 1983.
Bang, Billy, and Charles Tyler. *Live at Green Space*. Anima Productions, 1982.
Barbecue Bob. *Atlanta Moan/Doin' the Scraunch*. Columbia, 1931.
Barbecue Bob and Laughing Charley. *It Won't Be Long Now*. Columbia, 1927.
Belgrave, Marcus. *Gemini II*. Tribe Records, 1974.
Billy Bang Quartet. *Rainbow Gladiator*. Soul Note, 1981.
Billy Bang Quintet. *Invitation*. Soul Note, 1982.
Black Unity Trio. *Al-Fatihah*. Salaam Records, 1969.
Bland, Bobby. *Little Boy Blue/Last Night*. Duke, 1958.
———. *Sometime Tomorrow/Farther Up the Road*. Duke, 1957.
Blythe, Arthur. *The Grip*. India Navigation, 1977.
Braxton, Anthony. *Five Pieces 1975*. Arista Records, 1975.
Burton Green Quartet. *The Burton Green Quartet*. ESP-Disk, 1966.
Center of the World. *Center of the World*, vol. 1. Center of the World, 1972.
———. *Volume 2: Last Polka in Nancy?* Center of the World, 1973.
———. *Volume 3: More or Less Few*. Center of the World, n.d.
———. *Volume 4: Adieu Little Man*. Center of the World, n.d.
———. *Volume 5: Inner Song*. Center of the World, 1978.
———. *Volume 6: Solos & Duets*. Center of the World, n.d.
———. *Volume 7: Solos & Duets*. Center of the World, 1975.
Chadbourne, Eugene, and Charles Tyler. *Ghost Legends*. House of Chadula, n.d.
Charles Gayle Quartet. *Always Born*. Silkheart, 1988.
———. *Homeless*. Silkheart, 1989.
———. *Spirits Before*. Silkheart, 1988.
Charles Tyler Ensemble. *Charles Tyler Ensemble*. ESP-Disk, 1966.
———. *Live at Sweet Basil*. 2 vols. Bleu Regard, 2006.
———. *Saga of the Outlaws*. Nessa Records, 1978.
Charles Tyler Quartet. *Definite*, vol. 1. Storyville, 1982.
———. *Definite*, vol. 2. Storyville, 1984.
Charles Tyler Solo. Live at Environ. April 21, 1978. Analog recording. Ras Moshe Burnett private collection.
Charles Tyler/Brus Trio. *Autumn in Paris*. Silkheart, 1988.
Coleman, Ornette. *Science Fiction*. CBS, 1972.

Daniel, Ted. *In the Beginning*. Altura Music, 1997.
Davis, Miles. *Milestones*. Columbia, 1958.
Delcloo, Claude, and Arthur Jones. *Africanasia*. BYG Records, 1969.
Detroit Artists' Workshop: *Community, Jazz, and Art in the Motor City 1965–1981*. Art Yard, 2022.
Dunbar, Richard. *Running Buddies*, vol. 1. Jahari, 1983.
Dunn, Roy. *Know'd Them All*. Trix, 1975.
Elliott Levin Quartet. *The Motion of Emotion*. Spirit Room 48. CIMP, 1998.
Ervin, Booker. *The In Between*. Blue Note, 1968.
Few, Bobby. *Continental Jazz Express*. Vogue, 1979.
———. *Few Coming Thru*. Sun Records, 1977.
Fasteau, Zusaan Kali, et al. *Expatriate Kin*. CIMP, 1997.
Fischer, John. *6x1=10 Duos for a New Decade*. ReEntry records, 1980.
Frank Wright Quartet. *Blues for Albert Ayler*. ESP-Disk, 2012.
———. *Church Number Nine*. Odeon, 1971.
———. Live in Amsterdam. Archival recording. December 1970. https://www.youtube.com/watch?v=PeMTENwtCCQ.
———. *Uhuru Na Umoja*. America Records, 1970.
———. *Your Prayer*. ESP-Disk, 1967.
Frank Wright Sextet. *Stove Man, Love Is the Word*. Sandra Music Productions, 1979.
Frank Wright Trio. *Frank Wright Trio*. ESP-Disk, 1966.
Georgia Cotton Pickers. *Diddle-da-Diddle/She's Coming Back Some Cold Rainy Day*. Columbia, 1931.
———. *I'm on My Way Home/She Looks So Good*. Columbia, 1931.
Globe Unity Orchestra. *Intergalactic Blow*. Japo Records, 1983.
———. *20th Anniversary*. FMP, 1993.
Gordon, Roscoe. *Booted/Love You 'Til the Day I Die*. Chess, 1951.
Greene, Burton. *Firmanence*. Fore, 1980.
Greene, Burton, and Alan Silva. *The Ongoing Strings*. Hat Hut Records, 1981.
Griot Galaxy. *Kins*. Black & White Records, 1982.
———. *Live at the D.I.A*. Entropy Stereo Recordings, 2003.
———. *Opus Krampus*. Sound Aspects Records, 1985.
Hammond, Doug, and David Durrah. *Reflections in the Sea of Nurnen*. Tribe, 1975.
Harrison, Wendell. *An Evening with the Devil*. Tribe, 1973.
Harrison, Wendell, and Phil Ranelin. *Message from the Tribe*. Tribe, 1972.
Howard, Noah. *Space Dimension*. America Records, 1971.
Howard, Norman. *Burn, Baby, Burn*. Homeboy Music, 1993.
Howell, Peg Leg. *Complete Recordings in Chronological Order*, vol. 1: *1926–27*. Matchbox Records, 1986.
ICP Tentet. *Tetterettet*. Instant Composers Pool, 1977.
INTERface. *Environ Days*. Konnex, 1991.
———. *Live at Environ*. ReEntry Records, 1977.
Jacques Coursil Unit. *Way Head*. BYG Records, 1969.
Jarman, Joseph. *Song For*. Delmark, 1967.
Johnson, Margaret. *When a 'Gator Holler, Folks Say It's a Sign of Rain/Graysom Street Blues*. Victor, 1926.
Jones, Arthur. *Scorpio*. BYG Records, 1971.
Lateef, Yusuf. *Jazz and the Sounds of Nature*. Savoy Records, 1958.
Little Brenda Duff. *The Army's Got Me Crying/Tell Me Where're You Going*. Downbeat, n.d.
Lyman Woodard Organization. *Saturday Night Special*. Strata Records, 1975.
Marion Brown Quartet. *Marion Brown Quartet*. ESP-Disk, 1966.
Marion Brown Septet. *Juba-Lee*. Fontana, 1967.

Marzette Watts Ensemble. *Marzette Watts Ensemble*. Savoy Records, 1969.
McKinney, Harold. Voices and Rhythms of the Creative Profile. Tribe, 1974.
Michel Pilz Quartet. *Jamabiko*. M.P., 1984.
Midnight Sky. *Captain Midnight/So Real*. Skylife Production, 1983.
Mixed Bag. *Mixed Bag's First Album*. Tribe, 1976.
Modern Jazz Quartet. *Music from "Odds Against Tomorrow."* United Artists Records, 1959.
Moholo-Moholo, Louis, et al. *Spiritual Knowledge and Grace*. Ogun, 2011.
Mumin, Yusuf. *Sketches of the Invisible*. Self-released, 2021.
Negro Folk Music of Alabama: Religious. Folkways Records, 1956.
The New Wave in Jazz. Impulse!, 1966.
Noah Howard Quartet. *Noah Howard Quartet*. ESP-Disk, 1966.
Ornette Coleman Double Quartet. *Free Jazz*. Atlantic, 1961.
Parker, Charlie. *No. 3*. Dial Records, 1949.
Peter Brötzmann Group. *Alarm*. FMP, 1983.
Phillips, Joseph. *Burn, Baby, Burn*. ESP-Disk, 2007.
Ranelin, Phil. *The Time Is Now!* Tribe Records, 1974.
———. *Vibes from the Tribe*. Tribe, 1976.
Reed, Dock, and Vera Hall Ward. *Negro Folk Music of Alabama*, vol. 5: *Spirituals*. Ethnic Folkways Library, 1960.
Saheb Sarbib Quartet. *Live in Europe*, vol. 2. Marge, 1976.
Schlippenbach Quartet. *Anticlockwise*. FMP, 1983.
———. *Das Hohe Lied*. Po Torch Records, 1991.
Steve Lacy Quartet Featuring Charles Tyler. *One Fell Swoop*. Silkheart, 1987.
Sunny Murray Quintet. *Aigu-Grave*. Marge, 1980.
Trio Hurricane. *Suite of Winds*. Black Saint, 1994.
Tyler, Charles. *Eastern Man Alone*. ESP-Disk, 1967.
———. *Folk and Mystery Stories*. Sonet, 1981.
———. *Live in Europe: Jazz Festival Umea*. AK-BA Records, 1977.
Wallenstein, Barry. Charles Tyler memorial concert at St. Peter's, New York, digital recording, n.d., Barry Wallenstein private collection.
———. *Taking Off*. AK-BA Records, 1982.
Ware, David S., et al. *Planetary Unknown*. AUM Fidelity, 2011.
———. *Planetary Unknown: Live at the Jazzfestival Saalfelden 2011*. AUM Fidelity, 2012.
Waters, Patty. *Sings*. ESP-Disk, 1966.
Weaver, Curly, and Fred McMullen. *Leg Iron Blues/DeKalb Chain Gang*. Perfect, 1933.
Weaver, Curly, et al. *Some Cold Rainy Day/Just Can't Stand It*. Perfect, 1933.
Wendell Harrison and the Tribe. *Farewell to the Welfare*. Tribe Records, 1975.
Wilber Morris Trio. *Collective Improvisations*. Bleu Regard, 1994.
Winstons, The. *Color Him Father*. Metromedia Records, 1969.
Wright, Frank. *Unity*. ESP-Disk, 2006.
Wright, Frank, and George Arvanitas. *Shouting the Blues*. Sun Records, 1977.
Yosuke Yamashita Trio. *Ghosts by Albert Ayler*. West Wind, 1990.

FILM

Finally Got the News. Dir. John Watson, 1970.

CORRESPONDENCE

Chusid, Irwin. Email to Andreas Vingaard. N.d.
Mumin, Yusuf. Email to author. February 7, 2022.
———. Email to author. August 12, 2022.

SECONDARY SOURCES

Abbott, Lynn, and Doug Seroff. *Ragged but Right: Black Traveling Shows, "Coon Songs," and the Dark Pathway to Blues and Jazz*. University Press of Mississippi, 2007.
Abdullah, Ahmed. *A Strange Celestial Road: My Time in the Sun Ra Arkestra*. Blank Forms, 2023.
"About Our City: Mr. Mayor . . . Set It Out!" *Tribe* 1, no. 4 (1973): 16–20.
Abrahams, Roger D. *Blues for New Orleans: Mardi Gras and America's Creole Soul*. The City in the Twenty-First Century. University of Pennsylvania Press, 2006.
Addison, Gayle, Jr., ed. *The Black Aesthetic*. Doubleday, 1971.
"The African POW Movement and Solidarity Day." *Tribe* 1, no. 3 (1973): 38–41.
Albert, Peter J., and Grace Palladino, eds. *The Samuel Gompers Papers*, vol. 8: *Progress and Reaction in the Age of Reform, 1909–13*. University of Illinois Press, 2001.
Alessandrini, Paul. "Freepop." *Jazz* 173 (December 1969): 28.
Alexander, J. Trent, et al. "Second-Generation Outcomes of the Great Migration." *Demography* 54, no. 6 (December 2017): 2249–71.
Allen, Ernest, Jr. "The League of Revolutionary Black Workers: An Assessment," in *Workers' Struggles Past and Present: A "Radical America" Reader*, ed. James Green, 288–92. Temple University Press, 1983.
Allen, William Francis, et al., eds. *Slave Songs of the United States*. New York: A. Simpson, 1867.
Arnesen, Eric. *Brotherhoods of Color: Black Railroad Workers and the Struggle for Equality*. Harvard University Press, 2001.
Astor, Aaron. "The Crouching Lion's Fate: Slave Politics and Conservative Unionism in Kentucky." *Register of the Kentucky Historical Society* 110, no. 3/4 (2012): 293–326.
Austin, Addell. "The Present State of Black Theatre." *TDR* 32, no. 3 (1988): 85–100.
Axton, W. F. *Tobacco and Kentucky*. University of Kentucky Press, 1975.
Babson, Steve, et al. *Working Detroit: The Making of a Union Town*. Adama, 1984.
Baldwin, Leland D. *Pittsburgh: The Story of a City, 1750–1865*. Repr. University of Pittsburgh Press, 1981.
Bancroft, Frederic. *Slave-Trading in the Old South*. J. H. Furst, 1931.
Baraka, Amiri. "You Think This Is About You?" In Albert Ayler, *Holy Ghost*. Revenant, 2004.
Barlow, William. *Looking Up at Down: The Emergence of Blues Culture*. Temple University Press, 1989.
Bastin, Bruce. "From the Medicine Show to the Stage: Some Influences Upon the Development of a Blues Tradition in the Southeastern United States." *American Music* 2, no. 1 (1984): 29–42.
———. *Red River Blues: The Blues Tradition in the Southeast*. University of Illinois Press, 1986.
Bates, Beth Tompkins. *The Making of Black Detroit in the Age of Henry Ford*. University of North Carolina Press, 2012.
Beckham, Christopher. "The Paradox of Religious Segregation: White and Black Baptists in Western Kentucky, 1855–1900." *Register of the Kentucky Historical Society* 97, no. 3 (1999): 305–22.
Beecher, John. "The Share Croppers' Union in Alabama." *Social Forces* 13, no. 1 (October 1934–May 1935): 124–32.
Belhomme, Guillaume. "All Wright: Souvenir de Music in My Soul," in *Free Fight: This Is Our (New) Thing*, ed. Guillaume Belhomme and Philippe Robert. Camion Blanc, 2012.

Benston, Kimberly W. *Baraka: The Renegade and the Mask*. Yale University Press, 1976.
Bigham, Darrel E. *On Jordan's Banks: Emancipation and Its Aftermath in the Ohio River Valley*. University Press of Kentucky, 2006.
———. "River of Opportunity: Economic Consequences of the Ohio." In *Always a River: The Ohio River and the American Experience*, ed. Robert L. Reid. Indiana University Press, 1991.
———. *We Ask Only a Fair Trial: A History of the Black Community of Evansville, Indiana*. Indiana University Press, 1987.
Binsfield, Edmund L. "The Negro Cemetery at Carthagena." *Northwest Ohio Quarterly* 32 (1959–1960): 30.
Bjorn, Lars, and Jim Gallert. "Teddy Harris: A Jazz Man in Motown," in *Heaven Was Detroit: From Jazz to Hip-Hop and Beyond*, ed. M. L. Liebler, 20–25. Wayne State University Press, 2016.
"Black Women Involved in Broadcast Communications." *Tribe* 2, no. 3 (1974): 15–21.
"Blacks in Communications." *Tribe* 2, no. 2 (1974): 10–16.
Blocker, Jack S. *A Little More Freedom: African Americans Enter the Urban Midwest, 1860–1930*. Ohio State University Press, 2008.
Bowles, Dennis. *Dr. Beans Bowles "Fingertips": The Untold Story*. Sho-nuff Productions, 2003.
Boyd, Herb. *Black Detroit: A People's History of Self-Determination*. Amistad, 2017.
———. "Of Black Republicans and Others." *Tribe* 1, no. 3 (1973): 11–14.
———. "The Year of the Jackal or Down the Revolutionary Path." *Tribe* 2, no. 1 (1974): 27–28.
Boyd, Melba Joyce. "The Problem Was the Police." In *Detroit 1967: Origins, Impacts, Legacies*, ed. Joel Stone, 165–72. Wayne State University Press, 2017.
———. *Wrestling with the Muse: Dudley Randall and the Broadside Press*. Columbia University Press, 2003.
Boyd, Melba Joyce, and M. L. Liebler, eds. *Abandon Automobile: Detroit City Poetry 2001*. Wayne State University Press, 2001.
Bradley, Cisco. *Universal Tonality: The Life and Music of William Parker*. Duke University Press, 2021.
Brooks, Janet. "Black Women in Broadcasting." *Tribe* 2, no. 1 (1974): 10–16.
———. "Unemployment and Inflation: Detroiter's Comment." *Tribe* 3, no. 2 (1975): 7–9.
Brooks, Pamela E. *Boycotts, Buses, and Passes: Black Women's Resistance in the U.S. South and South Africa*. University of Massachusetts Press, 2008.
Brown, Charles A. "Lloyd Leftwich, Alabama State Senator." *Negro History Bulletin* 26, no. 5 (February 1963): 161–2.
Brown, Roger S. "Atlanta Odds and Ends." *Living Blues* 14 (1973): 14.
Bryant, Jonathan M. "'We Defy You': Politics and Violence in Reconstruction Savannah." In *Slavery and Freedom in Savannah*, ed. Leslie M. Harris and Daina Ramey Berry, 161–84. University of Georgia Press, 2014.
Bush, Bryan S. *Butcher Burbridge: Union General Stephen Burbridge and His Reign of Terror over Kentucky*. Acclaim, 2008.
Butler, Diane S. "The Public Life and Private Affairs of Sherman M. Booth." *Wisconsin Magazine of History* 82, no. 3 (1999): 166–97.
Camp, Jordan T. *Incarcerating the Crisis: Freedom Struggles and the Rise of the Neoliberal State*. University of California Press, 2016.
Camp, Stephanie M. H. *Closer to Freedom: Enslaved Women and Everyday Resistance in the Plantation South*. University of North Carolina Press, 2004.
Campbell, Robert L., and Christopher Trent. *The Earthly Recordings of Sun Ra*. Cadence Jazz Books, 1994.
Campbell, Tracy. *The Politics of Despair: Power and Resistance in the Tobacco Wars*. University Press of Kentucky, 1993.
Cantor, Louis. *Wheelin' on Beale*. Pharos, 1992.
Carles, Philippe, and Jean-Louis Comolli. *Free Jazz/Black Power*. Edition Champs Libre, 1971.

Carter, Dan T. "The Anatomy of Fear: The Christmas Day Insurrection Scare of 1865." *Journal of Southern History* 42, no. 3 (August 1976): 345–64.

Caux, Daniel. "Apparitions of Albert the Great in Paris and Saint-Paul-de-Vence." Liner notes. Albert Ayler, *Holy Ghost*. Revenant, 2004.

———. "My Name Is . . . Albert Ayler." *Chroniques de l'Art Avant Vivant* 17 (February 1971): 24.

Chaloin, Marc. "Albert Ayler in Europe: 1959–62." Liner notes. Albert Ayler, *Holy Ghost*, Revenant, 2004.

"Charles Tyler." *Jazz* 12 (1965): 67.

Cherry, F. L. *A History of Opelika and Her Agricultural Tributary Territory*. Genealogical Society of East Alabama, 1996.

Clark, Daniel A. "'If Just One of the Boats Had Remained': The 1862 Battle of Augusta and Its Aftermath." *Register of the Kentucky Historical Society* 114, no. 1 (2016): 41–73.

Colding, Charles E. "Blacks and the Economy." *Tribe* 3, no. 1 (1975): 9.

Coleman, Kwami. "*Free Jazz* and the 'New Thing': Aesthetics, Identity, and Texture, 1960–1966." *Journal of Musicology* 38, no. 3 (2021): 261–95.

Collins, Willie. "The Moan-and-Prayer Event in African American Worship." In *In the Spirit: Alabama's Sacred Music Traditions*, ed. Henry Willett. Black Belt, 1995.

Cox, Kenneth L. "Cultural Colonization and the Self Determination Movement in Music." *Tribe* 2, no. 2 (1974): 26–27, 29–31.

Craig, Barry. *Kentucky Confederates: Secession, Civil War, and the Jackson Purchase*. University of Kentucky Press, 2014.

Cramer, Alfred. "Schoenberg's *Klangfarbenmelodie*: A Principle of Early Atonal Harmony." *Music Theory Spectrum* 24, no. 1 (2002): 1–34.

Crepon, Pierre. "The Blistering Cosmic Music of the Black Unity Trio." *The Wire*, March 2020, https://www.thewire.co.uk/in-writing/interviews/the-black-unity-trio-cleveland-ohio-1968-1969-interviews-hasan-shahid-pierre-crepon.

———. "The Summer of '69." *Chimurenga: Imagi-nation Nwar* (April 2021): 26, 28, 59, 61, 65, 67.

Crosby, Molly Caldwell. *The American Plague: The Untold Story of Yellow Fever, the Epidemic That Shaped Our History*. Berkeley, 2006.

Cruse, Harold. "On Domestic Colonialism." *Black America* 2, no. 2 (1964): 10.

Current, Richard N. "The Politics of Reconstruction in Wisconsin, 1865–1873." *Wisconsin Magazine of History* 60, no. 2 (1976–1977): 82–108.

Curtin, Mary Ellen. "'Negro Thieves' or Enterprising Farmers?: Markets, the Law, and African American Community Regulation in Alabama, 1866–1877." *Agricultural History* 74, no. 1 (2000): 19–38.

Curtis, Edward E., IV. "Islamism and Its African American Muslim Critics: Black Muslims in the Era of the Arab Cold War." *American Quarterly* 59, no. 3 (2007): 683–709.

Daniel, Pete. "The Metamorphosis of Slavery, 1865–1900." *Journal of American History* 66, no. 1 (June 1979): 88–99.

Davis, Charles L. "Racial Politics in Central Kentucky During the Post-Reconstruction Era: Bourbon County, 1877–1899." *Register of the Kentucky Historical Society* 108, no. 4 (2010): 347–81.

Davis, Thulani. *The Emancipation Circuit: Black Activism Forging a Culture of Freedom*. Duke University Press, 2022.

DeLeon, Joseph. "'A Vital Human Place' for the Counterculture: Fifth Estate and Amateur Film Culture in Detroit, 1965–1967." In *Global Perspectives on Amateur Film Histories and Culture*, ed. Masha Salazkina and Enrique Fibla-Gutierrez, 226–42. Indiana University Press, 2020.

"Detroit Jazz." *Tribe* 1, no. 3 (1973): 20–22.

DeVito, Chris, et al. *The John Coltrane Reference*. London: Routledge, 2008.

Dew, Charles B. "Black Ironworkers and the Slave Insurrection Panic of 1856." *Journal of Southern History* 41 (1975): 321–38.

Dinnella-Borrego, Luis-Alejandro. *The Risen Phoenix: Black Politics in the Post–Civil War South*. University of Virginia Press, 2016.

Diouf, Sylviane A. *Dreams of Africa in Alabama: The Slave Ship 'Clotilda' and the Story of the Last Africans Brought to America*. Oxford University Press, 2007.

Donaldson, Bobby J. "'The Fighting Has Not Been in Vain': African American Intellectuals in Jim Crow Savannah." In *Slavery and Freedom in Savannah*, ed. Leslie M. Harris and Daina Ramey Berry, 185–212. University of Georgia Press, 2014.

Dorsey, Allison. *To Build Our Lives Together: Community Formation in Black Atlanta, 1875–1906*. University of Georgia Press, 2004.

Drott, Eric. "Free Jazz and the French Critic." *Journal of the American Musicological Society* 61, no. 3 (2008): 541–81.

Du Bois, W. E. B. *Black Reconstruction in America*. 1935; repr. Free Press, 1998.

Dumond, Dwight L., ed. *Letters of James Gillespie Birney, 1831–1857*. Vol. 2. D. Appleton-Century, 1938.

Eagle, Bob. "Directory of African-Appalachian Musicians." *Black Music Research Journal* 24, no. 1 (2004): 7–71.

Elkins, Alex. "Liberals and 'Get Tough' Policing in Postwar Detroit." In *Detroit 1967: Origins, Impacts, Legacies*, ed. Joel Stone, 106–16. Wayne State University Press, 2017.

Ellison, Mary. "Echoes of Africa in 'To Sleep with Anger' and 'Eve's Bayou.'" *African American Review* 39, no. 1/2 (2005): 213–29.

Elmore, Bartow. "Hydrology and Residential Segregation in the Postwar South: An Environmental History of Atlanta, 1865–1895." *Georgia Historical Quarterly* 94, no. 1 (2010): 30–61.

English, Ron. "Jazz in Detroit: Strata Concert Gallery 46 Selden." *Tribe* 1, no. 3 (1973): 35–6.

Evans, Chris. *The Histories of the United Mine Workers of America*, vol. 2: *1890–1900*. Microfiche. Library Resources, 1970.

Evans, David. "Charley Patton: The Conscience of the Delta," in *Charley Patton: Voice of the Mississippi Delta*, ed. Robert Sacré, 23–137. University Press of Mississippi, 2018.

Federal Writers' Project. *Mississippi: The WPA Guide to the Magnolia State*. Viking Press, 1938; repr. University Press of Mississippi, 1988.

Feight, Andrew. "'Black Friday': Enforcing Ohio's Black Laws in Portsmouth, Ohio." Scioto Historical Society. http://www.sciotohistorical.org.

Fibre, Michel. *From Harlem to Paris: Black American Writers in France, 1840–1980*. University of Illinois Press, 1991.

Finch, Herbert. "Organized Labor in Louisville, Kentucky 1865–1914." PhD diss., University of Louisville, 1965.

Fine, Elizabeth C. *Soulstepping: African American Step Shows*. University of Illinois Press, 2003.

Fine, Sidney. *Violence in the Model City: The Cavanaugh Administration, Race Relations, and the Detroit Riot of 1967*. Michigan State University Press, 2007.

Finkenbine, Roy. "A Community Militant and Organized: The Colored Vigilant Committee of Detroit." In *A Fluid Frontier: Slavery, Resistance, and the Underground Railroad in the Detroit River Borderland*, ed. Karolyn Smardz Frost and Veta Smith Tucker, 154–64. Wayne State University Press, 2016.

Fishel, Leslie H., Jr. "Wisconsin and Negro Suffrage." *Wisconsin Magazine of History* 46, no. 3 (1963): 180–96.

Fitzgerald, Michael W. "The Ku Klux Klan: Property Crime and the Plantation System in Reconstruction Alabama." *Agricultural History* 71, no. 2 (1997): 186–206.

———. "'To Give Our Votes to the Party': Black Political Agitation and Agricultural Change in Alabama, 1865–1870." *Journal of American History* 76, no. 2 (September 1989): 489–505.

———. *Urban Emancipation: Popular Politics in Reconstruction Mobile 1860–1890*. Louisiana State University Press, 2002.

Foner, Philip S., and Ronald Lewis, eds. *The Black Worker*, vol. 2: *The Black Worker During the Era of the National Labor Union*. Temple University Press, 1978.

———. *The Black Worker: A Documentary History from Colonial Times to the Present*, vol. 5: *The Black Worker from 1900 to 1919*. Temple University Press, 1980.

———. *The Black Worker*, vol. 6: *The Era of Post-War Prosperity and the Great Depression, 1920–1936*. Temple University Press, 1981.

Ford, Bridget. "Black Spiritual Defiance and the Politics of Slavery in Antebellum Louisville." *Journal of Southern History* 78, no. 1 (February 2012): 69–106.

Foster, Emily. *The Ohio Frontier: An Anthology of Early Writings*. University Press of Kentucky, 1996.

Free Lance Poets and Prose Workshop. *The Muntu Poets of Cleveland*. United Black Artists of Cleveland, 1968, repr. 2016.

Frost, Karolyn Smardz. "Forging Transnational Networks for Freedom: From the War of 1812 to the Blackburn Riots of 1833." In *A Fluid Frontier: Slavery, Resistance, and the Underground Railroad in the Detroit River Borderland*, ed. Karolyn Smardz Frost and Veta Smith Tucker, 43–66. Wayne State University Press, 2016.

Fry, Gladys-Marie. *Night Riders in Black Folk History*. University of North Carolina Press, 2001.

Gabriel, Larry. "Rebirth of Tribe," in *Heaven Was Detroit: From Jazz to Hip-Hop and Beyond*, ed. M. L. Liebler, 26–37. Wayne State University Press, 2016.

General Catalogue of Oberlin College, 1833–1908, Including an Account of the Principal Events in the History of the College, with Illustrations of the College Buildings. Oberlin College, 1909.

Georgakas, Dan, and Marvin Surkin. *Detroit: I Do Mind Dying; A Study in Urban Revolution*. 3rd ed. Haymarket, 2012.

Gerstin, Julian. "Tangled Roots: Kalenda and Other Neo-African Dances in the Circum-Caribbean." *NWIG: New West Indian Guide* 78, no. 1/2 (2004): 5–41.

Gioia, Ted. *West Coast Jazz: Modern Jazz in California, 1945–1960*. Oxford University Press, 1992.

Gizenga, Mulele. "Africa: America's Next Vietnam?" *Tribe* 2, no. 1 (1974): 32–33.

———. "Phony Détente: South Africa Prepares for War." *Tribe* 3, no. 3 (1975): 8.

Goldman, Jon, and Martin Davidson. "Albert Ayler: Life and Recordings." *Cadence* 1, no. 4 (April 1976): 8–11.

Gregory, James N. *The Southern Diaspora: How the Great Migrations of Black and White Southerners Transformed America*. University of North Carolina Press, 2005.

Griffler, Keith P. *Front Line of Freedom: African Americans and the Forging of the Underground Railroad in the Ohio Valley*. University Press of Kentucky, 2004.

Grossman, James R. *Land of Hope: Chicago, Black Southerners, and the Great Migration*. University of Chicago Press, 2017.

Guthrie, Charles S. "Tobacco: Cash Crop of the Cumberland Valley." *Kentucky Folklore Record* 14 (1968): 38–43.

Guthrie, James W., and Gary Peevely. "King Cotton's Lasting Legacy of Poverty and Southern Region Contemporary Conditions." *Peabody Journal of Education* 85, no. 1 (2010): 4–15.

Hahn, Steven. *A Nation Under Our Feet: Black Political Struggles in the Rural South from Slavery to the Great Migration*. Belknap Press of Harvard University Press, 2003.

Hall, Suzanne M. "Working the Black Patch: Tobacco Farming Traditions, 1890–1930." *Register of the Kentucky Historical Society* 89, no. 3 (1991): 266–86.

Hamlin, Michael. *A Black Revolutionary's Life in Labor: Black Workers Power in Detroit*. Against the Tide, 2012.

Handy, W. C. *Father of the Blues: An Autobiography*. Macmillan, 1941.

Harbour, Jennifer R. *Organizing Freedom: Black Emancipation Activism in the Civil War Midwest*. Southern Illinois University Press, 2020.

Harrison, Lowell H. *The Antislavery Movement in Kentucky*. University of Kentucky Press, 1978.

Hartman, Saidiya. *Scenes of Subjection: Terror, Slavery, and Self-Making in Nineteenth-Century America*. Rev. ed. Norton, 2022.

Haveman, Christopher D. *Bending Their Way Onward: Creek Indian Removal in Documents.* University of Nebraska Press, 2020.

———. *Rivers of Sand: Creek Indian Emigration, Relocation, and Ethnic Cleansing in the American South.* University of Nebraska Press, 2020.

Hayden, René, et al., eds. *Freedom: A Documentary History of Emancipation, 1861–1867,* Series 3, Vol. 2: *Land and Labor, 1866–1867.* University of North Carolina Press, 2013.

Head, Holman. "The Development of the Labor Movement in Alabama Prior to 1900." MA thesis, University of Alabama, 1955.

Hearn, Lafcadio. *The Children of the Levee.* Ed. O. W. Frost. University of Kentucky Press, 1957.

Helgeson, Jeffrey. "Politics in the Promised Land: How the Great Migration Shaped the American Midwest." In *Finding a New Midwestern History,* ed. Jon K. Lauck et al., 111–26. University of Nebraska Press, 2020.

Heller, Michael C. *Loft Jazz: Improvising New York in the 1970s.* University of California Press, 2016.

Hentoff, Nat. "Albert Ayler—the Truth Is Marching In." *Down Beat,* November 17, 1966, 17.

———. Liner notes. Albert Ayler, *In Greenwich Village.* Impulse!, 1967.

Herd-Clark, Dawn. "Jane Deveaux and Her Secret School." In *Slavery and Freedom in Savannah,* ed. Leslie M. Harris and Daina Ramey Berry, 134–35. University of Georgia Press, 2014.

Heron, W. Kim. "Musician Interrupted: Faruq Z. Bey." In *Heaven Was Detroit: From Jazz to Hip-Hop and Beyond,* ed. M. L. Liebler, 47–59. Wayne State University Press, 2016.

Hill, Robert, ed. *The Marcus Garvey and Universal Negro Improvement Association Papers,* vol. 4. University of California Press, 1985.

Hines, Sandra. "Detroit Coalition Against Police Brutality." In *Why Detroit Matters: Decline, Hope, and Renewal in a Divided City,* ed. Brian Doucet, 283–88. Bristol University Press, 2017.

Hischak, Thomas S. *Enter the Players: New York Stage Actors in the Twentieth Century.* Scarecrow, 2003.

Holloway, Betty. "Here's Looking at Unemployment." *Tribe* 3, no. 1 (1975): 11–13.

———. "Rappin' with Butter." *Tribe* 3, no. 1 (1975): 24–25.

Holzhueter, John O. "Ezekiel Gillespie, Lost and Found." *Wisconsin Magazine of History* 60, no. 3 (1977): 178–84.

Hornstein, Julius. *Sites and Sounds of Savannah Jazz.* Gaston Street, 1994.

Howard, Victor B. *Black Liberation in Kentucky: Emancipation and Freedom.* University of Kentucky Press, 1983.

Howard, Walter T. *We Shall Be Free! Black Communist Protests in Seven Voices.* Temple University Press, 2013.

Howe, Henry. *Historical Collections of Ohio: Containing a Collection of the Most Interesting Facts, Traditions, Biographical Sketches, Anecdotes, etc., Relating to Its General and Local History; with Descriptions of Its Counties, Principal Towns and Villages.* Cincinnati: Derby and Bradley, 1847.

Howell, Elmo. *Mississippi Backroads: Notes on Literature and History.* Langford, 1998.

Hudson, Hosea. *Black Workers in the Deep South: A Personal Record.* International Publishers, 1972.

Hurston, Zora Neale. *Barracoon: The Story of the Last "Black Cargo."* Amistad, 2018.

Hutton, Randy. "Review of Rivbea Summer Music Festival." *Coda* 11, no. 11 (September 1974): 32.

Ingham, John N. "Building Businesses, Creating Communities: Residential Segregation and the Growth of African American Business in Southern Cities, 1880–1915." *Business History Review* 77, no. 4 (2003): 639–65.

Ingram, Jim. "The Economy and Detroit." *Tribe* 3, no. 2 (1975): 32–35.

———. "Mayor Coleman A. Young's First Year in Office: How Did It Go?" *Tribe* 3, no. 1 (1975): 14–17.

Isoardi, Steve. *The Dark Tree: Jazz and Community Arts in Los Angeles.* University of California Press, 2006.

Jacoby, Sanford M. *Modern Manors: Welfare Capitalism Since the New Deal.* Princeton University Press, 1997.

Jacques, Geoffrey. "Kalaparusha: Forces and Feelings." *Tribe* 1, no. 3 (1973): 45.
———. "The Nigger Beaters." *Tribe* 1, no. 3 (1973): 42.
Jamison, Phil. *Hoedowns, Reels, and Frolics: Roots and Branches of Southern Appalachian Dance*. University of Illinois Press, 2015.
Jay, Mark, and Philip Conklin. *A People's History of Detroit*. Duke University Press, 2020.
Jay, Mark, and Virginia Leavell. "Material Conditions of Detroit's Great Rebellion." *Social Justice* 44, no. 4 (2017): 27–54.
"Jazz Professor." *Ebony*, May 1970, 110–11.
Jeffries, Judson L. *Comrades: A Local History of the Black Panther Party*. Indiana University Press, 2007.
Jenkins, Ned T. *Mapping the Mississippian Shatter Zone: The Colonial Indian Slave Trade and Regional Instability in the American South*. University of Nebraska Press, 2009.
Johnson, Michael P. "Out of Egypt: The Migration of Former Slaves to the Midwest During the 1860s in Comparative Perspective." In *Crossing Boundaries: Comparative History of Black People in Diaspora*, ed. Darlene Clark Hine and Jacqueline McLeod, 223–45. Indiana University Press, 1999.
Jones, Leroi. *Black Music*. W. Morrow, 1967.
———. "The Changing Same (R&B and New Black Music)." In *The Black Aesthetic*, ed. Addison Gayle Jr. Doubleday, 1971.
———. "Don Cherry: Making It the Hard Way." *Down Beat* 30, no. 30 (November 21, 1963): 16–17, 39.
Jost, Ekkehard. *Free Jazz*. Universal Editions, 1975.
———. *Jazzmusiker: Materialen zur Soziologie der Afro-Amerikanischen Musik*. Ullstein, 1982.
Justus, Judith P. *Down from the Mountain: The Oral History of the Hemings Family*. Juskurtara, 1990.
Kagie, Rudie. "Avonturen in de New Thing." *Jazz Bulletin* 83 (June 2012): 37.
Kauppila, Paul. "'From Memphis to Kingston': An Investigation Into the Origin of Jamaican Ska." *Social and Economic Studies* 55, no. 1/2 (March/June 2006): 75–91.
Kaye, Anthony E. *Joining Places: Slave Neighborhoods of the Old South*. University of North Carolina Press, 2007.
Kean, J. Randolph. "The Development of the 'Valley Line' of the Baltimore and Ohio Railroad." *Virginia Magazine of History and Biography* 60, no. 4 (October 1952): 537–50.
Keil, Charles. *Urban Blues*. University of Chicago Press, 1966.
Kelley, Robin D. G. *Freedom Dreams: The Black Radical Imagination*. Rev. ed. Beacon, 2022.
———. *Hammer and Hoe: Alabama Communists During the Great Depression*. University of North Carolina Press, 2015.
Kelly, Joseph. "Showing Agency on the Margins: African American Railway Workers in the South and Their Unions, 1917–1930." *Labour/La Travail* 71 (2013): 123–48.
Kerr, Daniel. *Derelict Paradise: Homelessness and Urban Development in Cleveland, Ohio*. University of Massachusetts Press, 2011.
———. "'The Reign of Wickedness': The Changing Structures of Prostitution, Gambling, and Political Protection in Cleveland from the Progressive Era to the Great Depression." MA thesis, Case Western Reserve University, 1998.
Kirk, Russell. *John Randolph of Roanoke: A Study in American Politics, with Selected Speeches and Letters*. Regnery, 1964.
Klug, Thomas A. "The Deindustrialization of Detroit." In *Detroit 1967: Origins, Impacts, Legacies*, ed. Joel Stone, 65–75. Wayne State University Press, 2017.
Koloda, Richard. *Holy Ghost: The Life and Death of Free Jazz Pioneer Albert Ayler*. Jawbone, 2022.
Kopelowicz, Guy. "Impressions de New York." *Jazz Hot* 1 (1968): 21.
Kramer, Michael J. "'Can't Forget the Motor City': *Creem* Magazine, Rock Music, Detroit Identity, Mass Consumerism, and the Counterculture." *Michigan Historical Review* 28, no. 2 (2002): 42–77.
Kroll, Harry Harrison. *Riders in the Night*. University of Pennsylvania Press, 1965.
Kusmer, Kenneth L. *A Ghetto Takes Shape: Black Cleveland, 1870–1930*. University of Illinois Press, 1976.

Lamb, J. Parker. *Railroads of Meridian*. Indiana University Press, 2012.
LaRoche, Cheryl Janifer. *Free Black Communities and the Underground Railroad: The Geography of Resistance*. University of Illinois Press, 2014.
Laws, Terri, and Kimberly R. Enard. "'I AM What I AM': The Religion of White Rage, Great Migration Detroit, and the Ford Motor Company." In *The Religion of White Rage: Religious Fervor, White Workers, and the Myth of Black Racial Progress*, ed. Stephen C. Finley et al., 58–72. Edinburgh University Press, 2020.
Lawson, Elizabeth. "The Jobless Negro." In *The Black Worker, vol. 6: The Era of Post-War Prosperity and the Great Depression, 1920–1936*, ed. Philip S. Foner and Ronald L. Lewis, 483–88. Temple University Press, 1981.
Lester, Charles. "'You Can't Keep the Music Unless You Move with It': The Great Migration and the Black Cultural Politics of Jazz in New Orleans and Chicago." In *Escape from New York: The New Negro Renaissance Beyond Harlem*, ed. Davarian L. Baldwin and Minkah Makalani, 313–34. University of Minnesota Press, 2013.
Letwin, Daniel. "Interracial Unionism, Gender, and 'Social Equality' in the Alabama Coalfields, 1878–1908." *Journal of Southern History* 61, no. 3 (August 1995): 519–54.
Lewis, George E. *A Power Stronger Than Itself: The AACM and American Experimental Music*. University of Chicago Press, 2009.
Lewis, Ronald L. *Black Coal Miners in America: Race, Class, and Community Conflict, 1780–1980*. University Press of Kentucky, 1987.
Lichtenstein, Alexander C. "Was the Emancipated Slave a Proletarian?" *Reviews in American History* 26 (March 1998): 124–48.
———. *Twice the Work of Free Labor: The Political Economy of Convict Labor in the New South*. Verso, 1996.
Lieb, Sandra R. *Mother of the Blues: A Study of Ma Rainey*. University of Massachusetts Press, 1982.
Litweiler, John. *The Freedom Principle: Jazz After 1958*. Da Capo, 1984.
Logan, John R., et al. "Creating the Black Ghetto: Black Residential Patterns Before and During the Great Migration." *Annals of the American Academy of Political and Social Science* 660 (July 2015): 18–35.
Looker, Benjamin. *Point from Which Creation Begins: The Black Artists' Group of St. Louis*. Missouri Historical Society Press, 2004.
Loupien, Serge. *La France underground: Free jazz et rock pop, 1965/1979, les temps des utopies*. Rivages Rouge, 2018.
Lovett, Bobby L. "Memphis Riots: White Reaction to Blacks in Memphis, May 1865–July 1866." *Tennessee Historical Quarterly* 38, no. 1 (1979): 9–33.
Loyal. "Letter from Mississippi." *New National Era*, March 14, 1872.
Lucas, Marion B. *A History of Blacks in Kentucky: From Slavery to Segregation, 1760–1891*. University of Kentucky Press, 2003.
Lumumba, Chokwe. "Short History of the U.S. War on the R.N.A." *The Black Scholar* 12, no. 1 (January/February 1981): 72–81.
Lunsford, Anita. *The Conspiracy of John Randolph's Slaves*. Private pub., 2006.
Marshall, Anne E. *Creating a Confederate Kentucky: The Lost Cause and Civil War Memory in a Border State*. University of North Carolina Press, 2013.
Marshall, Suzanne. *Violence in the Black Patch of Kentucky and Tennessee*. University of Missouri Press, 1994.
Martin, Elizabeth Anne. *Detroit and the Great Migration, 1916–1929*. Bulletin no. 40. Bentley Historical Library, University of Michigan, Ann Arbor, 1993.
Martin, Grant. "All That Jazz." *Tribe* 3, no. 1 (1975): 30.
———. "Caught in the Act: The Creative Profiles 'Live and Well' at the Blackhorse." *Tribe* 2, no. 1 (1974): 43.
———. "The Immortal John Coltrane." *Tribe* 1, no. 4 (1973): 24–30.
———. "The Prodigal Son Returns: An Interview with Donald Byrd." *Tribe* 1, no. 3 (1973): 25–34.

———. "A Profile of Sun Ra." *Tribe* 3, no. 2 (1975): 20–23.
———. "Wendell Harrison and Tribe Present *An Evening with the Devil*." *Tribe* 1, no. 3 (1973): 46.
Massey, Douglas S., and Nancy A. Denton. *American Apartheid: Segregation and the Making of the Underclass*. Harvard University Press, 1993.
Mathes, Carter. *Imagine the Sound: Experimental African American Literature After Civil Rights*. University of Minnesota Press, 2015.
Mathias, Frank F. "John Randolph's Freedmen: The Thwarting of a Will." *Journal of Southern History* 39, no. 2 (May 1973): 263–72.
Matlin, Daniel. "'Lift Up Yr Self!': Reinterpreting Amiri Baraka (Leroi Jones), Black Power, and the Uplift Tradition." *Journal of American History* 93, no. 1 (June 2006): 91–116.
Mauldin, Erin Stewart. "Freedom, Economic Autonomy, and Ecological Change in the Cotton South, 1865–1880." *Journal of the Civil War Era* 7, no. 3 (September 2017): 401–24.
McCartin, Joseph A. *Labor's Great War: The Struggle for Industrial Democracy and the Origins of Modern American Labor Relations, 1912–1921*. University of North Carolina Press, 1997.
McCloud, Aminah Beverly. *African American Islam*. Routledge, 1995.
McGill, James. *The First One-Hundred Years of Upson County Negro History*. AuthorHouse, 2017.
McNeilly, J. S. "The Enforcement Act of 1871 and the Ku Klux Klan in Mississippi." Ed. Franklin L. Riley. *Publications of the Mississippi Historical Society* 9 (1906): 109–71.
McRae, Barry. "Avant Courier: Frank Wright—Working on." *Jazz Journal* 28, no. 8 (August 1978): 13.
Meyers, David, and Elise Meyers Walker. *Historic Black Settlements of Ohio*. History Press, 2020.
Miller, John G. *The Black Patch War*. University of North Carolina Press, 1936.
Miller, M. V., and S. Gilmore. *Revolution at Berkeley*. Laurel, 1965.
Mitchell, Martha. "Birmingham: A Biography of a City of the New South." PhD diss., University of Chicago, 1946.
"Monteith College: Roots of the Workshop." Detroid Artists' Workshop. https://www.detroitartistsworkshop.com/monteith-college-roots-of-the-workshop/.
Montgomery, David. *Workers' Control in America: Studies in the History of Work, Technology, and Labor Struggles*. Cambridge University Press, 1979.
Morrison, Allan. "A New Surge in the Arts: Younger Generation Enhances Long Tradition of Creative Expression." *Ebony*, August 1967, 136.
Morrison, Melanie S. *Murder on Shades Mountain: The Legal Lynching of Willie Peterson and the Struggle for Justice in Jim Crow Birmingham*. Duke University Press, 2018.
Moten, Fred. *Black and Blur*. Duke University Press, 2017.
———. *In the Break: The Aesthetics of the Black Radical Tradition*. University of Minnesota Press, 2003.
Mueller, Ulrich F. *Red, Black, and White: A History of Carthagena, Mercer County, Ohio*. 1934.
Muhammad, Sadiq. "Mathematics of Melody," *Solid Ground: A New World Journal* 1, no. 2 (1982): 32.
Murray, Williamson, and Wayne Wei-siang Hsieh. *A Savage War: A Military History of the Civil War*. Princeton University Press, 2018.
Nall, James O. *The Tobacco Night Riders of Kentucky and Tennessee, 1905–1909*. Standard Press, 1939.
Natambu, Kofi. "The Visionary Consciousness of Faruq Z. Bey and the Long Revolution of the Black Creative Music Tradition." *Sound Projections*. https://soundprojections.blogspot.com/2018/02/faruq-z-bey-1942-2012-legendary-iconic.html.
Neal, Larry. "New Grass/Albert Ayler." *Cricket* 3 (1969): 37–39.
Neal, Larry, et al., eds. *Visions of a Liberated Future: Black Arts Movement Writings*. Thunder's Mouth, 1989.
Nelson, Ed. "Concert Review." *Tribe* 4, no. 3 (May–June 1976): 23.
Nielson, Erik. "White Surveillance of the Black Arts." *African American Review* 47, no. 1 (2014): 161–77.
Obadele, Imari Abubakari. "The Struggle of the Republic of New Africa." *The Black Scholar* 5, no. 9 (June 1974): 32–41.

Obrecht, Jas. *Early Blues: The First Stars of Blues Guitar*. University of Minnesota Press, 2015.
Oda, James C. *An Encyclopedia of Piqua, Ohio*. M. T. Publishing, 2007.
O'Foran, Shelly. *Little Zion: A Church Baptized by Fire*. University of North Carolina Press, 2006.
Oliver, Paul. "Mining 'The True Folk Vein': Some Directions for Research in Black Music." *Black Music Research Journal* 5 (1985): 21–31.
Ongiri, Amy Abugo. *Spectacular Blackness: The Cultural Politics of the Black Power Movement and the Search for a Black Aesthetic*. University of Virginia Press, 2010.
Ostendorf, Berndt. "Celebration or Pathology? Commodity or Art? The Dilemma of African-American Expressive Culture." *Black Music Research Journal* 20, no. 2 (2000): 217–36.
Paisley, Clifton. "Madison County's Sea Island Cotton Industry, 1870–1916." *Florida Historical Quarterly* 54, no. 3 (January 1976): 285–305.
Parsons, Elaine Frantz. *Ku-Klux: The Birth of the Klan During Reconstruction*. University of North Carolina Press, 2015.
Paterson, David E. "Slavery in the Village: Urban Bondage in Microcosm." Unpublished manuscript.
——. "Slavery, Slaves, and Cash in a Georgia Village, 1825–1865." *Journal of Southern History* 75, no. 4 (November 2009): 879–930.
Pease, William H., and Jane H. Pease. "Organized Negro Communities: A North American Experiment." *Journal of Negro History* 47, no. 1 (January 1962): 19–34.
Penn, William A. *Kentucky Rebel Town: The Civil War Battles of Cynthiana and Harrison County*. University Press of Kentucky, 2016.
Peters, Jeremy. "Cultural and Social Mecca: Entrepreneurial Action and Venue Agglomeration in Detroit's Paradise Valley and Black Bottom Neighborhoods." *Artivate* 9, no. 1 (2020): 20–41.
Peterson, Joyce Shaw. "Black Automobile Workers in Detroit, 1910–1930." *Journal of Negro History* 64, no. 3 (1979): 177–90.
Phillips, Kimberly L. *AlabamaNorth: African-American Migrants, Community, and Working Class Activism in Cleveland, 1915–1945*. University of Illinois Press, 1999.
Pinelli, Joe. "Ayler on Record: Lyrical Rockets." *Change* 2 (1966): 111–13.
Pinotti, Emanuele. "Charles Lacy Tyler." *Improjazz*, February 1997, 20.
Pitts, Timothy J. "Hugh M. Dorsey and 'The Negro in Georgia.'" *Georgia Historical Quarterly* 89, no. 2 (2005): 185–212.
Powell, C. A., et al. "Transplanting Free Negroes to Ohio from 1815 to 1858." *Journal of Negro History* 1, no. 3 (June 1916): 302–17.
Price-Spratlen, Townsand. "Urban Destination Selection Among African Americans During the 1950s Great Migration." *Social Science History* 32, no. 3 (2008): 437–69.
Quattrrocchi, Angelo. "What Happened." In *The Beginning of the End*, ed. Angelo Quattrocchi and Tom Nairn. Panther, 1968; repr. Verso, 1998.
Ramage, James A., and Andrea S. Watkins. *Kentucky Rising: Democracy, Slavery, and Culture from the Early Republic to the Civil War*. University Press of Kentucky, 2011.
"A Rap with Melvin Van Peebles." *Tribe* 1, no. 3 (1973): 15.
Ratcliffe, Philip R. *Mississippi John Hurt: His Life, His Times, His Blues*. University Press of Mississippi, 2011.
Rayner, John A. *The First Century of Piqua, Ohio*. Magee Bros. Co., 1916.
Rikard, Marlene Hunt. *The Black Industrial Experience in Early Twentieth Century Birmingham*. Alabama Center for Higher Education, 1979.
Robenalt, James. *Ballots and Bullets: Black Power Politics and Urban Guerilla Warfare in 1968 Cleveland*. Lawrence Hill, 2018.
Robertson, Brian K. "'Will They Fight? Ask the Enemy': United States Colored Troops at Big Creek, Arkansas, July 26, 1864." *Arkansas Historical Quarterly* 66, no. 3 (2007): 320–32.
Rohrbough, Malcolm J. *Trans-Appalachian Frontier: People, Societies, and Institutions, 1775–1850*. 3rd ed. Indiana University Press, 2008.

Rosen, Hannah. *Terror in the Heart of Freedom: Citizenship, Sexual Violence, and the Meaning of Race in the Postemancipation South.* University of North Carolina Press, 2009.
Rowe, Jill E. *Invisible in Plain Sight.* Peter Lang, 2017.
———. "Mixing It Up: Early African American Settlements in Northwestern Ohio." *Journal of Black Studies* 39, no. 6 (July 2000): 924–36.
Ruef, Martin. *Between Slavery and Capitalism: The Legacy of Emancipation in the American South.* Princeton University Press, 2014.
Rusch, Bob. "Review: Bobby Few, Alan Silva, Frank Wright, *Solo et Duets* (Sun Records, 1975)." *Cadence* 2, no. 5 (February 1977): 35–36.
———. "Review: Frank Wright, *One for John* (BYG Records, 1970)." *Cadence* 5, no. 10 (October 1979): 29.
———. "Two: Ayler, Twice." *Hip*, 1970, 17.
Safane, Clifford Jay. "Charles Tyler: The Saga of a Saxophonist." *Music Journal*, September 1979, 18.
Salem, James M. "Death and the Rhythm-and-Bluesmen: The Life and Recordings of Johnny Ace." *American Music* 11, no. 3 (1993): 316–67.
Sandberg, David. "Bells." *Change* 2 (1966): 113–14.
Schapp, Alain, and Pierre Vidal-Naquet. *The French Student Uprising November 1967–June 1968: An Analytical Record.* Trans. Maria Jolas. Beacon, 1969.
Schweninger, Loren. "Prosperous Blacks in the South, 1790–1880." *American Historical Review* 95, no. 1 (February 1990): 31–56.
Share, Allen J. *Cities in the Commonwealth: Two Centuries of Urban Life in Kentucky.* University Press of Kentucky, 1982.
Sharp, Charles. "Seeking John Carter and Bobby Bradford: Free Jazz and Community in Los Angeles." *Black Music Research Journal* 31, no. 1 (2011): 65–81.
Shepp, Archie. Interview. https://www.youtube.com/watch?v=3BUzRl_fFiA.
Sinclair, Leni. *Motor City Underground: Photographs 1963–1978.* Museum of Contemporary Art Detroit, 2021.
———. *Participant Observer: Fotografien von 1960 bis 2000.* Mitteldeutscher Verlag, 2021.
Sisk, Glenn N. "Negro Migration in the Alabama Black Belt, 1875–1917." *Negro History Bulletin* 17, no. 2 (November 1953): 32–34.
———. "The Wholesale Commission Business in the Alabama Black Belt." *Journal of Farm Economics* 38, no. 3 (August 1956): 799–802.
Sledge, John S. *The Mobile River.* University of South Carolina Press, 2015.
Smith, Barbara Hughes. "Worship Waystations in Detroit." In *A Fluid Frontier: Slavery, Resistance, and the Underground Railroad in the Detroit River Borderland*, ed. Karolyn Smardz Frost and Veta Smith Tucker, 103–19. Wayne State University Press, 2016.
Smith, Demon. "Toward a Black Theatre Quintessence." *Tribe* 2, no. 1 (1974): 37–40.
Smith, Shannon M. "'They Met Force with Force': African American Protests and Social Status in Louisville's 1877 Strike." *Register of the Kentucky Historical Society* 115, no. 1 (2017): 1–37.
Sparks, Randy J. *On Jordan's Stormy Banks: Evangelicalism in Mississippi, 1773–1876.* Athens: University of Georgia Press, 1994.
Spellman, A. B. *Four Lives in the Bebop Business.* Limelight Editions, 1966.
Spencer, J. H. *A History of Kentucky Baptists from 1769 to 1855*, vol. 1. Cincinnati: J. R. Baumes, 1885.
Stuckey, Sterling. *Slave Culture: Nationalist Theory and the Foundations of Black America.* Oxford University Press, 1994.
Sugrue, Thomas J. "'Forget About Your Inalienable Right to Work': Deindustrialization and Its Discontents at Ford, 1950–1953." *International Labor and Working-Class History* 48 (1995): 112–30.
Sumler-Edmond, Janice L. "Free Black Life in Savannah." In *Slavery and Freedom in Savannah*, ed. Leslie M. Harris and Daina Ramey Berry, 124–39. University of Georgia Press, 2014.

Taylor, Derek. "Review: *Center of the World* (Center of the World, 1972, reissued Fractal, 1999) and *Last Polka in Nancy?* (Center of the World, 1973: reissued: Fractal, 1999)." *Cadence* 25, no. 11 (November 1999): 29.

Taylor, Jack. "Revolution at the Point of Production: An Interview with Mike Hamlin of DRUM and the League of Revolutionary Black Workers." *Spectrum: A Journal of Black Men* 2, no. 1 (2013): 99–112.

Taylor, W. Allen. "In Search of My Father: Walkin' Talkin' Bill Hawkins." *Walkintalkin.com*, 2007. http://www.walkintalkin.com/bios2.html.

Thomas, Lorenzo. "The Shadow World: New York's Umbra Workshop & Origins of the Black Arts Movement." *Callaloo* 4 (October 1978): 53–72.

Thompson, H. Paul. *A Most Stirring and Significant Episode: Religion and the Rise and Fall of Prohibition in Black Atlanta, 1865–1887*. Cornell University Press, 2013.

Thompson, Julius E. *Lynchings in Mississippi: A History, 1865–1965*. McFarland, 2011.

Thornbrough, Emma. *The Negro in Indiana: A Study of a Minority*. Indiana Historical Collections 37. Indiana Historical Bureau, 1957.

Threadgill, Henry, and Brent Hayes Edwards. *Easily Slip into Another World: A Life in Music*. Knopf, 2023.

Ticknor, Thomas James. "Motor City: The Impact of the Automobile Industry on Detroit, 1900–1975." PhD diss., University of Michigan, 1978.

Tolnay, Stewart E. "The African American 'Great Migration' and Beyond." *Annual Review of Sociology* 29 (2003): 209–32.

Tosches, Nick. *Unsung Heroes of Rock 'n' Roll*. Charles Scribner's Sons, 1984.

Tracy, Steven C. "To the Tune of Those Weary Blues: The Influence of the Blues Tradition in Langston Hughes's Blues Poems." *MELUS* 8, no. 3 (1981): 73–98.

Trotter, Joe William, Jr. *River Jordan: African American Urban Life in the Ohio Valley*. University Press of Kentucky, 1998.

Tucker, Veta Smith. "Uncertain Freedom in Frontier Detroit." In *Fluid Frontier: Slavery, Resistance, and the Underground Railroad in the Detroit River Borderland*, ed. Karolyn Smardz Frost and Veta Smith Tucker, 27–42. Wayne State University Press, 2016.

Uchimura, Kazuko. "Coal Operators and Market Competition: The Case of West Virginia's Smokeless Coalfields and the Fairmont Field, 1853–1933." *West Virginia History* 4, no. 2 (2010): 59–86.

Underwood, E. E. *A Brief History of the Colored Churches of Frankfort, Kentucky*. Bugle Pub. Co., 1906.

Van Pelt, Derek. "Albert Ayler's Ghost." *Cleveland Magazine*, December 1978, 43.

Vance, W. Silas. "The Marion Riot." *The Mississippi Quarterly* 27, no. 4 (1974): 447–66.

Vaughn, Vernon R. *Vaughn History*. Private pub., 1964.

Verrastro, Scott. "Frank Wright: Unity." *Jazz Times*, April 25, 2019.

Vidal-Naquet, Pierre. "Outline of a Revolution." in *The French Student Uprising November 1967–June 1968: An Analytical Record*, ed. Alain Schapp and Pierre Vidal-Naquet, tr. Maria Jolas, 1–48, Beacon, 1969.

Wade, Richard. "The Negro in Cincinnati, 1800–1830." *Journal of Negro History* 39 (January 1954): 43–57.

———. *Urban Frontier: Pioneer Life in Early Pittsburgh, Cincinnati, Lexington, Louisville, and St. Louis*. University of Chicago Press, 1959.

Waldrep, Christopher. "Planters and the Planters' Protective Association in Kentucky and Tennessee." *Journal of Southern History* 52, no. 4 (November 1986): 565–88.

Waller, Ray. "Creative Arts Collective Concert: Holland & Bey Explode the 'Classical Conceit.'" *Solid Ground: A New World Journal* 1, no. 3/4 (1983): 43.

Ward, Stephen M. *In Love and Struggle*. University of North Carolina Press, 2016.

Ward, Stephen M., ed. *Pages from a Black Radical's Notebook: A James Boggs Reader*. Wayne State University Press, 2011.

Washington, Salim. "'All the Things You Could Be by Now': Charles Mingus Presents Charles Mingus and the Limits of Avant-Garde Jazz." In *Uptown Conversation: The New Jazz Studies*, ed. Robert O'Meally et al., 27–49. Columbia University Press, 2004.

Weiman, David F. "Peopling the Land by Lottery? The Market in Public Lands and the Regional Differentiation of Territory on the Georgia Frontier." *Journal of Economic History* 51, no. 4 (December 1991): 835–60.

Weinstein, Norman. "Charles Tyler's *Saga of the Outlaws*: Jazz at the Threshold of a Shootout." *Noh Quarter* (1987): 43–44.

Weiss, Jason. *Always in Trouble: An Oral History of ESP-Disk, the Most Outrageous Record Label in America*. Wesleyan University Press, 2012.

Welding, Peter J. "I'm Peg Leg Howell." In *Nothing but the Blues*, ed. Mike Leadbetter. Michael Joseph, 1960.

Welty, Eudora. "Cindy and the Joyful Noise." *Eudora Welty Review* 5 (2013): 19–26.

Whiteis, David. *Southern Soul-Blues*. University of Illinois Press, 2013.

Wilkerson, Isabel. *The Warmth of Other Suns: The Epic Story of America's Great Migration*. Vintage, 2010.

Williams, David Leander. *Indianapolis Jazz: The Masters, Legends, and Legacy of Indiana Avenue*. History Press, 2014.

Williams, K. Leander. "Reissues." *Cadence* 19, no. 2 (February 1993): 19.

Williamson, Edward C. "Black Belt Political Crisis: The Savage-James Lynching, 1882." *Florida Historical Quarterly* 45, no. 4 (April 1967): 402–9.

Wilmer, S. E. *Theatre, Society, and the Nation: Staging American Identities*. Cambridge University Press, 2002.

Wilmer, Valerie. *As Serious as Your Life: The Story of the New Jazz*. Lawrence Hill, 1977.

——. "Spiritual Unity." Liner notes. Albert Ayler, *Holy Ghost*, Revenant, 2004.

Wilson, Bobby M. *America's Johannesburg: Industrialization and Racial Transformation in Birmingham*. New ed. Geographies of Justice and Social Transformation. University of Georgia Press, 2019.

Wilson, Peter Niklas. *Spirits Rejoice! Albert Ayler and His Message*. Trans. Jane White. Wolke Verlag Hofheim, 1996.

Wood, Nicholas. "John Randolph of Roanoke and the Politics of Slavery in the Early Republic." *Virginia Magazine of History and Biography* 120, no. 2 (2012): 106–43.

Woodrum, Robert H. "Race, Unionism, and the Open-Shop Movement Along the Waterfront in Mobile, Alabama." In *Against Labor: How U.S. Employers Organized to Defeat Union Activism*, ed. Rosemary Feurer and Chad Pearson, 104–28. University of Illinois Press, 2017.

Woods, Clyde. *Development Arrested: The Blues and Plantation Power in the Mississippi Delta*. New ed. Verso, 2017.

Woodson, Byron. *A President in the Family: Thomas Jefferson, Sally Hemings, and Thomas Woodson*. Praeger, 2001.

Worger, William H. "Convict Labour, Industrialists, and the State in the US South and South Africa, 1870–1930." *Journal of Southern African Studies* 30, no. 1 (March 2004): 63–86.

Worthy, William. "The Red Chinese American Negro." *Esquire*, October 1964, 23.

Wright, George C. *A History of Blacks in Kentucky*, vol. 2: *In Pursuit of Equality, 1890–1980*. Kentucky Historical Society, 1992.

——. *Life Behind a Veil: Blacks in Louisville, Kentucky, 1865–1930*. Louisiana State University Press, 1985.

——. *Racial Violence in Kentucky, 1865–1940: Lynching, Mob Rule, and "Legal Lynchings."* Louisiana State University Press, 1990.

Wright, Sally. "Black Nation in the Western Hemisphere." *Tribe* 1, no. 4 (1973): 38–40.

Wye, Christopher G. "The New Deal and the Negro Community: Toward a Broader Conceptualization." *Journal of American History* 59 (December 1972): 621–39.

Young, Ben. *Dixonia: A Bio-Discography of Bill Dixon*. Greenwood, 1998.
———. "Tracks." Liner notes. Albert Ayler, *Holy Ghost*. Revenant, 2004.
———. "Whence." Liner notes. Albert Ayler, *Holy Ghost*. Revenant, 2004.
———. "Witnesses." Liner notes. Albert Ayler, *Holy Ghost*. Revenant, 2004.
Zak, Albin J. *I Don't Sound Like Nobody: Remaking Music in 1950s America*. University of Michigan Press, 2010.
Zieger, Robert H. *For Jobs and Freedom: Race and Labor in America Since 1865*. University Press of Kentucky, 2007.

INDEX

A&M Records, 305
Abdullah, Ahmed (trumpeter), 304, 314, 318
Abdur-Razzaq, Hasan (saxophonist), 151
Aboriginal Society, 349
Abraham, Alton, and El Saturn Records, 238
Abrams, Muhal Richard (pianist), 190, 191, 221
academic poetry, 163
Ackamoor, Idris (saxophonist), 306, 354
Adelphia Records, 322
Africa, 247, 308; African tonal languages, 218; anticolonial and anticapitalist movements in, 252; and apartheid, 220; Black Muslims and, 130; dances and rhythms, 57, 250; and enslaved people, 34; Izulu Dance Theatre and, 229; jazz as a hybrid of African forms, 227; musicians, 259; and patting juba, 57–58; and pentatonic mode, 235; and primitive music, 216; and "rhythmic consonance," 215; and the Tribe, 243
African diaspora, 229, 259, 353
African internationalism, 8
African music/rhythms, 154, 200, 227, 229, 250, 288, 306, 308, 334, 335
African World Festival, 229
Africatown, 84
Afrika Bambaata, 229
Afro-American Festival, 219
Afro-American Institute, 126
Afrofuturism, 8, 10, 21, 223, 236
Ajaramu (drummer), 236
Akbar, Amin (bassist), 349

Akbar, Rashied Al (bassist), 354
AK-BA records, 313, 320
Akram, Wali, and the Black Muslim Movement, 130–131
Akruma (soprano saxophonist), 321
Alabama Black Belt, 20, 42, 48–55, 86, 93, 94, 133
Alabama Sharecroppers Union, 93, 96, 97
Alan Silva's Celestial Communications Orchestra, 327, 335
ALARM ensemble, 352
Albert Ayler Quartet, 271
Alexander, Joe (saxophonist), 122
Alexander, Newman (trumpeter), 272
Alexander von Schlippenbach's quartet, 353
Ali, Muhammad (boxer), 125, 153
Ali, Muhammad (drummer), 9, 22, 290, 329–354
Ali, Rashied (drummer), 184, 330, 331, 345, 349; and the Archie Shepp Quintet, 354; and the Michel Pilz Quartet, 354; and the Rashied Ali Quartet, 271; and the Saheb Sarbib Quartet, 354; and Survival Records, 238
Alim, Kamal Abdul (trumpeter), 120–121, 127, 144, 330; and Frank Wright, 143, 330, 351
Allen, Byron (saxophonist), 196, 340, 341
Allen, Geri (pianist), 214, 236
Allen, Henry, 284
Allen, Jimmy, 250
Allen, Marshall (saxophonist), 105, 106, 300
American apartheid, 241
American Center for Students and Artists in Paris, 338, 346, 347, 353

American experimental music, George Lewis and, 15
American Federation of Labor, 92
Ananda, Prana (percussionist), 229
Anderson, Eric (bassist), 220
Anderson, Fred (tenor saxophonist), 190
Antibes festival, 291
Archie Shepp Quintet, 191, 354
Armstrong, Louis, 54, 92, 105, 140, 164, 268, 269, 280, 284, 297
Art Ensemble of Chicago, 212, 222, 223, 339
art therapy, 353
artist communities, 20
Artists' Workshop, 285
Artists' Workshop Press, 167, 176
Arvanitas, Georges (pianist), 350
Ashby, Dorothy (harpist), 215
Association for the Advancement of Creative Musicians (AACM), 15, 191, 213, 221, 223, 227, 317
Atkins, Russell (poet), 144; Muntu Poets Workshop, 154
Atlanta, 20, 97–103
Atlanta University, 97
Austin, Wiliam (bassist), 244
avant-garde films, 353
avant-garde modernism, 8
avant-garde music/jazz, 163, 268, 338, 348, 349, 352; Artists' Workshop Society and, 172; Albert Ayler and, 274, 292; Ayler-Cherry band and, 268; David Baker and, 301–302; and Faruq Z. Bey, 21; John Coltrane, 282; and Detroit, 165, 171, 234, 238; and Griot Galaxy, 219, 223, 225, 227, 234; Yusuf Mumin and, 147; and musical visionaries, 9–11; studies of, 14; Charles Tyler and, 304, 308, 313, 314, 318; Frank Wright and, 143, 349; Roland P. Young and, 307
Avant-garde press, 12, 168
Ayler, Albert, (saxophonist), xi, 4, 8, 9, 20, 92, 93, 117, 137–141, 147, 190, 257–297, 345; Albert Ayler Quartet, 131, 132, 271; and Edward Ayler, 85, 131, 132; and Ethel Ayler, 84; and Suther "Suthey" Ayler, 48, 82, 83, 84, 85; and Bird Notes, 257; and Capitol Studios, 283; and John Coltrane, 282; death, 293–294; and Debut Records, 259; and Nils Edström, 258; and electronic music, 13; and Bobby Few, 334; and free jazz, 1; and Jessie Myrtle Hunter, 46, 131, 132; and Will Hunter, 48, 132; and Jeamel Lee, 244; and *New Grass,* 287–289, 290; and Bengt Nordström, 257; and Mary "Maria" Parks, 287, 290, 291, 292, 293; and Ferdinand Proctor, 50; and Tempy Proctor, 50; and Clyde Shy, 143–144; and John Sinclair, 177, 194; and Mutawaf Shaheed, 154; and spirituality, 272, 290; and spiritual power, 275; and Stockholm Academy of Arts, 259; and Augusta Thomas, 85, 131; and Charles Tyler, 10, 112, 299–300, 314–315, 322; and Frank Wright, 329–333, 343, 345;
Ayler, Donald, 10, 142, 143, 147, 148, 270, 280, 283, 286, 292, 300; in Cleveland, 275; and John Coltrane funeral, 282; and Bob McKelby band, 132; and mental illness, 290; and new music, 273; in New York, 261; and peace, 279; and spirituality, 272

Bacon, Trevor (singer), 69
Baker, David (cellist), 111, 301, 322, 323
Bakr, Rashid (drummer), 325
Baldwin, James, 143
Bandung Conference, 128
Bang, Billy (violinist), 10, 324
Baraka, Amiri (Leroi Jones), 14, 184, 190, 268, 296, 302, 331; and *Birdland,* 173; correspondence of, 167; and Jihad Productions, 238; *Kulchur,* 168; on language is logic, 218; plays of, 162, 211, 271, 273; and white power structure, 12
Barefield, A. Spencer (guitarist): and Art Ensemble of Chicago, 222; and Detroit, 356; and Griot Galaxy, 220–221, 227; and Anthony Holland, 236
Barker, Thurman (drummer), 191
Basie, Count (bandleader), 110, 163
Battle, Bobby (drummer), 250
Beale Street Blues, Boys, 113
Beau, Chicago (harmonica player), 335
bebop, 7, 8, 148, 165, 187, 190, 241, 244, 355; Muhammad Ali and, 331; anti-bebop, 212; Albert Ayler and, 260, 262, 274; David Baker and, 301; Brother John and, 150; Ornette Coleman and, 310; John Coltrane and, 270; Bobby Few and, 135, 329; Noah Howard and, 340; Charles Moore and, 186; J. C. Moses and, 62; David Murray and, 309; and musicians, 208; Charlie Parker and, 138; post-bop, 260; Jaribu Shahid and, 149; Archie Shepp and,

285; Clyde Shy and, 275; Freddie Webster and, 122; Wendell Harrison and, 240, 247
Bechet, Sidney (clarinetist), 138
Bee Bee King's Original Band, 113
Bee Bee's Jeebies, 113
Beer, Ronnie (alto saxophonist), 334
Belgrave, Marcus (trumpeter): creative profile, 240, 241, 249–250; and Griot Galaxy, 220; and Tribe record label, 10, 21, 242, 244–246, 248–249, 251, 253
Bennink, Hans (drummer), 353
Berkeley Jazz Festival, 332
Berlin Jazz Festival, 278
Betsch, John (drummer), 325
Bey, Abdul Jalil (alto saxophonist) (Aindido): and Detroit uprising, 210–212; and Griot Galaxy, 214, 219
Bey, Faruq Z. (Jesse Davis) (tenor saxophonist), 4, 10, 21, 48, 160, 202–236, 251, 295; and Jesse Saunders Davis, 52; and Mary Lee Davis, 52; and Griot Galaxy, 213–215; and Mizimu, 217; and Northwoods Improvisers, 236; and Sufism, 211
Bey, Sadiq Muhammad (euphonium player/congas/poetry), 10; and anti-bebop, 212; and Detroit uprising, 206, 210; and First African Primal Rhythm Arkestra, 211; and Griot Galaxy, 213, 218, 220, 222, 223, 228, 230
Bibbs, Leroi, 271
Big Maybelle, 240
Bimsheas (gatherings), 154
Bird Notes, 257
Black America, 128
Black Artist Group (St. Louis), Benjamin Looker and, 15
Black Arts Festival, 154
Black Arts Movement, 5, 8, 15, 178, 213, 271, 285–287, 288
Black Arts Repertory Theatre School (BARTS), 270, 271
Black Belt, 3, 4, 5, 16, 44–52, 61, 62, 80, 97, 100; Alabama Black Belt, 20, 42, 48–55, 86, 93, 94, 133
Black creativity festival, 318
Black cultural festival, 308
Black cultural production, x, 2, 12, 15, 16, 17, 18, 20, 120
Black experimentality, 5, 14
Black geographies, 1, 2, 6, 19, 43

Black liberation, 20; Black Liberation Movement, 203
Black Music Infinity, 309
Black musical-familial lineages, 2
Black Muslim Movement, 130–131
Black nationalist movements, 8, 117, 127, 130, 144, 150, 203, 207, 275; Black Nationalist Youth Movement, 128
Black Panther Party, 203; and Black Students Alliances (BSAs), 307; and Huey Newton, 307, 308, 310; and Bobby Seale, 128, 307, 308
Black Unity Quartet: Yusuf, Mumin and, 148; Chuck Smart and, 148; Abdul Wadud and, 148; Oliver "Olly" Wilson and, 148;
Black Unity Trio, 10, 20, 146, 150, 151, 153; Yusuf Mumin (Joseph Phillips) and, 145; Hasan Shahid and, 145; Abdul Wadud and, 145
Blackshaw, Billy (drummer), 137
Blackshaw, Sam (organ/drums), 137
Blackwell, Ed (drummer), 305, 335
Blairman, Allen (drummer), 292
Blake, Arthur (Blind Blake) (guitarist), 104
Blakey, Art, 164, 262
Bland, Bobbie "Blue," 113
Bleu Regard, 327
Bley, Clara (pianist), 305
Bley, Paul (pianist), 13, 184, 191, 196
Blind Log (Lord Raymond Byrd), 105
Blount, Herman. *See* Sun Ra
Blue Notes, 351
Bluiett, Hamiet, 318
Blythe, Arthur (alto saxophonist), 10, 306, 313, 314; and Black Music Infinity, 309; and Rivbea Summer Music Festival, 312; and Charles Tyler, 318
Boggs, James, 206
Boon, Frederick (percussionist), 251
Boone House, 162
Booth, Juini, 286
Booth, Sherman, 39
Borca, Karen (bassoonist), 325
Bottoms, Cleve (saxophonist/clarinet), 111
Bowie, Lester (trumpeter), 335
Boyd, Emil (composer), 122, 136, 304
Boykins, Ronnie (bassist): and Festival Umea, 314; and Rahsaan Roland Kirk, 312; and Sun Ra, 312; and Charles Tyler, 312, 313, 317, 318; and Charles Tyler Ensemble, 315; and Charles Tyler Quartet Jazz, 321

Brackeen, Charles (saxophonist), 305
Bradford, Bobby (trumpeter), 10, 305, 309, 310
Braxton, Anthony (multi-instrumentalist): and
    BYG's Actuel, 335; Faruq Z. Bey, 209; and
    David McMurray, 222; *Tribe*, 252
Breuker, William, 326
Brimfield, Bill (trumpeter), 190
Brinkley, Kent (bassist), 301, 302
Brooks, Ron, 242
Brooks, Roy (musical saw), 249
Brown, Clifford (trumpeter), 248
Brown, James, 205, 288
Brown, Lorenzo (bongos), 249
Brown, Marion (saxophonist), 185; *Change*, 195;
    and Juba, 85and John Sinclair, 184, 194; and
    Frank Wright, 330
Brown, Pearly (slide guitarist), 59
Brubeck, Dave (pianist), 163, 277, 335
Budd, Harold (composer/drummer/poet), 139
Burnham, Charles (violinist), 251
Burrell, Dave (pianist), xi, 19, 28, 34, 50, 71, 335;
    and Henry Burrell, 49; and Mary Eleanor
    Washington, 37
Burrell, Kenny, 249
BYG's Actuel imprint, 334, 335, 340, 341, 346
Byrd, Donald (trumpeter), 8, 158, 252
Byrd, Lord Raymond (Blind Log), 105

Calhoun, James (bassist), 187
Calloway, Cab, 105
Campbell, Choker, 240
Campbell, Roy, Jr. (trumpeter), 325, 352
Capitol Studios, Albert Ayler and, 283
Carey, Michael (saxophonist), 236
Carter, Betty, 240
Carter, Daniel (multi-instrumentalist), 314,
    325, 338
Carter, James (saxophonist), 234, 236
Carter, John, 305, 309
Cass Technical High School, 158, 161, 164, 214
Castell, Taylor, 12
Cecil Taylor Unit Core Ensemble, 312, 325
Celestial Communications Orchestra, 327, 335,
    336, 348, 353, 354
Center of the World, 9, 22, 343–348, 349, 352, 354
Chadbourne, Eugene (guitarist), 320, 321
Chambers, Paul (bassist), 158
Change: Charles Moore and, 195; John Sinclair
    and, 195, 196

Charles, Denis (drummer), 324, 327
Charles, Ray, 121, 248
Charles Tyler Ensemble, 315
Charles Tyler Quartet, 321
Charles Tyler Sextet, 306
Charmasson, Remy (guitarist), 328
Cherry, Don (trumpeter), 267–270, 305; and
    Albert Ayler, 261, 266, 294; and BYG's Actuel,
    335; and Festival Actuel, 339; and Nat Hentoff,
    13; and New York Contemporary Five, 62; and
    John Sinclair, 177; and Charles Tyler, 319
Chicago Jazz Festival, 326
churches, 5, 6, 7, 51, 68, 79, 84, 103, 119, 122, 134,
    154, 320; Baptist, 19, 42, 51, 63, 71, 84, 88, 104,
    109, 126, 131, 157, 203, 208, 268, 340, 350; Black
    Muslim, 126, 130–131, 211, 212, 215, 219, 220;
    Methodist, 19, 37, 41, 42, 51, 84, 86, 87, 122,
    126, 350; Pentecostal, 110, 350; Sanctified/
    Holy Roller, 286
Civil Rights, 5, 6, 125, 247
Clark, Charles (bassist), 190, 191
Clark, Curtis (pianist), 325, 327
Cleveland, 1, 3, 5, 6, 7, 9–11, 16, 19, 20, 21, 26, 27,
    34, 61, 81, 93, 97, 111, 112, 113, 117–155, 160, 236,
    249, 257, 261–262, 269, 275–277, 292, 295, 299,
    300, 304, 306, 328, 329, 330, 331, 332, 334, 349,
    354, 356; Cedar-Central, 119, 121, 133; and class
    politics, 120; immigrants in, 118, 119, 120; and
    Station Hope, 118
Cliff, Walter (bassist), 144, 148, 149
Cobbs, Harvey Call, Jr. (pianist/harpsichordist),
    28, 33, 34, 264, 291, 292; and Albert Ayler, 264,
    276, 283, 286, 291; and Alan Silva, 287
Coda, 168
Coe, Jimmy (saxophonist), 111
Cohran, Phil, 190, 221
Colbert, Reggie (trumpeter), 308
Coleman, Ornette (saxophonist): and Artists'
    Workshop Society, 180; and Albert Ayler, 13,
    140, 262, 291; and Albert Ayler Quartet, 271;
    and David Baker, 301; and Faruq Z. Bey, 209;
    and Sadiq Muhammad Bey, 224; and Black
    experimentalists, 14; *Change*, 196; and John
    Coltrane, 282; and freedom, 356; and group
    improvisation; 266; and Larry Hancock, 143;
    and Noah Howard, 340; and Charles Moore,
    163, 194; and new musical concepts, 13; and
    New York, 261, 305; and rebellion, 244; and
    Michel Samson, 277; and Clyde Shy, 138, 356;

and John Sinclair, 177; and Charles Tyler, 10, 310, 315
Coleman, Victor, 193
Colored Vigilant Committee, 157
Coltrane, Alice:, *Cosmic Music*, 150, 158
Coltrane, John, x, 8, 48; and Muhammad Ali, 331; and Artists' Workshop Society, 172, 173, 174–176; and avant-garde music, 14, 166; and Albert Ayler, 262, 264–266, 269–270, 275, 281–285, 290, 294, 297; and Amiri Baraka, 275; and Faruq Z. Bey, 209, 234–235; and Black nationalism, 127; and Black Unity Trio, 150; *Change*, 196; John Coltrane Quartet, 334; and cultural revolution, 13; death of, 9; and Detroit Contemporary 5 (DC5), 172, 180, 182, 183; and Don Ellis, 195; funeral of, 282; and Godseekers, 275; and Griot Galaxy, 212, 224; *Jazz*, 195; and Elvin Jones, 334; and Frank Kofsky, 294; and Jeamel Lee, 244; and Harold McKinney, 249; and David McMurray, 222; and Charles Moore, 165, 195; and musical mentors, 121; and Hasan Shahid, 152; and Jaribu Shahid, 214, 225; and Archie Shepp, 294; and John Sinclair, 166, 177; and Danny Spencer, 194; touring networks, 124, 164; *Tribe*, 252–253; and Charles Tyler, 302, 314, 325; vocabularies, 10; and Abdul Wadud, 146, 148; and White-Light Band, 200; and Frank Wright, 329–331, 330, 331, 341
Comer, B. B., 90
composition, 323
composers' workshop, 314
Concept East, 161, 162, 211
Congress of Racial Equality (CORE), 126, 128, 304
Connell, Will, 153
Contemporary Five, 62
contemporary folk forms, 184
coon songs, 286
Cooper, Jerome (drummer), 317
Cosenza, Marie, 327
Cosmic Music record store, 147, 153
Coursil, Jacques (trumpeter), 10, 330, 332
Cowell, Stanley (pianist), 164; and Detroit Contemporary (DC4/DC5), 180–183; and Barry Wallenstein, 319
Cox, Ida, 59
Cox, Kenny, 200, 214, 252; and Strata Records, 238
Crawford, Hank (alto saxophonist), 241

Creative Arts Collective (CAC), 222, 227
Creative Arts Festival, 191
Creative Profile, 240, 241, 249–250; Jimmy Allen and, 250; Bobby Battle and, 250; Marcus Belgrave and, 240; Darryl Dybka and, 250; Wendell Harrison and, 240; Ron Jackson and, 250; Kirk Lightsey and, 250; Harold McKinney and, 240; Charles Miles and, 250; Ed Pickens and, 250; Sam Sanders and, 250; O. C. Smith and, 250; Billy Turner and, 250
Creeley, Robert, 162, 190, 193
Cricket, The, 195
Cross, Earl (cornetist/trumpeter): Muhammad Ali and, 354 Charles Tyler and, 312, 313, 318; and Charles Tyler Ensemble, 315; and Charles Tyler Quartet, 321, 324
Crouch, Stanley, 13, 14, 309, 310
cultural spaces, 18, 25–41, 81–113
Cunningham, Bob (bassist), 122, 132, 135
Cyrille, Andrew (drummer), 333, 335, 352

Dameron, Tadd (pianist/composer/arranger), 122
Dana, John (bassist): Detroit, 164; and Detroit Contemporary 5 (DC5), 172–173, 182, 184; and David Durrah, 239; and First African Primal Rhythm Arkestra, 212; and Andrew Hill, 191; and Scott LaFaro, 194; and Tribe, 245; and Lyman Woodard Ensemble, 189; and Workshop Music Ensemble, 187
Daney, Ike (drummer), 244
Daniel, Ted (trumpeter), 314, 318
Daniels, Leslie (drummer), 248
Dar Islam movement, 131
Davidson, George (drummer), 245
Davis, Angela, 245
Davis, Clarence, 49
Davis, James (Thunderbird), 84
Davis, Jesse. *See* Bey, Faruq Z.
Davis, Miles, 13, 54, 110, 111, 163, 164, 172, 194, 293; and Richard Davis, 283; and Benny Miller, 138; Quintet, 124, 209; and Tani Tabbal, 221; Freddie Webster, 122
Dawkins, Hasan (soprano saxophonist), 314
Day, Bobby, 149
DC4/5: *See* Detroit Contemporary 4/5
Debut Records, 259
DeCorte, Ron, 224
Defenders of Human Rights, 126
De La Soul, x, 10

DeMyers, Clarence (pianist), 187
DePriest, Jimmy (conductor/composer), 139
desegregation, 20
Detroit, 3, 5, 6, 7, 9, 10, 16, 19, 20, 21, 26, 29, 48, 51, 52, 54, 64, 73, 76, 81, 113, 127, 128, 131, 153, 155, 156–253, 285, 356; Boone House, 162; Broadside Press, 161, 162; Concept East, 161, 162, 211; the Detroit Way, 158; *Inner City Voice*, 206, 207; sound, 237; uprising, 202–236
Detroit Art Space, 236
Detroit Artists Workshop, 156–201; Artists' Workshop Press, 167, 176; Free University of Detroit, 179, 198; John Sinclair and, 9, 10, 20; and *Vortex*, 198; Workshop Arts Quintet, 179; Workshop Music Ensemble, 186–189
Detroit Artists Workshop Society, 163, 179, 180
Detroit Contemporary (DC4/DC5), 172, 173, 180–186, 191, 194, 197, 201
Detroit Edison White-Light Band, 199
Detroit Institute of the Arts, 21, 241
Detroit Jazz Artists on Tour program, 221
Detroit Visionaries, 237
DeVaughn, Ronald. *See* Wadud, Abdul Khabir
Dickerson, Walt (vibraphonist), 322
Dixon, Bill (trumpeter), 14, 177, 179; and Jazz Composers' Guild, 170
Doblekar, Frank, 356
Dodds, Elreta (clarinetist), 158, 213, 214, 218
Dodge Revolutionary Union Movement, 207
Dodson, Anne Grace Horn, 49
Dolphy, Eric, 216, 305, 339; and Albert Ayler, 262, 269; *Change*, 196; and Detroit Contemporary (DC4/DC5), 180; and Festival Actuel, 339; and Yusuf Mumin, 148; and Pierre Rochon, 194; Abdul Wadud, 148
Domino, Fats, 121
Douglass, Charles H., 59
Down Beat, 12, 164, 168
Doyle, Arthur (saxophonist), 314, 353
Dresser, Mark (bassist), 309
Drew, Kenny (pianist), 268
Duff, Little Brenda, 149
Dunbar, Richard (French hornist), 314, 323, 324, 325
Dunn, Roy, 102
Durrah, David (pianist): and Black Panthers, 308; in Cleveland, 144; and Detroit uprising, 238, 239; and Tribe, 239, 242, 251; and Charles Tyler, 306; and Frank Wright, 143

Dybka, Darryl (synthesizer player), 249, 250
Dylan, Bob, 305, 327
Dynatones, 271

East Jazz Trio: Raymond Farris and, 136; Bobby Few and, 136; Cevera Jeffries and, 136, 330
Ebony, 303
Eckstine, Billy, 105
Eichele, Robin, 170, 172, 178, 179, 194, 197
Ellington, Duke, 54, 84, 102, 105, 110, 121, 163, 164
Elliot, Marcus (saxophonist), 158, 356
Ellis, Don, 195
El Ni, Haroun (alto saxophonist/percussionist), 245
El Saturn Records. Alton Abraham, 238; Sun Ra, 238
English, Ron (guitarist), 236; and Artists' Workshop, 179; and avant-garde, 163; and Detroit Contemporary 4/5 (DC5), 172, 180; and Ronald Johnson, 189; and M. L. Liebler, 236; and Lyman Woodard, 164
Ervin, Booker (saxophonist), 196, 334
ESP Record Label, 9, 147, 152, 196, 312, 266, 283, 329, 341, 345, 347, 349; Bernard Stollman and, 330
Eubanks, Charles (pianist), 244
Evans, Ahmed, and Republic of New Libya (RNL), 129

FAME Studios, 149
Farris, Raymond (drummer), 136
Fasteau, Zusaan Kali (multi-instrumentalist), 252
Fataah, Muneer Abdul (cellist), 325
Favors, Malachi (bassist), 335
FBI, 170; and Black Arts Repertoire Theatre School (BARTS), 271; COINTELPRO program, 128, 204; and Detroit Edison White-Light Band, 199; and Leonard Feather, 282; and Inner City Voice, 207; and Joseph Jarmon, 199; and Vahan Kapagihan, 199; and Don Moye, 199; and Republic of New Afrika, 208; and Republic of New Libya (RNL), 129; and Hasan Shahid, 153; and John Sinclair, 199; and Leni Sinclair, 199;
Ferrucci, Frank (pianist), 316, 317, 324, 326
Festival Actuel, 339–341
Festival Amougies, 340
Festival of AvantGarde Music, 187
Festival of People, 188, 189, 191
festivals, 221, 249, 292, 293, 316, 323, 324, 342; African World Festival, 229; Afro-American

Festival, 219; Antibes festival, 291; Berkeley Jazz Festival, 332; Berlin Jazz Festival, 278; Black arts festivals, 154; Black creativity festival, 318; Black cultural festival, 308; Chicago Jazz Festival, 326; Creative Arts Festival, 191; Festival Actuel, 339–341, Festival Amougies, 340; Festival of AvantGarde Music, 187; Festival of People, 188, 189, 191; Jazz Festival Umea, 314; Jazz Pulsations Festival, 346; Kool Jazz Festival, 325; Moers Festival, 321, 347, 351; Montreux-Detroit International Jazz Festival, 225; New York Musicians' Festival, 346; Newport Jazz Festival, 277, 282; Notre Dame Collegiate Jazz Festival, 301; PanAfrican Cultural Festival, 334; Paris Jazz Festival, 278, 334; Reims jazz festival, 348; Rivbea Summer Music Festival, 312, 316; Sound Unity Festival, 325, 351; WCUW Music Fair, 323; Willisau Jazz Festival, 347, 348, 351

Few, Bobby (Robert Lee Jr.), xi, 55, 57, 59, 61, 132, 143, 326, 329–354; as bebop player, 135; and Cleveland, 9, 20, 21, 117, 123, 135–137, 142, 148; displacement of, 61; and East Jazz Trio, 136; and Betty Few, 132; and Ellen Few, 57; and James Few, 57, 61; and Robert Lee Few Sr., 59, 132; and Simon Few, 59, 61, 132, 138, 139; and Simone Few, 135, 338, 339; and Winifred Raephena Towe Few, 132; and Langston Hughes, 136; and metronomes, 135; and Organization for the Development and Advancement of the Cultural Black Arts (ODACBA), 295; and Paris, 326; and Dick Shelton Quintet, 135; and Sheltonaires, 135; spiritual point of view, 344

Fields, Reginald (bassist/vocalist), 215, 245, 246
Finn, Julio (harmonica player), 335
First African Primal Rhythm Arkestra, 211, 214
Fischer, John (pianist), 318, 319
Fisk University, 128
Fitzgerald, Ella, 105
Florida Memorial University, 63
Floyd, Eddie, 208
Fogel, Jerry, 332, 333
Fractal Record, 343
France, 334–341
Franklin, Aretha, 208, 333
Frank Wright Organ Combo, 136
Frank Wright Orchestra, 137
Frank Wright Quartet, 136, 341, 342
Frank Wright Trio (album), 330
Frary, Jordan (flutist and violinist), 143
Free Black communities, 6, 18, 19, 25, 27, 28, 34
Freedman, Joel (cellist), 321; and Albert Ayler, 147, 270, 274, 280; and Charles Tyler, 300–301, 321
Freedom Fighters, 126
Freedom Now Party, 206
Freeform Improvisation Ensemble, 335
free jazz movement, 1, 2, 3, 4, 5, 7, 8, 9, 10, 11, 12, 13, 14, 15, 16, 17, 19, 20, 22, 26, 37, 80, 113, 124, 131, 134, 135, 143, 144, 147, 154, 155, 160, 162, 164, 171, 177, 179, 191, 192, 193, 194, 195, 200, 201, 224, 236, 241, 244, 251, 266, 276, 284, 287, 297, 299, 302, 303, 320, 325, 329, 331, 334, 336, 339, 341, 342, 343, 346, 348, 351, 352, 354, 355, 356
Freeman, Chico, 317, 318
Freeman, Don, 127, 128, 134, 357
Freeman, Earl (bassist), 335
Free University of Detroit, 179, 198
French leftist uprising, 336–338
Friend, Becky (flutist), 335, 353
"Frolics," 58, 62, 100

Gabriel, Larry, 252
Gaddy, Christopher (pianist), 191
Gales, Warren (trumpeter), 182–337
Garnett, George (trombonist), 187
Garrett, Donald (saxophonist/clarinetist), 346
Garrison, Jimmy (bassist), 190, 238, 283
Garvey, Marcus, 85, 122, 252
Gaye, Marvin, 240
Gayle, Charles, xi, 4, 48, 50, 51, 52, 104, 286
Geller, Janice, 316, 317
Georgia Black Belt, 55, 61, 62
Georgia Cotton Pickers, 100
Georgia Piedmont, 58, 59
Gibbs, Arthur, 105
Giddens, Gary, 317
Gillespie, Dizzy, 111, 122, 284
Gillespie, Ezekiel, 19; and Catharina Lucas Robinson, 39, 40, 41
Gillespie v. Palmer, 39
Gilmore, John (saxophonist), 209
Gleason, Ralph, 12, 14, 333
Glover, Joshua, 39
Godseekers, 275
Golding, Alan "Ali," (drummer), 236
Goodman, Benny, 137, 164

Gordon, Dexter, 132, 268, 339
Gordon, Rosco (vocalist), 113
Gordon, Amos Franklin, Jr. (Hasan Shahid), 92
Gordon Amos Franklin, Sr. (clarinet/saxophone), 92
Grandy, Erroll (pianist), 111
Graves, Milford (drummer), 271, 283, 285, 286, 287
Gray, Wardell (saxophonist), 158
Great Migration, 2, 3, 12, 16, 42, 81, 83, 157, 159, 355, 356; "southern diaspora," 11
Greater Ohio Valley, 3, 4, 5, 6, 7, 16, 17, 18, 19, 20, 21, 25, 27, 28, 38, 42, 44, 48, 62, 80, 81, 82, 103, 113, 115–254, 356
Green, Candy (pianist/singer), 257
Green, Grant, 240
Green, James K., 49
Green, Kenny (pianist), 236
Greene, Burton (pianist): and BYG's Actuel, 335; *Change*, 196; and Jazz Art Music Society, 184; and new music, 192; and Alan Silva, 353; and Leni Sinclair, 197
Greenlee, Charles (trombonist), 48
Greenwood, Lil, 84
Gregg, Jack, 326
Gresham, Paul (saxophonist), 61, 97, 103
Grimes, Henry (bassist): and Albert Ayler, 261–262, 273; and Charles Tyler, 300, 302; and Frank Wright, 330
Griot Galaxy, 10, 21, 160, 246; and Faruq Z. Bey, 202–236; European tour, 229, 234; spiritual and physical fusion, 224
Grjegian, Hack (pianist), 172
group improvisation, 266
Guinness, Jim (alto saxophonist), 187

Hadden, Skip, 356
Haden, Charles (bassist), 186, 191, 305
Hakim, Mubarak (percussionist), 213
Haley, Alex, 14
Hamilton, Hobb, 271
Hamlin, Michael, 76, 156, 157, 204; League of Revolutionary Black Workers, 203
Hammond, Doug (pianist/drummer), 212, 239, 242, 251
Hammond, John, 293
Hampton, Clark "Deacon," 111
Hampton, Duke (saxophonist), 111
Hampton, Lionel (bandleader), 137, 144, 301
Hampton, Locksley "Slide" (trombonist), 111

Hampton, Paula (drummer/vocalist), 111
Hancock, Herbie (pianist), 250
Hancock, Larry (drummer), 142, 143, 144, 261
Handy, W. C., 52, 157
Hardman, Bill (trumpeter), 122
Harlaque, Horace (electric guitarist), 214, 220
Harlem Renaissance, 271
Harris, Anthony (tenor saxophonist), 187
Harris, Barry (pianist), 240
Harris, Beaver (drummer), 291; and Albert Ayler, 138–139, 276, 278, 283, 290–291; and Archie Shepp Quartet, 191
Harris, Bill (poet/playwright), 158, 160, 176, 177, 178, 194, 204, 358
Harris, Craig (trombonist), 325
Harris, Eddie, 240, 250
Harris, Otis (alto saxophonist), 144, 251, 306, 323
Harrison, Wendell (saxophonist), 237; and Creative Profile, 240, 241, 249–250; and Detroit, 356; and Pat Harrison, 247; and Rebirth Records, 253; and Tribe, 10, 21, 238, 242, 243, 246–248, 251; and Jaribu Shahid, 214; and WenHa Records, 253
Hawkins, Bill (*Walking Talking*), 124
Hawkins, Coleman, 140
Hawkins, Erskine, 92, 105
Haynes, Albert, 271
Haynes, Roy (drummer), 221, 271
Heard, J. C. (drummer), 158
Hefty Records, 253
Hemphill, Julius (saxophonist), 148, 310, 314, 317, 318
Henderson, Chris, 326
Henderson, David, 271
Henderson, Earle (Earl), 97, 132, 133; and Albert Ayler, 10, 93, 262, 299
Henderson, Joe, 210
Henderson, Leon, 210, 239
Hendrix, Jimi, 284, 304, 333
Hernton, Calvin C., 271
Heron, Kim, 224, 225, 227, 228, 229
Hicks, Charlie (Charley Lincoln), 98, 100
Hicks, Robert (Barbecue Bob), 98, 100
Hicks, Rod (bassist), 248
Higgins, Billy (alto saxophonist), 177, 212, 261, 305
Hill, Andrew (pianist), 191, 192, 196, 305, 353
Hilliard, David, 307
Holiday, Billie, 138

Holland, Anthony (alto saxophonist), 220, 221, 222, 223, 227, 229, 236
Holley, Major, Jr. ("Mule") (bassist), 158
Hood, Ed (trumpeter), 189
Hood, Oscar (drummer), 149
Howard, Noah (alto saxophonist): and Muhammad Ali, 331; and Byron Allen, 340; and Festival Actuel, 339; and Dewey Redman, 340; and Sonny Simmons, 340; and Sun Ra, 341; Frank Wright Quartet, 341–343, 351, 352
Howard, Norman (trumpeter), 64, 133; and Albert Ayler, 10, 262, 301; and Yusuf Mumin, 148; and Nation of Islam, 125; and Charles Tyler, 142
Howard University. 148; Black Unity Trio, 10, 153
Howell, Joshua "Peg Leg," 98
Howlin' Wolf, 139
Hubbard, Freddie, 240, 253, 278
Huby, Barbara (Mama Hoo-doo) (percussionist), 312
Hughes, Langston, *Simply Heavenly*, 136
Hurt, John, 76
Hutcherson, Bobby (vibraphonist), 308

immigrants, 118, 119, 120, 132, 133, 338
Impulse!, 10, 190, 196, 283, 288, 289
improvised music, 2
infrastructure projects, 20
Inner City Voice, 206, 207
Institute for Art, Culture and Perception, 353
INTERface, 318
Ishak, Abu (bassist/poet), 210, 211
Islam, 92, 125, 126, 130, 131, 148, 149, 153, 154, 214, 215, 302, 304, 313; Islamic mysticism, 211; Islamic poetry, 211
Izulu Dance Theatre, 229

Jackson, Chuck, 240
Jackson, Harry "Pee Wee" (trumpeter), 122
Jackson, Ronald (drummer), 300
Jackson, Ronald Shannon, 317
Jacquet, Illinois (tenor saxophonist), 137, 265, 278
Jamal, Khan (vibraphonist), 349
James, C. L. R., 203, 206
Jami, Hakim (bassist), 236
Jarman, Joseph (saxophone): and Richard Abrams, 190; and avant-garde, 314; and Bill Brimfield, 190; and BYG's Actuel, 335; and Charles Clark, 190; and DC4, 185, 186; in Detroit, 190; and FBI, 199; and Fred Anderson, 190; and Christopher Gaddy, 191; and Steve McCall, 190; and Charles Moore, 191; and Barker Thurman, 191; and Workshop Music Ensemble, 191, 198
Jazz, 168, 195; Pauline Rivelli and, 167
Jazz Art Music Society, 184
jazz clubs, 125, 132, 136, 165, 237, 277
Jazz Composers' Guild, 170, 196, 335
Jazz Crusaders, 122
Jazz Festival Umea, 314
jazz lofts, 21, 153, 313, 317, 318, 320, 324; Michael Heller and, 15
Jazz 1965, 194
jazz poetry, 136
Jazz Pulsations Festival, 346
jazz-rock, 248
Jefferson, Eddie (vocalist/lyricist), 351
Jeffries, Cevera, Jr. (bassist), 136, 330
Jefta, Harold (alto saxophonist), 259
Jenkins, Bobo, 51
Jenkins, Leroy (violinist), 227, 335
Jihad Productions, 238
John Coltrane Quartet, 173, 208, 334
Johnson, Alonzo "Pookie" (saxophonist), 111
Johnson, Blind Willie, 59, 164
Johnson, Margaret (singer), 105
Johnson, Ronald (drummer): and Miles Davis, 194; and Detroit Contemporary (DC4/DC5), 197; and Shattering Effect, 200; and Danny Spencer, 164; and Tony Williams, 194; and Workshop Music Ensemble, 187; and Workshop Trio, 189, 191
Johnson, Ronnie (pianist), 184
Jones, Arthur (alto saxophonist), 10, 127, 133, 330, 332, 335, 351
Jones, Elvin, 48, 173, 174, 194, 283, 334
Jones, Ernest (tenor saxophonist, 133
Jones, Leroi. *See* Baraka, Amiri
Jones, "Philly" Joe (drummer), 335, 351
Jordan, Lewis (alto saxophonist), 308, 309, 325
Jordan, Spencer, 62
Jullian, Jean-Pierre (drummer), 328
J-V-R Recording Company: and Detroit sound, 237; and Joe Von Battle, 237

Kenny Cox's Contemporary Jazz Quintet, 200
Kentucky, 3, 18, 19, 25, 26, 28, 36, 37, 68, 69, 70, 71, 72, 81, 85, 105–106, 109, 133, 139, 145, 324, 327; Black Patch, 20, 42, 64–66, 107, 110

Kenyatta, Kamau (tenor saxophonist), 214, 227
Kettle, Rupert, 275
Khafiz, Dauud Abdul (bassist), 213, 219
King, B. B., 112, 239; Beale Street Blues, Boys, 113; Bee Bee King's Original Band, 113; Bee Bee's Jeebies, 113
King, Martin Luther, Jr., 129, 149, 239, 252
Kirk, Rahsaan Roland, 69, 70, 124, 139, 192, 312
Kool Jazz Festival, 325
Kowald, Peter (bassist), 325, 352
Krall, Jackson (drummer), 316
Ku Klux Klan (KKK), x, 46, 47, 50, 58, 60, 66, 76, 84, 107, 108, 157, 159
Kulchur, 168, 173
Kyo, Kuumba (bassist), 214

labor unions, 4, 81, 83, 93, 94, 95, 106, 107, 162, 337; American Federation of Labor, 92; Auto Workers Union, 159; Colored Association of Railway Employees, 92; International Longshoremen's Association, 84
Lacy, Steve, 196, 352; Steve Lacy Quartet, 327, 353
LaFaro, Scott, 194, 305
Lake, Oliver (saxophonist), 310, 314, 317, 318
Lancaster, Byard (flutist), 334, 339
Lanear, Patrick (trombonist), 212
Lasha, Prince (multi-instrumentalist), 172, 180
Lateef, Yusef (multi-instramentalist), 146
Lawson, Hugh (pianist), 158
League of Revolutionary Black Workers, Michael Hamlin and, 203
Leary, Timothy, 336
Lee, Jeamel (vocalist), 243, 244, 245, 248
Lee, Jeanne (vocalist), 335
Lee, Spike, 14
Leftwich, Lloyd, 51
Levallet, Didier (bassist), 327
Levine, Elliott (saxophonist), 303
liberation movements, 125–126
Liebler, M. L., 15; and Magic Poetry Band, 236
Lightsey, Kirk, 250
Lincoln, Abby, 127
Little Walter, 138, 139
Lloyd, Charles, 113, 180
Lowe, Frank, xi, 318, 323
Luke, Oliver, 310, 314, 317, 318
Lumumba, Patrice, 203, 252
Lyles, Byron (drummer), 187
Lyman Woodard Ensemble, 188, 189

lynching, 5, 47, 55, 60, 66, 72, 76, 84, 85, 94, 97, 107
Lyons, Jimmy (saxophonist), 259, 262, 325, 333

Magic Poetry Band, M. L. Lieber and, 236
Majors, Brent (saxophonist), 164, 173, 180
Maka, Jo (saxophonist), 253
Malcolm X, 125, 126, 127, 128, 130, 143, 183, 203, 206, 209, 241, 251, 252, 304
Malik, Raphe (trumpeter), 325, 344, 346
Malis, Michael, 356
Mama Hoo-doo. *See* Huby, Barbara
Mandingo Griot Society, 229
Mao Tse-Tung, 179, 203
Mapp, Eddie, 98, 100, 102
Marsalis, Wynton, 14
Martha and the Vandellas, 189
Martinez, Andre (drummer), 325
Massingale, Walter, 144
MC5, 191, 222; John Sinclair and, 201
McBee, Cecil (bassist), 319
McCall, Steve (drummer), 190, 335
McClintock, Harriet, 49
McCray, Betsie, 76
McDuff, Jack, 240
McGhee, Howard (trumpeter), 158
McIntyre, Dianne, 147
McIntyre, Kalaparusha Maurice (saxophonist), 252
McKenzie, Tom (bassist), 352
McKesson, Brent (bassist), 301, 302
McKibbon, Al (bassist), 158
McKinney, Harold (pianist): 253; and avant-garde, 163; and Creative Profile, 240, 241, 249–250; and Hayden DeMar, 71, 72; and Washington DeMar, 72, 73; and Winny DeMar, 71; and Clarence McKinney (vocalist), 249; and Earl McKinney, 249; and George Patterson McKinney, 63; and Gwen McKinney, 250; and Ishmael McKinney, 63, 64; and Jacob McKinney Sr., 62; and Ray McKinney, 249; and Tribe, 242; and Kiane Zawadi (Bernard McKinney), 249
McLean, Jackie, 180, 183, 340
McMillen, Wallace, 221, 227
McMullen, Fred, 98
McMurray, David (saxophonist/flutist): and Afrofuturistic performativity, 223; and Detroit avant-garde, 234; and funk, soul, and smooth jazz, 236; *Met-azzthetics*, 224; Pyramid +1 (Griot Galaxy), 221, 222, 223, 227, 228, 229

McRae, Barry, 347
McTell, Blind Willie, 98, 100, 101, 102, 105
McTell, Kate, 101, 102
Melody Maker, 274
Met-azzthetics (WDET), 224
Metropolitan Arts Complex, 240–243, 250
Michel Pilz Quartet, 354
Mickeel, Trevis (violinist), 251
Miles, Charles (alto saxophonist), 184, 189, 213, 250
Miles Davis Quintet, 124, 209
Miles Modern Poetry Workshop, 162
Milhaud, Darius, 224
Miller, Benny, 138
Milsap, Cornelius, 148, 149
Mingus, Charles, 177, 189, 190, 194, 196, 221, 248, 265, 302, 308
Mitchell, Billy (saxophonist), 158
Mitchell, Cindy "Scinda," 77; "Cindy's Band," 79
Mitchell, Roscoe (saxophonist), 190, 209, 213, 221, 222, 224, 236, 314, 335, 352
mobility, 2, 3, 4, 5, 6, 7, 11, 16, 43, 55, 59, 76, 81, 82, 83, 86, 113, 355
Mobley, Hank (saxophonist), 335
Moers Festival, 321, 347, 351
Moffett, Charles (drummer/vibraphonist), 274, 300, 301, 309
Moholo, Louis (drummer), 351
Moncur, Grachan, III (trombonist), 172, 180, 183, 184, 271, 335
Monk, Thelonious, x, 136, 172, 182, 221, 265, 304
Monroe, James, 71
Monteith College, 162, 163, 168
Monteith Journal, 178
Montgomery, Wes (guitarist), 111, 249
Montreal Jazz Workshop, 285
Montreux-Detroit International Jazz Festival, 225
Moore, Charles (cornetist): as anti–nuclear weapons activist, 163; and Betty Armstead, 52; and Robert Armstead, 52, 53; and Kathleen Beaufait, 180; and Ornette Coleman, 194; and Kenny Cox's Contemporary Jazz Quintet, 200; and Detroit Artists' Workshop, 10, 165, 168, 198; and Detroit Contemporary 5 (DC5), 172–174, 181–183, 197; and David Durrah, 238, 239; and free jazz/pure feeling, 194; and Wendell Harrison, 246; and Joseph Jarman, 191; and *Jazz*, 195; and liberation struggles, 20; and Eugene Moore, 53, 54; and Nettie Moore, 54; and *New University Thought*, 163; and Phil Ranelin, 244, 245; and Shattering Effect, 200; and John Sinclair, 193, 198; and Cecil Taylor, 194; and WDET, 200; and Workshop Music Ensemble, 186–189
Moore, Gene (alto saxophonist), 187
Morris, Lawrence "Butch" (trumpeter), 153, 305, 306, 308, 309, 325
Morris, Wilber (bassist), 305, 308, 309, 323, 324, 325, 327
Moses, J. C. (bebop pianist) 103, 104, 271; and Contemporary Five, 62
Moss, Buddy (guitarist), 98, 102; and Georgia Cotton Pickers, 100
Moten, Fred, 4, 297, 356
Moton v. Kessens, 34
Motown, 3, 11, 21, 189, 237, 238, 239, 240, 244, 249
Moye, Don (drummer), 199
Muhammad Speaks, 207
Mumin, Yusuf (Joseph Phillips) (saxophonist), 125, 136, 147, 148, 149, 152, 261; and Black Unity Trio, 10, 20, 145–146, 150, 151, 153
Muntu Poets Workshop, 154
Murphy, Paul (drummer), 352
Murray, David (saxophonist), 10, 236, 308, 309, 310, 314, 325
Murray, Sunny (drummer), 148, 343, 345; and Muhammad Ali, 331; and Albert Ayler, 10, 259, 264, 265, 266, 294; and Amiri Baraka, 273, 275; and BYG's Actuel, 335; and Festival Actuel, 339; and Godseekers, 275; and Paris Jazz Festival, 335; and Richard Raux, 348; and Alan Silva, 353; and Cecil Taylor Trio, 259, 262, 331; and Charles Tyler, 318; and Frank Wright, 334
Music and Migration Lab, Pratt Institute, 356
musical intelligence, 336
musical visionaries, 9–11
"Music Is the Healing Force of the Universe," 1, 290, 291, 293, 334
Mustevic Sound. Steve Reid, 314

Nakamura, Tatsuya (drummer), 314
Narmour, Willie (fiddler), 76
Nassoma, Kafi Patrice. *See* Williams, Patrice
National Association for the Advancement of Colored People (NAACP), 104, 126, 128
National Association for the Advancement of White People, 134
national jazz culture, 8

National Negro Congress, 159
Nation of Islam, 125, 127, 131, 142, 146, 150, 153, 160, 203, 207, 241, 307
Neal, Aaron (bass clarinetist), 246
Neal, Larry, 8, 271, 285, 286, 288, 296
New American Cinema, 172
New Grass, 287–289, 290
New Left, 179
New Music, 8, 13, 16, 153, 186, 188, 192, 194, 196, 284, 299, 304, 327, 331
Newport Jazz Festival, 277, 282
Newton, Huey, 307, 308, 310
Newton, James (flutist), 309, 310, 325
New University Thought. Otto Feinstein, 163
New wave music, 188
New York Arts Quartet, 179, 189, 196
New York Musicians' Festival, 346
Night Riders, 107, 108
Nkrumah, Kwame, 203, 252
Northwoods Improvisers, M. L. Lieber and, 236
Notre Dame Collegiate Jazz Festival, 301
Nozero, Larry (saxophonist), 164, 180, 251
Nur, Abdul (bassist), 219
Nyerere, Julius, 203

Oba, and Black Messengers, 246
Obadele, Gaidi, 207
October Revolution, 335
Ohio River Valley, 3, 4, 5, 6, 7, 17, 18, 19, 21, 25, 27, 28, 42, 44, 48, 62, 80, 81, 82, 103, 113, 115–117, 354
Olson, Charles, 162
On Guard for Freedom, 271
Orchestra of Two Continents, 352
Ore, John (bassist), 315, 318, 321, 322, 323
Organization for the Development and Advancement of the Cultural Black Arts (ODACBA), 295

Pan-African, 276; Pan-African Congress, 214; PanAfrican Cultural Festival, 334
Pan Afrikan Peoples Arkestra: and Steven Isoardi, 15; and Horace Tapscott, 306
Paris Jazz Festival, 278, 334
Parker, Charlie, 52, 110, 111, 138, 215, 240, 260, 269, 299, 340
Parker, Evan, 265
Parker, William (bassist), xi, 1, 312, 313, 317, 325, 340, 352, 358

Parks, Mary "Maria" (singer), 287, 290, 291, 291, 293
Patterson, Charles, 271
Patterson, William, 271
patting juba, 57–58
Patton, Charley, x, 7
Peacock, Gary (bassist), 264, 265, 266, 273, 302, 305
Pearce, Richard (bassist), 314
Penick, Bill (saxophonist), 111
Peters, Henry (saxophonist), 308
Peterson, Joel (bassist), 236
Phillips, Joseph. *See* Mumin, Yusuf
Pickens, Ed (bassist), 249, 250
Pierce, Darryl (drummer), 213, 220
Pierre Rochon Quartet, 194
Pope, Byron (saxophonist), 182
Powell, Bud (pianist), 136, 137, 304
Powell, Dempsey (soprano saxophonist), 304
Pratt Institute, Music and Migration Lab, 356
Prentice, Jackie (drummer), 306, 309
Prestige records, 313
Price, Lloyd (singer), 138, 240
Price, Tom (drummer), 330
Prophet Muhammad, 130
protests, 103, 119, 133, 186, 338
Pukwana, Dudu (alto saxophonist), 351
Pullen, Don (pianist), 318

racial profiling, 125
Rahim, Mustafa Abdul (tenor saxophonist), 321
Rainey, Ma (singer), 59
Randolph, John, 28
Ranelin, Phil (trombonist), 21, 70, 71, 238, 241, 248; and William Austin, 244; and Marcus Belgrave, 10, 21, 220, 240, 241, 242, 244, 245, 246, 248–249, 250, 251, 242, 253; and Ike Daney, 244; and Camilla Hayes, 109; and Ferney J. Hayes, 109; and Hefty Records, 253; and Arthur W. Kimbrough, 108, 109; and Isaac Kimbrough, 109; and Jeamel Lee, 243, 244, 245, 248; and Charles Moore, 10, 20, 52, 163, 165, 168, 172, 173, 180, 181, 182, 183, 186–189, 191, 193, 194, 195, 197, 198, 200, 238, 239, 244, 245, 246; and Helen Kimbrough Ranelin, 109, 110; and the Temptations, 239; and Time Is Now Productions, 246; and Wix Smith, 109
Raoul, Sigmond (pianist), 304
Rashied Ali Quartet, 271
Raskin, Phil, 356

Rauuf, Abdul (pianist), 214
Rawlings, Albert (tenor saxophonist), 143, 144
Rebirth Records, 253
Redding, Otis (singer), 59
Redman, Dewey (saxophonist), 329, 340
Reed, Adele "Vera" (singer), 49
Reed, Doc, 49
Reed, Henry, 49
Reed, Ishmael, 13, 271
Reid, Steve (drummer), 10, 312, 313, 315, 317, 318, 321, 322, 323, 324; and Mustevic Sound, 314
Reims jazz festival, 348
Republic of New Afrika (RNA), 129, 203, 207, 208, 214
Republic of New Libya (RNL), 130, 154; and Ahmed Evans, 129
resistance, 4, 5, 6, 14, 19, 26, 29, 41, 42, 43, 45, 103, 113, 118, 134, 156, 157, 159, 160, 202, 205, 278, 297
Revolutionary Action Movement (RAM), 126–128, 206; and *Black America*, 128; and Detroit, 203; and Fisk University, 128; Vladimir Lenin, 127; and Mao Zedong, 127; and Karl Marx, 127; and Max Stanford, 127
Riggs, Doug (bassist), 187
Rivbea Summer Music Festival, 312
Rivers, Sam (multi-instrumentalist), 310
Roach, Max (drummer), xi, 8, 110, 127, 248, 277, 345
Robertson, Carol, 149
Robertson, Oscar, 111
Robinson, Perry (clarinetist), 140
Rochon, Pierre (trumpeter), 164, 173, 187; Pierre Rochon Quartet, 194; Workshop Arts Quartet, 189; Workshop Trio, 189
Rock, The, 60, 61
Rollins, Sonny (saxophonist), 261, 268
Rosewoman, Michelle (pianist), 324
Ross, Kevin (bassist), 323
Roulette, Charles Jack (flutist), 144
Rudd, Roswell (trombonist), 191, 268
Ruffin, David, x
Russell, George (pianist), 301

Saheb Sarbib Quartet, 354
Samad, Tariq Abdul (drummer), 213, 219
Samson, Michel (violinist), 275, 276, 277, 279, 280, 282, 300
Sanchez, Sonia, 171

Sanders, Pharoah (saxophonist), 329; and Albert Ayler, 266, 285, 288; and Albert Ayler Quartet, 271; and Amiri Baraka, 266; and Marion Brown, 184; *Change*, 196; and John Coltrane Quintet, 208; and Godseekers, 275; and Nat Hentoff, 13; and New Music, 8; and Phil Ranelin, 240
Sanders, Sam, 239, 250
Santacruz, Bernard (bassist), 328
Schooner, Kenneth (harmonica), 184
Scott, William Walter, III, 204, 205, 206
Seale, Bobby, 128, 307, 308
Semark, Jim (poet/trombonist), 173, 176, 182, 199; and Workshop Music Ensemble, 186–189
Shabazz, Majid (drummer), 304
Shaheed, Mutawaf. *See* Shy, Clyde
Shahid, Hasan (Amos Franklin Gordon Jr.) (drummer), 55, 92, 236; and Black Unity Trio, 10, 20, 145–146, 150, 151, 153; and Stokely Carmichael, 149; and Cosmic Music, 152; and Augustus J. Gordon, 86, 87, 88; and Eliza Gordon, 86; and Griot Galaxy, 221–225, 227, 228; and Howard University, 149; and Islam, 214; and Malcolm X, 149; and Roscoe Mitchell, 236; and Pan-African Congress, 214; and Republic of New Afrika, 214; and Bayard Rustin, 149; and SNCC, 149; and Sun Ra, 236
Shahid, Jaribu, (bass guitarist), 213, 229, 356
Shakur, Tupac, 14
Sharon Edmonds Dancers, 246
Sharpe, C., 271
Shattering Effect, and Charles Moore, 200
Shelton, Skeeter (saxophonist), 236
Shepp, Archie (saxophonist), x, xi, 193; and Albert Ayler, 260, 294; and Artists' Workshop Society, 179, 190; and avant-garde bands, 282; and Ayler-Cherry band, 268; and Amiri Baraka, 266; and Marion Brown, 184, 185; and *Change*, 196; and John Coltrane, 330; and Festival Actuel, 339; and free jazz/pure music, 194, 244, 266; and Charles Greenlee, 48; and identity politics, 12; and LSD and music, 170; and Charlie Moore, 186, 194; and new musical concepts, 13; and New York Contemporary Five, 62; and poetry, 212; and rebellion, 244; and Archie Shepp Quintet/Quartet, 35, 191; and Alan Silva, 334; and John Sinclair, 177, 194; and Danny Spencer, 186; and student organizations, 285

Shoo-Bee-Do (Reggie Fields) (bassist), 214, 215
Shorter, Wayne (saxophonist), 196, 214, 271
Shure, Carl (painter), 165
Shy, Clyde (Mutawaf Shaheed) (bassist), 38, 62, 123, 142, 276, 356; and Albert Ayler, 10, 138, 144, 261; and Amiri Baraka, 266; and bimsheas (gatherings), 154; and Black nationalism, 127; and Black Ohio, 28; and free jazz lineages, 134; and freedom, 117, 356; and Georgia Black Belt, 61; and Larry Hancock, 143; and Nation of Islam, 130, 131; and revolution, 275; and Charles Tyler, 304; and Underground Railroad, 37
Silva, Alan (bassist), xi, 9, 22, 262, 274, 280, 283, 284, 287, 288, 327, 329–354; and art therapy, 353; and Celestial Communications Orchestra, 327, 335, 336, 348, 353, 354; and Freeform Improvisation Ensemble, 335; and Globe Unity Orchestra, 353; and Institute for Art, Culture, and Perception, 353; and October Revolution, 335; and Alexander von Schlippenbach's quartet, 353
Simmons, Sonny (saxophonist), 177, 340
Simon, Joe (singer), 240
Simon, Ken (saxophonist), 317, 325
Simon, Martin (cellist), 146
Sinclair, David (poet), 173
Sinclair, John (poet), 9, 10, 20, 163, 164, 166, 176, 178, 182, 183, 186, 187, 190, 194, 196, 197, 198, 199, 242; as alto saxophonist, 87; and MC5, 191, 201, 222; and White Panther Party, 201
Sissle, Noble (singer), 122
Sixth World Congress of the Communist International, 93
Smart, Chuck (drummer), 143, 144, 148
Smart, Syndey "Syd" (drummer), 143
Smith, Bessie, 59
Smith, Cladys "Jabbo" (trumpeter), 105
Smith, Harold E. (drummer), 346
Smith, Jimmy, 164
Smith, Judd (guitarist), 100
Smith, Melvin (guitarist), 314
Smith, Michael (pianist), 352
Smith, Nehemiah (guitarist), 100
Smith, O. C. (singer), 250
Smith, Shell (fiddler), 76
Smith, Wadada Leo (trumpeter), 317, 318
Snow, Michael, 267

Socialist Workers Party, 275
Soft Machine, 339
Soulsonic Force, 229
Sound & Fury (magazine), 12, 168
Sound Unity Festival, 325, 351
Southern Christian Leadership Conference (SCLC), 128, 149, 164, 206
Southern Worker, 94, 95, 96, 97
Space Music, 223
Spaulding, James (flutist), 111
Spearman, Glenn (saxophonist), 309, 325, 346, 350, 351, 352
Spellman, A. B., 173, 175, 193
Spencer, Danny (drummer), 164, 172, 173, 180, 186, 194, 197, 239, 251
Spero, 168
Spiritual Principle, 285
spirituality, 305
Squires, David (tenor saxophonist), 189
Stanford, Max, and Revolutionary Action Movement (RAM), 127
Star Theater, 105
Stephens, Charles (trombonist), 314
Steve Lacy Quartet, 327, 353
Stockholm Academy of Arts, 259
Stollman, Bernard, 266; ESP, 190, 330
Strata Records. Kenny Cox, 200, 238
Streep, Harry, III, 316, 317, 324
STRESS (Stop the Robberies Enjoy Safe Streets), 204, 247
Strickland, Donald (reeds player), 142, 144, 304
Student Non-Violent Coordinating Committee (SNCC), 128, 206
student unions, 151, 310
Studio Rivbea festival, 316
Sufism, 211
Sun Ra (Herman Blount), 92, 341; and Dorothy Ashby, 215; and Albert Ayler, 271; and Amiri Baraka, 275; and Faruq Z. Bey, 209; and Sadiq Muhammad Bey, 224, 225; and big band music, 318; and James Brown, 288; and Marion Brown, 184; and *Change*, 196; and cultural revolution, 13; and David Durrah, 307; and El Saturn Records, 238; and Godseekers, 275; and Griot Galaxy, 223, 228; and Wendell Harrison, 240; and Noah Howard, 341; Myth Science Arkestra, 105, 271, 326; and philosophies and aesthetics, 214; and Ronnie Boykins, 312; and Jaribu Shahid, 214, 236; and

Tani Tabbal, 221, 222; and Tribe, 252; and Charlie Tyler, 326
Supreme Court, US, 34
Survival Records, and Rashied Ali, 238

Tabbal, Tani (drummer/tabla player), 221–225, 227–299, 236; Pyramid, 221
Taj Mahal, 229
Tapscott, Horace (pianist), 153, 305, 306
Tatum, Art (pianist), 124
Tatum, James, 208
Taylor, Art (drummer), 341
Taylor, Cecil, xi, 266, 288, 333, 352; and Artists' Workshop Society, 179, 190; *Change*, 196; and Stanley Crouch, 14; and free jazz concepts, 331; and Anthony Holland, 222; and Charles Moore, 194; and Yusuf Mumin, 148; and Sunny Murray, 10, 331; and new musical concepts, 13; in New York, 261, 262; and Alan Silva, 343, 344, 345; and John Sinclair, 177; and Cecil Taylor Trio, 259; and Cecil Taylor Unit Core Ensemble, 312; and Charles Tyler, 310, 318, 325; and Abdul Wadud, 148; and Frank Wright, 332, 343, 344, 352
Taylor, Jessie (saxophonist), 149
Tchicai, John (saxophonist), 177, 190, 212, 266, 330
Temptations, 239
Terroade, Kenneth (tenor saxophonist), 334, 335
Theater Owners' Booking Agency (TOBA), 59, 60, 102, 104
Theodore Finney's Orchestra, 157
Thornton, Clifford (trumpeter), 335
Thiele, Bob, 282, 283, 284, 287; and Impulse Records, 190
Thomas, Ken (pianist), 214
Thomas, Luther, 310
Thomaston Sax Horn Band, 58
Thompson, Lucky (saxophonist), 158
Time Is Now Productions. Phil Ranelin, 246
Tintweiss, Steve (bassist), 266, 277, 292, 293, 330, 331
Trayler, Thomas "Turk" (percussionist), 251
Tribe (magazine), 251–252
Tribe Records, 237–253; Marcus Belgrave and, 10, 21, 220, 240, 241, 242, 244, 245, 246, 248, 249, 250, 251, 242, 253; Frederick Boon and, 251; Ron Brooks and, 242; Roy Brooks and, 249; Lorenzo Brown and, 249; Charles Burnham and, 251; Hank Crawford and, 241; John Dana and, 164, 172, 173, 182, 184, 187, 189, 191, 194, 212, 239, 245; George Davidson and, 245; David Durrah and, 143, 144, 238, 239, 242, 251, 306, 308; Darryl Dybka and, 249; Haroun El Ni and, 245; Reggie Fields (Shoo Bee Do) and, 215, 245, 246; Doug Hammond and, 212, 239, 242, 251; Otis Harris and, 251; Wendell Harrison and, 10, 21, 214, 237, 238, 240, 241, 242, 243, 246, 246, 247, 248, 249, 250, 251, 253, 356, 357; and jazz-rock, 248; Harold McKinney and, 62, 64, 71, 163, 240, 242, 249–250, 253; Trevis Mickeel and, 251; Charles Moore and, 10, 20, 52, 163, 165, 168, 172, 173, 180, 181, 182, 183, 186–189, 191, 193, 194, 195, 197, 198, 200, 238, 239, 244, 245, 246; Aaron Neal and, 246; Larry Nozero and, 164, 180, 251; Ed Pickens and, 249; Phil Ranelin and, 10, 21, 70, 71, 108, 109, 110, 214, 238, 240, 241, 242, 243, 244, 245, 246, 248, 249, 251, 253; and Rebirth Records, 253; Danny Spencer and, 164, 172, 173, 180, 186, 194, 197, 239, 251; Thomas "Turk" Trayler and, 251; Billy Turner and, 245, 246, 249; Keith Vreeland and, 245, 246; and WenHa Records, 253
Triplett, Sam (trumpeter), 308
Tuck, Jane Ritchie, 36
Turner, Billy (drummer), 245, 246, 249, 250
Turner, Roger (drummer), 353
Turrentine, Stanley (tenor saxophonist), 139
Tyler, Charles (saxophonist/clarinetist), xi, 10, 21, 64, 66, 68, 69, 107, 110, 111, 112, 117, 125, 142, 143, 144, 153, 270, 273, 274, 294, 298–328; and A&M Records, 305; and AK-BA records, 313, 320; and Adelphia Records, 322; and Bleu Regard record label, 327; and Cadiz, 324; compositions, 323; and Marie Cosenza, 327; death of, 328; in France, 326–328; and INTERface, 318; and *Klangfarbenmelodie*, 301; and loft jazz, 317; "The Mysteries of the Dark Blue Depths of the Pale Blue Planet," 324; and spirituality/spiritual philosophy, 305, 313; and Inez Argleo Tinsley, 107; and William Tinsley, 66; and Dick Tyler, 68; with Tyler and the Vulcans, 304; and U.S. Army Band, 112; and WCUW Music Fair, 323
Tyler and the Vulcans, 304

Tyner, McCoy (pianist), 172, 173, 180, 249
Tysh, George, 162, 165, 173, 176, 178, 195

UHURU, 206
Ulmer, James (Blood), 212, 229, 349
Umbra, 271
Underground Musicians and Artists Association, 305
United Freedom Movement (UFM), 126
Universal Negro Improvement Association (UNIA), 85, 122
urban folk music, 223
urbanization, 19, 69, 71, 81–113, 159

Vajava. Black Messengers, 246
Vaughan, Sarah (singer), 221
Van Peebles, Melvin, 252
Vestine, Henry (guitarist), 291
Vietnam War, 153
Village Voice, 14
Vision Festival, 325
Von Battle, Joe, and J-V-B Recording Company, 237
voting, 26, 32, 37, 39, 44, 47, 49, 61, 96, 103, 149
Vreeland, Keith (pianist), 245, 246

Wadud, Abdul (Ronald DeVaughn) (saxophonist), 147, 148, 149, 152, 306; and Black Unity Trio, 10, 20, 145–146, 150, 151, 153
Wajid, Ibrahim Abdul (bassist), 304
Walden, Donald (saxophonist), 220
Walker, Thomas, 40
Wallenstein, Barry 314, 319, 320, 322, 323, 328
Ward, Carlos (saxophonist), 330
Ward, John, 71
Ware, David S. (saxophonist), 354
Washington, Darryl, 103
Washington, Grover, Jr., 104
Waters, Muddy (guitarist/singer), 139, 274
Watson, John, 207
Watts Poets, 153
Wayne State University, 151, 161, 162, 163, 164, 172, 176, 178, 180, 183, 184, 185, 191, 192, 195, 199, 214, 215, 222, 248
Weaver, Curley, 98, 100, 101, 102
Weaver, Lloyd, 302, 303
Weaver, Savannah "Dip," 100
Webster, Freddie (trumpeter), 122
Weinstein, Norman, 316

WenHa Records, 253
West, Cornel, 14
Weston, Kim, 246
Weston, Randy (pianist), 334
Whitecage, Mark, 317
white mob violence, 47
white oppression, 270
White Panther Party, 201
white supremacy, 20
Wilderman, Michael (saxophonist), 308
Williams, Art, 195
Williams, Arthur (trumpeter), 304
Williams, David, 110
Williams, Martin, 12
Williams, Patrice (Kafi Patrice Nassoma) (flutist/harpist), 213, 215, 218, 219
Williams, Richard (bassist), 321, 322
Williams, Tony (drummer), 173, 194
Willisau Jazz Festival, 347, 351
Wilmer, Valerie, 15, 292, 338, 339
Wilson, Benny (baritone saxophonist), 349
Wilson, Gerald, 158
Wilson, Oliver (Olly) (bassist), 148, 306
Wilson, Phillip, 317
Winkler, Adolf, 353
Wollny, Frank (guitarist), 352
Wonder, Stevie, 121
Woodard, Lyman (pianist/organist), 164, 194; and Lyman Woodard Ensemble, 188, 189; and Martha and the Vandellas, 189; and Motown, 189; and Workshop Music Ensemble, 186–189
Woodson, Thomas, 40
Workman, Reggie (bassist), 351
Workshop Arts Quartet, 189
Workshop Arts Quintet, 179
Workshop Music Ensemble, 186–189
Workshop Trio: Ronald Johnson in, 189; Tommy Dorsey in, 189
workshops, 121, 171, 240, 308, 309, 318
Works Progress Administration, 133
Worrell, Lewis (bassist), xi, 140, 270
Wright, Frank, xi, 10, 74, 77, 79, 112, 113, 117, 131, 135–137, 142, 143, 148, 329, 331, 332, 333, 334, 336, 338, 339, 340, 343–348, 349, 350; and ALARM ensemble, 352; and Blue Notes, 351; and Center of the World, 9, 22, 343–348, 349, 352, 354; in Cleveland, 20, 21; and ESP Records, 330, and Fractal Record, 343; and

Sarah Gary 74, 77; and Orchestra of Two Continents, 352; and Frank Wright Quartet, 341–342; and Frank Wright Trio, 330

Young, Coleman, 159, 162, 204, 252
Young, Lester (saxophonist), 137, 269
Young, Roland P. (clarinetist/saxophonist), 312, 322; and KSAN-FM, 307

Young, Steve, 271
young modernists, 257

Zagaria, Christian (violinist), 328
Zappa, Frank, 222
Zawadi, Kiane (Bernard McKinney) (trombonist), 62, 64, 71, 249
Zorn, John (saxophonist), 320

GPSR Authorized Representative: Easy Access System Europe, Mustamäe tee 50, 10621 Tallinn, Estonia, gpsr.requests@easproject.com

www.ingramcontent.com/pod-product-compliance
Lightning Source LLC
Chambersburg PA
CBHW022024290426
44109CB00014B/732